lonely planet

Vietna

LOOK FOR:
- __ Books
- __ Booklets
- __ CDs
- __ Charts
- __ DVDs
- __ Inserts
- __ Maps
- __ Music parts
- __ ____
- __ ____

Northern Vietnam p101

★ Hanoi p55

Central Vietnam p151

Siem Reap & the Temples of Angkor (Cambodia) p413

Southwest Highlands p279

Southeast Coast p231

● Ho Chi Minh City p305

Mekong Delta p353

Iain Stewart

Damian Harper, Bradley Mayhew, Nick Ray

Contents

WATER-PUPPET THEATRE P341, HO CHI MINH CITY

NADEZDA ZAVITAEVA/SHUTTERSTOCK ©

THANH TOAN BRIDGE P191, NEAR HUE

PETER STUCKINGS/SHUTTERSTOCK ©

Contents

COVID-19

We have re-checked every business in this book before publication to ensure that it is still open after the COVID-19 outbreak. However, the economic and social impacts of COVID-19 will continue to be felt long after the outbreak has been contained, and many businesses, services and events referenced in this guide may experience ongoing restrictions. Some businesses may be temporarily closed, have changed their opening hours and services, or require bookings; some unfortunately could have closed permanently. We suggest you check with venues before visiting for the latest information.

SPECIAL
FEATURES

Right: Hon May Rut,
An Thoi Islands (p379)

CRAVENA/SHUTTERSTOCK ©

WELCOME TO

Vietnam

I first visited Vietnam in 1991 when Hanoi was a socialist city of bicycles, faded French buildings and near-silence after dark. Times have changed. Today Vietnam's capital is booming, as a metro network is constructed underground and glass-and-steel monuments of commerce puncture the night sky. The raw energy of the country is addictive, and I find myself returning every year to admire the Vietnamese people's sheer lust for life, to feast on the best seafood in the world and to seek out that elusive, perfect cove beach.

By Iain Stewart, Writer
🐦 @iaintravel
For more about our writers, see p512

Vietnam

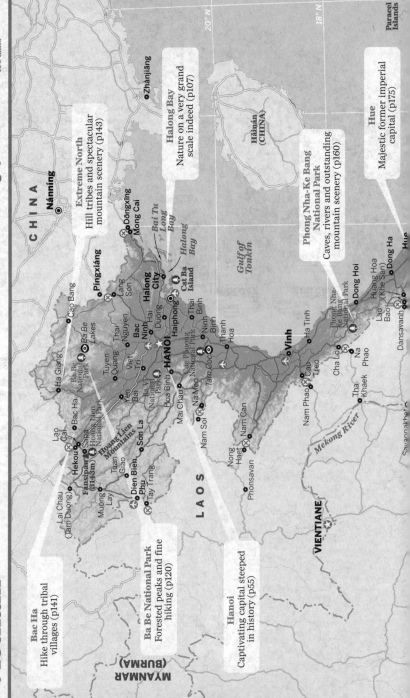

Bac Ha
Hike through tribal villages (p141)

Extreme North
Hill tribes and spectacular mountain scenery (p143)

Halong Bay
Nature on a very grand scale indeed (p107)

Phong Nha-Ke Bang National Park
Caves, rivers and outstanding mountain scenery (p160)

Hue
Majestic former imperial capital (p175)

Ba Be National Park
Forested peaks and fine hiking (p120)

Hanoi
Captivating capital steeped in history (p55)

CHINA

Nánníng

Zhànjiāng

Hǎinán (CHINA)

Gulf of Tonkin

Paracel Islands

20°N

18°N

Dōngxīng
Mong Cai

Pingxiáng

Lang Son

Cao Bang

Ha Giang

Bai Tu Long Bay

Halong Bay

Halong City

Cat Ba Island

Haiphong

Thai Binh

Ninh Binh

Ba Be Lakes

Ba Be National Park

Bac Kan

Thai Nguyen

Hai Duong

Tuyen Quang

Viet Tri

HANOI

Phuong

Ninh Hoa

Cuc Phuong National Park

Tam Coc

Thanh Hoa

Yen Bai

Ba Vi National Park

Hoa Binh

Na Meo

Lao Cai

Bac Ha

Hekou

Fansipan (3143m)

Hoang Lien Sapa National Park

Hoang Lien Mountains

Tuan Giao

Lai Chau (Tam Duong)

Muong Lay

Dien Bien Phu

Tay Trang

Son La

Mai Chau

Nam Soi

Nam Can

Nong Haet

Phonsavan

LAOS

Mekong River

VIENTIANE

Na Phao

Cau Treo

Vinh

Ha Tinh

Cha Lo

Na Phao

Tha Khaek

Savannakhet

Phong Nha-Ke Bang National Park

Dong Hoi

Dong Ha

Huang Hoa (Khe San)

Lao Bao

Dansavanh

Hue

MYANMAR (BURMA)

N

0   200 km
0   100 miles

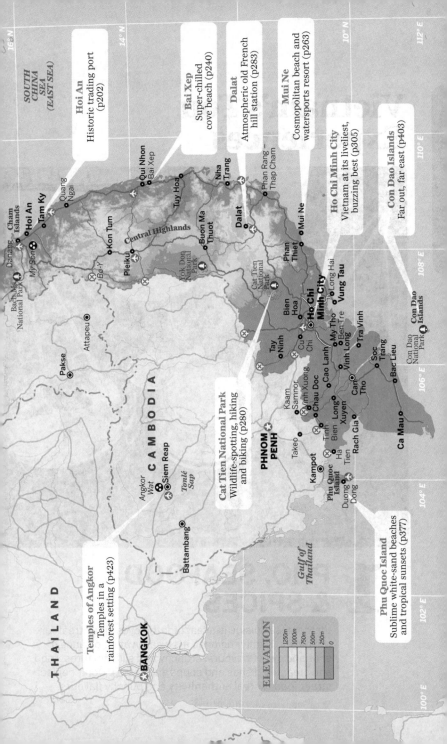

Hoi An
Historic trading port (p202)

Bai Xep
Super-chilled cove beach (p240)

Dalat
Atmospheric old French hill station (p283)

Mui Ne
Cosmopolitan beach and watersports resort (p263)

Ho Chi Minh City
Vietnam at its liveliest, buzzing best (p305)

Con Dao Islands
Far out, far east (p403)

Cat Tien National Park
Wildlife-spotting, hiking and biking (p280)

Temples of Angkor
Temples in a rainforest setting (p423)

Phu Quoc Island
Sublime white-sand beaches and tropical sunsets (p377)

SOUTH CHINA SEA (EAST SEA)

16° N
14° N
10° N

112° E
110° E
108° E
106° E
104° E
102° E
100° E

THAILAND

CAMBODIA

BANGKOK

Battambang

Siem Reap
Angkor Wat
Tonlé Sap

PHNOM PENH

Pakse

Attapeu

Takeo
Kaam Samnor
Kampot
Phu Quoc Island
Duong Dong

Gulf of Thailand

Vinh Xuong
Chau Doc
Tinh Bien
Ha Tien
Rach Gia

Cao Lanh
Long Xuyen

Can Tho

Ca Mau

Bac Lieu
Soc Trang
Tra Vinh
Vinh Long
My Tho
Ben Tre

Con Dao National Park
Con Dao Islands

Tay Ninh
Cu Chi
Bien Hoa
Ho Chi Minh City
Long Hai
Vung Tau

Cat Tien National Park

Phan Thiet
Mui Ne

Phan Rang – Thap Cham

Dalat

Buon Ma Thuot

Nha Trang

Central Highlands

Pleiku
Kon Tum

Yok Don National Park

Bo Y

Tuy Hoa

Qui Nhon
Bai Xep

Quang Ngai

Bach Ma National Park
Danang
My Son
Cham Islands
Hoi An
Tam Ky

ELEVATION

1250m
1000m
750m
500m
250m
0

Vietnam's Top Experiences

1 PHO, SEAFOOD & SPICES

Vietnamese cuisine is a feast for the eyes and a treat for the palate. Highly regional, it's a captivating balance of sour and sweet flavours, crunchy and silky textures, fried and steamed dishes and soups and salads. Don't neglect street food for real authenticity and punchy flavours.

Above: Street vendor, Hoi An (p202)

Northern Classics

Up north the climate is cooler and the influence from China more obvious, with soy sauce replacing *nuoc mam* (fish sauce) as the dominant condiment. *Pho bo* is the classic Northern dish, a richly satisfying beef broth best tried in Hanoi. Look out too for noodle dishes and *bun cha* (barbecued pork with rice vermicelli). p47

Right: *Pho bo*

Central Specialties

The home of Vietnamese imperial cuisine (in the city of Hue), central Vietnam food is incredibly diverse. Local specialities such as the exquisite 'white rose' mini-dumpling unique to Hoi An just have to be sampled, while savoury pancakes such as *banh xeo* and *banh khoai* are real street-food treats. p47

Above: Vendor preparing *banh xeo*

Southern Comfort

Tropical and sultry, southern Vietnam is renowned for its seafood and use of coconut and spices – here the influence of India and Siam is evident. For surf-fresh fish and fine value, the authentic seafood markets of Duong Dong and Vung Tau can't be beat. p47

Above: Coconut curry

2 METROPOLITAN BUZZ

Vietnam's two metropolises, Hanoi and Ho Chi Minh City, have a visceral energy that will delight urbanites. Few places on earth are as dynamic and exciting, yet you don't have to dig too deep to uncover tradition, for a step or two off the grand boulevards are *hem* (alleys) home to street kitchens and craft industries. In contrast, Danang is a modern, less-frenetic coastal city boasting a sparkling shoreline and imposing riverside.

Ho Chi Minh City

The heat is always on in HCMC (Saigon), so loosen your collar and enjoy: this is Vietnam at its most raucous and thrilling. Dive in and you'll be rewarded with a wealth of history, fine museums and a vibrant nightlife that sets the standard for the nation. p305

Right: Nightlife on Đ Bui Vien (p338), Pham Ngu Lao

Hanoi

Explore the streets of Hanoi's captivating Old Quarter, sipping drip coffee and slurping a hearty bowl of *bun rieu cua* (a sour crab noodle soup). Don't miss the crumbling decadence of the French Quarter or a wander along the shores of Hoan Kiem Lake. p55

Above: Diners at a street-food stall, Old Quarter (p79)

Danang

With a sweeping promenade flanked by sandy beaches and a glittering riverfront spanned by a roster of landmark bridges, Danang is a city on the up. It's far smaller (and less polluted) than Hanoi and HCMC, and boasts an ever-improving array of dining options. p193

Left: The Han River illuminated at night

3 CULTURAL HEARTLAND

Central Vietnam encompasses two historic cities, a couple of hours' travel apart, which should be on the itinerary of every visitor. Hue, the capital of the nation in the 19th and early 20th centuries, has an incredible Imperial legacy to investigate. Smaller Hoi An is a perfectly preserved ancient trading port, complete with a cosmopolitan array of dining and retail options.

Above: Imperial Enclosure (p175), Hue

Hoi An

Explore on foot and immerse yourself in history in the warren-like lanes of Hoi An's Old Town and tour the temples and pagodas. Dine like an emperor on a peasant's budget. Then hit glorious An Bang Beach, wander along the riverside and bike the back roads. p202

Left: Old Town (p203)

Hue

Hue's position on the banks of the Perfume River is sublime and its cuisine justifiably famous. And that's without the majesty of the Hue Citadel, replete with royal residences and elegant temples, formidable walled defences and gateways. On the city's fringes are some of Vietnam's most impressive pagodas and royal tombs, many in wonderful natural settings. p175

Below left: Thien Mu Pagoda (p187); Below: *Bun bo Hue* (p47)

4 BIG NATURE

Vietnam offers nature on a very grand scale indeed, particularly in the north, home to impressive limestone peaks and thousands of craggy karst islands. Elsewhere, the monumental cave complexes in Phong Nha-Ke Bang are off the charts, with dozens to explore. National parks are dotted around the nation, with primates, birdlife and croc sightings possible in Cat Tien.

Phong Nha-Ke Bang National Park

Perhaps the world's most exciting caving destination, Phong Nha-Ke Bang has towering hills shrouded in rainforest, and cathedral-like chambers to explore, including Hang Toi (Dark Cave) and the other-worldly beauty of Paradise Cave. p160

Below: Hang Son Doong (p162)

JUNPHOTO/SHUTTERSTOCK ©

Halong Bay

Halong Bay (pictured above) is a combination of karst limestone peaks and sheltered, shimmering seas and is one of Vietnam's top draws, but with more than 2000 islands, there's plenty of superb scenery to go around. p107

Cat Tien

Cat Tien National Park (pictured right) is set on a bend in the Dong Nai River, and there's something vaguely *Apocalypse Now* about arriving here. You can trek, cycle and spot wildlife: the Wild Gibbon Trek is a must. p280

5 ON TWO WHEELS & TWO FEET

BEN WASSINK/SHUTTERSTOCK ©

HANOI PHOTOGRAPHY/SHUTTERSTOCK ©

QUANG NGUYEN VINH/SHUTTERSTOCK ©

Brushed with every shade of green in the palette, the mountainous terrain of northern Vietnam offers superb trekking trails and epic rides with spectacular vistas at every turn. The north is also home to dozens of hill tribes, providing a fascinating glimpse into the nation's cultural diversity. Down south, Dalat is the best base for cycling, hiking and a myriad of other adventure sports.

Extreme North

Ha Giang province (pictured above) is an emerging destination for the intrepid, with towering karst peaks and colossal granite outcrops. With improved roads, new trekking routes and minority markets, Vietnam's final frontier is really opening up. p143

Bac Ha

Our favourite hiking location is Bac Ha, where you can overnight in Tay, Flower Hmong and Dzao homestays on treks and explore bucolic rural lanes on two wheels. p141

Dalat

Laid-back Dalat is a fine base for adventure sports including abseiling, canyoning, mountain biking, hiking, rafting and kayaking. The town also has charm, dotted with grand colonial-era villas and set amid pine groves. p283

6 BEACH LIFE

Vietnam boasts a stunning coastline, blessed with oceanic beaches and idyllic coves, towering sand dunes and offshore islands dotted with hidden bays. Northern Vietnam has some fine stretches of sweeping sands, but during the winter months the sea is usually too rough for safe swimming and temperatures can be cool. Head south between October and March for balmy weather.

STUDIOLOCO/SHUTTERSTOCK ©

FABIO LAMANNA/SHUTTERSTOCK ©

Con Dao Islands

Once hell on earth for a generation of political prisoners, Con Dao (pictured top left) is now a heavenly destination of remote beaches, compelling dive sites and wildlife-rich rainforests. p403

Bai Xep

The tiny sheltered cove of Bai Xep (pictured above left) has grown exponentially in popularity over the past few years thanks to its fine sandy shoreline, azure waters and barefoot vibe. p240

Mui Ne

The upmarket beach resort of Mui Ne (pictured above) is a kitesurfing capital, with world-class wind and more than 20km of beachfront that stretches invitingly along the shores of the South China Sea. p263

7 QUENCH THAT THIRST

SALAJEAN/SHUTTERSTOCK ©

DMITRY BURLAKOV/SHUTTERSTOCK ©

BULLSTAR/SHUTTERSTOCK ©

Beer Ahoy

Vietnam has a deep-rooted beer-drinking culture. Seek out *bia hoi* – fresh draught beer – which is brewed daily, incredibly cheap and consumed on street terraces. There's also a dynamic craft-beer scene in the big cities. p49

Top left: Patrons drinking *bia hoi* with a meal, Hanoi

Coffee Time

Indigenous Vietnamese coffee culture runs deep. Vietnamese drip coffee can be served hot or iced (a real treat in summer), either treacle-thick or with milk (usually sweetened and condensed). p49

Left: Drip coffee

Vietnam is a great country to enjoy a tipple or two, with a wide selection of beers, imported wines and potent *ruou* (rice wine liquor). Tropical fruit juices are sublime. Coffee lovers rejoice: virtually every neighbourhood has a little cafe where locals go to de-stress from the office, the family or simply the traffic. Most are located on quiet side streets with copious greenery to promote relaxation.

Need to Know

For more information, see Survival Guide (p471)

Currency
Dong (d)

....

Language
Vietnamese

....

Visas
Standard tourist visas are valid for a calendar-month stay. Stays for nationalities not requiring a visa are mostly 15 days.

....

Money
Cash is most useful, and ATMs can be found across the country. Many hotels take debit and credit cards.

....

Mobile Phones
Buy a local SIM card to make local and international calls.

....

Time
Vietnam is seven hours ahead of GMT/UTC.

When to Go

Warm to hot summers, mild winters
Tropical climate, wet & dry seasons

Sapa •
GO Mar–May & Sep–Nov

• Hanoi
GO Mar–May & Sep–Nov

• Danang
GO Mar–Sep

• Ho Chi Minh City
GO Nov–Feb

High Season
(Jul & Aug)

➡ Prices increase by up to 50% by the coast; book hotels well in advance.

➡ All Vietnam, except the far north, is hot and humid, with the summer monsoon bringing downpours.

Shoulder
(Dec–Mar)

➡ During Tet (late January or early February), the whole country is on the move and prices rise.

➡ North of Nha Trang can get cool weather. Chilly conditions in the north.

➡ In the far south, clear skies and sunshine are the norm.

Low Season
(Apr–Jun, Sep–Nov)

➡ Perhaps the best time to tour the whole nation.

➡ Typhoons can lash the central and northern coastline until November.

Useful Websites

Saigoneer (https://saigoneer.com) Based in Ho Chi Minh City (HCMC) but with excellent nationwide cultural features.

Vietnam Coracle (http://vietnamcoracle.com) Excellent independent travel advice, including lots of back-roads adventure.

Vietcetera (https://vietcetera.com) Classy magazine-style site with lots of articles relevant to travellers.

Oi Vietnam (http://oivietnam.com) Travel, arts and news.

Rusty Compass (www.rustycompass.com) Useful online travel guide with itineraries and videos.

Lonely Planet (lonelyplanet.com/vietnam) Destination information, hotel bookings, traveller forum and more.

Important Numbers

To call Vietnam from outside the country, drop the initial 0 from the area code.

Country code	84
International access code	00
Directory assistance	116
Police	113
General information service	1080

Exchange Rates

Australia	A$1	17,900d
Canada	C$1	19,100d
Euro	€1	28,100d
Japan	¥100	21,100d
New Zealand	NZ$1	16,700d
UK	£1	32,600d
US	US$1	23,000d

For current exchange rates, see www.xe.com.

Daily Costs

Budget: Less than US$40

➡ Glass of *bia hoi* (draught beer): from US$0.30

➡ One hour on a local bus: US$1–1.50

➡ Cheap hotel: US$9–18, dorms less

➡ Simple noodle dish: US$1.50–2.50

Midrange: US$40–100

➡ Comfortable double room: US$25–50

➡ Meal in a restaurant: from US$7

➡ One-hour massage: US$7–20

➡ Ten-minute taxi ride: US$2.50–5

Top end: More than US$100

➡ Luxury hotel room: from US$80

➡ Gourmet dinner: from US$20

➡ Internal flight: US$35–100

Opening Hours

Hours vary little throughout the year.

Banks 8am to 3pm weekdays, to 11.30am Saturday; some take a lunch break

Offices and museums 7am or 7.30am to 5pm or 6pm; museums generally close on Monday; most take a lunch break (roughly 11am to 1.30pm)

Restaurants 11am to 9pm

Shops 8am to 6pm

Temples and pagodas 5am to 9pm

Arriving in Vietnam

Tan Son Nhat International Airport (HCMC) Taxis to central districts (150,000d to 200,000d) take about 30 minutes; a Grab cab is around 100,000d. There are also very regular Route 152 (6000d), the yellow 109 (20,000d) and 49 buses (40,000d); all are air-conditioned.

Noi Bai International Airport (Hanoi) Taxis to the centre cost 450,000d and take around 50 minutes. Vietnam Airlines minibuses and VietJet Air shuttle buses (both 40,000d) run roughly hourly. The Route 17 public bus to Long Bien bus station is 9000d.

Getting Around

Buses are the main mode of transport for locals in Vietnam, but travellers tend to prefer planes, trains and automobiles.

For much more on **getting around**, see p484

First Time Vietnam

For more information, see Survival Guide (p471)

Checklist

➡ Check out the visa situation; you may need to apply in advance

➡ Make sure your passport is valid for at least six months past your arrival date

➡ Check your immunisation history

➡ Arrange appropriate travel insurance

➡ Prebook internal flights and trains

➡ Inform your debit-/credit-card company

What to Pack

➡ Good footwear – Vietnam's streets are bumpy and lumpy

➡ Photocopies of passport and visa details

➡ Good mosquito repellent with DEET

➡ Rain jacket

➡ Electrical adaptors

➡ Extra phone-charging cables

➡ Torch (flashlight)

➡ Flip-flops or sandals

➡ Vietnamese phrasebook

➡ Fleece or jumper if travelling to the north

Top Tips for Your Trip

➡ Expect crazy driving: traffic can come at you every which way, and in the cities swarms of motorbikes reach biblical proportions. When crossing busy urban roads maintain a slow, deliberate walking pace.

➡ Try not to lose your temper; shouting and aggression cause a loss of face for both parties.

➡ The more 'local' you eat, the more authentic the food.

➡ Vietnam has more than its fair share of scams; most concern overcharging. Though very rare, more serious dangers (such as unexploded ordnance) can be a real concern.

➡ In towns such as Hue and Sapa, and on beaches popular with tourists, expect plenty of hustle from street vendors and the like. Off the beaten track there's little or no hassle.

➡ Prepare your bargaining head before you arrive.

➡ Very few locals speak English away from tourist centres; try to learn a few words of Vietnamese.

What to Wear

There are no serious cultural concerns about wearing inappropriate clothing in Vietnam. In religious buildings and government offices (or if attending a formal dinner), legs should be covered and sleeveless tops avoided.

Yes, Vietnam is in the tropics, but visit anywhere north of Hoi An between November and March and it can be cool, so pack some layers (a fleece or two). The rest of the year, and in the south, flip-flops or sandals, a T-shirt and shorts are likely to be your daily uniform.

Etiquette

Feet Avoid pointing your feet at people or sacred objects (eg Buddhas).

Heads Don't pat or touch an adult (or child) on the head.

Homes Remove your shoes when entering a private house.

Meals When dining with Vietnamese people, it's customary for the most senior diner to pay for everyone. It is still polite to offer to pay at least once.

Bargaining

Bargaining is essential in Vietnam, but not for everything and it should be good-natured – don't shout or get angry. Discounts of 60% or more may be possible; in other places it may only be 10% – or prices may be fixed. Haggle hard in marketplaces and most souvenir stores, and for *cyclos* and *xe om* (motorbike taxis). Many hotels offer a discount; restaurant prices are fixed.

Tipping

Bars Never expected.

Guides A few dollars on day trips is sufficient, more for longer trips if the service is good.

Hotels Not expected. Leave a small gratuity for cleaning staff if you like.

Restaurants Not expected; 5% to 10% in smart restaurants or if you're very satisfied. Locals don't tip.

Taxis Not necessary, but a little extra is appreciated, especially at night.

Language

English is not widely spoken in Vietnam. In the tourist areas, most staff in hotels and restaurants will speak a little, but communication problems are very common. A few key phrases of Vietnamese go a long way.

See p496 for our Language chapter.

An entrance to the Imperial Enclosure (p175), Hue

Sleeping

Accommodation is superb value for money. As tourism is booming it's usually best to book a day or two in advance (most places can be booked online), or several weeks ahead in the high season (the Tet holiday in late January to mid-February, July to August, and around Christmas).

Camping Options are extremely limited, but new facilities are opening in southern Vietnam.

Guesthouses Usually family run and less formal than hotels.

Hostels Popular in the main tourism centres, but rare elsewhere.

Hotels Range from simple, functional mini-hotels to uber-luxurious.

Eating

It's rarely necessary to reserve a table, except in national park restaurants (where food has to be purchased ahead), and upmarket places in Hanoi, Hoi An and Ho Chi Minh City (HCMC).

Cafes May have a snack or two available, but rarely meals.

International restaurants In tourist areas many serve up Western and Asian food; often the Vietnamese food is toned down and not as authentic.

Local restaurants Vietnamese restaurants tend to have functional decor and may look scruffy, but if they're busy, the food will be fresh and delicious.

Street food Pavement kitchens offer cheap, often incredibly tasty, local grub.

What's New

Vietnam has one of the world's most dynamic economies and even boasted strong growth figures in pandemic-hit 2020. Vast swathes of the coastline are being developed into tourist mega-resorts and Hanoi and Ho Chi Minh City (HCMC) are becoming truly cosmopolitan cities. But the nation remains a one-party state and environmental issues are pressing.

District Chic

For long an exclusive preserve of wealthy locals and expats, HCMC's leafy District 2 (p322) is drawing more and more travellers thanks to a waterbus link to the centre. Compared to the city centre, it's far less congested and polluted and has an expanding range of restaurants, cafes and bars.

Quy Nhon & Bai Xep

Emerging as an alternative to Nha Trang, Quy Nhon (p236) is going from strength to strength, with new hotels, guesthouses, cafes and bars adding to this city-by-the-sea's beachy allure. Neighbouring Bai Xep (p240) is also on the up, and fast becoming a mecca for independent travellers.

Metro Progress

Vietnam's two metro projects, in Hanoi and HCMC, have both been cursed by lengthy delays. However there's now clear light visible at the end of the tunnel, and the capital's elevated Line 2A should commence service in late 2021, with Line 3 to follow. Meanwhile in HCMC, most construction is complete on the first line, with trains set to roll (at up to 110kph) by 2022 or 2023.

Ha Giang Loop

This remote mountain route (p144) is fast becoming the north's must-do trip and increasing numbers of Vietnamese are heading here. For much of the year, you won't find a room in remote Dong Van on Saturday nights without a reservation. Reliable motorbikes are now available for rent from local experts QT, and off-the-beaten-track detours like Du Gia are taking off too.

Walking Streets

A simply stroll can be quite challenging in Vietnam, where the motorbike is king and traffic regulations rarely observed. Recently implemented pedestrianisation schemes (called 'Walking Streets' locally) in Hanoi,

---

LOCAL KNOWLEDGE

WHAT'S HAPPENING IN VIETNAM

Iain Stewart, Lonely Planet writer

The Vietnamese government's response to the COVID-19 pandemic was swift and successful, involving border closures and contact tracing so effective that nationwide lockdowns were avoided. Indeed, the Lowy Institute ranked the nation's efforts as the second-best in the world (behind New Zealand). By late-March 2021 only 35 COVID-related deaths had been recorded.

Certain sectors, including manufacturing and agriculture, fared well during 2020, though tourism was hit particularly hard as international visitor arrivals plummeted. When the situation improves, the nation remains an incredibly enticing destination and investment in infrastructure, particularly regional airports, has meant that getting around has never been easier.

Hoi An, HCMC and Hue have improved things to a degree, however these areas tend to be small and only operate at certain times of day. Plans to expand HCMC's pedestrian-friendly zones will transform the city for travellers, if implemented.

Golden Bridge

From a distance, this long walkway up in the clouds of Ba Na Hill Station seems to be supported by a pair of huge stone hands (they're actually fibreglass and wire mesh). On a cloudy day the Golden Bridge (p202) is perhaps a fogged-out let-down, but if the Vietnam sun has its hat on, the panoramas are astonishing (though working around the crowds of Instagrammers isn't easy).

New Wave Coffee

Vietnam has a centuries-old coffee culture and it's easy to find a life-affirming traditional drip-fed local coffee anywhere. But exciting new cafes are revolutionising the caffeine scene using high-tech hardware and barista expertise.

Bosgaurus Coffee (p339) Setting the standard in HCMC.

La Viet Coffee (p291) Cafe, coffee farm and factory in Dalat.

Sound of Silence (p225) Oceanic vistas and perfect coffee.

Chat Coffee Roasters (p339) Backstreet hipster cafe in HCMC.

Espresso Station (p216) Run by Hoi An's finest barista.

Little Plan Cafe (p87) Boho Hanoi cafe; try the iced coconut coffee.

Can Tho Takes Off

Long the unofficial capital of the Mekong Delta thanks to its sophisticated hotels and restaurants and nearby floating markets, Can Tho (p365) is now well and truly on the map thanks to a network of domestic flights that connect it to the blissful beaches of Phu Quoc and Con Dao, as well as Dalat, Danang, Hai Phong and Hanoi. International budget airlines offer direct links to Bangkok and Kuala Lumpur.

Cham Islands Visitor Cap

In a bid to preserve the ecosystem of the Cham Islands (p225) and ease pressure on scarce water resources, a 3000-person per

LISTEN, WATCH & FOLLOW

For inspiration and up-to-date news, visit www.lonelyplanet.com/Vietnam/articles.

Vietcetera (https://vietcetera.com/en) Great cultural, travel and cuisine content. Based in HCMC but relevant to the whole nation.

The Bureau (https://thebureauasia.com) Fine restaurant and bar reviews.

Saigoneer (https://saigoneer.com) This excellent website produces a superb weekly podcast covering all things Vietnam.

VnExpress (https://twitter.com/vietnam english) Tweets in English about Vietnamese issues, with an independent tone.

Another Side of Vietnam (www.facebook.com/groups/21346846424) Looking at the quirky side of life in Vietnam.

FAST FACTS

Food trend Contemporary street food

Ethnic groups In addition to the Kinh majority, 54 minority groups are recognised

Pop 97.9 million

POPULATION PER SQ KM

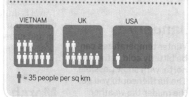

VIETNAM   UK   USA

≈ 35 people per sq km

day visitor limit has been imposed. Authorities hope that this action (combined with an admission price hike) will help counter overtourism and environmental damage.

A Bird's-Eye View over An Thoi

Soaring high above the An Thoi Islands off the southern tip of Phu Quoc, the Hon Thom Cable Car (p382) is the world's longest over-sea cable car. The views over the fishing fleet of An Thoi and the hidden coves and bays of the islands below are stunning and not to be missed. A major water park called Aquapolis adds to Hon Thom's allure.

Month by Month

January

Winter temperatures can be bitterly cold in the far north, with snow possible. The further south you go, the milder the weather.

✿ Dalat Flower Festival

Held early in the month, this is always a wonderful occasion, with huge elaborate displays. It's become an international event, with music and fashion shows and a wine festival.

February

North of Danang, chilly 'Chinese winds' usually mean overcast conditions. Conversely, sunny, hot days are the norm in the southern provinces.

☆ Quang Trung

Wrestling competitions, lion dances and human chess take place in Hanoi on the fifth day of the first lunar month at Dong Da Mound (p75).

✿ Tet (Tet Nguyen Dan)

Tet falls in late January or early February. Vietnamese Lunar New Year is like Christmas, New Year and birthdays all rolled into one. Travel is difficult at this time, as transport is booked up and many businesses close. (p458)

March

Grey skies and cool temperatures can affect anywhere north of Hoi An, but towards the end of the month the thermometer starts to rise. Down south, the dry season is ending.

✿ Buon Ma Thuot Coffee Festival

Caffeine cravers should make for the highlands during March, as Buon Ma Thuot plays host to an annual coffee festival. Growers, grinders, blenders and addicts rub shoulders in the city's main park.

April

Generally an excellent time to cover the nation, as the winter rainy season should have subsided.

✿ Holiday of the Dead (Thanh Minh)

It's time to honour the ancestors with a visit to graves of deceased relatives to tidy up and sweep tombstones. Offerings are presented. It's held on the first three days of the third moon.

✿ Hue Festival (Biennial)

Vietnam's biggest cultural event is held every two years, with events in 2022 and 2024. Most of the art, theatre, music, circus and dance performances are held inside Hue's Citadel.

May

A fine time to tour the centre and north, with a good chance of clear skies and warm days. Sea temperatures are warming up nicely and it's a pretty quiet month for tourism.

✿ Buddha's Birth, Enlightenment and Death (Phong Sinh)

A big celebration at Buddhist temples with lively

street processions and lanterns used to decorate pagodas. Complexes including Chua Bai Dinh (p155) and HCMC's Jade Emperor Pagoda (p316) host lavish celebrations. Fifteenth day of the fourth lunar month.

✨ Ba Chua Xu Temple Festival

Held in the Mekong Delta town of Chau Doc, this impressive festival at the Ba Chua Xu temple features elaborate ceremonies and classical theatre.

June

A great time to tour Vietnam as it's just before the peak domestic season. Humidity can be punishing at this time of year, so spend some time by the coast.

✨ Nha Trang Sea Festival (Biennial)

This lively event, held every two years in early June (the next in 2023), includes a street festival, photography exhibitions, sports events, embroidery displays and kite-flying competitions.

☆ Danang International Fireworks Festival

Danang's riverside explodes with sound, light and colour during this spectacular event, which features pyrotechnic teams from around the world. (p196)

✨ Summer Solstice Day (Tet Doan Ngo)

Offerings are made to the spirits, ghosts and the God of Death on the fifth day of the fifth moon. Sticky rice wine (ruou nep) is consumed in industrial quantities.

August

The peak month for tourism with domestic and international tourists. Book flights and accommodation well ahead. Prices rise and beaches are busy. Weatherwise it's hot, hot, hot.

✨ Children's (or Mid-Autumn) Festival, Hoi An

This is a big event in Hoi An and Hanoi, when citizens celebrate the full moon, eat moon cakes and beat drums. Children are fully involved in the celebrations.

✨ Wandering Souls Day (Trung Nguyen)

Second in the pecking order to Tet is this ancient Vietnamese tradition. Huge spreads of food are left out for lost spirits who, it's believed, wander the earth on this day. Held on the 15th day of the seventh moon.

September

Excellent time to tour the whole nation. The coastal resorts are less crowded and there are fewer people on the move. Temperatures and humidity levels drop.

✨ Vietnam's National Day

Big parades and events are held across Vietnam on 2 September. Celebrated with a rally and fireworks at Ba Dinh Sq, Hanoi, and there are also boat races on Hoan Kiem Lake.

✨ Hanoi Pride

Held in late September with events including film screenings, exhibitions, discussions and workshops.

October

A good time to visit the far north, with a strong chance of mild temperatures. Winter winds and rain begin to affect the centre, but down south it's often dry.

✨ Cham Kate Festival

Celebrated at Po Klong Garai Cham Towers in Thap Cham on the seventh month of the Cham calendar. The festival commemorates ancestors, Cham national heroes and deities. (p261)

🏃 Khmer Oc Bom Boc Festival

The Mekong Delta's Khmer community celebrates on the 15th day of the 10th moon of the lunar calendar with boat races at Ba Dong Beach in Tra Vinh province and on the Soc Trang River.

✨ Mid-Autumn Festival (Trung Thu)

A fine time for foodies, with moon cakes of sticky rice filled with lotus seeds, duck-egg yolks, raisins and other treats. Also known as the Full Moon Festival, it's celebrated on the 15th day of the eighth moon and can fall in September or October.

December

From mid-December the popular tourist resorts get increasingly busy. Steamy in the south, but can get chilly up north.

✨ Christmas Day (Giang Sinh)

Not a national holiday, but this is celebrated throughout Vietnam, particularly by the sizeable Catholic population.

Plan Your Trip
Itineraries

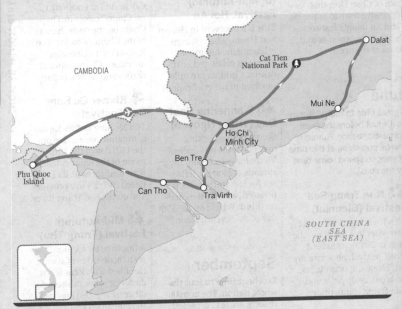

Dalat

Cat Tien
National Park

CAMBODIA

Mui Ne

Ho Chi
Minh City

Ben Tre

Phu Quoc
Island

Can Tho

Tra Vinh

SOUTH CHINA
SEA
(EAST SEA)

2 WEEKS Deep South

This itinerary takes in an offshore island blessed with wonderful sandy bays, the nation's main watersports centre and some fascinating floating villages. If tropical sunsets and white-sand beaches are high on your agenda, it's probably best not to plan this trip during the southern rainy season (roughly May to October). There's frequent public transport to all the main places.

After a couple of days enjoying the urban delights and compelling energy of **Ho Chi Minh City** (HCMC), head into the Mekong Delta, stopping at **Ben Tre** to explore canalside lanes by bike and islands by boat. Then hop aboard a cargo ship for a slow, scenic journey to **Tra Vinh** and take in the town's colourful pagodas. Next it's a short trip to **Can Tho**, where it's worth lingering a couple of days to visit the bustling floating markets, the city museum and a temple or two. Then head to **Phu Quoc Island** for three days of well-earned beach time on some of Vietnam's best sandy shores and seafood feasts at night.

Cai Rang Floating Market (p365), Can Tho

From Phu Quoc, fly (or bus it) back to HCMC, then head north into the south-central highlands via a night in **Cat Tien National Park**, home to gibbons, croco-diles and bountiful birdlife. Next up it's the hill station of **Dalat** for a tour of its quirky sights, and the opportunity to get stuck into some adventure sports such as canyoning, mountain biking or kayaking.

The road trip from Dalat down to **Mui Ne** is one of the nation's finest, negotiat-ing highland ridges and plunging through valleys and pine forests; it's ideally done on the back of a motorbike (consider hiring an Easy Rider). You can then rest up by the beach in Mui Ne for two or three days – a tropical idyll with towering sand dunes and a laid-back vibe – or for those with the stamina, get stuck into some crazy kite-surfing or a sailing course.

Round the trip off in style with a night in **HCMC**, perhaps with a meal at Hum Lounge followed by drinks somewhere atmospheric such as BiaCraft.

2 WEEKS From South to North

This route covers the nation's essential cultural sights and is bookended by its two greatest cities. You'll have an opportunity for some beach time, too. Definitely consider taking internal flights (or overnight trains) to save time.

The adventure begins in the cauldron of commerce that is **Ho Chi Minh City** (HCMC). Spend two to three days hitting the markets, browsing museums and eating some of Asia's best cuisine.

Then it's a plane or train up to **Danang** to access the cultured charmer and culinary hotspot that is **Hoi An**. This town certainly warrants three or four days, such is its allure. Enjoy Hoi An's unique ambience, touring its temples and Old Town, and visit the nearby beach of An Bang. Then it's on to the old imperial capital of **Hue** for two to three nights to explore the citadel, pagodas and tombs (and nearby beaches, in season).

Next it's a long journey by train (or a flight) to **Hanoi** to check out the capital's evocative Old Quarter, munch some street food and view the city's elegant architecture and cultural sights. From Hanoi book a tour to incomparable **Halong Bay**, which boasts more than 2000 limestone islands, before returning to Hanoi.

Above: Streets of Hoi An (p202)
Below left: Boat to Perfume Pagoda (p97), near Hanoi
Below: Tomb of Khai Dinh (p189), Hue

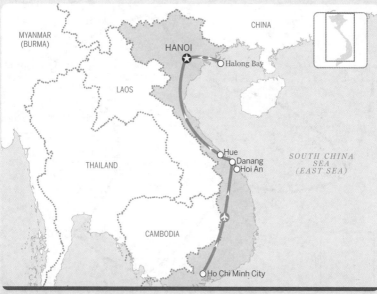

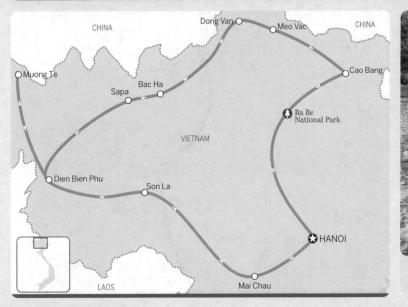

 Northern Mountains

Northern Vietnam is a world unto itself: a land of brooding mountains, overwhelming beauty and a mosaic of ethnic minorities. It's ideal terrain to cover on two wheels, with light traffic and breathtaking views, though, with a patient attitude, most of the region can be tackled by public transport.

Leaving **Hanoi**, head west to **Mai Chau**, home to the White Thai people, for your first two nights; it's a perfect introduction to ethnic minority life. Northwest, where the road begins to climb into the Tonkinese Alps, a logical overnight stop is **Son La**, a sleepy town where restaurants serve minority dishes.

Continue on for two nights at **Dien Bien Phu**, a name that resonates with history as it was here that the French-colonial story ended in defeat. Tour the military sights and impressive museum then continue north through stunning scenery up the Tram Ton Pass. If you're looking to get off the beaten track, consider a one- or two-night detour to **Muong Te**, a predominately White Thai enclave in the country's northwesternmost corner.

Sapa is the premier destination in the northwest, thanks to the infinite views (on a clear day!), and an amazing array of minority peoples. Explore the area on two feet or two wheels for around three days before heading to **Bac Ha** for four nights to experience the best of the region's markets. .

From Bac Ha, move east to Ha Giang province, taking it slowly through stunning scenery and towns including Yen Minh, Dong Van and Meo Vac. Explore remote destinations such as the Lung Cu flag tower and the Vuong Palace from **Dong Van**. Onwards towards the vertiginous Mai Pi Leng Pass and **Meo Vac**, there's no public transport (so you'll need to hire a car or *xe om* – motorbike taxi). The route then loops down to the riverside junction town of Bao Lac.

Local buses run from Bao Lac to **Cao Bang** and on to **Ba Be National Park**. Spend about three nights around Ba Be, staying at local Tay homestays and exploring the park by trekking or kayaking. From Ba Be buses run back south to Hanoi.

Top: Ban Gioc Waterfall (p124), Cao Bang
Above: Underground trench, A1 Hill (p128), Dien Bien Phu

Off the Beaten Track: Vietnam

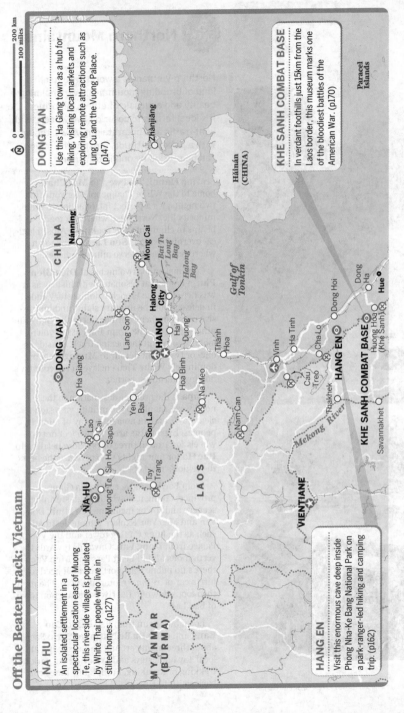

DONG VAN

Use this Ha Giang town as a hub for hiking, visiting local markets and exploring remote attractions such as Lung Cu and the Vuong Palace. (p147)

KHE SANH COMBAT BASE

In verdant foothills just 15km from the Laos border, this museum marks one of the bloodiest battles of the American War. (p170)

NA HU

An isolated settlement in a spectacular location east of Muong Te, this riverside village is populated by White Thai people who live in stilted homes. (p127)

HANG EN

Visit this enormous cave deep inside Phong Nha-Ke Bang National Park on a park-ranger-led hiking and camping trip. (p162)

0   200 km
0   100 miles

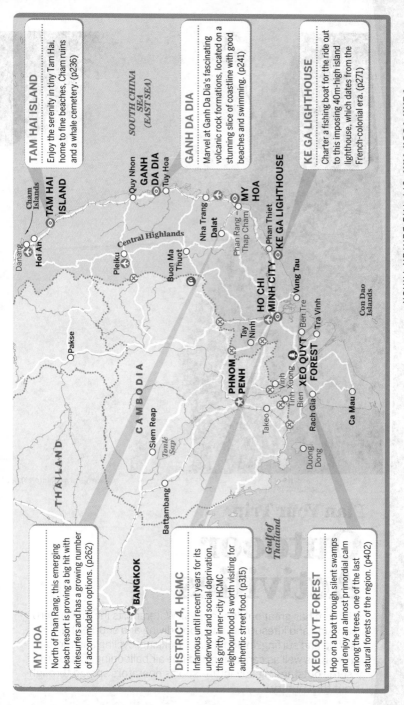

TAM HAI ISLAND

Enjoy the serenity in tiny Tam Hai, home to fine beaches, Cham ruins and a whale cemetery. (p236)

GANH DA DIA

Marvel at Ganh Da Dia's fascinating volcanic rock formations, located on a stunning slice of coastline with good beaches and swimming. (p241)

KE GA LIGHTHOUSE

Charter a fishing boat for the ride out to this imposing 40m-high island lighthouse, which dates from the French-colonial era. (p271)

MY HOA

North of Phan Rang, this emerging beach resort is proving a big hit with kitesurfers and has a growing number of accommodation options. (p262)

DISTRICT 4, HCMC

Infamous until recent years for its underworld and social deprivation, this gritty inner-city HCMC neighbourhood is worth visiting for authentic street food. (p315)

XEO QUYT FOREST

Hop on a boat through silent swamps and enjoy an almost primordial calm among the trees, one of the last natural forests of the region. (p402)

Canyoning, Datanla Falls (p286), near Dala

Plan Your Trip

Outdoor Activities

Vietnam has great outdoor appeal. Watersports include superb kayaking and kitesurfing, and good diving and snorkelling, sailing and surfing. Inland there's trekking, cycling and motor-biking, as well as canyoning and hot-air ballooning. There are some outstanding adventure-sports operators spread through-out the country.

Best Outdoors

Best Diving & Snorkelling

Con Dao Islands Remote, but the best.

Phu Quoc Visibility can be a challenge, but some nice coral gardens.

Nha Trang Professional scuba schools and many dive sites.

Best Trekking

Bac Ha Spectacular highland hiking incorporating village homestays.

Dong Van Trails in dramatic mountain scenery.

Mai Chau Sublime landscapes and tribal villages.

Kon Tum Treks to Sedang and Jarai minority hamlets.

Best Cycling

Dalat Base camp for numerous mountain trails.

Mekong Delta Back roads beside waterways.

Hoi An Flat terrain to explore craft villages and cut across rice paddies.

Best Kayaking

Cat Ba Island Paddle through spectacular limestone outcrops.

Ba Be National Park Explore this superlative lake district.

Hoi An Offers some superb riverside scenery.

Phong Nha-Ke Bang National Park Excellent trips along the region's rivers.

When to Go

Whether you're a committed kitesurfer or a warm-water diver, some careful planning is essential – Vietnam's climate is extremely variable and monsoon-dependent.

The action peaks for kitesurfers in winter (November to April). Surfing is also best at this time of year. Divers take note that water visibility is best in the calm months of June, July and August.

It would be foolish to attempt an ascent of Fansipan in the height of the rainy season, from May to September. Snorkelling and diving is not that rewarding between November and April when visibility drops.

Trekking

Vietnam offers excellent trekking and less strenuous walks. The scenery is often remarkable, with plunging highland valleys, tiers of rice paddies and soaring limestone mountains. Anything is possible, from half-day hikes to assaults on Fansipan, Vietnam's highest mountain.

Generally northern Vietnam is your best bet: its dramatic mountain paths and fascinating minority culture are huge draws. Elsewhere, national parks and nature reserves have established trails (and usually guides available to keep you on them).

Northern Vietnam

The region north of Hanoi is truly spectacular. Sapa (p131) is Vietnam's trekking hub, full of hiking operators and hire stores (renting out sleeping bags, boots and waterproof gear). Maps detailing trails are available, as are guides. The scenery is wonderful, with majestic mountains, impossibly green rice paddies and some fascinating tribal villages. But prepare yourself – the main trails are incredibly popular and some villages see hiking groups on an hourly basis. To trek remote paths you'll have to find an expert local guide.

At a lower elevation is Bac Ha (p141), less rainy and the trails are not heavily trampled. It's very picturesque, but it slightly lacks Sapa's drama in terms of high mountains. You will find great hikes to Flower Hmong and Nung villages.

High-altitude Ha Giang province (p143), in the extreme north of Vietnam, is the nation's Tibet. Hikers can hook up with guides in Ha Giang city, or head out to Dong Van where there are exciting trekking opportunities. Self-guided day hikes are a snap in and around the towns of Dong Van and Meo Vac.

If you're spooked by the prospect of climbing hills, Mai Chau (p125) offers great, fairly easy walking in an idyllic valley setting.

Elsewhere, Ba Be National Park (p120) has a network of rugged trails through spectacular karst scenery to minority villages, and Cat Ba (p107) boasts a popular 18km hike (and shorter alternatives such as Butterfly Valley).

Central Vietnam

Some outstanding treks and numerous trails have been developed between the limestone hills of Phong Nha-Ke Bang National Park (p160) by outfits such as Jungle Boss Trekking (p164), which offers hikes to the Abandoned Valley area and Ma Da. Many routes combine trekking with some caving or tubing. Vietnam's most famous trek is to the world's largest cave, Hang Son Doong, but numbers are strictly limited and it costs US$3000.

You'll find excellent trails inside Cuc Phuong National Park (p157) through superb forest and past ancient trees and caves to a minority village.

Close to Danang, Bach Ma National Park (p191) has some good hikes, while the Ba Na Hill Station (p202) has short trails and awesome views. Adventure-tour operators in Hoi An also offer some intriguing treks in the tribal areas west of town.

Southern Vietnam

With a bit of luck you might glimpse one of the dozens of mammals present in Yok Don National Park (p297) near Buon Ma Thuot. You'll need to hire a guide to make the most of Cat Tien National Park (p280),

where crocodiles can be seen and night hikes are possible; the Wild Gibbon Trek here is highly popular. Over in Dalat, adventure-tour operators including Phat Tire Ventures (p287) and Pine Track Adventures (p287) offer hikes: one rewarding area is the Bidoup Nui Ba National Park (p286).

Further south there's little for hikers to get excited about – the climate is perennially hot and humid and the landscape largely flat. Con Son (p407) is one curious exception, an island with cooling sea breezes and hikes through rainforest and mangroves.

Cycling

Bikes are a popular mode of transport in Vietnam, so cycling is an excellent way to experience the country. Basic bicycles can be rented for US$1 to US$3 per day, and good-quality mountain bikes for US$7 to US$18. E-bikes can also be rented in some places (from US$10).

The flat lands of the Mekong Delta region are ideal for long-distance rides down back roads. Good routes include the country lanes around Chau Doc, and the quiet road that runs along the Cambodian border from Chau Doc to Ha Tien (with a possible detour to Ba Chuc). There's also some nice cycling on the islands off Vinh Long.

Avoid Hwy 1 as insane traffic makes it tough going and dangerous. Consider the inland Ho Chi Minh Hwy (Hwys 14, 15 and 8), which offers some stunning scenery and little traffic. Hoi An is an excellent base for exploring craft villages and rural lanes, and there are several recommended tour operators running cycling tours. Hue is also a great place for cyclists, with temples, pagodas and the Perfume River.

In the southwest highlands, Dalat has lots of dirt trails and is the base camp for the dramatic two-day descent to Mui Ne.

Heading further north, the highly scenic region fringing Phong Nha-Ke Bang National Park is beginning to open for cycling. And in the far north the highland lanes around Ba Be National Park and Bac Ha offer fine riding.

ALT HIGHWAY 1

Highway 1's heavy traffic and trucks don't make for great motorbiking or bicycling. It's possible, with some careful planning, to loop off Hwy 1 at regular intervals and use coastal back roads:

➡ east of Hue between Thuan An and Vin Hien

➡ between Chi Thanh and the Hon Gom peninsula

➡ south of Nha Trang to the Cam Ranh airport

➡ between Phan Thiet and Vung Tau

➡ linking Phan Thiet, Mui Ne and Tuy Phong

Rice terraces surrounding Sapa (p131)

Motorbiking

Motorbiking through Vietnam is an unforgettable way to experience the nation. It's the mode of transport for most Vietnamese. Two wheels put you closer to the countryside – its smells, people and scenery – compared with getting around by car or bus. For those seeking true adventure, there is no better way to go.

However, obtaining a valid licence (p487) and travel insurance is tricky. Many travellers decide to risk it, but if you're in an accident you may not be covered. It's comparatively cheap to hire someone to drive a bike for you (from US$30 per day). Easy Riders is one such scheme.

Unless you relish getting high on exhaust fumes and barged by trucks, avoid too much time on Hwy 1. The inland Ho Chi Minh Hwy running the spine of the country from north to south is one alternative, though of course you miss out on the ocean. The stretch from Duc Tho to Phong Nha offers wonderful karst scenery, forests, little traffic and an excellent paved road.

Two of the most dramatic rides in the southern half of the country are the Hai Van Pass, featuring hairpin after hairpin and ocean views, and the spectacular road between Nha Trang and Dalat, which cuts through forests and takes in a 1700m pass.

There's more fine riding around the dramatic limestone hills that characterise both the Phong Nha-Ke Bang National Park and Ninh Binh region. Both areas have tour operators offering guided motorbiking excursions.

Further north, there's glorious mountain scenery, river valleys and tribal villages around Sapa and Dien Bien Phu. The route through Ha Giang province through Ha Giang, Dong Van and Bao Lac is the ultimate, with superlative vistas and stupendous mountain roads.

Surfing

There's surf most times of the year in Vietnam, though it isn't an acclaimed destination – the wave scene in *Apocalypse*

Now was shot in the Philippines. Dedicated surf shops are rare, but the odd guesthouse and adventure-sport tour operator have boards for hire.

Surf's up between November and April when the winter monsoon blows from the north. Several typhoons form in the South China Sea (East Sea) each year, and these produce the biggest wind swells.

The original GI Joe break, Danang Beach is a 30km stretch of sand, which can produce clean peaks greater than 2m, though watch out for pollution.

North of Quy Nhon, the stretch of coastline heading up towards Quang Ngai also has fine potential, though little or nothing in the way of facilities. Contact Haven (p241) for information in this area.

In high season, head to Bai Dai beach, 27km south of Nha Trang, where's there's a good left-hand break. Boards can be rented at Coco's Surf Kitchen Lounge (p259).

Beginners can head to Mui Ne, with multiple breaks around the bay, including short right- and left-handers. Further south, Vung Tau is inconsistent, but offers some of Vietnam's best waves when conditions are right. There's a watersports (p274) centre here.

Anyone searching for fresh waves in remote locations should be extremely wary of unexploded ordnance. Garbage, storm-water run-off and industrial pollution are other hazards.

BEST BEACHES

Drawing up a list of Vietnam's best beaches is a near-impossible task (there are a dozen idyllic coves in Phu Quoc alone) but here are our picks:

Northern and central coastlines Minh Chau Beach, An Bang Beach, Thuan An Beach

Southeast coastline Bai Mon, Quy Nhon, Mui Ne, Bai Xep, Doc Let

Island beaches Sao Beach, Phu Quoc, Bai Dat Doc, Con Dao Islands

---

Kitesurfing, Windsurfing & Sailing

Windsurfing and kitesurfing are taking off. Mui Ne Beach is a windchasers' hotspot in Asia with competitions and a real buzz about the place. My Hoa (p262), north of Ninh Chu Beach, is an emerging kitesurfing destination with a couple of kitesurf camps and a barefoot vibe. Nha Trang and Vung Tau are other possibilities.

Two-hour beginner lessons start at US$100; it's hard to get your head around all the basics (and also tough on your body!).

The best conditions in Mui Ne and My Hoa are between November and April. Mornings are ideal for beginners, while in the afternoon wind speeds regularly reach 35 knots.

Also based in Mui Ne, Manta Sail Training Centre (p265) is a very professional sailing outfit run by an Englishwoman, which offers training and boat rentals. In Phu Quoc, Viet Sail (p383) has dinghies and catamarans for training and excursions.

Diving & Snorkelling

Vietnam is not a world-class dive destination but it does have some fascinating dive sites. If you've experienced reefs in Indonesia or Australia, prepare yourself for less sea life and reduced visibility. The most popular scuba-diving and snorkelling is around Nha Trang (p251), where there are several reputable dive operators. Hoi An's dive schools head to the Cham Islands (p225), where macro life can be intriguing. Phu Quoc Island (p382) is another popular very spot.

Two fun dives typically cost US$65 to US$80; expect to pay US$25 to US$35 for snorkelling day trips. PADI or SSI Open Water courses cost between US$300 and US$475.

The Con Dao Islands offer unquestionably the best diving and snorkelling in Vietnam, with diverse (but not bountiful) marine life, fine reefs and even a wreck dive. However, prices are high (around US$160 for two dives).

Above: Hang Son
Doong (p162)

Right: Snorkelling off
Phu Quoc Island (p377)

Note that Vietnam is home to some dodgy dive shops, some of which have fake PADI credentials. Nha Trang in particular has several such places. Stick to reputable, recommended dive schools with good safety procedures, qualified instructors and well-maintained equipment.

Kayaking & SUP

Kayaking is very popular around Halong Bay. Many tours now include a spot of kayaking or stand-up paddleboarding through the karst islands, or you can choose a specialist and paddle around limestone pinnacles before overnighting on a remote bay.

Other key destinations include Cat Ba Island, Ba Be National Park, the Con Dao Islands, Phong Nha, Dalat, Cat Tien National Park and rivers in the Hoi An region. You can also rent sea kayaks and SUPs on many beaches including Nha Trang, Tam Hai, Mui Ne and Bai Xep.

Operators include Cat Ba Ventures (p110), SUP Monkey (p211), Hoi An Kayak Tours (p211) and Phat Tire Ventures (p287).

Whitewater Rafting

Rafting is in its infancy in Vietnam. Several outfits in Dalat offer trips, including Phat Tire Ventures (p287), which runs a tour down the Da Don River with Class II and III rapids, depending on the season, priced from US$69. Bike-rafting trips from Dalat to Nha Trang are also recommended. Rafting trips are also possible from Nha Trang with Shamrock Adventures (p252).

Caving

There are stupendous cave trips at Phong Nha-Ke Bang National Park (p160), many of which involve some hiking, swimming (there are a lot of river caves) and a short climb or two.

Specialist Oxalis Adventure Tours (p163) is the only operator licensed to take you to the wonders of Hang Son Doong, the world's largest cave. But if your budget won't stretch to this, other excellent options include Hang Toi (Dark Cave), which you can visit independently; this is a memorable day out that takes in some zip lining, cave swimming and kayaking. Cave expeditions are also offered by Phong Nha Farmstay Tours (p163).

You can also trek 7km inside remarkable Paradise Cave and there's the lovely swim-through Tu Lan cave system.

Rock Climbing & Canyoning

Cat Ba is the capital of the Vietnam climbing scene, with Langur's Adventures (p110) offering rope climbing on karst hills, deep-water soloing and climbing/kayaking combo excursions. In Hoi An, Phat Tire Ventures (p211) offers climbing and rappelling on a marble cliff.

Canyoning involves descending river valleys using a mixture of rappelling, scrambling, hiking and swimming. It's very popular in Dalat. Don't compromise on safety; only book canyoning trips through reputable, well-established companies. Sadly, travellers have died in canyoning accidents around Dalat.

Market stall, Hoi An (p202)

Plan Your Trip

Eat & Drink Like a Local

Showcasing fresh and vibrant flavours, excellent street food and elegant restaurants in restored colonial architecture, Vietnam is packed with superb opportunities for eating and drinking. Cookery classes, market visits and walking tours make it easy to discover the country's culinary heritage.

The Year in Food

Festivals and seasonal fresh fruit are the highlights of Vietnam.

19 January to 20 February

Tet (Vietnamese New Year) is a week of feasting with friends and family. Traditional dishes include *banh tet* (sticky rice with pork and egg) and *mut* (dried and sugared fruits).

March to June

Luscious mangoes from Cao Lanh in the Mekong Delta.

Mid-June to early July

Fresh lychees are sold across northern Vietnam.

June to July

Fragrant durian (and other fruit) is in season across the Mekong.

May to October

Fresh rambutan is popular during the rainy season.

August to November

Pomelos fill the markets of central Vietnam.

8 September to 7 October

Traditional moon cakes are eaten during Tet Trung Thu, the annual Full Moon Festival.

Food & Drink Experiences

Plan your travel around these tasty recommendations and understand the essence of Vietnamese cuisine.

Introducing Vietnamese Food

Welcome to your first night in Vietnam. Here's where to go to get up to speed with the country's cuisine.

Quan Bui (p331) Vietnamese flavours to seriously savour in Ho Chi Minh City (HCMC).

Chim Sao (p84) For terrific Viet salads and minority dishes from the north in Hanoi.

Street-Food Tours

Pull up a squat plastic stool and discover what makes Vietnam's street food exceptional.

Saigon Street Eats (p324), HCMC

Funtastic Danang Food Tour (p196), Danang

Eat Hoi An (p214), Hoi An

Hue Flavor (p182), Hue

Hanoi Street Food Tours (p74), Hanoi

Dalat Happy Tours (p287), Dalat

Best Fusion Restaurants

Discover the culinary intersection between Western flavours and Vietnamese cuisine at these elegant restaurants.

Nu Eatery (p215) Delivering Vietnamese and global flavours with aplomb in Hoi An.

La Badiane (p84) French flavours blend with Vietnamese in this leafy colonial villa in Hanoi.

Blanc Restaurant (p335) Classy HCMC restaurant putting a winning twist on Viet classics.

Mango Mango (p216) Superchef Duc's riverside restaurant is one of Hoi An's most creative.

Saigonese (p385) Celebrity-chef-worthy dishes elevate Vietnamese flavours on Phu Quoc Island.

Xu (p332) Stylish HCMC restaurant-lounge with an inventive Vietnamese-inspired fusion menu.

Vegetarian & Vegan Food

Com chay (vegetarian) restaurants serving vegan food can be found across Vietnam, often adjacent to Buddhist temples. Around the first and 15th days of the Buddhist calendar month, some food stalls substitute tofu in their dishes.

Hum Vegetarian Cafe & Restaurant (p334) Gourmet vegetarian cuisine in an elegant HCMC environment.

Vegan Zone (p213) Hoi An mecca of vegan eating.

V's Home (p81) This fine Hanoi restaurant is staffed by deaf people.

Street-food vendor

Au Lac (p255) Excellent plates of the day at this simple backstreet place in Nha Trang.

Lien Hoa (p185) Featuring flavour-packed dishes with aubergine and jackfruit; Hue.

Chay Garden (p335) A beautiful garden setting for a memorable vegetarian meal; HCMC.

Viet Chay Sala (p235) Excellent selection of tempting dips and sauces in Quang Ngai.

Minority Flavours

Curious travellers should seek out the food of Vietnam's ethnic minority groups. Look forward to occasionally challenging, but always interesting, dishes.

Hill Station Signature Restaurant (p138) Modern decor combines with dishes influenced by traditional Hmong cuisine in Sapa.

Chim Sao (p84) Hanoi favourite for terrific hill-tribe cuisine.

Pleiku (p298) Popular local street foods include *pho kho* (two-dish noodle) and *thit bo nuong ong* (beef cooked in bamboo pipe).

Quan Kien (p84) Dishes inspired by Hmong, Thai and Muong cuisine in Hanoi.

Vietnamese Coffee

Try these places to get your caffeine fix.

Cafe Duy Tri (p85) Dripping with heritage, and virtually unchanged for more than 75 years; Hanoi.

Cafe Pho Co (p85) Negotiate your way to a hidden balcony overlooking Hanoi's Hoan Kiem Lake.

K'Ho Coffee (p286) Sample coffee and buy freshly roasted beans at this highland plantation near Dalat.

Sound of Silence (p225) Sip a coconut coffee and gaze over an island-studded horizon.

TEA TOO

Northerners favour hot green tea, while in the south the same is often served over big chunks of ice. Chrysanthemum and jasmine infusions are also popular. Particularly delicious is a fragrant noncaffeinated tea made from lotus seeds. In the cities, bubble tea is wildly popular with young Viets.

Local market (p72) on P Gia Ngu, Hanoi

Vietnamese Flavours

Vietnamese palates vary from north to south, but no matter where they are, local cooks work to balance hot, sour, salty and sweet flavours in each dish.

Saltiness

Vietnamese food's saltiness comes from, well, salt, but also from the fermented seafood sauces that grace the shelves of every Vietnamese pantry. The most common is *nuoc mam* (fish sauce), which is made from small fish (most often anchovies) that are layered with salt in large containers, weighted to keep the fish submerged in their own liquid, and left in a hot place for up to a year. As they ferment, the fish release a fragrant (some might say stinky) liquid. The first extraction, called *nuoc mam cot*, is dark brown and richly flavoured – essentially an 'extra virgin' fish sauce reserved for table use. The second extraction, obtained by adding salted water to the already fermented fish, is used for cooking. Phu Quoc Island is famous for its *nuoc mam*, though some cooks prefer the milder version made around coastal Phan Thiet.

Sweetness

Sugar's centrality to the cuisine is best illustrated by the ever popular *kho*, a sweet-savoury dish of fish or meat simmered in a clay pot with fish sauce and another oft-used seasoning – bitter caramel sauce made from cane sugar. Vietnamese cooks also use sugar to sweeten dipping sauces, desserts and, of course, coffee.

Sourness

Sweetness is countered with fruity tartness, derived from lime (to squeeze into noodle soups and dipping sauces) and from *kalamansi* (a small, green-skinned, orange-fleshed citrus fruit), the juice of which is combined with salt and black pepper as a delicious dip for seafood, meats and omelettes. In the south, tamarind is added as a souring agent to a fish-and-vegetable soup called *canh chua*, and to a delectable dish of whole prawns coated with sticky, sweet-and-sour sauce called *tom rang me*. Northern cooks who seek sourness are more likely to turn to vinegar. A clear, yellowish vinegar mixed with chopped ginger is often served alongside snail specialities such as *bun oc* (rice noodle and snail soup).

Herbs

Vietnamese food is often described as 'fresh' and 'light' owing to the plates heaped with gorgeous fresh herbs that seem to accompany every meal. Coriander, mint and anise-flavoured Thai basil will be familiar to anyone who's travelled in the region. Look also for green-and-garnet *perilla* leaves; small, pointy, pleasantly peppery, astringent *rau ram* leaves; and *rau om* (a rice-paddy herb), which has delicate leaves that hint of lemon and cumin. *Rau om* invariably shows up atop bowls of *canh chua*. Shallots, thinly sliced and slowly fried in oil until caramelised, add a bit of sweetness when sprinkled on salad and noodle dishes.

Chilli & Pepper

Vietnamese cooking uses less hot chilli than Thai cuisine, though it's a key ingredient in central Vietnamese meals. Local chillies vary from the mild-flavoured, long, red, fleshy variety that appears in many southern dishes and is served chopped to accompany noodles, to the smallish pale-chartreuse specimen served as an accompaniment in restaurants specialising in Hue cuisine. Beware: the latter really packs a punch. Dried ground chillies and spicy chilli sauces are tabletop condiments in many a central Vietnamese eatery.

Vietnam is a huge peppercorn exporter, and ground black and white peppercorns season everything from rice porridge to beef stew. Vietnamese black peppercorns put what's sold in supermarkets back home to shame; if your country will allow it in, a 500g bag makes a fine edible souvenir.

Fish Flavours

When it comes to fermented fish products, *nuoc mam* is only the tip of the iceberg. *Mam tom* is a violet (some would also say violent!) paste of salted, fermented shrimp. It's added to noodle soups, smeared onto rice-paper rolls, and even served as a dip for sour fruits such as green mango. It also lends a pungent salty backbone to specialities such as *bun mam* (a southern fish-and-vegetable noodle soup). *Mam tom* has many versions in Vietnam, including ones made from crabs, shrimp of all sizes and various types of fish. Try to get past the odour and sample a range of dishes made with it: the flavour it lends to food is much more subtle than its stench might imply.

Fish flavours also come from dried seafood. Vietnamese cooks are quite choosy about dried shrimp, with market stalls displaying up to 15 grades. You'll also find all sorts and sizes of dried fish, and dried squid.

Sauces, Spices & Curries

Vietnamese cooks use quite a few sauces, such as soy, oyster and fermented soybean – culinary souvenirs of China's almost 1000-year rule over the country's north.

RICE

Rice, or *com*, is the very bedrock of Vietnamese cuisine. In imperial Hue, rice with salt was served to distinguished guests by royal mandarins; these days locals eat at least one rice-based meal every day and offer a bowl of rice to departed ancestors.

If a Vietnamese says, 'An com' (literally 'let's eat rice'), it's an invitation to lunch or dinner. You can also get your fill of the stuff, accompanied by a variety of stir-fried meat, fish and vegetable dishes, at specialised, informal eateries called *quan com binh dan*.

Cooked to a soupy state with chicken, fish, eel or duck, rice becomes *chao* (rice porridge); fried in a hot wok with egg, vegetables and other ingredients, it's *com rang;* and 'broken' into short grains, steamed, topped with barbecued pork, an egg, and sliced cucumber, and accompanied by *nuoc cham* (a dipping sauce of sweetened fish sauce), it's *com tam*. Tiny clams called *hen* are sautéed with peppery Vietnamese coriander and ladled over rice to make *com hen*.

Sticky or glutinous rice (white, red and black) is mixed with pulses or rehydrated dried corn, peanuts and sesame seeds for a filling breakfast treat called *xoi (ngo* in central Vietnam). It can also be mixed with sugar and coconut milk then moulded into sweet treats, or layered with pork and steamed in bamboo or banana leaves for *banh chung*, a Tet speciality.

Soaked and ground into flour, rice becomes the base for everything from noodles and sweets to crackers and the dry, round, translucent 'papers' that Vietnamese moisten before using to wrap salad rolls and other specialities.

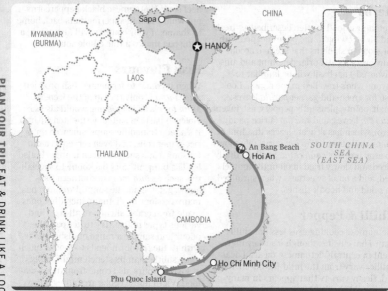

The Ultimate Vietnamese Food Tour

Start in **Ho Chi Minh City**, Vietnam's energetic southern hub, and negotiate the city's street-food scene with Saigon Street Eats (p324) or Vespa Adventures (p324). Adjourn to BiaCraft (p339) for artisan ales.

Consider a southern sojourn on **Phu Quoc Island**, taking in grilled seafood at the Phu Quoc Night Market (p385), before heading north to **Hoi An**. Once one of Asia's most cosmopolitan ports, Hoi An now hosts international visitors at the town's many cookery schools. Learn the secrets of local cuisine at the Red Bridge Cooking School (p214), and uncover street-food flavours with the Eat Hoi An (p214) food tour.

Detour to nearby **An Bang Beach** for excellent seafood by the sand, then try Hoi An's signature dish *cao lau* (Japanese-style noodles with herbs, salad greens, bean sprouts and roast pork) at Streets (p215). Continue north to **Hanoi**, and negotiate the bustling labyrinth of the Old Quarter with Hanoi Street Food Tours (p74). Iconic Hanoi dishes to try include *cha ca* (grilled fish with turmeric and dill) at Cha Ca Thang Long (p80), *pho bo* (beef noodle soup) and hotpots; head to P Truc Bach (p80) for the latter.

Learn about northern Vietnamese cuisine at the Hanoi Cooking Centre (p73), try dishes inspired by Vietnam's ethnic minorities at Quan Kien (p84) or Chim Sao (p84), and then head north to **Sapa**, the heartland region of minority groups including the Hmong and the Red Dzao. Experience Hmong-inspired dishes at Hill Station Signature Restaurant (p138), book in for its cooking class, and toast your new knowledge of Vietnamese cuisine with a *ruou* (rice wine) tasting set.

For more itineraries, see our Itineraries chapter on p26.

Warm spices such as star anise and cinnamon are essential to a good *pho*.

Curries were introduced to Vietnam by Indian traders; now they're cooked up using locally made curry powder and paste packed in oil. Vietnamese curries, such as *ca ri ga* (chicken curry cooked with coconut milk and lemongrass) and *lau de* (curried goat hotpot), tend to be more aromatic than fiery.

PLAN YOUR TRIP EAT & DRINK LIKE A LOCAL

> ### BANH MI
>
> A legacy of the French, *banh mi* refers to the crackly crusted rice- and wheat-flour baguettes sold everywhere, and the sandwiches made with them, stuffed with meats, veggies and pickles. If you haven't tried stuffed *banh mi*, you haven't eaten in Vietnam.

Regional Specialities

Travelling north to south is a Vietnamese journey that, geographically and gastronomically, begins in China and ends in Southeast Asia. Differences in history, culture and geography combine for many techniques, ingredients and tastes, all linked by the Vietnamese love for vibrant flavours, fresh herbs, noodles and seafood.

Northern Vietnam

Northern Vietnamese food bears the imprint of centuries of Chinese occupation. Comforting noodle dishes, mild flavours and rustic elegance underpin the region's cuisine. Soy is used as frequently as fish sauce, vinegar adds sourness rather than lime juice or tamarind, chillies give way to black pepper, and long cooking times coax maximum flavour from unpretentious ingredients.

Banh cuon These rolls are made from rice-flour batter that's poured onto a piece of muslin cloth stretched over a steamer; once firm, the noodle sheet is scattered with chopped pork, mushrooms and dried shrimp, then rolled up, sprinkled with crispy shallots, and served alongside a tangle of bean sprouts, slivered cucumber and chopped fresh herbs, with a saucer of *nuoc cham* (dipping sauce) for drizzling. In the far north, the dish is served with a small bowl of broth, which is seasoned and used for dipping.

Bun cha This street favourite features barbecued sliced pork or pork patties served with thin rice vermicelli, fresh herbs and green vegetables, and a bowl of lightly sweetened *nuoc mam* with floating slices of pickled vegetables. The Hanoi version combines sliced pork belly and pork patties formed from chopped pork shoulder.

Pho bo A northern culinary highlight is *pho bo* (beef noodle soup). A good *pho* hinges on the broth, which is made from beef bones boiled for hours with shallot, ginger, fish sauce, black cardamom, star anise and cassia. Hard-core northern

pho lovers frown upon adding lime, basil and bean sprouts to their bowls.

Banh da cua This combination of hearty, dark rice noodles in a clear broth with pork balls, shrimp and morning glory is a breakfast staple and the signature dish of Haiphong.

Central Vietnam

Positioned between culinary extremes, the food of central Vietnam combines moderation and balance – except where it concerns the locals' love of chilli. People cook from the land, transforming modest resources into fare fit for an emperor. Everything seems smaller; baguettes and herbs are miniature versions of their southern selves, while Hue's imperial cuisine showcases dainty, delicate dishes. One edible legacy of the royal court is easily found on the street: *banh beo*, delicate steamed cakes made from rice flour. The central Vietnamese like gutsy and spicy flavours, including briny shrimp sauce and spritely lemongrass.

Banh khoai These dessert-plate-sized crêpes are made with rice-flour batter and cooked with oil in special long-handled pans. With a spare filling of shrimp, pork, egg and bean sprouts, they are encased with fresh herbs in lettuce, and then dunked in a sauce based on earthy fermented soybeans.

Bun bo Hue This rice-noodle soup with beef and pork exemplifies the central Vietnamese proclivity for spicy food. Tinged yellow-orange by chillies and annatto, the broth is laden with lemongrass notes and anchored by *mam tom* (savoury shrimp sauce).

Com hen Rice is served with the flesh of tiny clams, their cooking broth, and garnishes including roasted rice crackers, crisp pork crackling, peanuts, sesame seeds, fresh herbs and vegetables.

Southern Vietnam

Southern cuisine emphasises the region's abundance and tends to be on the sweet side. Vendors at southern markets display

JOANNATKACZUK/SHUTTERSTOCK ©

Above: *Banh xeo*
Left: Vietnamese
ingredients

VIETNAMESE COFFEE COMBOS

Enjoying a Vietnamese coffee is a tradition that can't be rushed. A glass tumbler, topped with a curious aluminium lid is placed before you while you crouch on a tiny blue plastic chair. A layer of condensed milk on the bottom of the glass is gradually infused with coffee lazily drip, drip, dripping from the aluminium top. Minutes pass, and eventually a darker caffeine-laden layer floats atop the condensed milk. Stir it together purposefully – maybe pouring it over ice in a separate glass – and it's definitely an energising ritual worth waiting for. And while you're drip-watching, consider the *caphe* variations usually on offer in a Vietnamese cafe.

Caphe sua da Iced coffee with condensed milk.

Caphe da Iced coffee without milk.

Caphe den Black coffee.

Caphe sua chua Iced coffee with yoghurt.

Caphe trung da Coffee topped with a beaten egg yolk.

lush, big-leafed herbs, colourful fruits and the freshest fish. Coconut milk infuses mild curries and lends richness to sweets. The southern love of fresh herbs, fruit and vegetables comes to the fore in refreshing *goi* (salads) of green papaya, grapefruit-like pomelo or lotus stems.

Canh chua ca This soup is the Mekong Delta in a bowl: snake head or catfish; fruits such as tomato and pineapple; and vegetables including bean sprouts, okra and *bac ha* (taro stem), all in a broth that's tart with tamarind and salty with *nuoc mam*.

Banh mi This baguette sandwich is a legacy of French and Chinese colonialism, but it's 100% Vietnamese. The filling might be a smearing of pâté or a few slices of silky sausage, mayonnaise moistens the bread and soy sauce imparts *umami* (savoury) goodness.

Banh xeo This giant crispy, chewy rice crêpe is crammed with pork, shrimp, mung beans and bean sprouts. Take a portion and encase it in lettuce or mustard leaf, add some fresh herbs, then dunk it in *nuoc cham*.

Drinks

Spirits

Vietnam distills a number of its own spirits. Distilled sticky-rice wine called *ruou* is often flavoured with herbs, spices and fruits (and even animals such as lizards). Travel to the northern highlands and you may be offered *ruou can*, sherry-like rice wine drunk through long bamboo straws from a communal vessel.

Beer

Beer is ubiquitous in Vietnam. Sooner or later every traveller succumbs to *bia hoi* ('fresh' or draught beer) – local brews served straight from the keg for a pittance (from 5000d) from specialist streetside bars. If you're looking to pay a little more, Saigon and Huda brands are decent, and La Rue, brewed on the central coast, is quite good. Expect to pay 20,000d to 25,000d for a beer in an ordinary bar, and maybe double that in a lounge.

The craft-beer scene is strongest in HCMC and Hanoi, where you'll find many specialist pubs and bars perfect for quaffing an IPA, dark ale or wheat beer. Prices start at around 50,000d a glass.

Coffee & Tea

Vietnam is the world's second-biggest coffee producer. Whiling away a morning or an afternoon over endless glasses of iced coffee is something of a ritual for Vietnam's male population. Espresso coffee is also available in cities and tourist destinations.

The preparation, serving and drinking of tea (*tra* in the south and *che* in the north) has a social importance. Serving tea in the home or office is more than a gesture of hospitality; it is a ritual.

Juices

Interesting local options include *mia da*, a freshly squeezed sugar-cane juice that's especially refreshing served over ice with a squeeze of *kalamansi*. *Sinh to* are fresh-fruit smoothies blended to order.

Regions at a Glance

Vietnam is incredibly varied – physically, climatically and culturally. Jagged alpine peaks define the northern provinces and a pancake-flat river delta enriches the endless rice paddies of the far south. Cave-riddled limestone hills loom over the central belt and there are dense rainforests along its western border.

The northern half of the nation experiences a much cooler winter, and the cuisine, lifestyle and character of the people reflect this. As you head south, the country has more of a tropical feel, with coconut trees outnumbering bamboo plants and fish sauce replacing soy sauce on the menu. The southern provinces are always humid, hot and sticky, their food sweet, spicy, aromatic and complex.

Top: Ta Prohm (p428), Angkor, Cambodia
Centre: Nha Trang Beach (p246)
Bottom: Rush hour, Ho Chi Minh City (p305)

Hanoi

Food
Temples
Cafe Culture

Spectacular Street Food

Dine in elegantly restored colonial villas, or pull up a stool and chow down on street-food classics including *pho bo* (beef noodle soup) or *bun cha* (barbecued pork with rice vermicelli).

Religion Before Communism

A millennium of history including periods of Chinese and French occupation has left a legacy of religious and spiritual tradition evident in Hanoi's many surviving temples and churches.

Cafe Cool

Hanoi's coffee scene is endlessly diverting, with a heady mix of charming cafes in heritage buildings and time-honoured, family-owned coffee shops. When in town, it's mandatory to sink a Hanoi egg coffee.

p55

Northern Vietnam

Landscapes
Culture
Adventure

Limestone Peaks

Halong Bay's majestic islands are perhaps best observed shrouded in morning mist, which gives them an ethereal air. To the north, the sublime mountainous scenery of Ha Giang province is arguably even more spectacular.

Local Life

The cascading rice paddies around Sapa and Bac Ha are a spectacular hub for trekking and homestays with ethnic minorities, including the colourful Dzao and Flower Hmong people.

Active Adventures

Adventurous detours in northern Vietnam include rock climbing on Cat Ba Island or kayaking to hidden coves and sandy beaches in nearby Lan Ha Bay.

p101

Central Vietnam

Food
History
Landscapes

Local Flavours

Partner with local foodies to discover flavour-packed street food unique to Hoi An and Hue – including Hue's famed Imperial cuisine – before dining at sophisticated restaurants helmed by international chefs crafting innovative fusion menus.

Centuries of History

The storied layers of history in this diverse, compelling region include Hue's enchanting imperial Citadel, wartime sites of the DMZ and ancient Cham temples of My Son.

Stunning Scenery

The area around Ninh Binh is typified by sublime limestone mountains. Further south, Phong Nha-Ke Bang National Park offers more of the same, plus several immense cave systems.

p151

Southeast Coast

Beaches
Temples
Watersports

Inspiring Coastlines

Vietnam's coastline at its most enticing. Mui Ne and Nha Trang are the big hitters, but do investigate less hyped beaches such as Bai Xep and the secret coves of the Con Dao Islands.

Ancient Temples

The kingdom of Champa once held sway over much of this region. Its legacy is still visible in a host of ancient brick temples, including the Po Nagar towers (Nha Trang) and the Po Klong Garai towers (Thap Cham).

Life on the Ocean Wave

This is undoubtedly the best region in Vietnam for watersports: kitesurfing is king in Mui Ne and My Hoa; Con Dao and Nha Trang draw scuba divers; and you'll also find surf breaks about.

p231

Southwest Highlands

Wildlife
Adventure
Culture

National Parks

Explore some of Vietnam's leading national parks where the wild things are. Cat Tien is home to endangered primates and the innovative Wild Gibbon Trek. Yok Don, easily accessible from Buon Ma Thuot, is where elephants roam.

Adrenaline Rush

Dalat is the place to sign up for waterfall canyoning, mountain biking, rafting and hiking, but also consider Cat Tien National Park for jungle walks.

Meet the Locals

Leave the lowlanders behind on the coast and meet the high-ground minority people. Get to know them better with a traditional village homestay around Kon Tum.

p279

Ho Chi Minh City

Eating & Drinking
History
Tours

Food & Drink

This is Vietnam at its most cosmopolitan and cool. HCMC has interesting cafes and the country's best international restaurants, most stylish cocktail bars and liveliest craft breweries.

Military History

The fall/liberation of Saigon was one of the 20th century's defining moments. Explore sites associated with the American War, from the tunnels at Cu Chi to the War Remnants Museum and Reunification Palace.

Metropolitan Buzz

From an after-dark street-food exploration on two wheels to quirky walking tours uncovering street art and hip cafes hidden in heritage apartments, HCMC has a fascinating array of fun and informative tours.

p305

Mekong Delta

Beaches
Boat Trips
Sanctuaries

White Sands

The white sands of gorgeous Sao Beach and graceful Long Beach on Phu Quoc Island are the Mekong Delta's trump cards. The island's a world away from the muddy riverbanks of the delta. Don't forget your beach gear.

Waterways

Boat trips are essential for understanding how water defines this part of Vietnam, a region where children don life jackets to swim all day and the river can get so wide that you almost lose sight of either bank.

Nature Reserves

Only the sound of paddling water interrupts the bird calls as you glide through the superb wetlands of Tra Su Bird Sanctuary in Chau Doc.

p353

Siem Reap & the Temples of Angkor (Cambodia)

Temples
Dining
Activities

Khmer Kingdoms

It's not all about Angkor Wat. True, the 'city that is a temple' is one of the world's most iconic buildings, but nearby are the enigmatic faces of the Bayon, the jungle temple of Ta Prohm and the inspirational carvings of Banteay Srei.

Foodie Heaven

Contemporary Khmer, spiced-up street food, fine French and a whole host more, plus legendary Pub St – Siem Reap is where it's happening.

Culture Fix

When not visiting temples, you can see Angkor by helicopter, zip line through the jungle or quad bike through rice fields and villages. For a slower pace, take a cooking class or unwind with a massage.

p413

On the
Road

**Northern
Vietnam**
p101
⭐ **Hanoi**
p55

**Central
Vietnam**
p151

**Siem Reap & the
Temples of Angkor
(Cambodia)**
p413
●

**Southwest
Highlands**
p279

**Southeast
Coast**
p231

● **Ho Chi
Minh City**
p305

**Mekong
Delta**
p353

AT A GLANCE

POPULATION
8 million

**UNESCO WORLD
HERITAGE SITE**
Imperial Citadel of
Thang Long (p67)

**BEST LOCAL
SEAFOOD**
Đuong Thuy
Khue (p80)

BEST HOSTEL
Tomodachi
House (p76)

**BEST HILLTRIBE
CUISINE**
Chim Sao (p84)

WHEN TO GO
Jan–Apr Cooler
days collide with the
energy and colour of
the Tet festival.

Jun–Aug Heavy heat
and humidity signals
low season in Hanoi:
bargains on hotel
suites abound.

Oct–Dec Clear,
sunny days and
cooler temperatures
make this the ideal
time to visit Hanoi.

Temple of Literature (p65)
CHARLIE TONG/GETTY IMAGES ©

Hanoi

Vietnam's capital is a city with one foot buried in a fascinating past, while the other strides confidently towards tomorrow. With five million motorbikes, it surges with the incessant din of blaring horns, while historical nuggets from periods of French and Chinese rule glint in the haze, overlooking crowded intersections or stuffed down hidden alleyways. Explore the streets and alleys of the Old Quarter, where farmers hawk their produce while city folk breakfast on noodles, practise t'ai chi at dawn or play chess with goateed grandfathers. Devour divine food at every corner, sample market wares, uncover an evolving arts scene and hunt down the perfect Hanoi egg coffee. Meet the people, delve into the past and witness the awakening of a Hanoi on the move.

History

The site where Hanoi stands today has been inhabited since the Neolithic period. Emperor Ly Thai To moved his capital here in AD 1010, naming it Thang Long (Ascending Dragon).

The decision by Emperor Gia Long, founder of the Nguyen dynasty in 1802, to rule from Hue relegated Hanoi to the status of a regional capital for a century. The city was named Hanoi by Emperor Tu Duc in 1831, from the words 'Ha' meaning 'river' and 'Noi' meaning 'inside', referring to its position within a bend of the Song Hong (Red River).

From 1902 to 1953, Hanoi served as the capital of French Indochina and was proclaimed capital of the Democratic Republic of Vietnam by Ho Chi Minh during the August Revolution of 1945. The French restored control and the First Indochina War ensued until 1954. Following the Geneva Accords of the same year, the Viet Minh, having driven the French from the city, were able to return.

During the American War, heavy US bombing destroyed parts of Hanoi and killed hundreds of civilians. One of the prime targets was the 1682m Long Bien Bridge. US aircraft repeatedly bombed this strategic point, yet after each attack the Vietnamese managed to improvise replacement spans and return road and rail services. It is said that the US military ended the attacks when US prisoners of war (POWs) were put to work repairing the structure. Today the bridge is renowned as a symbol of the tenacity and strength of the people of Hanoi.

It's hard to believe that Hanoi's millions of motorbikes and scooters would have been an uncommon sight as recently as the early 1990s, when most people got around on bicycles and the occasional Soviet-era bus. Today Hanoi's conservationists fight to save historic structures, as the city struggles to cope with a booming population, soaring pollution levels and inefficient public transport that is only now being invigorated with a metro system.

The city remains richly decorated with colonial architecture, hidden-away temples and tempting little alleyways that honeycomb town; while voracious modernisation may have drowned out much of Hanoi's vibrant palette of Vietnamese, French, Russian and American influences, many tempting islets of heritage remain in the churning sea of modern construction.

◉ Sights

◉ Old Quarter

Hanoi's historic heart, the 'Old Quarter', is home to over 1000 years of trade, commerce and activity, with no signs of slowing down. While its name tends to evoke images of ancient lamp-lit streets lined with the wooden storefronts of traditional artisans, merchants and craftspeople, you'll find the reality of the Old Quarter perhaps more busy than romantic, though you'll sense a charm here, and if you keep your eyes peeled you'll spot temples poking out of nowhere, sometimes down slender alleyways, and festooned with *chu nho* Chinese characters. The Old Quarter is what Hanoi is all about, and much of the enticement is the perception of a thriving and pulsing community.

The Old Quarter evolved between the Song Hong and the smaller To Lich River, which once flowed through the city centre in an intricate network of canals and waterways. Waters could rise as high as 8m during the monsoon. Dykes, which can still be seen along Tran Quang Khai, were constructed to protect the city.

In the 13th century, Hanoi's 36 guilds established themselves here, each taking a different street – hence the Vietnamese '36 Pho Phuong' (36 Guild Sts). There are more than double that many streets in the area today, typically named Pho Hang (Merchandise St), followed by the word for the product traditionally sold there. Some of the specialised streets include P Hang Quat, with its red candlesticks, funeral boxes, flags and temple items; and the more glamorous P Hang Gai, with its silk, embroidery, lacquerware, paintings and water puppets. Street names today do not always reflect the type of businesses in operation, however, and are historic in meaning and association.

Exploring the maze of backstreets is fascinating: some open up while others narrow into a warren of alleys. The area is known for its tunnel (or tube) houses, so called because of their narrow frontages and long rooms, developed to avoid taxes based on the width of their street frontage. By feudal law, houses were also limited to two storeys and, out of respect for the king, could not be taller than the royal palace. Today, as Old Quarter real-estate prices are

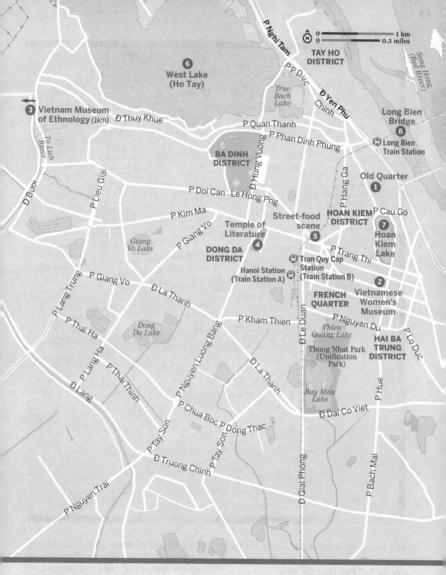

Hanoi Highlights

1 **Old Quarter** (p56)
Experiencing Asia at its
rawest, pulsating best in the
labyrinthine streets.

2 **Vietnamese Women's
Museum** (p63) Celebrating
the strength and heroism of
the country's women.

3 **Vietnam Museum of
Ethnology** (p71) Piecing

together Vietnam's ethnic
mosaic.

4 **Temple of Literature**
(p65) Stepping into history at
this Confucian retreat.

5 **Street-food scene** (p80)
Getting an authentic taste of
the city on its food streets.

6 **West Lake** (p71) Escaping the hustle and bustle on

a walking path around the
waters.

7 **Hoan Kiem Lake** (p61)
Waking at dawn to ease
peacefully into another Hanoi
day with the t'ai chi buffs.

8 **Long Bien Bridge** (p59)
Contemplating the atrocities
of war and the resilience of the
Vietnamese.

HANOI SIGHTS

Greater Hanoi

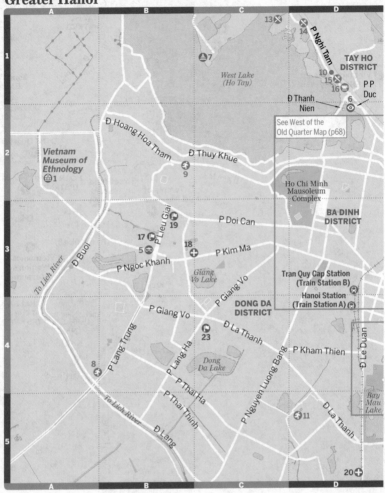

at a premium, most of the streets are lined with narrow and skinny, hastily constructed, six- to 10-storey buildings.

A stroll through the historic Old Quarter can last from an hour to a whole day, depending on your pace and demeanour, during which there are opportunities to dispense with your fistfuls of Vietnamese dong.

⭐**Bach Ma Temple**   TEMPLE
(Den Bach Ma; Map p60; cnr P Hang Buom & P Hang Giay; ⏰ 8-11am & 2-5pm Tue-Sun) FREE In the heart of the Old Quarter, the small Bach Ma Temple (literally 'White Horse Temple')

is said to be the oldest temple in the city, though much of the current structure dates from the 18th century and a shrine to Confucius was added in 1839. It was originally built by Emperor Ly Thai To in the 11th century to honour a white horse that guided him to this site, where he chose to construct his city walls.

Pass through the wonderful old wooden doors of the pagoda to see a statue of the legendary white horse, as well as a beautiful red-lacquered funeral palanquin. At the time of research the temple was shut for restoration.

Long Bien Bridge BRIDGE
(Cau Long Bien; Map p58) A symbol of the tenacity and resilience of the Hanoian people, the Long Bien Bridge (built between 1899 and 1902) was bombed on several occasions during the American War, and each time quickly repaired by the Vietnamese. Designed by Gustave Eiffel (of Eiffel Tower fame), the bridge, used by trains, mopeds and pedestrians, is undergoing reconstruction to restore its original appearance. It's colourfully illuminated at night.

Dong Xuan Market MARKET
(Cho Dong Xuan; Map p60; cnr P Hang Khoai & P Dong Xuan; ⊙6am-7pm) The largest covered market in Hanoi was originally built by the French in 1889 and almost completely destroyed by fire in 1994. Almost everything

★**Heritage House** HISTORIC BUILDING
(Ngoi Nha Di San; Map p60; 87 P Ma May; 10,000d; ⊙9am-noon & 1-6pm) One of the Old Quarter's best-restored properties, this traditional merchants' house is sparsely but beautifully decorated, with rooms filled with fine furniture set around two courtyards. Note the high steps between rooms, a traditional design incorporated to stop the flow of bad energy around the property. There are crafts and trinkets for sale here, including silver jewellery, basketwork and Vietnamese tea sets, and there's usually a calligrapher or another craftsperson at work too.

Old Quarter

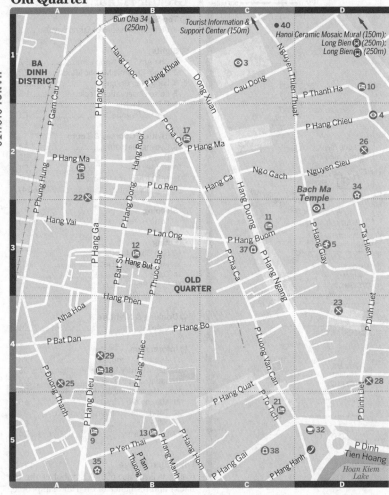

you can think of, from fresh (and live) produce to cheap clothing, souvenirs, consumer goods and traditional arts and crafts, can be found inside. Stalls continue selling outside on Friday, Saturday and Sunday nights.

Hanoi Ceramic Mosaic Mural PUBLIC ART
(Con Duong Gom Su; Map p58; ⏱24hr) FREE
Spanning almost 4km along the Song Hong dyke, from its terminus at the Long Bien Bridge, this mural project holds the Guinness World Record for being the largest ceramic mosaic on the planet. The colourful mural lines busy roads, uses ceramics produced at nearby Bat Trang and depicts

different periods in Vietnam's history. Local and international artists commenced work on the project in 2007; it was completed in 2010 for Hanoi's 1000th-birthday celebrations. New sections have recently been added and the mural continues to grow.

Old East Gate LANDMARK
(Cua O Quan Chuong; Map p60) Of the former 16 medieval gates to the city, only this single stone and brick gate remains. The portal – still used by scooter traffic – is inscribed on the north side with the *chu nho* characters 東河門 (East River Gate).

◉ Around Hoan Kiem Lake

Extending south of the Old Quarter is the city's most attractive and photogenic lake: Hoan Kiem Lake, which serves as a handy cartographic reference point for the rest of the city. The area can be explored at any time, though sunset is a particularly romantic time for lake-shore wanderers and photographers. The twin bell towers of St Joseph Cathedral – Hanoi's most imposing chunk of church heritage and one of the city's most-visited sights – rises up to the west of the water; take in the scene of the church and the plaza in front through the steam of a cappuccino from an assortment of artfully positioned cafes. Riddled with small lanes, the bustling area around the church similarly abounds with restaurant choice. Southwest of the lake lies a further, important piece of Hanoi heritage: the Hoa Lo Prison Museum, sarcastically known by its American wartime occupants as the 'Hanoi Hilton'.

★ Hoan Kiem Lake LAKE

(Map p64) Legend claims that, in the mid-15th century, heaven sent Emperor Ly Thai To a magical sword, which he used to drive the Chinese from Vietnam. After the war a giant golden turtle grabbed the sword and disappeared into the depths of this lake to restore the sword to its divine owners, inspiring the name Ho Hoan Kiem (Lake of the Restored Sword).

The area is best from Friday to Sunday: nearby traffic is banned between 7pm and midnight and a public-square, funfair vibe takes over.

Every morning at around 6am local residents practise t'ai chi on the shore. Sunset is a lovely time to explore the lake too, and can make for some sublime photographs as the sun sets.

The ramshackle **Thap Rua** (Turtle Tower; Map p64; Hoan Kiem Lake), on an islet near the southern end, is often used as an emblem of Hanoi. A number of elegant pagoda-like stone gateways can be found around the lake, inscribed with *chu nho* Chinese characters, including **Hoa Phong Pagoda** (Thap Hoa Phong) near the southeast of the lake shore.

You may often bump into small groups of Hanoi university and high-school students out interviewing foreigners to practise their English. They are invariably polite, often very interesting to talk to and provide an opportunity to interact with local youngsters, while they get the chance to improve their language skills (which the Vietnamese are highly ambitious about).

★ Hoa Lo
Prison Museum HISTORIC BUILDING

(Map p64; ☎ 024-3934 2253; cnr P Hoa Lo & P Hai Ba Trung; adult/child 30,000d/free; ⊙ 8am-5pm) This thought-provoking site is all that remains of the former Hoa Lo Prison, ironically nicknamed the 'Hanoi Hilton' by US POWs during the American War. Most exhibits relate to the prison's use up to the

Old Quarter

mid-1950s, focusing on the Vietnamese struggle for independence from France. A gruesome relic is the ominous French guillotine, used to behead Vietnamese revolutionaries. There are also displays focusing on the American pilots who were incarcerated at Hoa Lo during the American War.

These pilots include the late Pete Peterson (the first US ambassador to a unified Vietnam in 1995) and Senator John McCain (the Republican nominee for the US presidency in 2008). McCain's flight suit is displayed, along with a photograph of Hanoi locals rescuing him from Truc Bach Lake after being shot down in 1967.

The vast prison complex was built by the French in 1896. Originally intended to house around 450 inmates, records indicate that by the 1930s there were close to 2000 prisoners. Hoa Lo was never a very successful prison, and hundreds escaped its walls over the years – many squeezing out through sewer grates.

Polyglots might notice that the French signs are watered down compared with the English equivalents.

The name 'Hoa Lo' means 'stove' or 'furnace'. Most of the prison was demolished in the 1990s and high-rises (including the Somerset Grand Hanoi; p78) and other developments were built upon its land, though the section in a corner of the plot containing the museum survives.

★ **National Museum of Vietnamese History**　MUSEUM
(Bao Tang Lich Su Quoc Gia; Map p64; ☑ 024-3825 2853; www.baotanglichsu.vn; 1 P Trang Tien; adult/student 40,000/10,000d, camera 15,000d; ⊙ 8am-noon & 1.30-5pm, closed 1st Mon of month) Built between 1925 and 1932, this architecturally impressive museum was formerly home to the École Française d'Extrême-Orient. Its architect, Ernest Hebrard, was among the first in Vietnam to incorporate a blend of Chinese and French design elements.

Exhibit highlights include bronzes from the Dong Son culture (3rd century BCE to 3rd century CE), Hindu statuary from the Khmer and Champa kingdoms, jewellery from imperial Vietnam, and displays relating to the French occupation and the Communist Party. The audio guide is free.

★ **Vietnamese Women's Museum** MUSEUM
(Bao Tang Phu Nu Viet Nam; Map p64; ☑ 024-3825 9936; www.baotangphunu.org.vn; 36 P Ly Thuong Kiet; adult/student 30,000/15,000d; ☺ 8am-5pm) This excellent and highly informative museum showcases the roles of women in Vietnamese society and culture. Labelled in English and French, exhibits cover everything from marriage customs to childbirth, but it's the memories of the wartime contribution by individual heroic women that are most poignant.

If the glut of information sometimes feels repetitive, for visual stimulation there is a stunning collection of propaganda posters, as well as costumes, tribal basketware and fabric motifs from Vietnam's ethnic minority groups. Check the website for special exhibitions.

Ngoc Son Temple BUDDHIST TEMPLE
(Den Ngoc Son; Map p64; Hoan Kiem Lake; adult/student 30,000/15,000d, child under 15yr free; ☺ 8am-6pm) Meaning 'Temple of the Jade Mountain', Hanoi's most visited temple sits on a small island in the northern part of Hoan Kiem Lake, connected to the lakeshore by an elegant scarlet bridge (called Cau The Huc), constructed in classical Vietnamese style. The temple is dedicated to General Tran Hung Dao (who defeated the Mongols in the 13th century), La To (patron saint of physicians) and the scholar Van Xuong.

St Joseph Cathedral CHURCH
(Nha To Lon Ha Noi; Map p64; P Nha Tho; ☺ 8am-noon & 2-6pm) **FREE** Hanoi's neo-Gothic St Joseph Cathedral was inaugurated in 1886, and has a soaring facade that faces a little plaza that's usually stuffed with selfie sticks and posses of preening photographers. The church's most noteworthy features are the looming twin bell towers, elaborate altar and fine stained-glass windows. Entrance via the main gate is only permitted during Mass: times are listed on a sign on the gates to the left of the cathedral.

At other times, enter via the Diocese of Hanoi compound, a block away at 40 P Nha Chung. When you reach the side door to the cathedral, to your right, ring the small bell high up on the right-hand side of the door.

An array of cafes and restaurants are artfully placed with views to the cathedral, including La Place (p81), Eden Cafe (p86) and Cong Caphe (p86).

HANOI IN...

One Day

Rise early for a morning walk around misty **Hoan Kiem Lake** (p61) before a classic Hanoi breakfast cup of egg coffee at **Loading T Cafe** (p86). Get up to speed on Uncle Ho with a visit to the **Ho Chi Minh Mausoleum Complex** (p66) and nearby **Ho Chi Minh Museum** (p67). Explore the dynastic remains at the **Imperial Citadel of Thang Long** (p67) before grabbing a cab for a strong Vietnamese coffee at **Cong Caphe** (p86) and admiring the ecclesiastical lines of **St Joseph Cathedral** (p63). Grab lunch at nearby **Hanoi Social Club** (p81) then discover the organised chaos and backstreets of the **Old Quarter** (p56), or contemplate history at the **Vietnamese Women's Museum** (p63). Stop for a refreshing glass of *bia hoi* (draught beer) and catch a **water-puppets performance** (p88) or walk around the lake at sunset, before din-dins at **Grandma's Restaurant** (p79).

Two Days

Head to the suburbs to the excellent **Vietnam Museum of Ethnology** (p71). Back in the city have lunch at **Koto** (p81) before exploring the Confucian introspection of the **Temple of Literature** (p65) and perusing either the collection at the **Fine Arts Museum of Vietnam** (p65) or delving into the **Vietnam Military History Museum** (p64). Roll up your sleeves to dine at superb **Cha Ca Thang Long** (p80) or **Old Hanoi** (p81), then head to **Nola** (p85) for drinks.

Around Hoan Kiem Lake

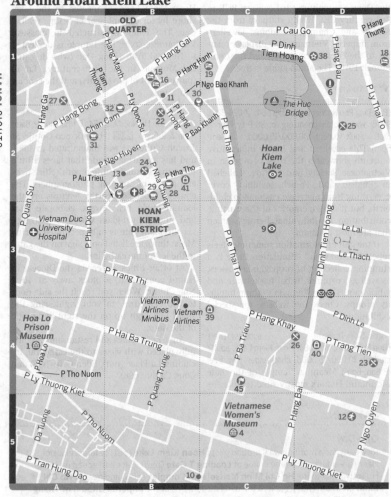

Martyrs' Monument   MONUMENT
(Tuong Dai Quyet Tu Cho To Quoc Quyet Sinh;
Map p64; P Dinh Tien Hoang) This dramatic
monument depicts a woman with a sword
and one man holding a rifle and another a torch. It was erected as a memorial
to those who died fighting for Vietnam's
independence.

**Vietnam Military
History Museum**   MUSEUM
(Bao Tang Lich Su Quan Su Viet Nam; Map p68;
📞 024-6253 1367; www.btlsqsvn.org.vn; 28a P
Dien Bien Phu; 40,000d, camera fee 20,000d;

⊗8-11.30am daily & 1-4.30pm Tue-Thu, Sat & Sun)
Easy to spot thanks to a large collection of
weaponry at the front, the Military Museum
displays Soviet and Chinese equipment
alongside French- and US-made weapons
captured during years of warfare.

The centrepiece is a Soviet-built MiG-21
jet fighter, triumphant amid the wreckage
of French aircraft downed at Dien Bien
Phu, and a US F-111. Adjacent is the hexagonal **Flag Tower** (Map p68; ⊗9am-5pm), one
of the symbols of Hanoi. Tower-only admission is free via the adjacent Highlands
coffee shop.

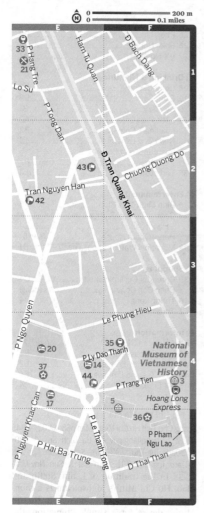

West of the Old Quarter

Embracing the districts of Ba Dinh and Dong Da, this wide-ranging region of Hanoi contains many major sights linked to the imperial heritage of the city as well as its more recent political history. The imposing gate and significant remains of the Imperial Citadel of Thang Long can be explored, as well as the august and often serene Temple of Literature, a deeply important seat of Confucian learning. To the northwest ranges Ba Dinh Sq and sights associated with Ho Chi Minh, including Ho Chi Minh's Mausoleum

and the Ho Chi Minh Museum, as well as some grand examples of French-colonial architecture, such as the imposing Presidential Palace.

Running north–south just west of the Old Quarter is the train line that popularised itself in recent years as Hanoi Train Street, though the sudden influx of cafes has, at the time of research, seen it shut down by city authorities. Other sights in the area include the Fine Arts Museum of Vietnam and the One Pillar Pagoda: you'll need to give yourself a couple of days to do the area justice.

★**Temple of Literature** CONFUCIAN TEMPLE
(Van Mieu; Map p68; ☑024-3845 2917; P Quoc Tu Giam; adult/student 30,000/15,000d; ☉8am-6pm) A rare example of well-preserved traditional Vietnamese architecture, the Temple of Literature honours Vietnam's finest scholars. Founded in 1070 by Emperor Le Thanh Tong, the attractive complex is dedicated to the Qufu-born philosopher Confucius (Khong Tu) and was the site of Vietnam's first university, Quoc Tu Giam (1076). The altars are popular with students praying for good grades, while the halls, ponds and gardens of the five courtyards make picturesque backdrops for student graduation photos. It is depicted on the 100,000d note.

Originally university admission was exclusively for those born of noble families, but after 1442 it became more egalitarian. Gifted students from all over the nation headed to Hanoi to study the principles of Confucianism, literature and poetry. In 1484 Emperor Le Thanh Tong ordered that stelae be erected to record the names, places of birth and achievements of exceptional scholars: 82 of 116 stelae remain standing, mostly atop turtle statues. Paths lead from the imposing tiered gateway on P Quoc Tu Giam through formal gardens to the Khue Van pavilion, constructed in 1802.

**Fine Arts Museum
of Vietnam** MUSEUM
(Bao Tang My Thuat Viet Nam; Map p68; ☑024-3733 2131; www.vnfam.vn; 66 P Nguyen Thai Hoc; adult/child 40,000/20,000d; ☉8.30am-5pm) The excellent Fine Arts Museum is housed in two buildings that were once the French Ministry of Information. Treasures abound, including ancient Champa stone carvings and some astonishing effigies of Quan Am, the thousand-eyed, thousand-armed

Around Hoan Kiem Lake

Goddess of Compassion, worshipped across the Far East. Look out for the lacquered statues of Buddhist monks from the Tay Son dynasty and the collection of contemporary art and folk-naive paintings. Most pieces have English explanations, but guided tours (150,000d) are useful (they don't run between 11.30am and 1.30pm).

Ho Chi Minh
Mausoleum Complex HISTORIC SITE
(Map p68; ☑ 024-3845 5128; www.bqllang.gov.vn; entrance cnr P Ngoc Ha & P Doi Can) The Ho Chi Minh Mausoleum Complex is an important place of pilgrimage for many Vietnamese. A traffic-free area of botanical gardens, monuments, memorials and pagodas, it's usually crowded with groups of Vietnamese who come from far and wide to pay their respects to 'Uncle Ho'. Within the complex are Ho Chi Minh's Mausoleum, Ho Chi Minh's Stilt House, the Ho Chi Minh Museum, the Presidential Palace and the One Pillar Pagoda.

➡ Ho Chi Minh's Mausoleum
(Lang Chu Tich Ho Chi Minh; Map p68; ☑ 024-3845 5128; www.bqllang.gov.vn; Ba Dinh Sq; ⊗ 7.30-10.30am Tue-Thu, 7.30-11am Sat & Sun Apr-Oct, 8-11am Tue-Thu, 8-11.30am Sat & Sun Nov-Mar) FREE In the tradition of Lenin, Stalin and Mao, Ho Chi Minh's Mausoleum is a monumental marble edifice. Contrary to Ho Chi Minh's desire for a simple cremation, the mausoleum was constructed from materials gathered from all over Vietnam between 1973 and 1975. Set deep in the bowels of the building in a glass sarcophagus is the frail, pale body of Ho Chi Minh. The mausoleum is usually closed from 4 September to 4 November while his embalmed body goes to Russia for maintenance.

Dress modestly: wearing shorts, sleeveless T-shirts or hats is not permitted. You may be requested to store day packs, cameras and phones before you enter. Talking, putting your hands in your pockets and photography are strictly prohibited in the mausoleum. The queue usually snakes for several hundred metres to the mausoleum entrance and inside, filing past Ho's body at a slow but steady pace.

If you're lucky you'll catch the changing of the guard outside the mausoleum – the pomp and ceremony displayed here rivals the British equivalent at Buckingham Palace in London.

The app Into Thin Air 2 (www.facebook.com/intothinairhanoi) is well worth downloading to listen to the sound work relating to the mausoleum.

➡ Ho Chi Minh's Stilt House

(Nha San Bac Ho & Phu Chu Tich Tai; Map p68; So 1 Ngo Bach Thao; 25,000d; ⊙8-11.30am daily & 2-4pm Tue-Thu, Sat & Sun) This humble, traditional stilt house where Ho lived intermittently from 1958 to 1969 is set in a well-tended garden adjacent to a carp-filled pond and has been preserved just as Ho left it. The clear views through the open doorways and windows permit insights more fascinating than many museum displays. The stilt house is now used for official receptions and isn't open to the public, but visitors may wander the grounds if sticking to the paths.

➡ Ho Chi Minh Museum

(Bao Tang Ho Chi Minh; Map p68; ☎024-3846 3757; www.baotanghochiminh.vn; 19 P Ngoc Ha; 40,000d; ⊙8am-noon daily & 2-4.30pm Tue-Thu, Sat & Sun) The huge concrete Soviet-style Ho Chi Minh Museum is a triumphalist monument dedicated to the life of the founder of modern Vietnam. The often-confusing exhibition is a mixed bag; highlights include mementos of Ho's life, and some fascinating photos and dusty official documents relating to the overthrow of the French and the onward march of revolutionary socialism. Photography is forbidden and you may be asked to check your bag at reception.

An English-speaking guide costs around 100,000d, and given the quite surreal nature of the exhibition it's a worthwhile investment.

➡ Presidential Palace

(Map p68; 2 Đ Hung Vuong) This opulent restored colonial pile was flung up in 1906 as the Palace for the Governor General of Indochina. The yellow (a colour of communism) beaux-arts palace is now used for official receptions and isn't open to the public. There's a combined entrance gate to the stilt house and Presidential Palace grounds on P Ong Ich Kiem inside the mausoleum complex. When the main mausoleum entrance is closed, enter from Đ Hung Vuong near the palace building.

➡ One Pillar Pagoda

(Chua Mot Cot; Map p68; P Ong Ich Kiem; 25,000d; ⊙8-11.30am daily & 2-4pm Tue-Thu, Sat & Sun) The One Pillar Pagoda was originally built by the Emperor Ly Thai Tong who ruled from 1028 to 1054. According to the annals, the heirless emperor dreamed that he met Quan The Am Bo Tat, the Goddess of Mercy, who handed him a male child. Ly Thai Tong then married a young peasant girl and had a son and heir by her. As a way of expressing his gratitude for this event, he constructed a pagoda here in 1049.

★ Imperial Citadel of Thang Long   HISTORIC SITE

(Hoang Thanh Thang Long; Map p68; www.hoangthanhthanglong.vn; 19c P Hoang Dieu; adult/child 30,000d/free; ⊙8am-5pm Tue-Sun) Added to Unesco's World Heritage List in 2010, Hanoi's Imperial Citadel was the hub of Vietnamese military power for over 1000 years. Ongoing archaeological digs continue on-site, revealing remains of ancient palaces, grandiose pavilions and imperial gates. The **main gate** (Doan Mon) is named after one of the gates of the Forbidden City in Beijing. Further back is the imposing and colonnaded French **Caserne de la Compagnie d'Ouvriers**. At the rear is the **Princess Pagoda** (Hau Lau), which probably housed imperial concubines.

There are also fascinating military command bunkers from the American War – complete with maps and 1960s communications equipment – used by the legendary Vietnamese general Vo Nguyen Giap. The leafy grounds are also an easy-going and quiet antidote to Hanoi's bustle. Guided tours are 150,000d or you can download the Hoang Thanh Thang Long mobile app.

Ambassadors' Pagoda   BUDDHIST TEMPLE

(Chua Quan Su; Map p68; 73 P Quan Su; ⊙8-11am & 1-4pm) **FREE** The official centre of Buddhism in Hanoi, the wonderfully maintained and otherwise peaceful Ambassadors' Pagoda attracts quite a crowd on holidays. During the 17th century there was a guesthouse on-site for the ambassadors of Buddhist countries. Today about a dozen monks and nuns are based here.

HANOI SIGHTS

West of the Old Quarter

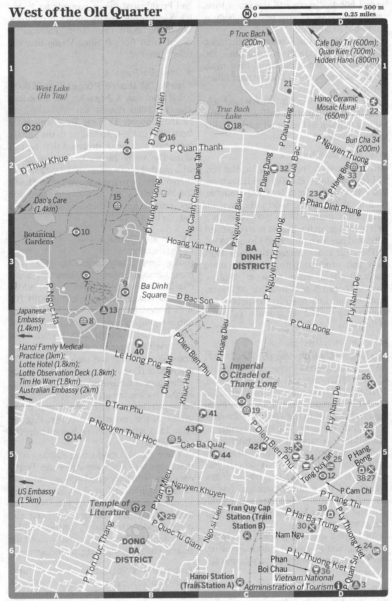

Quan Thanh Temple   TAOIST TEMPLE
(Tran Vu Quan; Map p68; P Quan Thanh; 10,000d;
⊙7am-5pm) Shaded by huge trees, Quan
Thanh Temple was established during the
Ly dynasty (1010–1225) and was dedicated to

Tran Vo (God of the North), whose symbols
of power were the tortoise and the snake. A
bronze statue and bell date from 1677 and
there's a fascinating copy of an ancient map
of old Hanoi in *chu nho* (Chinese characters)

West of the Old Quarter

and *chu nom* (Vietnamese script) in the main hall. The temple is on the shores of Truc Bach Lake, near the West Lake.

◉ French Quarter

Despite its evocative moniker, today's French Quarter lacks the style and elegance of days past. Its once-glamorous villas, annexed by the Communist Party for government offices and repatriation housing, stand in disrepute, desperate for restoration. Many, occupying some of Hanoi's prime development sites, have already been demolished in favour of taller, shinier things. Those that have been best maintained serve as the offices for Hanoi's foreign embassies and diplomatic outposts. In a way, there's some sense of a cycle completing itself here: in creating a Parisian-style city befitting their new area of governance, the French colonialists appropriated and razed whatever traditional Vietnamese dwellings and monuments stood in their way.

Occupying an area just south of Hoan Kiem Lake, west of the Song Hong as far as Hanoi Train Station (depending on whom you talk to), south until Thong Nhat Park (Reunification Park) and east to Hanoi Opera House, this quieter part of town is well worth a visit and is blessed with wide traffic-free pavements. Stroll among the embassies and crumbling villas, contemplating what once was and what once could have been.

★ **Hai Ba Trung Temple** BUDDHIST TEMPLE
(Map p70; P Tho Lao; ☺6am-6pm Mon-Sat) Two kilometres south of Hoan Kiem Lake, this temple was founded in 1142. A statue shows the two Trung sisters (from the 1st century CE) kneeling with their arms raised in the air. Some say the statue shows the sisters, who had been proclaimed the queens of the Vietnamese, about to dive into a river. They are said to have drowned themselves rather than surrender in the wake of their defeat at the hands of the Chinese.

French Quarter

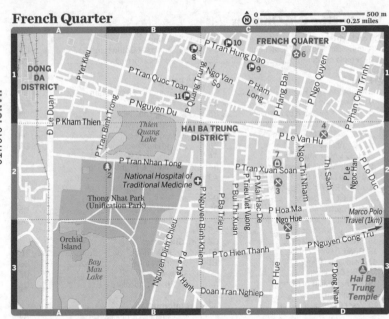

French Quarter

◉ Top Sights
1 Hai Ba Trung Temple D3

◉ Sights
2 Thong Nhat Park B2

✕ Eating
3 Banh Mi Pho Hue C2
4 Bun Cha Huong Lien D2
5 Chim Sao C3

✪ Entertainment
6 August Cinema D1

▣ Shopping
7 Hom Market C2

ⓘ Information
8 Cambodian Embassy B1
9 French Embassy C1
10 Indian Embassy C1
11 Laotian Embassy B1

Hanoi Opera House   HISTORIC BUILDING
(Nha Hat Lon Ha Noi; Map p64; ☎ 024-3993 0113, tours 093 815 0111; http://hanoioperahouse.org. vn; 1 P Trang Tien) This glorious neoclassical centrepiece of Hanoi's French Quarter is unmissable with its Gothic pillars and domes. The French-colonial 900-seat venue was built in 1911, and on 16 August 1945 the Viet Minh–run Citizens' Committee announced that it had taken over the city from a balcony in this building. For some drama today, book ahead for a performance here, or take a 50-minute tour (at 2.30pm, 3.30pm or 4.30pm). Most weekends you'll see Hanoi wedding couples getting photographed on the elegant front steps.

◉ Greater Hanoi

Hanoi sprawls beyond the central districts, where the distances begin to pile up and a taxi will most likely be your preferred form of transport (unless you've hired a scooter). Despite their size, however, these neighbourhoods lay claim to some top sights, including the endlessly rewarding Vietnam Museum of Ethnology, an assortment of historic Buddhist pagodas, a thought-provoking art space, vistas of the city from the Lotte Observation Deck, and placid lakes that encourage breezy bicycle outings.

★ **Vietnam Museum of Ethnology** MUSEUM
(Map p58; ☑024-3756 2193; www.vme.org.vn; Đ Nguyen Van Huyen; adult/concession 40,000/15,000d, guide 100,000d; ⊘8.30am-5.30pm Tue-Sun) This fabulous collection relating to Vietnam's ethnic minorities features well-presented tribal art, artefacts and everyday objects gathered from across the nation, and examples of traditional village houses. Displays are well labelled in Vietnamese, French and English. If you're into anthropology, it's well worth the Grab motorbike-taxi fare (approximately 40,000d each way) to the Cau Giay district, about 7km from the city centre, where the museum is located.

Otherwise local bus 14 (4000d) departs from P Dinh Tien Hoang on the east side of Hoan Kiem Lake and passes within a couple of blocks (around 600m) of the museum; get off at the Nghia Tan bus stop and head to Đ Nguyen Van Huyen.

West Lake LAKE
(Ho Tay; Map p68) The city's largest lake, West Lake is 15km in circumference and ringed by upmarket suburbs, including the predominantly expat Tay Ho district. On the south side, along Đ Thuy Khue, are seafood restaurants, and to the east, the Xuan Dieu strip is lined with restaurants, cafes, boutiques and luxury hotels. The atmosphere makes a calm change from the chaos of the Old Quarter. A pathway circles the lake, making for a great bicycle ride.

Tay Ho Pagoda BUDDHIST TEMPLE
(Phu Tay Ho; Map p58; Đ Thai Mai; ⊘8am-8pm) **FREE** Jutting into West Lake, beautiful Tay Ho Pagoda is perhaps the most popular place of worship in Hanoi. Throngs of people come here on the first and 15th day of each lunar month in the hope of receiving good fortune from the Mother Goddess, to whom the temple is dedicated.

Lotte Observation Deck VIEWPOINT
(Map p58; ☑024-3333 6016; www.lottecenter.com.vn; 54 P Lieu Giai, Ba Dinh; adult/student day 230,000/170,000d, night 130,000/110,000d; ⊘9am-10pm) The city's best views can be found on the 65th-floor 360-degree Observation Deck of the landmark Lotte Center in the western corner of Hanoi's Ba Dinh district. From this uninterrupted vantage point, high above Hanoi's hustle and bustle, you can compare the size of the Old Quarter relative to the sheer scale of Hanoi's voracious growth. Glass-floor sky walks allow you to walk out over the precipitous drop. There's also a rooftop bar on the same floor as an alternative.

The tower also houses a hotel, all manner of restaurants and a department store on its lower floors. The Lotte Center is around 20 minutes by taxi from the Old Quarter.

Manzi Exhibition Space & Artist Residency GALLERY
(Map p68; ☑024-3716 3397; www.facebook.com/manzihanoi; 2 Ngo Hang Bun; ⊘9am-7pm) Just round the corner from its namesake cafe (p85), gallery and shop, this art space and gallery hosts exhibitions and open studios for local and international artists, connecting with overseas art institutions and promoting intellectual and artistic debate in Hanoi.

Tran Quoc Pagoda BUDDHIST TEMPLE
(Chua Tran Quoc; Map p68; Đ Thanh Nien) One of the oldest pagodas in Vietnam, Tran Quoc Pagoda looks new with its clean orange bricks. What gives it a photogenic advantage is the backdrop of the eastern shore of West Lake. It's just off Đ Thanh Nien, which divides this lake from Truc Bach Lake. A stela here, dating from 1639, tells the history of this site. The pagoda was rebuilt in the 15th century and again in 1842.

Truc Bach Lake LAKE
(Ho Truc Bach; Map p68) Separated from West Lake only by Đ Thanh Nien, this lake is lined with flame trees. During the 18th century the Trinh lords built a palace on the lakeside; it was later transformed into a reformatory for wayward royal concubines, who were condemned to spend their days weaving pure white silk. It's not much to look at but makes for a quiet stroll.

🏃 **Activities**

Sports

Hash House Harriers RUNNING
(Map p64; www.hanoih3.com; 21 P Hai Ba Trung, American Club; run per adult/child 150,000/50,000d; ⊘from 1.30pm Sat) For the uninitiated, the 'hashers' are drinkers with a running problem. To get to the sightseeing walks/runs just outside of Hanoi, there's an included bus that departs from the American Club south of Hoan Kiem Lake. Check the website for details. Female runners can also ask about the Harriettes. Runs are followed by a dinner in town.

🏃 City Walk
Old Quarter

START NGOC SON TEMPLE
END P NHA THO
LENGTH 3.5KM; MINIMUM TWO HOURS

Start at the **1 Ngoc Son Temple** (p63) on Hoan Kiem Lake. Return over the red **2 Huc Bridge**, to the photogenic **3 Martyrs' Monument** (p64). Follow P Dinh Tien Hoang to the **4 Municipal Water Puppet Theatre** (p88). Head north on P Hang Dau, but don't get too sucked in by all the cheap shoes in the **5 shoe shops**. Cross P Cau Go to P Hang Be for the **6 local market** on P Gia Ngu.

Back on P Hang Be, continue north to P Hang Bac: look out for artisans hand carving intricate **7 gravestones**. Next, head up to the **8 Heritage House** (p59) on P Ma May, the street to come to for nightlife.

Return to P Hang Bac, passing **9 jewellery shops**, to **10 house 102**, which includes a fully functioning temple at the end of the corridor. Retrace your steps and head up narrow **11 P Ta Hien**, popular for more after-dark bars. Turn left on P Hang Buom to the **12 Bach Ma Temple** (p58), and

continue to the well-preserved **13 Old East Gate** (p60) for an obligatory photograph. Continue north to the **14 street market** on P Thanh Ha, then veer right to **15 Dong Xuan Market** (p90).

Backtrack south on Nguyen Thien Thuat and turn right on to P Hang Chieu, past **16 shops** selling straw mats and rope. This becomes **17 P Hang Ma**, where imitation 'ghost money' is sold for burning in Buddhist ceremonies. Follow your ears to the **18 blacksmiths** near the corner of P Lo Ren and P Thuoc Bac. Continue along Lan Ong to the pungent fragrances of **19 herb merchants**.

Double back to P Thuoc Bac and head south past the **20 tin-box makers**, opposite the **21 mirror shops** on P Hang Thiec. Continue left towards shops selling **22 Buddhist altars and statues** along P Hang Quat.

Head south along P Luong Van Can, famed for its **23 toy shops**, and continue along P Hang Gai for elegant **24 silk shops**. Head south on P Ly Quoc Su to **25 St Joseph Cathedral** (p63), and the cafes on P Nha Tho and P Au Trieu.

Spa & Massage

You might be overwhelmed by the countless promises of mind-blowing massages as you wander the streets of the Old Quarter. For something a little different and likely to please even the most discerning of clients, try our top picks for Hanoi's best massages.

★ **Omamori Spa** MASSAGE

(Map p68; ☑024-3773 9919; www.omamorispa.com; 52a P Hang Bun, Ba Đình; 1hr massage from 300,000d) This wonderful spa is operated by a not-for-profit organisation that provides training and employment opportunities for the blind. Masseuses here are vision impaired and speak excellent English. The trained therapists give massages with a level of gentleness and body awareness that differs from traditional practitioners. Tips are not accepted; pricing and service are excellent. There are three branches in town, including this one.

Dao's Care SPA

(Map p58; ☑024-3722 8316; www.daoscare.com; 351 Đ Hoang Hoa Tham; herbal bath from 150,000d; ☺9am-9pm) This welcoming and friendly spa is a very therapeutic experience, with well-trained therapists who are either visually impaired or blind. There's a caring family feel here that customers respond well to, with options from herbal baths to Dao, Swedish or foot massage and much more. The spa supports members of the Red Dao ethnic minority in Sapa. A 'no tips' policy is in effect.

Yakushi Center MASSAGE

(Map p58; ☑024-3719 1971; www.yakushicenter.com; 20 P Xuan Dieu, Quang An, Tay Ho; treatments from 250,000d; ☺8.30am-8pm) In the fashionable expat-centric suburb of Tay Ho you'll find this fabulous clinic that specialises in a range of traditional Vietnamese and Chinese medicine practices, as well as therapeutic and relaxing massages, including Swedish massage. Bookings are essential: your English-speaking practitioner conducts a brief consultation with you prior to commencing your treatment.

Huong Sen MASSAGE

(Map p68; ☑024-3927 1330; www.huongsenhealthcare.com; 78 Đ Yen Phu; massage from 250,000d; ☺9am-10.30pm) A wide range of beauty treatments and services, including Jacuzzi and steam baths, are available at this professional outfit with good facilities and English-speaking staff. A full menu is available to view on the website. There are three other branches in Hanoi.

Courses

Zo Project ARTS & CRAFTS

(Map p64; ☑0366 602 928, 0168 432 9379; www.zopaper.com; 26 Tho Xuong; workshops from 700,000d; ☺store 9am-7pm) If you love traditional Vietnamese paper, then this workshop-store is the place to come for handcrafted paintings, postcards and even artistic lampshades. Workshops here include papermaking, calligraphy, bookbinding, watercolour painting and jewellery making, and there are paper-making tours to Hoa Binh. Zo's location right on the much-photographed train track towards Sapa adds to the allure. Profits help ethnic minority craftspeople in northern Vietnam.

Blue Butterfly Cooking Class COOKING

(Map p60; ☑0944 852 009; www.bluebutterflyrestaurant.com; 69 P Ma May; per person from US$55; ☺8.30am & 2.30pm) In this popular four-hour cooking class you'll meet your chef/teacher in the restaurant kitchen, and be accompanied on a shopping trip to the Dong Xuan Market, before returning to the kitchen where you'll be instructed in the preparation and cooking of three dishes. After the class you can enjoy the fruits of your labour in the restaurant.

Hidden Hanoi COOKING, LANGUAGE

(Map p58; ☑0987 240 480; www.hiddenhanoi.com.vn; 147 P Nghi Tam, Tay Ho; cooking classes per person from US$25; ☺classes 9am-5pm) Offers cooking classes from its kitchen near the eastern side of West Lake (Ho Tay). Options include seafood and village-food menus. Walking tours (per person US$25) exploring Hanoi street food are available. Hidden Hanoi also offers a language-study program (per person from US$200), including 18 hours of tuition and two field trips, or a short Vietnamese course of two hours (US$20).

Hanoi Cooking Centre COOKING

(Map p68; ☑024-3715 0088; www.hanoicookingcentre.com; 44 P Chau Long; per person from 1,380,000d; 🖮) Excellent interactive classes, including market visits, along with a special Kids' Club – handy if your children are aspiring chefs. Cookery classes conclude with a shared lunch in its elegant restaurant. The

CHOO-CHOO! HANOI TRAIN STREET HITS THE BUFFERS

Becoming an overnight sensation at the start of 2019, Hanoi Train Street had already begun luring visitors to a line of cafes that had clustered alongside the train tracks in early 2018. Before then, the train track was like any other, but all of a sudden it became a celebrity, drawing Instagrammers from far and wide.

The original cafe here was The Railway Hanoi (p85), set up – with a slow start – by the enterprising Thao Quach in 2017. Coffee-quaffers would gather to watch the train rumble past in the evening. Word spread, more travellers began appearing, copycat cafes followed and so did the customers. Restrictions were imposed by nervous authorities and then lifted as The Railway Hanoi cafe set about winning local hearts with projects for the train-track community, including free English lessons for the kids. Locals became more involved in the new life of the Train Street and cafes began popping up in living rooms.

Then, as noted by food-tourer and blogger Fabienne Fong Yan (www.a-fab-journey.com), in the Christmas of 2018, Hanoi Train Street went viral on social media and the floodgates opened. Arguing that the railway track posed a danger to its new fan base, the authorities suddenly closed the Train Street in October 2019, and it remains closed to pedestrians. Its fate remains unknown, but you can still visit Thao and her fantastic team at The Railway Hanoi 2 (p85), around the corner, where staff entice you with chirpy calls of 'Choo-choo'.

Hanoi Cooking Centre also runs a highly recommended walking tour exploring Hanoi's street-food scene.

👉 Tours

⭐ **Hanoi Free Tour Guides**　　WALKING
(📱0988 979 174; www.hanoifreetourguides.com)
There's no better way to experience the real Hanoi than with this not-for-profit organisation run by volunteer staff and guides comprising students and ex-students, speaking a multitude of languages. A variety of suggested tours is available, or you can work with your guide to tailor an itinerary. Although the service is free, you pay the small cost of the guide's transport, admission fees and meals. Book online.

⭐ **Gay Hanoi Tours**　　WALKING
(📱0947 600 602; www.facebook.com/gayhanoi
tour; tours from US$65) The inimitable Tuan offers personal and small-group walking (or scooter) tours exploring lesser-known, real-life corners of the ancient city. Popular tours cover food, architecture, design, classic sights and night tours. While tours aren't gay themed, Tuan, a gay Hanoian man, offers a unique perspective on his beloved home town and Vietnamese food, regardless of your sexuality.

⭐ **Hanoi Street Food Tours**　　WALKING
(📱0904 517 074; www.streetfoodtourshanoi.
blogspot.com.au; tours from US$75) There's a local company running tours under the same name, but we continue to recommend this pricier, private option, run by Van Cong Tu and Mark Lowerson, a couple of passionate Hanoi foodies. Whet your appetite with their individual social-media photos. Tours can be customised to different interests.

Vietnam in Focus　　TOURS
(📱0795 150 522; www.vietnaminfocus.com; per person with/without own camera from US$70/100) Journalists Colm Pierce and Alex Sheal run photographic tours exploring Hanoi life, including the Old Quarter, night-time Hanoi, the railway area, Tho Ha handicraft village and further-away places such as Ninh Binh, Danang, the Hai Van Pass, Ho Chi Minh City and the railway network. Tours can be suited to photographers of all levels, even beginners.

Friends of Vietnam Heritage　　WALKING
(www.fvheritage.org; tours from 70,000d) Staffed mainly by volunteers from the international expat community, this not-for-profit organisation produces various publications, hosts events, and conducts fun and informative walking tours aimed at preserving Hanoi's heritage and culture.

Vietnam Awesome Travel　　WALKING
(Map p60; 📱0904 123 217; www.vietnamawesome
travel.com; 64 P Nguyen Huu Huan; tours from US$18) A wide range of good-value walking tours, including the popular Food on Foot (US$25) street-food walking tours around

the Old Quarter. A variety of day trips and longer guided tours are also available. See the website for details.

Hanoi Kids
WALKING

(☑ 0976 217 886; www.hanoikids.org; by donation; ⊕) This volunteer organisation partners visitors with Hanoi teens and young adults wishing to improve their English-language skills. Tours are customised to the needs of visitors and can include Hanoi sights like the Temple of Literature and Hoa Lo Prison Museum, or street-food and market visits. It's best to arrange tours online a couple of weeks before you arrive in Hanoi.

Festivals & Events

Tet
CULTURAL

(Tet Nguyen Dan, Vietnamese Lunar New Year; ⊗ late Jan or early Feb) The lunar year is Vietnam's mega festival to celebrate with family members and commemorate the dearly departed. The holiday lasts up to a week, when many shops are closed and the whole country can seem to be on the move, so booking transport in advance is highly advisable. Finding accommodation in Hanoi is generally fine.

Plan on staying put and enjoying a walk around a lake, watching some fireworks and eating too much. If you want to be in the thick of it, join the throngs at the Perfume Pagoda (p97). During the week preceding Tet there's a flower market on P Hang Luoc. There's also a colourful, two-week flower exhibition and competition, beginning on the first day of the new year, that takes place in Thong Nhat Park near Bay Mau Lake.

The word Tet is just a shortened form of Tet Nguyen Dan, and the word 'tet' itself simply means 'festival'.

Quang Trung Festival
CULTURAL

(⊗ Feb or Mar) Wrestling competitions, lion dances and human chess take place on the fifth day of the first lunar month at Dong Da Mound, site of the uprising against the Chinese led by Emperor Quang Trung (Nguyen Hue) in 1788.

Hanoi Pride
LGBT

(www.fb.me/VietPride.vn; ⊗ 1 week in Jul-Sep) The annual Hanoi Pride festival is a colourful week of parties, film screenings, talks and a bicycle rally. It is held over one week between July and September; check the website for details. It has changed and grown since the first parade in 2012, which was Vietnam's first Pride event.

Vietnam's National Day
CULTURAL

(⊗ 2 Sep) Celebrated with a rally and fireworks at Ba Dinh Sq, in front of Ho Chi Minh's Mausoleum. There are also boat races on Hoan Kiem Lake.

Full Moon Festival
CULTURAL

(Tet Trung Thu; ⊗ mid-Sep or early Oct) This festival, also known as the Mid-Autumn Festival *(tet trung thu)*, begins on the 15th day of the eighth month of the lunar calendar – usually in mid-September or early October. Singing, dragon dances, and the giving and receiving of moon cakes and money are some of the reasons why this lively festival is so popular with children.

Sleeping

An extra US$10 to US$20 makes a massive difference in Hanoi accommodation: you could easily move from a windowless room to a larger space with a view, so splurge if you can. Expect to pay US$20 to US$30 for a compact budget room. For around US$30 to US$50 you'll get more space, a smart TV and minibar. For US$75 to US$100 you should get a 'junior suite' in a contemporary boutique hotel with stylish appointments, bathtub and balcony. Over US$100 buys international four- to five-star standards.

Always check that your hotel has a fire escape, as the rush to convert buildings to hotels has left some hotels with no means of escape in the event of a conflagration.

Old Quarter

The main advantages of staying in the Old Quarter – the most popular area – are that you get an overwhelming range of options and proximity to attractions. The disadvantages are also an overwhelming range of options and it's busy and noisy.

Be sure to look beyond a hotel's foyer – many Old Quarter hotels look flash downstairs at reception, but rooms can be small and average. Some guests will prefer paying extra to stay in the quieter French Quarter.

Backpacker accommodation in Hanoi is plentiful, and a new breed of flashpackers and boutique hostels has brought luxury touches to the Old Quarter. For US$8 to US$10 you can get a soft, clean dorm bed with a modern shared bathroom.

TACKLING THE OLD QUARTER

Initially, you're likely to find negotiating the narrow streets of the Old Quarter an intimidating experience. Waves of motorbikes compete with cars and pedestrians pushing their way through the maze full of countless cheap hotels, shopfronts of knock-off wares and hawkers with their sizzling baskets, amid an ever-present tumult of horns and the heady aromas of exhaust fumes, street food and sweat.

Employ strategy and determination to cross the street, and remember to look up when you can: glimpses of the old and the very old peek out occasionally from behind garish modern facades. You'll gain your confidence soon enough, and when you do, there's no better way to spend time here than to wander, soaking up the sights, sounds and smells, and immersing yourself in the unique flavours of Hanoi's street-side kitchens.

Remember to carry your hotel's calling card, and if you get lost, it's only a cheap cab, Grab taxi or *xe om* (motorbike taxi) ride back.

★ **Tomodachi House** HOSTEL $
(Map p68; ☑ 024-3266 9493; 5a Tong Duy Tan; dm/d from US$9/27; ❋ @ 🛜) This quiet and clean Japanese-styled flashpacker sits on the snazzier western edge of the Old Quarter, near hip all-night eating and drinking. Large, restful dorm beds have their own USB charging, shelf space, privacy curtain and chunky locker. A great breakfast (included) and very friendly, welcoming and helpful staff seal the deal.

★ **Nexy Hostel** HOSTEL $
(Map p60; ☑ 024-7300 6399; www.nexyhostels. com; 12 P To Tich; dm/tw/tr from US$7/35/40; ❋ 🛜) Flashpackers Nexy has modern, clean dorms and bathrooms, soft beds with privacy curtains, quality linen and ample locked storage, plus staff who speak excellent English and are helpful with travel tips. This boutique hostel is also in a standout location near Hoan Kiem Lake, and has a calm bar, a games room, a small lounge and rooftop zones.

Cocoon Inn HOSTEL $
(Map p60; ☑ 024-3885 3333; www.cocooninn.com; 116-118 P Hang Buom; dm US$8-10, tw US$38-45; ❋ @ 🛜) This attractive, resourceful hostel has good dorms, a decent cocktail bar and a lovely rooftop terrace on the 7th floor. Privacy curtains indeed create a cocoon around plush, clean beds that come with personal lamps, fans and power points. An entourage of helpful staff can organise tours, airport transfers and visa extensions. It's on a busy street full of restaurants and bars.

Hanoi Hostel HOSTEL $
(Map p60; ☑ 0462 700 006; www.vietnam-hostel.com; 91c P Hang Ma; dm/d US$5.50/25,

homestay US$30; ❋ 🛜) This small, quiet, privately owned hostel is nicely located away from Hanoi's conglomeration of hostels. It's popular, well run and clean, with tours on tap and plenty of information about onward travel to China or Laos. The homestay option puts you in a family-owned house in the Old Quarter.

Central Backpackers Hanoi HOSTEL $
(Map p60; ☑ 024-3928 2899; www.centralbackpackershostel.com; 16 P Thanh Ha; dm from US$6, s/d/tw US$20/25/25; @ 🛜) This decent hostel enjoys a good Old Quarter location, with private rooms as well as dorms. Not for the withdrawn, reclusive traveller, it's an easily excitable, social spot, with free pub crawls and walking tours, and a nightly free-beer happy hour from 7pm to 8pm.

★ **La Beauté de Hanoi** HOTEL $$
(Map p60; ☑ 024-3935 1626; www.la-beaute hanoihotel.com; 15 Ngo Trung Yen; d/ste from US$60/ 96; ❋ 🛜) This very pleasant and stylish 35-room boutique hotel has a fresh white-and-cream palette with red accents, and small private balconies attached to larger suites and family rooms. It's in an excellent location on a quiet lane just a hop, skip and a jump from all the action on P Ma May.

★ **Golden Art Hotel** HOTEL $$
(Map p60; ☑ 024-3923 4294; www.goldenart hotel.com; 6a P Hang But; d & tw US$45, s US$75; ➲ ❋ @ 🛜) Golden Art enjoys a quiet location on the western edge of the Old Quarter. Well-equipped rooms are stylish and relatively spacious, with a work desk and clean shower; there's a can-do attitude from the friendly staff too. Breakfast (included in the price) features warm baguettes, omelettes,

pho (noodle soup) and fresh fruit. Nab a room here in the low season for US$30.

★**Hanoi House Hostel**   HOTEL $$
(Map p60; ☑024-3935 2571; www.hanoiguest house.com; 85 P Ma May; dm/s/d/tr from US$5/24/26/50, ste US$40; ✳@🛜) On bustling P Ma May, this winning choice has excellent, comfortable rooms and decent beds in the six-bed dorms, but it's the super staff that give it a real shine. The central location in the middle of the action is an added bonus, with bars, restaurants, travel agencies and shopping right outside. Good breakfast too (included in the cost of all rooms, apart from dorms).

Art Boutique Hotel   HOTEL $$
(Map p60; ☑024-3923 3868; 63 P Hang Dieu; r from US$50; ✳@🛜) The young, friendly, helpful crew at the Art Hotel make this well-located spot really stand out. Rooms are spacious, with very clean bathrooms and wooden floors, and within a 30m radius you'll find some of the best opportunities for partaking in the city's great street food.

Hanoi Little Town Hotel   HERITAGE HOTEL $$
(Map p60; ☑024-3828 3525; www.hanoilittletown. com; 77 P Hang Luoc; d & tw US$35, tr US$65, f US$85; ✳@🛜) Little Town has kept things old-fashioned. Dark, ornate furniture, some massive rooms, white cotton bedding, high ceilings and spacious bathrooms seem from another era. English-speaking staff also display classic good service, but with youthful enthusiasm, and breakfast is excellent. Front rooms have balconies; quieter rear rooms look to nearby Dong Xuan Market. There's a huge family room on the top floor.

Golden Moon Suite Hotel   HOTEL $$
(Map p60; ☑0982 971 918; www.goldenmoon suitehotel.com; 12a P Hang Manh; d US$35-60; ☺✳🛜) The balconies at this mini 18-room hotel give a fascinating bird's-eye view on local life in narrow P Yen Thai, dotted with greengrocers, butchers and colourful flags. Nights are quiet, but if you're bothered by morning hubbub, opt for inner rooms. Witnessing Hanoi awaken from the rooftop terrace at breakfast is a huge reason to stay here, along with the small but very comfortable rooms.

Hanoi Elite   HOTEL $$
(Map p60; ☑024-3828 1711; www.hanoielitehotel. com; 10/50 Dao Duy Tu; r from US$50; ✳@🛜) It's often surprising what you can find in the narrowest, most hidden-away lanes in the Old Quarter. Hanoi Elite features cool and classy decor, fine rooms, top-notch and ever-helpful staff, tasty breakfasts cooked to order and an escape from the more chaotic roads nearby. Low season sees prices fall to around US$40.

Hanoi Rendezvous Hotel   HOTEL $$
(Map p60; ☑024-3828 5777; www.hanoirendez voushotel.com; 31 P Hang Dieu; d/tw/tr US$37/37/50; ✳🛜) Deliciously close to several brilliant street-food places, Hanoi Rendezvous is a very solid choice, with huge old rooms, friendly staff and good breakfasts. It organises well-run tours to Halong Bay, Cat Ba Island and Sapa. Good deals are often available.

★**La Siesta Classic Ma May Hotel**   BOUTIQUE HOTEL $$$
(Map p60; ☑024-3926 3641; www.lasiesta hotels.vn/mamay; 94 P Ma May; d & tw US$135, tr US$195, ste from US$235; ✳🛜) La Siesta is a top choice for its excellent service and elegant rooms, which come in a wide variety of sizes (including some snazzy bi-level suites), while its cracking location on P Ma May means that scores of restaurants, bars and things to do are right on your doorstep. If that's all a bit too hectic for you, chill out in the day spa.

🛏 Around Hoan Kiem Lake

Although the Old Quarter is often referred to specifically as the area north of Hoan Kiem Lake, the area to the west of the lake has a high concentration of hotels and is still considered to be part of the neighbourhood. Here you'll find P Ngo Huyen with its glut of cheap dorms, and nearby, the calmer, atmospheric streets around St Joseph Cathedral – light sleepers be warned, the cathedral bells start tolling every quarter hour from 5am. This popular area sees a high turnover of guests (read: wear and tear) and hostel facilities are basic at best. Getting around is straightforward, however, and you'll be central (if anything's too far to walk, get a Grab taxi).

★**Golden Lotus Luxury Hotel**   HOTEL $$
(Map p64; ☑024-3828 5888; www.goldenlotus hotel.com.vn; 53-55 P Hang Trong; d/ste from US$55/100; ✳@🛜✖) Rooms at this stylish, atmospheric hotel have attractive wooden finishes, fine silk trims, local art and high technology. Standard rooms lack natural

light, but oversized suites have generous terraces. And there's a rooftop pool! Its older sister property, the **Golden Lotus Hotel** (Map p64; ☑024-3938 0901; www.golden lotushotel.com.vn; 39 P Hang Trong; d/ste from US$45/89; ❄@☎⍚), is marginally cheaper, and you can still use the pool here if staying there.

Madame Moon Hotel GUESTHOUSE **$$**
(Map p64; ☑024-3938 1255; www.madam moonguesthouse.com; 17 P Hang Hanh; d & tw from US$30; ❄☎) Keeping it simple just one block from Hoan Kiem Lake, Madame Moon has surprisingly chic rooms and a (relatively) traffic-free location in a street filled with local cafes and bars. Note that there are three hotels belonging to Madame Moon (this review is for the property on P Hang Hanh).

La Siesta Classic Lo Su Hotel HOTEL **$$$**
(Map p64; ☑024-3935 1632; 32 P Lo Su; r from US$105) There's a high degree of comfort at this good-looking and elegant hotel with a spa and super rooftop bar with excellent views over Hoan Kiem Lake – a top spot for sunset cocktails. The hotel has an excellent location and rooms are stylish and comfortable, though the cheapest have no windows; upgrade to a deluxe room for a view.

🛏 French Quarter

The French Quarter is the area just south of Hoan Kiem Lake, west of the Song Hong as far as Hanoi Train Station, and south of Thong Nhat Park. Cheaper digs are less common here – this is quite a classy area and the preserve of boutiquey choices and historic hotels. You're further away from the action, but taxis are plentiful and you're never far from a decent dinner.

★Somerset Grand Hanoi APARTMENT **$$**
(Map p68; ☑024-3934 2342; www.somerset.com; 49 P Hai Ba Trung; apt from US$130; ❄☎⍚) Rates vary dramatically due to the nature and location of this sprawling apartment-hotel tower, but bargains can be found if you book ahead. For the central location and amenities alone, the selection of studio to three-bedroom apartments with full kitchen and laundry facilities can't be beat. Outside high season the rates drop to around US$100 for a one-bed 64-sq-metre apartment.

★Sofitel Legend Metropole Hotel HOTEL **$$$**
(Map p64; ☑024-3826 6919; www.sofitel-legend -metropole-hanoi.com; 15 P Ngo Quyen; r from US$220; ❄@☎⍚) Hanoi's finest hotel is a slice of colonial history, with its restored French-colonial facade, mahogany-panelled reception rooms and haute cuisine. Rooms in the Heritage Wing have unmatched colonial style and have hosted Charlie Chaplin and Graham Greene – the latter wrote *The Quiet American* while staying here. The modern Opera Wing has sumptuous levels of comfort, if not the same character.

Even if you're not a guest here, pop in for a poolside cocktail at the Bamboo Bar, which is surprisingly reasonably priced.

★Conifer Boutique Hotel HOTEL **$$$**
(Map p64; ☑024-3266 9999; www.coniferhotel. com.vn; 9 P Ly Dao Thanh; d/ste from US$95/140; ❄☎) This is a fantastic little hotel tucked away on a pleasant French Quarter side street, opposite a wonderfully dilapidated French-colonial mansion. Rooms are on the smaller side but are functional and well thought out. Be sure to pay extra for a street-facing room with a generous, enclosed balcony: perfect for watching afternoon storms. Otherwise, aim for one of the suites.

Hotel de l'Opera BOUTIQUE HOTEL **$$$**
(Map p64; ☑024-6282 5555; www.hoteldelopera. com; 29 P Trang Tien; r from US$145; ❄@☎⍚) The chic Hotel de l'Opera effortlessly combines French-colonial style with a sophisticated design aesthetic. Rooms are trimmed in silk and Asian textiles, and splurge-worthy features include a spa and the late-night live-jazz vibe of the bar La Fée Verte (Green Fairy) at the end of the lobby. If you're wondering, Green Fairy is a reference to absinthe. There's a pool on the 3rd floor.

🛏 Greater Hanoi

Fraser Suites Hanoi APARTMENT **$$$**
(☑024-3719 8877; http://hanoi.frasershospi tality.com; 51 Xuan Dieu, Tay Ho; apt from US$187; ❄☎⍚) These sumptuous, fully equipped serviced apartments in buzzing lakeside Tay Ho are the perfect choice for the discerning traveller staying a few days or more. There's a gym and children's play areas, and the gorgeous, landscaped outdoor pool is the city's most alluring.

Lotte Hotel HOTEL $$$
(Map p58; ☑024-3333 1000; www.lottehotel. com; 54 Lieu Giai, Ba Dinh, Lotte Center; d/ste from US$150/197; ☎☒) Hanoi's highest hotel rooms on the upper floors of the 65-storey Lotte Center are lauded by the pretty, young and self-conscious travelling set for their elegant design, sophistication, spaciousness and incomparable sense of loftiness. Facilities include two pools, a gym, spa, four restaurants and two bars, with views as standard. It's located a 20-minute drive from the Old Quarter.

✖ Eating

Hanoi is an international city, and whatever your budget or tastes, it's available here. If you've just flown in, dig into the fragrantly spiced local cuisine – the city's street food is an essential experience.

If you've been up in the hills of northern Vietnam subsisting on noodles and rice, the capital's cosmopolitan dining will be a welcome change.

✖ Old Quarter

★**Bun Cha 34** VIETNAMESE $
(Map p58; ☑0948 361 971; 34 P Hang Than; meals 35,000d; ⊙8.30am-5pm; ☎) Best *bun cha* (barbecued pork with rice vermicelli) in Vietnam? Many say 34 is up there. No presidents have eaten at the plastic tables, but you get perfectly moist chargrilled pork, zesty fresh herbs and delicious broth to dip everything in. The *nem* (seafood spring rolls) are great too. Aim for noon for patties straight off the coals.

New Day VIETNAMESE $
(Map p60; ☑024-3828 0315; 72 P Ma May; meals 50,000-100,000d; ⊙9.30am-11pm) Busy New Day attracts locals, expats and travellers alike with its broad menu. The eager staff always find space for new diners, so look forward to sharing a table with some like-minded fans of Vietnamese food. It's not advertised, but evening diners can point and choose from selections for a mixed plate for about 100,000d.

Com Pho Co VIETNAMESE $
(Map p60; ☑024-2216 4028; 16 Nguyen Sieu; meals 60,000-140,000d; ⊙10am-9.30pm) This large, bustling restaurant attracts a mixed crowd for its long menu of simple, good Vietnamese dishes such as *ga nuong xa* (lemongrass chicken) and Hanoi *pho cuon*

(steamed rice rolls filled with mango, vegetables and shrimp). The four-course set meals (US$6) are good value and can include surprisingly tasty crème caramel. Choose the internal leafy courtyard for some peace.

Banh Mi Hoi An SANDWICHES $
(Bami Bread; Map p60; ☑0981 043 144; 98 P Hang Bac; banh mi 15,000-25,000d; ⊙6.30am-10.30pm) Dense, toasted baguettes with flavoursome pâté and fillings like *ga nuong xa* are what keeps this tiny *banh mi* (filled baguettes) place busy into the night. They often sell out before closing time.

Banh Mi Pho Hue SANDWICHES $
(Map p70; 118 P Hue; banh mi 25,000-55,000d; ⊙6.30am-7pm) *Banh mi* vendors abound in Hanoi, although this baguette phenomenon is less popular than in Ho Chi Minh City. Open since 1978, this place is usually packed with locals – always a good sign.

Banh Cuon VIETNAMESE $
(Map p60; 14 P Hang Ga; meals from 35,000d; ⊙8am-3pm) Don't even bother ordering here; just squeeze in, and a plate of gossamer-light *banh cuon* (steamed rice pancakes filled with minced pork, mushrooms and shrimp) will be placed in front of you.

Hung Lau VIETNAMESE $
(Map p68; ☑024-3828 8700; 6 Ngo Tram; meals 50,000d; ⊙8.30am-3.30pm) This small spot with metal tables does simply delicious *bun cha* – very affordable and very scrummy indeed. The spring rolls are yummy, too.

★**Blue Butterfly** VIETNAMESE $$
(Map p60; ☑0944 852 009, 024-3926 3845; www. bluebutterflyrestaurant.com; 69 P Ma May; meals 195,000-400,000d; ⊙9.30am-11pm) Blue Butterfly floats above its weight with the lamp-lit dark-wood stylings of a heritage house and a good-value menu of Vietnamese classics, from *bun cha* (barbecued pork) to duck with tamarind sauce. Staff offer knowledgeable suggestions and demonstrate how to tackle dishes such as *nem lui* (pork grilled on lemongrass skewers, wrapped in rice paper and dipped in peanut sauce).

★**Grandma's Restaurant** VIETNAMESE $$
(Map p68; ☑024-3537 8666; www.grandmares taurant.com; 6a P Duong Thanh; meals 300,000d; ⊙11am-2pm & 5-10pm; ☎) With dark-wood furniture, concrete walls and lanterns, staff dressed in white and a limited menu of artfully presented dishes, Grandma's

SPECIALITY FOOD STREETS

To combine eating with exploration, head to these locations crammed with interesting restaurants and food stalls.

Ngo Cam Chi (Map p68) This narrow lane is packed with local eateries turning out cheap, tasty food for a few dollars. Ngo Cam Chi translates as 'Forbidden to Point Alley' and dates from centuries ago. It is said that the street was named as a reminder for the local residents to keep their curious fingers in their pockets when the king and his entourage went through the neighbourhood. Ngo Cam Chi is about 500m northeast of Hanoi Train Station. Adjoining Tong Duy Tan is also crammed with good eating.

Đuong Thuy Khue (Map p68) Near the southern bank of West Lake, Đ Thuy Khue features dozens of outdoor seafood restaurants. The level of competition is evident by the daredevil touts who literally throw themselves in front of oncoming traffic to steer people towards their tables. You can eat well here for about 150,000d per person.

Pho Ly Van Phuc (Map p68) More commonly known as 'Chicken Street', Pho Ly Van Phuc is devoted to barbecued, grilled and roast chicken, usually dished up brushed with honey and served with bread, potatoes, vinegar dip, chilli sauce and lashings of cold beer (to taste).

Pho Truc Bach (Map p58) A quieter waterfront scene is around the northeast edge of Truc Bach Lake. Many *lau* (hotpot) restaurants are huddled together in an almost continuous strip for a few hundred metres. Grab a few friends and settle in at one of the dinky lakeside tables for a DIY session of fresh seafood, chicken or beef. It's perfect on a cool Hanoi night.

Cho Am Thuc Ngoc Lam (Map p58) Across the Song Hong (Red River), in Long Bien, this sprawling riverfront food street is popular with locals and heavy on seafood. There are excellent views of the Chuong Duong and Long Bien bridges. Beware the cluster of *thit cho* dog-meat restaurants at the start of the strip (Hanoi is aiming to make the city dog-meat free by 2021, so these restaurants should soon disappear under the planned city-wide ban).

is worth savouring for its ravishing beef, chicken, duck and seafood dishes. The sea bass with pepper sauce sounds spicy, but is actually quite sweet, and lovely. Finish with the excellent handmade coconut ice cream. There's a good wine list too. Reserve ahead.

Cha Ca Thang Long　　　VIETNAMESE $$
(Map p60; ☑ 024-3824 5115; www.chacathanglong. com; 19-31 P Duong Thanh; cha ca fish meals 180,000d; ☺10am-3pm & 5-10pm) Bring along your DIY cooking skills and grill your own succulent *cha ca* fish dish in a pan with a little shrimp paste and plenty of veggies, herbs and peanuts. *Cha ca* is an iconic Hanoi dish heavy on turmeric and dill; staff will show you what to do. You may get taken across the road to the overspill restaurant.

Zaika　　　INDIAN $$
(Map p60; ☑ 0913 221 971, 0913 221 972; 13 P Hang Dieu; meal 180,000-250,000d; ☺11am-10pm; ☏🅿️) With a cinnabar interior, this buzzing spot delivers a measure of elegance on top of its warm and welcoming service. The North Indian menu is a tantalising and ambitious affair, from *palak paneer* (cottage cheese in spinach) through to barbecue tandoori shrimps, searing chicken vindaloo and smooth, slow-cooked black lentils. The flavours are superb and vegetarians find themselves well catered for.

🍴 Around Hoan Kiem Lake

Kem Trang Tien　　　ICE CREAM $
(Map p64; 35 P Trang Tien; ice cream from 8000d; ☺8am-10pm) It's barely possible to walk down the road to get to this parlour on hot summer nights, such is its popularity with local teens and families. Prices are so low that many try multiple flavours, like coconut milk, chocolate, green bean or taro. Most popular are the scoops, served in the main hall inside, where it's tempting to join the queue again and again.

Pho Thin　　　NOODLES $
(Map p64; 61 Dinh Tien Hoang; meals 50,000d; ☺6am-1pm & 5-10.30pm; 🅿️) This slender,

crammed hole-in-the-wall place directly east of Hoan Kien Lake has narrow tables and stools where it's all elbows and chatter. The place has been going since 1955, serving steaming bowls of beef noodle *pho* in three sizes (small, big and jumbo); extra beef costs from 30,000d and a poached egg thrown in is 5000d.

Vegetarians can just ask for egg; add chilli according to taste.

Jalus Vegan Kitchen   VEGAN $
(Map p64; ☑ 024-3266 9730; 2nd fl, 46 Hang Trong; meals 30,000-60,000d; ☺10am-10pm Tue-Sun; ☏⏚) Pull up a pine table at this modern, comforting and quiet hidden-away gem to sink a delicious blueberry smoothie and feast on veggie burgers, vegan soup of the day, potato curry with red rice, spinach pasta and more. There are definite Vietnamese twists, with lemongrass and spice, and sometimes special all-Vietnamese menus.

Bun Rieu Cua   VIETNAMESE $
(Map p64; 40 P Hang Tre; bun rieu 25,000d; ☺7-9.30am) Get to this incredibly popular spot early, as its sole dish of *bun rieu cua* (noodle soup with beef in a spicy crab broth) is only served for a couple of hours from 7am. A Hanoi classic.

La Place   CAFE $
(Map p64; ☑ 024-3928 5859; 4 P Au Trieu; meals from 70,000d; ☺7.30am-10.30pm; ☏) This popular cafe/restaurant with balcony views straight over St Joseph Cathedral has an East–West menu and walls decorated in propaganda art. Plenty of wine by the glass is on offer and the coffee has a real kick. Reserve ahead for a balcony table, but you'll need to sit side by side. Breakfasts are also good.

★Poke Hanoi   HAWAIIAN $$
(Map p64; ☑0903 483 218; 11b P Hang Khay; meals 180,000d; ☺11am-9pm Mon-Sat; ☏) Just the ticket for a good-looking detox in a neat and wholesome well-furnished space with an outside terrace and parasols. Choose your rice base, fish (salmon, spicy tuna, octopus etc) or tofu, sauce, topping and a crispy sprinkling, all added to a large bowl, and enjoy. For views of the lake you'll need to fight for the table in the terrace corner.

★Hanoi Social Club   CAFE $$
(Map p68; ☑024-3938 2117; www.facebook.com/TheHanoiSocialClub; 6 Hoi Vu; meals 95,000-175,000d; ☺8am-11pm; ⏚) On three levels

with retro furniture, the Hanoi Social Club is an artist hub and the city's most cosmopolitan cafe. Dishes include potato fritters with chorizo for breakfast, and pasta, burgers and wraps for lunch or dinner. Vegetarian options feature a tasty mango curry, and the quiet laneway location is a good spot for an egg coffee (60,000d), beer or wine.

The Hanoi Social Club also hosts regular gigs and events. Check its Facebook page for what's on.

V's Home   VEGETARIAN $$
(Map p64; ☑0888 011 074; P Duong Thanh; meals 125,000d; ☺10am-10pm; ⏚) ✿ Blink and you'll miss the slim alleyway opening leading to this excellent upstairs restaurant, with diners attended to by hearing- and speech-impaired staff. The relaxing space is elegant and charming, with a gorgeous tiled floor, graceful arches and green foliage. The dishes with organic ingredients are lovely and there's a good vegan selection. Profits are contributed to community initiatives.

The restaurant also purveys various goods – soaps, peanut oil, handmade goods – all made with environmentally friendly ingredients. Some of the Vietnamese dishes, such as *bun cha gio* (vermicelli with spring rolls) and *banh mi xiu mai dau ga* (Vietnamese bread with steamed chickpea meatballs in tomato sauce), are only served on Thursdays. V's Home has a small (if rather disorganised) store of goods for sale at 8 Nguyen Che Nghia, south of Hoan Kiem Lake.

✕ West of the Old Quarter

★Old Hanoi   VIETNAMESE $$
(Map p68; ☑024-3747 8337; www.oldhanoi.com; 18 Ton That Thiep; meals 90,000-179,000d; ☺10am-2pm & 5-10pm) This sophisticated eating spot in a restored French-colonial villa has a pleasant casual courtyard outside and starched white tablecloths inside. Once host to celebrity chef Gordon Ramsay, it serves traditional Hanoian and Vietnamese specialities with aplomb; you'll enjoy the selection and find the best value for money if you dine in a group.

Koto   CAFE $$
(Nha Hang Koto Van Mieu; Map p68; ☑024-3747 0338; www.koto.com.au; 59 P Van Mieu; meals 160,000d; ☺7.30am-10pm, closed dinner Mon) Ranging over four floors with a terrace

Street-Food Spotter's Guide

Deciphering Hanoi's street-food scene can be bewildering, but it's worth persevering and diving in.

1. Bun cha

Barbecued pork with rice vermicelli. Visiting Hanoi and missing out is a big food no-no. Try it at Bun Cha 34 (p79).

2. Pho

Almost synonymous with Vietnamese food; ensure you down bowl upon bowl of Vietnam's most celebrated noodle dish. Have some at Pho Thin (p80).

3. Banh cuon

Steamed rice crêpes with minced pork, mushrooms and shrimp, wrapped up in a gossamer-light skin. Squeeze into Banh Cuon (p79) to sample some.

4. Banh mi

The go-to on-the-spot sandwich responsible for much of the city's calorific intake. You can find it everywhere, but Banh Mi Pho Hue (p79) is a goodie.

5. Banh goi

Delectable deep-fried pastries crammed with pork, vermicelli and mushrooms.

6. Bun bo nam bo

Rice noodles with beef; mix in bean sprouts, garlic, lemongrass and green mango for a filling treat.

7. Banh tom

A crispy and crunchy shrimp and sweet potato fritter – once bitten, forever smitten.

8. Bun rieu cua

Moreish, hunger-slaying noodle soup with beef in a spicy crab broth. Pop into Bun Rieu Cua (p81), east of Hoan Kiem Lake.

9. Caphe trung

OK, not street food per se, but egg coffee is the city's signature drink, served all over town. Head to Cafe Giang (p85) for the original and very best.

and bar, this superb modernist cafe-bar-restaurant overlooking the Temple of Literature features neat interior design and exceptionally sweet staff, with daily specials chalked up on a blackboard. The short menu has everything from excellent Vietnamese food, including braised pumpkin in a creamy sauce with mushroom, to yummy pita wraps and beer-battered fish and chips.

Koto was started by Vietnamese Australian Jimmy Pham as a not-for-profit project providing career training and guidance to disadvantaged children and teens.

🍴 French Quarter

★ Chim Sao   VIETNAMESE $
(Map p70; ☑024-3976 0633; www.chimsao. com; 63-65 Ngo Hue; meals 45,000-120,000d; ☺9.30am-11pm; 🖉) Sit at tables downstairs or grab a more traditional spot on the floor upstairs and discover excellent Vietnamese food, with some dishes inspired by the ethnic minorities of Vietnam's north. Definite standouts are the hearty and robust sausages, zingy and fresh salads, and duck with star fruit (carambola). Even simple dishes are outstanding. Come with a group to sample the full menu.

Bun Cha Huong Lien   VIETNAMESE $
(Map p70; ☑0966 962 683; 24 P Le Van Hu; meals from 40,000d; ☺10am-8pm) Bun Cha Huong Lien was launched into stardom thanks to Barack Obama, who dined here with celebrity chef Anthony Bourdain in May 2016. Customers fill the four storeys to sample the grilled-pork-and-noodle delicacy while staff call out 'Obama *bun cha!*' to passers-by. The 'Combo Obama' gets you a bowl of *bun cha,* a fried seafood roll and Hanoi beer for 90,000d.

★ La Badiane   INTERNATIONAL $$$
(Map p68; ☑024-3942 4509; www.labadiane -hanoi.com; 10 Nam Ngu; meals from 280,000d; ☺11.30am-2pm & 6-10pm Mon-Sat) This stylish bistro is set in a restored, whitewashed French villa arrayed around a breezy central courtyard. French cuisine underpins the menu – La Badiane translates as 'star anise' – but Asian and Mediterranean flavours also feature. Menu highlights include sea-bass tagliatelle with smoked paprika, and prawn bisque with wasabi tomato bruschetta. Two-/three-course lunches (395,000/485,000d) are on the menu along with an evening degustation (1,890,000d).

🍴 Greater Hanoi

Oasis   DELI $
(Map p58; ☑024-3719 1196; www.oasishanoi. net; 24 P Xuan Dieu; pizza slices 25,000d; ☺7am-8pm) This Italian-owned deli has excellent bread, cheese and salami, as well as home-made pasta and sauces and other items. It's north of central Hanoi in the Tay Ho restaurant strip on P Xuan Dieu. It delivers too (20,000d between 8am and 7pm).

★ Tim Ho Wan   DIM SUM $$
(Map p58; ☑024-3333 1725; 36th fl, Lotte Center, 54 P Lieu Giai, Ba Dinh; dim sum 69,000-95,000d; ☺11.30am-10pm) Do yourself a favour and reserve a window table at the Hanoi branch of this legendary Hong Kong dim sum chain, high above the city on the 36th floor of the Lotte Center. Bring a friend or six and an empty stomach – we guarantee you won't regret it.

Maison de Tet Decor   CAFE $$
(Map p58; ☑0966 611 383; www.tet-lifestyle -collection.com; 156 Tua Hoa, Nghi Tam, Tay Ho; meals from 120,000d; ☺7am-10pm) Sumptuous, healthy and organic (when possible) wholefoods are presented with aplomb in one of Hanoi's loveliest settings, an expansive, airy villa overlooking West Lake.

Quan Kien   VIETNAMESE $$
(Map p58; ☑024-6297 2021; 143 P Nhgi Tam; meals 80,000-130,000d; ☺9am-11pm) Quan Kien is an interesting spot for cuisine from the Hmong, Muong and Thai ethnic minorities – try the grilled chicken with wild pepper – traditional Vietnamese *ruou* (wine) made from apricots or apples, and more challenging snacks like grilled ants' eggs and crickets. If insects aren't your thing, it's still a fun night sitting at the low tables eating excellent Vietnamese dishes.

🍷 Drinking & Nightlife

Hanoi's eclectic drinking scene features grungy dive bars, Western-style pubs, one gay bar, sleek lounge bars, craft-beer houses, cafes and hundreds of *bia hoi* (draught beer) joints.

The best places for a bar crawl include traveller-friendly P Ta Hien in the Old Quarter, and P Ngo Bao Khanh near the northwest edge of Hoan Kiem Lake. An alternative scene, popular with expats, is on P Xuan Dieu in the West Lake area.

HANOI'S COFFEE CULTURE

Western-style cafes and coffee shops are widespread in Vietnamese cities, but many pale in comparison to traditional Vietnamese family-run cafes dotted around central Hanoi. Here's where to go and what to order for an authentic local experience. Most cafes are open from around 7am to 7pm, but hours sometimes vary. On the eastern edge of the Old Quarter, P Nguyen Huu Huan is lined with good cafes, most with free wi-fi.

Cafe Duy Tri (Map p58; ✆ 024-3829 1386; 43a P Yen Phu; ⊗ 8am-6pm) In the same location since 1936, this caffeine-infused labyrinth is a Hanoi classic. You'll feel like Gulliver as you negotiate the tiny ladders and stairways to reach the 3rd-floor balcony. Delicious *caphe sua chua* (iced coffee with yoghurt) may be your new favourite summertime drink. It's a couple of blocks east of Truc Bach Lake.

Cafe Pho Co (Map p60; ✆ 024-3928 8153; 4th fl, 11 P Hang Gai; ⊗ 8am-11pm) One of Hanoi's most hidden cafes, this place has plum views over Hoan Kiem Lake. Enter through the silk shop, and continue through the antique-bedecked courtyard up to the top floor for the mother of all vistas. You'll need to order coffee and snacks before tackling the final winding staircase. Try sweet *caphe trung da* (40,000d), coffee topped with silky-smooth beaten egg yolk.

Cafe Lam (Map p60; ✆ 024-3824 5940; www.cafelam.com; 60 P Nguyen Huu Huan; ⊗ 6.30am-7.30pm) A classic multiroom cafe and beautiful space of wooden tables that's been around for years – long enough to build up a compact gallery of modern and traditional paintings left behind by talented patrons who couldn't afford to pay their tabs during the American War. These days you might spy Vespa-riding youth refuelling on wickedly strong *caphe den* (black coffee).

Cafe Giang (Map p60; 39 P Nguyen Huu Huan; ⊗ 7am-10pm) The originator of Hanoi's egg coffee is still running in this time-worn family establishment, serving the best in town since 1946 at *egg-sellent* prices... Head upstairs and order up a superb regular egg coffee (25,000d), or varieties of egg coffee with chocolate, cinnamon, Coke, rum or beer. Other non-egg coffees and teas are available. You get a plastic tab and pay downstairs.

Hanoi has a surfeit of superb cafes; beyond those listed here, check out Hanoi Hideaway (www.hanoihideaway.com) for more caffeine-loaded ideas.

★ **The Railway Hanoi 2** CAFE
(Map p68; www.therailwayhanoi.com; 65 P Ton That Thiep; ⊗ 9am-9pm) Choo-choo! Thao and her fun and exceedingly amiable staff woo-woo passers-by to this stand-in for the owner's other cafe by the railway line (p74). The cafe serves excellent egg coffee, craft beer and food, teaches English to local kids (which you can join in with) and runs food tours. Vietnamese classes are in the pipeline too.

The Railway Hanoi CAFE
(Map p68; www.therailwayhanoi.com; 26/10 Đ Dien Bien Phu; ⊗ 9am-9pm) Closed at the time of research, with authorities shutting down all the cafes along the railway line (p74), this was the original and best of all the cafes on the tracks. If it has not reopened by the time you read this, stop by the excellent Railway Hanoi 2 just around the corner.

★ **Tadioto** BAR
(Map p64; ✆ 024-6680 9124; www.facebook.com/tadiotohanoi; 24b P Tong Dan; ⊗ 9am-11.45pm Sun-Thu, from 8am Fri & Sat; 🛜) Attracting a well-dressed clientele, Nguyen Qui Duc's unofficial clubhouse for the underground art and literary scene is this dark, quirky colonial bar in the French Quarter. Obligatory red accents (seat covers, wrought-iron grille on the doors), reworkings of art-deco furniture and plenty of recycled ironwork feature heavily. The highlight of the cool cocktail list is the sweet mojito.

★ **Nola** BAR
(Map p60; 89 P Ma May; ⊗ 10am-11.30pm Mon-Sat, to 11pm Sun) Retro furniture and art are mixed and matched in this bohemian multilevel labyrinth tucked away from Ma May's tourist bustle. Pop in for a coffee and banana bread in a quiet section, or return after dark to one of Hanoi's best little bars.

Manzi Art Space BAR
(Map p68; ✆ 024-3716 3397; www.facebook.com/manzihanoi; 14 Phan Huy Ich; ⊗ 8am-10.30pm) Part

cool art exhibition space, part chic cafe and bar, Manzi is worth seeking out north of the Old Quarter. A restored French villa hosts diverse exhibitions of painting, sculpture and photography, and the compact courtyard garden is perfect for a cup of coffee or glass of wine. There's also a small shop selling works by contemporary Vietnamese artists.

Just round the corner is a second branch of Manzi Art Space, which operates solely as an exhibition space.

Loading T Cafe
CAFE

(Map p64; ☑ 0903 342 000; 2nd fl, 8 Chan Cam; ⊙ 8am-10pm; 🛜) Architecture lovers will appreciate this charmer of an upstairs cafe converted from a room in a crumbling French-colonial house. The ornate tiled floor, vintage fans, huge window, mismatched period furniture and other design gems capture Hanoi's faded glamour. Homemade cakes, fresh juices and coconut or yoghurt coffee are on the menu. The egg coffee is a winner, while the music is all French ballads. There's a mezzanine loft, up the stairs.

Pasteur Street Brewing Company
BAR

(Map p64; ☑ 024-6294 9462; www.pasteurstreet. com; 1 P Au Trieu; ⊙ 11am-midnight; 🛜) A curious lack of character stalks this two-floor bar, although the terrace is good. The beer menu is pricey, but the superb choice of IPAs, fruity ales, Belgian-style ales and stouts are the draw if you need to flush the ever-present taste of Hanoi beer from your palate. Try the Double IPA, a hoppy brew with a 8.7% ABV (alcohol by volume) punch.

Bluebird's Nest
CAFE

(To Chim Xanh; Map p68; 19 P Dang Dung; ⊙ 8am-10.30pm; 🛜) Truly a satisfying two-floor haven of peace in a bustling city, this cute, book-stuffed cafe feels like a quiet library; it's a superb choice for some tranquillity and space to read a book, zip out a few emails, check your Instagram feed, zone out, hide from the noise and unwind. It's down an alley off P Dang Dung.

Eden Cafe
CAFE

(Map p64; 2 P Nha Tho; ⊙ 8am-10pm; 🛜) Spectacular views extend right over to the facade of St Joseph Cathedral from upstairs at easy-going Eden Cafe, a comfortable space arrayed with chairs, sofas and cushions and bedecked with colourful murals. Sink a refreshing smoothie, juice, hot chocolate, coffee or an evening cocktail and soak up the vista outside. Beer is also served.

Cong Caphe
CAFE

(Map p64; www.congcaphe.com; 27 P Nha Tho; ⊙ 7am-11pm) Settle in to the eclectic beats and kitsch Communist memorabilia at hip Cong Caphe with a *caphe sua da* (iced coffee with condensed milk), *caphe nong* (hot coffee with condensed milk), a latte, cappuccino or *tra* (tea), and take in the views of St Joseph Cathedral opposite. Service is usually superb. There are tons of branches about town; check the website.

GC Bar
GAY & LESBIAN

(Map p64; ☑ 024-3825 0499; 5 P Ngo Bao Khanh; ⊙ 5pm-midnight Sun-Thu, to 2am Fri & Sat; 🛜)

BIA AHOY!

'Tram phan tram!' Remember these words, as all over Vietnam, glasses of *bia hoi* are raised and emptied, and cries of *'tram phan tram'* ('100%' or 'bottoms up') echo around the table.

Bia hoi is Vietnam's very own draught beer or microbrew. This refreshing, light-bodied pilsner was first introduced to Vietnam by the Czechs in a display of Communist solidarity. Brewed without preservatives, it is meant to be enjoyed immediately and costs as little as 5000d a glass.

Hanoi is the *bia hoi* capital of Vietnam and there are microbars on many Old Quarter street corners. A wildly popular place unofficially known as 'Bia Hoi junction' and 'Beer Corner' is at the corner of P Ta Hien and P Luong Ngoc Quyen, in the heart of the Old Quarter. It's now packed with backpackers and travellers though, and has lost most of its local charm.

An alternative, more local *bia hoi* junction is where P Nha Hoa or P Bat Dan meets P Duong Thanh on the western edge of the Old Quarter. For something to go with the beer, **Nha Hang Lan Chin** (Map p64; ☑ 024-3824 1138; cnr P Hang Tre & P Hang Thung; ⊙ 9.30am-10pm) is famed for *vit quay* (roast duck); and you can't go past **Quan Bia Minh** (Map p60; 7a P Dinh Liet; meals 90,000-130,000d; ⊙ 7.30am-late) for well-priced Vietnamese food and excellent service led by the eponymous Mrs Minh.

Hanoi's long-standing (25 years and counting), only established gay bar – and unofficial LGBT HQ – might seem small and vanilla midweek, but it gets pumped on weekend nights. Reasonably priced drinks make it popular with a mixed local crowd and it's easy for gay visitors to drop by. It's casual, so shorts and smoking indoors are common.

Little Plan Cafe
CAFE
(Map p64; www.facebook.com/thelittleplan.cafe; 11 P Phu Doan; ⊙8am-10pm) Tucked away down a very tight alley off Phu Doan, Little Plan possesses a charming ambience, steeped in an old-world feel beneath a whirling ceiling fan, with bygone photos, time-worn furniture, a friendly cat and aged TV sets and analogue cameras lying about. It's all set to relaxing music, with a balcony outside and a cosy mezzanine loft.

The Rooftop
BAR
(Map p68; ☑0913 706 966; www.therooftop.vn; 19th fl, Pacific Place, 83b P Ly Thuong Kiet; ⊙noon-midnight) For views of the city, pop in for an expensive beer or cocktail and enjoy the vista. It's very popular with a glittering array of Hanoi's cashed-up youth, especially late in the evening when DJs play.

☆ Entertainment

There is plenty of Vietnamese folk and traditional theatre aimed at visitors here. If water puppets and showy costumes are not your thing, seek out small cafes that double as performance spaces where jazz, live music and more are performed up close.

Cinemas

August Cinema
CINEMA
(Rap Thang 8; Map p70; 45 P Hang Bai; ⊙024-3825 3911) One of the oldest cinemas in town, with architecturally significant, modernist lines. It occasionally shows English-language films.

Centre Culturel Français de Hanoi
CINEMA
(Map p64; www.institutfrancais-vietnam.com; 24 P Trang Tien) Set in the sublime L'Espace building near the Hanoi Opera House, the Centre Culturel offers a regular program of French films. Musical events are also staged; check the website for what's on. French lessons are also offered.

Music

Traditional music is usually performed daily at the Temple of Literature (p65).

CURFEW

Hanoi is certainly not a clubbers' paradise, and the often-enforced curfew means dancing is pretty much confined to bar-clubs in and around the Old Quarter. The no-fun police supervise strict opening hours and regularly show up to compel the closure of bars and clubs that flout this law. This makes for minimal action after midnight during the week. Weekends are getting busier now that the Old Quarter is allowed to stay open until 2am on Fridays, Saturdays and Sundays. In any case, lock-in action after curfew does occur; ask around in Hanoi's hostels to find out which bars are currently staying open beyond the witching hour.

★ Binh Minh Jazz Club
JAZZ
(Map p64; ☑024-3933 6555; www.minhjazzvietnam.com; 1a P Trang Tien; ⊙performances 9pm-midnight) This atmospheric venue tucked behind the Opera House is the place in Hanoi to catch live jazz. There's a full bar, a food menu and high-quality gigs featuring father-and-son team Minh and Dac, plus other local and international jazz acts. There's no cover charge, so the small, smoky venue fills quickly – get there early.

★ Thang Long Ca Tru Theatre
LIVE MUSIC
(Map p60; ☑0122 326 6897; www.catruthanglong.com; 28 P Hang Buom; ⊙8pm Thu & Sat) Concerts of traditional Vietnamese music are held in this intimate restored house in the Old Quarter. *Ca tru* is indigenous to the north of Vietnam, and concerts feature a selection of the 100 or so *ca tru* melodies. The art form has been recognised as an endangered 'intangible cultural heritage' by Unesco.

Hanoi Opera House
OPERA
(Map p64; ☑0913 489 858, 024-3993 0113; www.ticketvn.com; 1 P Trang Tien) Evening performances of classical music, opera and ballet are periodically held at the grand Hanoi Opera House. Check the website for details of upcoming performances.

Music Cafe
LIVE MUSIC
(Nhac Cafe; Map p60; ☑024-3935 2580; www.fb.me/nhaccafehn; 7 Hang Thung; ⊙7am-11pm, shows 8.30pm Thu-Sun) This intimate cafe and bar shows off its style with vintage-music

DON'T MISS: PUNCH & JUDY IN A POOL

The ancient art of water puppetry (roi nuoc) was virtually unknown outside of northern Vietnam until the 1960s. It originated with rice farmers who worked the flooded fields of the Red River Delta. Some say they saw the potential of the water as a dynamic stage; others say they adapted conventional puppetry during a massive flood. Whatever the real story, the art form is at least 1000 years old. Performances take place at the Municipal Water Puppet Theatre.

The farmers carved the human and animal puppets from water-resistant fig-tree timber (sung) and staged performances in ponds, lakes or flooded paddy fields. Today a tank of waist-deep water is used for the 'stage'. The glossy, painted puppets are up to 50cm long and weigh as much as 15kg. Some puppets are simply attached to a long pole, while others are set on a floating base, in turn attached to a pole. In the darkened auditorium, it appears as if they are walking on water. If used continually, each puppet has a lifespan of about four months: puppet production provides several villages outside Hanoi with a full-time livelihood.

Eleven puppeteers, each trained for a minimum of three years, are involved in the performance. Their considerable skills were traditionally passed only from father to son, for fear that daughters would marry outside the village and take the secrets with them.

Traditional live music is as important as the action on stage. Each memorable performance consists of a number of vignettes depicting pastoral scenes and legends. One scene tells of the battle between a fisherman and his prey, which is so electric it is as if a live fish were being used. There are also fire-breathing dragons (complete with fireworks) and a flute-playing boy riding a buffalo.

The water puppets are both amusing and graceful, appearing and disappearing as if by magic. Spectators in front-row seats can expect a bit of a splash!

paraphernalia. It's best with a cocktail in hand in the evening, when vocalists croon in Vietnamese about lost loves, with accompanying acoustic guitar or violin. Check the website for the performance calendar. The coffee is good and so's the food.

Theatre

**Municipal Water
Puppet Theatre**   PUPPET THEATRE
(Map p64; ☑024-3824 9494; www.thanglong waterpuppet.org; 57b P Dinh Tien Hoang; tickets 100,000-200,000d) Water-puppetry shows are a real treat for children. Multilingual programs allow the audience to read up on each vignette as it's performed. Although there are five afternoon performances daily, book well ahead, especially from October to April. The first/last performances are at 3pm/8pm.

**Vietnam National
Tuong Theatre**   THEATRE
(Map p60; ☑024-837 0046; www.vietnam tuongtheatre.com; 51 P Duong Thanh; tickets 150,000d; ☺6pm Mon & Thu) Hat tuong is a uniquely Vietnamese variation of Chinese opera that enjoyed its greatest popularity under the Nguyen dynasty in the 19th century. Performances at this theatre used to be by invitation only but are now open to locals and visitors. A night watching hat tuong is an interesting traditional alternative to Hanoi's wildly popular water puppets.

🛍 Shopping

For Vietnamese handicrafts, including textiles and lacquerware, head to the stores along P Hang Gai, P To Tich, P Hang Khai and P Cau Go in the Old Quarter. P Hang Gai and its continuation, P Hang Bong, are good places to look for embroidered tablecloths, T-shirts and wall hangings. P Hang Gai is also a fine place to buy silk and have clothes custom-made.

★**Craft Link**   ARTS & CRAFTS
(Map p68; ☑024-3733 6101; www.craftlink.com. vn; 43-51 P Van Mieu; ☺9am-6pm) A not-for-profit organisation near the Temple of Literature that sells quality tribal handicrafts, textiles and weavings at fair-trade prices. The bags are quite beautiful and richly coloured – explore them over two floors. There's another branch a little further down the road.

Tan My Design CLOTHING
(Map p60; 024-3938 1154; www.tanmydesign.com; 61 P Hang Gai; 8am-8pm) Stylish clothing, jewellery and accessories, with the bonus of a cool cafe when you need a break from shopping. The homewares and bed linen are definitely worth a look.

Three Trees FASHION & ACCESSORIES
(Map p64; 024-3928 8725; http://threetrees.com.vn; 15 P Nha Tho; 9am-7pm) Stunning, very unusual designer jewellery, including many delicate necklaces and beautiful brooches of insects and animals wrought from silver and opals: they make for special gifts.

Cerender Ceramic Shop CERAMICS
(Map p64; 0938 632 481; 11a P Trang Thi; 9am-9pm) The truly delightful handmade ceramics on show here are a joy. Wonky, weird, winsome and wonderful; if ceramics are right up your street, this place will be too.

Bookworm BOOKS
(Map p68; 024-3715 3711; www.bookwormhanoi.com; 44 P Chau Long; 9am-7pm) Bookworm stocks over 20,000 new and used English-language books over two floors. There's plenty of fiction and it's good on South Asian history and politics as well as children's books and general nonfiction. There's a couple of long couches upstairs for a comfortable sit-down with whatever gems you find on the packed shelves.

Pheva Chocolate CHOCOLATE
(Map p68; 024-3266 8579; www.phevaworld.com; 8b P Phan Boi Chau; 8am-7pm) Pheva sells decidedly moreish artisanal dark and white chocolate produced from organic and free-trade cacao and stylishly wrapped. There's a tantalising and surprising range of flavours, including ginger, white pepper, sesame and peanuts, cinnamon, orange peel, black pepper, and pistachio and raisins.

Chan Con Cong VINTAGE
(Map p64; www.facebook.com/chan.con.cong; 8 Chan Cam; 8am-8pm) This charmingly small vintage shop stuffed away beneath Loading T Cafe sells delightful vintage long dresses and classic togs. There's another, larger branch at 14 Đ Thanh.

Mekong+ ARTS & CRAFTS
(Map p60; 024-3926 4831; https://mekong-plus.com; 13 P Hang Bac; 8am-8pm) Beautiful quilts handcrafted by rural women working in a not-for-profit community-development program.

Mai Gallery ART
(Map p68; 0936 368 367, 024-3938 0568; www.maigallery-vietnam.com; 113 P Hang Bong; 9am-7pm) With some very attractive, elegant and thought-provoking art hanging from its walls, this gallery, run by resident artist Mai, is a good place to learn more about Vietnamese art before making a purchase.

ART IN HANOI

Modern Vietnamese artists are highly technically trained – many could copy a photographic portrait by hand with remarkable detail and accuracy, in a short space of time. Prior to the Communist Party takeover, Vietnam had over 900 years of artistic heritage, which to this day provides many young Vietnamese with an exceptional creative skill set. That said, the Communist Party still curbs freedom of expression, forcing some artists and artisans to work underground. However, with an influx of tourism and interest from the West in recent years, Hanoi's art scene in particular is gaining attention from the outside world. Ever so slowly, talented Vietnamese artists are getting the chance to expand their horizons and broaden their skills.

For visitors interested in art, this means a burgeoning art scene begging for appreciation. Keen shoppers can pick up an original work on canvas by a local artist from as little as US$40 in any one of the Old Quarter's many private galleries – Mai Gallery is a good start. Kick back and check out the vibe at Tadioto (p85) and Manzi Art Space (p85): you'll lock in with like-minded arty folk in no time at all. Better still, go on **Sophie's Art Tour** (0798 303 742; www.sophiesarttour.com; tours from $75). **Into Thin Air 2** (www.facebook.com/intothinairhanoi) is an augmented-reality art exhibition that you download as an app to visit locations around the city accompanied by sound pieces and performance works detailing Hanoi's history.

Thang Long
BOOKS

(Hieu Sach Thang Long; Map p64; ☑ 024-825 7043; 53-55 P Trang Tien; ☻9am-6pm) One of the biggest bookshops in town, with some English and French titles, international newspapers and magazines, and a good selection of titles on the history of Hanoi plus a large choice of books in Vietnamese.

Markets

Dong Xuan Market
MARKET

(Map p60; Dong Xuan; ☻6am-7pm) This large, nontouristy market is located in the Old Quarter, 900m north of Hoan Kiem Lake. There are hundreds of stalls here and lots of the goods are household items or tat, but it's a fascinating place to explore to catch the flavour of local Hanoian life. The area around it also has loads of bustling shops, and more stalls appear at night.

Hom Market
MARKET

(Map p70; cnr P Hue & P Tran Xuan Soan; ☻6am-5pm) On the northeast corner of P Hue and P Tran Xuan Soan, this is a good general-purpose market that's also excellent for local fabric if you plan to have clothes made.

Night Market
MARKET

(Map p60; P Hang Ngang; ☻7pm-midnight Fri-Sun) This market runs north–south through the Old Quarter along P Hang Ngang (P Hang Dao near Hoan Kiem Lake). Content-wise there is spillover from the area's shops, with cheap clothing, souvenirs, street food and plenty of junk, but at least the streets are closed to traffic and prices are low (after haggling). Watch out for pickpockets here.

❶ Information

SAFE TRAVEL

Hanoi is generally a safe city to explore, and serious crimes against tourists are extremely rare, but it's pertinent to exercise some caution.
➡ While it's generally safe to walk around the streets of the Old Quarter at night, it's best to avoid the darker lanes after around 10pm. It's sensible for solo female travellers to take a metered taxi with a reputable company or a Grab taxi when travelling across the city at night.
➡ Beware of pickpockets around market areas and unwanted baggage 'helpers' in crowded transport terminals – particularly when boarding night trains.

Scams

While there's no need to be paranoid, Hanoi is riddled with scams, many of them inextricably linked. Most problems involve budget hotels and tours, and occasionally things can get nasty. We've received reports of verbal aggression and threats of physical violence towards tourists who've decided against a hotel room or a tour. Stay calm and back away slowly or things could quickly flare up.

The taxi and minibus mafia at the airport shuttle unwitting tourists to the wrong hotel. Invariably, the hotel has copied the name of another popular property and will then attempt to appropriate as much of your money as possible. Taxi swindles are also becoming increasingly common. Try to avoid the taxis loitering at Hanoi's bus stations; many have superfast meters. Similarly be careful at the airport; stick to recommended taxi companies (p96).

Some shoeshine boys and *cyclo* (pedicab or bicycle rickshaw) drivers attempt to add a zero or two to an agreed price for their services; stick to your guns and give them the amount you originally agreed upon. Other hawkers will shove food into your hands so you then feel obliged to buy it – just hand it back.

Watch out for friendly, smooth-talking strangers approaching you around Hoan Kiem Lake (but don't confuse them with the legitimate students out practising English!). Be very wary if they suggest a drink or a meal. Gay men are also targeted in this way. Your new friend may then suggest a visit to a karaoke bar, snake-meat restaurant or some other venue and before you know it you're presented with a bill for hundreds of dollars. Be careful and follow your instincts, as these crooks can seem quite charming.

Keep your wits about you, and try to stay in a group if you're returning from a bar late at night.

Traffic & Pollution

Traffic and pollution are other irritants. The city's traffic is so dense and unrelenting that simply crossing the street can be a real headache, and weaving a path through a tide of motorbikes (five million and counting) can be a hairy experience. Our advice is to walk slowly and at a constant pace, allowing motorcyclists sufficient time to judge your position and avoid you. Don't try to move quickly, as you'll just confuse them. Keep your wits about you as you explore the Old Quarter, as motorbikes come from all directions and pavements are obstructed by cooking stalls and more parked motorbikes – despite recent police efforts to keep them clear. Pollution levels can be punishing and the air quality is poor.

EMERGENCY

The emergency services should be able to transfer you to an English-speaker.

Ambulance	☑ 115
Fire	☑ 114
Police	☑ 113

LGBTIQ+ TRAVELLERS

There are very few gay venues in Hanoi, but plenty of places that are gay friendly. Official attitudes have greatly improved in recent years, in part helped by the openly gay former US ambassador to Vietnam, Ted Osius, and his husband, who served until 2017.

The LGBTIQ+ community still keeps a low profile, apart from the annual festival Hanoi Pride (p75), when there's partying, film screenings, talks and a colourful bicycle rally. It's held over one week between July and September.

To get a handle on gay life in Hanoi, join one of the tours with Gay Hanoi Tours (p74): Tuan will happily field any questions you might have. The GC Bar (p86) is the only truly established gay bar in Hanoi, and it's a good place to find out about the most happening new places in town. Accommodation-wise, the Art Boutique Hotel (p77) and Golden Art Hotel (p76) – there's an art theme here! – are gay friendly.

Hanoian contemporary artist Truong Tan is considered Vietnam's first openly gay visual artist, and sometimes exhibits in Hanoi.

The website www.utopia-asia.com has up-to-date information about gay Hanoi.

INTERNET ACCESS

➡ Wi-fi access is virtually ubiquitous in the city's cafes and bars, and pretty much every budget and midrange hotel has it available for free.

➡ If you're staying longer than a week, it's worth getting a prepaid SIM card to stay connected on your (unlocked) device. Prepaid SIM cards are very cheap in Vietnam. Your hostel can arrange one for you (perhaps for a slight price hike), otherwise **Viettel** (Map p60; http://international.viettel.vn; 51 Luong Van Can; ⊗8am-8pm) will sell and set up a SIM from around US$7 to US$10 (the latter option should get you 2GB per day). You can then top up as required. You can also buy a SIM at the International Postal Office. Your passport may be required as ID.

MONEY

Hanoi has many ATMs. On the main roads around Hoan Kiem Lake are international banks where you can change money and get cash advances on credit cards.

POST

Domestic Post Office (Buu Dien Trung Vong; Map p64; ☑024-3825 7036; 75 P Dinh Tien Hoang; ⊗7am-9pm) For internal postal services in Vietnam; also sells philatelic items.

International Postal Office (Map p64; ☑024-3825 2030; cnr P Dinh Tien Hoang & P Dinh Le; ⊗7am-8pm) The entrance is to the right of the Domestic Post Office.

TOURIST INFORMATION

Tourist Information & Support Center (Map p58; ☑24hr English hotline 0941 336 677, Vietnamese 0911 081 968; 28 P Hang Dau; ⊗8am-5pm Wed-Sun) Hanoi finally has an official tourist information desk, although the location near the Long Bien Bridge might put off those staying south around Hoan Kiem

Lake. It offers four free walking tours, themed by architecture, history, Hoan Kiem Lake and Hanoi's craft streets.

Tourist Information Center (Map p60; ☑024-3926 3366; P Dinh Tien Hoang; ⊗9am-7pm) Has city maps and brochures, but is privately run with an emphasis on selling tours. In the cafes and bars of the Old Quarter, look for the excellent local magazine *The Word*.

American Club (Map p64; ☑024-3824 1850; www.facebook.com/AmClubHanoi; 19-21 P Hai Ba Trung; ⊗8am-11pm) A source of contacts for the American expat community. Features a good restaurant and bar, and also a children's playground.

TRAVEL AGENCIES & TOUR OPERATORS

Hanoi has hundreds of travel agencies and plenty are of ill repute, operating with pushy staff out of budget Old Quarter hotels. Some hotels have been known to evict guests who book tours elsewhere: it's all about the commission.

The agencies we recommend have professional, knowledgeable staff and coordinate well-organised trips with a high rate of guest satisfaction: most run small groups, use their own vehicles and guides, and offer trips away from the main tourist trail.

If you choose to book elsewhere, beware of clones of popular agencies. It's common for shysters to set up shop close to a respected agency and attempt to cream off a slice of their business. Visit online forums like the Thorn Tree (www.lonelyplanet.com/thorntree) to check the latest travellers' buzz.

Cuong's Motorbike Adventure (☑0918 763 515, 024-3632 0682; www.cuongs-motorbike-adventure.com) This highly recommended operator conducts motorbike tours all around the north.

ⓘ CATCHING THE BUS TO CHINA

Three daily services (at 7.30am, 9.30am and 11.30am) to China's Nanning ('Nam Ninh' in Vietnamese; 480,000d, nine hours) in Guangxi province leave from 206 Ð Tran Quang Khai. Tickets should be purchased in advance through a reputable travel agency. Be sure you have the correct Chinese visa.

The bus runs to the border at Dong Dang, where you pass through Chinese immigration. You then change to a Chinese bus, which continues to the Lang Dong Bus Station in Nanning. Reports from Nanning-bound travellers indicate that this route is less hassle and quicker than the 13-hour trip by sleeper train from Gia Lam Railway Station (p95), which is an eight-minute walk north of Gia Lam Bus Station.

Electric Smiles (www.electric-smiles.com; 33 Nhat Chieu Tay Ho; ☺8am-5pm Sun-Fri, to 7pm Sat) For e-bike tours in and around Hanoi plus e-bike rental too.

Ethnic Travel (Map p60; ☑024-3926 1951; www.ethnictravel.com.vn; 35 P Hang Giay; ☺7am-8pm Mon-Sat, 7am-7pm Sun) Off-the-beaten-track trips across the north in small groups; some are activity-based (including hiking, cycling and cooking).

Handspan Adventure Travel (Map p60; ☑024-3926 2828; www.handspan.com; 78 P Ma May; ☺9am-8pm) Excellent, innovative community-based tourism projects in northern Vietnam. Handspan also has offices in Sapa and Ho Chi Minh City.

Marco Polo Travel (Map p58; ☑0913 571 687; www.marcopoloasia.com; Rm 107b, N14-49 Nguyen Khoai; ☺9am-5pm) Runs kayaking trips around Halong Bay and Ba Be Lakes.

Mr Linh's Adventure Tours (Map p60; ☑024-3642 5420; www.mrlinhadventure.com; 83 P Ma May) A professional, well-meaning outfit, specialising in off-the-beaten-track and adventure travel in Vietnam's remote north.

Ocean Tours (Map p60; ☑0983 234 628; www.oceantours.com.vn; 82 P Ma May; ☺7am-9pm) Professional tour operator based in Hanoi, with Ba Be National Park options, tours of Halong Bay, and adventures around the northeast.

Vega Travel (Map p60; ☑024-3926 2092; www.vegatravel.vn; cnr P Ma May & 24a P Hang Bac; ☺8am-8pm) Family-owned and operated company offering well-run tours around the north and throughout Vietnam.

TRAVEL WITH CHILDREN

Hanoi is a fun and eye-opening city for most kids, but language barriers, the organised chaos of the Old Quarter and the raw, earthy nature of Hanoi's street food can pose some challenges. The friendliness of the Vietnamese people, however, generally helps to diffuse any stresses you might encounter. There's no shortage of things to keep youngsters engaged as you wander around the Old Quarter, with plenty of ice-cream vendors and fruit markets for treats

along the way. Most kids love the chance to get hands-on at the special Kids' Club sessions at the Hanoi Cooking Centre (p73), and a tour with the gang at Hanoi Kids (p75) is a great cross-cultural opportunity.

A trip to the Lotte Observation Deck (p71) should also be on the menu. Boating is a fun family activity; you have the choice of bigger boats on West Lake (p71) or pedal-powered boats in **Thong Nhat Park** (Unification Park; Map p70; P Tran Nhan Tong). Come evening, it's essential to catch a water-puppet show at the Municipal Water Puppet Theatre (p88) – a *Punch & Judy* pantomime on water. Hanoi Train Street (p74) – to watch the train rumble by – was shut at the time of research, but may reopen. In the meantime, kids (and grown-up kids) should love The Railway Hanoi 2 (p85). For ice cream, take your young ones to Kem Trang Tien (p80).

If you're in town for a few days and travelling as a family, you can't beat the apartments at Somerset Grand Hanoi (p78) for price, location and value.

ⓘ Getting There & Away

Hanoi is one of the major entry points into Vietnam, with plenty of direct international flights. Trains connect with southern China and to cities along the whole length of the country to Ho Chi Minh City (HCMC) – though buses are an easy option for Nanning in China. Many open-ticket buses travelling through Vietnam start or finish in Hanoi, allowing you to make stops in cities along the way.

AIR

Hanoi has fewer direct international flights than HCMC, but with excellent connections through Singapore, Hong Kong or Bangkok you can get almost anywhere easily.

Vietnam Airlines (Map p64; ☑1900 545 486; www.vietnamair.com.vn; 25 P Trang Thi; ☺8am-5pm Mon-Fri) Links Hanoi to destinations throughout Vietnam, with direct flights to Europe, China, Japan, South Korea, Laos, Singapore and Taiwan. Popular routes include

Dalat, Danang, Dien Bien Phu, HCMC, Hue, Nha Trang and Phu Quoc Island, all served daily.

Jetstar Airways (www.jetstar.com) Operates low-cost flights to Danang, HCMC, Dalat and Hong Kong.

VietJet Air (www.vietjetair.com) This low-cost airline has flights to Phu Quoc, Danang, Dong Hoi, Bangkok, Seoul, Taipei and Tokyo.

BUS & MINIBUS

Hanoi has three main long-distance bus stations of interest to travellers: Giap Bat, Gia Lam and My Dinh. They are fairly well organised, with ticket offices, fixed prices and schedules, though they can be crowded and at times chaotic. Consider buying tickets the day before you plan to travel on the longer-distance routes, to ensure a seat. It's often easier to book through a travel agent, but you'll obviously be charged a commission.

Tourist-style minibuses can be booked through most hotels and travel agents. Popular destinations include Halong Bay and Sapa. Prices are usually about 30% to 40% higher than the regular public bus, but include a hotel pickup.

Many open-ticket tours through Vietnam start or finish in Hanoi.

Giap Bat Bus Station (☑ 024-3864 1467; Đ Giai Phong) Serves points south of Hanoi, and offers more comfortable sleeper buses. It is 7km south of Hanoi Train Station. There are irregular services two or three times per month to Dalat (470,000d, 35 hours). For Danang, an alternative is to take the bus (350,000d) to HCMC (leaving at 1.30pm, 3pm, 6pm and 6.30pm; dinner included) and get off in Danang. The same bus goes through Dong Hoi (250,000d), Dong Ha (300,000d), Hue (350,000d) and Nha Trang (700,000d).

BUSES FROM HANOI
Giap Bat Bus Station

DESTINATION	DURATION (HR)	COST (D)	FREQUENCY
Danang	13-14	350,000	4pm & 5pm
Dong Ha	9	300,000	4pm & 5pm
Dong Hoi	8	250,000	4pm & 5pm
HCMC	36-38	920,000	1.30pm, 3pm, 6pm & 6.30pm
Hue	12	350,000	4pm & 5pm
Nha Trang	24-28	700,000	4pm & 6pm
Ninh Binh	2	70,000	frequent 6am-6pm

Gia Lam Bus Station

DESTINATION	DURATION (HR)	COST (D)	FREQUENCY
Bai Chay (Halong City)	4-4½	110,000-130,000	frequent 6am-6pm
Hai Phong	1½	100,000	every 40min 6am-7pm
Lang Son	4	100,000	every 45min 8am-8.30pm
Lao Cai	4-5	250,000	6 daily 8am-7pm
Mong Cai	7	200,000	irregular, no fixed times
Sapa	6	250,000	8pm & 9pm

My Dinh Bus Station

DESTINATION	DURATION (HR)	COST (D)	FREQUENCY
Cao Bang	7-8	180,000-200,000	hourly to 1pm, sleeper at 9pm
Dien Bien Phu	9-9½	320,000-415,000	7am, 7.30am, 1.30pm, 4pm & 5.45pm
Ha Giang	7½	200,000	hourly 5.30am-9pm
Hoa Binh	2	47,000-90,000	hourly 4am-6pm
Lang Son	4	100,000	frequent to 6pm
Son La	5½	220,000-270,000	10.45am & 4.45pm

Gia Lam Bus Station (📞 024-3827 1569; 132 P Ngo Gia Kham) Has buses to regions north and northeast of Hanoi. It's located 3km northeast of the city centre across the Song Hong.

My Dinh Bus Station (📞 024-3768 5549; Đ Pham Hung) This station 7km west of the city provides services to the west and the north, including sleeper buses to Dien Bien Phu for onward travel to Laos. It's also the best option for buses to Ha Giang, Mai Chau and Lang Son. In addition to the times listed here, for Song La you can also take the Dien Bien Phu bus and disembark at Son La.

CAR

Car rental is best arranged via a travel agency or hotel and is useful for trips out of town. Generally this will always mean hiring a car with a driver, as rental firms will not usually rent to a foreign driver even with an International Driving Permit. The Grab app (www.grab.com) can arrange chauffeured cars at a decent rate.

Costs start at about US$110 a day (including a driver and petrol). Make sure the driver's expenses are covered in the rate you're quoted.

MOTORBIKE

Offroad Vietnam (Map p60; 📞 024-3926 3433, 0913-047 509; www.offroadvietnam. com; 36 P Nguyen Huu Huan; ⊘8am-6pm Mon-Sat) For reliable Honda off-road bikes (150cc from US$20, 250cc from US$40 daily) and 150cc road bikes (US$15). Booking ahead is recommended. Offroad's principal business is running excellent tours, mainly dealing with travellers from English-speaking countries. Tours are either semi-guided,

excluding meals and accommodation, or all-inclusive fully guided tours.

TRAIN

Trains depart from four main stations in Hanoi, where you can purchase tickets. We recommend buying your tickets at least a few days before departure to ensure a seat or sleeper; the website www.baolau.vn is a very useful booking engine, though you can go to the station for the lowest fares. For full departure times and at-counter ticket prices, consult the website of the **Vietnam Railway Corporation** (www.dsvn.vn).

Tickets can also be purchased from most travel agencies (their commission may be worth it to avoid the language hassle of buying tickets at the train station, though there is a booth at the station where English is spoken). Travel agencies often have preferential access to tickets to popular destinations such as Hue, Ho Chi Minh City (HCMC) and Lao Cai (for Sapa).

Southbound Trains to Danang, Hue & Nha Trang

Trains to southern destinations go from the main **Hanoi Train Station** (Ga Hang Co, Train Station A; 📞 024-3825 3949; 120 Đ Le Duan; ⊘ticket office 7.30am-12.30pm & 1.30-7.30pm) at the western end of P Tran Hung Dao. To the left of the main entrance is the ticket office, with adjacent posters displaying train departure times and fares. Take a ticket and look out for your booth number on the screens. It's a good idea to write down your train number, departure time and preferred class in Vietnamese. Southbound trains depart at 6.15am, 9am, 1.15pm, 7pm and 11pm.

TRAINS FROM HANOI
Southbound Trains

DESTINATION	HARD SEAT (D)	SOFT SEAT (D)	HARD SLEEPER (D)	SOFT SLEEPER (D)
Danang	from 412,000	from 554,000	from 751,000	from 804,000
HCMC	from 695,000	from 1,049,000	from 1,410,000	from 1,580,000
Hue	from 358,000	from 438,000	from 707,000	from 799,000
Nha Trang	from 607,000	from 905,000	from 1,209,000	from 1,305,000

Northbound & Eastbound Trains

DESTINATION	STATION	DURATION (HR)	HARD SEAT/ SLEEPER (D)	SOFT SEAT/ SLEEPER (D)	FREQUENCY
Beijing	Gia Lam	18	-	6,400,000	9.20pm Tue & Fri
Hai Phong	Gia Lam	2	65,000	70,000	6.16am, 9.48am, 3.45pm & 6.46pm
Hai Phong	Long Bien	3	60,000	70,000	9.20am, 3.30pm & 6.26pm
Nanning	Gia Lam	12	-	752,000	9.20pm

❶ HANOI TO CAT BA ISLAND

Direct buses (US$14) run to Cat Ba Town on Cat Ba Island from Hanoi, generally including hotel pick-up. Buses first run to the wharf on the island of Cat Hai, lashed to Hi Phong by bridge; passengers then take a short ferry ride to Cat Ba Island to continue by minibus to Cat Ba Town. Companies running buses include Good Morning Cat Ba (www.goodmorningcatba.com), Daiichi Travel (https://daiichitravel.net), Cat Ba Express (www.catbaexpress.com) and Cat Ba Discovery (www.catbadiscovery.com). Unicharm (Map p60; ☑ 024-3823 8476; www.unicharmcruise.com; 4th fl, 24a P Hang Bac; per person from US$138) offers transport through, and exploration of, Cat Ba Island en route to or from its cruise ship in secluded Lan Ha Bay. Hoang Long Express (Map p64; ☑ 022-5392 0920; www.hoanglongasia.com; 5 P Pham Ngu Lao) also sells combination bus and high-speed-boat tickets (single/return US$13/24, 4½ hours) to Cat Ba, with buses leaving from Nuoc Ngam Bus Station (1 Ngoc Hoi) or, more conveniently for travellers, from 34 Tran Nhat Duat, near Long Bien Railway Station.

Journey times from Hanoi given here are approximate, but check when you book, as some trains are quicker than others: Hue (11 hours), Danang (13½ hours), Nha Trang (24½ hours), HCMC (31 hours). Note that different departures have different fare structures and available classes; check www.dsvn.vn or www.baolau.vn.

Northbound Trains to Lao Cai (for Sapa), China & Hong Kong

Some northbound trains for Lao Cai leave from either Hanoi Train Station (Station A) or **Tran Quy Cap Station** (Train Station B; ☑ 024-3825 2628; P Tran Quy Cap; ☺ ticket office 4-6am & 4-10pm), just behind Hanoi Train Station. Soft-sleeper northbound trains to Nanning, Guilin (for Yangshuo) and Beijing in China depart from **Gia Lam Railway Station** (Ga Gia Lam). For Hong Kong, change at Nanning for a high-speed train to Guangzhou and then the high-speed train south to Hong Kong.

Eastbound Trains to Hai Phong

As well as those heading northwards, eastbound (Hai Phong) trains depart from Gia Lam Railway Station on the eastern side of the Song Hong, or from **Long Bien Railway Station** on the western (city) side of the river. Be sure to check which station you need.

❶ Getting Around

TO & FROM NOI BAI INTERNATIONAL AIRPORT

Hanoi's **Noi Bai International Airport** (☑ 024-3827 1513; www.hanoiairportonline.com) is about 35km north of the city, around 45 minutes away along a modern highway. If you're planning to use public or airline buses to get to the airport, be sure to allow plenty of time before your flight. Many hotels and accommodation options can arrange pick-up for competitive prices.

Bus

Public bus 17 (9000d, 5.30am to 10.30pm, 75 to 90 minutes) from outside the domestic (not international) arrivals hall runs to/from **Long Bien Bus Station** (Map p58; ☺ 5am-9pm) on the northern edge of the Old Quarter. Luggage is free unless larger than the luggage cage.

Express bus 86 (35,000d, one hour, every 20 to 30 minutes, 5.05am to 9.40pm from Hanoi Train Station; 6.18am to 10.58pm from the airport) is a comfortable service that runs from Hanoi Train Station, and the north side of Hoan Kiem Lake outside the tourist information centre (buses do not stop here Friday to Sunday from 5pm, diverting instead to 6c Phan Chu Trinh, opposite Hanoi Opera House), to the international and then domestic airport terminals, via Long Bien Bus Station. From domestic Terminal 1, follow the orange signs for bus 86. From international Terminal 2, take bus 86 from opposite stand 02.

Minibus & Shuttle Bus

Vietnam Airlines Minibus (Map p64; 1 P Quang Trung; 40,000d) Links Hanoi from their branch on Quang Trung not far south of Hoan Kiem Lake in the centre of town to Noi Bai International Airport (one hour). Look for the minibus with the price written on the side. This service runs every 45 minutes from 5am to 7pm, but is not very reliable as it only departs when full.

Vietjet Air Shuttle Bus (www.hanoiairportshuttle.com/transportation/vietjet-air-shuttle-bus-hanoi; 40,000d; ☺ 4am-9pm) This bright-red shuttle bus runs every one to two hours between 4am and 9pm. The bus runs to P Tran Nhan Tong in the French Quarter around 1.5km south of Hoan Kiem Lake. If you are staying in the Old Quarter, ask to be dropped off at the P Nguyen Thai Hoc or Quang Trung stop and if you need to, get a Grab cab.

Taxi

Airport Taxi (✆ 024-3873 3333) charges US$20 for a door-to-door taxi ride to or from Noi Bai International Airport. From the terminal, look out for the official taxi drivers who wear bright-yellow jackets. They do not require that you pay the toll for the bridge you cross en route. Some other taxi drivers do require that you pay the toll, so ask first. There are numerous airport scams involving taxi drivers and dodgy hotels. Don't use freelance taxi drivers touting for business – the chances of a rip-off are too high. If you've already confirmed accommodation, you're well advised to book an arrival transfer through your hotel, which is easy to arrange. App-based Grab cabs (https://www.grab.com) are also available.

BICYCLE

Many Old Quarter guesthouses and cafes rent out bikes for about US$3 per day. Good luck with that traffic – be safe! You can rent an e-bike from **Electric Smiles** (www.electric-smiles.com; 33 Nhat Chieu Tay Ho; 2hr from US$10; ⊙ 8am-5pm Sun-Fri, to 7pm Sat); week-long rentals (US$200) are also possible. Cycling Vietnam (p98) also rents out bikes.

BUS

Hanoi has an extensive public bus system, though few tourists take advantage of the low trip cost (7000d). If you're game, pick up the *Xe Buyt Ha Noi* (Hanoi bus map; 5000d) from the bookshop Thang Long (p90).

CYCLO

A few *cyclo* drivers still frequent the Old Quarter, though many deal with tour groups. If you're only going a short distance, it's a great way to experience the city (despite the fumes). Settle on a price first and watch out for overcharging – a common driver's ploy when carrying two passengers is to agree on a price, and then *double*

it upon arrival, gesturing 'no, no, no...that was per person'.

Aim to pay around 50,000d for a shortish journey; night rides cost more. Few *cyclo* drivers speak English so take a map and your hotel calling card with you.

ELECTRIC BUS

Hanoi's golf-buggy-esque ecofriendly tours with **Electric Bus** (Dong Xuan; per buggy of 6 passengers per hour 300,000d; ⊙ 8.30am-10pm) are actually a pretty good way to get your bearings in the city. They traverse a network of 14 stops in the Old Quarter and around Hoan Kiem Lake, parting the flow of motorbikes and pedestrians like a slow-moving white dragon.

Nothing really beats haphazardly discovering the nooks and crannies of the Old Quarter by foot, but if you're feeling a tad lazy, the hop-on, hop-off bus is worth considering. The main **departure point** (Map p60) is on P Dinh Tien Hoang at the northern end of Hoan Kiem Lake, and there's another departure point outside **Dong Xuan Market** (Map p60). A full journey around the Old Quarter takes around an hour, with a recorded English-language commentary as you ride.

MOTORBIKE TAXI

You won't have any trouble finding a *xe om* (motorbike taxi) in Hanoi, though much of their market share has been stolen by green-jacketed Grab drivers; download the Grab app (www.grab.com) and start hailing your nearest motorbike (you can pay in cash). The advantage is that the fares are fixed at a cost-effective price and you don't need to negotiate the fare with a *xe om* driver.

An average journey by *xe om* in the city centre costs around 15,000d to 20,000d, while a longer trip to Ho Chi Minh's Mausoleum is around 35,000d to 40,000d. For two or more people, a Grab taxi or metered taxi is usually cheaper and more convenient than a convoy of *xe om*.

TAXI

App-based **Grab** (www.grab.com/vn/en/transport/taxi) operates taxi-like cars in Hanoi, including from the airport, offering good rates and reliability. Uber sold its ride-hailing service to Grab in 2018 so no longer has a presence in Vietnam, but Grab works in a similar fashion and you can pay with cash if you want.

Otherwise, reliable taxi companies include **Mai Linh** (✆ 024-3822 2666), which offers metered cabs. Flagfall is around 20,000d, which takes you 1km to 2km; every kilometre thereafter costs around 15,000d. Some dodgy operators may have high-speed meters, so stick to Grab or Mai Linh.

AROUND HANOI

The region around Hanoi abounds in opportunities for exploration and to flee the occasionally polluted city air. The nearby Tam Dao National Park offers trekking, clean mountain air, rare plant life and animal-spotting. At Tam Dao Hill Station the weather is refreshingly cool year-round. Hanoi is also within reach of several important and venerated Buddhist pagodas, including the Perfume Pagoda, accessible on a popular day trip.

Perfume Pagoda
BUDDHIST PAGODA

(Chua Huong; Huong Son, My Duc; entry incl return boat trip 100,000d) This striking complex of pagodas and Buddhist shrines is built into the karst cliffs of Huong Tich Mountain (Mountain of the Fragrant Traces). Among the better-known sites are Chua Thien Chu (Pagoda Leading to Heaven); Chua Giai Oan Chu (Purgatorial Pagoda), where the faithful believe deities purify souls, cure suffering and grant offspring to childless families; and Huong Tich Chu (Pagoda of the Perfumed Vestige). It's extremely popular with Vietnamese tourists from February to April, but otherwise remarkably peaceful.

The complex is located about 60km southwest of Hanoi; getting here requires a journey first by road, then by river, then on foot or by cable car. The journey is half the fun, but don't try and do it without a guide: most tour operators offer day-return trips here from US$30 to US$50.

Travel from Hanoi by car for two hours to My Duc, then take a small boat, rowed by women from the local village, to the foot of the mountain. This entertaining boat trip takes an hour and travels along scenic waterways between limestone cliffs. Allow a couple more hours to climb to the top and return. The path to the summit is steep in places, and if it's raining the ground can get very slippery. There's also a cable car to the summit (one way/return 100,000/160,000d); a smart approach is to take the cable car up and walk down.

WORTH A TRIP

THAY & TAY PHUONG PAGODAS

Stunning limestone outcrops loom up from the emerald-green paddy fields, while the Tay Phuong and Thay Pagodas cling to the cliffs about 20 minutes apart from each other by road.

The pagodas are about 30km west of Hanoi in Ha Tay province. Hanoi travel agents and tour operators offer day trips that take in both pagodas. Expect to pay US$48 to US$72 per person for two people.

Also known as Sung Phuc Pagoda, **Tay Phuong Pagoda** (Pagoda of the West; Thach Xa, Thach That district; 10,000d) consists of three single-level structures built in descending order on a hillock that is said to resemble a buffalo. Figures representing 'the conditions of man' are the pagoda's most celebrated feature – carved from jackfruit wood, many date from the 18th century. The earliest construction dates from the 8th century.

Take the steep steps up to the main pagoda building, then find a path at the back that loops down past the other two pagodas and wander through the adjacent hillside village.

Also known as Thien Phuc (Heavenly Blessing), **Thay Pagoda** (Chua Thay, Master's Pagoda; Sai Son, Quoc Oai district; 10,000d) is dedicated to Thich Ca Buddha (Sakyamuni, the historical Buddha). To the left of the main altar is a statue of the 12th-century monk Tu Dao Hanh, the master in whose honour the pagoda is named. To the right is a statue of King Ly Nhan Tong, who is believed to have been a reincarnation of Tu Dao Hanh.

In front of the pagoda is a small stage built on stilts in the middle of a pond where water-puppet shows are staged during festivals. Follow the path around the outside of the main pagoda building and take a steep 10-minute climb up to a beautiful smaller pagoda perched high on the rock. Thay Pagoda is a big and confusing complex for non-Buddhists – consider hiring a guide.

The pagoda's annual festival is held from the fifth to the seventh days of the third lunar month (approximately March). Visitors enjoy watching water-puppet shows, hiking and exploring caves in the area.

Co Loa Citadel HISTORIC SITE

(Co Loa Thanh; per person/car 10,000/20,000d; ☺ 8am-5pm) Located 16km north of Hanoi's Old Quarter and dating from the 3rd century BCE, Co Loa Citadel was the first fortified citadel in Vietnamese history and became the national capital during the reign of Ngo Quyen (939–44 CE). Only vestiges of the ancient ramparts, which enclosed an area of about 5 sq km, remain.

In the centre of the citadel are temples dedicated to the rule of King An Duong Vuong (257–208 BCE), who founded the legendary Thuc dynasty, and his daughter My Nuong (Mi Chau). Legend tells that My Nuong showed her father's magic crossbow trigger (which made him invincible in battle) to her husband, the son of a Chinese general. He stole it and gave it to his father. With this not-so-secret weapon, the Chinese defeated An Duong Vuong, beginning 1000 years of Chinese occupation.

Public bus 46 (7000d, 45 minutes) runs here every 15 minutes from My Dinh Bus Station in Hanoi. A taxi here is about 120,000d; a *xe om* is 50,000d. From the Co Loa Bus Station, cross the bridge, turn left and walk for around 500m.

Ho Chi Minh Trail Museum MUSEUM

(Bao Tan Duong Ho Chi Minh; ☑ 034-382 0889; Hwy 6, towards Hoa Binh; 20,000d; ☺ 7.30-11am & 1.30-4.30pm Mon-Sat) A throwback to the 1980s, this graphic museum, about 13km southwest of Hanoi's Old Quarter, is dedicated to the famous supply route from Vietnam's Communist North to the occupied South. The displays, including an abundance of American ammunition and weaponry as well as some powerful photography, document all too clearly the horrors of the American War, from a distinctly Vietnamese viewpoint. A short film fills you in on the details and English captions are good, while the recreated tunnels are well worth exploring.

If you have an interest in the American War, you're best advised to hire a local guide from a reputable travel agency to bring you here on a half-day tour. Local bus 02 runs here from the Temple of Literature.

Cycling Vietnam CYCLING

(Map p58; www.vietnamcycling.com; 4th fl, 2/62 Nguyen Chi Thanh, Hanoi) Specialises in cycling tours from Hanoi, some taking in the Thay and Tay Phuong Pagodas and nearby handicraft villages, as well as into central and northern Vietnam.

The tours also avoid having to struggle through Hanoi's ferocious traffic, as a minibus takes the strain through the suburbs. Cycling Vietnam also rents out bikes.

❶ Getting There & Away

Hanoi is the gateway to this region, well connected by air to plenty of international cities. Tours and rental vehicles with drivers and guides are affordable and are the best choices for reaching distant sights outside the city.

Tam Dao Hill Station

☑ 0211 / ELEV 930M

Nestling below soaring forest-clad peaks, Tam Dao is a former French hill station in a spectacular setting northwest of Hanoi. Today it's a popular summer resort – a favoured weekend escape for Hanoians, who come here to revel in the temperate climate and make merry in the extensive selection of restaurants and bars. Founded in 1907 by the French, most of its colonial villas were destroyed during the Franco–Viet Minh War, only to be replaced with brutalist concrete architecture. Tam Dao is a useful base for hiking, but the town itself is an unattractive sprawl of hotel blocks.

Remember that it is cool up in Tam Dao, and this part of Vietnam has a distinct winter. Don't be caught unprepared.

The best time to visit is between late April and mid-October, when the mist sometimes lifts and the weather can be fine. Visit on a weekday to avoid the crowds.

Tam Dao National Park NATURE RESERVE

(25,000d) Tam Dao National Park was designated in 1996 and covers much of the area around the town. With a Chinese etymology, Tam Dao means 'Three Islands', and the three summits of Tam Dao Mountain, all about 1400m in height, are sometimes visible to the northeast of the hill station, floating like islands in the mist.

There are at least 64 mammal species (including langurs) and 239 bird species in the park, but you'll need a good local guide and have to be prepared to do some hiking to find them. Illegal hunting remains a big problem.

Hikes vary from the 30-minute return to the waterfall to day treks taking in bamboo forest and primary tropical forest. A guide, essential for the longer hikes, can be hired from 400,000d; ask at the Mela Hotel (☑ 0211-382 4321).

Huong Lien Hotel HOTEL $

(☑ 0211-382 4282; r weekday/weekend 250,000/
350,000d; ☜) Offering decent value for the
price, most of the rooms here have balconies
to make the most of those misty mountain
views. There's a little restaurant as well
(mains 135,000d to 200,000d).

❶ Getting There & Away

Tam Dao is 85km northwest of Hanoi in Vinh
Phuc province. Buses to the town of Vinh Yen
(55,000d, frequent from 6am to 4pm) leave
from Hanoi's Gia Lam Bus Station. From Vinh
Yen hire a *xe om* (one way around 80,000d) or
a taxi (160,000d) to travel the 24km road up to
Tam Dao.

On a motorbike from Hanoi the journey takes
around three hours, and the last part of the ride
into the national park is beautiful. A taxi from
Hanoi is about 750,000d one way.

AT A GLANCE

POPULATION
Haiphong: 2 million

BIGGEST TOURIST ATTRACTION
Halong Bay (p107)

BEST RICE WINE
Can Cau Market (p143)

BEST VISTA
Quan Ba Pass (p146)

BEST RUSTIC LODGE
Little Mai Chau Homestay (p126)

WHEN TO GO

May The month before high season has sunny days aplenty yet few crowds.

Late Aug & Sep Hike Sapa and Bac Ha during rice harvest season.

Nov Blue skies, calm seas; the perfect time for Halong Bay.

Rice terraces, Sapa (p131)
TRACY BEN/SHUTTERSTOCK ®

Northern Vietnam

The north is home to Vietnam's largest landscapes: a place of rippling mountains, cascading rice terraces and the surreal karst topography for which the region is famed. Halong Bay's seascape of limestone towers is the prime view, but the karst connection continues inland, to Ba Be's sprawling lakes, Cao Bang's remote valleys and the dramatic gorges and peaks of Ha Giang. In this heartland of hill-tribe culture, stilt houses snuggle between paddy-field patchworks and the scarlet headdresses of the Dzao and the Black Hmong traders add dizzying colour to fabulous highland markets.

Northern Vietnam Highlights

❶ Halong Bay (p107) Kayaking around karst cliffs, and into lagoons and hidden beaches.

❷ Ha Giang province (p143) Winding your way across mountain passes and karst scenery on the north's greatest road trip.

❸ Cat Ba Island (p107) Diving into northern Vietnam's action-adventure centre;

hiking, cycling and climbing your way around the island.

❹ Bac Ha (p141) Exploring a less-seen slice of the north, trekking the countryside speckled with hill-tribe villages.

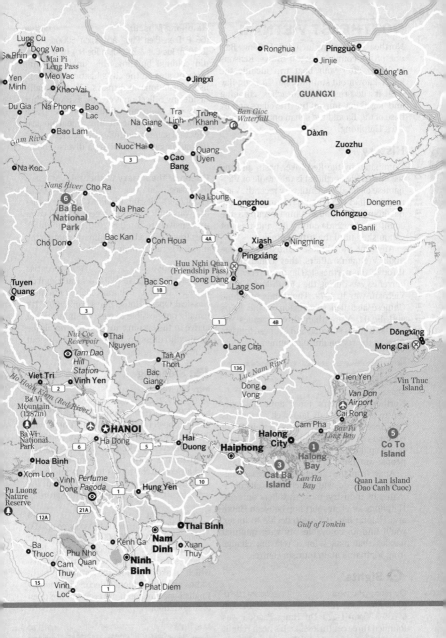

Co To Island (p117)
Joining your local counterparts on white-sand beaches.

Ba Be National Park (p120) Gliding across tranquil lakes and soaking up the scenery of shoreline villages and mountain peaks.

Sapa (p131) Trekking mountain trails through sublime scenery to hill-tribe villages, while avoiding the crowds.

Mai Chau (p125) Recharging your travel batteries after the Hanoi hustle by meandering through green checkerboards of rice paddies.

NORTHEAST VIETNAM

Northeast Vietnam includes Halong Bay, one of the county's biggest draws. Reasons to linger after your boat trip include the lesser-known but stunning Bai Tu Long Bay with its deserted island beaches, climbing and kayaking fun at the traveller-friendly base of Cat Ba and the urban options in laid-back Haiphong.

History

Dominated by the Red River basin and the sea, the fertile northeast is the cradle of Vietnamese civilisation. Until very recently, Vietnam has had challenging relations with the neighbouring Chinese. China occupied the country in the 2nd century BC, and was not vanquished until the 10th century.

Any time the Chinese wanted to advance upon Vietnam's affairs, they could do so through the northeast. The most recent occurrence was during the month-long China-Vietnam war in 1979. Thousands of ethnic Chinese also fled this region in the 1970s and 1980s. More than three decades on, border trade is surging, and Chinese tourists flock to the region during summer.

Haiphong

☎0225 / POP 2 MILLION

Northern Vietnam's most appealing city centre has a distinctly laid-back air with its tree-lined boulevards host to a bundle of colonial-era buildings and hip cafes where tables spill onto the pavements – perfect for people-watching.

Apart from the cafe culture, there's actually not a lot to do, with much of the city dominated by industry; most travellers only use Haiphong as a transport hop between Hanoi and Halong Bay. If you do decide to linger, you'll find an enjoyable city with minimal hassles that makes for a relaxing change from Vietnam's main tourism centres.

Sights

Du Hang Pagoda BUDDHIST TEMPLE

(Chua Phuc Lam; 121 P Chua Hang; ⏲5-11.30am & 1.30-9.30pm) FREE Du Hang Pagoda was founded three centuries ago. It's been rebuilt several times, but remains a fine example of traditional Vietnamese architecture and sculpture, chock-a-block with golden Buddhas, jade dragons and artful bonsai. The pagoda is 1.5km southwest of Haiphong's main street, P Dien Bien Phu; a *xe om* (motorbike taxi) here costs 30,000d.

Haiphong Museum MUSEUM

(66 P Dien Bien Phu; admission 5000d; ⏲8-10.30am Tue-Sun & 2-4.30pm Tue-Fri) In a splendid colonial building, this small museum concentrates on the city's history, with English translations on displays. The front hall's taxidermy collection is creepy, as always, but there are interesting finds from the Trang Kenh and Viet Khe Tombs archaeological sites and some beautiful ceramic pieces. The museum's garden harbours a diverse collection of war detritus.

Queen of the Rosary Cathedral CATHEDRAL

(P Hoang Van Thu; ⏲dawn-dusk) FREE Haiphong's elegant Roman Catholic cathedral was built in the 19th century and comprehensively restored in 2010. The building's grey towers are a local landmark, though the interior is rather plain.

Opera House HISTORIC BUILDING

(P Quang Trung) FREE With a facade embellished with white columns, Haiphong's neoclassical Opera House dates from 1904. It's usually not possible to view the interior, but arrive in the evening and you can watch the locals who dress up and pose for photos out front.

Sleeping

May Hostel HOSTEL $

(☎0866 777 436; www.facebook.com/may.hostel; 35 P Le Dai Hanh; dm 160,000d; ❄📶) This modern hostel hits all the right notes, with a central location, a good rooftop bar, gated motorcycle parking and everything you need from a dorm bed – from bathrooms and air-con in the rooms to plugs and lights by each bed. Prices fluctuate throughout the week by 40,000d or so, peaking on Saturday.

Bao Anh Hotel HOTEL $

(☎0225-382 3406; www.hotelbaoanh.com; 20b P Minh Khai; r 400,000-600,000d; ❄📶) The Bao Anh has a great location in a leafy street surrounded by good restaurants, which makes up for the cramped bathrooms and old-fashioned decor. The friendly English-speaking staff at reception are open to negotiation.

Maxim's HOTEL $$

(New Wind Hotel; ☎0225-374 6540; maximshotelhp@gmail.com; 3k P Ly Tu Trong; d 500,000-700,000d, ste 900,000d; ❄📶) Maxim's has been going for years, but remains a fine lower-midrange choice. The cheapest rooms come without a window, so it's worth upgrading, but all rooms are fresh and comfortable.

Haiphong

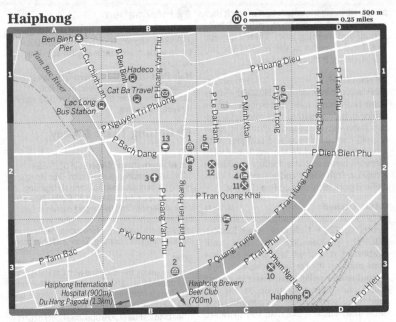

Haiphong

◎ Sights
1 Haiphong Museum	B2
2 Opera House	B3
3 Queen of the Rosary Cathedral	B2

🛏 Sleeping
4 Bao Anh Hotel	C2
5 Manoir Des Arts Hotel	C2
6 Maxim's	C1
7 May Hostel	C3
8 Monaco Hotel	B2

🍴 Eating
9 BKK	C2
10 Co Yen	C3
11 Indian Kitchen	C2
12 Nam Giao	C2

🍸 Drinking & Nightlife
13 Cong Ca Phe	B2

Spacious suites come with a kitchenette and microwave. The ground-floor cafe-restaurant is handy, though the location on a quiet side street is central enough for local restaurants.

Monaco Hotel　　　　　　　　　　HOTEL **$$**
(☏ 0225-374 6468; www.haiphongmonacohotel. com; 103 P Dien Bien Phu; r incl breakfast US$30-57; ❇🛜) Modern, reliable and central, though somewhat dull, the Monaco features an imposing lobby with professional staff who speak a little English. The theme carries on into the rooms, which are comfy and spotless, with good bathrooms.

**★Manoir Des
Arts Hotel**　　　　　　　HISTORIC HOTEL **$$$**
(☏ 0225-883 1522; www.manoirdesartshotel.com; 64 P Dien Bien Phu; d 2,500,000d; ❇🛜🏊) The

Manoir serves up just the right amount of classy, colonial French vibe, with brilliant white columns, black-and-white tiled floors and lush green foliage, combined with modern facilities, in a building dating from 1943. The pool is the size of a birdbath, but the surrounding terrace is a great place to relax. Garden-facing twins are the quietest option.

The classy and reasonably priced restaurant is a great place for dinner, even if you aren't staying here. Online room discounts of 25% are standard.

🍴 Eating

★Co Yen　　　　　　　　　　VIETNAMESE **$**
(P Pham Ngu Lao; meals from 20,000d; ⊙ 6-10am) This streetside stall sells one thing only: *banh da cua*, Haiphong's signature breakfast

noodle dish. It's a combination of thick dark rice noodles in a clear broth with pork balls, shrimp and morning glory. There's no sign; look for the vendor at the head of the tiny side street off P Pham Ngu Lao.

★**Nam Giao** VIETNAMESE $$
(22 P Le Dai Hanh; meals from 180,000d; ⊙8am-11pm) Haiphong's most atmospheric dining choice is hidden within this colonial building. Rooms are a colourful clutter of Asian art, old carved cabinets and antiques, with a cool bar area, while the small but well-executed menu includes a tangy sea bass in a passion-fruit sauce and a succulent caramelised pork belly cooked in a clay pot.

Indian Kitchen INDIAN $$
(☑0225-384 2558; www.facebook.com/Indiankitchen22D; 22d P Minh Khai; meals 100,000-160,000d; ⊙9.30am-11pm; ☑) This well-established restaurant is run by Keralans from India so it's the real deal, with puk-ka (authentic) milky chai, lassis (a yogurt drink) and Bollywood music on the TV. Everything is good, from fish coconut curry to the tasty chicken Mughlai, and there are plenty of vegetarian options.

BKK THAI $$
(☑0225-382 1018; 22 P Minh Khai; meals from 180,000d; ⊙11.30am-10pm; ☑) At this restored town house, authentic Thai dishes are beautifully prepared and presented – try the *lab moo* (pork salad) or pepper squid; there are good vegetarian options, too. Choose from the outdoor teak deck or classy interior.

🍷 Drinking & Nightlife

★**Haiphong Brewery**
Beer Club BEER HALL
(16 Đ Lach Tray; ⊙10am-10pm) Picture an open-air German beer hall with a rowdier crowd, and you've got the vibe of this fun venue. Couple the surprisingly tasty draught brews (7000d to 25,000d; try the Amber Ale) with a menu of Vietnamese drinking snacks, and remember that *tuoi* means 'draught' in Vietnamese. It's a short taxi ride or 15-minute walk southeast of the city centre, in the shadow of the Mercure Hotel.

Cong Ca Phe CAFE
(84 P Dien Bien Phu; ⊙7am-11pm; 🛜) Haiphong has a branch of everybody's favorite retro-themed cafe, complete with effortlessly cool vintage decor. Stop in for excellent Vietnamese-style coffee drinks, fresh juices and other drinks (from 30,000d).

ⓘ Information

Haiphong International Hospital (☑0225-395 5888; http://hih.vn; 124 P Nguyen Duc Canh) Modern, with some English-speaking doctors.

Main Post Office (3 P Nguyen Tri Phuong; ⊙8am-6pm Mon-Fri) A grand old yellow dame on the corner of P Hoang Van Thu and P Nguyen Tri Phuong.

ⓘ Getting There & Away

AIR

Cat Bi International Airport (☑0225-397 6408; www.haiphongairport.com; Đ Le Hong Phong) is 6km southeast of central Haiphong; a taxi to the centre is around 80,000d. Jetstar, Vietnam Airlines and the largest carrier at Cat Bi, VietJet, offer flights to most cities in central and southern Vietnam. International destinations include Bangkok, Kunming, Seoul and Shenzhen.

BOAT

A bridge linking the mainland with Cat Hai Island, next door to Cat Ba Island, has reduced the number of boats from Haiphong and most people now take the cheaper and more frequent bus.

Boats to Cat Ba (180,000d, one hour) depart from Haiphong's **Ben Binh Pier** (Đ Ben Binh) at 9am and 1pm, arriving at Cat Ba Town Pier. The frequency of boat departures increases from May to August.

BUS

Haiphong has three long-distance bus stations, but **Lac Long Bus Station** (P Cu Chinh Lan), the closest to Haiphong city centre, has departures for most destinations.

The exception is buses to Cat Ba (100,000d, two hours), which depart from nearby Đ Ben Binh. **Cat Ba Travel** (☑0769 206 069; Đ Ben Binh) and **Hadeco** (☑0912 810 555; www.hadeco.vn; Đ Ben Binh) each have a half-dozen departures between 6am and 4pm.

For Cai Rong (Van Don Island) take one of the frequent buses from Lac Long to Cua Ong (120,000d, two hours), then change for a local minibus to Cai Rong (10,000d, 15 minutes), from where you can catch a *xe om* to the dock.

For Halong City (Bai Chay; 100,000d, one hour) take one of the Mong Cai (200,000d, four hours) minivans, which leave every 15 minutes.

Buses to Hanoi's Giap Bat station (100,000d, two hours) leave frequently.

TRAIN

A spur-line service travels three times daily between Haiphong Train Station and Hanoi's Long Bien station (75,000d to 85,000d, 2½ to 3½ hours, 9.05am, 3pm and 6.40pm). Some trains continue to Hanoi's central train station. If the timings work for you, it's a comfortable way to travel.

Halong Bay

Designated a World Heritage site in 1994, Halong Bay's scatter of almost 2000 limestone islands, dotted with wind- and wave-eroded grottoes, rising from the emerald waters of the Gulf of Tonkin, is a vision of ethereal beauty and, unsurprisingly, northern Vietnam's number-one tourism hub.

Most visitors opt for cruise tours from Hanoi that include sleeping on board within the bay, while a lot of independent travellers eschew the main bay completely, heading straight for Cat Ba Island to see less-visited but equally alluring Lan Ha Bay.

Halong translates as 'where the dragon descends into the sea' and legend tells that this mystical seascape was created when a great mountain dragon charged towards the coast, its flailing tail gouging out valleys and crevasses. As the creature plunged into the sea, the area filled with water, leaving only the pinnacles visible. The geological explanation of karst erosion may be more prosaic, but doesn't make this seascape any less poetic.

ⓘ When To Go

➡ Halong Bay attracts visitors year-round, with peak season for Vietnamese tourists between late May and early August.

➡ January to March is often cool and drizzly, and the ensuing fog can make visibility low, but adds bags of eerie atmosphere.

➡ From May to September tropical storms are frequent, and year-round tourist boats sometimes need to alter their itineraries, depending on the weather.

➡ October's and November's sunny blue-sky days, lack of crowds and discounted hotel rates make these months the best time here.

⊙ Sights

Most cruises and day-tripper boats include at least a couple of caves, an island stop-off and a visit to one of Halong Bay's **floating villages**.

Popular caves to visit include **Hang Trong** (Drum Grotto), **Hang Thien Cung** and the three-chambered **Hang Sung Sot** (Surprise Cave). The huge 25m-tall **Hang Dau Go** (Cave of Wooden Stakes) derives its name from the role it played during 13th-century battles with the Mongolians when locals stored wooden stakes, used to destroy invading ships, in its third chamber.

Visitors must purchase an entry ticket for the national park (40,000d) as well as separate admission tickets for some caves and fishing villages (30,000d to 50,000d), so check what's included in your cruise.

ⓘ Getting There & Away

Most travellers elect to experience Halong Bay on a cruise prearranged in Hanoi, which usually includes transfers to/from the bay.

Alternatively, head directly to Cat Ba Island from Hanoi by bus and arrange a boat trip from there to explore Lan Ha Bay.

ⓘ Getting Around

Tuan Chau Pier, 13km southwest of Halong City, is the jumping-off point for passenger boats to Cat Ba Island. Boats to Quan Lan Island depart from Hon Gai Pier, across the suspension bridge from Halong City, and boats to Quan Lan and Co To Islands depart from Cai Rong, on Van Don Island.

Cat Ba Island

☑ 0225 / POP 13,500

Rugged, craggy and jungle-clad Cat Ba, the largest island in Halong Bay, is the most popular destination for independent tourists. The central hub of Cat Ba Town is now framed by a wall of hotels along its once-lovely bay, and large hotel projects are under construction in nearby bays, but the rest of the island is largely untouched and as wild as ever. Cat Ba is the single best place to sign up for climbing, kayaking and hiking trips, most of which take place in idyllic Lan Ha Bay, just offshore.

Almost half of Cat Ba Island (with a total area of 354 sq km) and 90 sq km of the adjacent waters were declared a national park in 1986 to protect the island's diverse ecosystems.

⊙ Sights

First impressions of Cat Ba Town are not great, but the commercial strip only extends for a street or two behind the promenade. A **Ho Chi Minh monument** (off Đ Nui Ngoc) stands up on Mountain No 1, the hillock opposite the pier in Cat Ba Town. The **market** (⊙ 6am-7pm) is located at the northern end of the harbour.

Rent a motorbike or taxi and head out of town for the island's best sights.

★ **Lan Ha Bay** ⠀⠀⠀⠀⠀⠀⠀⠀⠀⠀BAY
(40,000d) Lying south and east of Cat Ba Town, the 300-or-so karst islands and limestone outcrops of Lan Ha are just as beautiful as those of Halong Bay but feel more

Halong Bay & Bai Tu Long Bay

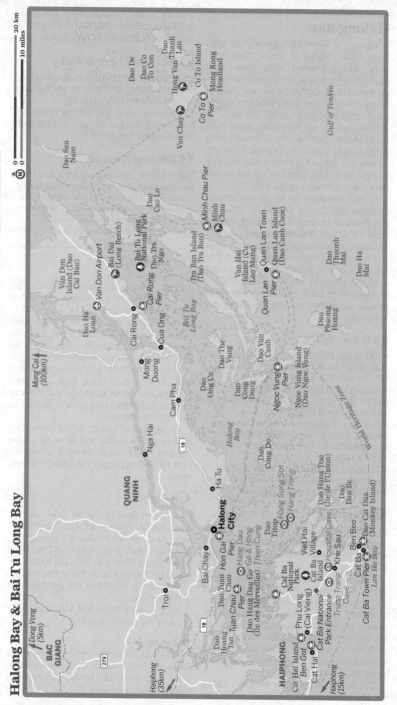

BAC GIANG

HAIPHONG

QUANG NINH

Dong Vong (5km)

Haiphong (35km)

Cat Hai

Dao Hoang Tan

Cat Ba Island Ben Got

Phu Long (Cai Vieng)

Cat Ba National Park Entrance

Trung Trang Cave

Dao Hang Dau Go & Hang (Ile des Merveilles) Thien Cung

Tuan Chau Pier

Dao Tuan Chau

Bai Chay

Troi

Nga Hai

Cam Pha

Mong Duong

Cua Ong

Cai Rong

Cai Rong Pier

Van Don Airport

Van Don Island (Dao Cai Bau)

Dao Ha Loan

Mong Cai (100km)

Bai Dai (Long Beach)

Bai Tu Long National Park

Dao Tra Ngo

Dao Cao Lo

Minh Chau Pier

Minh Chau

Van Hai Island (Cu Lao Mang)

Tra Ban Island (Dao Tra Ban)

Quan Lan Town

Quan Lan Pier

Quan Lan Island (Dao Canh Cuoc)

Dao Van Canh

Dao Ha Mai

Dao Thuonh Mai

Dao Phuong Hoang

Ngoc Vung Island (Dao Ngoc Vung)

Ngoc Vung Pier

World Heritage Zone

Dao De

Dao Co To Con

Hong Van Thanh Lan

Co To Island

Mong Rong Headland

Co To Pier

Van Chay

Dao Sau Nam

Gulf of Tonkin

Hon Gai Pier

Hang Dau

Halong City

Ha Tu

Dao Cong Do

Bai Tu Long Bay

Dao The Vang

Dao Ong Ca

Halong Bay

Dao Cong Dong

Hang Sung Sot

Hang Trong

Dao Titop

Viet Hai Village

Hospital Cave

Khe Sau

Cat Ba Island

Cat Ba National Park

Cat Ba Town Pier

Lan Ha Bay

Ben Beo

Dao Cat Dua (Monkey Island)

Dao Dau Be

Dao Hang Trai (Ile de l'Union)

Haiphong (15km)

18

18

279

isolated and untouched, and have the additional attraction of numerous white-sand beaches. Sailing and kayak trips here are easily organised in Cat Ba Town.

Geologically, Lan Ha is an extension of Halong Bay but sits in a different province. Around 200 species of fish, 500 species of mollusc, 400 species of arthropod (prawns, crabs) and numerous hard and soft corals live in the waters here, while larger marine animals in the area include seals and three species of dolphin.

The bay's admission fee is normally incorporated into the cost of tours.

★ **Cannon Fort**   HISTORIC SITE
(40,000d; ⊙ sunrise-sunset) For one of the best views in Vietnam, head to Cannon Fort, where there are astounding panoramas of Cat Ba Island's jungle-clad hills, the harbour and the karst-punctuated sea. The entrance gate is a steep 10-minute walk from Cat Ba Town, and it's then another stiff 20-minute walk to the fort, or take a *xe om* from town (15,000d).

Cat Ba National Park   NATIONAL PARK
(☑ 0225-216 350; 80,000d; ⊙ sunrise-sunset) Cat Ba's beautiful national park is home to 32 species of mammal, including most of the world's 65 remaining golden-headed langurs, the world's most endangered primate. There are some good hiking trails here, including a two-hour return trip to Ngu Lam peak and a day-long hike to Viet Hai village. To reach the roadside **park headquarters** at Trung Trang, hop on the Song Tung bus from Cat Ba Town, or hire a *xe om* (around 80,000d one way) or a car (US$30 return).

A guide is not mandatory but is definitely recommended. Many visitors opt to visit the park on an organised tour from Cat Ba Town, but you can also arrange guides at the park headquarters.

The short but strenuous hike to the top of **Ngu Lam peak** (park guide 200,000d) brings views over the surrounding jungle. The challenging 9km hiking trail through the park (starting just north of the park entrance) to the village of **Viet Hai** is best done with a guide (500,000d to 700,000d). Lunch and homestays are available in Viet Hai. From here you can walk, rent a bicycle (75,000d) or take an electric vehicle for 5km to the pier, where taxi boats shuttle back to Ben Beo Pier (300,000d to 500,000d per boat) near Cat Ba Town until 4pm. An elusive shared public ferry (50,000d per person, one hour) should depart from Ben Beo

at 11am and 4pm, and from Viet Hai at 7am and 1pm but check these times.

Take proper hiking shoes, a raincoat and a generous supply of water for the Viet Hai hike. This is not an easy walk, and best avoided during the wet season or after rain.

Of the mammals present in the park, the more commonly seen include macaques, deer, civets and several species of squirrel, including the giant black squirrel. Seventy bird species have been spotted here, including hawks, hornbills and cuckoos.

Trung Trang Cave   CAVE
(Hang Trung Trang; park admission 80,000d; ⊙ 7.30am-5pm) Within Cat Ba National Park but accessed from a separate roadside entrance 2km north of Hospital Cave, the multichambered Trung Trang Cave is fun to explore. The entry fee covers both the cave and the main park.

Hospital Cave   HISTORIC SITE
(40,000d; ⊙ 8am-5pm) Hospital Cave served both as a secret bomb-proof hospital during the American War and as a safe house for Viet Cong (VC) leaders. Built between 1963 and 1965 (with assistance from China), this incredibly well-constructed three-storey feat of engineering was in constant use until 1975.

The cave is about 10km north of Cat Ba Town, on the road to Cat Ba National Park entrance.

The cave spans 17 rooms, including an old operating theatre (complete with patient mannequins) and a huge natural cavern that was used as a cinema (and even had its own small swimming pool).

Cat Co Cove   BEACH
A 10-minute walk southeast from Cat Ba Town, the three Cat Co Cove beaches have the nearest sand to town, though all are being developed with hotel construction. **Cat Co 3** is the closest, with a small and popular sliver of sand. From there a walking trail, cut into the cliff and offering gorgeous sea views, winds its way to **Cat Co 1**, dominated by a resort, then onwards to the pretty white-sand swathe of **Cat Co 2**.

You can also follow the road uphill straight to Cat Co 1 and 2, or take the tourist 'train' (basically an oversized golf cart; 10,000d) that trundles over the hill during the summer months.

Kayaks and jet skis are available to rent at Cat Co 1. Note that the beaches get packed on summer weekends.

🏃 Activities

Kayaking

Kayaking among the karsts is one of the highlights of Lan Ha Bay and most cruises offer an hour's paddling through limestone grottoes or to a floating village in the bay.

Due to shifting, strong currents, more intrepid exploring is best done with a guide, particularly if you're not an experienced kayaker.

You're no longer allowed to kayak straight from Ben Beo Harbour, so most kayak rentals or tours include a water-taxi shuttle.

Cycling

A few hotels can arrange bicycles (around US$6 per day). Blue Swimmer offers better-quality mountain bikes for US$15 per day.

One possible bicycle (or motorbike) route traverses the heart of the island, past Hospital Cave and the entrance to Cat Ba National Park, down to the west coast's mangroves and crab farms, and then in a loop back to Cat Ba Town past tidal mudflats and deserted beaches. Figure on half a day with stops for the 32km cycle.

👉 Tours

Boat trips around Lan Ha Bay are offered by nearly every hotel on Cat Ba Island. Typical prices start at around US$25/80 for a day/overnight tour that takes in some swimming, kayaking and a visit to Monkey Island. A two-day trip allows you to get to the remoter, less-visited islands and hidden beaches of northern Lan Ha Bay.

★ Cat Ba Ventures   ADVENTURE

(☑0912 467 016, 0225-388 8755; www.catbaventures.com; 223 Đ 1-4, Cat Ba Town; overnight boat tour per person from US$136; ☉7.30am-8pm) Locally owned and operated company offering boat trips around Lan Ha and Halong Bays, one-day kayaking trips (US$29) and guided hikes in Cat Ba National Park (US$18 to US$29). Excellent service from Mr Tung is reinforced by multiple reader recommendations.

Langur's Adventures   ADVENTURE SPORTS

(☑0225-388 7789; www.langursadventures.com; Đ 1-4; ☉8am-9pm) Well-run agency that focuses on kayaking, rock climbing and hiking. Trips include a half-day introduction to top-rope climbing (US$39), a boat-supported kayaking day trip (US$29), deep-water soloing and a climbing/kayaking day combo, plus multi-activity overnight trips (US$110 to US$167 per person).

Cat Ba Kayak Adventures   KAYAKING

(☑0976 713 082; www.catbakayakadventures.com; Cai Beo; kayak rental single/double US$35/45) Self-guided kayak rentals include a drop off and pickup by water taxi, or take a guided day trip with lunch for $45 per person. Most interesting are the overnight tours (US$160 per person) into more secluded parts of Lan Ha Bay, overnighting on a junk or in an island bungalow.

Blue Swimmer   ADVENTURE

(☑0225-368 8237, 0915 063 737; www.blueswimmersailing.com; Ben Beo Harbour; overnight sailing trip per person from US$190; ☉8am-8pm) This environmentally conscious outfit was established by Vinh, one of the founders of respected tour operator Handspan Adventure Travel (p92). Superb sailing and kayaking trips, and trekking and mountain-biking excursions (some with overnight homestay accommodation), are offered. Enquire at the office just before Ben Beo Harbour.

🛏 Sleeping

Room rates on Cat Ba Island fluctuate wildly; in June and July they can double from the rates listed here. At other times some hotels raise rates a little on Friday and Saturday nights. From May to July, it's definitely worth booking ahead.

CAT BA TOWN

Most basic hotels are clustered on (or just off) the waterfront in Cat Ba Town. Nearby Đ Nui Ngoc lacks the views but is quieter, with good-value accommodation.

Central Backpackers Hostel   HOSTEL $

(☑0225-627 4888; www.centralbackpackershostel.com; Dap Nuoc Lake; dm 117,500d, r 423,000d; ❈ 🛜 🌊) One of a new breed of modern hostels, this well-run and spotlessly clean place on the western edge of town has dorms and a few comfortable private rooms. The garden area and small pool provide a social hub, or take the evening shuttle bus to party in town (returning at 1am).

Rates include breakfast and a free evening beer. Motorbike rental and tours available.

Cat Ba Tropicana Homestay   GUESTHOUSE $

(☑0938 934 338; 21 Alley 1, Đ Nui Ngoc; r US$13; ❈ 🛜) Clean, good-value rooms and a quiet but central location away from the busy coastal strip are a great start, but what really elevates this place is the unbelievably helpful owner, Tien, who can arrange anything from bus tickets and motorbike rental to cruises.

CRUISING THE KARSTS

The most popular way to experience Halong Bay's karst scenery is on a cruise. Fortunately everyone, their grandmother and their friendly family dog wants to sell you a Halong Bay tour in Hanoi. Unfortunately, shoddy operators abound.

Every year we receive complaints from travellers about poor service, bad food and rats running around boats on ultra-budget cruises, and more expensive trips where itinerary expectations didn't meet what was delivered.

Tours sold out of Hanoi start from a rock-bottom US$60 per person for a dodgy day trip, and can rise to around US$220 for two nights. For around US$110 to US$130, you should get a worthwhile overnight cruise. From Cat Ba a day cruise starts at around US$25.

At the other end of the scale, cruising the karsts aboard a luxury Chinese-style junk is hard to beat, but be aware that paying top dollar doesn't necessarily equate to heading away from the crowds. If you want to experience less-crowded karst views, consider cruises focused on Lan Ha Bay (p107), near Cat Ba Island. Several activity-based cruises here combine kayaking, climbing and swimming.

Most cruises include return transport from Hanoi, Halong Bay entrance fees and meals. A decent overnight tour usually includes kayaking. Drinks and even water are extra, payable in cash only.

This is one destination where it definitely pays to do your homework beforehand. Here are some suggestions to help make Halong Bay memorable for the right, rather than wrong, reasons:

➡ It can be a false economy to sign up for an ultra-cheapie tour. Spend a little more and enjoy the experience a whole lot more.

➡ At the very least, check basic onboard safety standards. Life jackets should be provided. If kayaking is included, make sure it's guided.

➡ Realise that most Halong Bay cruises follow a strict itinerary, with stops at caves often at the same time as other boats. On an overnight trip there's simply not the time to stray far from Halong City.

➡ Make sure you know what you're paying for to avoid disappointment. Many cruises marketed as 'two-day' trips actually involve less than 24 hours on board.

➡ Ascertain in advance what the tour company's refund policy is if the cruise is cancelled due to bad weather.

Cruise operators to consider:

Cat Ba Ventures (p110) Overnight tours set out from Cat Ba Island and concentrate on the Lan Ha Bay area.

Handspan Adventure Travel (p92) Operates the only true sailing ship on the bay.

Indochina Sails (☑ 0982 042 426; www.indochinasails.com) Cruise Halong on a traditional junk with great viewing decks and cabins kitted out to a three-star standard.

Unicharm (p955) Tranquil cruises into remoter corners of Lan Ha Bay, with snorkelling, kayaking and cooking classes on the menu.

Vega Travel (p92) Good-value overnight tours of Halong Bay, with comfortable cabins. Two-night tours also explore Lan Ha Bay and Cat Ba Island, including kayaking, cycling and hiking.

Note that until construction work finishes next door, you might end up staying in the equally comfortable Hai Binh Hotel two minutes' walk away.

Thu Ha HOTEL $
(☑ 0225-388 8343; www.thuhahotel.com; 205 Đ 1-4; s/d 250,000/300,000d; ❄ 🛜) This small family-run place has basically furnished,

clean rooms, some with four beds (600,000d). Negotiate hard for a front room and wake up to sea views; otherwise, head to the 11th-floor shared balcony.

Sea Pearl Hotel HOTEL $$
(☑ 0225-368 8567; www.seapearlcatbahotel.com. vn; 219 Đ 1-4; r incl breakfast 600,000-1,000,000d; ❄ @ 🛜 ⓢ) The Sea Pearl is a solid, if

Cat Ba Town

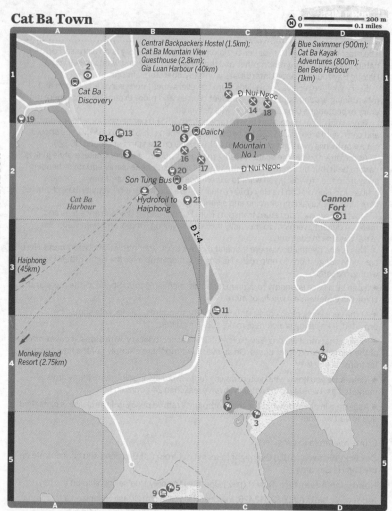

somewhat old-fashioned, choice. Deluxe rooms are comfortable and spacious and have fine bay views (standard rooms are smaller with no view), and staff are professional and helpful. Views from the 13th-floor Sky Bar and pool are excellent.

Hung Long Harbour Hotel　　　HOTEL **$$**
(☑0225-626 9269; www.hunglonghotel.vn; 268 Đ 1-4; r 900,000-1,500,000d; ❀ 🛜) At the quieter southeastern end of Cat Ba Town, the towering, three-star Hung Long Harbour has spacious rooms, many with harbour views. Don't bother upgrading to a superior room, as the standards are the ones with balconies.

AROUND THE ISLAND

There are some interesting options on other parts of Cat Ba Island, and offshore on isolated islands in Lan Ha Bay.

Woodstock Beach Camp　　　HOTEL **$**
(☑0225-388 599; www.facebook.com/wood stockbeachcamp; Phu Cuong; dm 80,000-150,000d, tr/q 350,000/400,000d; ❀ 🛜) As the name might suggest, basic Woodstock has some dirt under its fingernails, but if you want a uniquely old-school hippy backpacker crash pad, there's no better place. Dorm beds can be as simple as a mattress on the balcony or a tent on the beach, but

Cat Ba Town

there are a few air-con rooms in the main structure. It's located on the main road, 9km west of Cat Ba Town, with a free daily shuttle into town.

Whisper of Nature   HOTEL **$$**
(☑0987 989 094; https://whisper-nature-bun galow.business.site; Viet Hai village; bungalow incl breakfast US$32-38; ❋ 🛜) Whisper of Nature is a simple place where nature lovers can kick back and enjoy some downtime, or engage in hiking and swimming. Little concrete-and-thatch bungalows are set on the edge of the forest in the centre of Cat Ba Island. Getting here is an adventure in itself, with a boat ride from Ben Beo and then a 4km bicycle ride.

Cat Ba Mountain View Guesthouse   BUNGALOW **$$**
(☑0225-368 8641; https://catbamountainview. business.site; 452 Đ Ha Sen, Ang Soi village; dm 150,000d, cabin 350,000d, bungalow 500,000-1,000,000d; 🛜❇) Removed from the hustle of town, this collection of roadside bungalows and basic hilltop cabins made from pallets offers simple accommodation but great views over two bays from the small but dramatic hilltop pool. Laundry and bike hire available. It's on the main road, 3km (a 50,000d taxi ride) from Cat Ba Town.

Cat Ba Eco Lodge   RESORT **$$**
(☑0973 238 686; www.catbaecolodge.com; Xuan Dam village; r incl breakfast 950,000-1,500,000d; ❋@🛜) This resort boasts a rural location 12km from Cat Ba Town and 2km off the main road. Spacious, simple and somewhat overpriced wooden stilt houses sit around a breezy bar and restaurant, while more stylish but smaller A-frame cabins with

a balcony are surrounded by pine forest. There's a relaxing pool, and activities include riding bicycles to a beach 2km away, plus nearby hiking trails.

It runs two daily shuttles to/from Cat Ba Town. If coming by bus from Hanoi, ring for a lift from the main road.

Cat Ba Sunrise   RESORT **$$$**
(☑0225-388 7360; www.catbasunriseresort.com; Cat Co 3; r US$95-108; ❋@🛜❇) This beachfront resort is tastefully planned, with low-rise, tiled-roofed blocks sitting below green cliffs. The rooms are relatively spacious and smart (more expensive rooms come with sea-view balconies), but the real highlights are the beachside facilities, including a swimming pool and beach bar. A five-star annexe, with its own beach access and swimming pools, is in the works.

Monkey Island Resort   RESORT **$$$**
(☑0981 222 028, 0439 260 572; www.monkey islandresort.com; Cat Dua Island; r & bungalow incl breakfast US$70-160; ❋@🛜) Although the wood-and-thatch standard bungalows are tiny for the asking price, and could do with some TLC, the island location and strip of beach are truly lovely. There's a nice social vibe, and a nightly seafood buffet and kayaking and hiking activities are offered. Free 10-minute boat transfers from Ben Beo Harbour are provided. Discounts of 60% are common outside of May to August.

🍴 Eating

★**Casa Bonita**   INTERNATIONAL **$**
(www.facebook.com/casabonita.vn; 82 Đ Nui Ngọc; meals from 85,000d; ⊙7am-11pm; 🛜☑) This is one of our Cat Ba favourites for its

DON'T MISS

CLIMBING THE KARSTS

If you've ever been tempted to climb, Cat Ba Island is a superb place for it – the karst cliffs offer exceptional climbing amid stunning scenery. Most climbers in Cat Ba are complete novices, but as the instruction is excellent, many leave Cat Ba completely bitten by the bug.

The karst limestone here is not too sharp and quite friendly on the hands, and as many of the routes are sheltered by natural overhangs that prevent the climbable portion of the rock from getting wet, climbing is almost always possible, rain or shine.

Climbing opportunities are located on walls inland on Cat Ba Island or out in beautiful Lan Ha Bay and there are several experienced operators in Cat Ba Town, including Langur's Adventures (p110). You'll be kitted up with a harness and climbing shoes, given instruction and taught the fundamentals of top-rope climbing and belaying techniques, then given a demonstration. Then it's over to you, with your climbing instructor talking you through each move and anchoring you. Most people are able to complete a couple of climbs at Hai Pai and Moody Beach, which are both ideal for beginners.

The vertical cliffs of Halong and Lan Ha Bays are also perfect for **deep-water soloing**, which is basically climbing alone, without ropes or a harness, and using the ocean as a waterbed in case you fall. This is obviously only for experienced climbers with an experienced local crew, and it's essential to know the depth of water and tidal patterns. It's customary to finish a solo climb with a controlled free fall (or 'tombstone') into the sea and a swim back to the shore, or your boat.

Experienced climbers should check out the locally produced guidebook *Ha Long Bay Climbing* by Luca Di Giorgi.

combination of good service, tasty mains (try the seafood curry or fish in a clay pot), lighter options such as the chicken, avocado and mango salad, plenty of vegetarian and vegan choices, and a lovely rooftop garden. Start the day right with a smoothie bowl with house-made granola.

Little Leaf   INTERNATIONAL $
(91 Đ Nui Ngoc; meals 70,000-120,000d; ⊘7am-11pm; 🗲🖉) Attentive service and smart decor, set around a central cafe counter, are the draws here, with tasty Chinese-style dishes (try the braised mushroom and pepper) and Vietnamese-style grilled fish with lemongrass and chilli, plus crunchy *banh mi* for lunch and sweet mango crêpes for dessert.

Yummy 2   INTERNATIONAL $
(7 Đ Nui Ngoc; meals 40,000-80,000d; ⊘8am-10pm; 🖉) This backpacker-oriented family restaurant serves a menu of pan-Asian dishes – think Indian curries, pad thai and Vietnamese standards. Not exceptional, but capable and convenient. There's a more ramshackle **branch** (www.facebook.com/yummy catba; ⊘8am-10pm) a block nearer to the sea, serving an identical menu.

Vien Duong   SEAFOOD $$
(12 Đ Nui Ngoc; meals 150,000-200,000d; ⊘11am-11pm) Justifiably one of the most popular of

the seafood spots lining Đ Nui Ngoc, and often heaving with Vietnamese tourists diving into local crab, squid and steaming seafood hotpots. Definitely not the place to come if you're looking for a quiet night.

🍷 Drinking & Nightlife

Bia Hoi Stalls   BAR
(Đ 1-4; ⊘4-10pm) For a cheap and cheerful night out, with pretty great views of Cat Ba Town's harbour, head to this strip of open-air *bia hoi* (draught beer) stalls. Food is available if you can negotiate the Vietnamese menu.

Bigman   BAR
(www.facebook.com/thebigmanbar; Noble House, Đ 1-4; ⊘noon-late; 🗲) This bar has a real vibe and goes until late most nights, making it probably the most popular nightspot in town. It comes fully equipped with pool tables and harbour views.

Oasis Bar   BAR
(Đ 1-4; ⊘noon-1am; 🗲) A free-use pool table, smiley staff and tables spilling out onto the pavement slap in the centre of the seafront strip make Oasis one of the most popular spots to plonk yourself down for a beer or two, especially during the generous happy hour (5.30pm to 9.30pm).

ⓘ Information

For tourist information, Cat Ba Ventures (p110) is helpful. Most hotels and travel agencies sell bus tickets to Hanoi.

Agribank (Đ Nui Ngoc; ☺8am-3pm Mon-Fri, to 11.30am Sat)

Agribank ATM (Đ 1-4; ☺24hr)

Main Post Office (Đ 1-4; ☺7am-noon & 1.30-6.30pm Mon-Fri)

ⓘ Getting There & Away

Buses from Hanoi and Haiphong take the road bridge to Ben Got dock on Cat Hai Island, where passengers take a 15-minute speedboat ride to Phu Long (Cai Vieng) Pier on Cat Ba Island. Passengers are then generally put on a waiting minibus, though some buses cross on the larger car ferry (motorcycles allowed).

TO/FROM HAIPHONG

The fastest way to Haiphong is on the twice-daily direct hydrofoil from central Cat Ba pier to Ben Binh dock (180,000d, one hour), leaving at 10am and 2pm.

Buses are more frequent, running direct every hour or so from Cat Ba to Haiphong (100,000d, two hours) from the square in front of Cat Ba pier.

Check your bus or boat is headed to central Ben Binh, not the inconvenient Dinh Vu port.

TO/FROM HALONG CITY

Scenic car ferries run three times a day between Halong City's Tuan Chau Pier and Cat Ba Island's Gia Luan Harbour on the north side of the island, 40km from Cat Ba Town.

From Gia Luan ferries depart for Tuan Chau (per person/motorbike 80,000/20,000d, 1½ hours) at 9am, 1pm and 4pm. **Son Tung buses** (☑0353 422 342; Đ 1-4) run from Cat Ba to meet all ferries (30,000d, 40 minutes); catch the 7.45am, 9.15am, 11am or 3pm bus from outside Cat Ba Ventures to connect with the boat. There are additional ferries at 11.30am and 3pm between late May and early August.

TO/FROM HANOI

Companies such as **Daiichi Travel** (www.daiichitravel.com; 19 Đ Nui Ngoc), **Cat Ba Discovery** (☑0988 558 392; www.catbadiscovery.com; 5 Tung Dinh), **Good Morning Cat Ba** (www.goodmorningcatba.com) and **Cat Ba Express** (www.catbaexpress.com) each offer four or five comfortable direct services from Hanoi's Old Quarter (four hours, between 7.30am and 4pm) a day, making this the easiest way to get to/from Cat Ba. Coming from Hanoi the companies will pick you up anywhere in the Old Quarter. Fares vary from 200,000d to 270,000d, depending on the season. Your hotel in Cat Ba can book any of these.

TO/FROM OTHER DESTINATIONS

Daiichi and Cat Ba Discovery offer sleeper-bus connections to other destinations in Vietnam, including Ninh Binh (250,000d, 8am, 9am, 12.30pm and 4pm, five hours) Sapa (450,000d, 8am and 4pm, 11 hours), Ha Giang (400,000d, 4pm, 12 hours) and Hue (450,000d, 4pm, 16 hours).

ⓘ Getting Around

Cat Ba's Son Tung bus trundles between Cat Ba and Gia Luan Harbour (30,000d) in the north of the island, passing Hospital Cave, Trung Trang Cave and the national park headquarters en route; pick it up outside Cat Ba Ventures (p110).

Services leave Cat Ba Town at 7.45am, 9.15am, 11am and 3pm, returning from Gia Luan around 45 minutes later, once the ferry arrives. During the peak holiday period of June and July, more departures are added.

Bicycle and motorbike hire (both around 150,000d per day) is available from most Cat Ba hotels. If you're heading out to the beaches or national park, pay the 5000d parking fee for security.

Halong City

☑0203 / POP 221,580

Despite enjoying a stunning position on the cusp of Halong Bay, Halong City (known locally as Bai Chay) is a gritty town with pockets of high-rise hotel development dotting the shoreline.

Many travellers opt to skip Halong City completely, preferring to spend a night out in Halong Bay itself. Increased competition for a dwindling clientele means budget hotel rates are some of the cheapest in Vietnam, especially outside of June and July. Chinese and Korean visitors are now more prevalent, preferring to enjoy terra firma attractions such as casinos and karaoke after a day exploring the bay.

⊙ Sights

For a relaxing early morning or late-afternoon stroll, head to wide and sandy **Beach No 1**, accessible behind the Sunworld complex.

Sunworld CABLE CAR
(☑0203-223 8888; www.halongcomplex.sunworld.vn/en; Đ Halong; cable car adult/child 350,000/250,000d; ☺2-10pm Mon-Fri, 9am-10pm Sat & Sun) Vietnamese and cruise-ship tourists flock to this cable car that spans the Cua Luc inlet, offering dramatic views over Halong Bay. The views are particularly impressive at dusk, though the cabins can get

Halong City

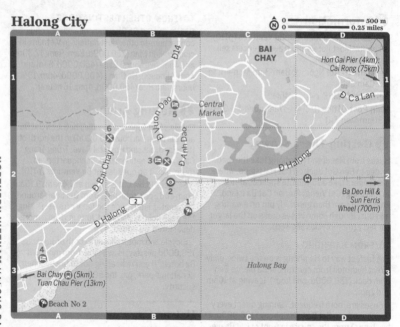

Halong City

⊙ Sights

🛏 Sleeping

✗ Eating

uncomfortably cramped at peak times. Your ticket includes a ride on the **Sun Ferris Wheel** on the far Ba Deo Hill and there are lots of other less-interesting attractions.

Families might be interested in the roller-coasters of **Dragon Park** and the seasonal **Typhoon Water Park** on the Bay Chay side, but check which rides are open before buying a ticket. Admission prices for these sights fluctuate seasonally.

🛏 Sleeping

★ **Light Hotel**   HOTEL $
(☑0203-384 8518; www.thelighthalong.vn; 108a Đ Vuon Dao; r incl breakfast 220,000-400,000d; ❄🛜) The good-sized, modern and clean rooms here are excellent value, especially the spacious triples with one large and one small bed. Chuck in the fact that the extremely helpful staff speak English and you've got Halong City's best budget find. Laundry service and motorbike rental available.

Fancy Hostel   HOSTEL $
(☑0868 150 290; 27, Lane 1, Đ Vuon Dao; dm 70,000-115,000d, r 280,000d; ❄🛜) A very central location, cheap laundry and a free bottle of beer are sweeteners at this hostel, and the dorm rooms are clean and spacious. It's down an alley off Đ Vuon Dao.

Novotel   HOTEL $$$
(☑0203-384 8108; www.novotelhalongbay.com; 160 Đ Halong; r US$74-120; ❖❄@🛜🏊) The Novotel fuses Asian influences with contemporary details, resulting in stunning rooms with teak floors, marble bathrooms and sliding screens to divide living areas. Facilities include an oval infinity pool and a good restaurant. It's a great place to start or finish a top-end cruise.

✗ Eating

Linh Dan Restaurant   SEAFOOD $
(☑0914 634 598; 104 Đ Bai Chay; meals from 70,000d, seafood 150,000-200,000d; ⊙11am-9pm; 🛜) Airy and spacious, Linh Dan offers

great local seafood dishes away from the touts of the town's seafront restaurants. The fish in clay pot with lemongrass and ginger is a standout, but there are plenty of other options and the English-speaking owner elevates it beyond the ordinary.

Tuan Huong　　　　　　　　SEAFOOD **$**
(✍0203-384 4651; 1 Ð Vuon Dao; meals from 100,000d, noodles 35,000d; ⊙10am-10pm) A simple local place with an English menu that specialises in fresh seafood. You can also pick your fish, squid or crab from the tanks outside, but make sure you check the price (calculated by weight) first.

❶ Getting There & Away

BOAT

From **Hon Gai Pier** (Ð Le Thanh Tong), next to Hon Gai Market, on the east side of the suspension bridge across from Halong City, there is a daily speedboat to Quan Lan Island (200,000d, 1½ hours, 1.30pm). A taxi/xe om from Halong City costs 80,000/35,000d.

From **Tuan Chau Pier** (Tuan Chau Island), 13km southwest of central Halong City, there are car ferries to Cat Ba Island's Gia Luan Harbour at 8am, 11.30am and 3pm (per person/motorbike 80,000/20,000d, one hour), with two additional services between late May and early September.

A taxi or Grab from the centre costs 160,000d. Tuan Chau is a major starting point for cruises into Halong Bay.

BUS

All buses leave from **Bai Chay bus station** (off Hwy 18), 6km west of central Halong City, though hotels can often book pricier services that pick up at your hotel.

For Cai Rong on Van Don Island (where ferries depart for the islands of Bai Tu Long Bay) take minibus number 1. For the sleeper bus to Sapa head to the Phuc Xuyen ticket office at the back of the bus-station yard. Note that many buses to Halong City will be marked 'Bai Chay'.

Bai Tu Long Bay

✍0203

There's much more to northeast Vietnam than Halong Bay. The sinking limestone plateau, which gave birth to the bay's spectacular islands, continues for some 100km to the Chinese border. The area immediately northeast of Halong Bay is part of **Bai Tu Long National Park**.

Bai Tu Long Bay is every bit as beautiful as its famous neighbour. In some ways it's actually more enjoyable, since it's only in its early stages as a destination for travellers. Improved boat transport to the scattering of resorts here means the area is quickly growing in popularity with domestic tourists, but the bay and its islands are still relatively undeveloped. Come outside the domestic high season of late April to August and you'll likely have the beaches and bays to yourself.

Accommodation rates on Co To and Quan Lanh Islands are highly seasonal. Rates peak between May and August but also rise slightly on Friday and Saturday night in other months.

Co To Island

Despite being the furthest inhabited island from the mainland, Co To Island has boomed in recent years, and today it's a popular destination for domestic tourists between May and August. This should hardly come as a surprise, as the island is home to some of Bai Tu Long Bay's best beaches and its widest spread of accommodation and restaurants. Yet despite all this, the island sees very few foreign faces.

◉ Sights

⭐**Hong Van Beach**　　　　　　　BEACH
Most Vietnamese visitors make a beeline for Hong Van Beach – and justifiably so. It's nearly 3km of fine, white sand lapped

BUSES FROM HALONG CITY

DESTINATION	COST (D)	DURATION (HR)	FREQUENCY
Cai Rong (Van Don Island)	27,000	1½	frequent 5.30am-6pm
Haiphong	70,000-100,000	1	frequent 6.30am-9pm
Hanoi	120,000	3	frequent 5.30am-7pm
Lang Son	110,000	5	every 30min 5.30am-noon
Mong Cai	100,000	4	every 40min 5.30am-noon
Ninh Binh	120,000	4	frequent 5.30am-4.30pm
Sapa	370,000	10	6.45am, 11.15am, 2.45pm & 8.45pm

by blue water and backed by a few season-al restaurants. It's so long you'll never feel crowded.

Van Chay Beach
BEACH

Located in the northwestern corner of Co To Island is broad Van Chay Beach. During the summer months it's home to lots of food stalls, as well as kayak rental.

Mong Rong Headland
VIEWPOINT

(Dragon's Claw) For coastal scenery beyond the beaches, head south from town for 3km, bearing left at the pond, to the flagpole and headland of Mong Rong, where walking trails offer dramatic cliff-side views down to the crashing coast.

Sleeping

Co To Island is home to Bai Tu Long Bay's widest spread of accommodation. Most is found in Co To Town, a brief walk from the island's pier, but there are also many small beachside hotels in other parts of the island.

Coto Hotel Group
HOTEL $

(☑ 0981 336 337, 0203-388 9678; cotohotelgroup@gmail.com; P Chang Son, Co To Town; r 400,000d; ❄☎) It's a mixed bag at this tall waterfront structure in Co To Town – two rooms on every floor have great sea views, while the other two have no exterior windows at all. No English is spoken here, so communicating can be tricky.

Coto Center Homestay
GUESTHOUSE $

(☑ 0962 616 898; No 66 Hai Tien village; r 400,000d; ❄☎) There are just six comfortable, modern rooms in this well-run homestay in the middle of the island. The location is rural, 4km from the ferry and 2km from Van Chay Beach, so you'll need to rent its scooter to get around. Contact owner Miss Hue for a free pickup from the ferry, and book a delicious seafood dinner (150,000d) while you're at it.

★ Starlight Boutique Hotel
HOTEL $$

(☑ 0964 085 500, 0203-350 0501; www.starlightcoto.com; Co To Pier; r US$25-55; ❄☎) Spacious, spotless modern rooms and staff that go above and beyond the call make this the top place in town, with a dockside location that's handy for an early morning ferry. The top-floor rooms with large tiled terraces are quite luxurious. From October to March rooms can be discounted to 500,000d or lower.

Coto Life
RESORT $$

(☑ 0988 722 688; www.facebook.com/cotoresorts; Hong Van Beach; bungalows 800,000-1,200,000d;

❄☎) This strip of rustic, wood and bamboo stilt bungalows is probably the best place near Hong Van Beach, though it's somewhat overpriced. The more expensive rooms are outfitted with spacious open-air bathrooms and a deck. It's on the western lagoon side of the spit on the northeastern side of the island, 300m from Hong Van Beach.

Eating

Quan Ngon 98
VIETNAMESE $

(P Ngyuen Cong Tru, Co To Town; meals 50,000d; ☺10am-1pm & 5-10pm) At the southern end of the town's main street is this simple but delicious shop selling point-and-choose dishes served over rice. The owner's son speaks English.

Sen Viet Restaurant
SEAFOOD $$

(P Chang Son, Co To Town; meals from 150,000d; ☺8am-10pm) There's not much English spoken at this popular seafood place, so you'll have to get the dictionary out or point at the tanks of shrimp, crabs, shellfish and fish out front (it also has barbecue pork). It's located on Co To Town's bay-front restaurant strip, with pleasant outdoor tables overlooking the beach.

❶ Information

Agribank ATM (cnr P Hoang Hoa & P Hai Ba Trung; ☺24hr)

❶ Getting There & Around

Cai Rong Pier, on Van Don Island, is the launching point for boats to/from Co To Island (250,000d, 1½ hours). Boats depart from Cai Rong at 7am, 9am, 11.30am and 1.30pm; you'll need to register your passport when buying a ticket. In the opposite direction, boats leave from Co To Pier at 8.30am, 9am, 11am and 1pm, with additional services on weekends during high season.

Electric cars, linked to the various resorts, shuttle visitors to/from a number of locations and can be hired for approximately 400,000d per day. Alternatively, most hotels have motorcycles for hire for around 150,000d per day.

Quan Lan Island

If you want to slide right off the typical traveller trail, Quan Lan Island (Dao Canh Cuoc) ticks the boxes. The island's only real hub is the sleepy three-street settlement of **Quan Lan Town**, 3km from the town pier and separated from the sea by a hem of mangroves. A handful of simple hotels and restaurants lines the main street.

Apart from hanging out on the beach and tootling around the island by bicycle or motorbike, there really is very little to do, which is the charm of the place if that's what you're looking for.

⊙ Sights

Minh Chau Beach   BEACH
The beautiful 1km-long crescent-moon sweep of Minh Chau Beach, 12km from Quan Lan town on the northeastern coast, is the island's main drawcard. Between May and August there are several beer and seafood restaurants and kayaks for hire; at other times, and especially midweek, the beach is all yours. There are several other small, blissful beaches on the island's eastern seaboard.

Quan Lan Pagoda   BUDDHIST TEMPLE
(Linh Quang Tu; ⊙ dawn-dusk) The only attraction within Quan Lan Town itself is this beautiful 200-year-old pagoda, flanked by the town's communal house and a temple, all of which are open to visitors. Opposite the complex is the town's main **fish market** (⊙ 4am-7am).

⫞ Sleeping & Eating

Nam Phong Hotel   GUESTHOUSE **$**
(⬚ 0988 961 358; s/d 200,000/300,000d; ✲ 🛜) Conveniently close to Quan Lan Town Pier (2km) but walkable to the town (1km), this welcoming, family-run place offers clean, spacious and excellent-value rooms (back rooms with a balcony are best), plus useful motorbike rental.

Ask English-speaking Phuong about his idyllic seafood **restaurant** (meals 100,000d to 200,000d) on a lovely stretch of beach 10 minutes' walk away.

Ann Hotel   HOTEL **$$**
(⬚ 0203-387 7889; www.annhotel.com.vn; Quan Lan Town; r incl breakfast 650,000d; ✲ 🛜) The well-run Ann Hotel, in the centre of town, offers spacious rooms with gleaming bathrooms. The best rooms at the back have balconies with ocean views.

Tuan Thuy Restaurant   VIETNAMESE **$**
(Quan Lan Town; meals 50,000-100,000d; ⊙ 8am-9pm) A decent selection of all the usual noodle and rice dishes is available at this simple family-run outfit, which is one of the few restaurants still open at dinnertime (and with an English menu). It's on Quan Lan Town's main street. It also offers spacious, comfortable and good-value rooms (double 200,000d) and rents scooters.

ⓘ Getting There & Away

TO/FROM CAI RONG
Boats from Cai Rong (on Van Don Island) dock at two places: Quan Lan Town Pier, 3km from the main township on the island's southern tip; and near Minh Chau Beach, on the island's northeastern tip.

Fast boats to **Minh Chau Pier** (140,000d, one hour) depart at 7.30am and 1.30pm. Returning to Cai Rong, boats depart at 7am and 1.30pm.

Fast boats to **Quan Lan Town Pier** (150,000d, one hour) depart Cai Rong at 7.30am and 1.30pm. From Quan Lan Town Pier boats make the return journey to Cai Rong (150,000d to 200,000d, one hour) at 7am and 1pm.

TO/FROM HALONG CITY
An alternative route to Quan Lan Town Pier is from Hon Gai Pier, across the suspension bridge from Halong City. A speedboat (200,000d, 1½ hours) leaves daily at 1.30pm, via Ngoc Vung Island, returning at 7am.

ⓘ Getting Around

Quan Lan is a surprisingly large island, and if you're staying in Quan Lan Town you'll need some kind of transport to get to the beach.

There are plenty of bicycles (US$4 per day) and motorbikes (150,000d per day) for hire in Quan Lan Town.

Electric cars and *xe lam* shuttle between Qan Lan Town Pier and Quan Lan Town for 20,000d and can also be hired to do tours of the island.

Van Don Island

Van Don (Dao Cai Bau) is the largest (around 30 sq km) and most populated island in the Bai Tu Long archipelago. Now linked to the mainland by a series of bridges, it's chiefly useful as the jumping-off point for ferries to Co To and Quan Lan Islands.

Van Don's main town is scruffy **Cai Rong** (pronounced 'cai zong'), about 8km north of the bridge to the mainland, with the pier a further 2km from the main road junction. If you're forced to overnight before catching a morning ferry, there are lots of accommodation and food options, and some dramatic limestone rock formations just offshore.

⫞ Sleeping

Luc Xoan Hotel   HOTEL **$**
(⬚ 0964 314 358; Cai Rong Pier; d 400,000d; ✲ 🛜) Steps from Cai Rong Pier is this bright green, perfectly located dockside hotel. 'I think clean is very important', the friendly,

English-speaking owner told us, and we tend to agree. The ground-floor seafood restaurant is handy.

❶ Getting There & Away

AIR

Van Don Airport (☑ 0203-390 1111; www.vdia.com.vn; Van Don Island) opened in 2019, with VietJet, Bamboo Air and Vietnam Airlines offering daily flights to Ho Chi Minh City. An expressway runs to Halong City, 50km away.

BUS

From Cai Rong Pier you'll have to take a *xe om* (20,000d) 2.5km northwest to the main road, just south of the post office, where you can find frequent minibuses to Halong City (also known as Bai Chay; 27,000d, 1¾ hours, 5am to 6pm). Buses to Hanoi (130,000d, five hours, 5.30am, 6am and 9am) depart from here and sometimes from the pier itself.

If you're heading north from Cai Rong, take the Halong City–bound bus for 8km to the Cua Ong turn-off (10,000d), where buses to Mong Cai and Lang Son pick up passengers.

BOAT

Cai Rong Pier has boats bound for Quan Lan Island – both to Quan Lan Town Pier (150,000d, one hour, 7.30am and 1.30pm) and Minh Chau Pier (140,000d, one hour, 7.30am and 1.30pm).

Boats leave for Co To Island (250,000d, 1½ hours) at 7am, 9am, 11.30am and 1.30pm.

For Co To you'll need to register your passport with the border police next to the ticket counter.

Northern Vietnam & the Chinese Border

Travellers' highlights towards the northern border with China include the lakes and caves of Ba Be National Park, the stunning karst scenery around Cao Bang and the sublime Ban Gioc Waterfall, and a couple of offbeat overland crossings into China's Guangxi province.

Ba Be National Park

☑ 0209

Often referred to as the Ba Be Lakes, **Ba Be National Park** (☑ 0281-389 4721; entry 46,000d; ☉ 5am-9pm) was established as a national park in 1992. The scenery plunges from limestone mountains peaking at 1554m down into lush valleys wrapped in dense evergreen forests and speckled with waterfalls and caves. The lakes dominate the very heart of the park.

The park is a rainforest area with more than 550 named plant species. The hundreds of wildlife species here include 65 mammals, 353 butterflies, 106 species of fish, four kinds of turtles and the highly endangered Vietnamese salamander. The 233 bird species include the spectacular crested serpent eagle and the oriental honey buzzard. Hunting is forbidden, but villagers are permitted to fish, and the government subsidises the villagers not to cut down the trees.

The region is home to 13 villages, most belonging to the Tay minority plus smaller numbers of Dzao and Hmong.

◉ Sights & Activities

Guesthouse owners can organise excursions. Boat trips (up to 12 passengers) are the most popular activity – figure on 550,000d for a half-day to **Dau Dang Waterfall** (Thac Dau Dang), or 600,000d to Hang Puong. **Mr Sinh** (☑ 0653 224 214) is a keen, English-speaking boat conductor. There are also opportunities for kayaking, cycling and trekking.

Hiking routes can take in Hmong, Tay and Dzao villages scattered through the park. Costs depend on the number of people, starting at about US$30 per day for a solo traveller, less for a group.

Ba Be Lake   LAKE

(Ba Be National Park) Rimmed by limestone peaks, Ba Be (meaning Three Bays) is in fact three linked lakes, with a total length of 8km and a width of about 400m. Most boat excursions around the lakes visit the **An Ma Pagoda**, on an islet in the middle of the lake, and the 300m-long, tunnel-like **Hang Puong** (Puong Cave), full of stalactites and stalagmites and home to as many as 7000 bats (belonging to 18 species).

Other Ba Be Lake stops can include the pretty Tay village of **Cam Ha** and the startling, circular, jungle-rimmed lagoon of **Ao Tien**. Two of the lakes are separated by a 100m-wide strip of water called Be Kam, sandwiched between high walls of chalk rock.

Hua Ma Cave   CAVE

(22,000d; ☉ 7am-5pm) One of Ba Be's most popular off-the-water sights is this 800m-long cave complex with a pathway leading down into a soaring 50m-high cavern. It's 6km southeast of Pac Ngoi and easily reachable on motorbike.

Tours

Ba Be Tourism Centre ADVENTURE
(☎0209-389 4721; www.babenationalpark.com.vn; Bo Lu village) Essentially a travel agency run by Mr Linh's Homestay, this helpful, English-speaking office can arrange kayaking, boating, hiking and cycling trips (or a combo of all four) for around US$45 per day. It specialises in multiday treks (from US$83 for two days) and amazing caving adventures in nearby Lo Mo Cave.

Sleeping & Eating

The village of Pac Ngoi, 2km from the ferry, has two dozen simple guesthouses (rooms 100,000d to 180,000d) that offer simple private rooms, shared hot-water bathrooms and meals (100,000d). There's not much to differentiate them, so just see what appeals when you get there. The low-key settlements of Bo Lu and Coc Toc, nearer the ferry, have a few quieter guesthouses.

Hai Dang Lodge GUESTHOUSE $
(☎0977 568 434; www.babelakeview.com; Bo Lu; r 150,000-600,000d; ❄☜) The Hai Dang is raised above the main road in Bo Lu village and so has great views from its terrace towards Ba Be Lake. Rooms are comfortable, some with en suite bathrooms and air-con, and the food is excellent.

Mr Linh's Homestay GUESTHOUSE $$
(☎0209-389 4894, 0989 587 400; www.mrlinhhomestay.com; Coc Toc village; dm US$8, r with shared bathroom US$25-30, r US$30-40; ❄☜) A step up in amenities from Ba Be's homestays, this lakeside place in Coc Toc village consists of lovely sitting areas linking bamboo and wood-panelled rooms – the newer ones have a bathroom and concrete bathtub. Visitors are well looked after by friendly, English-speaking staff. All rates include breakfast.

Information

There is no bank or ATM in Ba Be National Park. Bring all the cash you'll need with you.

Getting There & Away

Ba Be National Park is 240km from Hanoi, 61km from Bac Kan and 18km from Cho Ra.

Most people visit Ba Be as part of a three- or four-day tour from Hanoi, or as part of an adventurous motorbike trip.

The park entrance fee is payable at a checkpoint about 15km before the park headquarters, just beyond the town of Cho Ra.

BUS

From Hanoi the most direct route to Ba Be's lakeside homestay villages of Pac Ngoi, Bo Lu and Coc Toc is the local bus to Cho Don (130,000d, four hours), via Thai Nguyen, run by Thuong Nga bus company. It leaves My Dinh bus station at 10am. At Cho Don you hop on a connecting minibus (run by the same company) to Pac Ngoi, Bo Lu and Coc Toc (40,000d).

A more roundabout route is to head into the park via Cho Ra. There are daily buses to Cho Ra at 6am and 2pm from Hanoi's My Dinh bus station (180,000d, six hours). A direct bus (90,000d, five hours) also departs from Cao Bang for Cho Ra at 7am. There are also regular bus services from Thai Nguyen and Cho Don to Cho Ra. Once in Cho Ra, you can arrange a *xe om* (about 150,000d) to cover the last 18km into the park, or wait for a passing bus from Phu Thong.

Buses normally drop passengers at the **ferry** (adult/motorbike 10,000/20,000d) on the north side of the lake; accommodation is all on the south side.

GETTING TO CHINA: MONG CAI TO DONGXING

Getting to the border Rarely used by travellers, the **Mong Cai/Dongxing border crossing** is around 2km from the Mong Cai bus station. There are frequent buses to Mong Cai from Hanoi (seven hours), Halong City (five hours) and Lang Son (five hours). From the station, it's around 20,000d on a *xe om* or 40,000d in a taxi to the border.

Overnighting at Mong Cai If your budget allows it, aim for the plush **Mong Cai Grand Hotel** (☎0203-377 6555; www.grandmongcaihotel.vn; 23 P Hung Vuong; r incl breakfast US$28-44; ❄☜), 2km from the border; otherwise the budget **Hoang Hiep** (☎0203-388 7999; 12 Đ Hoang Quoc Viet; r 350,000-400,000d; @☜) is a minute's walk from the Chinese border.

At the border The border is open daily between 7am and 8pm Vietnam time. Note that China is one hour ahead of Vietnam. You'll need to have a prearranged visa for China.

Moving on Across the border in Dongxing, frequent buses run to Nanning in China's Guangxi province.

Departing Ba Be's lakeside villages, there are minibuses to Cho Don at 6am and 1.30pm. If you're heading northeast from Ba Be, you can take a local bus headed to Phu Thong or Thai Nguyen and get off at the Na Phac junction (50,000d, one hour), from where there are frequent through services to Cao Bang (100,000d, two hours).

Mr Linh's Adventure Tours (p92) and **QBus** (www.qbustravel.jimdofree.com) are trying to arrange a direct daily morning bus (US$13 to US$20) between Hanoi and Ba Be so it's worth contacting them to see if it's operating.

Lang Son

📞 0205 / POP 148,000

Lang Son is a booming city set next to tranquil Phai Loan Lake and surrounded by green karst peaks. Most travellers pull through town on their way to or from China – the border is 18km north, just outside Dong Dang – but there are a couple of attractions if you decide to overnight.

Lang Son was partially destroyed in February 1979 by Chinese forces. Although the border is still heavily fortified, both Lang Son and Dong Dang have been rebuilt and Sino–Vietnamese trade is in full swing again.

◎ Sights

Nhi Thanh Cave   CAVE
(adult/child 20,000/10,000d; ⊙6am-6pm) Paths follow the Ngoc Tuyen River through this beautiful cave for about 1km. The entrance has a series of poems carved in Chinese characters by the cave's 18th-century discoverer, a soldier called Ngo Thi San. There's also an intriguing carved stone plaque commemorating an early French resident of Lang Son. It's a five-minute drive south of Tam Thanh Cave.

Tam Thanh Cave   CAVE
(off P Tam Thanh; adult/child 20,000/10,000d; ⊙6am-6pm) Tam Thanh Cave is vast and seductive, with a water pool inside and natural 'window' offering a sweeping view of the surrounding rice fields.

A few hundred metres above the cave exit are the ruins of the Mac Dynasty Citadel, but the trail is very overgrown and it's a hard slog. It's a lovely, deserted spot, with stunning rural views.

🛌 Sleeping & Eating

★Song Long Hotel   BUSINESS HOTEL $
(📞0205-389 5588; www.songlonghotel.com; 122 Ly Thuong Kiet; r 350,000-600,000d; ❋🖧🛈) This excellent-value hotel has spotless midrange rooms for upper-budget prices. The spacious doubles are better value than the cheaper superior rooms. Motorbike rental is possible if you have a licence, but you must leave your passport as a deposit. It's just east of the town centre.

Van Xuan Hotel   HOTEL $
(📞0205-371 0440; lsvanxuanhotel@yahoo.com. vn; 147 Đ Tran Dang Ninh; r 360,000-550,000d; ❋@🛈) The simple and central Van Xuan has helpful staff and old-fashioned but neat rooms that lead out to a communal balcony overlooking the eastern edge of Phai Loan Lake. The cheaper rooms have interior windows looking on to the corridor.

Quan Nga Tue   VIETNAMESE $
(P Minh Khai; meals from 40,000d; ⊙10am-10pm; 🖉) P Minh Khai, a couple of blocks north of Lang Son's market, is home to several *com binh dan* (point-and-choose dishes served

---

ⓘ GETTING TO CHINA: LANG SON TO NANNING

Getting to the border The Friendship Pass at the Dong Dang–Pingxiang border crossing is the most popular crossing in the far north. The border post itself is at Huu Nghi Quan (Friendship Pass), 3km north of Dong Dang Town. From Lang Son, a train passes through from Hanoi to Dong Dang at 11.25am (15,000d, 20 minutes), or take a bus bound for That Khe (50,000d, every 45 minutes) and get off in Dong Dang. Easiest is a taxi (160,000d) or *xe om* (70,000d) from Lang Son directly to the border.

Note that direct international buses (p92) and trains (p95) also run between Hanoi and Nanning.

At the border The border is open from 7am to 8pm daily Vietnam time. Note that China is one hour ahead of Vietnam. To cross the 500m to the Chinese side, you'll need to catch one of the electric cars (12,000d). You'll also need a prearranged visa for China.

Moving on On the Chinese side, it's a 20-minute drive to Pingxiang by bus or shared taxi. Pingxiang is connected by train and bus to Nanning (three hours).

over rice) restaurants. Quan Nga Tue is typical of the lot, and meat-free dishes are available.

ℹ Getting There & Away

BUS

Buses depart from the northern bus station, about 2km north of central Phai Loan Lake. Buses run frequently to Hanoi (100,000d, three hours) until 5pm. There are also buses to Mong Cai (95,000d to 120,000d, 5½ hours, nine departures from 5.15am to 4.30pm), Cao Bang (100,000d, four hours, eight departures from 5.15am to 1.45pm) and sleeper buses to Ha Giang (240,000d to 280,000d, 10 hours, 7.30am and 6pm).

TRAIN

The DD5 train from Hanoi to Lang Son departs daily at 7am (78,000/89,000d for hard/soft seat, four hours), continuing on to the border town of Dong Dang. The return to Hanoi leaves Lang Son at 3.30pm.

Cao Bang

☑ 0206 / POP 51,386

This eponymous provincial capital isn't unpleasant – the climate is mild, there's a fine central market and the location on the banks of the Bang Giang River is striking – but you'll most likely use the city as a base to explore rural Cao Bang province, one of the most beautiful regions in Vietnam.

◉ Sights

War Memorial MONUMENT
(off Đ Pac Bo) There's not a whole load to do in Cao Bang Town itself, but there are great 360-degree views from the town's hilltop war memorial. Head up the second lane off Đ Pac Bo, go under the entrance to a primary school and you'll see the steps leading up the hill.

🛏 Sleeping

★Thanh Loan Hotel HOTEL $
(☑ 0948 173 336, 0206-385 7026; www.thanhl oanhotel.com; 131 P Vuon Cam; d incl breakfast 400,000-450,000d; ❋ 🛜) This well-run place with English-speaking staff features spacious rooms with high ceilings, some with a balcony, and a useful location near the main market and several restaurants.

Duc Trung Hotel HOTEL $
(☑ 0206-385 3424; www.ductrunghotel.com.vn; 85 P Be Van Dan; r 400,000-500,000d; ❋ 🛜) A solid

Cao Bang

option with spacious, business-style rooms, some with floor-to-ceiling windows, on a quiet street off Cao Bang's main drag.

✖ Eating

In the mornings look out for stalls selling *banh cuon* – freshly steamed, stuffed, lasagne-like noodles, served with a bowl of hot broth.

★Thu Ngan VIETNAMESE $
(21 P Vuon Cam; meals 40,000-60,000d; ☺ 8am-9pm; 🛜 🍴) One of our favourite *com binh dan* joints in northern Vietnam. Enter to find a reliable spread of appetising dishes, including a handful of meat-free options, and a cold beer in your hand before you even find your seat.

ℹ Getting There & Away

Cao Bang's main **bus station** (Hwy QL3) is inconveniently located around 7km northwest of the centre. A taxi here costs a hefty 100,000d.

Morning and afternoon limousine vans to Hanoi (300,000d) sidestep the bus station by picking you up from your hotel, making them a simpler and faster option.

If you are headed to the Ha Giang region, note that there is no reliable public transport between Bao Lac and Meo Vac. You'll have to hire a taxi in Bao Lac.

ℹ Getting Around

QT Motorbikes & Tours (☑ 0975 278 711; www.qtmotorbikesandtours.com.vn; 54 Cau Bang Giang, P Hop Giang), a branch of the excellent Ha Giang operation, is the best place to hire a motorbike. It rents scooters

BUSES FROM CAO BANG

DESTINATION	COST (D)	DURATION (HR)	FREQUENCY
Ban Gioc Waterfall	70,000	2	half-hourly 5.30am-6pm
Bao Lac	120,000	4	6 departures 6am-5pm
Cho Ra (Ba Be National Park)	100,000	5	7am, 9am & noon
Hanoi	200,000	7	hourly 6.30am-1pm; sleepers 4pm & 7.30pm
Lang Son	100,000	3	7 departures 6am-noon

(150,000d to 200,000d per day) and larger motorbikes (380,000d to 650,000d), along with optional protective gear and bike-damage insurance. You can return the bike in Ha Giang for a surcharge.

Around Cao Bang

★ **Ban Gioc Waterfall**   WATERFALL
(40,000d, plus 5000d insurance; ⊙ 7.30am-5pm) Ban Gioc is one of Vietnam's best-known waterfalls, and its image adorns the lobby of many a cheap guesthouse. The falls, fed by the Quay Son River that marks the border with China, are an impressive sight in a highly scenic location. Aim to visit around lunchtime when the upstream dam is opened to allow full flow.

Boat owners here will punt you on bamboo rafts (50,000d) close enough to the waterfall so you can feel the spray on your face. Rafts on the Vietnamese side have blue canopies; on the Chinese side canopies are green.

For a fine overview of the falls and the entire karst valley, head back towards Cao Bang for 1km and climb left to the hillside **Phat Tich Truc Lam Ban Gioc Pagoda** (⊙ dawn-dusk).

Frequent buses link Cao Bang and the waterfall (70,000d, two hours, hourly from 5.30am to 6pm). Catch them just east of the **Bang Giang Bridge** in Cao Bang.

The police station at the waterfall sometimes requires foreigners to buy a border permit (200,000d for up to 10 people) to visit the falls, though we weren't asked during our visit. Bring your passport just in case.

Nguom Ngao Cave   CAVE
(45,000d; ⊙ 7am-5.30pm) About 4km from Ban Gioc Waterfall, 2km up a side valley, Nguom Ngao Cave is one of the most spectacular cave systems in Vietnam. Created by an underground river, it extends for several kilometres underground; villagers sheltered

here during the 1979 war with China. Visitors are permitted in one section, where a 1km-long concrete path and lighting have been installed.

Buses between Cao Bang and Ban Gioc can drop you at the valley turn-off, where you can look for a *xe om* for the remaining 2km.

For an overnight stay here, head to one of the eight rustic **homestays** (from 100,000d per person, plus 100,000d for dinner) in the charming stone village of Khoi Ky, 1.5km before the cave.

NORTHWEST VIETNAM

Northwest Vietnam, with its rocky, cone-like mountains, high vistas and deep valleys, encompasses some of the most extreme geography in the country – if not all of Southeast Asia.

Northwest Vietnam's people and culture are additional draws, and the mountains are home to a variety of ethnic groups living in scenic villages with colourful markets.

Travelling to more remote parts of the region takes time and effort, which is perhaps one reason why travel by motorcycle is a particularly popular way to see the region. The rising star of the area is Ha Giang, with its stunning karst scenery, but there are plenty of places to explore, particularly the Hoang Su Phi region between Ha Giang and Bac Ha.

History

The history of the northwest differs to lowland Vietnam. The Vietnamese traditionally avoided mountains, believing the terrain was not suitable for large-scale rice production. For many centuries the area remained inhabited only by a mosaic of regional ethnic groups, joined in the 19th century by migrants from Yunnan, China, and Tibet. For decades this was the 'badlands', a buffer zone of bandits between China and

Vietnam, where opium production was rife. During Ho Chi Minh's leadership, the North Vietnamese experimented with limited autonomy in 'special zones', but these were abolished after reunification.

ℹ Getting There & Away

The region's main airport is at Dien Bien Phu, but most travellers take the train from Hanoi to Lao Cai, the gateway to Sapa. Given the scenery, this is a great place to consider hiring a car and driver, or riding a motorbike.

To undertake the northwest loop, some travellers head for Mai Chau, then Dien Bien Phu via Son La, continuing north to Sapa and then back to Hanoi. Allow a week for this journey (more if using local buses).

Many travellers are now skipping Sapa and taking the sleeper bus from Hanoi direct to Ha Giang to focus on the spectacular four-day motorcycle loop from there.

Travellers can cross from Laos into Vietnam at the Tay Tran–Sop Hun border crossing, 34km from Dien Bien Phu, or from China at Lao Cai, near Sapa.

Mai Chau

📞 0218 / POP 12,000

Set in an idyllic valley, hemmed in by misty mountains, the Mai Chau area is a world away from Hanoi's hustle. The small town of Mai Chau itself is unappealing, but the patchwork of rice fields begins just 100m away, speckled by tiny Thai villages where visitors can bunk down for the night in traditional stilt houses and wake up to a rural soundtrack defined by gurgling irrigation streams and birdsong.

The villagers are mostly White Thai, distantly related to tribes in Thailand, Laos and China. Most no longer wear traditional dress, but the Thai women are masterful weavers, producing plenty of traditional-style textiles. Locals do not employ strong-arm sales tactics here: polite bargaining is the norm.

If you're looking for hardcore exploration, Mai Chau is not the place, especially on the busy weekends, but for midweek cycling, hiking and relaxation, the calm area fits the bill nicely.

◉ Sights & Activities

Most visitors come simply to stroll (or cycle) the paths through the rice fields to the surrounding villages. Most stilt-house homestays rent bikes to explore the valley at your own pace.

Many hotels offer guided day-hiking options that take you by motorbike to Pa Co market or southeast to Pu Luong Nature Reserve to spend a half-day exploring rural paths and remote villages.

The excursions desk at Mai Chau Lodge (p126) also offers kayaking on Song Da Reservoir, cooking classes ($23 per person) and mountain-biking excursions.

Many travel agencies in Hanoi run inexpensive trips to Mai Chau.

Pa Co Market MARKET
(◷ 6-10am Sun) This interesting weekly market, 30km northwest of Mai Chau, makes for a fine excursion. The back section has a small but high-quality section of batiks and embroideries made by the local Black Hmong people. The market is in Xi Linh, 500m south of the main Hoa Binh–Son La highway; turn off opposite the petrol station.

On the way back to town, pop into Mai Chau's own **Sunday market** (◷ 6am-3pm).

🛏 Sleeping & Eating

Mai Chau is an extremely popular weekend getaway for locals from Hanoi, and huge school groups often flood the numerous stilt guesthouses in the tiny village of Lac/Pom Coong; try to come midweek if possible.

WORTH A TRIP

MUONG CULTURAL MUSEUM

One potential stopover between Hanoi and Mai Chau is this **centre** (Khong Gian Van Hoa Muong; 📞 0218-389 3688, 0913 553 937; www.muong.vn; 202 Đ Tay Tien; admission 50,000d; ◷ 7.30am-5.30pm Tue-Sun) founded by Hanoi artist Vu Duc Hieu to showcase the culture of the local Muong ethnic minority and the quirky art and sculpture of the owner. There's a collection of Muong artefacts, but the highlight is the sprawling 5-hectare complex itself, which is home to traditional buildings and open-air art pieces.

The museum is 8km southwest of Hoa Binh (3km off the main highway to Mai Chau); a xe om costs around 50,000d and a taxi 80,000d.

Simple **accommodation** (📞 0913 553 937; www.muong.vn; 202 Đ Tay Tien; dm 100,000d; r 300,000-500,000d; 🖧) is available at the museum.

Most people eat where they stay. Establish the price of meals first as some places charge up to 200,000d for dinner.

★ Little Mai Chau Homestay
GUESTHOUSE $

(☑ 0973 849 006; littlemaichauhomestay@gmail.com; Na Phon village; dm 100,000d, r 300,000-500,000d; ❋ ☎) It's hard to beat this collection of thatched bamboo bungalows, backing onto karst cliffs, with balconies overlooking the paddy fields, 2km west of Mai Chau. The secluded family bungalow in particular is perfect for couples. It's very well set up, with free bicycles, motorbike rental (150,000d per day) and sociable shared dinners (80,000d).

Owner Heung speaks English and can arrange anything.

Ban Van Guest House
GUESTHOUSE $

(☑ 0218-386 7182; Ban Van village; r 300,000-400,000d; ❋ ☎) Ban Van village is only 800m east of central Mai Chau, but is noticeably less developed for tourism. Three or four stilt-house homestays dot the village, but this modern guesthouse is a step up, offering comfortable and modern rooms, some with balconies overlooking the rice fields. The pleasant cafe across the road has more lounging potential.

Hotel Mai Chau Valley View
HOTEL $$

(☑ 0218-386 7080; www.maichauvalleyview.com; Hwy 15; r 700,000-800,000d; ❋ ☎) This small and professionally run place of just six rooms combines the convenience of being in town with rural views of the paddy fields from the balconies of the smart, modern rooms. Bonuses include a ground-floor cafe-restaurant and helpful, switched-on staff.

★ Mai Chau Eco Lodge
RESORT $$$

(☑ 0218-381 9888; www.maichau.ecolodge.asia; Na Thia village; bungalows incl breakfast 2,900,000-3,430,000d; ❋ ☎ ☒) 🏊 Located on a slight hill surveying the surrounding rice fields is this village-like compound. Step inside the thatched-roof bungalows and you'll find they're both modern and rustic, with attractive tiled floors, local design touches and attempts to recycle water and use solar electricity. Easily the most sophisticated place to stay in the area, so book ahead.

Mai Chau Lodge
HOTEL $$$

(☑ 0218-386 8959; www.maichaulodge.com; Hwy 15; r 1,900,000-2,140,000d, ste 2,590,000d; ❋ @ ☎ ☒) This tour-group favourite has handsome rooms decked out in local textiles, a refreshing plunge pool and a nice bar area overlooking the local pond. It's at the turn-off to Lac village, a short walk from the rice fields. Discounts of 40% are standard during the week.

Three Sisters Restaurant
VIETNAMESE $

(meals 50,000-120,000d; ⊙ 6am-10pm; ☎) The eponymous three sisters here run a friendly local joint that's a step up from other places in town. House specials include red pumpkin soup with rice, a banana-flower salad and local rice wine served with honeycomb, plus lots of smoothies and juices. It's 300m down a side street west of Mai Chau's main road, near the central market.

❶ Getting There & Around

Direct buses to Mai Chau (90,000d, 3¾ hours) leave Hanoi's My Dinh Bus Station (p94) at 6am, 8.30am and 11am. You'll be dropped off at the crossroads, just a short stroll from Lac village.

To Hanoi and Hoa Binh (50,000d, two hours), buses leave from along Hwy 15 every hour or so until 5pm. One limousine minivan (US$12) runs directly to Hanoi's Old Quarter at 3.30pm. **Thai's Travel Bus** (☑ 0972 058 696; www.thaitravelbus.com) operates a daily tourist bus to Ninh Binh/Tam Coc (285,000d, 3½ hours) at 8.30am. Homestay owners can book these and arrange for you to be picked up from your guesthouse.

For Son La or Dien Bien Phu you'll have to take a *xe om* to the main road, 5km north, and flag down a through bus.

Several guesthouses rent out bicycles for free; others charge 40,000d per day.

Son La

☑ 0212 / POP 66,500

Sprawling Son La has prospered as a logical transit point between Hanoi and Dien Bien Phu. For many travellers it's not high on the list of places to visit, but a few minor diversions could occupy you for half a day.

The region is one of Vietnam's most ethnically diverse, being home to more than 30 different minorities, including Black Thai, Meo, Muong and White Thai.

◉ Sights

Old French Prison & Museum
MUSEUM

(Nha Tu Son La; ☑ 0212-385 0221; Khau Ca; admission 30,000d; ⊙ 7.30-11.30am & 1.30-5.30pm) Son La's old prison was a French penal colony

MUONG TE & NA HU

An unassuming district capital, Muong Te gets its charm from its remote location, beautiful setting and Thai inhabitants. It's a great place to get off the beaten track en route between Dien Bien Phu and Sapa.

One place to get a taste of local White Thai culture is Na Hu village, 9km east of Muong Te, where residents live in elevated stilt houses in a bucolic setting at the edge of the Boum River.

To overnight in Muong Te, try the spacious rooms and hard beds of **Dung Phu Hotel** (☑0213-388 2555, 0977 026 217; Đ 127, Muong Te; r 200,000-350,000d) at the far western end of town.

For dinner try the *bun dau mam tom* (deep-fried tidbits, noodles and herbs that are dipped in shrimp paste) at **Toi Ben** (Đ 127, Muong Te; meals from 50,000d; ⏰10am-10pm), a few blocks south of Muong Te's bus station.

Buses from Muong Te run three times a day to Dien Bien Phu (150,000d, six hours), twice in the afternoon to Hanoi (400,000d, 12 hours, sleeper bus) and hourly to Lai Chau (100,000d, four hours).

where anticolonial revolutionaries were incarcerated from 1908. It was destroyed by the 'off-loading' of unused ammunition by US war planes after bombing raids, but is now partially restored. Rebuilt turrets stand guard over claustrophobic underground cells and a famous lone surviving peach tree, planted by To Hieu, a 1940s inmate.

Lookout Tower   VIEWPOINT
(off Hwy 106; ⏰daylight hours) FREE For an overview of Son La, follow the stone steps to the left of the Trade Union (Cong Doan) Hotel in the north of town. It's a 20-minute uphill walk to reach the lookout.

Son La Market   MARKET
(Đ Chu Van Thinh; ⏰6am-2pm) You'll find woven shoulder bags, scarves, silver buttons and necklaces and other hill-tribe crafts at this market in the north of town.

Thuan Chau Craft Market   MARKET
(Thuan Chau; ⏰7am-1pm) Take a local bus or *xe om* to Thuan Chau, about 35km northwest of Son La, early in the morning, when its daily market swells with colourfully dressed hill-tribe women.

Sleeping

★**Cosy Hotel**   HOTEL $
(☑0334-911 919, 0212-366 6789; www.cosyhotel sonla.com.vn; No 2, 4 KDT Lam Son, Dau Cau Nam La; r 300,000-600,000d; ☀☎) This gleaming hotel in the north of town is your best choice, whatever your budget. The poky 300,000d rooms don't have windows but all other rooms are spacious and well decorated, with comfy beds and rain showerheads.

There's a ground-floor cafe and you can take in the surrounding karst scenery from the rooftop bar or common balcony.

Drinking

Trung Nguyen Cafe   CAFE
(P Ba Thang Hai; ⏰8am-10pm; ☎) This smart cafe-bar has a relaxing, tree-shaded garden at the front and serves up some of Son La's best coffee.

Getting There & Away

Son La is 340km from Hanoi and 140km from Dien Bien Phu.

From the **bus station** (AH 13), 5km southeast of town, there are frequent buses (mostly sleepers) to Hanoi between 5am and 11pm (165,000d to 220,000d, eight hours); Dien Bien Phu, with eight departures from 5am to 4.45pm (110,000d, four hours); and Ninh Binh (185,000d to 250,000d, nine hours, 5.10am and 8.15pm).

For Mai Chau take a Hanoi bus, get off at the junction 5km from the town and look for a *xe om* (or through bus); you'll likely have to pay the fare to Hanoi.

To get to the bus station from the town centre, jump on one of the red-and-white number 3 minibuses heading south on the main street (10,000d), or take a taxi (50,000d).

Dien Bien Phu

☑0215 / POP 46,362

Dien Bien Phu (DBP) plays a starring role in Vietnam's modern history. It was in the surrounding countryside, on 7 May 1954, that the French colonial forces were defeated by the Viet Minh in a decisive battle that served as the nail in the coffin of the French Indochina empire.

The town sits in the heart-shaped Muong Thanh Valley, surrounded by heavily forested hills. The scenery along the way here is stunning, with approach roads scything through thick forests and steep terrain. Tay, Hmong and Si La people live in the surrounding mountains, but the city and valley are mainly inhabited by ethnic Vietnamese.

Previously just a minor settlement, DBP was elevated to provincial capital in 2004. It's a pleasant stop for fans of (predominantly French) military history or those heading to northern Laos.

Sights

★ Dien Bien Phu Museum   MUSEUM

(279 Đ 7-5; 15,000d; ⊙7-11am & 1.30-6pm) This well-laid-out museum, contained in a space-agey modern structure, features an eclectic collection that commemorates the 1954 battle. Alongside weaponry and guns, there's a bathtub that belonged to the French commander Colonel de Castries, a bicycle capable of carrying 330kg of ordnance, and the testimony of Vietnamese who were there.

★ A1 Hill   MONUMENT

(Đ 7-5; 15,000d; ⊙7-11am & 1.30-5.30pm) This vantage point was crucial in the battle of Dien Bien Phu. There are tanks and a monument to Viet Minh casualties on this former French position, known to the French as Eliane and to the Vietnamese as A1 Hill. The elaborate trenches at the heart of the French defences have also been recreated. Little background information is given on-site.

Market   MARKET

(P Be Van Dan; ⊙6am-5pm) Dien Bien Phu's liveliest quarter is this bustling produce market on the east bank of the Ron River, just east of the old Muong Thanh Bridge.

Men Village   VILLAGE

(Ban Men; ⊙24hr) FREE Dien Bien Phu is ringed by Tay villages, and this one, 5km north of the city, has been deemed a 'culture and tourism village', ostensibly because of its traditional wooden stilt homes and textile industry. There's little to do other than wander around and appreciate the architecture, but it's a pleasant insight into Tay culture and there are no tour groups. Get a taxi or *xe om* here from the bus station.

THE BATTLE OF DIEN BIEN PHU

In early 1954 General Henri Navarre, commander of the French forces in Indochina, sent 12 battalions to occupy the Muong Thanh Valley in an attempt to prevent the Viet Minh from crossing into Laos and threatening the former Lao capital of Luang Prabang. The French units, of whom 30% were ethnic Vietnamese, were soon surrounded by Viet Minh forces under General Vo Nguyen Giap. The Viet Minh outnumbered the French by five to one, and were equipped with artillery pieces and anti-aircraft guns, painstakingly carried by porters through jungles and across rivers. The guns were placed in concealed, carefully camouflaged positions overlooking the French troops.

When the guns opened fire, French Chief Artillery Commander Pirot took his own life. He'd assumed there was no way the Viet Minh could get heavy artillery to the area. A failed Viet Minh assault against the French was followed by weeks of intense artillery bombardments. Six battalions of French paratroopers were parachuted into DBP as the situation worsened, but bad weather and the impervious Viet Minh artillery prevented sufficient French reinforcements from arriving. The elaborate series of French trenches and bunkers were overrun by the Viet Minh after the French decided against the use of US conventional bombers and the Pentagon's proposal to use tactical atomic bombs. All 13,000 French soldiers were either killed or taken prisoner, and Viet Minh casualties were estimated at 25,000.

Just one day before the Geneva Conference on Indochina was set to begin in Switzerland, Viet Minh forces finally overran the beleaguered French garrison after a 57-day siege. This shattered French morale, and the French government abandoned all attempts to re-establish colonial control of Vietnam.

Dien Bien Phu Cemetery
CEMETERY

(Đ 7-5; ⊙24hr) **FREE** The immaculately maintained Dien Bien Phu Cemetery commemorates the Vietnamese who died in the battle of Dien Bien Phu, with each gravestone bearing the gold star of the Vietnamese flag and a clutch of incense sticks.

Bunker of Colonel de Castries
MONUMENT

(off P Nguyen Huu Tho; 15,000d; ⊙7-11am & 1.30-6pm) West of the Ron River, the dank command bunker of Colonel de Castries has been recreated, though there's little to actually see. A discarded tank and some mortar guns linger nearby. You might see Vietnamese tourists mounting the bunker and waving the Vietnamese flag, re-enacting an iconic photograph taken at the battle's conclusion.

French War Memorial
MEMORIAL

(off P Nguyen Huu Tho; ⊙daylight hours) **FREE** The unsigned French War Memorial, erected on the 30th anniversary of the 1954 battle, commemorates the 3000 French troops buried under the rice paddies.

Victory Monument
MONUMENT

(Đ 1-4; admission 15,000d; ⊙7-11am & 1.30-6pm) The epic hilltop Victory Monument, commemorating the 1954 battles, presides heroically over Dien Bien Phu's main road. Road access leads around the back of the hill, or you can climb the steps for fine views.

🛏 Sleeping

Nam Ron Hotel
HOTEL $

(☑0946 251 967; Đ Trang Dang Ninh; r 250,000-400,000d, VIP r 500,000d; ❉🛜) At the edge of the Ron River is this characterless but tidy place. By Vietnamese standards, the rooms feel tight (except for the spacious VIP rooms) but are functional and comfortable, and the VIP rooms come decked out with retro sofas. Motorbike rental is possible.

Phadin Hotel
HOTEL $

(Quan Kha 2; ☑0215-655 8888; www.facebook.com/phadinhoteldienbien; 63 Đ Trang Dang Ninh; d/tr 400,000/550,000d, VIP r 800,000d; ❉🛜) Bright-feeling but plain rooms in a large three-star hotel complex one minute's walk from the bus station. All rooms come with a balcony and the VIP rooms are huge with lots of natural light. The attached coffee shop is excellent and there's a large supermarket next door. Rooms come with breakfast.

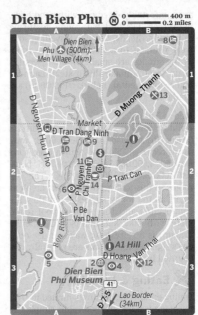

Dien Bien Phu

⭐ Ruby Hotel
HOTEL $$

(☑0913 655 793; www.rubyhoteldienbien.com; off P Nguyen Chi Thanh; r incl breakfast 560,000-900,000d; ❉🛜) The best deal in Dien Bien Phu is this friendly hotel, down a quiet, riverside alleyway. The 31 rooms are comfortably fitted out with good beds, flat-screen TVs and bathrooms featuring rain showerheads. If you're travelling solo, treat yourself to a spacious double room as the singles are small. Online discounts of up to 50% make this a steal. Laundry and scooter rental (half-day 100,000d) are available.

Muong Thanh
Holiday Hotel   HOTEL $$$
(Muong Thanh Grand; ☑ 0215-381 0043; www. muongthanh.com; 514 Đ Vo Nguyen Giap; r incl breakfast 1,600,000-1,800,000, ste incl breakfast 2,000,000-3,100,000d; ❈ 🛜 ☸) The 148 rooms in this tour-group favourite aren't as smart as the lobby suggests, but they are comfortable and the outdoor pool (complete with fake karst cliffs and concrete dragon) is a refreshing way to rinse off a day's sightseeing. Rooms are generally discounted by 50%.

🍴 Eating & Drinking

Dining options are relatively limited in DBP, but there is a line of good-value, simple restaurants along P Nguyen Chi Tranh, all with pick-and-choose counters (40,000d) where you can tuck into everything from chicken to fried locusts.

★**Yen Ninh**
Vegetarian Restaurant   VEGETARIAN $
(☑ 0989 887 513; www.dbpcity.wixsite.com/ yenninh; 257 Group 9, Ton Thanh ward; meals 35,000-50,000d; ☺ 8am-10pm; 🛜 ✎) This is an unexpected find down a nondescript residential alley in the commercial northwest of town – a family home doubling as a bookshop that serves up light and fresh vegan food to a stream of grateful backpackers. Tuck into fresh spring rolls and mango banana smoothies, while the family goes about its daily business around you. Ever-helpful English-speaking boss Yen also rents out motorbikes (half-day 80,000d).

Bia Hoi Restaurants   VIETNAMESE $
(Đ Hoang Van Thai; meals from 30,000d; ☺ noon-10pm) Meet the locals at the *bia hoi* (draught beer) gardens along Đ Hoang Van Thai. There's decent and cheap grilled food as well.

Moc Quan   CAFE
(P Tran Can; ☺ 10am-10pm; 🛜) Moc Quan is one of several appealing modern cafes on this street, but we like the smiling staff and airy design here. It serves Vietnamese coffee and good fruit shakes, as well as ice cream.

ℹ Information

Agribank (Đ 7-5; ☺ 8am-3pm Mon-Fri, to 11.30am Sat, ATM 24hr)
Main Post Office (896 Đ 7-5; ☺ 8am-6pm Mon-Fri)

ℹ Getting There & Away

AIR
Dien Bien Phu Airport is 1.5 km north of the town centre along the road to Muong Lay; a taxi to town costs 50,000d. Vietnam Airlines operates two flights daily to/from Hanoi (from 1,600,000d, one hour) through its subsidiary Vasco Airlines.

BUS
DBP's **bus station** (Hwy 12) is at the corner of Đ Tran Dang Ninh and Hwy 12.

ℹ Getting Around

Renting a scooter or hiring a *xe om* for a half-day is the best way to see the town's sights, which are fairly spread out.

BUSES FROM DIEN BIEN PHU

DESTINATION	COST (D)	DURATION (HR)	FREQUENCY
Hanoi	255,000-345,000, VIP (9.30pm) 570,000	11½	7am, then frequent sleepers 4.30-9.30pm
Lai Chau	145,000	8	hourly 5am-4pm
Muong Lay	70,000	3	2.30pm & 4pm
Muong Te	150,000	6	7am & 8.15am
Sapa	230,000	8	6.30am, 9am & 11.30am, sleepers 5pm, 5.30pm & 6.30pm
Sin Ho	120,000	5	6.30am
Son La	110,000-120,000	4	9 departures 4.30am-2pm

ⓘ GETTING TO LAOS: DIEN BIEN PHU TO MUANG KHUA

....

Getting to the border A bus from Dien Bien Phu to Muang Khua (115,000d, five hours) in Laos leaves daily at 5.30am. It's advisable to book your ticket the day before travelling. This bus takes you through the **Tay Trang–Sop Hun border crossing**. Other destinations in Laos from DBP include Bo Keo (560,000d, 6.15am), Luang Prabang (495,000d, 6.45am and 7.30am), Luang Nam Tha (350,000d, 6.30am and 7am), Phongsali (345,000d, 7.15am) and Udomxai (230,000d, 6am).

At the border The Tay Trang–Sop Hun border, 34km from Dien Bien Phu, is open daily between 7am and 4.30pm. Crossing into Laos, most travellers can get a 30-day visa on arrival (US$30 to US$42). Have two passport photos and additional small US dollar bills on hand for occasional local administrative fees.

Moving on From Muang Khua there are buses to Udomxai.

Sin Ho

📞 0213 / POP 4000

Sin Ho is a scenic mountain town that's home to a large number of ethnic minorities. Few travellers make it here, but a hotel and decent road access mean it's an interesting detour if you're keen to see an authentic local market very different from those at Sapa and Bac Ha, which are now firmly on the tour-bus route.

◉ Sights

Sin Ho Market   MARKET

(Đ 128; ⊗ 6am-2pm) Sin Ho has markets on Saturday and Sunday; the wildly colourful Sunday market is the more impressive of the two. It's a better place to buy livestock than ethnic handicrafts, but that's its charm.

🛏 Sleeping & Eating

Thanh Binh Hotel   HOTEL $

(📞 0213-387 0366; Đ 128; r 250,000-450,000d; ❄ ❀ ⊛) The ageing, government-run Thanh Binh has 17 tired but passable rooms at the north end of town, but staff are rarely troubled by any guests. The upper-floor rooms are best. There's a restaurant on-site if you order in advance.

Jumong Quan   VIETNAMESE $

(Đ 128; meals from 50,000d; ⊗ 8am-10pm) At the southern end of Sin Ho, by the edge of the lake, is this large, friendly *com,* one of the few places in town open for dinner.

ⓘ Getting There & Away

From the south, the turn-off uphill to Sin Ho is 1km north of Chan Nua on the main road from Muong Lay to Lai Chau. Definitely ask about the state of this road and the road north to Lai

Chau before you leave, as sections are subject to landslides.

Sin Ho has at least one bus departure for Dien Bien Phu at 8am (120,000d, five hours), and five departures a day to Lai Chau (60,000d, 1½ hours) between 6.30am and 4pm. For Sapa change in Lai Chau.

A *xe om*/taxi from Lai Chau to Sin Ho costs a negotiable 300,000/800,000d

There's no formal bus station in Sin Ho, so ask your accommodation to book a seat.

Sapa

📞 0214 / POP 9000 / ELEV 1650M

Established as a hill station by the French in 1922, Sapa today is the major tourism centre of the northwest. The town is oriented to make the most of the spectacular views emerging on clear days – it overlooks a plunging valley, with mountains towering above on all sides. If you were expecting a quaint alpine town, recalibrate your expectations. Modern tourism development has mushroomed chaotically in Sapa and much of the centre is under seemingly endless reconstruction.

But you're not here to see the town. Sapa is northern Vietnam's premier hiking base, from where hikers wind through the surrounding countryside of cascading rice terraces and hill-tribe villages. Rough roads, ugly development and overtourism have blighted many parts of the countryside around Sapa, but if you look hard enough there are still some sublime corners of traditional village architecture framed by golden terraced fields. This is the Sapa you've come to see.

Sapa offers quite different charms throughout the year. The best weather in general is in March and April. June to September offers views of flooded, sky-reflecting

🛈 LAI CHAU

If you are taking public transport between Sapa, Sin Ho, Dien Bien Phu or Muong Te, you might well find yourself changing buses in the sprawling provincial capital of Lai Chau.

Lai Chau bus station has minibuses to Sin Ho (60,000d, two hours) at 5am, 6am, 7am, 9am and 1pm, to Dien Bien Phu (130,000d, six hours) hourly until 12.45pm and then at 5pm, and hourly to Lao Cai (120,000d, three hours) via Sapa.

If you have to overnight, there are a half-dozen acceptable hotels around the bus station, or try the better **Minh Son Hotel** (☑ 0213-387 8431; cnr P Nguyen Thi Minh Khai & P Ton Phong; r 250,000-400,000d; ❄ ☎), 2km northwest, with spacious, modern rooms and fine views from the upper floors.

rice terraces and ripening yellows later in August, plus waterfalls are at their peak, but the weather is hot and rainy.

September to January is generally most popular with foreigners, though cloud and fog are common in October and November.

👁 Sights

Sapa Museum   MUSEUM

(103 P Cau May; ⊙ 7.30-11.30am & 1.30-5pm) FREE An excellent showcase of the history and ethnology of the Sapa area, including the French colonial era. Dusty exhibitions overview the various ethnic groups around Sapa, with information on the region's rich handicrafts, so it's worth a quick visit when you first arrive in town. Located above a handicrafts shop behind the Tourist Information Center (p140).

Fansipan Cable Car   CABLE CAR

(☑ 0214-381 8888; www.fansipanlegend.sunworld. vn; return adult/child 700,000/500,000d; ⊙ 7am-4.30pm, last car from summit 6pm) Towering above Sapa are the Hoang Lien Mountains, once known to the French as the Tonkinese Alps and now a national park. These mountains include the often-cloud-obscured Fansipan (3143m), Vietnam's highest peak, regularly dubbed 'The Roof of Indochina'. Fansipan's wild, lonesome beauty has been somewhat shattered with the opening of a 6292m-long cable car, taking people across the Muong Hoa Valley and up to near the summit in 15 minutes.

Buy tickets at the **ticket office** (Đ Phan Xi Pang, Sun Plaza) in Sapa's main square, from where a funicular train (50,000d return) shuttles passengers to the lower cable-car station. After the cable-car ride you still face 600 steps to the summit, or you can take another funicular (70,000d one way) from Do Quyen, passing a series of pagodas and Buddhas to the summit. Expect crowds or clouds, depending on the weather.

Sapa Market   MARKET

(Đ Ngu Chi Son; ⊙ 6am-2pm) Turfed out of central Sapa and now in a purpose-built modern building near the bus station, Sapa Market is still interesting, and hill-tribe people from surrounding villages come here most days to sell handicrafts. Saturday is the busiest day.

Tram Ton Pass   VIEWPOINT

The road between Sapa and Lai Chau crosses the Tram Ton Pass on the northern side of Mt Fansipan, 15km from Sapa. At 1900m it's Vietnam's highest mountain pass, and acts as a dividing line between two climatic zones. The lookout points here have fantastic views in clear weather.

On the Sapa side it's often cold and foggy, but drop a few hundred metres onto the Lai Chau side and it can be sunny and warm. Surprisingly, Sapa is the coldest place in Vietnam, but Lai Chau can be one of the warmest.

Most people also stop at 100m-high **Thac Bac** (Silver Waterfall, admission 20,000d), 12km from Sapa. A one-way/return xe om here costs 80,000/150,000d.

Sapa Church   CHURCH

(Đ Ham Rong; ⊙ Mass 6am Sun) Sapa's small stone church was built by the French and is still a central landmark. It opens for Mass on Sunday and on certain evenings for prayers.

🏃 Activities

Hiking

You won't step too far out of your hotel in Sapa before being accosted with offers to guide you on hikes.

For longer treks with overnight stays in villages, it's important to hook up with someone who knows the terrain and culture and speaks the language. We recommend using local minority guides, as this offers them a means of making a living. Always go through a reputable tour agency.

The villages surrounding Sapa now all have admission fees. Some have been transformed by tourism and host dozens of

Sapa

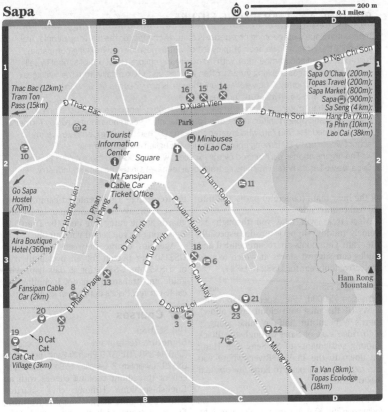

NORTHERN VIETNAM SAPA

Sapa

homestays, restaurants and souvenir shops, linked to Sapa by dusty roads – not quite what you trekked to see. If you head down valley to heavily commercialised villages such as Lao Chai and Ta Van you will want to be sure you have a guide that can take you

BUILDING A BETTER HMONG FUTURE

Inherent in Sapa's burgeoning prosperity is cultural change for the hill-tribe people. Traditionally the Hmong have been employees of Vietnamese-owned trekking companies, restaurants and accommodation, with many Hmong children kept out of school to sell handicrafts or act as trekking guides, often walking up to 10km daily from their villages to Sapa to earn money. A new generation, though, is now focused on securing a more independent and positive future for their people.

Sapa O'Chau, meaning 'thank you Sapa' in the Hmong language, is focused on providing training and opportunities to Hmong young people. The organisation is run by former handicraft peddler Shu Tan, who created the Sapa O'Chau Learning Centre, a live-in school where up to 20 Hmong children can learn English and Vietnamese.

The organisation is part funded by the excellent walks, treks and tours it runs around Sapa, as well as its hotel, which helps train local teenagers in the hospitality industry.

off the busy main (concrete) paths and into the real countryside.

Most treks will take you through extremely muddy, slippery terrain, especially after rain. Gumboots are recommended and guides can suggest stores at which to rent protective footwear for US$2 to US$4.

Sa Seng & Hang Da HIKING
(admission 75,000d) For spectacular valley views (if the mist and cloud gods allow), there's a beautiful half-day hike along a high ridge east of Sapa through the Black Hmong settlements of Sa Seng and Hang Da down to the Ta Van River, where you can get transport back to Sapa (xe om/taxi 80,000/200,000d).

Ta Phin HIKING
(admission 75,000d) A very popular day hike from Sapa is to Ta Phin village, home to Red Dzao people, about 10km north of Sapa. Most people take a taxi (around 200,000d) to a starting point about 8km from Sapa, and then make a 14km loop through the area, passing through Black Hmong and Red Dzao villages.

Mt Fansipan HIKING
To fully earn the views from the summit of Fansipan, you can hike to the summit. Tour agencies in Sapa offer all-inclusive overnight camping trips, but some fit and experienced trekkers hike up in a long day (set off at dawn) and catch the cable car down the same day. It's a tough hike.

Be aware that the terrain is rough and slippery and adverse weather is frequent. Bring warm clothes and plenty of water. Don't attempt an ascent if Sapa's weather is poor, as limited visibility on Fansipan can be treacherous.

There are a few rudimentary shelters en route, but these are very basic so it's bet-

ter to arrange a fully catered camping trip if overnighting. Guides are mandatory and guards at the entry gate near the Tram Ton Pass won't let you set off without one.

Agencies charge between US$112 and US$150 per person for an overnight trip, or US$55 to US$65 for a day trip, with guide and transport but not including the cable-car fee. Prices depend on group size.

☕ Courses

Hill Station
Signature Restaurant COOKING
(☑0214-388 7111; 37 Đ Phan Xi Pang; per person US$29, minimum 2 people; ⊙9am-noon) Excellent three-hour cooking classes with an English-speaking Hmong chef, starting with a 30-minute market tour and featuring five local dishes, including homemade tofu, smoked buffalo and banana-flower salad, as well as tasting local rice wine. Book the evening before.

Indigo Cat ART
(☑0982 403 647; www.indigocat.shop; 46 Đ Phan Xi Pang; class 400,000d; ⊙10am) Craft shop Indigo Cat runs morning workshops where you can learn traditional Hmong batik-dyeing techniques. The half-day classes take place in the village of Ta Van, 8km away, so add on 500,000d for a taxi, plus 75,000d per-person village-entry fee. Call into the lovely Sapa shop (p139) for details.

☞ Tours

Many visitors arrive on tour packages pre-arranged in Hanoi, but there are a couple of standout local operators in town that are well worth looking into.

★ Sapa O'Chau HIKING
(☑0915 502 589; www.sapaochau.org; 3 Le Van Tam; ⊙7.30am-6.30pm) ✔ Excellent local

company offering day walks (from US$30 per person), longer homestay treks (around US$38 per day), Bac Ha market trips and Fansipan hikes. It also runs culturally immersive tours that focus on handicrafts and farmstays. Profits provide training to Hmong children in a learning centre.

Sapa Sisters HIKING

(☑ 0904 567 985; www.sapasisters.com; 9 Đ Phan Xi Pang; ☺ 7am-5pm) Run by a group of savvy and knowledgeable Hmong women, Sapa Sisters offers customised private day hikes (from US$37 per person) and longer village homestay treks (from US$74), some staying in their Zao's House guesthouse in Ta Van. English and French are spoken.

Topas Travel HIKING

(☑ 0214-387 1331; www.topastravel.vn; 15 Le Van Tam) High-quality trekking, mountain-biking and village encounters, based around a stay in Topas Ecolodge (p138) or the **Topas Riverside House** (☑ 0214-3715 1005; www.topas riversidelodge.com; Nam Cang village; d half-board with shared bathroom US$87). Book in advance.

Handspan Travel ADVENTURE SPORTS

(☑ 0214-387 2110; www.handspan.com; Chau Long Hotel, 24 Đ Dong Loi; ☺ 8am-8pm) This nationwide agency offers trekking and mountain-biking tours to villages and markets.

🛏 Sleeping

Many hotels raise rates on Fridays and Saturdays with the weekend influx of domestic tourists.

Sapa can be busy, so if there's somewhere in particular you want to stay, prebook directly with the hotel itself for the best rate.

🛏 In Town

Construction, touts and weekend crowds mean that staying in Sapa itself can be a hectic experience. That said, if you need some pampering before or after a trek, there are some excellent-value places to stay.

Sapa O'Chau HOTEL $

(☑ 0214-387 1890; www.sapaochau.org; 3 Le Van Tam; dm US$6, r US$20-30; ✳ ⚡) The hotel attached to the excellent tour agency exists to train locals in hotel management, so be patient. The best rooms enjoy spacious lake views and a small balcony, but even the six-bed dorms come with their own bathroom. Rates include breakfast on the rooftop, and staff rent out motorbikes. Sign up for a trek and you'll get a room discount.

Auberge Hotel HOTEL $

(☑ 0214-387 1243; www.aubergedangtrunghotel. com; 31 P Cau May; r incl breakfast US$15-35; ⚡) An old-school yellow villa with porticoes, terrace seating and a garden restaurant, the Auberge retains a vaguely colonial vibe. Rooms are comfortable but can be damp on the lower floors, so book an upper-floor or family room. It's close to the main strip but off the road, so quieter than most hotels. French-speaking owner Mr Manh runs a tour agency and can arrange anything you need, including trekking tours and motorcycle rental.

Thai Binh Hotel HOTEL $

(☑ 0214-387 1212; www.thaibinhhotel.com; 45 Đ Ham Rong; r incl breakfast 500,000d; ⚡) You'll likely feel at home here from the minute you enter the lobby to see the hotel cat dozing in front of the crackling fireplace. Rooms are spacious and clean, particularly the front-facing ones with a balcony, and the quiet location near Sapa's church is a bonus. The English-speaking owners provide a nice family touch.

Go Sapa Hostel HOSTEL $

(☑ 0214-871 198; www.gosapahostel.com; 25 Đ Thac Bac; dm 110,000-130,000d; r 300,000-360,000d; @⚡) Up the hill from central Sapa, this well-run hostel has a multitude of six- and eight-bed dorms (with lockers) set around a communal courtyard and lots of pleasant sitting areas. The two private rooms come with their own terrace and are a great deal. Motorbike hire, bus tickets and laundry are available.

Elegance Hotel HOTEL $$

(☑ 0214-389 8868; www.sapaelegancehotel.com; 3 Hoang Dieu; r incl breakfast 500,000-800,000d; ✳⚡) The spacious, well-furnished deluxe rooms with balcony here are one of the best deals in Sapa, especially given the perfect central location. Helpful staff can arrange bus tickets and motorbike rental, and the breakfast features deliciously crunchy baguettes. The cheapest old-block rooms in the separate villa-style back garden lack the views but are still pleasant.

Sapa Dragon Hotel HOTEL $$

(☑ 0214-871 363; www.sapadragonhotel.com; 1a Đ Thac Bac; r incl breakfast US$55-60; ✳⚡) Professional staff, a quiet neighbourhood and stylish interior design give this hotel a reassuring vibe. The 20 rooms are handsome and spacious and come with balconies, though there aren't any real mountain views. Without online discounts it's a bit overpriced, but get a deal and it's a fine option.

KEVIN MILLER/GETTY IMAGES ©

1. Traditional *rong* house (p302), Kon Tum **2.** Boating along the Ngo Dong at Tam Coc (p156) **3.** Paradise Cave (p162), Phong Nha-Ke Bang National Park **4.** Rice terraces at Fansipan (p132)

EFIRED/SHUTTERSTOCK ©

Caves & Highlands

Vietnam is blessed with some of the world's most awe-inspiring cave systems. Its northern and western highlands, topped by ghostly, shape-shifting clouds and mist, form the heartland of the nation's minority people.

Highland Culture

Dotted around the southwest highlands town of Kon Tum (p299), Bahnar villages are wonderful places to experience minority culture. Marvel at the soaring *rongs* (thatched community houses), go fishing with locals and watch kids swim their herds of cattle across rivers.

Karst Mountains

Vietnam's highlands are characterised by spectacular limestone outcrops known as karst formations. These remarkable peaks stretch from the far northeastern mountains in Ha Giang (p143) and Cao Bang (p123) provinces down towards the Laos border.

Phong Nha-Ke Bang National Park

The western side of this national park (p160) is home to highland jungle that includes the highest concentration of tigers in Vietnam. But Phong Nha is best known for its simply extraordinary cave systems, which include Hang Son Doong, the world's largest cave.

Tonkinese Alps

The spectacular Tonkinese Alps soar skywards along the rugged, uncompromising edges of the country and include Fansipan (p132), Vietnam's highest peak. From sinuous and spidery ridges, rice terraces cascade down into river valleys home to ethnic minority villages of Hmong, Red Dzao and Giay peoples.

Botanic Sapa
HOTEL $$

(☑0912 480 433; http://botanicsapa.com; 8a Cau May Alley; r US$25-35; ☎) The cosy Botanic stands out mostly due to friendly husband-and-wife owners Minh and Van, who are wonderful hosts. There are only four rooms, brightened with local textiles, fresh white linen and modern bathrooms, and everything is kept spotlessly clean. Twin rooms are best. The back-alley location, down a steep staircase off P Cau May, won't suit everyone.

Cat Cat View Hotel
HOTEL $$

(☑0214-387 1946; www.catcathotel.com; 46 Đ Phan Xi Pang; r incl breakfast 500,000-1,000,000d; apt 2,000,000-3,600,000d; ❄@☎) There's plenty of choice at this rambling, family-run spot with comfortable pine-trimmed rooms over nine floors and two wings, with the upper floors opening out onto communal terracotta terraces and a restaurant. The spacious apartments are a great option for travelling families or groups of friends.

Aira Boutique Hotel
HOTEL $$$

(☑0214-377 2268; www.airaboutiquesapa.com; 30 P Hoang Lien; r incl breakfast US$75-95; ❄☎❄) Located at the edge of a cliff, and offering fantastic views of the valley below, is this fresh, modern hotel. Front-facing rooms with views are the most expensive, but all are decked out in rich chocolate-brown decor, with particularly inviting bathrooms and balconies attached to all but the cheapest rooms. Rates include afternoon tea.

Amazing Hotel
HOTEL $$$

(☑0214-386 5888; http://amazinghotel.com.vn; Đ Dong Loi; r 2,930,000-4,800,000d; ❄❄@❄) Amazing might be an exaggeration, but this striking, modern, four-star hotel offers comfortable rooms and impressive views from some of them. A rooftop gym and pool are nice perks, but be sure to ask for a room away from the basement nightclub. Book online for discounts of 30%.

Victoria Sapa Resort
RESORT $$$

(☑0214-387 1522; www.victoriahotels.asia; P Hoang Dieu; r incl breakfast US$130-150; ❄☎❄) This alpine-style hotel gets top marks for its attentive service and charming garden, terrace and restaurant areas decorated with local weavings. The rooms themselves are on the small side but have private balconies, with deluxe rooms offering the better views. Facilities include a fine adjoining spa (open to the public).

Outside of Town

Head a few kilometres out of town and the landscape reveals itself, beautiful and rural. It's also home to the area's most unique accommodation options.

★ Sapa Clay House
HOTEL $$$

(☑0965 288 160; www.sapaclayhouse.com; Hwy 152, Y Linh Ho; r/bungalow incl breakfast US$105/125, ste US$155-170; ❄☎❄) Located 3km southeast of Sapa is this charming compound of adobe rooms and bungalows. Perched on a hillside with views of the rice terraces below, its accommodation is handsomely rustic, but the bungalows offer a bit more privacy and large open-air bathrooms. The infinity pool and spa bring a splash of luxury. A taxi here costs 80,000d.

Topas Ecolodge
RESORT $$$

(☑0214-387 2404; www.topasecolodge.com; bungalows incl breakfast from US$235; ❄) Overlooking a plunging valley 18km from Sapa, this resort has stone-and-thatch bungalows with front balconies to make the most of the truly breathtaking views. Bungalows don't have TVs, but a stunning infinity pool, and hiking, cycling and market tours are available.

Eating

Sapa has northern Vietnam's widest range of restaurants, with plentiful choice along P Cau May. Look out for hill-tribe specialities using Sapa's wild mushrooms and herbs, and local trout.

Hotpot & Roast Piglet Restaurants
VIETNAMESE $

(Đ Xuan Vien; meals from 60,000d; ☺11am-11pm) This strip is home to several similar places serving Vietnamese-style *lau* (hotpot; meat stew cooked with local vegetables, cabbage and mushroom) and roast piglet (a speciality of Sapa; look for the rotisserie grills).

★ Hill Station Signature Restaurant
VIETNAMESE $$

(☑0214-388 7111; www.thehillstation.com; 37 Đ Phan Xi Pang; meals from 120,000d; ☺11am-10pm; ❄☎☑) A showcase of Hmong cuisine with cool Zen decor and superb views. Dishes include flash-cooked pork with lime, ash-baked trout in banana leaves, and traditional Hmong-style black pudding. Tasting sets of local rice and corn wine are also of interest to curious travelling foodies. Don't miss trying the delicate, raw rainbow-trout rice-paper rolls; think of them as 'Sapa sushi'.

NORTHERN VIETNAM SAPA

Le Gecko
INTERNATIONAL $$

([phone] 0214-377 1504; Đ Xuan Vien; meals 90,000-170,000d, steaks 220,000d; [hours] 7am-11pm; [wifi]) This French-owned place has classy service and a menu of flavoursome country cooking that jumps from French *tartiflette* casserole with potato, cheese and bacon to pan-fried wild Sapa mushrooms and good steaks, all washed down with French wine by the glass. Save room for the amazing chocolate mousse.

Le Petit Gecko
INTERNATIONAL $$

(15 Đ Xuan Vien; meals 90,000-150,000d; [hours] 7am-10pm) A smaller, more intimate version of Le Gecko, just a few doors away, with cabana-style architecture and slightly cheaper prices for almost the same menu. There's more of an emphasis on Hmong dishes, such as grilled wild pork with cardamom and smoked buffalo, along with the same wonderful French-inspired desserts.

Nature View
VIETNAMESE $$

(61 Đ Phan Xi Pang; meals 100,000-125,000d; [hours] 7am-10pm; [wifi][veg]) This place stands out for great service and superb valley views from the windows. Come for decent Vietnamese and European food, good-value set meals and just maybe Sapa's best fruit smoothies. Anyone unconvinced by the merits of bean curd should try the grilled tofu with lemongrass and prepare to be converted.

Viet Emotion
INTERNATIONAL $$

(www.vietemotion.com; 27 P Cau May; snacks/meals from 80,000/190,000d; [hours] 7am-11pm; [wifi]) This intimate bistro is recognisable by its colourful exterior lanterns. The menu rambles from pizza, pasta and steaks to Vietnamese with a couple of Sapa specialities, such as herbal-medicine hotpot for two (with lemongrass and mountain mushrooms). There's also a a branch at 17 Đ Xuan Vien.

[icon] Drinking & Nightlife

Hill Station Deli
CRAFT BEER

(www.thehillstation.com; 7 Đ Muong Hoa; [hours] 7am-10.30pm; [wifi]) With half a dozen craft beers (105,000d) on tap, sharp modern decor and snacks such as cheese and charcuterie plates and local smoked trout, the Hill Station is the most sophisticated drinking spot in town. Try a four-beer taster for 195,000d or opt for our favourite, the jasmine-infused IPA. The beer isn't cheap but happy hour gets you two for one between 2pm and 6pm.

Cafe in the Clouds
BEER GARDEN

([phone] 0214-377 1011; 60 Đ Phan Xi Pang; [hours] 6am-11pm; [wifi]) The large upper terrace of this bar is a great corner of Sapa in which to pause and soak in the valley or, equally often, the wandering mist at eye level. Drinks are priced reasonably.

Color Bar
BAR

(56 Đ Phan Xi Pang; [hours] 4pm-1.30am; [wifi]) Owned by a Hanoi artist, this atmospheric thatched hut ticks all the boxes with reggae, table football, shisha and ice-cold Bia Lao Cai. A great refuelling option on the steep walk up from Cat Cat village.

Mountain Bar & Pub
BAR

(2 Đ Muong Hoa; [hours] noon-11pm; [wifi]) Dangerously strong cocktails, cold beer (30,000d) and a mellow reggae off beat make this welcoming old-school bar Sapa's go-to place for a great night out. Try the warm apple wine for some highland bliss.

Hmong Sisters
BAR

([phone] 0915 042 366; 31 Đ Muong Hoa; [hours] 4pm-1am; [wifi]) With liquor sold by the bottle and shots by the metre (!), this is the place for serious late-night drinking. Earlier in the evening the spacious bar has a mellower vibe, with pool tables, an open fire and pretty decent music.

[icon] Shopping

Lots of the minority women and girls have gone into the souvenir business, and Sapa's streets are packed with handicraft peddlers. The older women in particular are canny traders and known for their strong-arm selling tactics. When negotiating prices, hold your ground, but avoid aggressive bargaining.

Note that on some cheaper textiles, the dyes used are not set, which can turn anything the material touches (including your skin) a muddy blue-green colour. Wash the fabric separately in cold salted water to stop the dye from running, and wrap items in plastic bags before packing them in your luggage.

If you've arrived in town with insufficient warm clothing, stores along P Cau May sell lots of 'brand-name' walking shoes, fleeces and coats. Some of it might be authentic, but don't count on it; haggle accordingly.

Indigo Cat
ARTS & CRAFTS

(www.indigocat.shop; 34 Đ Phan Xi Pang; [hours] 9am-9pm) This Hmong-owned, family-run handicrafts shop offers a wonderful selection of interesting local crafts, including bags, clothing, cushion covers, jewellery and a fun DIY embroidered-bracelet kit for children. Many items have hip design touches unique to the store and the set-price labels are a relief if you have haggling fatigue.

🅘 GETTING TO CHINA: LAO CAI TO KUNMING

Getting to the border The Chinese border at the **Lao Cai/Hekou crossing** is about 3km from Lao Cai train station, a journey done by *xe om* (motorbike taxi; around 25,000d) or taxi (around 50,000d).

At the border The border is open daily between 7am and 10pm Vietnam time. China is one hour ahead of Vietnam. You'll need to have a prearranged visa for China. China is separated from Vietnam by a road bridge and a separate rail bridge over the Song Hong (Red River). Note that travellers have reported Chinese officials confiscating Lonely Planet *China* guides at this border, so you may want to try masking the cover or take a PDF. Be wary of getting short-changed by black-market currency traders, especially on the Chinese side. If you do need to change money, just make it a small amount.

Moving on The Hekou bus station is around 6km from the border post. There are regular departures to Kunming, including sleeper buses that leave at around 7.30pm, getting into Kunming at around 7am. There are also four daily trains.

🅘 Information

Many hotels and businesses will change euros and US dollars.

Agribank (P Cau May; ⊙ 8am-3pm Mon-Fri, ATM 24hr)

BIDV Bank (Đ Ngu Chi Son; ⊙ 8am-3pm Mon-Fri, to 11am Sat, ATM 24hr)

Main Post Office (Đ Thach Son; ⊙ 8am-6pm Mon-Fri)

Tourist Information Center (📋 0214-387 3239; www.sapa-tourism.com; 103 Đ Xuan Vien; ⊙ 7.30-11.30am & 1.30-5.30pm) Helpful English-speaking staff offering details about transport and trekking; its website is also a great source of information.

🅘 Getting There & Away

The gateway to Sapa is Lao Cai, 38km away along a well-maintained highway.

BUS & MINIBUS

Sapa's **bus station** (Đ Luong Dinh Cua) is north-east of the town centre, behind the market, though the major bus companies have their own offices in town; your hotel can help book these. To Hanoi there are frequent sleeper buses (250,000d, six hours) between 7am and 10.30pm, as well as faster limousine vans (415,000d).

Yellow-and-red **minibus number 1** (Đ Ham Rong) to Lao Cai train station (30,000d, 45 minutes) leaves every 30 minutes between 6am and 6pm from a bus stop near Sapa Church.

For Bac Ha it's easiest to take the minibus to Lao Cai train station and change there or at the nearby **Lao Cai inter-provincial bus station** (Pha Dinh Phung). There is said to be a direct bus (150,000d) from Sapa bus station at 1pm, though it seems somewhat unreliable.

For Dien Bien Phu (300,000d, 8am) or Lai Chau (100,000d, hourly until 11am) head to the junction of Xuan Vien and Dien Bien Phu roads

near the northeast of Sapa Lake and flag down a through bus from Lao Cai.

TRAIN

There's no direct train line to Sapa, but there are regular services between Hanoi and Lao Cai, 45 minutes away. Hotels and travel agencies can book train tickets, or you can book them online.

🅘 Getting Around

The best way to get around compact Sapa is to walk. For excursions, motorbikes are available to rent for about 150,000d a day. If you've never ridden a motorbike before, this is not the place to learn. The weather can be wet and treacherous at any time of year, and roads are steep and often clogged by thundering construction trucks. If you do ride, be aware of the one-way system in town.

Consider hiring a *xe om*. Local drivers hang out on the corner of P May Cai and Đ Phan Xi Pang and prices are posted there.

Lao Cai

📋 0214 / POP 98,360

Lao Cai is squeezed limpet-like onto the Vietnam–China border. The border crossing slammed shut during the 1979 Chinese invasion, when the town was badly damaged, and only reopened in 1993. Now it's a bustling spot fuelled by growing cross-border trade.

For travellers, Lao Cai is the jumping-off point when journeying between Hanoi and Sapa by train, and a transit stop when heading further north to Kunming in China. With Sapa just a 45-minute hop away, few linger, but it offers everything China-bound travellers might need for an overnight stay.

🛏 Sleeping & Eating

Nam Anh Hotel
HOTEL **$**

(📞 0944 485 989; 69a Đ Phan Dinh Phung; s/d/tr 300,000/350,000/450,000d; 🌐🛜) Basic budget rooms a short walk from the train station; you'll find lots of similar places along this strip. You can pop in and take a shower for 100,000d.

Thien Hai Hotel
BUSINESS HOTEL **$$**

(📞 0214-383 3666; www.thienhaihotel.com; 306 P Khanh Yen; r incl breakfast from 500,000d; 🌐🛜) Towering over Lao Cai's train station, the Thien Hai is a solid option with big business-brisk-style rooms and professional staff. Rates shoot up on Saturdays.

Pineapple
CAFE **$**

(47 Đ Phan Dinh Phung; meals from 90,000d; ⏲7am-10pm; 🌐🛜) A Sapa-esque cafe. Try the full English breakfast, pasta options or good Vietnamese dishes. To find it from the train station, cross the main road and head west down the street directly in front of you for around 100m.

Viet Emotion
CAFE **$**

(65 Đ Phan Dinh Phung; meals from 100,000d; ⏲7am-10pm; 🌐🛜) This branch is an offshoot of the successful Sapa cafe, with a handy location near the train station. It does good breakfasts and sandwiches and decent pizza.

ⓘ Information

There are two ATMs by the train station. **BIDV Bank** (Đ Thuy Hoa; ⏲8am-3pm Mon-Fri, to 11.30am Sat), on the west bank of the river, changes cash.

ⓘ Getting There & Away

BUS & MINIBUS

Lao Cai's **inter-provincial bus station** (off Hwy 4E; ⏲24hr) is a whopping 10km southeast of town; a taxi there will cost about 150,000d. Most people avoid it by travelling direct to other destinations from Sapa.

Yellow-and-red minibuses for Sapa (30,000d, 45 minutes) leave every 30 minutes between 5.10am and 6pm from the car park in front of Lao Cai train station.

TAXI

A taxi to Sapa costs about US$25; it's around US$50 to Bac Ha.

TRAIN

Virtually everyone travelling to and from Hanoi uses the train, the safest and most comfortable option. There are daily services to Hanoi (Station B) from Lao Cai train station at 8.55pm and 9.40pm (eight hours). Tickets cost 150,000d for a reclinable seat or 385,000d in a four-berth soft sleeper cabin.

Luxury four-berth cabins (US$35 per berth) are also operated on these trains by private companies such as **Livitrans** (www.livitrans.com) and **Oriental Express** (www.orienttrainticket.com), with a superluxury US$84 service run by **Victoria Express** (www.victoriahotels.asia).

It's possible to transport your motorbike on the train as freight. You'll need to buy a ticket (around 240,000d, depending on the size of bike), fill out a form, show the bike's blue ownership card and get a receipt. Staff will drain your bike of fuel.

Bac Ha

📞 0214 / POP 7400

Sleepy Bac Ha wakes up for the riot of colour and commerce that is its Sunday market, when its lanes fill and villagers flock in from the hills and valleys. Once the bartering, buying and selling is done and the day-tripper tourist buses from Sapa have left, the

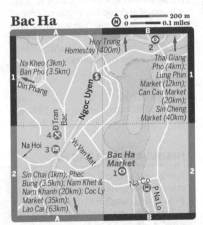

Bac Ha

Bac Ha

◎ **Top Sights**
  1 Bac Ha Market...................................... B2

◎ **Sights**
  2 Vua Meo...B1

⊕ **Activities, Courses & Tours**
  Ngan Nga Bac Ha ....(see 3)

⬤ **Sleeping**
  3 Ngan Nga Bac Ha Hotel....................... A2

⊗ **Eating**
  4 Hoang Yen Restaurant A2

town rolls over and goes back to bed for the rest of the week. If you can, overnight in Bac Ha on Saturday and get to the market early before the day trippers start arriving.

Despite being surrounded by countryside just as lush and interesting as Sapa's, Bac Ha has somehow flown under the radar as a trekking base. That's one reason we prefer it.

Sights

★ Bac Ha Market MARKET
(off Đ Tran Bac; ⊙ sunrise-2pm Sun) This Sunday market is Bac Ha's big draw. There's an increasing range of handicrafts for sale, but it's still pretty much a local affair. Bac Ha Market is a magnet for the local hill-tribe people, above all the Flower Hmong.

Vua Meo NOTABLE BUILDING
('Cat King' House; ĐT 153; 20,000d; ⊙ 7.30am-5pm) The outlandish Vua Meo, built in 1921 by the French to keep the Tay chief Hoang A Tuong happily ensconced in style, is a bizarre palace constructed in a kind of 'Eastern baroque' style on the northern edge of Bac Ha. There's not much to see, other than the architecture itself, but the ground floor has a shop selling excellent-quality embroideries and traditional clothes.

Tours

Ngan Nga Bac Ha HIKING
(☎ 0969 658 080; www.bachatrip.com; 117 Đ Ngoc Uyen; ⊙ 8am-9pm) Inside the Ngan Nga Bac Ha Hotel, Mr Dong offers a great range of day hikes and longer treks with authentic village homestays. Figure on US$55/85 for one/two people for a two-day trek. He also rents out motorbikes (120,000d to 150,000d per day) and can organise trips to outlying markets.

Sleeping & Eating

Room rates tend to increase by about 20% on Saturday nights due to the Sunday market.

Ngan Nga Bac Ha Hotel HOTEL $
(☎ 0214-880 286; www.nganngabachahotel.com; 117 P Ngoc Uyen; r incl breakfast Mon-Fri 250,000-400,000d, Sat & Sun 460,000-690,000d; ❄ ☎) Rooms here are a solid budget deal; they are a decent size and are decked out with a few homey touches, with a good ground-floor restaurant for a post-hike beer. Bag a room on the 4th floor and above for maximum natural light.

★ Huy Trung Homestay GUESTHOUSE $$
(☎ 0979 776 288; huytrung@gmail.com; r 400,000-600,000d, ste 1,200,000d; ☎ ❄) This well-designed place is clearly signposted in a residential district to the north of town and walkable from the centre. The five rooms are immaculate, and the secure parking, rooftop viewing platform, motorbike rental and seasonal plunge pool push the place into a league of its own. The three-bed

---

HIKING AROUND BAC HA

Hiking trails around Bac Ha lead to villages that are home to 11 hill-tribe groups. The colourful Flower Hmong are the most visible, but other ethnic groups in the area include Dzao, Giay (Nhang), Han (Hoa), Xa Fang, Lachi, Nung, Phula, Tay, Thai and Thulao.

For a short stroll from town head to the Nung village of **Sin Chai** and Hmong village of **Phec Bung**.

Overnights in village homestays are possible on longer treks. Trails can be hard to find and language obstacles an issue, so hiking here is best done with a local guide. Trails include:

Thai Giang Pho to Na Lo The looping track that winds from Bac Ha, through the hills and down to the rice terraces that surround the Flower Hmong village of Thai Giang Pho, then onward to the Tay village of Na Lo, is home to some of the finest rural vistas you'll see anywhere in northern Vietnam. It's about an 8km round trip.

Ban Pho to Na Kheo The Flower Hmong village of Ban Pho and the Nung settlement of Na Kheo make a good 7km day hike from Bac Ha. The locals of Ban Pho are renowned for their skill in making potent *ruou* corn liqueur, and the scenery of rolling hillscapes between the villages is superbly verdant.

Nam Det to Nam Khanh The 10km hike through rice fields, cinnamon forests and rolling hills to the Black Dzao village of Nam Det and onward to the Dzao village of Nam Khanh is a popular option for a night in a village homestay.

MARKETS AROUND BAC HA

Bac Ha's Sunday market is firmly stamped on the day-trip agenda from Sapa, though it's hardly been trussed up for tourists and is full of local flavour. But if you want to head further out to other markets, try these on for size:

Can Cau Market (☉6am-1pm Sat) This small market, spilling down a hillside 20km north of Bac Ha, attracts a growing number of visitors. It's a magnet for local Flower Hmong and Blue Hmong traders (look out for the striking zigzag costume of the latter). Some tours combine a visit here with a hike to the nearby village of Fu La.

Coc Ly Market (☉8.30am-1.30pm Tue) The impressive Coc Ly market attracts Dzao, Flower Hmong, Tay and Nung people from the surrounding hills. It's about 35km southwest of Bac Ha. Operators in Bac Ha can arrange tours that include a 2½-hour river trip.

Lung Phin Market (☉6am-1pm Sun) Lung Phin market is between Can Cau market and Bac Ha, about 12km from town. It's less busy than other markets, with a really local feel, and is a good place to move on to once the tour buses arrive in Bac Ha from Sapa.

Sin Cheng Market (☉5am-2pm Wed) This market, in the remote border area of Si Ma Cai, 40km from Bac Ha, is a vibrant and chaotic weekly hub for the local Nung and Thulao ethnic minorities.

family suite with balcony is the best room in town and a worthy splurge.

Hoang Yen Restaurant VIETNAMESE **$**
(Đ Tran Bac; meals 60,000-120,000d; ☉7am-10pm; 🛜) Hoang Yen's simple menu includes decent breakfast options and a set menu for 200,000d. Cheap beer is also available.

ℹ Information

Agribank (P Ngoc Uyen; ☉8am-3pm Mon-Fri, to 11am Sat, ATM 24hr)

ℹ Getting There & Away

Tours to Bac Ha from Sapa cost around US$20 per person; on the way back you can bail out in Lao Cai and catch the night train to Hanoi.

Bac Ha's **bus station** (P Na Lo) is southeast of the town centre, across the Na Co River. Sleeper buses run to Hanoi (300,000d, eight hours) at 7am, 12.30pm, 3pm and 8.30pm.

Minibuses to Lao Cai (70,000d, two hours) depart hourly from the square just south of the Ngan Nga Bac Ha Hotel until 4pm.

If you're heading east to Ha Giang, there are two options – check the latest information with Mr Dong at Ngan Nga Bac Ha. Option one is to catch a taxi from Bac Ha 35km northeast to Xin Man (800,000d, 2½ hours), then take the 12.30pm bus from Xin Man to Ha Giang (150,000d, four hours). Option two is the bus south from Bac Ha to Bac Ngam (50,000d, 30 minutes, frequent from 7am to 2pm), followed by another bus from Bac Ngam to Ha Giang (250,000d, five hours, 7.30am and 12.30pm). The bus from Bac Ngam always waits for the bus from Bac Ha to arrive before leaving.

Ha Giang Province

Ha Giang is the final frontier in northern Vietnam, an amazing landscape of limestone pinnacles and swooping gorges. The far north of the province has some of the most spectacular scenery in the country – if not Southeast Asia – and the trip between Yen Minh and Dong Van, and then across the Mai Pi Leng Pass to Meo Vac, is quite mind-blowing.

In 2011 Unesco designated the Dong Van Karst Plateau as one of its National Geoparks – Vietnam's first – due to the spectacular nature of its limestone geology.

Ha Giang's secret is well and truly out of the bag and visitor (and motorcycle) numbers have gone through the roof in the last few years. That said, there are plenty of quiet back roads and stunning corners to explore and tourist infrastructure is improving, making travel easier every year.

ℹ Permits

Travel permits (US$10) are technically required to travel on the road north from Tam Son to Dong Van and Meo Vac, but neither police nor hotels ask to see them. If required, it's possible to get one in 10 minutes at the immigration office (p146) in Ha Giang, or from whichever hotel you choose to overnight in along the way.

ℹ Getting Around

The province is best visited with a car and driver or, better still, by motorbike. If you're going to splurge on private transport just once during your trip, this is the place to do it.

MOTORCYCLING THE HA GIANG LOOP

Renting a motorbike for the four-day Ha Giang Loop has become *the* must-do adventure in northern Vietnam, but there are several important things to consider before revving up. Firstly, these are winding mountain roads, full of sheer drop-offs and blind corners, and minibuses and trucks think nothing of hogging both lanes, especially on tight bends. The bottom line: this is not the place to learn how to ride a motorbike. Crashes involving foreign riders are disturbingly common, and several tourists have died in bike accidents in recent years. If you do have an accident, know that it is unlikely that your travel insurance will cover you, unless you or your driver has a Vietnamese motorcycle licence. The golden rule: take it easy and always keep your eyes on the road, regardless of how eye-catching the scenery may be.

Petrol stations are frequent on the main Ha Giang to Dong Van road, but much less so on the minor roads. Bring bungy cords and a plastic bag/cover for your backpack and buy a rain poncho (available everywhere in Vietnam) for yourself.

Safety

Lower your risks with the following tips:

➡ At a minimum wear a full-face helmet, sturdy trousers and a jacket. It's possible to hire knee and shin armour from bike-rental companies.

➡ Be particularly careful of hairpin turns and patches of gravel at the edge of the road.

➡ Use your engine to slow you down on descents and get used to using your back brake rather than the front to avoid slides.

➡ Don't take pillion passengers if you aren't used to it.

➡ If you want to take in the scenery, pull off the road completely and enjoy the views safely.

➡ Most guesthouses can advise on secure parking or will bring your bike inside for the night.

Motorbike Rental

Several agencies in Ha Giang rent motorbikes, with optional bike damage insurance (100,000d to 150,000d per day), and organise motorbike tours. Most are very helpful in helping you plan an itinerary. The most professional agency, QT Motorbikes & Tours even offers useful one-way rental between Ha Giang and Cao Bang.

The better agencies have a range of bikes for hire, from scooters (150,000d per day) to 150cc manual Suzukis (400,000d), and even the occasional trials bike (600,000d). You'll appreciate a manual motorbike, rather than a simple scooter, on these mountain roads. If you are nervous about riding yourself, Easy Rider–style trips (where you ride pillion) are available and cost from 700,000d to 900,000d per day, including motorbike rental, fuel, driver and your driver's costs.

Itineraries

The most popular itinerary is a four-day loop from Ha Giang taking in Yen Minh, Dong Van and Meo Vac, and then returning on minor roads to Tan Son and Ha Giang. The main highway to Dong Van is quite busy and minor roads offer much more enjoyable riding, particularly the back roads to Du Gia (p147). If you are an experienced rider and want to get off the beaten track, consider the less-travelled roads to Hoang Su Phi, Ba Be National Park or Cao Bang (which offers particularly good opportunities for exploration).

For advice on routes check out the excellent website of Vietnam Coracle (www.vietnam coracle.com).

Public transport is patchy but it's relatively simple to journey by bus from Ha Giang city to Dong Van. At the time of writing there was still no reliable public transport from Dong Van onward to Meo Vac. However, there are buses, along the low road, between Meo Vac and Ha Giang city, so by hiring a *xe om* or taxi in Dong Van for the stretch to Meo Vac, it is entirely possible to do a loop back to Ha Giang city. Heading east from Meo Vac to Cao Bang continues to be a headache, as there is no public transport from Meo Vac to Bao Lac.

Ha Giang

📞 0219 / POP 72,000

This surprisingly large town, bisected by the broad Lo River, is a provincial capital with clean streets and an understated ambience. It's the place to organise your motorbike trip to Dong Van, and while there's little to keep you in town itself, the spectacular limestone outcrops soaring skywards over the suburbs hint at the amazing scenery in the surrounding hinterland.

The main drag is P Nguyen Trai, which runs north–south, paralleling the west bank of the Lo for 3km or so. You'll find some hotels and banks on this road but more on the east bank of the river.

🏃 Tours

★ QT Motorbikes & Tours   MOTORCYCLE RENTAL

(📞0975 278 711, 0365-506 9696; www.qtmotorbikesandtours.com.vn; Lam Dong, Phuong Thien) QT is the most reliable place in Ha Giang for motorbike rentals and tours, offering excellent off-the-beaten-track route advice. All the bikes are less than two years old and insurance is offered, along with protective equipment. One-way rentals to its Cao Bang office (p123) are possible for a premium.

Kiki's House   MOTORCYCLE RENTAL

(📞0968 722 242; www.kikishouse.com.vn; 134b Ly Tu Trong) Arrange motorbike rental (150,000d to 500,000d per day), bike damage insurance, motorbike tours and local day tours at this budget operation, plus there is an on-site hostel and hotel accommodation.

🛏 Sleeping

As the busy provincial capital, there are lots of places to stay in Ha Giang.

Huy Hoan Hotel   HOTEL $

(📞0219-386 1288; www.huyhoanhotel.com; 395 Đ Nguyen Trai; r 350,000-600,000d; ❋🐾) Run by a friendly family, the central Huy Hoan (pronounced 'Hwe Hwan') offers large, clean, well-kept rooms that represent excellent value. The communal balcony at the back of each floor looks out over a limestone cliff. The secure parking is useful for motorcyclists.

QT Guest House   GUESTHOUSE $

(📞0349 354 144; www.qtmotorbikesandtours.com; Lam Dong, Phuong Thien; dm 60,000d, d 270,000-360,000d, tr 450,000d; ❋🐾) This welcoming guesthouse run by nearby QT Motorbikes & Tours has clean, spacious eight-bed dorms and comfortable doubles (the back-facing twins are best). Its location near the bus station is super convenient if you are arriving from Hanoi for a motorcycle tour or rental; less so if you plan to spend much time in town.

Bong Hostel   HOSTEL $

(📞0888 526 606; www.bongbackpacker.com; 9a Nguyen Thai Hoc; dm/d 90,000/300,000d; ❋🐾) A popular central hostel that is always full of people embarking on, or returning from, Ha Giang motorbike loop. It rents a range of motorbikes, books bus tickets, offers luggage storage and has a sociable downstairs bar with pool table. One gripe: the basement showers could be hotter. Rates include breakfast.

Truong Xuan Resort   RESORT $$

(📞0219-386 2268; www.hagiangresort.com; Km 5, P Nguyen Van Linh; r incl breakfast US$30-45; ❋🐾❋) A relaxing place sitting along the bank of the Lo River, 5km north of town, with spacious thatched duplex bungalows set in lush grounds. You'll want one of the deluxe riverside bungalows (US$45) to make the most of the view. From the bus station, a taxi costs 90,000d.

🍴 Eating & Drinking

Bong Restaurant   INTERNATIONAL $

(115 Đ Minh Khai; meals 110,000-135,000d; ⏱9am-11pm; 🐾) A foreigner-friendly place with enthusiastic service, pleasant outdoor seating

NORTHERN VIETNAM HA GIANG PROVINCE

WORTH A TRIP

PAN HOU VILLAGE

This **ecolodge** (📞0219-383 3535; www.panhou-village.com; Pan Hou village; s/d/tr incl breakfast US$45/55/75; 🐾) is tucked away in a hidden river valley in the High Song Chau mountains, with simple, solar-powered bungalows set in a riot of tropical gardens and fronted by a thatched restaurant pavilion (meals US$11). Traditional spa treatments and baths, infused with medicinal healing herbs, are available, and day hikes and longer treks to ethnic-minority villages can be arranged.

From Tan Quang village, 45km south of Ha Giang, head northwest on road DT177 towards Hoang Su Phi for 18km then branch left up a gorgeously scenic, twisty-turny mountain road for another 12km, turning right en route at Thong Nguyen village.

and a wide menu of Asian and Western comfort food. Our sautéed beef, mushroom and onion and the coconut chicken curry were both excellent.

Duc Giang 2 Restaurant
VIETNAMESE $$

(Đ Nguyen Trai; meals from 100,000d; ⊗11am-11pm) Vast, buzzy (read: loud), hall-like restaurant serving hotpot and other Vietnamese dishes. Be careful what you order blindly off the (Vietnamese only) menu: *ba ba* is tortoise, *ran* is snake, *ech* is frog and *nhong ong* is pupae (yes, pupae...). It's just north of central Ha Giang, west of the Lo River.

Tung Duong Cafe
CAFE

(Đ Hoang Hoa Tham; ⊗7.30am-11.30pm) A cosy coffee shop popular among locals and domestic tourists. Come for superstrong coffee drinks and tasty smoothies. Its convenient location near several excellent pho shops makes it an easy breakfast choice.

❶ Information

Agribank (Đ Tran Hung Dao; ⊗8am-3pm Mon-Fri, to 11.30am Sat, ATM 24hr)

Immigration Office (296 Đ Tran Phu; ⊗7.30-11.30am & 1.30-5.30pm Mon-Sat, 7.30-11.30am Sun) The place to get a travel permit (p143) for the Ha Giang loop, if you decide to get one.

Vision Travel (☑0902 093 223; www.vision-travelagent.com; 50 Đ Hai Ba Trung; ⊗8am-8pm) Arranges excellent motorbike and car tours and is a great source of local information. Car rental costs US$57 to US$67 per day with driver and petrol. Contact Mr Minh.

❶ Getting There & Away

Ha Giang's **bus station** (Hwy 2) is located 3km south of the city centre; a *xe om* to/from the centre costs about 15,000d; a taxi 25,000d.

If you're heading to Bac Ha, you'll have to take the Lao Cai–bound minibus to the junction at

Bac Ngam (180,000d, five hours), from where you can flag down an hourly Bac Ha–bound bus (50,000d, 30 minutes).

In addition to the normal sleeper buses to Hanoi, there are also limousine minivans (300,000d) at 7am and 4pm, and a luxury cabin sleeper bus (400,000d) at 8.30pm

Tam Son

The small town of Tam Son lies in a valley at the end of the **Quan Ba Pass** (Heaven's Gate; Hwy 4C), about 40km from Ha Giang and one of the loop's most dramatic sights.

On Sundays there's a good market with various ethnic minorities, including White Hmong, Red Dzao, Tay and Giay people.

Tam Son has the decent **Nha Nghi Nui Doi** (☑0219-651 0789; P Tran Hung Bao, Tam Son; r 250,000-400,000d; ✸🛜) guesthouse on the main drag, but a nicer place to stay is Nam Dam villlage, 6km up a side road, and home to over a dozen homestays. The most stylish of these is the traditional-style **Dao Lodge** (☑0943 466 8488; www.daolodge.com; Nam Dam village; d 660,000d, dinner 150,000d; 🛜), built with natural wood, bamboo and tamped earth and with only five rooms, all with modern bathrooms.

From Ha Giang, all buses trundling the high road to Dong Van and the low road to Meo Vac pass through Tam Son.

Tam Son to Dong Van

From Tam Son, Ha Giang province's main mountain pass road connects to Dong Van, first passing through the sleepy town of **Yen Minh**. The **Thao Nguyen Hotel** (☑0219-385 2297; thaonguyenym.hotel@gmail.com; So Nha 140 to 3, Yen Minh; d 300,000-350,000d; tr/q 400,000/600,000d; ✸🛜), on the main street through town, opposite the **Agribank** (Yen Minh; ⊗24hr) ATM, has

BUSES FROM HA GIANG

DESTINATION	COST (D)	DURATION (HR)	FREQUENCY
Dong Van	110,000	4½	every 90min 5am-1pm
Haiphong	240,000-255,000	8	6pm & 8pm
Halong City	320,000	10	4pm, 6pm & 7pm
Hanoi (My Dinh)	200,000	6	every 2hr 5am-4pm, 8pm & 9pm
Lao Cai	150,000	6	6am, 7.30am, 9.30am & noon
Meo Vac	110,000	5	every 2hr 5am-1pm
Sapa	200,000-250,000	7	7.30am, 9.30am & 8pm

WORTH A TRIP

ROUTES TO DU GIA

If you have a motorbike and want to get off the main highway, the quiet back roads to Du Gia are a great option. From Yen Minh and Meo Vac, roads meet at Mao Due junction, where the scenic DT176 road climbs south past rice terraces, picturesque villages and pine forest to crest a ridge and descend past karst hills to the ruins of a French fort by the junction near Lung Ho (32km from Yen Minh).

From here you can continue south over another pass to reach tiny **Du Gia** village, 14km from the junction. Du Gia village has a petrol pump and half a dozen homestays, including the excellent **Du Gia Homestay** (☑ 035-772 0252; www.dugiahomestay.com; Du Gia village; dm 120,000d, r 250,000-500,000d; ☏), a collection of ramshackle bungalows set around a stilt house on the eastern edge of town.

From Du Gia the road south is beautiful, but the main QL34 road it joins to Ha Giang is in terrible shape, so most bikers head back to Lung Ho junction and then branch west on DT181 for 36km through a beautiful valley and over a pass to eventually join the main road near Tam Son. From here it's a couple of hours riding back to Ha Giang.

well-kept, colourful rooms, but it's worth pushing on to overnight in Dong Van. In Yen Minh, **Phuc Cai** (Yen Minh; meals from 30,000d; ⊘ 7am-10pm) is a popular spot for lunch – coming from Ha Giang, turn left at the corner before the Thao Nguyen Hotel to find it.

Around 5km east of Yen Minh, a road meanders southeast to Meo Vac, but the recommended route is the northern fork to Dong Van, with the mountain road rubbing shoulders with the Chinese border and vast vistas of green valleys rolling on below.

If you're travelling by public transport, you can flag down buses to Dong Van (via the northern fork) and Meo Vac (low road) as they pass through.

The northern fork heads past the intriguing **Vuong Palace** (Sa Phin; admission 20,000d; ⊘ 8am-5pm), a grandiose two-storey mansion built by the French for a local Hmong king in the 1920s. Set in a hidden valley just off the main road, the Chinese-Hmong-style building is a fascinating sight in such a remote region of the country. Vuong Palace is at Sa Phin, around 15km west of Dong Van, and the scenery of conical peaks through to Dong Van is quite incredible.

A major detour 2.5km before Dong Van runs north to **Lung Cu** (25,000d; ⊘ 8am-5pm), a massive flag tower erected in 2010 next to the Chinese border to mark the northernmost point of Vietnam. The summit is reached by almost 300 steps, and the views across rural villages are stunning. The flag is 54 sq metres, to represent Vietnam's 54 official nationalities.

Dong Van

☑ 0219 / POP 7000

Dong Van is the Ha Giang region's most popular overnight stop and, not coincidentally, is home to some solid accommodation and food. But the real reason to come is for the Sunday market, one of the region's biggest and most colourful. The town is also a good base for day treks around nearby minority villages.

◉ Sights & Activities

The owner of the Hoang Ngoc Hotel (p148) has put together a surprisingly detailed trekking map of the area surrounding Dong Van.

★**Dong Van Market**   MARKET

(Đ Vao Cho; ⊘ 6am-2pm Sun) Once a week, local villagers from the surrounding hills, including the Hmong, Tay, Nung and Hoa ethnic groups, flood into Dong Van for the Sunday market. It's an entirely local affair full of colour, with several food stalls plus Hmong jackets and berets for sale. The rest of the week the market is open, but quiet.

French Fort   RUINS

(⊘ 24hr) FREE At the top of the karst peak that overlooks central Dong Van are the dramatic ruins of a French fort. It's possible to scale the peak, using the path that starts just east of the old market square. It's a sweaty half-hour to the top, from where you're rewarded with stunning views of the town and the patchwork of rice fields and peaks that hem it.

ℹ SOUTH TO BAO LAC & CAO BANG

Heading south from Meo Vac, you'll soon pass the turn-off to Khau Vai and a high pass, before dropping to a bridge across the Nho Que River at Na Phong (Ly Bon).

Around 75km from Meo Vac is the town of Bao Lac. Here, at the northern end of town, the **Song Gam Guesthouse** (☑ 0206 387 0269; Khu 11, Bao Lac; r 250,000-350,000d, VIP r 400,000d; ❋ ☎) has a spacious terrace overlooking the namesake river and is popular with motorbike tours. The **Bao Lac Homestay & Hostel** (☑ 0912 849 915; www.facebook.com/baolachomestay; Bao Lac; dm 120,000d, r 350,000-450,000d; ❋ ☎) is another good choice, with a rooftop terrace bar and fresh private rooms a couple of doors down. The English-speaking owner is helpful with transport information.

Heading on, buses pull through town every couple of hours to Cao Bang (100,000d, four hours). On a motorbike it's worth stopping en route at the Mausoleum to Ho Chi Minh and the hanging valley above Tinh Tuc, and then the Dragon Back Panorama – the name given to a dramatic panorama of high karst peaks. The 125km ride to Cao Bang takes 3½ hours.

Sky Path HIKING

This path high above Ma Li Peng Pass offers the chance to view the stunning gorge scenery away from the Dong Van–Meo Vac road. The path starts from the Youth Volunteer Movement monument at Xeo Sa Lung, 8km southeast of Dong Van, and skirts the karst cliffs of the Co Tien mountains down to the roadside Panorama Restaurant, 8km (two to three hours) away.

To do the hike you'll need to arrange transport. Green Karst offers a car, guide and packed lunch for two for US$65, or a car alone for US$20.

🛌 Sleeping

Dong Van gets insanely busy on Saturday nights in October and November, when it's not uncommon for every single bed in town to sell out. Be sure to book a room in advance.

★ Lam Tung Hotel HOTEL $

(☑ 0219-385 6789; lamtunghotel@gmail.com; Đ Vao Cho; r 350,000-450,000d; ❋ ☎) Just off Dong Van's main road, and overlooking the Sunday market, the Lam Tung has surprisingly smart modern rooms with soft mattresses, friendly English-speaking staff and motorbikes for hire (150,000d to 200,000d per day).

Nha Nghi Ly Hoan HOTEL $

(☑ 0974 598 241; daolydv34@gmail.com; Dong Van Market; dm 80,000d, r 200,000-300,000d; ❋ ☎) At the western edge of the market, this family-run budget place combines clean rooms and dorms in a shophouse.

Hoang Ngoc Hotel HOTEL $$

(☑ 0219-385 6020; www.hoangngochotel.vn; Đ 3-2; r 500,000-700,000d; ❋ ☎) A solid choice on Dong Van's main road, the Hoang Ngoc features spacious, sparkling-clean back rooms and older, cheaper, front-facing rooms with balcony (400,000d). Staff can arrange trips to local sights and can usually rustle up motorbikes to rent (200,000d per day).

🍴 Eating

The market halls in Dong Van's old market plaza, in the centre of town, have been turned into open-air cafes, which are great for atmospheric coffee and snacks.

★ Green Karst INTERNATIONAL $

(☑ 0968 098 619; www.greenkarst.com; Đ Vao Cho; meals 80,000-150,000d; ⊙ 6.30am-10pm; ☎ ☑) This friendly restaurant serving Vietnamese and Western dishes is fast becoming Dong Van's hub for foreign travellers. The couple who run it have lots of experience in the restaurant world and are an excellent source of local information. It's open early for breakfast, and late at night it functions as a rooftop pub.

Owner Tan Phan runs tours and treks, as well as a nearby hostel, can arrange transport and motorbike rental (200,000d per day), and is a great source of local information.

★ Ba Ha VIETNAMESE $

(31 P Co; meals from 30,000d; ⊙ 6-9am) Where the locals go for breakfast in Dong Van. The menu begins and ends with *banh cuon* – freshly steamed and filled noodles – served

the northern way with a small bowl of broth that you season yourself.

Quang Dung Restaurant VIETNAMESE $
(19 P Co; meals 50,000-150,000d; ⊙7am-10pm; ◪) Opposite the old market plaza, in the centre of town, Quang Dung has an English menu featuring good breakfasts and hearty Vietnamese staples. The balcony at the front is a great place to chill out with a juice or beer after a long drive.

❶ Information

Dong Van's only **ATM** (Đ1-3; ⊙24hr) is on the main road, a couple of blocks east of the Sunday market.

❶ Getting There & Away

Buses to Ha Giang (100,000d, 4½ hours) leave from the central square every hour or so from 6am to 3.30pm.

In theory there is a daily 6am bus from Dong Van to Na Phong (Ly Bon; on the road to Bao Lac), via Meo Vac (50,000d), but it's somewhat unreliable. A *xe om* to Meo Vac should cost around 250,000d, and a taxi around 400,000d. Most hotels in Dong Van can arrange this for you and can also help organise private transport to Vuong Palace and Lung Cu.

Meo Vac

🕿 0219 / POP 5000
Meo Vac is a small but charming district capital hemmed in by steep karst mountains and, like many towns in the northwest, it is steadily being settled by Vietnamese from elsewhere.

The journey here, over the spectacular **Mai Pi Leng Pass**, which winds for 22km from Dong Van, is the main attraction. The road has been cut into the side of a cliff, with a view of rippling hills tumbling down to the distant waters of the Nho Que River and its striking gorge. At the pass a lookout point offers a stop to take in the scenery.

◉ Sights

Market MARKET
(Đ Loc Vien Tai; ⊙6am-noon) Meo Vac has a good Sunday market. The timing and its proximity with Dong Van's Sunday market means that it's easy enough to combine the two by *xe om*.

Viewpoint VIEWPOINT
Head south of town, branching off on the road left towards Khau Vai, and you'll soon get to a homestay and a series of steps that lead up to fabulous views of Meo Vac and the surrounding valley. It's 1km from the centre.

🛏 Sleeping & Eating

There's a useful line of cafes and juice bars opposite the Hoa Cuong Hotel.

Don't be surprised if you're offered a slug of a local speciality, 'bee wine', while you're in town. It's a bracing drink on a chilly Meo Vac night.

Hoa Cuong Hotel HOTEL $
(🖉0219-387 1888; Đ Loc Vien Tai; r 450,000-600,000d; ✴🕿) Centrally located, opposite Meo Vac's Sunday market, this stately hotel has vast, neat rooms with soft beds and big TVs. A comfortable choice, though bring earplugs for the nearby karaoke on Saturday and Sunday nights.

★**Auberge de Meo Vac** BOUTIQUE HOTEL $$
(🖉0219-387 1686; aubergemeovac@gmail.com; dm/r with shared bathroom 330,000/1,320,000d; 🕿) This is a unique stay in a lovingly restored Hmong house dating from the 19th century, with clay exterior walls, lots of natural timber and a spacious inner courtyard. Expect to hear your neighbours through the creaky wooden walls. Breakfast (US$5) and dinner (US$11) are available.

It's located northeast of the town centre, hidden down an alley just east of Hwy 4C.

May Co Quan VIETNAMESE $
(46 Đ Nguyen Du; meals from 60,000d; ⊙6am-10pm) Recommended by locals, this place does the usual point-and-choose dishes served over rice, and a few noodle dishes. It's located just around the corner (west) from the Hoa Cuong Hotel.

❶ Information

Meo Vac is home to one **Agribank** (Đ Minh Khai; ⊙24hr) ATM, around the corner from the Hoa Cuong Hotel.

❶ Getting There & Away

Buses head west to Ha Giang hourly from 5.30am to 3pm (100,000d, five hours), via Yen Minh (40,000d, 1½ hours).

There is no public transport southeast to the transport hub of Cao Bang. Instead catch a *xe om* (600,000d) or taxi (1,200,000d) to Bao Lac, where there is accommodation and daily buses to Cao Bang or Bao Lam.

A *xe om*/taxi to Dong Van costs around 200,000/400,000d.

Thai Hoa Palace (p178), Hue
SUCHART BOONYAVECH/SHUTTERSTOCK ©

Central Vietnam

Central Vietnam is stuffed with historic sights and cultural appeal, and blessed with ravishing beaches and outstanding national parks. Marvel at Hue and its sublime Imperial Citadel, royal tombs and superb street food. Savour the unique heritage grace of riverside jewel Hoi An, and tour the more recent military remains of the Demilitarised Zone (DMZ). Check out Danang, fast emerging as one of the nation's most dynamic cities. A must-visit destination is the extraordinary Phong Nha region, home to three gargantuan cave systems (including the world's largest cave), and a fascinating war history concealed amid stunning scenery. Enjoy downtime on the golden sands of An Bang Beach or learn to cook central Vietnamese cuisine, the nation's most complex.

Central Vietnam Highlights

❶ **Hoi An** (p202) Meandering amid a throng of ancient sights in this stunningly historic port town.

❷ **Phong Nha-Ke Bang National Park** (p160) Going underground in one of the world's foremost caving destinations.

❸ **Hue** (p175) Treading in the footsteps of emperors, from the Purple Forbidden City to the imperial tombs.

❹ **An Bang** (p221) Taking it easy and eating well at this relaxed beach near Hoi An.

❺ **Danang** (p193) Putting your finger on the pulse of this exciting and fast-growing city.

❻ **My Son** (p227) Standing in amazement amid these glorious yet war-blighted Cham ruins.

❼ **Trang An** (p155) Exploring a World Heritage–listed riverine wonderland.

❽ **Vinh Moc Tunnels** (p170) Discovering the poignant, war-torn sights of the Demilitarised Zone (DMZ).

History

This region's seen them all: kings and king-makers, warriors and occupiers, and a history of warfare and conflict. The ancient kingdom of Champa began here in the 2nd century and flourished for more than a thousand years. Myriad Cham towers and temples dot the landscape; the most renowned are at My Son. The Vietnamese subdued Champa in the 15th century, while in subsequent centuries European, Japanese and Chinese traders established footholds in Hoi An.

In 1802 Vietnam's final royal dynasty, the Nguyens, set up court at Hue, which became the centre of political intrigue, intellectual excellence and spiritual guidance. Later emperors were subdued by expanding French ambitions in Vietnam, and by the time of independence the locus of national power had shifted back to Hanoi.

In 1954, Vietnam was fatefully partitioned into North and South, creating a DMZ that saw some of the heaviest fighting of the American War. Thousands of lives were lost in bloody battles as entire cities, including Vinh and most of Hue's Imperial Enclosure, were flattened. Vast tracts of countryside around Dong Hoi and Dong Ha remain littered with lethal ordnance. Historic Hoi An was one of the few places spared.

Today, tourism drives Hue and Hoi An, and Danang is expanding with energy and investment, but the region's north remains relatively undeveloped.

NORTH-CENTRAL VIETNAM

The karst limestone landscapes around Ninh Binh are ideal for exploring by boat or bicycle, and there are stellar opportunities for caving and trekking amid the fast-developing travellers' scene of the Phong Nha-Ke Bang National Park. Dong Hoi, the coastal gateway to Phong Nha, also has an enjoyable low-key beach scene and good restaurants.

Ninh Binh Province

South of Hanoi, Ninh Binh province is blessed with natural beauty, cultural sights and the Cuc Phuong National Park. Highlights include boat trips amid karst landscapes at Tam Coc and the Unesco World Heritage-listed Trang An grottoes. Note that the region is very popular with domestic travellers and many attractions are commercialised, with an abundance of hawkers.

Ninh Binh City

☎ 0229 / POP 160,000

Bustling Ninh Binh City is lacking in sights and not a destination in itself, but it makes a decent base for exploring some quintessentially Vietnamese limestone scenery close by. Western tourists are far outnumbered by Vietnamese, who flock to nearby sights, including the nation's biggest pagoda and the Trang An grottoes.

The region has significant natural allure, but insensitive development has placed giant cement factories right next to nature spots.

☞ Tours

Hotels book tours around Ninh Binh province and also to Cuc Phuong National Park.

Chookie's Tours OUTDOORS
(☎ 0229-361 8897; www.chookiestravel.com; per person 400,000-1,500,000d) Regular departures exploring the area's attractions by motorbike, with tours to the Trang An grottoes, photogenic sunset scooter tours and the Cuc Phuong National Park. Chookie's also does day tours (US$70) of Tam Coc from Hanoi, with pickup from your hotel.

Truong Nguyen TOURS
(☎ 0915 666 211, 0165 348 8778; truong_tour@yahoo.com) Freelance guide Truong offers escorted motorbike trips around Ninh Binh using country back roads, and trekking in Pu Luong Nature Reserve, a forested area across two mountain ridges, where you can stay in Thai and Hmong homestays. He also runs trips to the northern Ha Giang province, and operates the excellent Friendly Home hotel in town.

🛏 Sleeping

Go Ninh Binh Hostel HOSTEL $
(☎ 0229-387 1186; www.goninhbinhhostel.com; 1 Đ Hoang Hoa Tham; dm US$5, weekday/weekend d US$20/24; ✳@🛜) In the city's former railway station, Go Ninh Binh has OK dorms, doubles with en-suite bathrooms, and plenty of shared areas including hammocks. A library, bar, pool table and dartboard are also popular, and the team at reception can help with ideas for exploring the broader Ninh Binh area.

★**Friendly Home** HOTEL $$
(☎ 0229-388 3588; 5 60/45 Đ Hai Thuong Lang On; s US$16, d US$22-35, f $42; ✳@🛜) This excellent, very friendly and tidy hotel has six spotless en-suite rooms, buffet breakfasts and free use of bicycles. It's owned and operated by local guide Truong Nguyen, so handy information is available on local sights, bus timetables and tours around the Ninh Binh region. Motorbikes can be hired if you're keen to explore the region independently.

🍴 Eating & Drinking

Plan to eat early as not much is open after 9pm. The local speciality is *de* (goat meat) served with fresh herbs and rice paper. Around 3km out of town, the road to Trang An is lined with goat-meat restaurants.

Chookie's Hideaway CAFE $
(☎ 0919 103 558; www.chookiestravel.com; 147 Đ Nguyen Hue; meals 40,000-70,000d; ⊘9am-10pm; 🛜🍴) This vast place with a pool table and beer on tap serves good-value Vietnamese and Western food and has plenty of local information on what to do and see in the region as the company runs tours. Burgers, wood-fired pizzas, wraps and a few vegetarian options all feature, along with smoothies, cocktails, craft beers

Ninh Binh

Ⓝ 0 —————— 400 m
0 —————— 0.2 miles

North-Central Vietnam

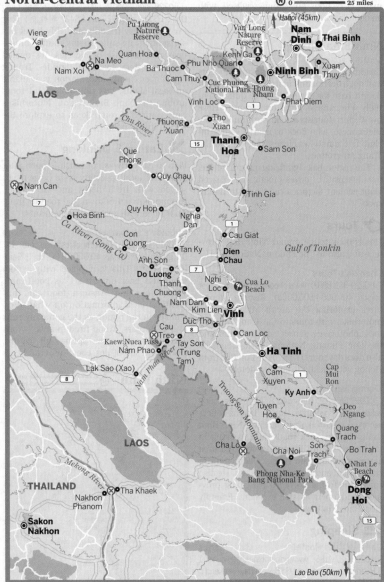

and a wine and gin menu. Local beer by the bottle starts at 20,000d; Magners cider is also at hand for apple fans.

Trung Tuyet VIETNAMESE $
(14 Đ Hoang Hoa Tham; meals 60,000-100,000d; ⏰8.30am-9.30pm; 🍽) Expect very large por-

tions, options for vegetarians, and a warm welcome from the host family at this busy little place that's popular with travellers. The owners will even drop you off at the nearby train station if you're moving on after your meal.

❶ Information

Ninh Binh General Hospital (Benh Vien Da Khoa Ninh Binh; ☑ 0229-387 1030; Đ Tue Tinh; ⊘ 24hr) Main city hospital.

Vietin Bank & ATM (Đ Tran Hung Dao; ⊘ 7am-2.30pm Mon-Fri, 7.30am-noon Sat) One of two branches on this street.

Main Post Office (Đ Tran Hung Dao; ⊘ 7am-6pm Mon-Fri, to 5pm Sat & Sun)

❶ Getting There & Away

BUS

Ninh Binh's **bus station** (Đ Le Dai Hanh) is located near Lim Bridge. Public buses leave every 15 minutes until 7pm for the Giap Bat bus station in Hanoi (from 75,000d, 2½ hours), and there are regular buses to Hai Phong (95,000d, three hours, every 1½ hours) and twice-daily connections to Halong City (140,000d, 3½ hours).

Ninh Binh is also a stop for open-tour buses between Hanoi (US$7, two hours) and Hue (US$15, 10 hours). Hotel pickups and drop-offs are available.

TRAIN

The **train station** (Ga Ninh Binh; 1 Đ Hoang Hoa Tham) is a scheduled stop on the main north–south line, with destinations including Hanoi (from 62,000d, two to 2½ hours, four daily), Vinh (from 93,000d, six hours, six daily) and Hue (from 261,000d, 12½ to 13½ hours, five daily).

❶ Getting Around

Most hotels rent out bicycles (around US$2 per day) and motorbikes (US$5 to US$10 per day). Motorbike drivers charge around US$12 a day.

Around Ninh Binh City

◉ Sights & Activities

★ **Van Long**
Nature Reserve   NATURE RESERVE
(entry 20,000d, boat 60,000d; ⊘ 7am-5pm) Set amid glorious limestone pinnacles, this tranquil reserve comprises a reedy wetland that's popular with birdwatchers. Among the bird species that have been spotted here are the rare black-faced spoonbill, cotton pygmy goose and white-browed crake. Van Long is also one of the last wild refuges of the endangered Delacour's langur (population roughly 120), partly because the wetlands keep predators and poachers at bay. Langurs are not easy to spot; try your luck early in the morning or in the evening.

Rowboat rides (90 minutes, maximum two people per boat) around the reserve are a more relaxed alternative to occasional hawker hassles on the Tam Coc boat trips. Ninh Binh hotels can arrange tours. Van Long is 2km east of Tran Me, 19km from Ninh Binh along the road to Cuc Phuong.

Trang An   CAVE
(⊘ 7.30am-4pm) **FREE** Rowboats bob along the Sao Khe River through limestone caves. It's a relaxing trip, but many caves have also been enlarged to accommodate boats. Boat trips (200,000d per person, or 800,000d for your own boat) take two hours, and there are two possible routes, both visiting caves and temples. Bring a hat and sunscreen as the boats lack shade. Trang An is 7km west of Ninh Binh. You'll pass it on the way to the Chua Bai Dinh.

A trip out here makes for a fun bike or scooter journey from town.

Mua Cave   CAVE
(Hang Mua; 100,000d; ⊘ 7am-4pm) Down a sleepy road between rice paddies, this cave (the name means 'Cave of Dance') is not terribly impressive, but there are panoramic views from the peak above. A stone staircase beside the cave entrance zigzags through the karst (beware the goat droppings) and it's almost 500 steps to a simple altar to Quan The Am Bo Tat (the Goddess of Mercy). Look west for the Ngo Dong River winding through Tam Coc.

The climb is paved but steep in sections, so bring water and allow an hour return. Mua Cave is 5km from Ninh Binh and is a popular stop on Tam Coc tours.

Chua Bai Dinh   BUDDHIST SITE
(www.chuabaidinhninhbinh.vn; pagoda 50,000d, train 30,000d; ⊘ 7am-5.45pm) **FREE** Chua Bai Dinh is a bombastic Buddhist complex, built on a vast scale, that rises up a hillside near Ninh Binh. Construction was completed in 2014, and it's now a huge attraction for Vietnamese tourists. The entrance leads to cloistered walkways past 500 stone *arhat* (enlightened Buddhists) lining the route to the main triple-roofed Phap Chu Pagoda. This contains a 10m, 100-tonne bronze Buddha, flanked by two more gilded Buddha figures.

Steps behind lead to a viewpoint, a 13-storey pagoda and a giant Buddha. The compound's central area features more temples, including one showcasing a 36-tonne bell, the largest in Vietnam. Most structures use natural materials, and the complex's impressive bronzework, lacquerwork and stone-carving was crafted by local artisans.

Chua Bai Dinh is 11km northwest of Ninh Binh, and attracts many visitors. Think twice if you're after a spiritual experience. Tours arrive at the main car park where an electric train continues to the main entrance. If you arrive independently by bicycle you'll still be directed to the car park to catch the train.

Hoa Lu Temples TEMPLE

(20,000d) Yen Ngua Mountain provides a scenic backdrop for Hoa Lu's two surviving temples, both spaces dominated by dark-red lacquered pillars. The first, Dinh Tien Hoang, was restored in the 17th century and is dedicated to the Dinh dynasty. At the front of the main temple building is the stone pedestal of a royal throne; inside are bronze bells and a statue of Emperor Dinh Tien Hoang with his three sons. The second temple is dedicated to monarch Le Dai Hanh.

For a great perspective of the ruins, hike 20 minutes (around 1.5km) to the tomb of Emperor Dinh Tien Hoang. Access is via the hill opposite the ticket office. Hoa Lu is 12km northwest of Ninh Binh; turn left 6km north of town on Hwy 1. There is no public transport, but tours leave from Ninh Binh.

Bich Dong Pagoda BUDDHIST TEMPLE

(Jade Grotto) FREE This charming sequence of cave temples is a couple of kilometres west of Ninh Hai village. The Lower Pagoda is located at the base, from which 100 steps lead to the Middle Pagoda, where there's a shorter but steep ascent to the Upper Pagoda. Inside each cave temple are looming statues peering from the haze of burning incense. Outside there are incredible countryside views.

Tam Coc Boat Trips BOATING

(Dinh Cac Pier, Ninh Hai village; boat base fare 150,000d, plus entry adult/child 120,000/60,000d; ⏱ 7am-3.30pm) Tam Coc boasts surreal karst beauty along the Ngo Dong River, and it is immensely popular with domestic tourists. Consider visiting early morning or late afternoon when things are quieter. Rowers use their feet to propel the oars, as the route (around two hours) negotiates Tam Coc's three caves. There's a maximum of two people per boat.

Unfortunately the area is now overshadowed by giant cement factories, which you can't see from the river, but air quality and pollution are concerns. Boats leave from the pier in Ninh Hai village (known as Tam Coc, but also called Van Lan). The name Tam Coc derives from the old Chinese: Tam (three) Coc (caves), and is also given to the general area around the caves.

🛏 Sleeping

Anna Tham Hotel View HOTEL $

(☎ 0229-361 8522; annathanhotelview@gmail. com; Tam Coc–Bich Dong Rd; r US$20; ❄ 🛜) This decent and friendly family-owned hotel is in a quiet area just a short walk from Bich Dong Pagoda. Rice-paddy views, spacious rooms and a warm welcome combine here, close to simple village eateries. Bicycles are free to use and the hotel can also help out with motorbike and scooter hire.

Nguyen Shack BUNGALOW $$

(☎ 0229-361 8678; www.nguyenshack.com; near Mua Cave, Hoa Lu district; bungalows US$22-45; 🛜) With a riverside setting around 5km from Tam Coc, Nguyen Shack's easygoing, lazy-days thatched bungalows are the perfect antidote to the bustle of Hanoi. Lie in a hammock, drop a fishing rod off your rustic terrace, or grab a bicycle and go exploring. There's an on-site restaurant and bar, too.

Limestone View Homestay GUESTHOUSE $$

(☎ 0918 453 761; www.limestoneview.com; Đ Xuan Thanh, Xuan Ang village, Hoa Lu district; d US$57-98, tr from US$65, ste from US$118, apt from US$159; ⊜❄🛜) With superb mountain vistas from a village location convenient for Tam Coc (5km), Hoa Lu (5km) or Trang An (2km), Limestone View has very comfortable rooms, suites and an apartment – along with the company of a very friendly family. Bicycle use is free if you want to go exploring.

Mua Cave Ecolodge LODGE $$

(☎ 0229-361 8754; Khe Ha village, Hoa Lu district; s/d from 550,000/800,000d; ❄🛜) Surrounded by rice paddies and karst limestone, this quiet choice has spacious rooms and bungalows with a tinge of heritage style. A quirky highlight is the restaurant and bar located within a cave. Half- and full-day tours are available around the area. It's relatively isolated, so you'll need to count on eating at the lodge as well.

★ Tam Coc Garden BOUTIQUE HOTEL $$$

(☎ 024 6273 3615, 037 825 3555; www.tamcoc garden.com; Hai Nham village, Hoa Lu district; d US$145-175; ⊜❄🛜▣) The most Zen place to stay around Ninh Binh is this lovely boutique hotel. In a private location with a sea of rice paddies at your balcony, it has eight stone-and-timber 50-sq-metre bungalows set in a luxuriant garden, as well as other hotel rooms. Following a day of cycling or exploring nearby attractions, there's a swim in the compact pool to look forward to.

Phat Diem

Home to a huge cathedral, combining Sino-Vietnamese and European architecture, Phat Diem makes an intriguing half-day excursion from Ninh Binh.

During colonial times, Phat Diem's bishop ruled the area with his private army, until French troops moved in and took over in 1951.

◉ Sights

Phat Diem Cathedral   CHURCH
Built in 1892, the cathedral's wooden interior has a vaulted ceiling supported by massive columns. Vietnamese-looking cherubs swarm above the granite altar, while Chinese-style clouds drift across the blue ceiling. Beneath are icons of the martyrs slaughtered by Emperor Tu Duc during the 1850s anti-Catholic purges. Opposite the cathedral's main doors is the free-standing bell tower; stone slabs are where mandarins used to observe Catholic Mass. Between the tower and the cathedral is the tomb of the Vietnamese founder, Father Six (Tran Luc).

Dong Huong Pagoda   PAGODA
Dong Huong Pagoda is the area's largest Buddhist pagoda, and many of its congregation are minority Muong people. Turn right at the canal at the north of town and continue alongside the water for 3km.

Ton Dao Cathedral   CHURCH
A Gothic counterpoint to Phat Diem's is this cathedral at Ton Dao, along Rte 10 about 5km from Phat Diem. At the rear, a statue of the Virgin Mary keeps unexpected company with porcelain images of Quan The Am Bo Tat (the Goddess of Mercy).

❶ Getting There & Away

Phat Diem, sometimes known by its former name Kim Son, is 121km south of Hanoi and 26km southeast of Ninh Binh. There are direct buses here from Ninh Binh (25,000d, one hour); *xe om* (motorbike taxi) drivers charge about 200,000d (including waiting time) for a return trip.

Cuc Phuong National Park

⏱ 030 / ELEV 150-656M
With 336 species of bird, 135 species of mammal, 122 species of reptile and more than 2000 species of plant, **Cuc Phuong National Park** (☑091 566 6916, 0229-384 8018; www.cucphuongtourism.com.vn; adult/child 60,000/30,000d) is one Vietnam's most important protected areas. Established as a national park in 1962, Cuc Phuong spans two karst limestone mountain ranges and three provinces. Its highest peak is Dinh May Bac (Silver Cloud Peak), at 656m.

Unfortunately, poaching and habitat destruction plague the park. Improved roads have led to illegal logging, and many native species – such as the Asiatic black bear, Siamese crocodile, wild dog and tiger – have now vanished from the area. Other wildlife is notoriously elusive, so manage your expectations accordingly.

The park is home to the minority Muong people, whom the government relocated from the park's central valley to its western edge in the late 1980s.

❶ When to Go

The best time to visit is in the dry months from November to February. From April to June it becomes increasingly hot, wet and muddy, and from July to October the rains arrive, bringing lots of leeches. Visitors in April and May may see millions of butterflies in a simply astonishing sight. Note that weekends can be busy with Vietnamese families.

◉ Sights

Cuc Phuong's conservation centres offer glimpses into the animals they're helping. Arrange for a guide (no charge) from the visitor centre to escort you to the Endangered Primate Rescue Center and the Turtle Conservation Center, both around 2km from the entrance. Volunteers can offer to work at both centres, or in tree-planting in the park (write to volunteer@eprc.asia or cucphuong np@gmail.com for more information).

Endangered Primate Rescue Center   WILDLIFE RESERVE
(☑0229-384 8002; www.eprc.asia; 30,000d; ⊙9-11am & 1.30-4pm) The Endangered Primate Rescue Center is supervised by the Frankfurt Zoological Society, and is home to around 180 primates (15 species in total), including 12 kinds of langur, plus three species of gibbon and two loris. All the centre's animals

were either bred here or rescued from illegal traders. Tours with a nature-conservation focus are on offer. Volunteers (experience not necessary, just enthusiasm) are encouraged to get in touch; tasks include preparing animal feed and cleaning enclosures. Your entry ticket also allows access to the Turtle Conservation Center.

Turtle Conservation Center (TCC) WILDLIFE RESERVE

(☑ 024 7302 8389, 030 384 8090; www.asianturtle program.org; 30,000d; ☉ 9-11am & 2-4.45pm) The Turtle Conservation Center houses more than 600 terrestrial, semiaquatic and aquatic turtles representing 19 of Vietnam's 25 native species. Many have been confiscated from smugglers who have been driven by demand from the domestic and Chinese markets – eating turtle is thought to aid longevity. Visitors can see turtles in tanks and incubators, as well as in ponds in near-wild settings. Signs in English about the endangered turtles are informative. Your entry ticket also allows access to the Endangered Primate Rescue Center.

🏃 Activities

Cuc Phuong offers excellent hiking. Short walks include a 220-step trail up to the Cave of Prehistoric Man. Human graves and tools found here date back 7500 years, making it one of Vietnam's oldest sites of human habitation.

Popular hikes include a 6km-return walk to the massive 1000-year-old 'old tree' (Tetrameles nudiflora), and a longer four-hour (around 12km) walk to Silver Cloud Peak. There's also a strenuous 15km (approximately five-hour) hike to Kanh, a Muong village. You can stay overnight here with local families and raft on the Buoi River (around 100,000d).

Park staff can provide basic maps, but a guide is recommended for day trips and is mandatory for longer treks. The two-hour escorted night hike to spot nocturnal animals and the Silver Cloud Peak hike both cost US$25 (for up to five people). The Deep Jungle trek (US$60) gets into remote terrain where you might spot flying squirrels. See the park's website for other one-day and overnight options.

🛏️ Sleeping & Eating

There is accommodation in the park, and one luxury resort nearby. It's advisable to book for weekends and public holidays.

Camping (per person US$4) is also available at the visitor centre or Mac Lake. Simple homestays (per person US$10) with Muong families can be organised by park staff.

There are simple restaurants and snack shops at the park headquarters and Mac Lake, but prices are not very cheap and all meals must be ordered well in advance.

Park Headquarters GUESTHOUSE $

(s US$16-35, d US$27-50, stilt houses US$14, bungalows US$23) This accommodation beside the national park entrance includes 'modern' rooms, a stilt house and a private bungalow. Standard rooms are quite dark, but still adequate.

Mac Lake BUNGALOW $

(bungalows US$16-27) Attractive bungalows overlooking Mac Lake are 2km inside the park, and though the location is quiet, it's also rather isolated and the restaurant can be undersupplied.

Cuc Phuong Resort RESORT $$$

(☑ 030 384 8886; www.cucphuongresort.com; Dong Tam village; bungalows/villas from US$108/ 167, s/d from US$97; ⊛ @ 🛜 🏊) This resort is near a natural spring, enabling mineral-rich water to be pumped into wooden bathtubs in each room. There are (spring-fed) indoor and outdoor pools, tennis courts, and an impressive spa; breakfast is included. It's 2km from the park entrance. Rooms are cheapest from Sunday to Thursday. Non-guests can use the pools for 130,000d per person.

ℹ️ Information

The park visitor centre has English-speaking staff, and can arrange guides and tours, as well as accommodation.

ℹ️ Getting There & Away

Cuc Phuong National Park is 45km from Ninh Binh. The turn-off from Hwy 1 is north of Ninh Binh and follows the road that runs to Kenh Ga and Van Long Nature Reserve.

Buses (two hours, 90,000d) from Hanoi's southern Giap Bat bus station depart to the town of Nho Quan near Cuc Phuong regularly from 8am to 4pm, with return buses to Hanoi from 7am to 3pm. From Nho Quan to the park, catch a xe om (around 120,000d) or taxi (250,000d). There's also a direct bus from Giap Bat to Cuc Phuong departing at 9am, returning to Hanoi at 3pm.

From Ninh Binh, catch a xe om (around 250,000d return) or taxi to the park; alternatively, rent a motorbike. A bus also runs from Ninh Binh (20,000d).

Hanoi tour companies offer trips to Cuc Phuong, usually combined with other sights in the Ninh Binh area. It's also possible to book trips to Cuc Phuong at travel agencies, and at accommodation in Ninh Binh.

Vinh

 0238 / POP 502,000

Practically obliterated during the American War, Vinh was rebuilt with East German aid – hence the brutalist concrete architecture dominating downtown. The only reasons to stop here are if you're a Ho Chi Minh devotee (he was born in a nearby village), or if you're heading to Laos.

Vinh is a major transport hub with regular buses to Ho Chi Minh City (HCMC), Hanoi, Danang and Dien Bien Phu, and trains to all stops north to Hanoi and south to HCMC. Open-tour buses pass through town between Hanoi and Hue, and while it's easy to ask to jump off here, it's difficult to arrange a pickup.

 Sights

Ho Chi Minh Pilgrimage Spots   HISTORIC SITE

(⊙7-11.30am & 2-5pm Mon-Fri, 7.30am-noon & 1.30-5pm Sat & Sun) FREE Ho Chi Minh's birthplace in Hoang Tru, and the village of Kim

---

ⓘ GETTING TO LAOS: VINH TO PHONSAVAN & LAK SAO

The following are our recommended routes into Laos. An alternative crossing is from the Vietnamese city of Thanh Hoa to Sam Neua in Laos, but this route is plagued by reports of rampant overcharging of non-Vietnamese travellers by taxi drivers and bus companies.

Vinh to Phonsavan

Getting to the border The often mist-shrouded **Nam Can/Nong Haet border crossing** is 250km northwest of Vinh. Buses leave at 6am Mondays, Wednesdays, Fridays and Saturdays for Luang Prabang (750,000d, 22 hours) via Phonsavan (410,000d, 12 hours). It's possible to travel independently from Vinh to Muong Xen by bus and then haggle for a motorbike (around 180,000d) uphill to the border, but we strongly recommend you take the direct option to avoid overcharging and hassle.

At the border The border post is open from 7.30am to 5.30pm. Vietnamese visas aren't available, but Lao visas are available for most nationalities for between US$30 and US$40.

Moving on Travellers not on the direct bus face numerous challenges, so it is highly advisable to go by bus. In Laos, transport to Nong Haet is erratic, but once you get there you can pick up a bus to Phonsavan. On the Vietnam side, firstly you'll have to haggle over a motorbike ride from the border to the nearest town, Muong Xen. The route is breathtaking (but it's only 25km downhill and should cost around 120,000d, though drivers may ask for up to 300,000d). From Muong Xen there are irregular buses to Vinh (150,000d, six hours). Note that some buses from Phonsavan claim to continue to Hanoi or Danang, but unceremoniously discharge all their passengers in Vinh.

Vinh to Lak Sao

Getting to the border The **Cau Treo/Nam Phao border crossing** has a dodgy reputation with travellers on local nondirect buses; they often report chronic overcharging and hassle (such as bus drivers ejecting foreigners in the middle of nowhere unless they cough up extra bucks). Stick to direct services. Most transport to Phonsavan in Laos uses the Nan Can/Nong Haet border further north. Buses leave Vinh at 6am (on Mondays, Wednesdays, Fridays and Saturdays) for Vieng Khan in Laos (280,000d). There are also regular local buses from Vinh to Tay Son (70,000d, two hours), and then irregular services from Tay Son on to the border at Cau Treo. Otherwise, *xe om* (motorbike taxis) charge around 170,000d for the ride.

At the border The border is open from 7.30am to 5.30pm. Lao visas are available.

Moving on If you're not on a direct bus, expect rip-offs. Upon entering Vietnam bus drivers quote up to US$40 for the ride to Vinh. A metered taxi costs about US$50, a motorbike about 320,000d. Some buses from Lak Sao claim to run to Danang or Hanoi, but in fact terminate in Vinh. On the Laos side, a jumbo or *sawngthaew* (truck) between the border and Lak Sao runs to about 60,000 kip (bargain hard).

Lien, where he spent some of his formative years, are 14km west of Vinh. Although these are popular pilgrimage spots for the party faithful, there's little to see other than recreated houses of bamboo and palm leaves, dressed (barely) with a few pieces of furniture. From Vinh, *xe om* drivers charge around 150,000d (including waiting time), and taxis around 300,000d.

🛏 Sleeping & Eating

As a major provincial capital, Vinh has accommodation across all price ranges. Cheaper digs are gathered around the train station.

Dining selections are found around Vinh's main street, Nguyen Trai, with cheaper options near the bus and train stations.

Than An Hotel   HOTEL **$**
(☑0238-384 3478; 168 Đ Nguyen Thai Hoc; r 250,000-350,000d; ❄@☎) Enjoys a convenient location 300m south of the bus terminal. Rooms have attractive wooden furniture and good beds. Near-zero English is spoken at reception.

ⓘ Getting There & Away

AIR
Vinh International Airport is 8km north of the city. There are regular flights linking Vinh to HCMC with Vietnam Airlines and Bamboo Airways (both also fly to Hanoi), and VietJet and Jetstar. VietJet flies to Dalat, Can Tho and Nha Trang; Jetstar flies to Nha Trang.

BUS
Vinh's centrally located bus station has a reasonably modern booking office (including a departures board and price list).

Buses for Hanoi leave very regularly until 4.30pm, and 10 sleeper buses also run. Services go to all four Hanoi bus terminals. For Ninh Binh (800,000d, four hours) take a Hanoi-bound bus. There are also six daily buses to Dien Bien Phu (600,000d, 16 hours).

Open-tour buses pass through town between Hanoi and Hue, and while it's easy to ask to jump off here, it's harder to arrange a pickup.

TRAIN
Vinh train station is on the northwestern edge of town. There are regular departures on the Reunification Express to destinations including Hanoi, Ninh Binh, Dong Hoi and Hue.

Phong Nha-Ke Bang National Park
☑0232

Designated a Unesco World Heritage Site in 2003, the remarkable **Phong Nha-Ke Bang National Park** (☑052 367 7021; www.phongnhakebang.vn/en) ❂**FREE** contains the oldest karst mountains in Asia, formed approximately 400 million years ago, as well as the **world's largest cave**. Riddled with hundreds of cave systems – many of extraordinary scale and length – and spectacular underground rivers, Phong Nha is a speleologists' heaven on earth.

The Phong Nha region is changing fast. Son Trach town (population 3000) is the main centre, with an ATM, a rapidly mushrooming range of accommodation options and a growing choice of restaurants, and improving transport links with other parts of central Vietnam.

The caves are the region's absolute highlight, but the above-ground attractions of forest trekking, the regional war history, and rural mountain biking mean it deserves a stay of around three days, but you could explore for weeks.

Serious exploration of the park's amazing caves only began in the 1990s, led by the British Cave Research Association and Hanoi University. Cavers first penetrated deep into Phong Nha Cave, one of the world's longest systems. In 2005 Paradise Cave was discovered, and in 2009 a team found the world's largest cave – Hang Son Doong (p162). In 2015 public access to two more cave systems was approved.

Above the ground, most of the mountainous 885 sq km of Phong Nha-Ke Bang National Park is near-pristine tropical evergreen jungle, more than 90% of which is primary forest. It borders the biodiverse Hin Namno reserve in Laos to form an impressive, continuous slab of protected habitat. More than 100 types of mammal (including 10 species of primate, plus tigers, elephants and saola, a rare Asian antelope), 81 types of reptile and amphibian, and more than 300 varieties of bird have been logged in Phong Nha.

⊙ Sights

The Phong Nha region is exploding in popularity, and it's recommended that you book overnight caving tours for Tu Lan, Hang Va and Hang En in advance if possible, as well

Phong Nha-Ke Bang National Park

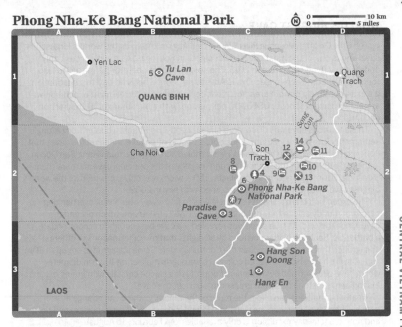

Phong Nha-Ke Bang National Park

as the four-day Hang Son Doong expedition. Note that most of the adventure caves are closed during the wet season from around mid-September to either late November or late December.

In the past, access to the national park was limited and strictly controlled by the Vietnamese military. Access is still quite tightly controlled, for good reason (the park is riddled with unexploded ordnance). Officially you are not allowed to hike here without a licensed tour operator. You can, however, travel independently (on a motorbike or car) on the Ho Chi Minh Hwy or Hwy 20, which cut through the park.

⭐ **Tu Lan Cave**   CAVE
(www.oxalis.com.vn; 1-day tour per person 1,800,000d, 2-day tour per person 5,500,000d; ⊘ mid-Nov–mid-Sep) Tu Lan cave trips begin with a countryside hike, then a swim (with headlamps and life jackets) through two

WORLD'S BIGGEST CAVE

Hang Son Doong (Mountain River Cave; ⊘ Feb-Aug) is known as the world's largest cave, and is one of the most spectacular sights in Southeast Asia, with access only approved by the government in 2013. The sole specialist operator permitted to lead tours here is Son Trach–based Oxalis Adventure Tours. This is no day-trip destination; it's in an extremely remote area. You must book a four-day/three-night expedition with around 16 porters. It costs US$3000 per person, with a maximum of 10 trekkers on each trip.

This enormous cave was discovered quite recently. Ho Khanh, a hunter from a jungle settlement close to the Vietnam–Laos border, would often take shelter in the caves that honeycomb his mountain homeland. He stumbled across gargantuan Hang Son Doong in the early 1990s, but the sheer scale and majesty of the principal cavern (more than 5km long, 200m high and, in some places, 150m wide) was only confirmed as the world's biggest cave when British explorers returned with him in 2009.

The expedition team's biggest obstacle was to find a way over a vast overhanging barrier of muddy calcite they dubbed the 'Great Wall of Vietnam', which divided the cave. Once they did, its true scale was revealed – a cave big enough to accommodate a battleship. Sections of it are pierced by skylights that reveal formations of ethereal stalagmites that cavers have called the Cactus Garden. Some stalagmites are up to 80m high. Cavers have also discovered colossal cave pearls measuring 10cm in diameter, which have been formed by millennia of drips, fusing calcite crystals with grains of sand. Magnificent rimstone pools are present throughout the cave.

Weather conditions can affect the route of the itinerary, which can change at short notice. Check availability on the website's calendar (be aware it's a popular expedition) and note the four-day excursion is only available from February to August.

spectacular river caves, before emerging in an idyllic valley. Then there's more hiking through dense forest to a 'beach' where rivers merge; this is an ideal campsite for the two-day tour. There's more wonderful swimming here in vast caverns. Moderate fitness levels are necessary. Tu Lan is 65km north of Son Trach and can only be visited on a guided tour.

★ Hang En   CAVE

(2-day tour per person 7,600,000d; ⊘ late Dec–mid-Sep) This gigantic cave is very close to Hang Son Doong; both have been featured in a *National Geographic* photographic spread. Getting here involves a trek through dense jungle, valleys and the Ban Doong minority village, a very remote tribal settlement (with no electricity or roads). You stay overnight at a campsite in the cave or in a minority village. Tours can be booked via Oxalis Adventure Tours or local accommodation.

★ Paradise Cave   CAVE

(Thien Dong; adult/child under 1.3m 250,000/125,000d; ⊘ 7.30am-4.30pm) Surrounded by forested karst peaks, this staggering cave system extends for 31km, though most people only visit the first kilometre. The scale is breathtaking, as wooden staircases plunge into a cathedral-like space with vast alien-looking stalagmites and stalactites. Get here early to beat the crowds, as during peak times (early afternoon) tour guides shepherd groups using megaphones. Paradise Cave is about 14km southwest of Son Trach. Electric buggies (per person one way/return 15,000/25,000d) ferry visitors from the car park to the entrance 1km away.

From the buggie drop-off, it's a further 600m-plus sweaty climb up to the cave entrance. To explore deep inside the cave beyond the barrier at the end, and with luck see the eyeless cave fish that are part of its ecosystem, book a 7km Paradise Cave tour (2,650,000d, minimum two people), which includes a swim through an underground river (there's a boat if you can't swim) and lunch under a light shaft. Bookings can be made through Phong Nha Farmstay (p164) and Easy Tiger (p164).

Hang Toi   CAVE

(Dark Cave; per person 450,000d) Incorporating an above-water 400m-long zip line, followed by a swim into the cave and then exploration of a pitch-black passageway of oozing mud, it's little wonder Hang Toi is the cave experience you've probably already heard about from other travellers. Upon exiting the cave, a leisurely kayak paddle heads to a jetty where there are more into-the-water zip-line thrills to be had. Don't take any valuables into the cave.

Hang Tien   CAVE
(www.oxalis.com.vn; day trip per person 2,000,000d; ⊘ Mon, Wed-Fri & Sun Dec–mid-Sep) The largest part of the Tu Lan cave system, this moderately challenging dry cave was opened to visitors in 2016. The 10- to 12-hour adventure includes a jungle walk, and the cave is studded with astonishing calcite formations and rimstone pools. Two- and three-day explorations are also available (6,500,000d and 8,500,000d respectively).

Phong Nha Cave & Boat Trip   CAVE
(adult/child under 1.3m 150,000/25,000d, boat up to 14 people 320,000d; ⊘ 7am-5pm) The spectacular boat trip through Phong Nha Cave is an enjoyable though touristy experience beginning in Son Trach town. Boats cruise past buffalo, limestone peaks and church steeples to the cave's gaping mouth. The engine is then cut and the boats are negotiated silently through cavern after garishly illuminated cavern. On the return leg there's the option to climb (via 330 steps) up to the mountainside **Tien Son Cave** (60,000d), with the remains of 9th-century Cham altars and inscriptions.

Hang Va   CAVE
(www.oxalis.com.vn; per person 8,000,000d; ⊘ Feb-Aug) Discovered in 2012, and opened to visitors in 2015, Hang Va is explored on a two-day/one-night excursion that initially travels along an underground river in Hang Nuoc Nut. Tours stay overnight in a jungle camp at the entrance to Hang Va, where the cave's highlight is a spectacular stalagmite field partly submerged in crystalline waters. Ropes and harnesses are used extensively.

🏃 Activities

Beyond the attractions of the caves, there's a growing range of options to explore the jungle scenery and the history of this interesting area. Most activities can be booked through your accommodation.

Nuoc Mooc Ecotrail   WALKING
(basic access adult 80,000d, full access 180,000d; ⊘ 7am-5pm) A lovely riverside retreat inside Phong Nha-Ke Bang National Park, the wooden walkways and paths of the Nuoc Mooc Ecotrail extend over a kilometre through woods to the confluence of two rivers. It's a beautiful place for a swim, where you can wallow hippo-style in turquoise waters with a limestone-mountain backdrop. Attractions include an exciting rope bridge and kayaking on a weir on the river.

Lemon Tree Spa   MASSAGE
(☑ 0977 234 874; www.facebook.com/lemon.tree.spa.phongnha; Son Trach; massage from 125,000d; ⊘ 8am-11.30pm) Relax with spa, cosmetic and massage services after you've been jungle trekking, mountain biking or caving. There's also a very pleasant garden cafe on-site.

👉 Tours

Tours of Phong Nha are available from Dong Hoi, but as the region offers so much, it's best to stay near the national park. Tours can be set up through most accommodation and the specialist tour operators. Don't even consider a day trip from Hue, as you'll spend most of the time on the road.

★ Oxalis Adventure Tours   ADVENTURE
(☑ 0232-367 7678; www.oxalis.com.vn; Son Trach; ⊘ 8am-noon & 1.30-7.30pm Mon-Sat, 10am-7.30pm Sun) Oxalis is unquestionably *the* expert in caving and trekking expeditions, and is the only outfit licensed to conduct tours to Hang Son Doong. Staff are all fluent English speakers, and trained by world-renowned British cavers Howard and Deb Limbert. All excursions, from day trips to Tu Lan Cave to four-night/three-day expeditions to the world's largest cave, are meticulously planned and employ local guides and porters. You can discuss trips at Oxalis' riverside Expedition Cafe.

Pre-booking Son Doong for the following year is essential and, if possible, booking a few months ahead for expeditions in Tu Lan and Hang En is recommended to avoid disappointment. Consult the calendar on the excellent website and search for available slots.

★ Phong Nha Farmstay Tours ADVENTURE
(☑ 0232-367 5135; www.phong-nha-cave.com; Cu Nam) Phong Nha Farmstay's very popular National Park Tour (per person 1,350,000d) incorporates the Ho Chi Minh Trail (p293) with Paradise Cave and Hang Toi; there's also the option of swimming in and exploring Tra Ang Cave. Ask about exciting, informative customised tours (per person 2,500,000d) in the farmstay's vintage army jeep. Guests at the farmstay also get free motorbike-sidecar jaunts.

★ Jungle Boss Trekking   HIKING

(☑ 0917 800 805; www.jungle-boss.com; Phong Nha village, Son Trach; per person from 1,350,000d) English-speaking Dzung ('Jungle Boss') is an experienced guide who runs one- and two-day tours around the Ho Chi Minh Trail and the Abandoned Valley area of the national park with a good team. An excellent option (requiring a moderate to high fitness level) is exploring the remote Ma Da Valley, which includes a swim in the Tra Ang river cave and exploration of Elephant Cave.

The three-day and two-night Tiger Cave adventure is a more ambitious and strenuous trek, requiring considerable fitness, and includes Hang Over cave and Pygmy cave (despite the name, the latter is the fourth-largest cave in the world).

Hai's Eco Tours   HIKING

(☑ 0962 606 844; www.ecophongnha.com; Bamboo Cafe, Son Trach; per person adult/child under 10yr 1,450,000/1,100,000d) Rewarding day tours combine hiking in the jungle – you'll need to be relatively fit – with a visit to Phong Nha's Wildlife Rescue and Rehabilitation Centre, which rehabilitates rescued animals (mainly macaques from nearby regions, but also snakes and birds). Prices include a barbecue lunch, and there's an opportunity to cool off at the end of the day in a natural swimming hole.

A two-day/one-night option camping overnight in the Weapon Cave is also available for 3,200,000d.

Phong Nha
Adventure Cycling   MOUNTAIN BIKING

(☑ 0985 555 827; www.phongnhacycling.jimdo. com; per person US$65-87) Excellent mountain-biking tours with the irrepressible Private Shi. Options include biking sections of the Ho Chi Minh Trail, visiting local villages and lunch at a homestay.

Thang's Phong Nha Riders   TOURS

(www.easytigerhostel.com/thangs-phong-nha-riders; Son Trach) A day's hire of a motorbike with driver is around 350,000d to 400,000d; drivers are well versed in the sights of Phong Nha-Ke Bang National Park, and you'll be providing work for enthusiastic locals with basic English. Located beside Easy Tiger hostel, Thang's can also arrange motorbike transfers through absolutely stunning scenery to Hue or Khe Sanh, a very much recommended journey.

🛏 Sleeping

Accommodation options in the area have improved dramatically over recent years, and now range from simple village homestays through to lakeside bungalows and a luxury riverside resort. However, a glut of homestays has led to a surfeit of choice and widely varying standards as homestead owners rapidly convert their homes to accommodate travellers.

Easy Tiger   HOSTEL $

(☑ 0232-367 7844; www.easytigerhostel.com; Son Trach; dm from 120,000d; ✳ @ 🛜 🌊) Son Trach town's first hostel, this very popular place has four- and six-bed dorms, the great Jungle Bar (p166), a pool table and excellent travel information. A swimming pool and beer garden make it ideal for relaxation after trekking and caving. Ask about the free morning talk, and free bicycles and app to explore the Bong Lai valley and surrounding region.

Central Backpackers Hostel   HOSTEL $

(☑ 0232-6536 868; www.centralbackpackershostel.com; Son Trach; dm US$6, s/d/tr US$15/20/24; ✳ 🛜 🌊) The new kid on the block, in a new block, this place is a good-value addition to the town, with an appealing choice of clean and bright dorms, doubles and triples, an outside pool, friendly staff and free beer for an hour from 7pm.

★ Phong Nha Farmstay   GUESTHOUSE $$

(☑ 0232-367 5135; www.phong-nha-cave.com; Cu Nam; r 800,000-1,050,000d, f 2,000,000d; ⊖ ✳ @ 🛜 🌊) The place that really put Phong Nha on the map, the relaxed Farmstay enjoys peaceful views overlooking an ocean of rice paddies. Rooms are smallish but neat, with high ceilings and shared balconies. The excellent bar-restaurant serves Asian and Western dishes, and there's a social vibe, with movies and live music several nights a week. Local tours are superb (with free sidecar rides).

Chay Lap Farmstay   BUNGALOW $$

(☑ 0932 488 839; www.chaylapfarmstay.com; Chay Lap village; d from US$60; ⊖ ✳ 🛜 🌊) Accommodation in the leafy and peaceful grounds here includes an excellent variety of pleasant rooms and pine 'farmrooms' that are designed to float above floodwaters. A pool, an on-site herbal sauna and a decent restaurant and bar are welcome distractions after caving and hiking expeditions, and just a short walk away is the opportunity to kayak and paddleboard along the beautiful river at the farmstay's watersports centre.

Karst Villas
HOTEL $$

(📷 0232-360 6999, 0857 788 789; Co Giang village; d/f/ste 950,000/1,500,000/1,400,000d; ✳ 🛜 ⊠) Highly tranquil and surrounded by paddy fields, this good-looking and fresh hotel has a drop-dead gorgeous infinity-pool view across the sparkling waterlogged landscape to the sublime karst hills beyond; sunset from one's sun-lounger is off the register. Rooms are elegant, stylish and comfortable; rates includes breakfast, bicycles and a shuttle to Son Trach and back.

Jungle Boss Homestay
GUESTHOUSE $$

(📷 0886 077 780; www.jungle-boss.com; Son Trach; incl breakfast d 800,000d, f 1,000,000-1,200,000d; ✳ 🛜) Run by the friendly Dzung – a local trekking guide with excellent English – and his wife Huong, this place has simple but stylish rooms and bungalows, and two edge-of-the-village locations with rice-paddy views and an organic farm. Rates include free use of bicycles, and Dzung's Jungle Boss Trekking also offers caving and jungle-trekking trips. Family rooms are good value.

Phong Nha Mountain House
GUESTHOUSE $$

(📷 0935 931 009; www.phongnhamountainhouse. com; d/f incl breakfast US$40/50; @ 🛜) Owned by a hardworking local family, the Phong Nha Mountain House features four comfortable wooden stilt houses (including one with a family room), with private bathrooms and views of surrounding farmland. Pristine white bed linen contrasts with the warm sheen of the timber walls, and the elevated position means rooms are light and breezy. It's a flat 3km bike ride into Son Trach town.

Phong Nha Lake House Resort
RESORT $$

(📷 0232-367 5999; www.phongnhalakehouse.com; Khuong Ha; d US$42-60; ✳ 🛜 ⊠) Owned by an Australian-Vietnamese couple, this impressive lakeside resort has excellent rooms and spacious, stylish villas. A pool and lake-view bungalows make it one of the area's most comfortable place to stay. The wooden restaurant is a traditional structure from Ha Giang province in northern Vietnam. Kayaking on the lake is included, staff are lovely and breakfast is good.

Note that wi-fi in the lakeside bungalows can be weak. The Lake House is 7km east of Son Trach.

Pepper House
GUESTHOUSE $$

(📷 0918 745 950, 0167 873 1560; www.pepperhouse-homestay.com; Khuong Ha; d/f 950,000/1,300,000d; ✳ 🛜 ⊠) Run by long-term Aussie expat Dave (aka 'Multi') and his Vietnamese wife Diem, this rural place has double rooms in attractive villas arrayed around a compact swimming pool. It's located 6km east of Son Trach en route to the Bong Lai valley. The pool is open to visitors for 50,000d (or if you purchase the same value in food and drink).

Cooking classes are free for guests, or 100,000d if you're not staying here.

Ho Khanh's Homestay
HOMESTAY $$

(📷 0916 794 506; www.phong-nha-homestay.com; Son Trach; r 780,000-900,000d; ✳ 🛜) This homestay belongs to the legendary Ho Khanh, who discovered Son Doong, the world's largest cave. He's also a master carpenter, and has four refurbished wood-panelled rooms fitted out with air-conditioning and private bathrooms. Excellent newer private bungalows are worth the extra investment. There's also a river-view cafe and a compact sandy beach. Cash only.

★ Victory Road Villas
VILLA $$$

(📷 0232-367 5699; www.victoryroadvillas.com; 20 Victory Rd, Son Trach; villas from US$135; 🅿 ✳ 🛜 ⊠) Effortlessly raising the bar for accommodation around Phong Nha, Victory Road Villas combines a riverside location with stunning Asian-chic decor, hip and modern bathrooms, stellar shared public spaces including an 18m lap pool, and an excellent restaurant with sublime views. Accommodation options include one-bedroom villas complete with a lounge area and fully equipped kitchen, and a river-view penthouse offering a maximum of three bedrooms.

🍴 Eating

Eating options in the town of Son Trach include everything from bakeries and simple Vietnamese restaurants through to pizza, Indian cuisine and Western-style cafes. Explore the nearby Bong Lai valley by mountain bike where there are simple places selling barbecue duck and pork.

D-Arts Zone
VIETNAMESE, BARBECUE $

(www.facebook.com/dartphongnha; Son Trach; meals 50,000-90,000d; ⏰ 7am-10pm) Vintage jazz and blues often feature at this interesting spot co-owned by an artist and an architect. Menu highlights include decent salads, spicy northern Vietnamese sausage infused with smoke from the restaurant's barbecue grill and excellent *bun cha* (barbecued pork). The barbecue duck is also good. Sit out front at the rustic wooden tables and watch what's happening along Son Trach's main street.

Veggie Box
VEGETARIAN $

(Son Trach; meals 80,000-100,000d; ⊙7.30am-10pm; 🕸🚲) This popular brick-lined vegetarian restaurant packs in a lot of flavour for those on the run from meat and dairy, with banana and mango pancakes for breakfast and delicious smoothie bowls, veggie sushi, hotpots, spring rolls, meat-free kebabs, coconut fried rice, pumpkin cake and a lot more served daily to an enthusiastic crowd.

Bamboo Cafe
CAFE $

(www.phong-nha-bamboo-cafe.com; Son Trach; meals 40,000-80,000d; ⊙7am-10.30pm; 🕸🚲) This laid-back haven on Son Trach's main drag has colourful decor and well-priced food and drink, including excellent fresh-fruit smoothies and varied vegetarian options.

Pub with Cold Beer
BARBECUE $

(Bong Lai valley; meals from 40,000d; ⊙10am-sunset) Up a dirt track in the middle of nowhere (but well signposted), this spot owned by a farming family (with chickens, pigs and rabbits) does what it says on the tin – the beer is ice cold. Hungry? Order roast chicken with peanut sauce (all ingredients are farm fresh). A kilo of perfectly grilled chicken is around 200,000d. Volleyball and river tubing are other lazy-day distractions.

Moi Moi
VIETNAMESE $

(Bong Lai valley; snacks from 60,000d; ⊙7am-5pm) Moi Moi's super-relaxed and very rustic location is just the ticket for a lazy afternoon of playing pool, chilling in a hammock and snacking on interesting local dishes like *heo nuong cao tre* (pork barbecued in bamboo). A whole barbecued chicken is 300,000d. Pick up a Bong Lai valley map and go exploring.

ⓘ PHONG NHA ONLINE RESOURCES

Click on **Visit Phong Nha** (www.visit phongnha.com) for reams of useful info on the region and transport tips, too. There are also free downloadable maps and a link to a podcast introducing the history of the area.

Capture Vietnam
CAFE $

(www.facebook.com/CaptureVietnam; Son Trach; snacks & meals 60,000-200,000d; ⊙7am-10pm) This cafe has espresso coffee, homestyle baking and interesting Western and Vietnamese meals. Bagels with smoked salmon, good pizza and Mediterranean-style antipasti all add up to the area's most cosmopolitan spot. There's also an attached deli section selling local souvenirs – try the Phong Nha beef jerky – and takeaway beer, wine and cider.

🍷 Drinking & Nightlife

Bomb Crater Bar
BAR

(📱0166 541 0230; www.bombcraterbar.com; Cu Lac village; ⊙9am-7pm Nov-Sep) Ride a bike 3km from Son Trach to this riverside spot for cold beers, robust gin and tonics, and tasty Vietnamese snacks. Lying in a hammock, kayaking on the river, or chilling with the bar's resident water buffalo are all added attractions at this great place for a sundowner. The crater here was the result of a huge 2000lb US bomb targeting a nearby fuel depot.

East Hill
CAFE, BAR

(📱0948 953 925; ⊙11am-8pm) High on a grassy hillock, the open-sided East Hill is a laid-back spot for a sunset beer and Vietnamese snacks, and equally popular with travellers, and students from nearby Dong Hoi. Sit at the rustic shared wooden tables and take in great rural views. East Hill is around 8km east of Son Trach en route to the Bong Lai valley.

Jungle Bar
BAR

(Son Trach; ⊙7am-midnight; 🕸) The in-house bar/cafe at Easy Tiger (p164) is the most happening place in Son Trach, with cheap beer, pool tables and live music every night. Add to the growing display of national flags if you're feeling patriotic. There's loads of local information on hand, even if you're not staying at Easy Tiger.

ⓘ Information

There's an ATM in Son Trach, but occasional power cuts means it sometimes doesn't work, and it can run out of cash. It's wise to bring enough Vietnamese dong for your stay.

Hai at the Bamboo Cafe is a superb source of independent travel information, and the helpful staff at the Phong Nha Farmstay (p164) and Easy Tiger (p164) can assist with tours, information and transport. There's a tourist office opposite the jetty in Son Trach, but staff are not knowledgeable about independent travel.

❶ Getting There & Away

Son Trach town is 50km northwest of Dong Hoi. From Dong Hoi, head 20km north on Hwy 1 to Bo Trach, then turn west for another 30km.

Phong Nha-Ke Bang National Park abuts Son Trach and spreads west to the Lao border. Until 2011 access was tightly controlled by the Vietnamese state, and some areas remain off limits to independent travellers.

BUS

Local buses (35,000d, 90 minutes) shuttle between Dong Hoi's bus station and Son Trach, leaving pretty much hourly between 5.30am and 5pm. Look for bus number B4. Dong Hoi's railway station is around 1.3km from the bus station and the city is on the main north–south line.

From Hue (around 180,000d, five hours), the Hung Thanh open-tour bus leaves 49 Đ Chu Van An between 4.30pm and 5pm, and the Tan Nhat bus leaves from the Why Not? Bar on Đ Pham Ngu Lao around 6.30am to 7am. Also convenient is a daily bus (150,000d) leaving the DMZ Travel bar in Hue at 2pm, arriving at 6pm. This departure travels directly to Phong Nha. A local bus (between 90,000d and 150,000d, four hours) also leaves the south bus station in Hue for Phong Nha at 11.25am.

Open-tour buses also link Hanoi and Hoi An to Son Trach.

Tours from hotels in Hue to Paradise Cave and other caves cost around 800,000d, including lunch and admission, leaving at around 6.30am and returning by around 7.30pm, perhaps taking in some DMZ sights on the way.

CAR & MOTORCYCLE

Hotels can organise lifts in private cars from Dong Hoi (500,000d); they work together so rides can be shared between travellers to cut costs. A motorbike ride from Dong Hoi will cost from 200,000d. Phong Nha is also increasingly being offered by motorbike transfer services operating from Hanoi, Hue and Hoi An. Sit back and enjoy the ride.

❶ Getting Around

BICYCLE

Bicycling is recommended to explore Phong Nha's rural back roads, especially the quirky collection of rustic local restaurants and activities popping up around the nearby Bong Lai valley. Easy Tiger (p164) hires out bikes and can supply a handy map.

MOTORCYCLE

Motorcycling or scootering around the national park is not recommended for inexperienced riders – the area is not well signposted and every year there's an increasing number of injuries to

travellers. Check your travel insurance carefully as you may not be covered in case of an accident for two-wheeled journeys.

A good option is to book a tour with Thang's Phong Nha Riders (p164).

Dong Hoi

📞 0232 / POP 160,000

Dong Hoi is a pleasant port and seaside town in an attractive location clinging to the banks of the Nhat Le River, with beaches to the north and south. Easing off the travel accelerator and spending a couple of laid-back days here at quality oceanfront accommodation is recommended before or after visiting the Phong Nha-Ke Bang National Park.

As the main staging area for the North Vietnamese Army (NVA), Dong Hoi suffered more than most during the American War, but the town has since recovered as a bustling provincial capital.

◉ Sights

Tam Toa Church   CHURCH
(Đ Nguyen Du) **FREE** The Nhat Le River, which divides the city of Dong Hoi from a beautiful sandy spit, has a landscaped riverside promenade that features the haunting and gaunt, ruined facade of the Tam Toa Church, which was bombed in 1965. Only the steeple and a small section of wall survives, while saplings sprout from its uppermost brickwork.

Dong Hoi Citadel Gate   HISTORIC BUILDING
All that remains of Dong Hoi Citadel (Thanh Dong Hoi; 1825) are two restored and elegant brick and stone gates. The one close to the riverbank is inscribed with the *chu nho* (Chinese) characters 東門 (Dong Mon in Vietnamese, meaning 'East Gate'), the other is on Đ Quang Trung. Walking around the brick wall of the citadel alongside the moat is a fun and occasionally fascinating jaunt.

☞ Tours

Tour to the Caves   TOURS
(📞 0918 923 595; www.tourtothecaves.com; 63 Đ Nguyen Dinh Chieu; tours from 500,000d) Runs a variety of trips to Phong Nha and the DMZ (500,000d). Also gives out free local maps with suggested Dong Hoi self-guided walking tours.

Phong Nha Discovery   ADVENTURE
(📞 0232-385 1660; www.phongnhadiscovery.com; 63 Đ Ly Thuong Kiet; day tours from 1,050,000d) Daily tours from Dong Hoi to Paradise Cave

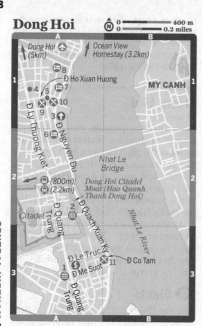

Dong Hoi

Ocean View Homestay GUESTHOUSE $

(☑ 0232-381 0686; www.oceanviewhomestay.com; Đ Truong Phap, Quang Phu village; dm/s/d/f from US$4.50/17/20/28, six-bed f US$38; ☻❄🖥) Around 4km north of the city, Ocean View Homestay is located about 150m from the beach. The savvy young owner speaks excellent English and the homestay's simple, colourful dorms and rooms are complemented by an excellent garden cafe. Tours and onward transport can be arranged.

Nam Long Hotel HOTEL $

(☑ 0918 923 595; www.namlonghotels.com; 22 Đ Ho Xuan Huong; dm US$6, d/tr/f US$20/26/30; ☻❄@🖥) A simply excellent budget hotel run by Nga and Sy, a welcoming, ever-helpful English-speaking couple. Rooms are bright and airy with enormous windows – book 301 for a river-view balcony. The eight-bed dorm is superb, with two en-suite bathrooms and its own balcony with great views. Breakfast is included, and Phong Nha tours and onward transport can be organised.

Nam Long Plus HOTEL $

(☑ 0918 923 595; www.namlonghotels.com; 28a Đ Phan Chu Trinh; d/tw/tr/f US$25/22/30/35; ☻❄🖥) A fine eight-storey hotel with spacious rooms and dorms, most with city or river views. A free hot breakfast is included, service is excellent and tours can be arranged. Check out the rooftop terrace to combine river vistas with a morning coffee or an afternoon beer.

Buffalo Hostel HOSTEL $

(☑ 0127 373 7373; www.facebook.com/buffalo pubandhostel; 4 Đ Nguyen Du; dm/d incl breakfast 100,000/200,000d; ❄🖥) Buffalo Hostel ticks all the boxes for the thrifty traveller: colourful six-bed dorms and five private rooms, loads of local information on where to kick on to next, and the promise of a cold beer and company at the downstairs Buffalo Pub. The friendly owners can also hook up travellers with various tours.

✖ Eating & Drinking

Local specialties include delicious savoury pancakes and excellent seafood, and there's an increasingly inventive range of international restaurants here including Japanese, Thai and Korean.

★ Tree Hugger Cafe CAFE $

(☑ 0935 983 831; www.treehugger-cafe.com; 30 Đ Nguyen Du; snacks 40,000-60,000d; ⏰7am-10pm; 🖥🍴) Splendid Tree Hugger's combo of

and Hang Toi (Dark Cave); also has multiday tours incorporating Tu Lan and Hang En and a combined jungle trek and cave tour.

🛏 Sleeping

Dong Hoi has an excellent) array of accommodation, from beachside hostels and guesthouses through to great-value hotels.

coffees, juices and Western-style snacks lures throngs of travellers and English-speaking Dong Hoi locals. There are also interesting organic and ecofriendly local products for sale, the information folders and wall maps are really worth investigating for onward travel, and excellent maps of Dong Hoi are at hand. Upstairs is a gallery/shop displaying arts and crafts from various minority peoples.

7th Heaven INTERNATIONAL $
(☑052 383 3856; www.7thheavenrestaurant. com; 39 Đ Duong Van An; meals 90,000-140,000d; ⊗10.30am-9pm Tue-Sun; ☑) This cosy, friendly restaurant and bar offers something for everyone, with everything from burgers and steaks to Thai curries and decent pizza, plus meat-free choices. The friendly service gives the place further appeal.

Tu Quy VIETNAMESE $
(17 Đ Co Tam; meals 25,000-80,000d; ⊗7am-8.30pm) This area is famous for its *banh khoai* (shrimp pancake) restaurants, of which Tu Quy is one of the best. It also does *banh cuon* (shrimp in steamed rice paper), *banh loc* (rice dumpling cake) and *nem lui* (grilled pork and lemongrass skewers). With street-side tables with the river in sight, it's in an interesting area near the market.

Buffalo Pub PUB
(www.buffalodonghoi.com; 4 Đ Nguyen Du; ⊗7am-11.30pm; ☎) This chilled spot with a penchant for natural timber is an amiable and gregarious venue for meeting other travellers over a cold beer. There's a pool table and occasional live music, or you can hijack the sound system with your own portable music device of choice. Upstairs, sleep is a short climb away at the attached hostel.

ℹ Information

Agribank (2 Đ Me Suot; ⊗7.30am-4pm Mon-Fri, to 12.30pm Sat) has an ATM and exchange services.

Tree Hugger Cafe offers tours and excellent travellers' resources, including information on local sights, and has a great map listing Vietnamese street eats plus wall maps of Phong Nha. Staff at both Nam Long hotels can organise motorbike and bicycle rentals, provide local maps and arrange bus and train tickets, while Buffalo Hostel can link you up with tours.

ℹ Getting There & Away

AIR

The airport is 6km north of town. For domestic flights, **Vietnam Airlines** (www.vietnamairlines. com) flies to/from Ho Chi Minh City and Hanoi, **Vietjet** (www.vietjetair.com) and **Jetstar Pacific Airlines** (www.jetstar.com) link Dong Hoi to HCMC.

Former air links to Hai Phong and the northern Thai city of Chiang Mai have been discontinued, but may restart at some stage.

BUS

Local buses to Phong Nha (35,000d, 90 minutes) leave from Dong Hoi's **bus station** (Đ Tran Hung Dao) from 6am to 5pm, and also run along Đ Tran Hung Dao and Đ Nguyen Du, past the Tree Hugger Cafe. Look for the blue-and-white signs and bus number B4. A taxi from Dong Hoi is around 450,000d.

From the bus station you can catch services south and north.

It's easy to leave an open-tour bus in Dong Hoi, but for a pickup go through a travel agency.

For Laos, buses leave for Vientiane daily (400,000d) and for Thakhek from Tuesday to Sunday (300,000d). Both nine-hour services run via the Cha Lo–Na Phao border crossing, where Lao visas are available.

For all up-to-date transport information, see Sy at the Nam Long Hotel or ask at the Tree Hugger Cafe (or download their app).

TRAIN

The **train station** (Ga Dong Hoi; Đ Thuan Ly) is 3km west of the centre. Trains leave for destinations including Hanoi (306,000d, 9½ to 11½ hours, six daily), Hue (104,000d, three to four hours, six daily) and Danang (168,000d, five hours, six daily): all prices quoted are for soft seats on express trains.

BUSES FROM DONG HOI

DESTINATION	COST (D)	TIME (HR)	FREQUENCY
Danang	170,000	5	5 daily
Dong Ha	60,000	2	frequent
Hanoi (via Ninh Binh)	230,000	9	4 daily
Hoi An	250,000	7	2 daily
Hue	150,000	4	frequent
Vinh	140,000	4	6 daily

SOUTH-CENTRAL VIETNAM

The highlights of south-central Vietnam include the vibrant city of Danang, the former imperial capital of Hue with its magnificent and sublime palace ruins and Confucian royal tombs, and the possibly overpopular (but undeniably stunning) historic port town of Hoi An. The best beach scenes can be found at An Bang near Hoi An and Lang Co near Danang, while for nature fans there is good hiking and birdwatching in Bach Ma National Park. Ancient Cham history is preserved in the astonishing temple architecture of My Son, while the compelling Demilitarised Zone showcases the poignant and tragic stories of the American War.

Demilitarised Zone (DMZ)

📋 0233

Most of the bases and bunkers have long vanished, but this 5km strip of land on either side of the Ben Hai River is still known by its American War moniker: the DMZ. From 1954 to 1975 it acted as a buffer between the North and the South. Ironically, the DMZ became one of the most militarised areas in the world. The area just south of the DMZ was the scene of some of the bloodiest battles in America's first televised war, turning Quang Tri, the Rockpile, Khe Sanh, Lang Vay and Hamburger Hill into household names.

There's not much left to see these day as most sites have been cleared, the land reforested or put back to use, planted with rubber and coffee. Only Ben Hai, Vinh Moc and Khe Sanh have small museums. Unless you're a veteran or military buff, you might find it a little hard to appreciate the place – which is all the more reason to hire a knowledgeable guide.

◉ Sights

★ **Vinh Moc Tunnels**   HISTORIC SITE
(40,000d; ⊘ 7am-5pm) A highly impressive complex of tunnels, Vinh Moc is the remains of a coastal North Vietnamese village that literally went underground in response to unremitting American bombing. More than 90 families disappeared into three levels of tunnels running for almost 2km, and continued to live and work while bombs rained down around them. Most of the tunnels are open to visitors and are kept in their original form (except for electric lights, a more recent addition).

Khe Sanh Combat Base   HISTORIC SITE
(museum 20,000d; ⊘ 7am-5pm) The site of the most famous siege of the American War, the USA's Khe Sanh Combat Base was never overrun, but it saw the bloodiest battle of the war. About 500 Americans, 10,000 North Vietnamese troops and uncounted civilian bystanders died around this remote highland base. It's eerily peaceful today, but in 1968 the hillsides trembled with the

---

WATCH YOUR STEP

Millions of tonnes of ordnance were dropped on Vietnam during the American War – it's estimated that about a third did not explode. Death and injury still tragically happen most days. At many places there's still a chance of encountering live mortar rounds, artillery projectiles and mines. Watch where you step and don't leave the marked paths. Never, ever touch any leftover ordnance.

It's not just the DMZ that's affected. It's estimated that as much as 20% of Vietnam remains uncleared, with more than 3.5 million mines and 800,000 tonnes of unexploded ordnance (UXO). Between 1975 and 2007, unexploded ordnance resulted in 105,000 injuries and over 45,000 deaths. Every year hundreds die and are injured – a disproportionate number of them children or people from ethnic minority groups.

The People's Army is responsible for most ongoing mine clearance. It's joined by foreign NGOs, such as the Mines Advisory Group (MAG; www.maginternational.org), who have been been clearing unexploded bombs in Vietnam for over two decades and whose efforts are well worth supporting. In 2018 alone, MAG released almost 25,000 sq metres of land by demining and destroyed almost 14,000 landmines and unexploded bombs. The US-based NGO Clear Path International also helps by assisting civilian victims of landmines and other unexploded ordinance.

Dong Ha has the excellent Mine Action Visitor Centre (p172). Do visit if you're in the area.

South-Central Vietnam

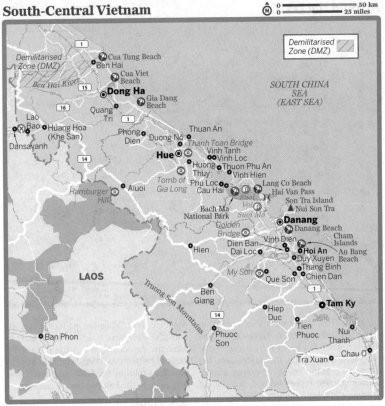

impact of 1000kg bombs, white phosphorus shells, napalm, mortars and endless artillery rounds, as desperate American forces sought to repel the North Vietnamese Army (NVA).

Quang Tri Citadel   HISTORIC SITE
(Nguyen Tri Phuong) Quang Tri once boasted an important citadel, but little of its old glory remains. In the Easter Offensive of 1972, North Vietnamese forces laid siege to and then captured the town. This provoked carpet bombing and artillery shelling by the US and South Vietnamese forces, which all but destroyed Quang Tri. Remnants of the ancient moat, ramparts and gates of the citadel remain, with cannons outside and a small museum. It's off Đ Tran Hung Dao, 1.6km north of Hwy 1.

Ben Hai River   MONUMENT
(museum 20,000d; ⊙7am-4.30pm) Once the border between North and South Vietnam, Ben Hai River's southern bank now has a grandiose reunification **monument**, its stylised palm leaves oddly resembling missiles. Cua Tung Beach's fine golden sands are just east of here. Ben Hai's northern bank is dominated by a reconstructed flag tower and a small **museum** full of war mementos. Ben Hai is 22km north of Dong Ha on Hwy 1.

Hamburger Hill   HISTORIC SITE
(Dong Ap Bia) Hamburger Hill was the site of a tumultuous battle in May 1969 between US forces and the North Vietnamese Army (NVA) over a 900m-high mountain – resulting in over 600 North Vietnamese and 72 American deaths. Today you need a special permit (US$25, obtained only in the town of Aluoi) and a guide to see the remaining trenches and bunkers. Hamburger Hill is 8km northwest of Aluoi, about 6km off Hwy 14, and less than 2km from Laos.

Truong Son National Cemetery   CEMETERY
(Nghia Trang Liet Si Quoc Gia Truong Son) A deeply evocative memorial to the legions of North Vietnamese soldiers who died along the Ho

Around the DMZ

Chi Minh Trail, this cemetery is a sobering sight. More than 10,000 graves dot these hillsides, each marked by a simple white tombstone headed by the inscription *liet si* (martyr). Many graves lie empty, simply bearing names, representing a fraction of Vietnam's 300,000 soldiers missing in action. It's 27km northwest of Dong Ha; the turn-off from Hwy 1 is close to Doc Mieu.

❶ Getting There & Around

Virtually everyone explores the DMZ on a tour. Standard tours are cheap (around US$15 to US$20 for a group day trip) and can be arranged in Hue or Dong Ha. Tam's Tours in Dong Ha is a recommended choice. Most take in the Rockpile, Khe Sanh, Vinh Moc and Doc Mieu, and leave Hue at between 6am and 7am, returning by about 6pm. From Hue, much more time is spent driving around 300km than sightseeing.

A superior experience is to see the DMZ independently. Reckon on US$120 for a car and expert guide. Leaving from Dong Ha rather than Hue means less time on the road.

Dong Ha

☑ 0233 / POP 94,000

Dong Ha is an important transport hub that sits at the intersection of Hwys 1 and 9. The town was completely flattened during the American War. While the main drag is dusty and traffic-plagued, the town does have its attractive aspects, with a string of riverside seafood restaurants. Dong Ha makes a useful base for exploring the DMZ and is the gateway town to the Lao Bao border crossing.

◉ Sights

Mine Action Visitor Centre   MUSEUM
(☑ 0935 211 281; Đ Ly Thuong Kiet; ⊗ 8am-5pm Mon-Fri, by appointment Sat & Sun) FREE Quang Tri province was the most heavily bombed part of Vietnam and it remains the most contaminated with ordnance. This museum provides an excellent historical overview – in English and Vietnamese – with photographs of the 1972 destruction of Quang Tri Citadel and of people attempting to deactivate mines with bamboo sticks. Other displays detail the tragic legacy of the defoliant Agent Orange. Call an hour ahead and Phu, the excellent English-speaking manager, will show you around the museum.

☞ Tours

DMZ Tours   MILITARY, ADVENTURE
(☑ 0914 017 835; www.dmztours.net; 113 Le Loi) Quality DMZ tours. Prices start at US$118 (two people) for a day's touring around the main war sites in a car.

★ **Tam's Tours** TOURS
(☎0905 425 912; www.tamscafe.jimdo.com; 211
Đ Ba Trieu, Tam's DMZ Cafe & Guesthouse) Excellent backpacker-priced DMZ tours using English-speaking war veterans. Tours cost US$35 to US$40 (per person per day) by motorbike, or from US$40 per car for two people or more. Tam also offers an evening street-food tour (US$15), and his DMZ Adventure Rider tours (US$55) combine spectacular scenery with motorbike transfers to and from destinations including Hue, Dong Hoi and Phong Nha.

Annam Tour HISTORY
(☎0905 140 600; www.annamtour.com) Outstanding tailor-made tours, guided by military historian Mr Vu (who speaks excellent English). Using iPads to show photographs and maps, the tours bring sights and battlegrounds to life. Trips cost around US$130 per day, and can be set up from Hue, too. Two- to three-day tours are also available.

🛏 Sleeping

**Tam's DMZ Cafe
& Guesthouse** GUESTHOUSE $
(☎0905 425 912; www.tamscafe.jimdo.com; 211
Đ Ba Trieu; s/d/tr US$7/10/15; ❈🛜) Simple but very good rooms feature at this riverside guesthouse operated by the helpful and friendly Tam, the best resource for English-speaking travellers to Dong Ha.

There's a decent cafe on-site, and Tam can arrange DMZ tours and onward transport by bus, motorbike or car. Book ahead and he'll pick you up when you arrive by bus or train at Dong Ha.

Saigon Dong Ha HOTEL $$
(☎0233-382 2276; www.saigondonghahotel.com; 20 Quach Xuan Ky; r incl breakfast from 900,000d; ❈🛜⊠) This smart hotel is a superb and stylish choice, with a decent riverside location as well as large, comfortable rooms, online specials and friendly service. The rooftop bar-cafe and the pool area (6am to 10pm) are top spots for a beer or a coffee, even if you're not staying here, while the riverside tennis courts out back are excellent for a workout.

🍴 Eating & Drinking

Dong Ha is famous for seafood. Head to the strip of riverside restaurants on Đ Hoang Dieu for wonderful *cua rang me* (crab in tamarind sauce), *vem nuong* (grilled clams) and steamed or roasted squid.

Tam's DMZ Cafe & Guesthouse CAFE $
(☎0905 425 912; www.tamscafe.jimdo.com; 211
Đ Ba Trieu; meals US$2-3; ⊙8am-10pm; 🛜) Vietnamese food, pizza, smoothies and juices all feature at this excellent spot, with decent accommodation too. It's run by the ever-helpful and friendly Tam, partly with the help of his brother.

GONE UNDERGROUND

In 1966 the USA began a massive aerial and artillery bombardment of North Vietnam. Just north of the Demilitarised Zone (DMZ), the villagers of Vinh Moc found themselves living in one of the most heavily bombed and shelled strips of land on the planet. Small family shelters could not withstand this onslaught, and villagers either fled or began tunnelling by hand and with simple tools into the red-clay earth.

The Viet Cong (VC) found it useful to have a base here and encouraged the villagers to stay. After 18 months of tunnelling, an enormous complex was established, creating new homes on three levels from 12m to 23m below ground, plus meeting rooms and even a maternity unit (17 babies were born underground). Whole families lived here, their longest sojourn lasting 10 days and 10 nights. Later, the civilians and VC were joined by North Vietnamese soldiers, whose mission was to keep communication and supply lines open to nearby Con Co island.

Other villages north of the DMZ also built tunnel systems, but none was as elaborate as Vinh Moc (p170). The poorly constructed tunnels of Vinh Quang village (at the mouth of the Ben Hai River) collapsed after repeated bombing, killing everyone inside.

US warships stationed off the coast consistently bombarded the Vinh Moc tunnels (craters are still visible), and occasionally the tunnel mouths that faced the sea were struck by naval gunfire. The only ordnance that posed a real threat was the 'drilling bomb'. It scored a direct hit once, but failed to explode, and no one was injured; the inhabitants adapted the bomb hole for use as an air shaft.

ⓘ GETTING TO LAOS: DONG HA TO SAVANNAKHET

Getting to the border The Lao Bao–Dansavanh border crossing, on the Sepon River (Song Xe Pon), is one of the most-popular and least-problematic border crossings between Laos and Vietnam. Buses to Savannakhet in Laos run from Hue via Dong Ha and Lao Bao. From Hue, there's a daily 7am air-conditioned bus (350,000d, 9½ hours) that stops at the Dong Ha bus station around 9.30am to pick up more passengers. It's also easy to cross the border on your own; Dong Ha is the gateway. Buses leave the town to Lao Bao (60,000d, two hours) roughly every 15 minutes. From here *xe om* charge 15,000d to the border. You can check schedules and book tickets at Tam's DMZ Cafe & Guesthouse (p173). Tam's also books tickets to Vientiane (14 hours), Thakhek (10 hours) and Pakse (10 hours); there is no longer a bus to Lao Bao from Pakse, however. The bus passes the nearby border of La Lay but there is no visa on arrival there (if you have a visa already, it's no problem). It's not possible to cross on motorbike from Vietnam at the Lao Bao border.

At the border The border posts (7am to 6pm) are a few hundred metres apart. Lao visas are available on arrival, but Vietnamese visas need to be arranged in advance. There are several serviceable hotels on the Vietnamese side. Try not to change large amounts of currency in Lao Bao: money changers offer terrible rates; the border accepts Laotian kip or US dollars for a Lao visa.

Moving on *Sawngthaew* head regularly to Sepon, from where you can get a bus or another *sawngthaew* to Savannakhet.

Hasa Restaurant   SEAFOOD $
(Nha Hang Hasa; www.facebook.com/nhahang hasa; cnr Đ Duy Tan & Đ Dai Co Viet; meals 80,000d; ⏰24hr; 🕐) This large, open and garrulous *hai san* (seafood) corner restaurant serves delicious fish, crab, prawn, mussels, sea snails and all manner of food from the briny depths, all well prepared and highly tasty. Best done as a group so you can all share platters and get into the sociable spirit: order up cheap beer as a liquid accompaniment.

Co Dau   VEGETARIAN $
(Quan Chay Co Dau; Hung Vuong Park; meals 50,000d; ⏰7am-11pm; 🍴) Vegetarians can avoid accidentally ordering pork, beef or chicken at this decent vegetarian restaurant in Hung Vuong Park (Cong Vien Hung Vuong). Dishes run from *mien xao* (fried vermicelli noodles) and *nem ran* (spring rolls) to *lau thai* (Thai hotpot), *nam kho to* (braised mushrooms), *ca tim ap chao* (pan-fried aubergine), *chao bot loc* (rice porridge) and much more.

ⓘ Information

Sacombank (43 Đ Tran Hung Dao) has a 24-hour ATM that takes foreign cards.

For impartial travel and tourist information, and a useful city map, head to Tam's DMZ Cafe & Guesthouse.

ⓘ Getting There & Away

BUS

Buses from the **Dong Hua Bus Station** (Ben Xe Khach Dong Ha; ☏ 053 385 1488; 68 Đ Le Duan) depart regularly to Hue (60,000d, 90 minutes), Danang (120,000d, 3½ hours), Khe Sanh (50,000d, 90 minutes) and Lao Bao (60,000d, two hours).

Buses to Dong Hoi (60,000d, two hours) pass through from Hue but you'll need to reserve a seat ahead. Direct buses for Son Trach and Phong Nha-Ke Bang National Park leave three times a day (170,000d, three hours). Bookings can be made through Tam's DMZ Cafe & Guesthouse.

CAR & MOTORCYCLE

A one-way car trip to the Lao Bao border will set you back US$45 and is a good option for three or more passengers. Motorbikes can be hired from US$6 per day. For motorcycle transfers to and from destinations including Hue, Dong Hoi and Phong Nha, contact Tam's Tours (p173) and ask about the DMZ Adventure Rider tours.

TRAIN

Dong Ha's **train station** (Ga Dong Ha; 2 Đ Le Thanh Ton), 2km south of the Dong Ha Bridge, has trains to destinations including Hanoi (sleeper from 622,000d, 11 to 14 hours, five daily), Dong Hoi (hard seat from 60,000d, 1½ to 2½ hours, six daily) and Hue (hard seat from 45,000d, 1½ to 2½ hours, six daily).

Hue

📞 0234 / POP 455,000

Pronounced 'hway', this deeply evocative capital of the Nguyen emperors still resonates with the glories of imperial Vietnam, even though many of its finest buildings were destroyed during the American War.

Hue owes its charm partly to its location on the Perfume River – picturesque on a clear day, atmospheric even in less-flattering weather. Today the city blends new and old, as sleek modern hotels contrast with the crumbling 19th-century Citadel walls and gates.

Hue remains a tranquil, conservative city with just the right concentration of nightlife.

History

In 1802, Emperor Gia Long founded the Nguyen dynasty, moved the capital from Hanoi to Hue in an effort to unite northern and southern Vietnam, and commenced building the Citadel. The city prospered, but its rulers struggled to counter the growing influence of France.

French forces responded to a Vietnamese attack in 1885 by storming the Citadel, burning the imperial library and removing every object of value. The emperors continued to reside in Hue, but were excluded from events of national importance.

The attention again shifted to Hue during the 1968 Tet Offensive. While the Americans concentrated on holding Khe Sanh, North Vietnamese and Viet Cong (VC) forces seized Hue, an audacious assault that commanded headlines across the globe.

During the 3½ weeks that the North controlled the Citadel, more than 2500 people (including soldiers from the Army of the Republic of Vietnam, wealthy merchants, government workers, monks, priests and intellectuals) were killed. The USA and South Vietnamese responded by levelling whole neighbourhoods, battering the Citadel and even using napalm on the imperial palace. Approximately 10,000 people died in Hue, including thousands of VC troops, 400 South Vietnamese soldiers and 150 US Marines – but most of those killed were civilians.

Late journalist Gavin Young's 1997 memoir, *A Wavering Grace,* is a moving account of his 30-year relationship with a family from Hue, and is a fine literary companion to the city.

⊙ Sights

Most of Hue's principal sights lie within the moats of its Citadel and Imperial Enclosure. Other museums and pagodas are dotted around the city. The royal tombs (p187) are south of Hue. A good-value 'package tour ticket' (adult/child 360,000/70,000d) is available that includes admission to the Citadel and the tombs of Gia Long (p191), Khai Dinh (p189) and Minh Mang (p189).

⊙ Inside the Citadel

Built between 1804 and 1833, the splendid and sublime Kinh Thanh (Citadel) is still the heart of Hue. Heavily fortified, it consists of 2m-thick, 10km-long walls, a moat (30m across and 4m deep) and 10 gateways.

The Citadel has distinct sections. The Imperial Enclosure and Purple Forbidden City (p179) formed the epicentre of Vietnamese royal life. On the southwestern side were temple compounds, while there were residences in the northwest, gardens in the northeast and, in the north, the Mang Ca Fortress (still a military base).

The following Citadel sights are presented as a walking tour, which takes an anticlockwise route around the enclosure.

At a leisurely stroll, many of the less-visited areas are highly atmospheric and sublime. It's best to choose a day with decent weather, with late afternoon (when there are fewer visitors and the sun is setting) a superb time to visit. There are little cafes and souvenir stands dotted around. Restoration and reconstruction are ongoing.

★**Imperial Enclosure**   HISTORIC SITE
(Huang Thanh; adult/child 150,000/30,000d; ⏱7am-6pm) The Imperial Enclosure or Imperial City is a citadel-within-a-citadel, housing the emperor's residence, temples and palaces, and the main buildings of state, within 6m-high, 2.5km-long walls. What's left is only a fraction of the original – the enclosure was badly bombed during the French and American Wars, and only 20 of its 148 buildings survived. Expect a lot of broken masonry, rubble, cracked tiling and weeds as you work your way around, but it's a fascinating site and easily worth half a day.

➡ Ngo Mon Gate

(Meridian Gate) The principal entrance to the Imperial Enclosure is Ngo Mon Gate, which faces the Flag Tower. The central

A B C D

1

Tinh Tam Lake

Đ Tinh Tam

Đ Nhat Le

Đ Ngo Si Lien

Đ Mai Thuc Loan

33

Đ Nguyen Dieu

Đ Le Thanh Ton

2

THE CITADEL

Đ Phung Hung

Đ Doan Thi Diem

Đ Dang Dung

Đ Nguyen Chi Dieu

Đ Han Thuyen

Đ Tue Tinh

Đ Dang Thai Than

3

Đ Dinh Cong Trang

3

Đ Le Truc

Đ Tong Duy Tan

10

6

Đ Le Truc

1

12

Imperial
Enclosure

14

7

Đ Ngo
Thoi Nhiem

4

13

Đ Nguyen
Thien Thuat

Đ Le Huan

Đ 23 Thang 8

4

*To Mieu
Temple
Complex*

8

Đ Tran Nguyen Han

2

Đ Dang Tran Con

34

*Phu Xuan
Bridge*

5

Đ Ton That Thiep

Đ Le Duan

6

An Hoa
(800m)

Đ Le Loi

Đ Le Lai

19

7

Đ Tran
Thuc

Đ Ngo Quyen

(150m);
Bao Quoc Pagoda (450m)

Đ Le Loi

Đ Nguyen Hue

A B C D

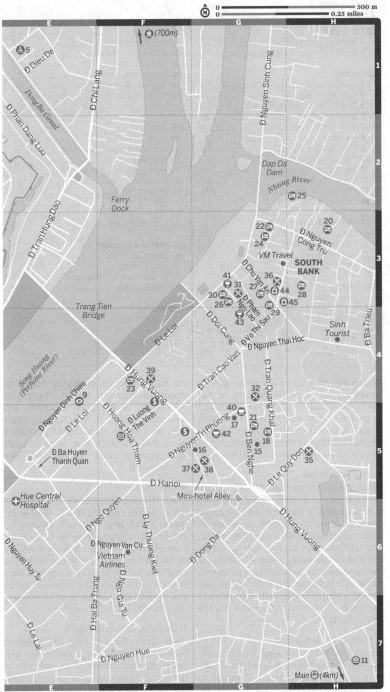

Hue

Top Sights
1 Imperial Enclosure ... B3
2 To Mieu Temple Complex ... B4

Sights
3 Co Ha Gardens ... B3
4 Dien Tho Residence ... A4
5 Dieu De National Pagoda ... E1
6 Emperor's Reading Room ... B3
7 Halls of the Mandarins ... B4
8 Ngo Mon Gate ... B4
9 Night Market ... E4
10 Purple Forbidden City ... B3
11 Royal Fine Arts Museum ... H7
12 Royal Theatre ... B3
13 Thai Hoa Palace ... B4
14 Truong San Residence ... A3

Activities, Courses & Tours
15 Bee Bee Travel Tours ... G5
16 Café on Thu Wheels ... G5
17 Hue Adventures ... G5
Stop & Go Café ... (see 39)

Sleeping
18 Alba Spa Hotel ... G5
19 Azerai La Residence ... C7
20 Canary Boutique Hotel ... H3
21 Cherish Hotel ... G5
22 Home Hotel ... G3
23 Hotel Saigon Morin ... F4
24 Hue Nino ... G3
25 Hue Riverside Villa ... H2
26 Moonlight Hotel Hue ... G3
27 Orchid Hotel ... G3
28 Poetic Hue Hostel ... H3
29 Rosaleen Boutique Hotel ... G3
30 Vietnam Backpackers' Hostel ... G3

Eating
31 Gecko Pub ... G3
32 Hanh Restaurant ... G4
33 Hong Mai ... C2
34 Les Jardins de la Carambole ... B5
35 Lien Hoa ... H5
36 Madam Thu ... G3
37 Nina's Cafe ... G5
38 Nook Cafe & Bar ... G5
39 Stop & Go Café ... F4

Drinking & Nightlife
40 Cong Caphe ... G5
41 DMZ Travel ... G3
42 La Boulangerie Française ... G5
43 Why Not? Bar ... G4

Shopping
44 Blue de Hue ... G3
45 Spiral Foundation Healing the Wounded Heart Center ... G3

passageway with its yellow doors was reserved for the use of the emperor, as was the bridge across the lotus pond. Others had to use the gates to either side and the paths around the pond. On top of the gate is Ngu Phung (Belvedere of the Five Phoenixes); on its upper level is a huge drum and bell.

➡ Thai Hoa Palace

(Palace of Supreme Harmony) This 1803 palace is a spacious hall with an ornate timber roof supported by 80 carved and lacquered columns. It was used for the emperor's official receptions and important ceremonies. On state occasions the emperor sat on his elevated throne, facing visitors entering via the Ngo Mon Gate. No photos are permitted, but be sure to see the impressive audiovisual display, which gives an excellent overview of the entire Citadel, its architecture and the historical context.

➡ Halls of the Mandarins

Located immediately behind Thai Hoa Palace, on either side of a courtyard, these halls were used by mandarins as offices and to prepare for court ceremonies. The hall on the right showcases intriguing old photographs (including boy-king Vua Duya Tan's coronation), gilded Buddha statues and assorted imperial curios. Behind the courtyard are the ruins of the Can Chanh Palace, where two wonderful long galleries, painted in gleaming scarlet lacquer, have been reconstructed.

➡ Royal Theatre

(Duyen Thi Duong; ☎054 352 4162; www.nhanhac.com.vn; performances 200,000d; ⏲40min performances 10am & 3pm) The Royal Theatre, begun in 1826 and later home to the National Conservatory of Music, has been rebuilt on its former foundations. When performances aren't on, it's free to sit in the plush chairs or examine the fascinating display of masks and musical instruments from Vietnamese theatre, with English descriptions.

➡ Emperor's Reading Room

(Royal Library, Thai Binh Lau) The exquisite (though crumbling) little two-storey Emperor's Reading Room was the only part of the Purple Forbidden City to escape damage during the French reoccupation of Hue in

1947. The Gaudí-esque, yin-yang roof mosaics outside are in stark contrast to the sombre, renovated interior, the circular hallway of which you can walk around on the small ground level. The exterior features poems by Emperor Khai Dinh on either side; the three *chu nho* characters above the main portico translate as 'Building of Great Peace'.

➡ Co Ha Gardens

(Royal Gardens) Occupying the northeast corner of the Imperial Enclosure, these delightful gardens were developed by the first four emperors of the Nguyen dynasty but fell into disrepair. They've been beautifully recreated in the last few years, and are dotted with little gazebo-style pavilions and ponds. They are an absolute picture and this is one of the most peaceful spots in the entire Citadel.

➡ Purple Forbidden City

(Tu Cam Thanh) In the very centre of the Imperial Enclosure, there's almost nothing left of the once-magnificent Purple Forbidden City. This was a citadel-within-a-citadel-within-a-citadel and was reserved solely for the personal use of the emperor – the only servants allowed into this compound were eunuchs, who would pose no threat to the royal concubines. The Purple Forbidden City was almost entirely destroyed in the wars, and its crumbling remains are now overgrown with weeds.

➡ Truong San Residence

(Cung Truong Sanh) In 1844, Emperor Thieu Tri described this as one of Hue's most beautiful spots, but it was devastated by war. Check out the superb entrance gate with prancing dragons and phoenixes, and the oval moat. The exterior has been restored, while the interior remains empty, except for its elaborate columns and tiles.

➡ Dien Tho Residence

(Cung Dien Tho) The stunning, partially ruined Dien Tho Residence (1804) once comprised the apartments and audience hall of the Queen Mothers of the Nguyen dynasty. The audience hall houses an exhibition of photos illustrating its former use, and there is a display of embroidered royal garments. Just outside, a pleasure pavilion above a lily pond has been transformed into a cafe worthy of a refreshment stop.

➡ To Mieu Temple Complex

Taking up the southwest corner of the Imperial Enclosure, this highly impressive walled complex has been beautifully restored. The imposing three-tiered **Hien Lam Pavilion** sits on the south side of the complex; it dates from 1824. On the other side of a courtyard is the solemn **To Mieu Temple**, housing shrines to each of the emperors, topped by their photos. Between these two temples are **Nine Dynastic Urns** *(dinh)* cast between 1835 and 1836, each dedicated to one Nguyen sovereign.

◉ Outside the Citadel

A selection of pagodas and museums belonging to Hue, yet outside the walls of the Citadel, lies sprinkled around town on either side of the river.

Dieu De National Pagoda   BUDDHIST TEMPLE
(Quoc Tu Dieu De; 102 Đ Bach Dang) FREE Overlooking Dong Ba Canal, this pagoda was built under Emperor Thieu Tri's rule (1841–47) and is celebrated for its four low towers, one on either side of the gate and two flanking the sanctuary. The pavilions on either side of the main sanctuary entrance contain the 18 La Han *(arhat),* whose rank is just below that of bodhisattva, and the eight Kim Cang, protectors of Buddha. In the back row of the main dais is Thich Ca Buddha, flanked by two assistants.

Royal Fine Arts Museum   MUSEUM
(150 Đ Nguyen Hue; ◷ 6.30am-5.30pm summer, 7am-5pm winter) FREE This museum is located in the baroque-influenced **An Dinh Palace**, commissioned by Emperor Khai Dinh in 1918 and full of elaborate murals, floral motifs and trompe l'oeil details. Emperor Bao Dai lived here with his family after abdicating in 1945. Inside you'll find some outstanding ceramics, paintings, furniture, silverware, porcelain and royal clothing, though information is a little lacking.

Bao Quoc Pagoda   BUDDHIST TEMPLE
(Ham Long Hill) FREE Founded in 1670, this hilltop pagoda is on the southern bank of the Perfume River and has a striking triple-gated entrance reached via a wide staircase. On the right is a centre for training monks, which has been functioning since 1940.

Night Market   MARKET
(Đ Nguyen Dinh Chieu; ◷ 7-10pm) This nightly market is mainly focused on local arts and crafts, but there are also simple cafes and bars perfect for a riverside snack and a drink.

Hue's Imperial Enclosure

EXPLORING THE SITE

An incongruous combination of meticulously restored palaces and pagodas, ruins and rubble, the Imperial Enclosure is approached from the south through the outer walls of the Citadel. It's best to tackle the site as a walking tour, winding your way around the structures in an anticlockwise direction.

You'll pass through the monumental **❶ Ngo Mon Gate**, where the ticket office is located. This dramatic approach quickens the pulse as you enter this citadel-within-a-citadel. Directly ahead is the **❷ Thai Hoa Palace**, where the emperor would greet offical visitors from his elevated throne. Continuing north you'll cross a small courtyard to the twin **❸ Halls of the Mandarins**, where mandarins once had their offices and prepared for ceremonial occasions.

To the northeast is the Royal Theatre, where traditional dance performances are held. Next you'll be able to get a glimpse of the Emperor's Reading Room, built by Thieu Tri and used as a place of retreat. Just east of here are the lovely Co Ha Gardens. Wander their pathways, dotted with hundreds of bonsai trees and potted plants, which have been restored.

Guarding the far north of the complex is the **❹ Tu Vo Phuong Pavilion**, from where you can follow a moat to the Truong San residence. Then loop back south via the **❺ Dien Tho Residence** and finally view the beautifully restored temple compound of To Mieu, perhaps the most rewarding part of the entire enclosure to visit, including its fabulous **❻ Nine Dynastic Urns**.

TOP TIPS

➡ Allow half a day to explore the Citadel.

➡ Drink vendors are dotted around the site, but the best places to take a break are the delightful Co Ha Gardens, the Tu Vo Phuong Pavilion and the Dien Tho Residence (the last two also serve food).

➡ Consider visiting later in the day to see the Citadel in late afternoon light.

Dien Tho Residence
This pretty corner of the complex, with its low structures and pond, was the residence of many Queen Mothers. The earliest structures here date from 1804.

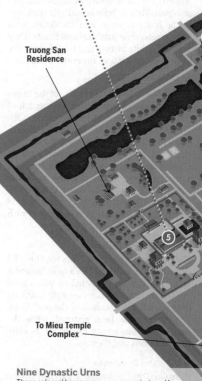

Truong San Residence

To Mieu Temple Complex

Nine Dynastic Urns
These colossal bronze urns were commissioned by Emperor Minh Mang and cast between 1835 and 1836. They're embellished with decorative elements including landscapes, rivers, flowers and animals.

Tu Vo Phuong Pavilion

The two-storey Tu Vo Phuong Pavilion, elevated above a moat, was once a defence bastion for the northern part of the Imperial Enclosure. It combines both European and Vietnamese architectural styles (note the elaborate roof dragons).

Halls of the Mandarins

Unesco-sponsored conservation work is ongoing in the eastern hall here to preserve the elaborate ceiling and wall murals.

Emperor's Reading Room

Co Ha Gardens

Royal Theatre

③

②

①

⑥

Ngo Mon Gate

A huge, grandiose structure that guards the main approach to the Imperial Enclosure, this gateway has a fortified lower level and a more architecturally elaborate upper part. It dates from 1833.

Thai Hoa Palace

Be sure to check out this palace's incredible ironwood columns, painted in 12 coats of brilliant scarlet and gold lacquer. The structure was saved from collapse by restoration work in the 1990s.

PERFUME RIVER BOAT TRIPS

Many sights around Hue, including Thien Mu Pagoda and several of the royal tombs, can be reached by boat via the Perfume River. Most hotels and travellers' cafes offer shared day tours from US$5 to US$20 per person. Better ones start with a morning river cruise, stopping at pagodas and temples, then after lunch a minibus travels to the main tombs before returning to Hue. On the cheaper options you'll often have to hire a motorbike to get from the moorings to the tombs, or walk in tropical heat.

At the moorings on the south side of the river you can theoretically negotiate your own route. Rates for chartering a boat start at US$10 for an hour's cruise, but these boats are slow. A full day is needed for the more impressive, distant tombs. Be clear on your requirements, preferably in writing.

🞂 Tours

You can hire a scooter to see many of the sights around town, otherwise there's no shortage of tour outfits that can help you explore in more comfort. A lot of the principal sights can be lassoed into a one-day expedition, taking in the Thien Mu Pagoda, the Tomb of Tu Duc, the Tomb of Khai Dinh and other imperial mausoleums and sights, but more ambitious multiday options also exist, extending to the Hai Van Pass, the DMZ and more distant destinations.

Tran Van Thinh   TOURS
(☑ 0905 731 537; www.tranvanthinhtours.com; half-day tours per person from US$15) Thinh is a knowledgeable local motorbike guide who can arrange local city tours and explorations of the royal tombs. A long-time resident of Hue, Thinh speaks excellent English and also runs DMZ tours (US$45), tours to Hoi An (US$50) and Ho Chi Minh Trail tours (US$70).

Oriental Sky Travel   ADVENTURE
(☑ 0985 555 827; www.orientalskytravel.com) Helmed by the experienced and friendly Shi, this Hue-based tour company arranges active trips including hiking in Bach Ma National Park, and also mountain biking, kayaking and caving around Phong Nha-Ke Bang National Park and the DMZ.

An epic eight-day/seven-night cycling tour down the Ho Chi Minh Trail from Dong Hoi to Hoi An starts at US$1188 per person, and other shorter trips can also be arranged.

A combined Hoi An–Hanoi trip followed by a Halong Bay cruise is also available.

Stop & Go Café   DRIVING
(☑ 0905 126 767; www.stopandgo-hue.com; 3 Đ Hung Vuong) Customised motorbike and car tours: a one-day tour of three Hue top sights is US$10 per person for four people; a DMZ car tour guided by a Vietnamese war veteran costs US$59 per person for four people. Guided trips to Hoi An stopping at beaches are also recommended. Note: there are similarly named, unrelated businesses elsewhere. Also has a travellers' cafe with quality food.

Hue Adventures   TOURS
(☑ 0905 771 602; www.hueadventures.com; 44 Đ Nguyen Tri Phuong) Well-regarded motorbike and jeep tours around Hue, and also motorbike transfers from Hue to Hoi An, the DMZ and Phong Nha.

Vietnam Motor Trail   TOURS
(☑ 0935 782 533; www.vietnammotortrail.com; tours from US$15) Quy is a friendly and trustworthy motorbike guide who can arrange scenic transfers via the Hai Van Pass to Hoi An, as well as local sightseeing around Hue and the DMZ, and longer trips exploring all parts of Vietnam.

Hue Flavor   FOOD & DRINK
(☑ 0905 937 006; www.hueflavor.com; per person US$49) Excellent street-food tours exploring the delights of Hue cuisine; more than 15 dishes are sampled across four hours, with two trips (one at 9am and the other at 2pm) including a visit to Dong Ba Market. Transport is by *cyclo* (pedicab).

Café on Thu Wheels   TOURS
(☑ 054 383 2241; 3/34 Nguyen Tri Phuong) Inexpensive cycle hire, and motorbike, minibus and car tours around Hue and the DMZ. Can also arrange transfers to Hoi An by motorbike (US$45) or car (US$55).

Bee Bee Travel Tours   WALKING
(☑ 0935 616 090; www.beebeetravel.com; 65 Ben Nghe; tours from US$17) A variety of walking tours, including a tour of the Imperial City at 6.30am and 2pm. The popular Hue Revolution Walking Tour (US$25) covers sights associated with the French occupation and the American War. Other tours delve into Hue's food scene, countryside tours and a cooking class. For every tour booked, US$1 goes to families affected by Agent Orange.

⚜️ Festivals & Events

Festival of Hue
PERFORMING ARTS

(www.huefestival.com; ☺ Apr, May or Jun) Held in even-numbered years, this biennial arts festival features local and international artists and performers.

🛏️ Sleeping

Hue accommodation rates are well below those in Hanoi or HCMC. The main tourist enclave is between Đ Le Loi and Đ Vo Thi Sau, and other good options are along Đ Nguyen Cong Tru. There's a decent selection of very affordable and quiet midrange hotels if you want a step up from the busier and more gregarious hostels.

Poetic Hue Hostel
HOSTEL $

(☎ 0918 342 138; 24/26 Đ Vo Thi Sau; dm/d/f from US$7/13/25; ❄🌐) In a whitewashed villa down a quiet back lane, this is a good alternative to Hue's busier hostels. Local families and birdsong give the location a neighbourhood ambience, but restaurants and bars are nearby and rooms are spacious and relaxing. Some rooms have balconies.

Canary Boutique Hotel
BOUTIQUE HOTEL $

(☎ 0234-393 6447; www.canaryboutiquehotel.com; Lane 8, 43 Đ Nguyen Cong Tru; r incl breakfast US$18-24; ❄🌐) This clean, budget place has professional staff, a great breakfast menu with free seconds, and competitively priced tours, with a bathtub the cherry on top after a long day at the Citadel or nearby bars. If you can't find the hotel's small lane, enquire at the sister Canary Hotel on the main road.

Home Hotel
HOTEL $

(☎ 0234-383 0014; www.huehomehotel.com; 8 Đ Nguyen Cong Tru; r US$17-25; ❄🌐) Run by a really friendly team, the welcoming Home Hotel has a youthful, hip vibe, and spacious rooms arrayed across several levels. Ask to book a room overlooking Đ Nguyen Cong Tru for a compact balcony, French doors and views of the river. The cheapest rooms come without windows. There's a gorgeous old staircase and a lovey owner, but no lift.

Hue Nino
GUESTHOUSE $

(☎ 054 382 2064; www.hueninohotel.com; 14 Đ Nguyen Cong Tru; r incl breakfast US$18-25; ❄🌐) This family-owned, warm and welcoming 16-room guesthouse has an artistic flavour, with stylish furniture, artwork and smallish rooms with minibar, cable TV and quality beds. There's a generous breakfast.

Vietnam Backpackers' Hostel
HOSTEL $

(☎ 0234-393 3423; www.vietnambackpackerhostels.com; 10 Đ Pham Ngu Lao; incl breakfast dm US$6-12, d/tr from US$15/20; ❄🌐) Thanks to its central location, eager-to-please staff, good info and sociable bar-restaurant that hosts happy hour and big sporting events, this place is a backpackers' mecca. Dorms are well designed, with air-conditioning and lockers, and a mix of single and double bunk beds and female-only dorms.

★ Hue Riverside Villa
BOUTIQUE HOTEL $$

(☎ 0905 771 602; www.hueriversidevilla.com; 16/7 Đ Nguyen Cong Tru; tw/d incl breakfast US$70-80, f US$95; ❄🌐) A short walk from decent restaurants, Hue Riverside Villa combines five whitewashed and red-brick bungalows with a relaxing and breezy shared garden and a quiet, absolute edge-of-the-river location. Adorned with warm timber, the bathrooms are especially pleasant, decor is crisp and modern, and the switched-on English-speaking owner offers tours and plenty of local information. Prices can drop to around US$36 per night in the low season.

★ Tam Tinh Vien
BOUTIQUE HOTEL $$

(☎ 054 3519 990, 091 4019 983; www.huehomestay.wevina.vn; Long Ha village; r US$49-56; ❄🌐) Around 6km from Hue in Long Ha village, tranquil and delightful Tam Tinh Vien is called a homestay but is really a delightful boutique guesthouse. Arrayed around a small pool and verdant garden, spacious villas with four-poster beds are imbued with a chic Asian aesthetic. Borrow a bike to make the 30-minute journey into Hue – a taxi is around 100,000d.

Rosaleen Boutique Hotel
BOUTIQUE HOTEL $$

(☎ 0234-394 6555; www.rosaleenhotel.com; 36 Đ Chu Van An; r/ste from US$40/60; ❄🌐) Renovations at the quiet 56-room Rosaleen have energised and smartened up this very decent central choice for travellers seeking a swimming pool and one of the city's best breakfast buffets. A stylish, heritage vibe lingers in the spacious rooms, and the team at reception are unfailingly friendly and helpful. Some of the deluxe rooms come with balcony.

Cherish Hotel
HOTEL $$

(☎ 0234-394 3943; www.cherishhotel.com; 57-59 Ben Nghe; r from US$50; ❄🌐) The very pleasant and quite elegant 98-room Cherish has smiling staff at reception, superb breakfasts, a 2nd-floor spa, a small pool, three restaurants, a bar, gym and a central location. Little touches, such as fruit waiting in your room when you arrive, make all the difference, while some doubles come with balconies.

Alba Spa Hotel
BOUTIQUE HOTEL $$

(☑ 0234-382 8444; www.albaboutiquehotels.com; 29 Đ Tran Quang Khai; r US$70-110; ⊝ ❄ ⓡ ☎) This lovely hotel combines cool and classy rooms with excellent service and a spa centre downstairs. The compact indoor pool is a welcoming choice after after a spa treatment, and the breakfast spread – including local Hue culinary specialities – is one of the city's best. The hotel's location is in a quiet back street, just a short walk from all the action.

Moonlight Hotel Hue
HOTEL $$

(☑ 054 397 9797; www.moonlighthue.com; 20 Đ Pham Ngu Lao; r US$60-80, ste US$120-150; ⊝ ❄ ⓡ ☎) This efficient Hue hotel charges modest bucks for very high-spec rooms with polished wooden floors, marble-clad bathrooms (with tubs) and lavish furnishings. Pay a bit more for a balcony with a Perfume River view. The pool area is small and covered, and there are good rooftop drinks in the Sirius bar.

Orchid Hotel
HOTEL $$

(☑ 054 383 1177; www.orchidhotel.com.vn; 30a Đ Chu Van An; r incl breakfast US$33-47; ⊝ ❄ ⓡ) This modern and central hotel delivers warm service – staff really make an effort. Accommodation is also excellent: all options have laminate flooring and bright scatter cushions, while some pricier rooms even have a Jacuzzi with city views. Your complimentary breakfast is decent (eggs are cooked to order) and children are well looked after.

★ Azerai La Residence
HOTEL $$$

(☑ 0234-383 7475; www.azerai.com/la-residence-hue; 5 Đ Le Loi; r from US$240; ⊝ ❄ ⓡ ☎) Now extensively renovated and run by Azerai, the former 122-room residence of the French Résident Superieur radiates art deco glamour, with original features and period detailing. You can gaze at the Perfume River from the 30m pool or be pampered in the heavenly spa. Rooms are sumptuously appointed, the restaurants are excellent and service is top-notch.

Hotel Saigon Morin
HISTORIC HOTEL $$$

(☑ 054 382 3526; www.morinhotel.com.vn; 30 Đ Le Loi; r US$90-120, ste US$170-500; ⊝ ❄ ⓡ ☎)

Built in 1901, this was the first hotel in central Vietnam and once the hub of French colonial life in Hue. The grand building is very classy, with accommodation set around inner gardens and a small pool. Rooms are lovely, with plush carpets and period detail; river-view rooms come at a premium. The hotel served as the University of Hue between 1957 and 1990.

✕ Eating

We have the famed fussy eater Emperor Tu Duc to thank for the culinary variety of Hue.

Vegetarian food has a long tradition in Hue. Stalls in Dong Ba Market serve it on the first and 15th days of the lunar month, while Lien Hoa is a super vegetarian choice every day.

Hue also has great street food. Consider a street-food tour with Hue Flavor (p182).

★ Madam Thu
VIETNAMESE $

(45 Đ Vo Thị Sau; meals 100,000d; ⊙ 8am-10pm) Ever-stuffed and frugal-looking Madam Thu draws in the crowds for its superb menu and lovely, very polite and helpful staff. The mushroom-and-carrot fried spring rolls (50,000d) are crispy and divine, while the peanut-topped tofu with vermicelli noodles and peanut sauce is up there with the very best. For every meal served the restaurant donates 2000d to underprivileged children in and around Hue.

★ Hanh Restaurant
VIETNAMESE $

(☑ 0905 520 512; 11 Pho Duc Chinh; meals 30,000-100,000d; ⊙ 10am-9pm) Newbies to Hue specialities should start at this busy restaurant. Order the five-dish set menu (120,000d) for a speedy lesson in banh khoai, banh beo (steamed rice cakes topped with shrimp and spring onions), and divine nem lui wrapped in rice paper and herbs. Ask the patient staff how to devour everything.

Nook Cafe & Bar
VIETNAMESE, CAFE $

(☑ 0935 069 741; www.facebook.com/nook cafebarhue; 7/34 Đ Nguyen Tri Phuong; meals 50,000-120,000d; ⊙ 8am-10pm; ⓡ ☑) Near a tangle of cheaper accommodation and travel agencies, Nook's breezy upstairs location is a good spot for well-executed Vietnamese dishes and Western comfort food like veggie burgers and toasted sandwiches. Top marks for the quirky decor, colourful tablecloths and lanterns, music (The B-52's!), charming staff and refreshing and rejuvenating fresh juices and smoothies.

Gecko Pub
CAFE $

(9 Đ Pham Ngu Lao; meals 40,000-110,000d; ☺8am-midnight; �📶) Harbouring a laid-back vibe (no football TV), this Pham Ngu Lao spot combines friendly service and Asian-chic decor along with the best street-side tables in town, while the food is a versatile mix of Western and Vietnamese favourites. Sit upstairs on the wooden terrace for views of the street and tuck into pizza, pad thai, pasta, steaks and burgers. Cocktails are truly top drawer.

Lien Hoa
VEGETARIAN $

(☎054 381 2456; 3 Đ Le Quy Don; meals 50,000-80,000d; ☺6.30am-9pm; ✎) This ever-popular and no-nonsense open-air vegetarian restaurant is renowned for filling food at bargain prices. Fresh *banh beo*, noodle dishes, crispy fried jackfruit and cauliflower fried with capsicum all deliver; wash it down with a *tra gung* (ginger tea). The menu has rough English translations. The restaurant's name means 'Lotus'.

Stop & Go Café
INTERNATIONAL $

(www.stopandgo-hue.com; 3 Đ Hung Vuong; meals 35,000-90,000d; ☺7am-10pm; 📶) This atmospheric and very friendly spot serves smiles and decent Vietnamese and backpacker fare: *banh beo*, *banh cuon*, beef noodle soup, spring rolls, tacos, pizza and pasta, and filling Western breakfasts. It's worth dropping by for the excellent travel information and helpful staff.

Hong Mai
VIETNAMESE $

(110 Đ Dinh Tien Toang; meals from 35,000d; ☺11am-8pm) After visiting the Citadel, try this excellent Vietnamese place with aluminium furniture that draws a local crowd for superior versions of two local street-food classics. The *banh khoai* are crammed with bean sprouts, and the *nem lui* go perfectly with a chilled Huda lager.

Les Jardins de la Carambole
FRENCH, VIETNAMESE $$

(☎0234-354 8815; www.lesjardinsdelacarambole.com; 32 Đ Dang Tran Con; meals 120,000-300,000d; ☺7am-11pm; 📶) This classy French restaurant occupies a gorgeous colonial-style building in the Citadel quarter. The menu majors in Gallic classics and there's a Vietnamese set menu popular with groups. Add a lengthy wine list and informed service, and it's just the place for a romantic meal – arrive by *cyclo* and it's easy to roll back the years to Indochine times.

ROYAL RICE CAKES

These savoury Hue specialities come in different shapes and sizes, but are all made with rice flour. The most common is the crispy fried, filled pancake *banh khoai* (smaller and denser than *banh xeo* pancakes). The other variations are steamed and like sticky rice, and are usually topped with shrimp and dipped in sweet fish sauce. Look for *banh beo*, which come in tiny dishes; banana-leaf-wrapped *banh nam*; transparent dumplings *banh loc*; and the leaf-steamed pyramids *banh it*, which can come in sweet mung-bean or savoury varieties.

Nina's Cafe
VIETNAMESE $$

(16/34 Nguyen Tri Phuong; meals 120,000d; ☺9am-10.30pm) Nina's is a friendly, painting-hung restaurant, around a corner at the end of an alley, where crowd-pleasing stir-fried, claypot, fried-rice and curry dishes are served to enthusiastic patrons. Top marks go to the vegetable curry loaded with carrots, potato and tofu. The vibrantly coloured Vietnamese tablecloths are for sale at the door, along with homemade chilli sauce (30,000d). Western breakfasts are also on the menu.

🍷 Drinking & Nightlife

Hue has a very active – if rather unimaginative – bar, pub and club scene. Most of the action happens along Đ Pham Ngu Lao and Đ Vo Thi Sau.

La Boulangerie Française
CAFE

(☎054 383 7437; www.laboulangeriefrancaise.org; 46 Nguyen Tri Phuong; ☺7am-8.30pm) Sit out on the slim terrace upstairs at this *petite boulangerie* for a delightful *petit déjeuner* with croissants, crêpes (from 20,000d) or *gaufres* (waffles), and a *café au lait* or a milkshake *glacé*. The *boulangerie* operates as a training school for young and disadvantaged Vietnamese who aspire to become bakers or chefs.

★ Cong Caphe
CAFE

(www.congcaphe.com; 22 Ben Nghe; ☺7am-11.30pm) With a lovely wood floor, concrete walls, colourful chairs and cushions and many a nook to escape to, Cong is a reassuring constant in a world of flux: here you are always guaranteed excellent service and a fun and fascinating communist-chic atmosphere, as well as grade-A coffee, thirst-busting coconut milk with peppermint, and iced coffee.

Why Not? Bar
BAR

(☑ 0903 583 812; www.whynot.com.vn; 26 Đ Pham Ngu Lao; ☺ 7am-midnight; 🛜) With a pool table, decent cocktails, food and sport on TV, plus a popular street-front terrace, rodeo pictures, saddles and cowboy paraphernalia, this Wild West–themed bar is a perennial favourite along Hue's backpacker way. Upstairs there's a good dorm and private-room accommodation, so you won't have to move far at the end of the night.

DMZ Travel
BAR

(☑ 0234-993 456; www.dmz.com.vn; 60 Đ Le Loi; ☺ 7am-2am; 🛜) This always-popular bar near the river has a free pool table, cold Huda beer, cocktails (try a watermelon mojito) and antics most nights. It also serves Western and local food till midnight, plus smoothies and juices. Happy hour is from 3pm to 8pm. Check out the upside-down map of the DMZ – complete with a US chopper – on the ceiling.

🛍 Shopping

Hue produces the finest conical hats in Vietnam. The city's speciality is 'poem hats', which, when held up to the light, reveal shadowy scenes of daily life. Hue is also known for its rice paper and silk paintings; there's no shortage of colourful shops where you can sift through a wide selection of gift items.

Blue de Hue
ANTIQUES

(43 Đ Vo Thi Sau; ☺ 7.30am-6.30pm) This antiques store is stuffed to the rafters with stonework, ceramics, calligraphy, laquerware, wooden carvings and all manner of intriguing pieces of art and decorative objects.

Spiral Foundation Healing the Wounded Heart Center
ARTS & CRAFTS

(☑ 0234-381 7643; 23 Đ Vo Thi Sau; ☺ 8am-10pm) Generating cash from trash, this shop stocks lovely handicrafts – such as quirky bags made from plastic, and picture frames made from recycled beer cans – all produced by artists with disabilities. Profits aid heart surgery for children in need.

ℹ Information

MEDICAL SERVICES

Hue Central Hospital (Benh Vien Trung Uong Hue; ☑ 0234-382 2325; 16 Đ Le Loi; ☺ 6am-10pm) Well-regarded local hospital.

MONEY

Vietcombank (78 Đ Hung Vuong; ☺ 8-11.30am Mon-Sat, 1-4pm Mon-Fri) This main branch has an ATM and foreign-currency exchange.

Vietin Bank ATM (12 Đ Hung Vuong) Centrally located ATM.

POST

Post Office (8 Đ Hoang Hoa Tham; ☺ 7am-5.30pm Mon-Sat)

TRAVEL AGENCIES

Most travel agencies and tour operators pool clients on their budget tours, so when you book a (standard) DMZ tour, you'll be on a large bus. Specialist bespoke trips are available but naturally cost far more.

A popular way to travel between Hue and Hoi An – or vice versa – is by motorbike or jeep. Trips often stop for a seafood lunch at Lang Co lagoon, and also at the Hai Van Pass. Count on around US$50 on the back of a bike, or about US$30 if you're comfortable being in charge of two wheels yourself.

DMZ Travel This bar arranges budget boat trips along the Perfume River, DMZ tours and tickets to Laos.

Sinh Tourist (☑ 0234-384 5022; www.thesinhtourist.vn; 37 Đ Nguyen Thai Hoc; ☺ 6.30am-8.30pm) Books open-tour buses, and buses to Laos.

VM Travel (☑ 0234-392 3747; www.vmtravel.com.vn; 67 Đ Vo Thi Sau) Books buses and private cars to Phong Nha, and tours of the caves there.

Other options include Café on Thu Wheels (p182) and Stop & Go Café (p182).

ℹ Getting There & Away

AIR

Jetstar (www.jetstar.com) has flights to HCMC and Dalat, **VietJet** (www.vietjetair.com) offers flights to/from HCMC and Hanoi, while **Vietnam Airlines** (☑ 0234-382 4709; www.vietnamairlines.com; 23 Đ Nguyen Van Cu; ☺ 8am-5pm Mon-Fri) has services to/from Hanoi and HCMC.

BUS

The main **Phia Nam Bus Station** (57 An Duong Vuong), 4km southeast of the centre, has connections to Danang and south to HCMC. **An Hoa Bus Station** (Ly Thai To), northwest of the Citadel, serves northern destinations.

DESTINATION	COST (D)	TIME (HR)	FREQUENCY
Danang	80,000	3	frequent
Dong Ha	60,000	2½	every 30min
Dong Hoi	100,000	4-5	frequent
Hanoi	330,000	13-16	9 daily
HCMC	500,000	19-24	9 daily
Ninh Binh	300,000	10½-12	8 daily

For Phong Nha (around 180,000d, five hours), the Hung Thanh open-tour bus leaves 49 Đ Chu Van An between 4.30pm and 5pm, and the Tan Nhat bus leaves from the Why Not? Bar on Đ Pham Ngu Lao around 6.30am to 7am. Also convenient is a daily bus (150,000d) leaving the DMZ Travel bar at 2pm. This departure travels directly to Phong Nha.

Hue is a regular stop on open-tour bus routes. Most drop off and pick up passengers at central hotels. Expect some hassle from persistent hotel touts when you arrive.

Sinh Tourist and Stop & Go Café (p182) can arrange bookings for buses to Savannakhet, Laos.

TRAIN

The **Hue Train Station** (☑ 0234-382 2175; 2 Đ Phan Chu Trinh) is at the southwestern end of Đ Le Loi. A taxi here from the hotel area costs about 70,000d.

DESTINATION	COST (US$)	TIME (HR)	FREQUENCY (DAILY)
Danang	2.50-6	2½-4	7
Dong Hoi	4-10	3-5½	6
Hanoi	15-35	12-15½	6
HCMC	20-43	19½-23	6
Ninh Binh	11-25	10-13	4

ⓘ Getting Around

To/from the airport Hue's Phu Bai Airport is 14km south of the city. Metered taxis cost about 300,000d to the centre; or take the Vietnam Airlines minibus service (60,000d) from outside the airport to their offices a 15-minute walk from the hotel area of Hue – taxis and xe om will be waiting here.

Bicycle Pedal power is a fun way to tour Hue and the royal tombs. Hotels rent out bicycles for around US$3 per day. Traffic around Hue can be busy, especially on the bridges crossing the river, so take care when cycling.

Car A car with driver costs US$50 to US$55 per day.

Cyclo Drivers usually quote extortionate prices in Hue, and a short ride begins at around 40,000d. It's normally cheaper and quicker to get a metered taxi.

Motorbike Rental from US$5 to US$10 per day.

Taxi Try the reliable company **Mai Linh** (☑ 0234-389 8989).

Around Hue

South of Hue are the extravagant and often glorious mausoleums of the rulers of the Nguyen dynasty (1802–1945), spread out along the banks of the Perfume River between 2km and 16km south of the city. Fine pagodas, elaborate temples, covered bridges, abandoned water parks, American bunkers, scenic lagoons and other sights dot the alluring landscape.

Almost all the royal tombs were planned by the emperors during their lifetimes, and some were also used as residences while they were still alive.

Most of the mausoleums consist of five essential elements. The first is a stele pavilion dedicated to the accomplishments, exploits and virtues of the emperor. Next is a temple for the worship of the emperor and empress. The third is an enclosed sepulchre, and fourth is an honour courtyard with stone elephants, horses, and civil and military mandarins. Finally, there's a lotus pond surrounded by frangipani and pine trees.

Most people visit on an organised tour from Hue, either by boat or by combining boat and bus, but it's possible to rent a *xe om* or bicycle and do a DIY tour.

Entry to the main sites costs 150,000/ 30,000d per adult/child per site, but discounted combination tickets including the Citadel are also available.

◉ Sights

★**Thien Mu Pagoda**   BUDDHIST TEMPLE

FREE Built on a small hill overlooking the Song Huong (Perfume River), 4km southwest of the Citadel, this seven-storey pagoda is an icon of Vietnam and as potent a symbol of Hue as the Citadel. The 21m-high octagonal tower, **Thap Phuoc Duyen**, was constructed under the reign of Emperor Thieu Tri in 1844. Each of its storeys is dedicated to a *manushi-buddha* (a Buddha that appeared in human form). Visit in the morning before tour groups show up.

Thien Mu Pagoda was originally founded in 1601 by Nguyen Hoang, governor of Thuan Hoa province. Over the centuries its buildings have been destroyed and rebuilt several times. Since the 1960s it has been a flashpoint of political demonstrations.

To the right of the brick pagoda tower is a pavilion containing a stele dating from 1715. It's set on the back of a massive marble turtle, a symbol of longevity. To the left of the tower is another six-sided pavilion, this one sheltering an enormous bell (1710), weighing 2052kg and audible from 10km away.

Beyond the pagoda tower is a gateway, on the upper floor of which sits an effigy of the Celestial Lady (Thien Mu) that the pagoda is named after. Above the central portal is a board with the Chinese characters 靈姥寺 (literally 'Divine Old Woman Temple'), in honour of the presiding deity of this plot of land.

The temple itself is a humble building in the inner courtyard, past the triple-gated entrance where three statues of Buddhist guardians stand at the alert. In the main sanctuary behind the bronze laughing Buddha are three statues: A Di Da, the Buddha of the Past; Thich Ca, the historical Buddha (Sakyamuni); and Di Lac Buddha, the Buddha of the Future.

For a scenic bicycle ride, head southwest (parallel to the Perfume River) on riverside Ð Tran Hung Dao, which turns into Ð Le Duan after Phu Xuan Bridge. Cross the railway tracks and keep going on Ð Kim Long. Thien Mu Pagoda can also be reached by boat.

Tomb of Tu Duc

TOMB

(Lang Tu Duc, Khiem Lang; adult/child 100,000/20,000d; ☉7am-5pm) This tomb (completed in 1867) is the most popular, imposing and impressive of the royal mausoleums, designed by Emperor Tu Duc himself before his death. The enormous expense of the tomb and the forced labour used in its construction spawned a coup plot that was discovered and suppressed. Tu Duc lived a life of imperial luxury and carnal excess, with 104 wives and countless concubines (though no offspring). The tomb is 5km south of Hue on Van Nien Hill in Duong Xuan Thuong village.

From the entrance, a path leads to Luu Khiem Lake. The tiny island to the right, Tinh Khiem, is where Tu Duc used to hunt small game. Across the water to the left is Xung Khiem Pavilion, where he would sit with his concubines, composing or reciting poetry.

Hoa Khiem Temple is where Tu Duc and his wife, Empress Hoang Le Thien Anh, were worshipped; today it houses royal artefacts. The larger throne was for the empress; Tu Duc was only 153cm tall. Minh Khiem Chamber, to the right behind Hoa Khiem Temple, was originally meant to be a theatre. Dress-up photo opportunities and cultural performances are available here. Directly behind Hoa Khiem Temple is the quieter Luong Khiem Temple, dedicated to Tu Duc's mother, Tu Du.

A FIERY PROTEST

Behind the main sanctuary of the Thien Mu Pagoda is the Austin motorcar that transported the monk Thich Quang Duc to the site of his 1963 self-immolation. He publicly burned himself to death in Saigon to protest against the policies of South Vietnamese President Ngo Dinh Diem. A famous photograph of this act was printed on the front pages of newspapers around the world, and his death inspired a number of other self-immolations.

The response of the president's notorious sister-in-law, Tran Le Xuan (Madame Nhu), was to crassly proclaim the self-immolations a 'barbecue party', saying: 'Let them burn and we shall clap our hands.' Her statements greatly aggravated the already substantial public disgust with Diem's regime. In November, both President Diem and his brother Ngo Dinh Nhu (Madame Nhu's husband) were assassinated by Diem's military. Madame Nhu was overseas at the time.

Another self-immolation sparked fresh protest in 1993. A man arrived at the pagoda and, after leaving offerings, set himself alight chanting the word 'Buddha'. Although his motivation remains a mystery, this set off a chain of events whereby the pagoda's leading monks were arrested and linked with the independent United Buddhists of Vietnam, the banned alternative to the state-sanctioned Vietnam Buddhists. This led to an official complaint to the UN by the International Federation of Human Rights, accusing the Vietnamese government of violating its own constitution, which protects freedom of religion.

Around the lake shore is the **Honour Courtyard**. You pass between a guard of elephants, horses and diminutive mandarins (even shorter than the emperor) before reaching the **Stele Pavilion**, which shelters a vast 20-tonne stele. Tu Duc drafted the inscriptions himself. He freely admitted he'd made mistakes and named his tomb Khiem (Modest). The **tomb**, enclosed by a wall, is on the far side of a tiny lagoon. It's a drab monument and the emperor was never interred here; where his remains were buried (along with great treasures) is not known. To keep it secret from grave robbers, all 200 servants who buried Tu Duc were beheaded.

★**Tomb of Khai Dinh** TOMB

(Lang Khai Dinh, Ung Lang; adult/child 100,000/20,000d; ⊙7am-5pm) This hillside monument is a synthesis of Vietnamese and European elements. Most of the tomb's grandiose exterior is covered in darkened, weathered concrete, with an unexpectedly Gothic air, while the interiors resemble explosions of colourful ceramic mosaic. Khai Dinh was the penultimate emperor of Vietnam, from 1916 to 1925, and widely seen as a puppet of the French. It took 11 years to construct his flamboyant tomb; it can be found 10km from Hue in Chau Chu village.

Steps lead to the **Honour Courtyard** where mandarin honour guards have a mixture of Vietnamese and European features. Up three more flights of stairs is the stupendous main building, **Thien Dinh**. The walls and ceiling are decorated with murals of the Four Seasons, Eight Precious Objects and the Eight Immortals. Under a graceless, gold-speckled concrete canopy is a gilt bronze statue (cast in Marseilles) of Khai Dinh, who is presumed to have been homosexual, though he did produce one heir. His remains are interred 18m below the statue. There's an audio guide in a dozen languages (70,000d).

Tomb of Minh Mang TOMB

(adult/child 100,000/20,000d) Planned during Minh Mang's reign (1820–40) but built by his successor, Thieu Tri, this majestic tomb, on the west bank of the Perfume River, is renowned for its architecture and sublime forest setting. The **Honour Courtyard** is reached via three gates on the eastern side of the wall; three granite staircases lead from here to the square **Stele Pavilion** (Dinh Vuong). Sung An Temple, dedicated to Minh

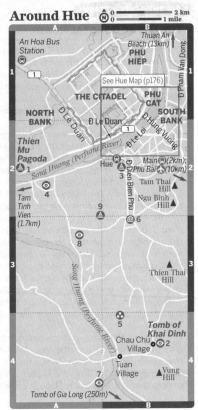

Around Hue

◎ **Top Sights**

◎ **Sights**

Mang and his empress, is reached via three terraces and the rebuilt Hien Duc Gate.

On the other side of the temple, three stone bridges span **Ho Trung Minh** (Lake of Impeccable Clarity). The central bridge was for the emperor's use only. **Toa Minh Lau** (Pavilion of Light) stands on the top of three superimposed terraces that represent the

OFF THE BEATEN TRACK

THE GREAT COASTAL ROAD

From the centre of Hue it's only 15km north to the coast, the road shadowing the Perfume River before you hit the sands of **Thuan An Beach**. Southeast from here there's a beautiful, quiet coastal road to follow with very light traffic (so it's ideal for cyclists). The route traverses a narrow coastal island, with views of the Tam Giang-Cau Hai lagoon and fish and shrimp farms on the inland side, and stunning sandy beaches and dunes on the other. This coastal strip is virtually undeveloped, but between September and March the water may be too rough for swimming.

From Thuan An the road winds past villages, alternating between shrimp lagoons and vegetable gardens. Thousands of colourful and opulent graves and family temples line the beach, most the final resting places of Viet Kieu (overseas Vietnamese) who wanted to be buried in their homeland. Tracks cut through the tombs and sand dunes to the beach. Pick a spot and you'll probably have a beach to yourself.

At glorious **Phu Thuan Beach** (about 7km southeast of Thuan An) is a hotel or two, some of which charge admission to the beach, but other areas of beach are accessible for free. A taxi from Hue to Phu Thuan is around 250,000d and a *xe om* (motorbike taxi) around 100,000d. Alternatively, hire a scooter from your hotel or rental outlet in Hue for more freedom of movement. You can also pop into little villages at will and explore (the word for a village is *làng*, and you will see each settlement announced by a large gate with the village name emblazoned on it). Almost all have bright and colourful, recently constructed temples. Keep an eye out for the occasional temple with Vietnamese script on the main gate that is artfully designed to resemble Chinese characters.

Around 8km past Beach Bar Hue, the remains of **Phu Dien**, a small Cham temple, lie protected by a glass pavilion in the dunes just off the beach. There are seafood shacks here, too.

Continuing southeast, a narrow paved road weaves past fishing villages, shrimp farms, giant sand dunes and the settlement of Vinh Hung until it reaches the mouth of another river estuary at Thuon Phu An, where there's a row of seafood restaurants. This spot is 40km from Thuan An. Cross the Tu Hien Bridge here and you can continue around the eastern lip of the huge Cau Hai lagoon and link up with Hwy 1.

'three powers': the heavens, the earth and water. To the left is the Fresh Air Pavilion, to the right, the Angling Pavilion.

From a stone bridge across crescent-shaped **Ho Tan Nguyet** (Lake of the New Moon), a monumental staircase with dragon banisters leads to Minh Mang's sepulchre. The gate to the tomb is opened only once a year on the anniversary of the emperor's death.

The tomb is in An Bang village, 12km from Hue.

Ho Quyen
HISTORIC SITE

FREE Wildly overgrown but evocative, Ho Quyen was built in 1830 for the royal pastime of watching elephants and tigers face off in combat. The tigers (and leopards) were usually relieved of their claws and teeth so that the elephants – a symbol of the emperor's power – triumphed every time. Climb up grassy ramparts and imagine the scene in the old arena – the last fight was held in 1904.

The south-facing section was reserved for the royal family, while diametrically opposite are the remaining tiger cages.

Ho Quyen is about 3km outside Hue in Truong Da village. Follow Đ Bui Thi Xuan west from the train station, then look out for the blue sign near the market that indicates the turn-off on the left. Follow this lane for about 200m to a fork in the road and go right.

Tu Hieu Pagoda
BUDDHIST TEMPLE

FREE Nestled in a pine forest, this pagoda was built in 1843 and later co-opted by eunuchs from the Citadel. Today 70 monks reside at Tu Hieu; they welcome visitors to the twin temples (one dedicated to Cong Duc, the other to Buddha). Listen to their chanting daily at 4.30am, 10am, noon, 4pm and 7pm. Tu Hieu Pagoda is about 5km from the centre of Hue, on the way to the tomb of Tu Duc (p188).

Tu Hieu is associated with Zen master Thich Nhat Hanh, who studied at the monastery in the 1940s, but lived in exile for more than 40 years and was only permitted to return to Vietnam in 2005.

Thanh Toan Bridge   BRIDGE

A classic covered Japanese footbridge in picturesque countryside, this makes a lovely diversion from Hue. The bridge is in sleepy Thuy Thanh village, 7km east of Hue. Head north for a few hundred metres on Ð Ba Trieu until you see a sign to the Citadel Hotel. Turn right and follow the bumpy dirt road for another 6km past villages, rice paddies and several pagodas.

Nam Giao Esplanade   HISTORIC BUILDING

This three-tiered esplanade was once the most important religious site in Vietnam, the place where the Nguyen emperors made animal sacrifices and elaborate offerings to the deity Thuong De. Ceremonies (last held in 1946) involved a lavish procession and a three-day fast by the emperor at the nearby Fasting Palace. The palace, located at the furthest end of the park, has photographs with English captions.

Chuon Lagoon   LAGOON

(Dam Chuon) Hire a scooter and head out to this picturesque spot on the edge of the lagoon either at sunrise or sunset, when there are beautiful views of the rising or setting sun across the fishing boats. To make a meal of it, dine on seafood at one of the stilted restaurants.

Ho Thuy Tien
Abandoned Water Park   RUINS

(Ho Thuy Tien; 20,000d) Closed for mysterious reasons in 2006, this long-abandoned water park outside Hue centres on a dramatic dragon head poking from the waters of Thuy Tien Lake (Ho Thuy Tien). Cross the bridges to the dragon's head, where you can climb up the internal stairs through a scene of graffiti-strewn dereliction and broken glass to great views from the dragon's mouth. Note this place is falling apart and potentially dangerous (an unofficial ticketing system exists whereby you pay the guard at the gate) – take appropriate care.

Tomb of Gia Long   TOMB

(Lang Gia Long; 100,000d; ⊙7am-5pm) `FREE`
Emperor Gia Long founded the Nguyen dynasty in 1802 and ruled until 1819. Both the emperor and his queen are buried here. Badly damaged during the American War, the now restored tomb is around 14km south of Hue and 3km from the west bank of the Perfume River. It can be reached by boat from the jetty near the Tomb of Minh Mang.

Bach Ma National Park

A French-era hill station, this national park reaches a peak of 1450m at Bach Ma mountain, only 18km from the coast. The cool climate attracted the French, who built over a hundred villas here. Not surprisingly the Viet Minh tried hard to spoil the holiday – the area saw heavy fighting in the early 1950s and again during the American War.

The national park, extended in 2008, stretches from the coast to the Annamite mountain range at the Lao border. More than 1400 species of plants, including rare ferns and orchids, have been discovered in Bach Ma, representing a fifth of the flora of Vietnam. There are 132 kinds of mammals, three of which were only discovered in the 1990s: the antelope-like saola, the Truong Son muntjac and the giant muntjac. Nine species of primates are also present, including small numbers of the rare red-shanked douc langur.

◉ Sights & Activities

Hiking

The **Rhododendron Trail** (from Km 10 on the road) leads to the upper reaches of a spectacular waterfall; head 689 steps down for a dip. The **Five Lakes Trail** passes pools for swimming before reaching a much smaller waterfall. The short **Summit Hike** leads to a viewpoint with magnificent views (on a clear day) over the forest, Cau Hai lagoon and the coast. Unexploded ordnance is still around, so ensure you stick to the trails.

Wildlife Spotting

As most of the park's resident mammals are nocturnal, sightings demand a great deal of effort and patience. Birdwatching is fantastic, but you need to be up at dawn for the best chance of glimpsing some of the 358 logged species, including the fabulous crested argus pheasant. It's hoped elephants will return to the park from the Lao side of the border.

⨾ Sleeping & Eating

At the visitor centre, arrange to eat at your accommodation before making your way to the summit. They may need time to send up ingredients.

There's limited camping, guesthouses near the entrance (though not very well maintained), and better villas near the summit. Arrange accommodation with the visitor centre before you ascend.

Summit Accommodation GUESTHOUSE $$
(☑054 387 1330; www.bachmapark.com.vn; d 650,000-1,050,0000d) Near the summit are four options, from the simple Kim Giao villa and Do Quyen villa to the more comfortable Phong Lan villa. All have private bathrooms, but note that not all villas may be available for booking. Call ahead and if you can book, also give at least four hours' notice if meals are needed. Accommodation is usually fully booked at weekends.

❶ Information

At the **visitor centre** (www.bachmapark.com. vn) by the park entrance there's an exhibition on the park's flora and fauna, and hiking booklets are available. You can book village and bird-watching tours and English-speaking guides (US$25 per day; recommended). Take insect repellent, waterproof clothing, sunscreen and strong trekking shoes.

The best time to visit is from February to September, particularly between March and June. Bach Ma is the wettest place in Vietnam, with the heaviest of the rain falling in October and November (bringing out the leeches). It's not out of the question to visit then, however, and the rainy season has been arriving later and later in recent years – check road conditions first though.

❶ Getting There & Away

Bach Ma is 28km west of Lang Co and 40km southeast of Hue. The turn-off is signposted in the town of Cau Hai on Hwy 1. You can also enter from the town of Phu Loc.

Buses from Danang (90,000d, two hours) and Hue (70,000d, one hour) stop at Cau Hai, where *xe om* drivers can ferry you the 3km (around 40,000d) to the entrance.

❶ Getting Around

From the visitor centre, it's a steep, serpentine 15km ascent, and the road almost reaches the summit. Walking down from the summit takes about three to four hours; you'll need water and sunscreen.

Private transport to the summit is available from the visitor centre, and a return same-day journey is around 800,000d to 1,000,000d for a minibus. At busy times, travellers can usually share the cost with other passengers.

For an overnight stay, transport to the summit is around 1,300,000d for six people. Note that cars are allowed in the park, so it's worth considering a tour here from Hue, or arranging a car and driver for around US$60 return. Motorbikes are not allowed in the park, but there is a secure parking area near the visitor centre.

A recommended Hue-based tour company is Oriental Sky Travel (p182), with regular overnight explorations of the park.

Lang Co Beach
☑0234

Lang Co is an attractive island-like stretch of palm-shaded white sand, with a turquoise lagoon on one side – Lap An Lagoon (Dam Lap An) – and 10km of beachfront on the other. As a beach resort it's more geared to Vietnamese day trippers than Western travellers, but if the weather's nice the ocean is certainly inviting. High season is April to July. From late August to November rains are frequent, and from December to March it can get chilly.

🍴 Sleeping & Eating

There are simple guesthouses and two-star hotels north of the town along the highway, but accommodation in nearby beachfront resorts is far superior. There are seafood restaurants alongside the lagoon for a memorably scenic meal.

Vedana Lagoon RESORT $$$
(☑0234-381 9397; www.vedanalagoon.com; Phu Loc; bungalows/villas from US$131/218; ☺❄@ ☎☒) Combining contemporary chic with natural materials, this remote but very comfortable lagoon-side spa hotel has gorgeous villas and bungalows with thatched roofs, modish furnishings and outdoor bathrooms. Some have private pools, others jut over the lagoon to maximise the views. The complex includes a wonderful wellness centre (for t'ai chi and yoga classes). Vedana is 15km north of Lang Co.

❶ Getting There & Away

Lang Co is on the north side of the Hai Van Tunnel and Danang.

Lang Co's **train station** (☑054 387 4423) is 3km from the beach, in the direction of the lagoon. Getting a *xe om* to the beach shouldn't be difficult. The train journey from here to Danang (30,000d, 1½ hours, four daily) is one of the most spectacular in Vietnam. Services also connect to Hue (30,000d, 1½ to two hours, four daily).

HAI VAN PASS & TUNNEL

The **Hai Van (Sea Cloud) Pass** (Deo Hai Van) crosses over a spur of the Truong Son mountain range that juts into the sea. About 30km north of Danang, the road climbs to an elevation of 496m, passing south of the Ai Van Son peak (1172m). It's an incredibly mountainous stretch of highway. The railway track, with its many tunnels, goes around the peninsula, following the beautiful and deserted shoreline.

In the 15th century, this pass formed the boundary between Vietnam and the kingdom of Champa. Until the American War, it was heavily forested. At the summit is a bullet-scarred French fort, later used as a bunker by the South Vietnamese and US armies. A large historic gate stands here with the *chu nho* characters 海雲關 (meaning 'Hai Van Pass').

If you cross in winter, the pass is a tangible dividing line between the climates of the north and south, protecting Danang from the fierce 'Chinese winds' that sweep in from the northeast. From November to March the exposed Lang Co side of the pass can be wet and chilly, while just to the south it's often warm and dry.

The top of the pass is the only place you can stop. The view is well worth it, especially if you climb up to the abandoned fort.

The 6280m-long **Hai Van Tunnel** bypasses the pass and shaves an hour off the journey between Danang and Hue. Motorcyclists and bicyclists are not permitted to ride through the tunnel (but you can pay to have your bike transported through in a truck). Sure it saves time, but on a nice day it really is a shame to miss the views from the pass.

Despite the odd hair-raising encounter, the pass road is safer than it used to be, but it is becoming very popular with selfie-taking locals on motorbikes, and increasing numbers of bus groups. Big trucks are also a hazard to be mindful of. If you can take your eyes off the highway, keep them peeled for the small altars on the roadside – sobering reminders of those who have died in accidents on this winding route.

Danang

🎵 0236 / POP 1.23 MILLION

Nowhere in Vietnam is changing as fast as Danang, Vietnam's fifth-most populous city. For decades it had a reputation as a quiet provincial town, but big changes have shaken things up. Stroll along the Han riverfront and you'll find gleaming new modernist hotels. Spectacular bridges span the river, and the entire Danang Beach strip is booming with tower-hotel and resort developments, including imposing projects such as Danang Times Square and the Wyndham Soleil Danang. Chinese tourism is a big driver, especially with Hoi An just down the coastline.

That said, the city itself still has few conventional sightseeing spots, except for a very decent museum, a handsome cathedral and a stunningly quirky bridge (or three). So for most travellers, a few days enjoying the city's beaches, restaurants and nightlife is probably enough. Book an after-dark tour to see Danang at its shimmering neon-lit best. The city's street-food scene also deserves close investigation.

History

Known during French-colonial rule as Tourane, Danang succeeded Hoi An as the most important port in central Vietnam during the 19th century, a position it retains to this day.

As American involvement in Vietnam escalated, Danang was where American combat troops first landed in South Vietnam – 3500 Marines in March 1965. Memorably, they stormed Nam O Beach in full battle gear, greeted by a bevy of Vietnamese girls in *ao dai* (the national dress) bearing cheerful flower garlands. A decade later, with the Americans and South Vietnamese in full retreat, the scene was very different as desperate civilians fled the city. On 29 March 1975, two truckloads of Communist guerrillas, more than half of them women, declared Danang liberated without firing a shot.

Today Danang hosts one of Vietnam's most vibrant economies, and is often dubbed 'Silicon City' due to its booming web sector.

🅞 Sights

⭐ **Museum of Cham Sculpture**　MUSEUM
(Bao Tang; 1 Đ Trung Nu Vuong; 40,000d; ⊘7am-5pm) This small but important museum contains the world's largest collection of

Danang

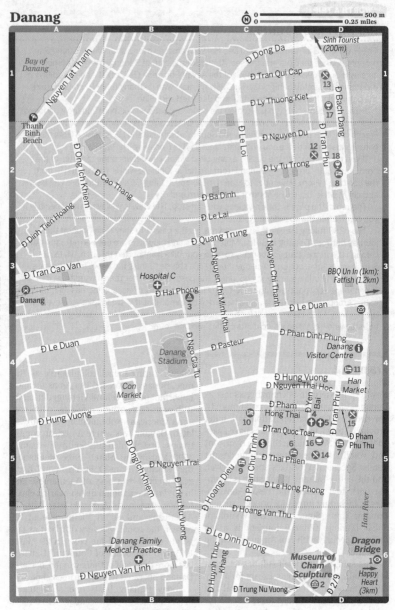

Cham artefacts, housed in buildings marrying French-colonial architecture with Cham elements. Founded in 1915 by the École Française d'Extrême Orient, it displays more than 300 pieces including altars, *lingas* (stylised phalluses representing Shiva),

garudas (griffin-like sky beings), *apsaras* (heavenly nymphs), Ganeshes and images of Shiva, Brahma and Vishnu, all dating from the 5th to 15th centuries. Explanations are slim. The audio guide is 20,000d (you'll need to show ID, passport or driving licence).

Danang

★ **Dragon Bridge**   BRIDGE
(Cau Rong) The biggest show in town every Saturday and Sunday night (at 9pm), this impressive dragon sculpture spouts fire and water from its head near the Han River's eastern bank. The best observation spots are the cafes lining the eastern bank to the north of the bridge; boat trips taking in the action also depart from Đ Bach Dang on the river's western bank. The colour-changing Dragon Bridge sees selfie-takers parking their scooters on the bridge every night.

Danang Cathedral   CHURCH
(Đ Tran Phu) Known to locals as Con Ga Church (Rooster Church) because of the weathercock atop the steeple, the candy-pink, photogenic Danang Cathedral was built for the city's French residents in 1923. Today it serves a Catholic community of over 4000, and is standing room only if you arrive late.

Cao Dai Temple   BUDDHIST TEMPLE
(63 Đ Hai Phong; ⊙ prayers 5.30am, 11.30am, 5.30pm & 11.30pm) FREE Central Vietnam's largest Cao Dai temple serves about 50,000 followers. A sign reading van giao nhat ly (all religions have the same reason) hangs before the main altar. Behind the gilded letters are the founders of five of the world's religions: Mohammed, Laozi (wearing Eastern Orthodox–style robes), Jesus, a Southeast Asian–looking Buddha and Confucius. Behind the main altar sits an enormous globe with the Cao Dai 'divine eye' symbol.

Convent of St Paul
de Chartres   CHRISTIAN MONASTERY
(Tu Vien Phao Lo; 47 Đ Yen Bai) You can't enter through the convent gate on the road be-hind the cathedral, but it's worth taking a look at the church architecture from the outside. The Sisters of St Paul de Char-tres date to the late 17th century and first arrived in Vietnam (in Saigon) in 1860, running orphanages and hospitals, and re-main active in working with the poor and disabled.

🗲 **Tours**

Hoi An Jeep Adventures   TOURS
(☏ 0905 101 930; www.vietnamjeeps.com; per person from US$96) Based in nearby Hoi An, but also offering fun jeep explorations of Danang's street-food and after-dark scenes. Inquisitive travelling foodies can look forward to really interesting street-food dis-coveries. Other Danang options include discovering Monkey Mountain by jeep and a day trip to the Hai Van Pass.

Danang Food Tour   FOOD & DRINK
(www.danangfoodtour.com) Excellent morning (US$35) and evening (US$45) explorations of the local food scene by passionate foodies. Doing both tours costs $75. The website has a great blog on the best of Danang.

Danang Free Walking Tour   WALKING
(☏ 0905 631 419; www.facebook.com/danang freewalkingtour; Vietnam Hostel, 22-24-26 Đ Hung Vuong; ⊙ 9am & 3pm) Run by local English-speaking students who are keen to practise their English, these walking tours are a de-cent introduction to the city. Donate what you think is appropriate at the end of the tour, and maybe sign up for one of the other (paid) specialised tours, including a street-food option. Tours leave from the Vietnam Hostel (the office is at the back).

Funtastic Danang Food Tour FOOD & DRINK
(☑0905 272 921; www.summerle.com/foodtour;
per person US$45) Very popular lunch and
evening street-food and restaurant tours
with Danang-born food blogger Summer Le,
who has been been featured in the *New York
Times*. Transport is by car and tours take in
five spots exploring a variety of Danang bites.

🎆 Festivals & Events

**Danang International
Fireworks Festival** FIREWORKS
(www.diff.vn/en; ⊙May-Jul) Held throughout
May, June and into July, with spectacular
displays from international fireworks teams
illuminating the river and bridges. Check the
website to see when displays are scheduled.

🛏 Sleeping

The sweet spot for eating and nightlife is
near the river west of the Dragon Bridge;
staying east across the Han River near My
Khe Beach saves you short taxi trips back
and forth, but things are definitely less exciting. Danang has a rapidly expanding selection of modern hotels along the riverside,
and a few much-needed new hostels.

★ Vietnam Hostel HOSTEL $
(☑0236-710 9228; www.vietnamhostel.com; 22-24-
26 Đ Hung Vuong; dm US$9, d/apt from US$17/65;
🌸🛜) With stylish brickwork and excellent
service, this clean, good-looking and hip
choice enjoys a very central location with a
wide variety of accommodation, from neat
and cool-looking dorms with sizeable bunks
to comfortable doubles and snazzy, fully
equipped apartments, plus a fine bar and rooftop terrace (with a cinema planned). It's also
the home of the Danang Free Walking Tour.

Memory Hostel HOSTEL $
(☑0236-374 7797; www.memoryhostel.com; 3 Đ
Tran Quoc Toan; dm US$7-8; 🌸🛜) Sweet memo-
ries are made of casual strolls to the Dragon
Bridge, restaurants and nightlife, all near
this hostel with a choice of four- to 12-bed
dorms, as well as a female six-bed dorm. If
you just want to stay in, the decor is arty and
eclectic, and beds have privacy curtains. An
excellent budget option. Also arranges tours.

Orange Hotel HOTEL $$
(☑0236-356 6177; https://danangorangehotel.
com; 29 Đ Hoang Dieu; d US$40-85; 🌸@🛜) This
family-owned hotel has a lemongrass aroma
in the lobby and sweet service instilled by
the friendly patriarch/boss, who's some-
times on hand at reception or in the rooftop

restaurant. Rooms are decorated with dark-
wood furniture and, despite the chintzy
feature here and there, the accommodation
is very clean. The expansive weekend break-
fast buffet features local dishes.

Sanouva BOUTIQUE HOTEL $$
(☑0236-382 3468; www.sanouvadanang.com; 68 Đ
Phan Chu Trinh; d from US$55; 🌸🌸@🛜) Bou-
tique mixes with business at the stylish
Sanouva, located in a bustling commercial street just a few blocks from Danang's
riverfront. An Asian-chic lobby is the introduction to relatively compact but modern
rooms, and the inhouse S'Spa and S'Ngon
restaurant are two good reasons to linger.

Dong Duong Hotel HOTEL $$$
(☑0236-363 1777; www.dongduonghotel.com.vn;
62 Đ Thai Phien; d/apt 1,800,000/3,200,000d;
🌸🛜🏊) The adorable staff at this large,
smart hotel (with apartments) are half the
appeal, while the lobby – with its classic cars
(including a bright-yellow convertible VW
Karmann Ghia, a scooter with sidecar and
a classic Citroën) and slightly kitsch faux
antiques – is a kind of marvel. Rooms are
very comfortable, the included breakfast is
superb and the service really shines.

**Novotel Danang
Premier Han River** HOTEL $$$
(☑0236-392 9999; www.novotel-danang-premier.
com; 36 Đ Bach Dang; r/ste from US$130/220;
🌸🌸@🛜🏊) This towering riverside landmark has stylish rooms with unmatched
views over the Han River towards the beach
and ocean. Staff are very welcoming and well
trained, and facilities include a pool, spa and
fitness centre. Those that enjoy the high life
should check out the 36th-floor sky bar.

🍴 Eating

Danang's restaurant scene is growing more
cosmopolitan by the day. Street food is also
great here, with copious *bun cha*, *com* (rice
and buffet) and *mi quang* (noodle soup)
stalls. Dedicated foodies should strongly
consider booking a food tour to really explore the Danang scene. Check out www.
danangcuisine.com for Danang tips and
tours by local blogger Summer Le.

Ngoc Chi VEGETARIAN $
(32 Đ Thai Phien; meals 35,000d; ⊙6am-10pm;
🍴) This highly affordable and affable modern vegetarian choice enjoys a central location in the buzzing Danang downtown, with
a tasty menu of classic fare from *banh canh*
(noodle soup) to *banh cuon, my xao mem*

(fried yellow noodles), fake-meat vegan dishes or just a bowl of curry with *banh mi* bread, a winner every time.

Vegan Ramen VEGAN $
(34 Đ An Thuong 5; meals 100,000d; ⊙11am-11pm; 📶🍴) Vegans can make a beeline for this tiny one-man ramen outlet for ample and satisfying bowls of *tantan men* (dandan noodles) with shiitake mushrooms, seaweed and sweat-inducing spiciness, plus coconut curry ramen, *shoyu* ramen, cold noodles and stir-fried noodles, each dish coupled with a dessert. All ramen dishes are loaded with flavour and goodness.

★Fatfish FUSION $$
(📱0236-394 5707; www.fatfishrestaurant.com; 439 Đ Tran Hung Dao; meals 110,000-330,000d; ⊙10am-11pm; 📶) This stylish restaurant and lounge bar has led the eating and drinking charge across the Han River on the eastern shore. Innovative Asian fusion dishes, pizza and wood-fired barbecue all partner with flavour-packed craft beers from Ho Chi Minh City's Pasteur Street Brewing Company (p338). Fatfish is good for a few snacks or a more leisurely full meal.

Waterfront INTERNATIONAL $$
(📱0236-384 3373; www.waterfrontdanang.com; 150-152 Đ Bach Dang; meals 150,000-350,000d; ⊙9.30am-11pm; 📶🍴) A riverfront lounge and restaurant that gets everything right on every level. It works as a stylish bar for a chilled glass of New Zealand sauvignon blanc or an imported beer, and also as a destination restaurant for a memorable meal (book the terrace deck for a stunning river vista). The menu features imported meats, Asian seafood, decent veg options and terrific 'gourmet' sandwiches.

BBQ Un In BARBECUE, VIETNAMESE $$
(📱0236-654 5357; www.bbqunin.com; 379 Đ Tran Hung Dao; meals 100,000-210,000d; ⊙11.30am-10.30pm) Vietnamese flavours and American barbecue combine at this fun place along the fast-expanding restaurant strip on the Han River's eastern bank. Shipping containers daubed with colourful street art provide the backdrop for fall-off-the-bone ribs, spicy grilled sausages, and hearty side dishes including sweetcorn and grilled pineapple. Order up a good-value beer tower if you're dining in a group.

Madame Lan VIETNAMESE $$
(📱0236-3616 226; www.madamelan.com; 4 Đ Bach Dang; meals 60,000-250,000d; ⊙6am-

10pm; 📶) In this huge restaurant in a French colonial-style building you can eat in an open courtyard or in one of the river-facing dining rooms. The menu has lots of alluring choices, including *bun cha cua* (crab sausage noodle soup), *hu tieu bo kho* (vermicelli with stewed beef), *bun cha*, and green papaya salad with shrimp and garlic.

Happy Heart CAFE $$
(📱0236-388 8384; www.facebook.com/happy heartdanang; 57 Ngô Thi Sỹ Bắc Mỹ An Ngū Hành Sơn; meals 95,000-160,000d; ⊙7.30am-9pm Mon-Sat; 📶🍴) ⏀ Hearing-impaired and ethnic-minority waiting staff deliver brilliant service at this cafe that helps to provide opportunities for people with disabilities in Danang. The food is excellent, with Western comfort food including burgers, lasagne and a terrific breakfast burrito plus MSG-free dishes. Good coffee, fruit-and-yoghurt smoothies and a selection of beers and ciders are further draws.

Mumtaz INDIAN $$
(www.mumtazrestvn.com; 69 Đ Hoai Thanh; meals from 140,000d; ⊙10am-10pm; 📶🍴) The music volume could go down a notch at Mumtaz, but the menu delivers. Select from an appealing and spicy array of fish and prawn dishes (including the excellent fish garlic tikka or prawn tandoori) and a strong showing of vegetable choices, including the smooth and appetising *daal makhini* (black lentils and kidney beans) and flavoursome *palak paneer* (cheese in a spinach sauce).

Bonjuk Lunchbox & Cafe KOREAN $$
(📱0236-353 8209; 2 Đ Ly Tu Trọng; meals 180,000d; ⊙7am-8.30pm; 📶) When you just need to satisfy those kimchi cravings, this simple and neat-looking Korean restaurant dishes up tasty sizzling stone-bowl bibimbap in a spectrum of flavour from spicy octopus to tuna or pork, a choice of *bulgogi* lunchboxes, plus seafood or kimchi noodles, stews and a whole host of fish, seafood, meat and vegetable porridge dishes.

🍺 Drinking & Nightlife

Luna Pub BAR
(www.facebook.com/LunaPubDanang; 9a Đ Tran Phu; ⊙11am-2am Mon-Wed, Fri & Sat, to 1am Thu & Sun; 📶) Half bar, half Italian restaurant, this hang-out is a warehouse-sized space with an open frontage, a DJ booth in the cabin of a truck, cool music, an amazing selection of drinks and and some shisha-smoking action. It's popular with the expat crowd for its authentic Italian food. Check its Facebook page for details of regular live gigs.

Golem Coffee
CAFE

(☑ 0915 857 079; www.facebook.com/golemdanang; 27 Đ Tran Quoc Toan; ⊘ 7am-10pm; 🛜) Hidden away from Danang's busy streets, this leafy and quiet garden cafe with a rustic but chic vibe is popular with younger locals cooling down with smoothies and gazing into smartphones. Try the refreshing coconut-and-yoghurt smoothie, and relax in the chilled interior, or on the teak daybeds or pleasantly mismatched furniture outside. The rooftop terrace is the place to be after dark.

Drop Coffee
CAFE

(41 Đ An Thuong 34; ⊘ 7am-9pm; 🛜) With its good-looking lines, neat and sharp white tiles, black stools, soft music and relaxed, unhurried rhythm, this spruce pocket-sized cafe is a welcome stop for some serious Danang unwinding and re-caffeination on the east side of the river. Cold brew and Italian coffees, Vietnamese brews, smoothies and teas are on the small menu.

Sky 36
COCKTAIL BAR

(☑ 0935 046 488; www.sky36.vn; Novotel Hotel, 36 Đ Bach Dang; ⊘ 6pm-midnight) This stylish and slick rooftop bar serves excellent cocktails and innovative bar snacks as well as the best after-dark views of Danang's river and neon-lit bridges. Note that a smart-casual dress code – including wearing closed-in shoes – applies to male visitors.

❶ Information

Agribank (111 Đ Phan Chu Trinh; ⊘ 24hr)

Danang Family Medical Practice (☑ 0236-358 2699; www.vietnammedicalpractice.com; 96-98 Đ Nguyen Van Linh; ⊘ 8am-7pm Mon-Fri, 8.30am-5pm Sat, 8.30am-12.30pm Sun) With in-patient facilities; run by an Israeli doctor.

Danang Visitor Centre (☑ 0236-355 0111; www.tourism.danang.vn; 108 Đ Bach Dang; ⊘ 8am-9.30pm) This visitor centre is really helpful, with English spoken and good maps and brochures, while the official Danang tourism website is one of Vietnam's best. Bicycles can be rented here.

Hospital C (Benh Vien C; ☑ 0511 382 1483; 122 Đ Hai Phong; ⊘ 24hr) The most modern of the four hospitals in town.

---

❶ ONLINE RESOURCES

The comprehensive **Danang Experience** (www.danangexperience.com) website has an expat leaning but is also good for visitors, with eating, drinking and accommodation recommendations.

Main Post Office (64 Đ Bach Dang; ⊘ 7am-5.30pm) Near the Song Han Bridge.

Sinh Tourist (☑ 0236-384 3259; www.thesinhtourist.vn; 16 Đ 3 Thang 2; ⊘ 7am-8pm) Books open-tour buses and tours, and offers currency exchange.

❶ Getting There & Away

Danang is the main gateway to Hoi An and one of the entry points to the Cham Islands, so it is well connected with trains and has an international airport. Staff at all hotels and hostels can help arrange transport to and from Hoi An, other sights and the airport. It's possible to arrange onward transport from the airport or train station direct to Hoi An.

Danang Airport (☑ 0236-3823 397; www.danangairport.vn/en) has international flights to China, South Korea, Japan, Macau, Hong Kong, Thailand, Cambodia, Singapore and Taiwan. It's also a major domestic hub with flights to Hanoi, Can Tho, HCMC, Hai Phong, Nha Trang and other regional Vietnamese airports. The main Vietnamese carriers are **Vietnam Airlines** (☑ 0236-382 1130; www.vietnamairlines.com), **VietJet Air** (www.vietjetair.com) and **Jetstar** (www.jetstar.com); destinations include Hanoi, HCMC, Nha Trang, Dalat and Hai Phong. **Silk Air** (www.silkair.com) has flights to/from Singapore.

❶ Getting Around

TO/FROM THE AIRPORT
Danang's airport is 2km west of the city centre. There is no airport bus; a taxi ride is around 60,000d to central Danang hotels.

BICYCLE
Bicycles can be rented from the Danang Visitor Centre for venturing across the bridge to Danang's beaches. Some hotels also lend out bicycles.

BUS
Danang's **intercity bus station** (☑ 0236-382 1265; Đ Dien Bien Phu) is 3km west of the city centre. A metered taxi to the riverside will cost around 90,000d. Frequent buses leave for all major centres including Dong Hoi (140,000d, six hours), Hanoi (320,000d, 16 hours), HCMC (400,000d, 22 hours), Hue (60,000d, three hours) and Nha Trang (250,000d, 12 hours).

Yellow public buses to Hoi An (20,000d, one hour, every 30 minutes to 6pm) travel along Đ Bach Dang. The price is usually posted inside the door; check it if you think the bus driver is attempting to overcharge.

Open-tour buses with Sinh Tourist pick up from the company office in the northern part of downtown twice daily for both Hue (90,000d,

MARBLE MOUNTAINS

Just off the Danang Beach coastal road, the Marble Mountains (Ngu Hanh Son) consist of five craggy marble outcrops topped with pagodas. Each mountain is named for the natural element it's said to represent: Thuy Son (water), Moc Son (wood), Hoa Son (fire), Kim Son (metal or gold) and Tho Son (earth). The villages that have sprung up at the base of the mountains specialise in marble sculpture, though they now astutely use marble from China rather than hacking away at the mountains that bring the visitors in.

Thuy Son (Water Mountain; 15,000d; ⊙7am-5pm) is the largest and most famous of the five Marble Mountains, with several natural caves in which first Hindu and later Buddhist sanctuaries have been built over the centuries. Of the two paths heading up the mountain, the one closer to the beach (at the end of the village) makes for a better circuit.

At the top of the staircase is a gate, Ong Chon, which is pockmarked with bullet holes, leading to Linh Ong Pagoda. Behind it, a path heads through two tunnels to caverns that contain several Buddhas and Cham carvings. A flight of steps also leads up to another cave, partially open to the sky, with two seated Buddhas in it. An elevator is also available if you want to give the steps a miss (or go up by elevator and descend the steps).

Immediately to the left as you enter Ong Chon Gate is the main path to the rest of Thuy Son, beginning with Xa Loi Pagoda, a beautiful stone tower that overlooks the coast. Stairs off the main pathway lead to Vong Hai Da, a viewpoint with a panorama of Danang Beach through scraggly trees. The stone-paved path continues to the right and into a mini-gorge. On the left is Van Thong Cave.

To reach other nearby caves near Thuy Son, exit the mini-gorge near Van Thong Cave through a battle-scarred masonry gate. A rocky path to the right leads to Linh Nham, a tall chimney-shaped cave with a small altar inside. Nearby, another path leads to Hoa Nghiem, a shallow cave with a Buddha. Left of here is cathedral-like Huyen Khong Cave, lit by an opening to the sky. The entrance to this spectacular chamber is guarded by two administrative mandarins (to the left) and two military mandarins (to the right).

Scattered about the cave are Buddhist and Confucian shrines; note the inscriptions carved into the stone walls. On the right, a door leads to a chamber with two stalactites – during the American War this was used as a VC field hospital. Inside is a plaque dedicated to the Women's Artillery Group, which destroyed 19 US aircraft from a base below the mountains in 1972.

Local buses between Danang and Hoi An (tickets 40,000d) can drop you at the Marble Mountains, 10km south of Danang. The site is also offered as a popular half-day tour by travel agencies in Hoi An and Danang.

2½ hours) and Hoi An (80,000d, one hour). Sinh Tourist can also advise on travel to Laos.

TAXI

Mai Linh (☑ 0511 356 5656) For reliable metered taxis. The Grab app can also be used in Danang to book cars but not motorbikes.

TRAIN

West of the city centre, Danang's **train station** (202 Đ Hai Phong) has services to all destinations on the north–south main line. Destinations from Danang include Dong Hoi (US$7 to US$20, 5½ to 8½ hours, six daily), Hanoi (US$19 to US$40, 14½ to 18 hours, six daily), HCMC (US$17 to US$36, 17 to 22 hours, six daily), Hue (US$2.50 to US$5, 2½ to four hours, seven daily) and Nha Trang (US$12.50 to US$30, nine to 12 hours, six daily).

The train ride to Hue is one of the best in the country – it's worth taking it as an excursion in itself to see the stunning coastline.

Around Danang

Danang makes an excellent base for day trips. The city is part of a long thin peninsula, at the northern tip of which is the more remote and spectacular coastal scenery of the Nui Son Tra (called Monkey Mountain by US soldiers). The rapidly evolving beach scene east of the river from My Khe down to An Bang is a draw, while the five Marble Mountains lie southeast of Danang.

Danang Beach

During the war, the Americans used the name China Beach to refer to this beautiful 30km sweep of fine white sand that starts at Monkey Mountain and ends near Hoi An to the south. Soldiers would be sent here for some R&R from bases all over the country.

Around Danang

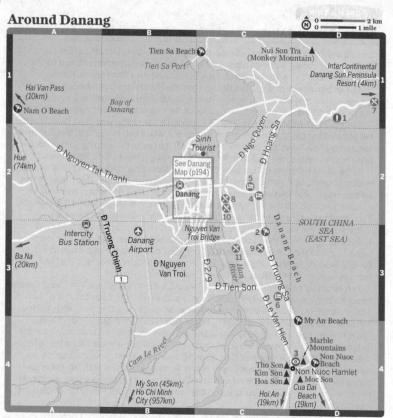

Around Danang

◎ Sights
1	Chua Linh Ung	D1
2	My Khe	C3
3	Thuy Son	D4

⬛ Sleeping
4	à la carte	C2
5	Frangipani Boutique Hotel	C2
6	Fusion Maia	C3

⊗ Eating
7	Bay Ban	D1
8	BBQ Un In	C2
9	Burger Bros	C3
10	Fatfish	C2
11	Mumtaz	C3
	Taco Ngon	(see 9)
	Vegan Ramen	(see 9)

⊕ Drinking & Nightlife
	Drop Coffee	(see 9)

The Vietnamese call sections of the beach by different names, including My Khe, My An, Non Nuoc, An Bang and Cua Dai. The northernmost stretch, My Khe, is now basically a mushrooming suburb of Danang, while in the south An Bang is considered Hoi An's beach. The area between is filled with a growing range of beach resorts; the beach at My Khe is busy with the manic construction of skyscraper hotel and apartment blocks, but the sand is clean and makes for pleasant strolls.

The best time for swimming is from April to July, when the sea is calmest. At other times the water can get rough. Note that lifeguards only patrol some sections of the beach. The surf can be good from around mid-September to December.

◎ Sights

My Khe
BEACH

Across the Song Han Bridge, My Khe is fast becoming Danang's easternmost suburb. In the early morning and evening, the beach fills up with city folk doing t'ai chi. Tourists emerge during peak suntanning hours, while locals prefer the evening; fishermen still cast off from the sands in their coracle boats. The water can have a dangerous undertow, especially in winter, however, it's protected by the bulk of Nui Son Tra. Construction is full-on alongside the beach.

🛏 Sleeping

**Frangipani
Boutique Hotel** BOUTIQUE HOTEL **$$**
(☑ 0236-393 8368; 8 Đ Nguyen Huu Thong; d US$45-50; ❄✳@🛜🏊) With just 11 rooms, and stylish common areas, the Frangipani is more like a classy European guesthouse. Rooms are spacious and modern with elegant decor, and it's just a short stroll to the sands of Danang Beach. There's a small indoor pool downstairs, bicycles are free to use, and there's also a pleasant on-site restaurant with courtyard seating.

à la carte DESIGN HOTEL **$$$**
(☑ 0236-359 9555; www.alacartedanangbeach. com; 200 Đ Vo Nguyen Giap; ste from US$183; ❄✳🛜🏊) The hotel à la carte dominates the beach's skyline, with 25 floors of all-suite accommodation, a spa and a fitness centre. The apartment-style suites are spacious and modern, with the best views at the front stretching effortlessly along the coast. An infinity pool sits in front of the hotel's very cool rooftop bar, and ground-floor restaurants include a deli and seafood bar.

Fusion Maia HOTEL **$$$**
(☑ 0236-396 7999; www.maiadanang.fusionresorts. com; Đ Vo Nguyen Giap, Khue My Beach; villas from US$466; ❄✳@🛜🏊) Contemporary beachfront hotel with an outstanding spa (all guests get a minimum of two treatments per day). And what a wellness zone it is, with treatment rooms, saunas and steam rooms set around a courtyard-style garden. One-, two- and three-bed villas all have minimalist decor and come with private pool. Free shuttle buses run to/from Hoi An.

🍴 Eating & Drinking

★ Taco Ngon TACOS **$**
(☑ 0906 504 284; www.facebook.com/tacongon; 19 Đ Tu Quan; tacos 39,000d; ⊙ 10.30am-10pm) This small spot thrust down a back street serves quite possibly Vietnam's best tacos. Tuck into fusion flavour combos like pork with wasabi coleslaw, fish with ginger and lime, or chicken with a tamarind barbecue sauce. Cool it all down with a cheap can of Larue beer or chuck in a tequila shot (30,000d).

Burger Bros BURGERS **$**
(☑ 0945 576 240; https://burgerbros.amebaownd. com; 18 Đ An Thuong 4; burgers 70,000-140,000d; ⊙ 11am-2pm & 5.30-10pm Tue-Sun) Owned by a Japanese surfer, Burger Bros is a cool spot for excellent gourmet burgers, plus well-priced beer and terrific french fries and coleslaw. Fish, shrimp and veggie patties also get the treatment, alongside blue-cheese beefburgers and the full-on My Khe burger.

❶ Getting There & Away

The My Khe section of Danang Beach is just 3km or so east of central Danang; it costs around 60,000d to get here by taxi.

Nui Son Tra

ELEV 850M

Jutting out into the sea, the Son Tra peninsula is crowned by the peak that the American soldiers called Monkey Mountain. Overlooking Danang to the south and the Hai Van Pass to the north, it was a prized radar and communications base during the American War. Until recently it was a closed military area, but now roads and beach resorts are opening up the peninsula.

The highlight of the area is the view from the summit of Nui Son Tra, which is stupendous on a clear day. All that remains of the American military presence are a couple of radar domes (still used by the Vietnamese military and a no-go for tourists) next to a helicopter pad, now a lookout point. The steep road to the summit is pretty deserted and road conditions can be iffy. If you're going on a motorbike, you'll need a powerful one to make it to the top. The turn-off to this road is about 3km before Tien Sa Port and marked by a blue sign that reads 'Son Tra Eco-Tourism'.

On the other side of Nui Son Tra, next to the port, is sheltered Tien Sa Beach. A memorial near the port commemorates an unfortunate episode of colonial history. Spanish-led Filipino and French troops attacked Danang in August 1858, ostensibly to end Emperor Tu Duc's mistreatment of Catholics. The city quickly fell, but the invaders were hit by sickness. By the summer of 1859, the number of invaders who had died of illness was 20 times the number who had been killed in combat.

WORTH A TRIP

BA NA HILL STATION

Around 40km west of Danang lies lush Ba Na. Originally established in 1919 by the French as a hill resort, the 200-odd old villas are now ruined, but the refreshingly cool weather and gorgeous countryside views make it a worthwhile trip from Danang.

Until WWII, the French were carried up the last 20km of rough mountain road by sedan chair, but now a 5.7km cable-car system has opened up access. The ride involves a rise of almost 1400m, a truly spectacular trip over dense jungle and waterfalls.

Around the resort, mountain tracks lead to waterfalls and viewing points. Near the top is the Linh Ung Pagoda (dating to 2004) and a colossal 24m-high white seated Buddha that's visible for miles around. At the top, attractions include the **Golden Bridge** (Cau Vang), a replica French provincial town, a funicular railway ascending even higher, and an exciting and fun downhill luge. The 150m-long Golden Bridge is designed to seem like it's supported by two massive stone (fibreglass and wire mesh, actually) hands. It's quite a sight and the views are superb, but it can get awfully crowded. Avoid public holidays.

Take an extra layer or two whatever time of year you visit – when it's 36°C on the coast, it could be 15°C on the mountain. Cloud and mist also cling to the hill top, so if you can try to visit on a clear day.

From the resort's carpark and entrance, the cable car (return 650,000d) ascends to the mountain resort. Travel agencies in Danang or Hoi An can arrange day tours (per person from US$60); a return taxi from Danang is around US$70.

⊙ Sights

Chua Linh Ung   MONUMENT
The major human-made draw on the peninsula is Chua Linh Ung, a temple whose name means 'Spirit Responding Temple'. The highlight is a simply colossal statue of the Bodhisattva Quan Am, or in her fuller name, Quan The Am Bo Tat (literally, the goddess who 'Listens to the cries of the world'). The towering, white statue is positioned on a lotus-shaped platform that looks south to Danang city. Note the signs not to feed the monkeys, which scamper through the trees.

🛏 Sleeping & Eating

**InterContinental
Danang Sun Peninsula Resort**   HOTEL **$$$**
(☑0236-393 8888; www.danang.intercontinental. com; Son Tra; r/ste from US$350/450; ☺❄🛜❄) Spilling down a hillside, this huge resort hotel dominates this corner of Son Tra, with golf buggies whisking its pampered guests around the landscaped grounds. There's an impressive spa, fully loaded fitness centre and a huge main pool.

Bay Ban   SEAFOOD **$$**
(☑0511 221 4237; Son Tra; meals 90,000-250,000d; ☺11am-9.30pm) This seafood restaurant is very popular with Vietnamese families on weekends and holidays, but is usually quiet otherwise. Eat right over the water in one of the thatched shelters in the bay. Fresh fish, spider crab, eel and shrimp dishes all feature.

ⓘ Getting There & Around

The peninsula and Monkey Mountain are best explored independently by motorcycle, and travel agencies in Danang and Hoi An also offer day tours incorporating sights including the Linh Ung Buddha statue.

Hoi An

☑0235 / POP 152,000

Graceful, historic Hoi An is Vietnam's most atmospheric and delightful town. Once a major port, it boasts the grand architecture and beguiling riverside setting that befit its heritage, and the 21st-century curses of traffic and pollution are almost entirely absent.

The face of the Old Town has preserved its incredible legacy of tottering Japanese merchant houses, elaborate Chinese guildhalls, ancestral halls and ancient tea warehouses – though, of course, residents and rice fields have been gradually replaced by tourist businesses. Lounge bars, boutique hotels, travel agents, a glut of tailor shops and vast numbers of Korean and Chinese tourists are very much part of the scene. And yet, down by the market and over on Cam Nam Island, you'll find that life has changed little. Travel a few kilometres further – you'll find some superb bicycle, motorbike and boat trips – and some of central Vietnam's most enticingly laid-back scenery and beaches are within easy reach.

History

The earliest evidence of human habitation here dates back 2200 years: excavated ceramic fragments are thought to belong to the late Iron Age Sa Huynh civilisation, which is related to the Dong Son culture of northern Vietnam. From the 2nd to the 10th centuries, this was a busy seaport of the Champa kingdom, and archaeologists have discovered the foundations of numerous Cham towers around Hoi An.

In 1306 the Cham king handed over Quang Nam province as a gift when he married a Vietnamese princess. When his successor refused to recognise the deal, fighting broke out and chaos reigned for the next century. By the 15th century, peace was restored, allowing commerce to resume. During the next four centuries, Hoi An – known as Faifoo to Western traders – was one of Southeast Asia's major ports. Chinese, Japanese, Dutch, Portuguese, Spanish, Indian, Filipino, Indonesian, Thai, French, British and American ships all came to call, and the town's warehouses teemed with treasures: high-grade silk, fabrics, paper, porcelain, areca nuts, pepper, Chinese medicines, elephant tusks, beeswax, mother-of-pearl and lacquer.

Chinese and Japanese traders left their mark on Hoi An. Both groups came in the spring, driven south by monsoon winds. They would stay in Hoi An until the summer, when southerly winds would blow them home. During their four-month sojourn in Hoi An, they rented waterfront houses for use as warehouses and living quarters. Some began leaving full-time agents in Hoi An to take care of their off-season business affairs.

The Japanese ceased coming to Hoi An after 1637 (when the Japanese government forbade contact with the outside world), but the Chinese lingered. The town's Chinese assembly halls (or guildhalls) still play a special role for southern Vietnam's ethnic Chinese, some of whom come from all over the region to participate in congregation-wide celebrations and worship folk deities of south China.

This was also the first place in Vietnam to be exposed to Christianity. Among the 17th-century missionary visitors was Alexandre de Rhodes, who devised the Latin-based *quoc ngu* script for the Vietnamese language.

Although Hoi An was almost completely destroyed during the Tay Son Rebellion, it was rebuilt and continued to be an important port until the late 19th century, when the Thu Bon River silted up. Danang (Tourane) to the north took over as the region's main port. Under French rule, Hoi An served as an administrative centre. It was virtually untouched in the American War, thanks to the cooperation of both sides.

Then in the 1990s, a tourism whirlwind swept through the town, transforming the local economy. The town was declared a Unesco World Heritage Site in 1999, and there are now very strict rules in place to safeguard the Old Town's unique heritage.

These days Hoi An's economy is booming, and at times the Old Town can struggle to contain the sheer number of selfie-stick-toting visitors.

◉ Sights

By Unesco decree, more than 800 historic buildings in Hoi An have been preserved, so much of the Old Town looks as it did several centuries ago. Eighteen of these buildings are open to visitors and require an Old Town ticket for admission; the fee goes towards funding conservation work.

Each ticket allows you to visit five different heritage attractions from a total selection of 22, including museums, assembly halls, ancient houses and a traditional music show at the **Handicraft Workshop** (9 Đ Nguyen Thai Hoc; entry with Old Town ticket). Tickets are valid for 10 days. As you enter each sight, a ticket stub will be removed.

Technically, the tickets are for access into the Old Town itself, but you won't normally be checked if you're just dining or shopping in the area. Keep your ticket with you just in case. You could be checked for a ticket as you cross the Japanese Covered Bridge, but insisting that you are just visiting shops nearby usually works. When the bridge is very busy with pedestrians, chances are you won't be asked either. If a ticket stub is clipped off when you cross the bridge, say you have had one removed already next time you cross, if the ticket collectors ask again.

All four museums are small. Displays are pretty basic and the information provided is rather minimal.

CENTRAL VIETNAM HOI AN

Hoi An

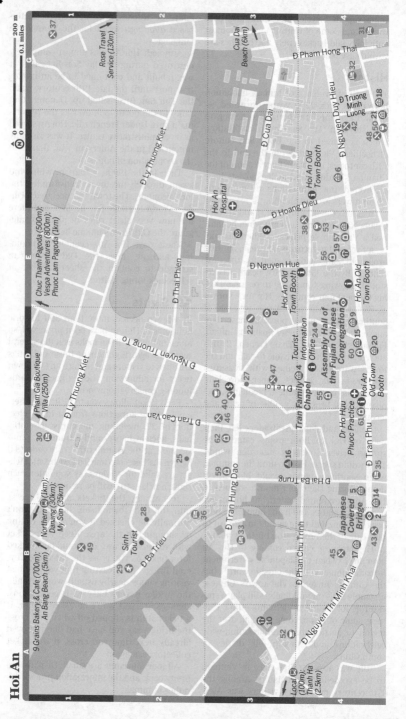

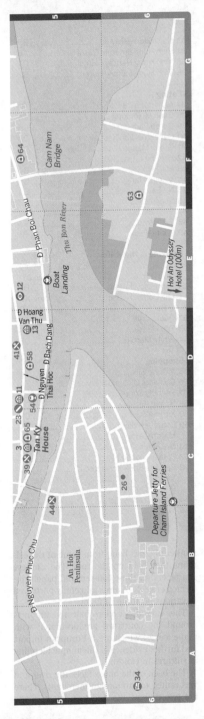

The Chinese who settled in Hoi An identified themselves according to their province of origin. Each community built its own assembly hall or guildhall, known as *hoi quan* in Vietnamese, for social gatherings, meetings and religious celebrations.

All the old houses, except Diep Dong Nguyen (p209) and Quan Thang (p208), offer short guided tours. They are efficient, if a tad perfunctory. You'll be whisked to a heavy wooden chair while your guide recites a scripted introduction to the house, and gives a souvenir soft sell. You're free to wander around the house after the tour.

One downside to putting these old houses on show is that what were once living spaces now seem dead and museum-like, the family having sequestered itself away from visitors' eyes. Huge tour groups can completely spoil the intimacy of the experience too, as they jostle for selfie shots.

Despite the number of tourists (South Koreans and Chinese in large numbers) who flood into Hoi An, it is still a conservative town. Visitors should dress modestly, especially since some of the old houses are still private homes.

★ **Japanese Covered Bridge**   BRIDGE
(Cau Nhat Ban; entry with Old Town ticket; ⏱24hr)
Emblematic of Hoi An, this beautiful bridge was first constructed in the 1590s by the Japanese community to link it with the Chinese quarters. Over the centuries the ornamentation has remained relatively faithful to the original Japanese design.

The structure is solidly constructed because of the threat of earthquakes. The entrances to the bridge are guarded by weathered statues: a pair of monkeys on one side, a pair of dogs on the other. According to one story, many of Japan's emperors were born in the years of the dog and monkey. Another tale says that construction of the bridge started in the year of the monkey and was finished in the year of the dog. The stelae, listing all Vietnamese and Chinese contributors to a subsequent restoration of the bridge, are written in *chu nho* (Chinese characters) – the Vietnamese *nom* script had not yet become popular.

The French flattened out the roadway for cars, but the original arched shape was restored in 1986.

★ **Tan Ky House**   HISTORIC BUILDING
(101 Đ Nguyen Thai Hoc; entry with Old Town ticket; ⏱8am-noon & 2-4.30pm) Built two centuries

Hoi An

ago by an ethnically Vietnamese family, this gem of a house has been lovingly preserved through seven generations. Look out for signs of Japanese and Chinese influences in the architecture. Japanese elements include the ceiling (in the sitting area), which is supported by three progressively shorter beams, one on top of the other. Under the crab-shell ceiling are carvings of crossed sabres wrapped in silk ribbon. The sabres symbolise force; the silk represents flexibility.

The interior is brightened by a beautiful detail: Chinese poems written in inlaid mother-of-pearl hang from some of the columns that hold up the roof. The Chinese characters on these 150-year-old panels are formed entirely of birds gracefully portrayed in various positions of flight.

The carved wooden balcony supports around the courtyard are decorated with grape leaves, which are a European import and further evidence of the unique blending of cultures in Hoi An.

The back of the house faces the river and was rented out to foreign merchants. There are two pulleys attached to a beam in the loft – in the past they were used for moving goods into storage, and today for raising furniture for safekeeping from floods.

The exterior of the roof is made of tiles; inside, the ceiling consists of wood. This design keeps the house cool in summer and warm in winter.

★ Assembly Hall of the Fujian Chinese Congregation TEMPLE

(Phuc Kien Hoi Quan; opposite 35 Đ Tran Phu; entry with Old Town ticket; ⊙ 7am-5.30pm) Originally a traditional assembly hall (or guildhall), this structure was later transformed into a temple for the worship of Thien Hau, a deity who protects seafarers. The green-tiled triple gateway dates from 1975. The mural on the right-hand wall depicts Thien Hau, her way lit by lantern light as she crosses a stormy sea to rescue a foundering ship. Opposite is a mural of the heads of the six Fujian families who fled from China to Hoi An in the 17th century.

The penultimate chamber of this guildhall contains a statue of Thien Hau. To either side of the entrance stand red-skinned Thuan Phong Nhi and green-skinned Thien Ly Nhan, deities who alert Thien Hau when sailors are in distress.

In the final chamber, the central altar contains seated figures of the heads of the six Fujian families. The smaller figures below them represent their successors as clan leaders. Behind the altar on the right are three fairies and smaller figures representing the 12 *ba mu* (midwives), each of whom teaches newborns a different skill necessary for the first year of life: smiling, sucking and so forth.

The goddess is also worshipped by childless couples who come to pray for offspring and leave fresh fruit as offerings.

Tran Family Chapel HISTORIC BUILDING

(21 Đ Le Loi; entry with Old Town ticket; ⊙ 7.30am-noon & 2-5.30pm) Built for worshipping family ancestors of the Tran (陳) clan, this chapel (more accurately an ancestral hall) dates back to 1802. It was commissioned by Tran Tu, a member of the clan who ascended to the rank of mandarin and served as an ambassador to China. His picture is to the right of the chapel as you enter. The architecture of the building reflects the influence of Chinese (the 'turtle'-style roof), Japanese (triple beam) and vernacular (bow-and-arrow detailing) styles.

The wooden boxes on the altar contain the Tran ancestors' stone tablets, with chiselled Chinese characters setting out the dates of birth and death, along with some small personal effects. On the anniversary of each family member's death, their box is opened, incense is burned and food is offered.

After a short tour, you'll be shown to the 'antique' room, where there are lots of coins for sale, and a side room full of souvenirs.

Assembly Hall of the Hainan Chinese Congregation HISTORIC BUILDING

(Hai Nam Hoi Quan; 10 Đ Tran Phu; ⊙ 8am-5pm) **FREE** Built in 1851, this assembly hall is a memorial to 108 merchants from Hainan Island who were mistaken for pirates and killed in Quang Nam province. The elaborate dais contains plaques to their memory. In front of the central altar is a fine gilded woodcarving of Chinese court life.

Phung Hung Old House HISTORIC BUILDING

(4 Đ Nguyen Thi Minh Khai; entry with Old Town ticket; ⊙ 8am-6pm) Just a few steps down from the Japanese Covered Bridge, this old house has a wide, welcoming entrance hall decorated with exquisite lanterns, wall hangings and embroidery. You can walk out onto a balcony and there's also an impressive suspended altar. Note that with all the photographing by the crowds that squeeze onto the balcony, the staff may control numbers to avoid the risk of it collapsing.

Confucius Temple CONFUCIAN TEMPLE

(Mieu Tho Khong Tu; Đ Tran Hung Dao) Behind an impressive gate emblazoned with Chinese *chu nho* characters that simply translate as 'Confucius Temple', this magnificent temple to the west of all the action is a colourful explosion of ceramic tiles. Look out for the spirit wall across the bridge that depicts a *ky lan*, a mythical chimerical creature often depicted in Confucian temples. At the rear is an effigy of Confucius (Khong Tu), venerated in the 'Great Achievement Hall'.

Assembly Hall of the Chaozhou Chinese Congregation HISTORIC BUILDING

(Trieu Chau Hoi Quan; opposite 157 Đ Nguyen Duy Hieu; entry with Old Town ticket or 10,000d donation; ⊙ 8am-5pm) Built in 1752, the highlights in this congregational hall are the gleaming woodcarvings on the beams, walls and altar – absolutely stunning in their intricacy. You could stand here for hours to unravel the stories, but if you're just popping by quickly, look for the carvings on the doors in front of the altar of two Chinese women wearing their hair in an unexpectedly Japanese style.

CENTRAL VIETNAM HOI AN

HOI AN HOUSES: A CLOSER LOOK

The historic buildings of Hoi An not only survived the 20th century's wars, they also retained features of traditional architecture rarely seen today. As they have been for centuries, some shopfronts are shuttered at night with horizontal planks inserted into grooves that cut into the columns that support the roof.

Some roofs are made up of thousands of brick-coloured *am* and *duong* (yin and yang) roof tiles – so called because of the way the alternating rows of concave and convex tiles fit snugly together. During the rainy season the lichens and moss that live on the tiles spring to life, turning entire rooftops bright green.

A number of Hoi An's houses have round pieces of wood with an *am-duong* symbol in the middle surrounded by a spiral design over the doorway. These *mat cua* ('watchful eyes') are supposed to protect the residents from harm.

Hoi An's historic structures are gradually being sensitively restored. Strict rules govern the colour that houses can be painted and the signs that can be used. To enhance the Old Town feel, lanterns are mandatory and fluorescent lights are banned.

It's not just individual buildings that have survived – it's whole streetscapes. This is particularly true around Đ Tran Phu and waterside promenade Đ Bach Dang. In the former French quarter to the east of Cam Nam Bridge, there's a whole block of colonnaded houses, painted in the mustard yellow typical of French colonial buildings.

Cam Kim Island   ISLAND

The master woodcarvers who crafted the intricate detail adorning Hoi An's public buildings and the historic homes of the town's merchants came from Kim Bong village on Cam Kim Island. Most of the woodcarvings on sale in Hoi An are produced here.

Boats to the island leave from the boat landing (p220) at Đ Bach Dang in town (35,000d, 30 minutes). The village and island, quite rural in character, are fun to explore by bicycle for a day.

Ba Le Well   LANDMARK

This square well's claim to fame is that it's the source of water for making authentic cao lau (p213), a Hoi An speciality. The well is said to date from Cham times and elderly people make their daily pilgrimage to fill buckets here. To find it, turn down the alley opposite 35 Đ Phan Chu Trinh and take the second laneway to the right.

Phuoc Lam Pagoda   BUDDHIST TEMPLE

(Thon 2a, Cam Ha; ⊘8am-5pm) This pagoda (founded in the mid-17th century) is associated with An Thiem, a Vietnamese prodigy and monk from the age of eight. When he was 18, he volunteered for the army so his brothers could escape the draft; he eventually rose to the rank of general. Later he returned to the monkhood, but to atone for his sins of war he volunteered to clean the Hoi An market for 20 years, then joined this pagoda as its head monk.

Chuc Thanh Pagoda   BUDDHIST TEMPLE

(Khu Vuc 7, Tan An; ⊘8am-6pm) Founded in 1454 by a Buddhist monk from China, this is the oldest pagoda in Hoi An. Among the antique ritual objects still in use are several bells, a stone gong that is two centuries old and a carp-shaped wooden gong said to be even more venerable. To get to Chuc Thanh Pagoda, go north all the way to the end of Đ Nguyen Truong To and turn left. Follow the lane for 500m.

Museum of Trading Ceramics   MUSEUM

(80 Đ Tran Phu; entry with Old Town ticket; ⊘7am-5.30pm) Occupies a restored wooden house and contains a small collection of artefacts from all over Asia, with oddities from as far afield as Egypt. While this reveals that Hoi An had some rather impressive trading links, it takes an expert's eye to appreciate the display. The exhibition on the restoration of Hoi An's old houses provides a useful crash course in Old Town architecture.

Quan Thang House   HISTORIC BUILDING

(77 Đ Tran Phu; entry with Old Town ticket; ⊘7am-5pm) This house is three centuries old and was built by a Chinese captain. As usual, the architecture includes Japanese and Chinese elements. There are some especially fine carvings of peacocks and flowers on the teak walls of the rooms around the courtyard, on the roof beams and under the crab-shell roof (in the salon beside the courtyard).

Museum of Sa Huynh Culture
& Museum of the Revolution   MUSEUM
(149 Đ Tran Phu; entry with Old Town ticket; ⊗7am-6pm) This two-floor museum has a collection of stone, bronze, gold, glass and agate jewellery, assorted ceramic fragments and burial jars dating from the early Dong Son civilisation of Sa Huynh.

Museum of Folklore in Hoi An   MUSEUM
(33 Đ Nguyen Thai Hoc/62 Đ Bach Dang; entry with Old Town ticket; ⊗7am-5.30pm) The exhibits at this 150-year-old Chinese trading house give some idea of local customs and culture. The view of the river from upstairs is very picturesque.

Assembly Hall of the Cantonese
Chinese Congregation   HISTORIC BUILDING
(Quang Trieu Hoi Quan; 176 Đ Tran Phu; entry with Old Town ticket; ⊗8am-5pm) Founded in 1786, this assembly hall has a tall, airy entrance, which opens on to a splendidly over-the-top mosaic statue of a dragon and a carp. The main altar is dedicated to Quan Cong, a revered Chinese general who represents many virtues, including sincerity, loyalty, integrity and justice. The garden behind has an even more incredible dragon statue. The goat statue at the rear is a symbol of Canton (Guangzhou), China.

Quan Cong Temple   CONFUCIAN TEMPLE
(Chua Ong; 24 Đ Tran Phu; entry with Old Town ticket; ⊗8am-5pm) Founded in 1653, this small temple is dedicated to Quan Cong, an esteemed Chinese general who is worshipped as a symbol of loyalty, sincerity, integrity and justice. His partially gilded statue, made of papier mâché on a wooden frame, is on the central altar at the back of the sanctuary. When someone makes an offering to the portly looking Quan Cong, the caretaker solemnly strikes a bronze bowl, making a bell-like sound.

Tran Duong House   HISTORIC BUILDING
(25 Đ Phan Boi Chau; 20,000d; ⊗9am-7pm) There's a whole block of colonnaded French colonial buildings on Đ Phan Boi Chau between Nos 22 and 73, among them the 19th-century Tran Duong House. It's still a private home, so a family member will show you around. There's some antique French and Chinese furniture, including a sideboard buffet and a sitting room with elaborate mother-of-pearl inlay. By contrast, the large, plain wooden table in the front room is the family bed.

Chinese All-Community
Assembly Hall   HISTORIC BUILDING
(Chua Ba; 64 Đ Tran Phu; ⊗8am-5pm) **FREE** Founded in 1773, this assembly hall was used by Fujian, Cantonese, Hainanese, Chaozhou and Hakka congregations in Hoi An. To the right of the entrance are portraits of Chinese resistance heroes in Vietnam who died during WWII. The well-restored main temple is a total assault on the senses, with smoking incense spirals, demonic-looking deities, dragons and lashings of red lacquer – it's dedicated to Thien Hau, the goddess protector of seafarers commonly worshipped along the south coast of China.

Diep Dong Nguyen House   HISTORIC BUILDING
(58 Đ Nguyen Thai Hoc; ⊗8am-noon & 2-4.30pm) **FREE** Built for a wealthy Chinese merchant in the late 19th century, this old house looks like an apothecary from another era. The front room was once a dispensary for *thuoc bac* (Chinese medicine); the medicines were stored in the glass-enclosed cases lining the walls.

Phap Bao Pagoda   BUDDHIST TEMPLE
(Đ Hai Ba Trung) Meaning the 'Treasure of the Law Temple', Phap Bao Pagoda has a colourful facade of ceramics and murals and an elaborate roof with snake-like dragons. There's a huge central courtyard containing hundreds of potted plants and bonsai trees.

🏃 Activities

Nomad Yoga   YOGA
(📞0777 184 604; www.nomadyogahoian.com; 22 Nguyen Du; class 200,000d, 1 week's unlimited classes 900,000d) 🏄 Classes are either held in a peaceful studio location surrounded by rice fields or, in the mornings at Salt Pub on An Bang Beach. Spa treatments and healing programs are also available, and the on-site cafe specialises in natural foods, tasty breakfast bowls and juice detox programs. Check the online schedule. Yoga teacher training and qigong are also offered.

Diving & Snorkelling
A trip to the Cham Islands (p225) is a superb excursion, and Hoi An's two dive schools offer packages including overnight camping and diving trips. The diving is not world class, but can be intriguing and the corals are healthy, with reefs being revived as the marine environment has improved over recent years.

VISITING THE CO TU

Living high in the mountains inland from Hoi An, the Co Tu people are one of the smallest and most traditional minority groups in Vietnam. Their villages comprise of stilt houses set around a *guol*, a community building used for meetings, rituals and performances. Until quite recently, facial tattoos were common, and traditional dress is still worn when cultural performances are given for visitors. In the French and American Wars, the Co Tu were feared and respected fighters, and visitors often get to meet community legends who fought bravely against the Americans.

One Co Tu settlement, **Bho Hoong**, has developed a fine community tourism project allowing visitors to stay in the village. Co Tu guides have been trained and income is ploughed back into the area. Accommodation is in very comfortable **bungalows** (www. bhohoongbungalows.com; d/tw from US$75; ☻) with classy Asian decor and spacious bathrooms trimmed with bamboo and river stones.

Independent overnight stays can be booked via online accommodation websites, and the village can also be visited on tours with Hoi An Jeep Adventures and Hoi An Motorbike Adventures. Two-day/one-night tours (per person from US$350) from Hoi An include meals and sightseeing around stunning scenery near the Lao border. Transport can be in a US jeep or an air-con car, and longer three-day/two-night tours (per person from US$525) are also available.

A PADI Discover Scuba dive costs US$65 and two fun dives are US$100, while Open Water courses start at around US$375. Snorkelling costs around US$50, including gear (overnight camping is also available).

It's usually only possible to dive or snorkel between February and September; the best conditions and visibility are from June to August.

Blue Coral Diving
DIVING
(☑ 0235-627 9297; www.divehoian.com; 33 Đ Tran Hung Dao) A friendly, professional outfit with an 18m dive boat and an additional speedboat. Cham Island snorkelling trips cost US$50 and there are Professional Association of Diving Instructors (PADI) courses, too; two dives cost US$100. Blue Coral is the only five-star IDC-certified PADI centre in central Vietnam. Overnight camping on the Cham Islands is also available.

Cham Island Diving Center
DIVING
(☑ 0235-391 0782; www.vietnamscubadiving. com; 88 Đ Nguyen Thai Hoc; snorkelling day trips 1,200,000d, overnight snorkelling/diving trips 2,300,000/3,000,000d; ☺ 9am-9.30pm) Run by a friendly, experienced team, this dive shop's mantra is 'no troubles, make bubbles'. It has a large boat and also a speedboat for zippy transfers. One-day and overnight trips to the Cham Islands are available. The centre also has a bar (Dive Bar) and restaurant.

Massage & Spa

There are many massage and treatment centres in Hoi An. Most are average, however, run by locals with minimal experience or training. A basic massage costs around US$12 an hour – there's a strip of places offering simple massages along Đ Ba Trieu. At the other end of the scale are indulgent places that offer a wonderful spa experience (with prices to match); these are mostly based in the luxury hotels.

Palmarosa
SPA
(☑ 0235-393 3999; www.palmarosaspa.vn; 48 Đ Ba Trieu; massages & treatments from 220,000d; ☺ 10am-9pm) This highly professional spa offers massages (including Thai, Swedish, Indian head massage and basalt hot-stone), scrubs and facials, as well as hand and foot care.

Tours

Vespa Adventures
TOURS
(☑ 0938 500 997; www.vespaadventures.com; Alley 22/2, 170 Đ Ly Thai To; per person $US69-80; ☺ 8am-5pm) Quite possibly the most fun and most stylish way to explore around Hoi An, Vespa Adventures offers the opportunity to ride pillion on classic retro two-wheelers with an Italian accent. There are morning and afternoon departures, and a popular after-dark 'Streets & Eats of Hoi An' option with lots of quality food and cold beer.

Hoi An Jeep Adventures
DRIVING
(☑ 0905 101 930, 0235-391 1930; www.vietnam-jeeps.com; Nguyen Chi Thanh; per person from US$96) Fun and fascinating half-day to three-day trips in classic US army and Russian jeeps taking in everything from My

Son, Monkey Mountain, the Hai Van Pass, Danang street food, the Co Tu village of Bho Hoong and the road to Hue. A daily jeep tour (US$65) over the Hai Van Pass to and from Hue leaves at 9am and arrives at 4pm, taking in sights en route.

Grasshopper Adventures   CYCLING
(✓0932 034 286; www.grasshopperadventures.com; 62 Đ Hai Ba Trung; per person US$37-47) Highly recommended biking tours on very well-maintained bikes. Options include a daytime countryside tour, a trip to My Son, combined biking and kayaking and an excellent sunset food tour. Longer multiday tours exploring Vietnam are also available.

Hoi An Motorbike Adventures   TOURS
(✓0905 101 930, 0235-391 1930; www.motorbiketours-hoian.com; Nguyen Chi Thanh; from US$50) Specialises in tours on hardy offroad motorbikes. The guides really know the terrain, and the trips make use of beautiful back roads and riverside tracks. Self-ride (with a licence) or back-of-the-bike pillion options are available, and some of the itineraries can also be done in a jeep.

Hoi An Free Tour   CYCLING
(www.freetour.com/hoi-an/free-bike-tours; 567 Đ Hai Ba Trung) Ride on a bike around the fringes of Hoi An with students. You get to meet the locals and see village life; they get to practise their English. Although tours are free, you will also need a reasonable 100,000d for bike rental, ferries and local community support.

Phat Tire Ventures   ADVENTURE
(✓0235-653 9839; www.ptv-vietnam.com; 80 Đ Le Hong Phong; per person from US$39) Offers a terrific mountain-bike trip to the My Son ruins that takes in country lanes and temple visits. Pickups from hotels are included. Also has adventure thrills via rappelling and rock climbing.

Hoi An Photo Tour   TOURS
(✓0905 671 898; www.hoianphototour.com; 42 Đ Phan Boi Chau; per person from US$40) Excellent tours with experienced photographer Etienne Bossot. Sunrise and sunset tours are most popular, harnessing Hoi An's delicate light for images of fishers and rice paddies. Experienced and newbie photographers are both catered for, and specialist private and night-time workshops are also available. Check the website for details of occasional three-day photography trips uncovering more remote areas around Hoi An.

You can book through the March Gallery, at the same address.

Hoi An Kayak Tours   KAYAKING
(✓0979 437 338; www.hoiankayaktours.com; Đ Tran Nhan Tong, Thuan Tinh Pier; kayak/paddleboard rental from US$10, kayak & paddleboard tours from $US29, bike & boat trips from US$25; ⊙8am-5pm) Has a wide range of kayak and paddleboard tours to explore the backwaters and riverine villages around Hoi An. Independent rentals of kayaks and paddleboards are also available, and long-tail boat tours coupled with bicycle tours incorporate sunsets and local food.

SUP Monkey   TOURS
(✓0125 593 1463; www.supmonkey.net; 250 Đ Cua Dai; per person US$30-120; ⊙9am-8pm Mon-Sat) Take to a stand-up paddleboard to explore the waterways around Hoi An. Options include a sunrise tour starting at An Bang Beach as well as a wilderness tour in the hills near My Son.

Heaven & Earth   CYCLING
(✓0235-386 4362; www.vietnam-bicycle.com; 61 Đ Ngo Quyen, An Hoi; tours from US$19) Heaven & Earth's cycling tours are well thought out and not too strenuous; they explore the Song Thu river delta area. Mountain-bike tours take in local dirt trails and rickety bamboo bridges.

⭐ Festivals & Events

Full Moon Festival   CULTURAL
(⊙5-11pm 14th day each lunar month) Hoi An is a delightful place to be on the 14th day of each lunar month, when the town celebrates a Full Moon Festival. Motorised vehicles are banned from the Old Town, while street markets sell handicrafts, souvenirs and food, and all the lanterns come out. Traditional plays and musical events are also performed.

🛏 Sleeping

Hoi An has good-value accommodation in all price categories. There are only a couple of hotels in the Old Town, but nightlife finishes early here so there is little need to be right in the middle of things when plenty of decent sleeping options are close by. The best places book up fast, so plan as far ahead as you can. Accommodation options have also opened around the town's periphery, as Hoi An expands to the fulfil the voracious tourism sector.

Many budget and midrange places are spread out to the northwest around Đ Hai Ba Trung and Đ Ba Trieu. Pretty An Hoi Peninsula and Can Nam island are also very close to the Old Town. Many luxury hotels are a few kilometres from town, on the beach, but all offer shuttle-bus transfers. Another option is staying at An Bang Beach.

Lazy Bear Hostel
HOSTEL $

(☏ 0905 025 491; www.facebook.com/lazybear hostel; 12 Đ Tran Quuc Toan; dm/d incl breakfast US$8/20; ❄ 🛜) This small family-owned hostel has a good location – the Old Town and Cua Dai Beach are both around 2.5km away – and lots of free inclusions, such as breakfast, bicycles and the occasional bar crawl and food tour. A relaxing garden and modern bathrooms in the private ensuite rooms seal the deal at one of Hoi An's best-value accommodation options.

Hoi An Backpackers Hostel
HOSTEL $

(☏ 0235-391 4400; www.vietnambackpackerhostels. com; 252 Đ Cua Dai; dm/tw/d incl breakfast US$12/ 40/40; ⊜ ❄ @ 🛜 ⛱) This purpose-built hostel (part of a hostel empire spanning the nation) offers decent and clean dorms and private en-suite rooms. A poolside bar and restaurant and plenty of quiet common areas add kudos. It's handily located between the Old Town and the beach, and bikes for exploring are available to hire.

⭐ Hoi An Odyssey Hotel
BOUTIQUE HOTEL $$

(☏ 0235-391 1818; www.hoianodysseyhotel.com; Đ Xuyen Trung, Cam Thanh; d from US$55; ⊜ ❄ 🛜 ⛱) In a semi-rural location across on Cam Thanh island – an easy 1.5km bike ride from the Old Town – the Odyssey is a great haven after a day's exploring. Rice-paddy and river views, a compact pool and stylish rooms all combine at one of Hoi An's best hotels. Bicycles and a handy shuttle to a private beach are both complimentary.

⭐ Nu Ni Homestay
GUESTHOUSE $$

(☏ 0235-392 7979; www.nu-ni-homestay.hoi-an -hotels.com/en; 131/12 Đ Tran Hung Dao; d/tr/f US$22/32/42; ⊜ ❄ 🛜) Hidden down a quiet lane just north of the Old Town, the Nu Ni Homestay has seven spacious and sparkling rooms – some with large balconies – and a positive can-do attitude from the friendly family owners. Modern bathrooms and a comfortable shared downstairs area all make Nu Ni a great choice. Breakfast is not included in the price.

Vinh Hung Emerald Resort
HOTEL $$

(☏ 0510 393 4999; www.vinhhungemeraldresort. com; Minh An, An Hoi; r US$50-80, ste US$95; ⊜ ❄ 🛜 ⛱) A beautifully designed hotel with a riverside location in An Hoi, and modernist rooms that represent good value for money. All rooms face the lovely central pool, or have a terrace facing the river. There's a fitness centre and small spa.

Pham Gia Boutique Villa
GUESTHOUSE $$

(☏ 0235-396 3963, 0914 085 075; www.pham giahoian.com; 73/1 Đ Phan Dinh Phung; d/ste from US$35/42; ⊜ ❄ 🛜 ⛱) Centred on its blue pool, Pham Gia edges into the boutique-guesthouse category. Blending colonial and local design, rooms are spacious and sunny, and the friendly owner is a Hoi An local with plenty of experience in the travel industry. Bikes are provided free of charge, and both the Old Town and An Bang Beach are just a short ride away.

Hoi An Garden Villas
HOTEL $$

(☏ 0510 393 9539; www.hoiangardenvillas.com; 145 Đ Tran Nhat Duat; d US$28-40, f US$65; ❄ 🛜 ⛱) Enjoying a tranquil location on a quiet, suburban lane, this eight-roomed hotel has attractive doubles and villa rooms, all with huge beds, bathtubs, a balcony or terrace with pool views, fine-quality furnishings and free bicycles. It's about 2km east of the centre.

Ha An Hotel
HISTORIC HOTEL $$

(☏ 0235-386 3126; www.haanhotel.com; 6-8 Đ Phan Boi Chau; r US$65-110; ❄ @ 🛜) Elegant and refined, the Ha An feels more like a colonial mansion than a hotel. All rooms have nice individual touches – textile wall hangings, calligraphy or paintings – and views fall over a gorgeous central garden. The helpful, well-trained staff make staying here a joy. It's about a five-minute walk from the centre of town (free bikes are available too). The hotel has a spa, a cafe and a bar.

Vinh Hung Library Hotel
HOTEL $$

(☏ 0235-391 6277; www.vinhhunglibraryhotel.com; 96 Đ Ba Trieu; r US$30-55; ❄ @ 🛜 ⛱) This fine minihotel has modish rooms with huge beds, dark-wood furniture, writing desks and satellite TVs; some rooms also have balconies, though the cheapest come without windows. All bathrooms are sleek and inviting, and the rooftop pool area is perfect for catching some rays or cooling off. The large, eponymous and browse-worthy library is on the ground floor.

Vinh Hung Heritage Hotel HISTORIC HOTEL **$$**
(☑0510 386 1621; www.vinhhungheritagehotel.
com; 143 Đ Tran Phu; r US$65-75; ⊛❋@�) For
heritage atmosphere, this hotel (occupying
a 200-year-old townhouse) is unmatched, its
whole timber structure simply oozing history
and mystique – you can almost hear echoes of
the house's ancestors as they negotiate spice
deals with visiting traders from Japan and
Manchuria. Of the two heritage suites, room
208 featured in the film *The Quiet American*.
Rooms at the rear are a little dark.

Ivy Villa HOTEL **$$**
(☑0235-391 0999; www.ivyvillahoian.com; 168a
Đ Nguyen Duy Hieu; r from US$32; ❋�❉) Out
of the thick of things on the eastern edge of
Hoi An, Ivy Villa is a professionally run and
welcoming choice set alongside a small, blue
rectangular pool. Rooms are modern, comfortable and decent value, while the breakfasts are excellent. The hotel can arrange
tours and offers free bike rental.

Almanity Hoi An BOUTIQUE HOTEL **$$$**
(☑0235-366 6888; www.almanityhoian.com; 326
Đ Ly Thuong Kiet; d US$140-220; ⊛❋�❉)
With a super-breezy foyer, heritage-style and
modern wellness-themed rooms, Almanity
may just be the most relaxing hotel in town.
Gardens and swimming pools create a laid-
back haven despite the central location,
happy hour in the bar often runs for three
hours, and there's a full menu of spa and
massage services. Check online for good-
value 'Spa Journey' packages.

Hoi An Chic Hotel HOTEL **$$$**
(☑0235-392 6899, 0235-392 6799; www.hoianchic.
com; Đ Nguyen Trai; r US$90-135; ⊛@�❉)
Surrounded by rice fields, halfway between
town and the beach, Hoi An Chic enjoys a
tranquil, near-rural location. The hip design features colourful furnishings, outdoor
bathrooms and an elevated pool. Staff are
very eager to please, and there's a free shuttle to town (in an original US jeep!). It's 3km
east of the centre.

Anantara Hoi An Resort RESORT **$$$**
(☑0235-391 4555; www.anantara.com; 1 Đ Pham
Hong Thai; r/ste from US$220/245; ⊛❋@�❉)
There's real attention to detail at this large
colonial-style 94-room resort. The accom-
modation is beautifully furnished, with a
contemporary look and superb bathrooms.
The expansive grounds are immaculately
maintained, and there are several restau-
rants, including an art-gallery dining space

and a riverside restaurant, plus a spa, sub-
lime pool and pool-side bar. Located in the
French Quarter, a short walk from the heart
of town. Activities include lantern-making
and river cruises.

Ana Mandara RESORT **$$$**
(☑0234-398 3333; www.anamandarahue-resort.
com; Thuan An; d from US$90, villas from US$169; ⊛❋
�❉) The breezy, naturally air-conditioned
lobby is a prelude to the comforts of this seaside resort, overseen by very helpful and gra-
cious staff. Situated by the sands of Thuan An
Beach east of Hue, this is the place for sunrise
views over the waves from your beachfront
villa. The resort has its own long length of
private beach, as well as an excellent spa.

✖ Eating

The special beauty of Hoi An is that you can
snag a spectacular cheap meal at the central
market and in casual eateries, or splash out
on a fine-dining restaurant experience. Hoi
An is also blessed with many international
dining choices as well as a growing number
of vegetarian and vegan options, while vegetarian dishes at more omnivorous places are
not difficult to find.

★ Vegan Zone VEGAN **$**
(☑0888 122 655; www.facebook.com/veganzone
hoian; 197 Đ Nguyen Duy Hieu; mains from 60,000d;
☺10am-9pm; �✐) This handsome-looking
restaurant in the east of town pulls out the

HOI AN TASTER

Hoi An is a culinary hotbed and there are
some unique dishes you should make
sure you sample. Most restaurants serve
these items, but quality varies widely.

Banh vac ('white rose') is a delicate,
subtly flavoured shrimp dumpling topped
with crispy onions; sample it at the restaurants White Rose (p214) and Streets
(p215) and at other eateries about town.
Banh bao is another steamed dumpling,
this one with minced pork or chicken, onions, eggs and mushrooms, which is said
to be derived from Chinese dim sum. *Cao
lau* is an amazing dish: Japanese-style
noodles seasoned with herbs, salad
greens and bean sprouts, and served with
slices of roast pork. Other local specialities are fried *hoanh thanh* (wonton) and
banh xeo (crispy savoury pancakes rolled
with herbs in fresh rice paper).

FOR FOODIES

Central Vietnamese cuisine is arguably the nation's most complex and flavoursome, combining fresh herbs (which are sourced from local organic gardens) with culinary influences from centuries of links with China, Japan and Europe.

Cooking

Hoi An has become an epicentre for Vietnamese cooking courses, with many restaurants offering classes. These range from a simple set-up in someone's backyard to purpose-built schools. The town does make an ideal place for budding chefs. There are many local specialities unique to the Hoi An region, but most are fiendishly tricky to prepare. Courses often start with a market visit to learn about key Vietnamese ingredients.

Green Bamboo Cooking School (☑ 0905 815 600; www.greenbamboo-hoian.com; 21 Đ Truong Minh Hung, Cam An; per person US$45) Directed by Van, a charming local chef and English speaker, these courses are more personalised than most. Groups are limited to a maximum of 10, and classes take place in Van's spacious kitchen. Choose what to cook from a diverse menu, including vegetarian choices. It's 5km east of the centre, near Cu Dai beach; transport from Hoi An is included.

Red Bridge Cooking School (☑ 0235-393 3222; www.visithoian.com/redbridge/cooking school.html; Thon 4, Cam Thanh; per person US$22-56) At this school, going to class involves a relaxing 4km cruise down the river. There are half-day and full-day courses, both of which include market visits. The half-day class focuses on local specialities, with rice-paper making and food-decoration tips thrown in for good measure. The full-day class instructs participants in the fine art of *pho* (noodle soup).

As an added sweetener, there's a 20m swimming pool at the school. It's 4km east of the centre on the banks of the Thu Bon River. An evening two-hour class is also available, including dinner, starting at 6pm.

Herbs and Spices (☑ 0235-393 6868, 0510 393 9568; www.herbsandspicesvn.com; 2/6 Đ Le Loi; per person US$35-58; ◷ 10.30am, 4.30pm & 8pm) These excellent classes have smaller, more hands-on groups than some other cookery classes, with three different menu options.

Tours

Eat Hoi An (Coconut Tours; ☑ 0905 411 184; www.eathoian.com; 37 Đ Phan Chu Trinh; per person US$45; ◷ 7am-10pm Mon-Fri, 8am-10pm Sat, 8am-11pm Sun) Lots of really authentic cuisine and the infectious enthusiasm of host Phuoc make this an excellent choice if you really want to explore the local grassroots street-food scene. Be prepared for lots of different foods and flavours; check the website for details of cooking classes held in Phuoc's home village.

Taste of Hoi An (☑ 0905 382 783; www.tasteofhoian.com; per person US$70) Walk the streets to meet the vendors, then munch your lunch at an ancient (though air-conditioned) Hoi An town house on this award-winning tour.

---

stops with a tantalising menu of vegan dishes, from potato cake through to *bun rieu* (rice noodle soup), lemongrass tofu, delicious vegan curry or steaming mushroom hotpot. Combine these with one of Vegan Zone's thirst-busting fruit juices, satisfying smoothies or a cider. Last dinner orders are at 8.30pm.

Banh Mi Phuong　　　　　　　VIETNAMESE $
(2b Đ Phan Chu Trinh; banh mi 20,000-30,000d; ◷ 6.30am-9.30pm) What makes the *banh*

mi (filled baguettes) at this cramped joint draw the stupendous crowds out front? It's the dense, chewy bread, the freshness of the greens and the generous serves of *thit nuong* (chargrilled pork), beef and other meat that seals the deal. A celebrity-chef endorsement helps, too.

White Rose　　　　　　　DUMPLINGS $
(☑ 0235-386 2784; www.facebook.com/bong hongtrang.hoian; 533 Đ Hai Ba Trung; dishes from 70,000d; ◷ 7am-8.30pm) White Rose has a

menu of just two dishes, so take half of each if you want, as many diners do. The choice is the (secret recipe) *banh bao banh vac* (shrimp dumpling) – so named as it resembles a white rose – and crispy *hoanh thanh chien* (fried wonton; also nicknamed Hoi An pizza). Both are delicious and the restaurant is frequently packed.

Streets VIETNAMESE **$**

(☑0235-391 1949; www.streetsinternational.org; 17 Đ Le Loi; meals from 110,000d; ☺8am-10pm) Do the meals taste exceptional here because Streets is for a good cause? Perhaps it helps to know that the staff are disadvantaged youths trained up in hospitality, but the textbook-good *cao lau* and 'white rose' dumplings deserve an A+ regardless. Although the place is busy, the service is warm and delightful.

Taco Ngon TACOS **$**

(www.tacongon.com; 316 Đ Cua Dai; tacos 45,000d; ☺10am-10pm) This creation from up north along the coast in Danang serves its immensely popular fusion-flavour tacos to satisfied Hoi An diners. Choice combos include fish with a tamarind barbecue sauce, pork with wasabi coleslaw or vegetables with ginger and lime, paired (if you wish) with an eye-watering shot of tequila (30,000d) for good measure.

★**Cargo Club** INTERNATIONAL **$$**

(☑0235-391 1227; www.tastevietnam.asia/cargo-cafe-restaurant-hoi-an; 109 Đ Nguyen Thai Hoc; meals 70,000-160,000d; ☺8am-11pm; 🛜) This remarkable cafe-restaurant, serving Vietnamese and Western food, has a terrific riverside location (the upper terrace has stunning views). A relaxing day here munching your way around the menu would be a day well spent. The breakfasts are legendary (try the eggs Benedict), the patisserie and cakes are superb, and fine-dining dishes and cocktails also deliver.

★**Tadioto** JAPANESE **$$**

(☑0869 997 586; www.facebook.com/tadioto hoian; 54 Đ Phan Boi Chau; meals 300,000d; ☺ for sushi 11am-2pm & 5-10pm, for coffee from 8am, bar to midnight) One of Hoi An's culinary secrets, Tadioto (owned and run by author, award-winning journalist and polylinguist Nguyen Qui Duc) belongs in its own charming world behind a rather dapper clothes store off Đ Phan Boi Chau. The tucked-away ambience is utterly compelling, amplifying the effects of the sushi and ramen on offer.

The menu is well worth reading for entertainment alone.

The list of gin (including Song Cai Distillery gin from Vietnam) and whisky (Scotch, Japanese, Irish and American) is particularly inspiring, but Tadioto is no slouch when it comes to wine, cocktails, beer, or indeed, coffee. An experience to savour.

★**Hill Station** INTERNATIONAL **$$**

(☑0235-629 2999; www.thehillstation.com; 321 Đ Nguyen Duy Hieu; platters 160,000-275,000d, mains 100,000-165,000d; ☺7.30am-10.30pm; 🛜) With a superb location in one of Hoi An's most charming and fascinating historic mansions, the Hill Station is ideal for a drink and snack after a busy day. Relax in the heritage armchairs and partner craft beer or wine with shared plates of Sapa charcuterie and Dalat cheeseboards, or take your Larue beer out front to people-watch from a roadside chair.

More robust options are interesting pasta dishes and Euro classics like *coq au vin*.

★**Sea Shell** FRENCH, SEAFOOD **$$**

(☑091 429 8337; 119 Đ Tran Cao Van; meals 90,000d; ☺noon-9pm Mon-Sat) Shaded by a decades-old banyan tree, Sea Shell is a flavour-packed offshoot of Nu Eatery in Hoi An's Old Town. Try snacks like tempura-prawn rolls and turmeric-catfish wraps, or mains like spicy pork noodles with a refreshing calamari and green-apple salad. A decent wine list covers Australia, France, Italy and South Africa.

Nu Eatery FUSION **$$**

(www.facebook.com/NuEateryHoiAn; 10a Đ Nguyen Thị Minh Khai; meals 130,000d; ☺noon-9pm Mon-Sat) Don't be deceived by the humble decor at this compact place near the Japanese Covered Bridge; there's a real wow factor to the seasonal small plates at this Hoi An favourite. Combine the pork-belly steamed buns (35,000d) with a salad of grilled pineapple, watermelon and pickled shallots (75,000d), and don't miss the homemade lemongrass, ginger or chilli ice cream (35,000d).

Ganesh Indian Restaurant NORTH INDIAN **$$**

(☑0235-386 4538; www.ganesh.vn; 24 Đ Tran Hung Dao; meals 70,000-155,000d; ☺11.30am-10.30pm; 🛜☑) This highly authentic, buzzing and fine-value North Indian restaurant is highly popular, but staff remain unfazed and very friendly; the tandoor oven pumps out perfect naan bread and the chefs' fiery curries don't pull any punches. Unlike many curry houses, this one has atmosphere, and also plenty of vegetarian choices. Slurp a lassi or slug a beer (a draught Tiger is 35,000d) and you're set.

Mai Fish
VIETNAMESE $$

(www.mangohoian.com/mai-fish; 45 Đ Nguyen Thi; meals 120,000-220,000d; ☺ 7am-10pm; ☎) A casual and laid-back place owned by well-known Vietnamese–North American chef Duc Tran, Mai Fish focuses on authentic and tasty versions of homestyle Vietnamese food. It's in a quiet location a short walk from the Japanese Covered Bridge. The seafood hotpot for two is superb, as are the Hoi An white rose dumplings and the Vietnamese prawn curry.

Green Mango
VIETNAMESE, INTERNATIONAL $$

(☑ 0235-392 9918; www.greenmango.vn; 54 Đ Nguyen Thai Hoc; meals 130,000-300,000d; ☺ 7am-10pm; ☎) The setting, inside one of Hoi An's most impressive traditional wooden houses, is beautiful, and the accomplished cooking (both Western and Eastern) matches the surrounds. There's also one of the only air-conditioned dining rooms in the Old Town upstairs.

Aubergine 49
FUSION $$$

(☑ 0235-221 2190; www.hoian-aubergine49.com; 49a Đ Ly Thai Tho; three-course menu 795,000d; ☺ 6-10pm Mon-Sat) This stylish restaurant, around five minutes north of central Hoi An by taxi, crafts excellent fusion combinations of Asian and Western cuisine. On top of the set menu and six-course degustation menu (1,750,000d) there are also à la carte options and a decent wine list; menu standouts include stuffed, roasted chicken breast, spiced wild red snapper and wild mushroom risotto.

Mango Mango
FUSION $$$

(☑ 0235-391 0839; www.themangomango.com; 45 Đ Nguyen Phuc Chu, An Hoi; meals US$18-23; ☺ 8am-10pm; ☎) Celebrity chef Duc Tran's most beautiful Hoi An restaurant enjoys a prime riverside plot and puts a global spin on Vietnamese cuisine, with fresh, unexpected combinations. Perhaps at times the flavour matches are just a little too out there, but the cocktails are some of the best in town, especially with an after-dark view of the river.

🍷 Drinking & Nightlife

Hoi An is not a huge party town, as the local authorities keep a fairly strict lid on late-night revelry with a curfew (last orders 11.45pm and no loud music after 10pm); the backstreets can be very dark after 10pm. However, there's lots of atmosphere and the Old Town is a great place to treat yourself to a cocktail or glass of wine.

An Hoi, across the river from the Old Town, offers more raucous action. Happy hours keep costs down considerably, and most places close around 1am. The most popular spots in An Hoi change on a regular basis. Turn right after crossing the bridge from Hoi An, and you'll soon see (and hear) where the backpacker action is currently happening along Đ Nguyen Phuc Chu.

9 Grains Bakery & Cafe
BAKERY

(☑ 0905 578 930; www.facebook.com/9grains hoianhbt; 441a Đ Hai Ba Trung; ☺ 7am-4pm) For baked goodies, 9 Grains gives it the whole nine yards: from granola at brekkie to the artisan bread, pain au chocolat, croissants, cakes and pastries, everything is superfresh and of tip-top quality. Totally moreish and worth the short journey it takes to get here (the coffee is decent, too).

Espresso Station
CAFE

(☑ 0905 691 164; www.facebook.com/TheEspresso Station; 28/2 Đ Tran Hung Dao; ☺ 7.30am-5.30pm; ☎) A slice of Melbourne-style coffee culture, albeit in a heritage Hoi An residence, the Espresso Station is where to go for the best flat whites and cold-brew coffees in town. There's a compact food menu with granola, muesli and sandwiches; relaxing in the arty courtyard is where you'll want to be.

Look for the sign on the main road and venture down the alley.

Queta Cafe
CAFE

(☑ 0907 355 339; www.facebook.com/pg/queta coffee/posts; 112 Phan Chu Trinh; ☺ 8am-10pm; ☎) ✐ Ensconce yourself in this bright, colourful, playful and unique cafe, surrounded by a sea of carved woodwork, from the tables to the statues, cups, effigies and stools. Drinks are served in bamboo cups with bamboo straws in an environmentally conscious, wholesome and quite delightful fashion. Coffees, cold-pressed juices and teas are on the menu. Pick up a pack of bamboo straws for 120,000d.

Tap House
CRAFT BEER

(☑ 0235-391 0333; 3 Đ Phan Chu Trinh; ☺ 9am-11pm) Craft beers from around Vietnam are the attraction at this Hoi An bar, but don't be surprised if you linger for the tasty charcuterie and cheeseboards as well. The

Platinum pale ale is a standout, but all the brews are fine and there are a couple of ciders. The interior could do with some character, though.

Mia Coffee House   CAFE
(www.facebook.com/miacoffeehouse; 20 Đ Phan Boi Chau; ⊙8am-5pm) One of our favourite spots for an espresso, latte or cappuccino. Mia's own coffee blend, sourced from Dalat arabica beans, is the standout brew, and be sure to try the coffee affogato, a delicious blend of dessert and hot beverage. There's appealing, wrap-around veranda seating, and decent food including grilled panini sandwiches, hearty baguettes and crispy fish burgers.

Dive Bar   BAR
(88 Đ Nguyen Thai Hoc; ⊙9am-midnight; 🛜) A top bar option in Hoi An within the Cham Island Diving Center (p210), with a great vibe thanks to the welcoming service, contemporary electronic tunes and sofas for lounging. There's also a cocktail garden and bar at the rear, pub grub and a pool table.

White Marble   WINE BAR
(✆0235-3911 862; www.facebook.com/whitemarble hoian; 99 Đ Le Loi; ⊙11am-11pm; 🛜) This wine bar/restaurant in historic premises has an unmatched selection of wines; many are available by the glass. Lunch and dinner tasting menus cost from US$20, and the corner location is a great place to watch the world go by or gaze over the river.

3 Dragons   PUB
(www.facebook.com/3DragonsSportsBar; 51 Đ Phan Boi Chau; ⊙8am-midnight; 🛜) An amiable half sports bar (where you can watch everything from Aussie Rules to Indian cricket) and half restaurant (serving burgers, steaks and local food), with seats at the rear looking onto the river. A pint of Tiger is 70,000d, a bottle of Larue is 40,000d, and ciders are at hand for variety.

Q Bar   LOUNGE
(94 Đ Nguyen Thai Hoc; ⊙noon-midnight; 🛜) Q Bar offers stunning lighting, electronica and lounge music, and excellent (if pricey, at around 120,000d) cocktails and mocktails. Draws a cool crowd.

🔒 Shopping

Hoi An has a long and celebrated history of flogging goods to international visitors, and today's residents haven't lost their commercial edge.

Pheva Chocolate   CHOCOLATE
(✆0235-392 5260; www.phevaworld.com; 74 Đ Tran Hung Dao; ⊙8am-7pm) 🌿 Excellent artisan chocolate crafted from organic and free-trade cacao from Vietnam's southern Ben Tre province. The dark chocolate spiked with Phu Quoc peppercorns is especially good, but there's everything from mango to pistachio, sesame and peanuts and puffed rice.

Clothes & Accessories

Clothes are the biggest shopping lure in Hoi An, long known for fabric production, and tourist demand has swiftly shoehorned many tailor shops (p218) into the tiny Old Town. Shoes, also copied from Western designs, and supposed 'leather' goods are also popular, but the quality is variable.

★Reaching Out   SOUVENIRS, CLOTHING
(✆0235-3910 168; www.reachingoutvietnam.com; 103 Đ Nguyen Thai Hoc; ⊙8.30am-9.30pm Mon-Fri, 9.30am-8.30pm Sat & Sun) 🌿 This excellent fair-trade gift shop stocks good-quality silk scarves, clothes, jewellery, hand-painted Vietnamese hats, handmade toys and teddy bears. The shop employs and supports artisans with disabilities, and staff are happy to show visitors through the workshop.

Metiseko   CLOTHING
(✆0235-392 9278; www.metiseko.com; 140-42 Đ Tran Phu; ⊙8.30am-9.30pm) 🌿 Winners of a sustainable-development award, this eco-minded store stocks gorgeous clothing (including kids' wear), accessories, and homewares such as cushions using natural silk and organic cotton. It is certified to use the Organic Content Standard label, and the company sources natural twill and Shantung and Habutai silk from within Vietnam.

Lotus Jewellery   FASHION & ACCESSORIES
(www.lotusjewellery-hoian.com; 82 Đ Tran Phu; ⊙8am-8pm) Lotus has very affordable and attractive hand-crafted pieces loosely modelled on butterflies, dragonflies, Vietnamese sampans, conical hats and Chinese zodiac symbols. There's another, smaller branch not far away at 53a Đ Le Loi.

Arts & Crafts

Hoi An has over a dozen art galleries; check out the streets near the Japanese Covered Bridge, along Đ Nguyen Thi Minh Khai. Woodcarvings are a local speciality: Cam Nam village and Cam Kim Island (p208) are the places to head to.

GETTING CLOTHES THAT MEASURE UP

Let's face it: the tailor scene in Hoi An is out of control. The estimated number of tailors working here is anywhere from 300 to 500. Hotels and tour guides all have their preferred partners – they'll promise you good prices before shuttling you off to their aunt/cousin/in-law/neighbour (from whom they'll earn a nice commission). You'll also be stopped on the street by friendly and persistent female conversationalists, who then turn out to be tailors as they lead you to their shop (or the shop of their aunt/cousin/in-law/neighbour).

The first rule of thumb is that while you should always bargain and be comfortable with the price, you also get what you pay for. A tailor who quotes a price much lower than a competitor's is probably cutting corners. Better tailors and better fabrics cost more, as do tighter deadlines.

Hoi An's tailors are, however, master copiers – show them a picture from a magazine, and they'll whip up a near-identical outfit. The shop assistants also have catalogues of many styles.

It helps to know your fabrics and preferences, right down to details such as thread colour, linings and buttons. When buying silk, make sure it's the real thing. The only real test is with a cigarette or match (synthetic fibres melt, silk burns). Similarly, don't accept on face value that a fabric is 100% cotton or wool without giving it a good feel for the quality. Prices hover at around US$25 for a man's shirt, or US$50 for a cotton dress. If a suit costs around US$100, make sure the fabric and handiwork is up to scratch.

Although many travellers try to squeeze in a clothing order within a 48-hour sojourn, that doesn't leave much time for fittings and alterations. Remember to check the seams of the finished garment; well-tailored garments have a second set of stitches that binds the edge, oversewing the fabric so fraying is impossible.

Shops can pack and ship orders to your home country. Although there are occasional reports of packages going astray or the wrong order arriving, the local post office's service is good.

In such a crowded field, these are places we regularly hear good things about (in alphabetical order): **A Dong Silk** (☑0235-391 0579; www.adongsilk.com; 40 Đ Le Loi; ⊗8am-9.30pm), **Hoang Kim** (☑0235-386 2794; 57 Đ Nguyen Thai Hoc; ⊗8am-9pm), **Kimmy** (☑0235-386 2063; www.kimmytailor.com; 70 Đ Tran Hung Dao; ⊗7.30am-9.30pm) and **Yaly** (☑0235-221 2474; www.yalycouture.com; 47 Đ Nguyen Thai Hoc; ⊗8am-9pm).

A few of Hoi An's tailors have now also diversified into making shoes and bags. See the **Friendly Shop** (☑093 521 1382; www.friendlyshophoian.com; 18 Đ Tran Phu; ⊗9am-9pm) for excellent shoes and bags, and quality work that is guaranteed.

Đ Phan Boi Chau east of Đ Hoang Dieu is a developing arts precinct, with galleries and a crafts museum. Look for the free map reinforcing the street as a **Rue des Arts** (Đ Phan Boi Chau) and showcasing the neighbourhood's French colonial heritage. Pick up a walking map from the March Gallery, **Precious Heritage** (☑0235-6558 382; www.facebook.com/precious.heritage.museum.art.gallery; 26 Đ Phan Boi Chau; ⊗8.30am-8.30pm) FREE or Mia Coffee House (p217) and start exploring.

★**Villagecraft Planet**   ARTS & CRAFTS
(www.facebook.com/VillagecraftPlanet; 59 Đ Phan Boi Chau; ⊗10am-5pm Fri-Sun & Wed, to 7pm Mon, Tue & Thu) 🖉 Shop here for intriguing and colourful homemade homewares and fashion, typically employing natural hemp,

indigo dye and beeswax-stencilled batik, and crafted with fair-trade practices by the Hmong, Black Thai and Lolo ethnic-minority people in the north of Vietnam.

March Gallery   ART
(☑0122 377 9074; www.marchgallery-hoian.com; 42 Đ Phan Boi Chau; ⊗10am-6pm) Owned by Yorkshire expat artist Bridget March, this gallery showcases her work – poignant watercolours, whimsical sketches and abstract works – and a slowly expanding range of pieces, including literature, from other Hoi An resident artists. Styles include fine lacquer paintings, but there is an affordable range of well-priced souvenir pieces and artisan jewellery as well. Check the website for art-related events.

Couleurs D'Asie Gallery   PHOTOGRAPHY, BOOKS
(www.facebook.com/couleurs.asie; 7 Đ Nguyen Hue;
☺ 8am-8pm) Superb and entrancing images
for sale of Vietnam, Asia and Cuba by Hoi
An–based photographer Réhahn. His portraits of the peoples of Vietnam are particularly stunning, and the best of his images are
collected in books, also for sale.

Books

Randy's Book Xchange   BOOKS
(☑ 093 608 9483; www.bookshoian.com; To 5 Thon
Xuyen Trung; ☺ 8am-7pm) Head to Cam Nam
Island and take the first right to get to this
two-floor bookshop. Set up like a personal library, it has stacks and rows of used (largely
paperback) books for sale or exchange, with
a low-ceilinged upstairs room.

ⓘ Information

MEDICAL SERVICES

Dr Ho Huu Phuoc Practice (☑ 0235-386 1419;
74 Đ Le Loi; ☺ 11am-12.30pm & 5-9.30pm)
English-speaking doctor.

Hoi An Hospital (☑ 0235-386 1364; 4 Đ Tran
Hung Dao; ☺ 6am-10pm) For serious problems,
however, go to Danang.

MONEY

Agribank (12 Đ Tran Hung Dao; ☺ 8am-4.30pm
Mon-Fri, 8.30am-1pm Sat) and **Vietin Bank**
(☑ 0510 386 1340; 4 Đ Hoang Dieu; ☺ 8am-
5pm Mon-Fri, 8.30am-1.30pm Sat) both change
cash and have ATMs.

POST

Main Post Office (6 Đ Tran Hung Dao;
☺ 6.30am-8pm) On the edge of the Old Town.

SAFE TRAVEL

Hoi An is one of Vietnam's safer towns, but
there are infrequent stories of late-night bag-
snatching, pickpockets and (very occasionally)
assaults on women. If you are a lone female, it
may be advisable to walk home with somebody
you know. Many street lights are turned off from
9.30pm. There have also been reports of drinks
being spiked in some bars, so keep a close eye
on your glass. It's also a good idea to call for a
taxi when leaving a bar and not rely on the local
xe om mafia (sometimes associated with incidents of violence).

Beach Safety

The ocean and waves can get rough east of
Hoi An, particularly between October and
March. Many local people get into trouble in
heavy seas; there are regular fatalities. Lifeguards now work the beaches, but be cautious
nonetheless.

Flooding

Hoi An's riverside location makes the town
vulnerable to flooding during the rainy season
(October and November). It's common for the
waterfront to be hit by sporadic floods of about
1m, and a typhoon can bring levels of 2m or more.

Police

Hoi An Police Station (☑ 0235-386 1204; 6 Đ
Ngo Gia Tu)

TOURIST INFORMATION

Tourist Information Office (☑ 0235-391 6961;
www.quangnamtourism.com.vn; 47 Đ Phan Chu
Trinh; ☺ 8am-5pm) Helpful office, with good
English spoken.

Hoi An Old Town Booths These booths sell Old
Town tickets and have limited information and
maps. Located at 30 Đ Tran Phu, 10 Đ Nguyen
Hue, 5 Đ Hoang Dieu and 78 Đ Le Loi (all are
open 7am to 6pm).

Coast Vietnam (www.coastvietnam.com)
Lots of colourful eating, drinking and activities
information from savvy Hoi An expats. Look for
the free and informative *Hoi An Travel Guide*
map, too.

TRAVEL AGENCIES

Competition is strong, so check out your options
and negotiate.

Rose Travel Service (☑ 0235-391 7567; www.
rosetravelservice.com; 37-39 Đ Ly Thai To;
☺ 7.30am-5.30pm) Tours around the area and
Vietnam, plus car hire and buses.

Sinh Tourist (☑ 0235-386 3948; www.thesinh
tourist.vn; 646 Đ Hai Ba Trung; ☺ 6am-10pm)
Books reputable open-tour buses.

ⓘ Getting There & Away

AIR

The closest airport is 45 to 60 minutes away in
Danang.

BUS

Most north–south bus services do not stop at
Hoi An, as Hwy 1 passes 10km west of the town,
but you can head for the town of Vinh Dien and
flag down a bus there.

More convenient open-tour buses offer regular
connections for Hue and Nha Trang.

For Danang (one hour), it is much more convenient to organise a bus (around 120,000d)
to pick you up at your accommodation. Yellow
buses to Danang (20,000d) leave from the
Northern Bus Station (Đ Le Hong Phong), a
15-minute walk or 15,000d *xe om* ride from
central Hoi An.

Local bus drivers for Danang sometimes try
to charge foreigners more, but the correct fare
is posted by the door and it helps to have the
correct change. Note the last bus back from

Danang leaves around 6pm. Accommodation can book transfers to/from Danang airport and train station.

CAR & MOTORCYCLE

To get to Danang (30km), head north out of town and join up with Hwy 1, or head east to Cua Dai Beach and follow the Danang Beach coastal road. Motorbikes charge about 180,000d for the trip to Danang. Taxis cost approximately 400,000d and are cheaper if you don't use the meter. Negotiate a price first.

A trip in a car to Hue starts from US$100 (depending on how many stops you plan to make along the way), while a half-day trip around the surrounding area, including My Son, is around US$60.

A popular way to transfer between Hoi An and Hue is on a motorcycle. A bike with driver is around US$45, and around US$25 if you're driving.

Roadtrippers Vietnam (☑ 0905 101 930; www.roadtrippersvietnam.com; per person US$65) offers jeep transfers from Hoi An to Hue – and vice versa – taking in the Hai Van Pass and lunch and beach stops along the way. Prices include hotel pickup and drop-off, leaving at 9am and arriving at 4pm.

TRAIN

The nearest train station is in Danang.

❶ Getting Around

Hoi An is really best explored on foot; the Old Town is compact and highly walkable.

Cars and motorbikes (but not bicycles) are banned from the central streets from 8am to 11am and from 3pm to 10pm. As start and finish times draw near, you will hear announcements on public loud speakers.

To go further afield, rent a bicycle (25,000d per day); these may available for free at your hotel. The route east to Cua Dai Beach is quite scenic, passing rice paddies and a river estuary, but has definitely become more developed with hotels and guesthouses.

A motorbike without/with a driver will cost around US$6/12 per day. Reckon on about 70,000d for a taxi to An Bang Beach. Motorbikes are a good way to reach My Son and most hotels can arrange rental.

BOAT

Boat trips on the Thu Bon River can be fascinating. A simple rowing boat (with rower) should cost about 100,000d per hour, and one hour is probably long enough. Some My Son tours include a return journey by boat back to central Hoi An.

Motorboats can be hired to visit handicraft and fishing villages for around 200,000d per hour. Boaters wait at the boat landing between the Cam Nam and An Hoi Bridges in central Hoi An.

BUS

The bus station, 1km west of the town centre, mainly covers local routes.

TAXI

Metered taxis are usually cheaper than *xe om*.
Hoi An Taxi (☑ 0510-391 9919) Good local operators.
Mai Linh (☑ 0235-392 5925) Local partners of a reliable Vietnam-wide taxi company.

Around Hoi An

The quintessentially Vietnamese country-side, rural lanes and beaches around Hoi An beg to be explored.

Motorbike and bicycle trips are popular and there's no better way to appreciate the countryside than on two wheels. Jeep tours are another option, and water-based activities include paddleboarding and kayaking. There are a number of recommended tour operators in Hoi An (p210).

The idyllic Cham Islands make another perfect day-trip destination during the March-to-September season. Hoi An dive schools Blue Coral Diving (p210) and Cham Island Diving Center (p210) run tours.

Cua Dai Beach

Heading east of Hoi An, new housing and hotels mix with older rice paddies, and the riverbank meanders for around 5km to sandy beaches. This palm-fringed coastline extends north to Danang, and despite the development, there are still a few quieter stretches. It's a good area to explore independently on two wheels and makes for a fun bike ride.

Nearest to Hoi An, Cua Dai Beach has a few big resorts. There's an ongoing problem with severe coastal erosion, however, exacerbated by the past building of hotels, so parts of the beach are lined with an unattractive sprawl of sandbags. If you're staying here, your daily swim may need to be in the hotel's pool – indeed the hotels are the main draw for sunbathers also seeking a radiant sunrise.

🛏 Sleeping

Hoi An Riverside Resort HOTEL $$$
(☑ 0235-386 4800; www.hoianriverresort.com; 175 Đ Cua Dai; r from US$70; ⊕ ✴ @ 🕸 🐾) Offers classy river-view rooms with hardwood floors and tasteful decor, many with balconies right over the water. It's a well-run

establishment, about a kilometre from the beach, with a decent restaurant, and massage and fitness facilities. A free shuttle bus connects the hotel with Hoi An and the hotel can arrange transport to Hue and other destinations.

Victoria Hoi An
Beach Resort & Spa   RESORT $$$

(☑ 0235-392 7040; www.victoriahotels.asia; Cua Dai Beach; r/ste from US$133/250; ❀ ❄ @ ⚲ ☲) This handsome 109-room hotel adopts a mix of French-colonial and traditional Hoi An design. Rooms are modern and immaculately presented, some with teak floors and Jacuzzis, and all with balconies. There's a 30m oceanside pool and a private beach, as well as good in-house dining and three bars.

ⓘ Getting There & Away

There's no public transport to the beach, but most accommodation will provide shared shuttle transport to Hoi An's Old Town. A taxi from Hoi An to the beach area is around 100,000d. Hiring a bicycle or a scooter from your hotel is a sensible idea.

An Bang Beach

Just 3km north of Hoi An, An Bang is one of Vietnam's most happening and enjoyable beaches. There's a wonderful stretch of fine sand and an enormous horizon (with less of the serious erosion evident at Cua Dai), and with only the distant Cham Islands interrupting the seaside symmetry. Staying at the beach and visiting Hoi An on day trips is a good strategy for a relaxing visit to the area.

There is a growing band of vendors selling souvenirs and food on the beach, and at the end of the day it gets very busy with local families heading down for a swim. A few watersports operators are also now offering parasailing and jet-ski hire. Note that safety standards for these activities may not be enforced as strongly as in other countries.

⊼ Activities

Heaven Garden Spa   SPA

(☑ 0796 229 432; www.facebook.com/Heaven GardenSpa; 118 Nguyen Phan Vinh; 1hr massage from 350,000d; ⊙ 8am-10pm) Owned and operated by a Vietnamese-New Zealand-Australian team, with treatments including body wraps, massages and facials. A 45-minute foot massage is 320,000d.

| WORTH A TRIP |

THANH HA
....

This small village has long been known for its pottery industry. Though most villagers have switched from making bricks and tiles to creating pots and souvenirs for tourist trades, artisans employed in this painstaking work are happy just to show off their work (but prefer it if visitors buy something). There's a 25,000d admission fee to the village.

Thanh Ha is 3km west of Hoi An and can be easily reached on bicycle.

🛏 Sleeping

An Bang is a decent alternative to staying in Hoi An. There's an expanding accommodation scene here, with stylish holiday rental houses making a fine option for families and friends travelling together. The area is much quieter in the winter months.

Under the Coconut Tree   BUNGALOW $

(☑ 0168 245 5666, 0235-651 6666; www.under thecoconuttreehoian.com; dm US$8, d US$25-30, f US$40; ☎) The most atmospheric place to stay in An Bang is this ramshackle garden collection of wooden and bamboo lodges and bungalows. For thrifty travellers, the Coconut Dorm House has outdoor showers and simple, shared accommodation in a breezy, open-sided pavilion, while the spacious Bamboo Family House accommodates four. The cosy Mushroom Hut is couple-friendly and has a private bathroom.

There's a cool bar/restaurant area for catching up with other travellers.

An Bang Seaside
Village Homestay   BUNGALOW, VILLA $$

(☑ 0911 111 101; www.anbangseasidevillage.com; cottage & villa d US$60-115; ❀ ❄ ☎) These cottages and villas are situated amid coastal trees on glorious An Bang Beach; it's one of Vietnam's best beachside locations. Each of the eight spacious options combines modern and natural materials, and are serviced daily, with breakfast included. The five-bedroom Lighthouse – right on the beach and with superb ocean views plus kitchen – can accommodate up to 10 people.

★ Chi Villa   RENTAL HOUSE $$$

(☑ 0935 310 875; www.chivilla.com; villas from US$430; ❀ ❄ ☎ ☲) Accommodating up to six, Chi Villa is An Bang's standout luxury

1. Bai Xep (p240) 2. White sand dunes (p265), Mui Ne
3. Aerial view of the floating villages around Cat Ba Island (p107)
4. Traditional basket boats, An Bang Beach (p221)

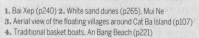

2 Islands & Beaches

Vietnam has an incredible coastline that's home to some of Asia's most sublime sandy beaches. Offshore islands – from mountainous Cat Ba in the north to tropical Phu Quoc in the south – also beg to be explored.

Bai Xep

South of Quy Nhon, this lovely sandy bay (p240) is drawing more and more travellers. It's one of the few places in Vietnam where you can bag a guesthouse room right on the shore with an ocean view. Bai Xep doubles as a fishing village, so it's also a good spot to interact with locals and enjoy some seriously chilled beach time.

Mui Ne

If you're touring Vietnam between November and April, the near-endless sands of Mui Ne (p263) come into their own at this time, for the climate on this stretch is reliably sunny and dry. Kite-surfers, windsurfers and sailors make use of the seasonal winds and there's an excellent selection of seafood restaurants.

Cat Ba Island

This rugged, forested island (p107), most of which is a national park, is a great base to for hiking, biking and adventure tourism. Trails across the island fringe the habitat of one of the world's rarest primates, the highly endangered Cat Ba langur. And Cat Ba is just a short boat ride from the spectacular karst islets of Lan Ha Bay.

An Bang Beach

A short ride from Hoi An, An Bang (p221) is a lovely expanse of pale sand backed by a protective emerald ribbon of casuarina trees. Away from the central section it's very low key, with local families providing sunloungers and serving drinks and snacks. The oceanic horizon is only fragmented by the craggy Cham Islands.

accommodation. Stylish Asian-chic decor fills the very spacious property, there's a full kitchen (including freshly prepared à la carte breakfasts every morning), and a beautiful pool area shaded by mango trees. Barbecue by the poolside or make the one-minute walk to beachfront restaurants. There's a two-night minimum stay.

Four Seasons Nam Hai HOTEL **$$$**
(☑0235-394 0000; www.fourseasons.com/hoian; Dien Duong village; villas from US$646; ❂✱@ ☎✉) About 8km north of An Bang and 15km from Hoi An, this beachfront temple of indulgence has it all: three tiers of infinity pools (one is heated), butler service, vast villas kitted out with neat gadgets and private plunge pools, excellent fitness facilities and a world-class spa. This all comes at an astonishing cost, but service is both thoughtful and excellent.

Recently brought under the uber-luxury Four Seasons brand, the Nam Hai remains one of the best hotels in Southeast Asia.

Hoi An Beach Rentals RENTAL HOUSE **$$$**
(www.hoi-an-beach-rentals.com; houses US$180-200; ✱☎) Asian-chic decor is the common theme of these lovely self-contained rental homes near the beach in An Bang village. Annam House (sleeps six; US$200) is a converted village home with three bedrooms and a beautiful garden. Nearby, CoChin House (sleeps four; US$180) is constructed in wood in heritage Vietnamese style, and has an expansive garden and a private lookout. Decorated with art and antiques, the Temple Beach House (US$230) incorporates temple elements into its seductive interior.

Hoi An Beach Bungalows RENTAL HOUSE **$$$**
(☑0908 117 533; www.hoianbeachbungalows.com; Lac Long Quan; apt from US$50-150; ❂✱☎) These rental homes in An Bang village are all super-comfortable, colourfully decorated and surrounded by lush gardens. Choose from Be's Beach Bungalow, with two bedrooms and a stylish self-contained kitchen, the two-bedroom Be's Bungalow, or the cosier, one-bedroom Be's Cottage in a renovated traditional Vietnamese home. More affordable is Be's Shack, with private garden, veranda and kitchen. Breakfast is additional.

✗ Eating

You'll find a growing selection of beachfront bar-restaurants here, as well as good eating options opening in the quieter lanes

a few streets back from the beach. Vendors comb the beach selling tasty quail eggs and other snacks, while stalls selling *banh mi* and *banh tom* (sweet potato and prawn fritters) are set up at the entrance to the beach.

7 Son Bakery & Coffee CAFE **$**
(☑090 519 9382; croissants 18,000d; ❂7am-7pm) This homely and rustic-textured spot is the top An Bang choice for baked goodies, with an on-site bakery taking care of fresh baguettes, cakes, croissants and pastries, served with quality cappuccinos and lattes infused from Vietnamese arabica coffee beans.

Purple Lantern VIETNAMESE **$$**
(meals 80,000-130,000d; ❂noon-10pm; ✎) Featuring a garden setting and decorated with colourful lanterns, Purple Lantern is a low-key family-owned restaurant a couple of streets back from the beach. Menu highlights include barbecue prawns with mango, and excellent seafood including grilled scallops. Partner them with a refreshing papaya salad.

Soul Kitchen INTERNATIONAL **$$**
(☑0906 440 320; www.soulkitchen.sitew.com; meals 90,000-180,000d; ❂10am-10pm Tue-Sun, to 6pm Mon; ☎) This oceanfront restaurant with a grassy garden and thatched dining area has a daily menu that may include tuna carpaccio, seafood salad or calamari. There's quality wine, strong cocktails and live music from 5.30pm Thursday to Sunday.

Salt Pub & Restaurant PUB FOOD **$$**
(www.saltpubhoian.com; Đ Nguyen Phan Vinh; meals 120,000-180,000d; ❂7.30am-late) With a beachfront location on the quiet side of the An Bang strip, this relaxed place offers craft beers on tap, espresso coffee and a tempting choice of Western and Vietnamese breakfasts and meals (try the pulled-pork burger). There's an ocean-facing terrace and stylish interior. For rooms, the pub has a sister hotel within stumbling distance across the road.

DeckHouse VIETNAMESE, SEAFOOD **$$**
(www.facebook.com/thedeckhouseanbang; meals 80,000-180,000d; ❂7am-10.30pm) This oceanfront place includes beachy decor with rustic timber, private cabanas, and a menu stretching from local flavours through to burgers and fresh seafood. The cocktail and wine list is equally eclectic, and there's often

good craft beers from Hanoi's Furbrew on tap. Check the Facebook page for details on occasional DJs and live music.

Drinking & Nightlife

Sound of Silence   CAFE
(📱0235-386 1101; www.facebook.com/soundof silencecoffee; 40 Đ Nguyen Phan Vinh; ⊙7.15am-4.30pm; 🛜) For excellent coffee (from 30,000d), Sound of Silence combines sure-fire barista skills with a rustic garden setting and ocean views. Fresh coconuts and crêpes crammed with tropical fruit are other distractions while you wonder about diving into the sea.

Juice House   JUICE BAR
(⊙7.30am-9pm; 🛜) Excellent juices, smoothies, salads and panini sandwiches are the highlights at this relaxed spot owned and operated by a switched-on young woman from the nearby Cham Islands. It's located at the right of the main intersection as you arrive at the beach.

Cham Islands
📞0236 / POP 3000

A breathtaking cluster of granite islands, set in aquamarine seas around 15km directly offshore from Hoi An, the Cham Islands make a wonderful excursion. The islands were once closed to visitors and under close military supervision, but now day trips, diving and snorkelling the reefs and even overnight stays are possible.

A rich underwater environment features 135 species of soft and hard coral, and varied macro life. The islands are officially protected as a marine park. Fishing and the collection of birds' nests (for soup) were traditionally the two key industries here, though many locals have moved into the tourism and ecotourism sector.

Overtourism has become another problem, however, as visitor numbers have swelled from just 17,000 in 2009 to a staggering 400,000 in 2018. A daily cap of 3000 visitors to the islands is in effect.

ⓘ When to Go
The serenity of the islands can be compromised – especially on weekends and Vietnamese holidays – by boatloads of tourists from the mainland, so plan your visit accordingly. It'll have to be between March and September, as the ocean is usually too rough at other times.

Sights

Only **Hon Lao**, the main island, is inhabited – the other seven Chams are rocky, forested specks. **Bai Lang**, Hon Lao's little port in the northwest of the island, is the main village (there are also two remote hamlets). A relaxed place with sleepy lanes, it has a leeward location that's long offered mariners protection from the rough waters of the South China Sea (East Sea). For a quieter and more authentic experience, **Bai Huong** is a tiny fishing village (population around 450) 5km southeast of Bai Lang. It's a more isolated spot with decent homestays.

Bac Beach   BEACH
A concrete path heads southwest from Bai Lang for 2km past coves to a fine, sheltered beach, where there's great swimming, powdery sand, and hammocks and thatched parasols beside seafood restaurants. During holiday times the beach is packed with boats coming and going. Trails lead into forested hills behind Bai Lang. Watersports, including parasailing, are more recent additions.

Ong Ngu   BUDDHIST TEMPLE
Bai Lang's only real sight is this modest temple dedicated to the whales (and whale sharks) once abundant around the Chams. Locals worshipped whales as oceanic deities who would offer them protection at sea. When a carcass washed ashore, they'd clean

---

DIVING THE CHAMS

Unsurprisingly divers and snorkellers are some of the main visitors to the Cham Islands. The diving may not be world class (visibility is sometimes poor, though strong efforts have been made to reverse overfishing, and coral reefs are being restored since the plastic-bag ban), however, it is very intriguing: five species of lobster, 84 species of mollusc and some 202 species of fish are endemic to the Chams. Dive trips and overnight stays can be arranged through dive centres in Hoi An, such as the Cham Island Diving Center (p210). A full-day trip that includes snorkelling, a short hike, lunch and beach time costs US$50 (an overnight option with camping on the beach is also available).

CENTRAL VIETNAM AROUND HOI AN

the bones and perform an elaborate ceremony at the temple before giving the bones a burial. Sadly, whales are very seldom seen around the Chams today.

Tours

Tour agencies charge US$30 to US$40 for island tours, but most day trips are very rushed and give you little time to enjoy the Chams. Speedboats are often crowded, time for snorkelling limited, and you may not get to see decent coral or marine life. Day trips by tourists staying in Danang are also becoming increasingly popular and pressure is being put on the islands. For the best one-day experience, book with one of the specialised dive operators in Hoi An. They can also arrange overnight camping stays, though the beach is not as quiet and serene as it once was, so this option has lost some popularity.

🛌 Sleeping

The Chams have simple guesthouses and a growing number of homestays in the villages of Bai Lang and Bai Huong; the latter has the better selection. Dive operators in Hoi An can also arrange overnight camping stays.

★ **Bai Huong Homestays**　　HOMESTAY $
(www.homestaybaihuong.com; per person 120,000d) Live with the locals in Bai Huong village. Visitors are given a bed with a mozzie net, and bathrooms have sit-down toilets and cold-water showers. Delicious home-cooked meals (30,000d to 70,000d) are available. The program works with nine families, generating income from community tourism. Note that little or no English is spoken by locals and there's usually electricity only from 6pm to 10pm.

Local families can take guests fishing or snorkelling (per person 150,000d) and trekking (per person 100,000d). Also available is a good-value three-day/two-night package (per person 880,000d) including all meals and snorkelling, fishing and trekking excursions. See the website for a two-day/one-night package (440,000d) as well. The project has helped fund education for Bai Huong's children, including scholarships and a local library.

Hammock Homestay　　HOMESTAY $
(☑ 0976 605 750; r 350,000-400,000d; ❋ 🛜) This homestay near the dock in Bai Lang is a very good choice. Spacious rooms,

with private bathrooms and breezy shared balconies, are clean and well looked after. The friendly English-speaking owner, Mrs Linh, can arrange boat and snorkelling trips (around 700,000d), and also a *xe om* driver to ride you around the island (around two hours, 200,000d). Evening meals and seafood barbecues can also be arranged (the food is good).

🍴 Eating

Dan Tri　　SEAFOOD $
(meals 80,000-120,000d; ⊙ 6am-2pm & 5-10pm) Not far from the jetty at Bai Lang, Dan Tri is a good choice for seafood noodles, grilled shrimps, braised cuttlefish, boiled squid with ginger, fried fish and a decent view over the harbour, especially as the sun sets. Limited English spoken.

ℹ️ Information

At the time of research holders of passports from China or Hong Kong are not permitted to stay overnight on the Cham Islands.

There is no ATM on Hon Lao, so make sure you bring enough cash.

ℹ️ Getting There & Away

Public boats to Cham Island dock at Bai Lang village. There's a scheduled daily connection from a jetty on Đ Nguyen Hoang in Hoi An (two hours, departing between 7am and 7.30am), west of the Hoi An Silk Marina Resort & Spa. Foreigners are routinely charged up to 150,000d. The ferry also stops at Cua Dai Pier at 8.30am; pay your 70,000d admission to the islands on board the ferry. A bike or a scooter is an additional 50,000d. Note that boats do not sail during heavy seas.

From Bai Lang, a return ferry back to Hoi An leaves between 11am and 11.30am. Speedboats also make the one-way trip to Bai Lang for around 300,000d, though returning by speedboat will depend on the availability of boats (less likely later in the day).

Alternatively, come on a day trip with a dive centre such as the Cham Island Diving Center (p210).

ℹ️ Getting Around

Local boats and *xe om* offer connections between Bai Lang and Bai Huong; the rate is about 30,000d for a boat and 120,000d for a *xe om*.

It's possible to take a bicycle or scooter on the public ferry (50,000d), and then ride up to terraced tea plantations or explore other areas of Hon Lao.

My Son

The site of Vietnam's most extensive Cham remains, My Son (the name means 'Beautiful Mountain') enjoys an enchanting setting in a lush jungle valley, overlooked by Cat's Tooth Mountain (Hon Quap). The Hindu temples are in poor shape – only about 20 structures survive where at least 68 once stood – but the intimate nature of the site, surrounded by gurgling streams and hills, is enthralling.

My Son was once the most important intellectual and religious centre of the kingdom of Champa and may also have served as a burial place for Cham monarchs. It was rediscovered in the late 19th century by the French, who restored parts of the complex, but American bombing later devastated the temples. My Son has been a Unesco World Heritage Site since 1999.

History

My Son (pronounced 'me sun') became a religious centre under King Bhadravarman in the late 4th century and was continuously occupied until the 13th century – the longest period of development of any monument in Southeast Asia. Most of the temples were dedicated to Cham kings associated with divinities, particularly Shiva, who was regarded as the founder and protector of Champa's dynasties.

Because some of the ornamentation work at My Son was never finished, archaeologists know that the Chams first built their structures and only then carved decorations into the brickwork.

During one period in their history, the summits of some of the towers were completely covered with a layer of gold. After the area fell into decline, many of the temples were stripped of their glory. The French moved some of the remaining sculptures and artefacts to the Museum of Cham Sculpture (p193) in Danang – fortuitously so, because the VC used My Son as a base during the American War and American bombing destroyed many of the most important monuments. Lots of the remaining statues are missing their heads.

◉ Sights

The ruins get very busy, so go early or late if you can. That way you can also avoid the intense, unsheltered daytime heat here. By departing from Hoi An at around 5am, you could arrive for sunrise and should be leaving when tour groups arrive.

Archaeologists have divided My Son's monuments into 10 main groups, uninspiringly named A, A', B, C, D, E, F, G, H and K. Each structure within that group is given a number.

Only a handful of the monuments at **My Son** (150,000d; ◷ 6.30am-4pm) are properly

---

KINGDOM OF CHAMPA

The kingdom of Champa flourished between the 2nd and 15th centuries. It first appeared around present-day Danang and later spread south to what is now Nha Trang and Phan Rang. Champa became Indianised through commercial ties: adopting Hinduism, using Sanskrit as a sacred language and borrowing from Indian art.

The Chams, who lacked enough land for agriculture, were semi-piratical and conducted attacks on passing ships. As a result they were in a constant state of war with the Vietnamese to the north and the Khmers to the southwest. The Chams successfully threw off Khmer rule in the 12th century, but were entirely absorbed by Vietnam in the 17th century.

They are best known for the many brick sanctuaries (Cham towers) they constructed throughout the south. The greatest collection of Cham art is in the Museum of Cham Sculpture (p193) in Danang but the major Cham site is at the astounding My Son, and other Cham ruins can be found in Quy Nhon and its surrounds, Tuy Hoa, Nha Trang, Thap Cham and the Po Shanu towers at Mui Ne.

Numbering around 140,000 people in Vietnam, the Cham remain a substantial ethnic minority, particularly around Phan Rang. Elements of Cham civilisation can still be seen in techniques for pottery, fishing, sugar production, rice farming, irrigation, silk production and construction throughout the coast. There are both Muslim and Hindu Cham living in Vietnam today, and the latter's towers in the south are still active places of worship.

My Son

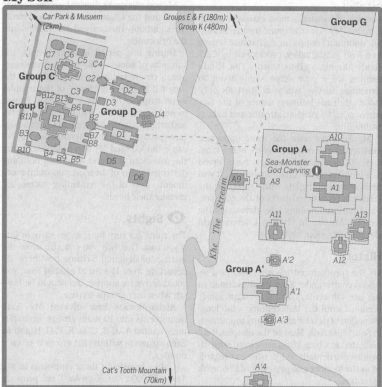

Car Park & Musuem (2km)

Groups E & F (180m); Group K (480m)

Group G

Group C

C7 C6 C5 C4
C1
C2
C3

Group B
B12 B13 B6
B11 B1 B2
B3 B7
B8
B10 B4 B9 B5

Group D
D2
D3
D4
D1
D5
D6

Khe The Stream

Group A
Sea-Monster God Carving
A9 A8
A10
A1
A11 A13
A12

Group A'
A'2
A'1
A'3
A'4

Cat's Tooth Mountain (70km)

labelled, but recent ongoing restoration has introduced a range of useful information panels outlining the history of the site. Resin from trees was used as an adhesive in the brickwork.

Group B HINDU TEMPLE

The main *kalan* (sanctuary), **B1**, was dedicated to Bhadresvara, which is a contraction of the name of King Bhadravarman, who built the first temple at My Son, combined with '-esvara', which means Shiva. The first building on this site was erected in the 4th century, destroyed in the 6th century and rebuilt in the 7th century. Only the 11th-century base, made of large sandstone blocks, remains.

The niches in the wall were used to hold lamps (Cham sanctuaries had no windows). The *linga* inside was discovered during excavations in 1985, 1m below its current position.

B5, built in the 10th century, was used for storing sacred books and objects used in ceremonies performed in B1. The boat-shaped roof (the 'bow' and 'stern' have fallen off) demonstrates the Malay-Polynesian architectural influence. Unlike the sanctuaries, this building has windows and the Cham masonry inside is original. Over the window on the outside wall facing **B4** is a brick bas-relief of two elephants under a tree with two birds in it.

The ornamentation on the exterior walls of **B4** is an excellent example of a Cham decorative style, typical of the 9th century and said to resemble worms. The style is unlike anything found in other Southeast Asian cultures.

B3 has an Indian-influenced pyramidal roof typical of Cham towers. Inside B6 is a bath-shaped basin for keeping sacred water that was poured over the *linga* in B1; this is the only known example of a Cham basin. **B2** is a gate.

Around the perimeter of Group B are small temples, **B7 to B13**, dedicated to *dikpalaka* (gods of the directions of the compass).

Group A   HINDU TEMPLE

Group A was almost completely destroyed by US bombs. According to locals, the massive **A1**, considered the most important monument at My Son, remained impervious to aerial bombing and was intentionally finished off by a helicopter-borne sapper team. All that remains today is a pile of collapsed brick walls. After the destruction of A1, Philippe Stern, an expert on Cham art, wrote a letter of protest to US president Nixon, who ordered US forces to stop damaging Cham monuments.

A1 was the only Cham sanctuary with two doors. One faced east, in the direction of the Hindu gods; the other faced west towards Groups B, C and D and the spirits of the ancestor kings reputedly buried there. Inside A1 is a stone altar. Among the ruins, some of the astonishingly precise brickwork (typical 10th-century style) is still visible. At the base of A1 on the side facing A10 (decorated in 9th-century style) is a **carving** of a small worshipping figure flanked by round columns, with *kala-makara* (a Javanese sea-monster god) above.

Group C   HINDU TEMPLE

The 8th-century **C1** was used to worship Shiva, portrayed here in human form. Inside is an altar where a statue of Shiva, now in the Museum of Cham Sculpture (p193) in Danang, used to stand. Note the motifs, characteristic of the 8th century, carved into the brickwork of the exterior walls. Given the massive bomb crater in front of this group, it's amazing that anything's still standing.

Other Groups   HINDU TEMPLE

Buildings **D1** and **D2** were once meditation halls and now house small displays of Cham sculpture. Preservation has now been completed at **Group G**, where a roof arches over the 12th-century temples, and an exhibition space with archaeological findings from the site can be found.

Group E was built between the 8th and 11th centuries, and renovation of this site is nearing completion, while **Group F** dates from the 8th century; both were badly bombed. Follow the path towards **K** – a stand-alone small tower – to loop back towards the car park.

My Son Museum   MUSEUM

(entry with My Son ticket; ⊙ 6.30am-4pm) My Son's impressive museum has many statues from the site, as well as information about the carvings, statues and architecture, and how the temples were constructed. Cham culture, religion and way of life are also explained.

❶ Getting There & Away

BUS & MINIBUS

Hotels in Hoi An can arrange day trips to My Son (around US$10 to US$15). Most minibuses depart at 8am to 8.30am and return between 1pm and 2pm. For a boat-ride option on the return leg, add an extra hour; lunch is sometimes served. 'Sunrise' trips departing at around 5am do not necessarily mean you'll see the first ray of morning light, but they do beat the crowds and much of the daytime heat. Most tours include an English-speaking guide, but the information provided may be rudimentary.

CAR & MOTORCYCLE

My Son is 55km from Hoi An. A hired car with driver costs around US$60. The site is adequately signposted for those with their own wheels.

CENTRAL VIETNAM AROUND HOI AN

AT A GLANCE

★

POPULATION
Nha Trang: 441,000

BUSIEST AIRPORT
Cam Ranh

BEST HOTEL POOL
Amanoi (p263)

BEST ROMANTIC MEAL SETTING
Sandals (p269)

BEST CRAB
Ganh Hao (p276)

📅

WHEN TO GO

Jul The perfect time to sample the delights of the region's beautiful beaches.

Oct See Cham people celebrate the *kate* festival at Po Klong Garai temple.

Dec Enjoy Christmas in Mui Ne with the best kitesurfing and windsurfing conditions.

Beach at Mui Ne (p263)
HUY THOAI/SHUTTERSTOCK ©

Southeast Coast

This stupendous coastline of ravishing white sands and azure bays is Vietnam's premier destination for beach holidays. If your idea of paradise is reclining in front of turquoise waters, weighing up the merits of a massage or a mojito, then you have come to the right place. On hand to complement the sedentary delights are activities to set the pulse racing, including scuba diving, snorkelling, surfing, windsurfing and kitesurfing. Nha Trang and Mui Ne attract the headlines, but the beach breaks come thick and fast in this part of the country. Explore further and you'll find that hidden bays, lonely lighthouses and a barefoot vibe are all in reach.

Quang Ngai

☑ 0255 / POP 128,700

Quang Ngai city is something of an over-grown village, and most visitors only drop by for a spot of grazing at lunchtime. The few travellers who venture here come to pay their respects to the victims of the most famous atrocity of the American War at nearby Son My.

Even before WWII, Quang Ngai was an important centre of resistance against the French. In 1962, the South Vietnamese government introduced its ill-fated Strategic Hamlets Program. Villagers were forcibly removed from their homes and resettled in fortified hamlets, infuriating and alienating the local population and increasing popular support for the Viet Cong (VC).

◉ Sights

★ Son My Memorial   MEMORIAL

(10,000d; ☺ 7am-4.30pm) This tranquil rural spot was the setting for one of the most horrific crimes of the American War, a massacre committed by US troops that killed 504 villagers, many of them elderly and children, on 16 March 1968. The deeply poignant Son My Memorial was constructed as a monument to their memory.

Centred on a dramatic stone sculpture of an elderly woman holding up her fist in defiance, a dead child in her arms, the monument rises high above the landscape.

Surrounding the main sculpture, scenes have been recreated in peaceful gardens to reflect the aftermath of that fateful day. Burnt-out shells of homes stand in their original locations, each marked with a plaque listing the names and ages of the family that once resided there. The concrete connecting the ruins is coloured to represent a dirt path, and indented with the heavy bootprints of American soldiers and the bare footprints of fleeing villagers.

Known as the My Lai massacre in the USA, the killing was painstakingly documented by an American military photographer, and these graphic images are now the showcase of a powerful on-site museum. The content is incredibly harrowing: villagers are shown cowering from troops, and there are corpses of children and limbless victims. The display ends on a hopeful note, chronicling the efforts of the local people to rebuild their lives afterwards. A section honours the GIs who

tried to stop the carnage, shielding a group of villagers from certain death, and those responsible for blowing the whistle.

The massacre was one of the pivotal moments of the Vietnam conflict, shaping public perceptions in the USA and across the world.

The best way to get to Son My is by motorbike (around 140,000d including waiting time) or regular taxi (about 360,000d return). From Quang Ngai, head north on Đ Quang Trung (Hwy 1) and cross the long bridge over the Tra Khuc River. Take the first right (eastward, parallel to the river) where a triangular concrete stela indicates the way and follow the road for 12km.

My Khe Beach   BEACH

A world away from the sombre atmosphere of the Son My Memorial, but only a couple of kilometres down the road, My Khe is a superb beach, with fine white sand and good swimming. It stretches for kilometres along a thin, casuarina-lined spit of sand, separated from the mainland by Song Kinh Giang, a body of water just inland from the beach.

If you avoid holidays and weekends you've a good chance of having this pretty beach largely to yourself. The shoreline's profile is gently shelving so it's great for children.

Dozens of seafood shacks are spread along the shore, all in a line, and gallons of beer are guzzled on warm weekends.

⊨ Sleeping

Thanh Lich   GUESTHOUSE $

(☑ 097 547 4930; 702 Đ Nguyen Van Linh; r 280,000-350,000d; ❄ 🎅) This guesthouse is run by a very welcoming couple, who speak near-zero English, though their daughter is learning fast. Rooms are well maintained and clean, with good air-conditioning, hot-water showers and solid wooden furniture; some have river views. Located on the north bank of the river, around 2km from central Quang Ngai. Scooters are available to hire.

My Khe Hotel   HOTEL $

(☑ 0255-384 3316; khudulichmykhe@gmail.com; My Khe; s/d/tr 400,000/500,000/600,000d; ❄ 🎅) On My Khe Beach, 17km from Quang Ngai, this midsized hotel has a slightly forgotten ambience, but good-value rooms, all with attractive furnishings and flat-screen TVs. Staff speak a little (broken) English. There's a restaurant at the front for meals, though the menu isn't that exciting.

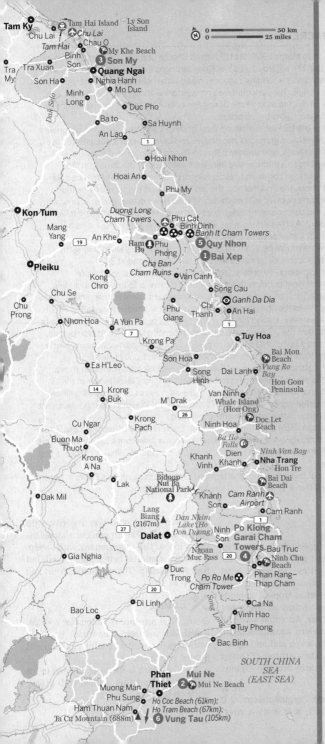

Southeast Coast Highlights

1 Bai Xep (p240) Chilling by the coast with fellow travellers and locals at this tranquil cove.

2 Mui Ne (p263) Chasing the wind by day and eating fresh fish at night in this kitesurfing mecca.

3 Son My Memorial (p232) Coming face-to-face with the horrors of war at this deeply moving memorial.

4 Po Klong Garai Cham Towers (p260) Admiring one of ancient Cham's greatest monuments.

5 Quy Nhon (p236) Enjoying the cafe and bar scene in this emerging coastal city.

6 Vung Tau (p273) Eating surf-fresh seafood by the waves.

MY LAI MASSACRE

At about 7.30am on 16 March 1968, the US Army's Charlie Company landed by helicopter in the west of Son My, regarded as a Viet Cong stronghold. The area had been bombarded with artillery, and the landing zone was raked with rocket and machine-gun fire from helicopter gunships. They encountered no resistance during the 'combat-assault', nor did they come under fire at any time during the operation; but as soon as their sweep eastward began, so did the atrocities.

As the soldiers of the 1st Platoon moved through Xom Lang, they shot and bayoneted fleeing villagers, threw hand grenades into houses and bomb shelters, slaughtered livestock and burned dwellings. Somewhere between 75 and 150 unarmed villagers were rounded up and herded to a ditch, where they were executed by machine-gun fire.

In the next few hours, as command helicopters circled overhead and American Navy boats patrolled offshore, the 2nd Platoon, the 3rd Platoon and the company headquarters group also became involved in the attacks. At least half a dozen groups of civilians, including women and children, were assembled and executed. Villagers fleeing towards Quang Ngai were shot. As these massacres were taking place, at least four girls and women were raped or gang-raped by groups of soldiers.

According to the memorial here, a total of 504 Vietnamese were killed during the massacre; US Army sources determined the total number of dead at 347.

Troops who participated were ordered to keep their mouths shut, but several disobeyed orders and went public with the story after returning to the USA, including helicopter pilot Hugh Thompson Jr who managed to rescue several women and children on that fateful day. When the story broke in the newspapers, it had a devastating effect on the military's morale and fuelled further public protests against the war. It did little to persuade the world that the US Army was fighting on behalf of the Vietnamese people. Unlike WWII veterans, who returned home to parades and glory, soldiers coming home from Vietnam often found themselves ostracised and branded 'baby killers'.

A cover-up of the atrocities was undertaken at all levels of the US Army command, eventually leading to several investigations. Lieutenant William Calley, leader of the 1st Platoon, was court-martialled and found guilty of the murders of 22 unarmed civilians. He was sentenced to life imprisonment in 1971 and spent three years under house arrest at Fort Benning, Georgia, while appealing his conviction.

Calley was paroled in 1974 after the US Supreme Court refused to hear his case. The case still causes controversy – many claim that he was made a scapegoat because of his low rank, and that officers much higher up ordered the massacres. What is certain is that he didn't act alone.

For the full story of this event and its aftermath, pick up a copy of *Four Hours in My Lai* (1992) by Michael Bilton and Kevin Sim, a fine piece of journalism.

★ **Cocoland River Beach Resort & Spa**   RESORT $$

(☎0255-222 5555; http://cocolandriverbeach.vn; Thu Xa, Xa Nghia village; r/villa from US$44/80; ✳❄☎✉) This very attractive resort hotel is the best luxury option in the area, with 76 rooms and villas set in tropical grounds studded with coconut palms on the banks of the Vuc Hong River. Attention to detail is excellent, with modern accommodation, a well-equipped gym, a spa and an impressive pool. Located 10km southeast of Quang Ngai. There's also a nearby beach to explore.

Song Tra Hotel   HOTEL $$

(☎0255-382 2204; http://songtrahotel.com; 2 Đ Quang Trung; r US$30-80; ✳@☎✉) A river-side tower that looms over the city, with chintzy touches like an opulent chandelier-heavy lobby. The rooms, many with sweeping views, could be better maintained, but they are spacious. There's a tennis court and large pool.

✗ Eating

Quang Ngai province is famous for *com ga*: boiled chicken over yellow rice (steamed with chicken broth) with mint, egg soup and pickled vegetables.

My Khe Beach is the place to head to for seafood; the shoreline is lined with places. Settle on prices in advance.

Viet Chay Sala
VEGETARIAN **$**

(83 Đ Cach Mang Thang Tam; meals 35,000-75,000d; ⊘6.30am-8.30pm; 🍴) This vegetarian restaurant offers a selection of tempting dishes – tofu, noodles, spring rolls and soups – all beautifully presented and served with dips and sauces. It's on a side street 300m south of the main drag, Đ Le Trung Dinh. No alcohol is served.

Nha Hang Hai San Sake
SEAFOOD **$**

(www.facebook.com/haisansakeqn; 109 Đ Pham Van Dong; meals from 65,000d; ⊘11.30am-10pm) A bustling barn of a place that's popular for seafood, including great squid dishes. There's a raucous atmosphere here on summer evenings, with beers flowing and a gregarious vibe.

❶ Getting There & Away

AIR
The nearest airport is Chu Lai (VCL), 36km north of Quang Ngai. Vietnam Airlines (www.vietnamairlines.com), Jetstar (www.jetstar.com), Bamboo Airways (www.bambooairways.com) and VietJet Air (www.vietjetair.com) offer flights to Ho Chi Minh City and Hanoi. A taxi to/from town is around 450,000d.

BUS
Quang Ngai Bus Station (Đ Le Thanh Ton) is situated to the south of the centre, 50m east of Đ Quang Trung. Regular buses head to all the major stops on Hwy 1, including Danang (from 55,000d, two hours) and Quy Nhon (from 85,000d, 3½ hours). Open-tour buses can drop you off here, but pick-ups are harder to arrange.

TRAIN
Trains stop at **Quang Ngai Train Station** (Ga Quang Nghia; 204 Đ Nguyen Chi Thanh), 1.5km west of the town centre. Destinations include Danang (from 89,000d, 2½ hours), Dieu Tri (for Quy Nhon; from 105,000d, three hours) and Nha Trang (from 235,000d, seven hours).

Cha Ban Cham Area

📞 0256

The former Cham capital of Cha Ban (also known as Vijaya) is located 25km northwest of Quy Nhon and 5km from Binh Dinh. While there are several important Cham monuments of archaeological importance, there's very little to see for the casual visitor.

⊙ Sights

Quang Trung Museum
MUSEUM

(Phu Phong, Tay Son district; 10,000d; ⊘7.30-11.30am & 1.30-5pm) This museum is built on the site of the Tay Son (p438) brothers' house and encompasses an ancient tamarind tree said to have been planted by the brothers. Displays include statues, costumes, documents and artefacts from the 18th century, most of them labelled in English. Especially notable are the elephant-skin battle drums and gongs from the Bahnar tribe. Demonstrations of *vo binh dinh,* a traditional martial art performed with bamboo sticks, take place here. It's 43km northwest of Quy Nhon.

Banh It Cham Towers
HINDU SITE

(Phuoc Hiep, Tuy Phuoc district; 10,000d; ⊘7-11am & 1.30-4.30pm) This group of four towers sits atop a wooded hilltop 16km northwest of Quy Nhon, just east of Hwy 1, with sweeping riverine views towards the distant South China Sea (East Sea). The architecture of each tower is distinct, although all were built around the turn of the 12th century. The smaller, barrel-roofed tower has the most intricate carvings, and there's a wonderfully toothy face looking down on it from the wall of the largest tower.

Duong Long Cham Towers
HINDU SITE

(1km south of My An village, Tay Son district; ⊘7-11am & 1.30-4.30pm) **FREE** These towers are hard to find, sitting in the countryside 35km northwest of Quy Nhon. Dating from the late 12th century, the largest of the three brick towers (24m high) is embellished with granite ornamentation representing *naga* (a mythical serpent being with divine powers) and elephants (Duong Long means 'Towers of Ivory'). Over the doors are bas-reliefs of women, dancers, monsters and various animals. The corners of the structure are formed by enormous dragon heads.

❶ Getting There & Around

The sights in this region are widely dispersed and best explored with your own wheels. Hiring a car and driver from Quy Nhon for a half-day trip costs US$60, or US$90 for a full day out. Reckon on US$30 for a day's hire of a *xe om* (motorbike taxi).

Hourly buses (15,000d, one hour) link Quy Nhon with Phu Phong, the location of the Quang Trung Museum.

WORTH A TRIP

TAM HAI ISLAND

A tiny (6km-wide), rarely visited island scattered with a handful of fishing villages and coconut palm-fringed beaches, Tam Hai is mellow, accessible and well worth a visit. Culturally, it's a fascinating place, with some minor Cham ruins, an ancient whale graveyard and some unique festivals.

Tam Hai Island is 45km north of Quang Ngai and is connected to the mainland by boat (5000d, frequent, 7am to noon and 1.30pm to 9.30pm) via three small ports. On arrival on Tam Hai Island you can hire bicycles and motorbikes from cafes and stores to tour the island.

In the main village (Tam Hai) you'll find simple seafood restaurants and stores. Heading north from here it's 2km to a **whale grave site**. Continuing west from the Tam Hai village you pass **Ban Than**, a spectacular 40m-high black rocky outcrop, below which there's a good snorkelling spot in the calmer summer months (April to August).

Before you make the hike up Ban Than, flag any of the coconut sellers down and ask them to take you to the **Cham well and temple ruin**, which is hidden down a narrow dirt track under a canopy of coconut trees, almost impossible to find on your own. The well water is considered the most sacred and pure on the island, so the islanders use it to make rice wine that locals believe can cure seasickness.

Ancient traditions run deep in Tam Hai, and islanders regularly gather to host a multitude of festivals connected with the sea. There's an annual **whale festival** on 20 January, and a large festival, **Le Khao Le The Linh**, celebrated annually on the March full moon to honour fisherfolk lost at sea. Village elders build miniature replicas of fishing boats, each with a small mannequin of the deceased and shamans chant prayers before the boats are cast out to sea along with hundreds of candles to guide the lost souls to safety.

If you like the island so much you want to stay, the peaceful **Le Domaine de Tam Hai** (☑0235-354 5105; www.tamhairesort.com; villa US$120; ❋☎☒) resort is just the ticket.

The nearest airport is Chu Lai, which has daily connections via Jetstar, VietJet and Vietnam Airlines to both HCMC and Hanoi. A taxi from the airport to Tam Quang Harbour on the mainland takes 20 minutes and costs 120,000d.

Quy Nhon

☑ 0256 / POP 337,000

A large, prosperous coastal city, Quy Nhon (pronounced 'hwee ngon') boasts a terrific beach-blessed shoreline and grand boulevards. Its seaside appeal and tidy, litter-free streets make it the kind of place that affluent Vietnamese couples choose to retire to, spending their final days ocean-gazing and promenade-walking.

The city is certainly a good spot to sample some fresh seafood, but for most travellers its attractions are perhaps less compelling. However, Quy Nhon is steadily shaking off its somewhat provincial reputation, and there's an emerging cafe and bar scene worth investigating.

Quy Nhon is also the main gateway to lovely Bai Xep, a pretty cove beach 13km to the south where there's a collection of fine guesthouses popular with independent travellers. Other fine beaches lie east of town along the Phuong Mai Peninsula, including Ky Co.

◉ Sights

★ Municipal Beach   BEACH

The long sweep of Quy Nhon's beachfront extends from the port in the northeast to distant wooded hills in the south. It's a beautiful stretch of sand and has been given a major facelift in recent years. There's little rubbish in evidence and good swimming at the southern end.

Thap Doi Cham Towers   HINDU TEMPLE

(Đ Tran Hung Dao; 20,000d; ⊙7am-8.30pm) This pair of Cham towers sits within the city limits in a pretty park. Steep steps lead up to the temples, which are open to the sky. Atypically for Cham architecture, they have curved pyramidal roofs rather than the usual terracing. The larger tower (20m tall) retains some of its ornate brickwork and remnants of the granite statuary that once graced its summit. The dismembered torsos of garuda (half-human, half-bird) can be seen at the corners of the roofs. Take Đ Tran Hung Dao west away from the centre and look out for the towers on the right.

Quy Hoa Beach & Leper Hospital
HISTORIC SITE

 Leprosy may not conjure up images of fun in the sun, but this really is a lovely shoreside spot. A former leper hospital, today it's more of a dermatology clinic, and encompasses a model village. There are not so many patients here these days, but the descendants of affected families continue to live together here in a well-kept community.

Fronting the village is Quy Hoa Beach, a lovely stretch of sand and a popular weekend hang-out.

The hospital grounds are well maintained, complete with numerous busts of distinguished and historically important doctors, both Vietnamese and foreign.

Depending on their abilities, patients work in the rice fields, in fishing, and in repair-oriented businesses. There's also a workshop here where prosthetic limbs and special shoes are crafted, though you'll probably need permission from the director of the institution to visit it.

Just up from the beach, there's a dirt path to the hillside tomb of Han Mac Tu, a mystical poet who died and was buried here in 1940.

If travelling by foot or bicycle, continue along the coast road past Queen's Beach until it descends to the hospital's entrance gates, about 2.5km south of Quy Nhon. Bus T11 passes by.

Binh Dinh Museum
MUSEUM

(28 Đ Nguyen Hue; ⊙ 7-11am & 2-5pm Apr-Sep, 7.30-11am & 1.30-4.30pm Oct-Mar) FREE This small museum concentrates on regional history and has some superb Cham sculpture. The entry hall focuses on local communism, while the room to the left has a natural-history section and exhibits devoted to tribal culture. Impressive Cham relics fill the rear room, including an astonishing 12th-century statue of the Goddess Mahishasuramardini. The room to the right is devoted to the American War.

Also check out the silk print (by Zuy Nhat, 1959) in the lobby showing an overweight French colonist sitting aloft mandarins, in turn supported by bureaucrats, and cruel bosses, with the struggling masses supporting the whole ensemble.

Ky Co Beach
BEACH

(Phuong Mai Peninsula; 100,000d) Backed by coastal cliffs, this drop-dead-gorgeous cove beach is 23km east of Quy Nhon. Ky Co's turquoise waters and fine pale sands have not gone unnoticed by the Instagram crowd, and it's wildly popular with day-tripping domestic tourists, so visit early or late in the day if possible. Note that access is tricky: from the car park above the beach via 4WD shuttle (60,000d per person), or on foot.

Long Khanh Pagoda
BUDDHIST TEMPLE

(off Đ Tran Cao Van) FREE It's hard to miss the 17m-high Buddha (built in 1972) heralding Quy Nhon's main pagoda, set back from the road by 143 Đ Tran Cao Van. The pagoda was founded in 1715 by a Chinese merchant, and the monks who reside here preside over the religious affairs of the city's active Buddhist community.

Mosaic dragons with manes of broken glass lead up to the main building, flanked by towers sheltering a giant drum (on the left) and an enormous bell.

Ong Nui Temple
BUDDHIST STATUE

(Phuong Binh village) FREE Located 25km north of Quy Nhon, the biggest seated Buddha in Southeast Asia enjoys a commanding hillside location with sweeping sea views. Access is via a vertiginous 600-step pathway lined with 18 statues of *arhats* (those who have attained nirvana).

🏃 Activities

Zen Spa
MASSAGE

(☑ 0256-652 5678; 270 Đ Nguyen Thi Dinh; 1hr body massage 250,000d; ⊙ 8.30am-9pm) A professional spa that employs well-trained, experienced staff and has clean, attractive premises. Facials, foot massages (180,000d per hour) and other body treatments are available, and rates are very moderate.

Quynhonkids English Club
TOURS

(☑ 090 630 2218; www.facebook.com/quynhonkids) This friendly bunch of locals loves to meet up with foreigners to chat in English. You're welcome to join them on beach clean-ups, countryside tours by motorbike, hillside hikes or for football games. You'll just need to contribute to fuel costs.

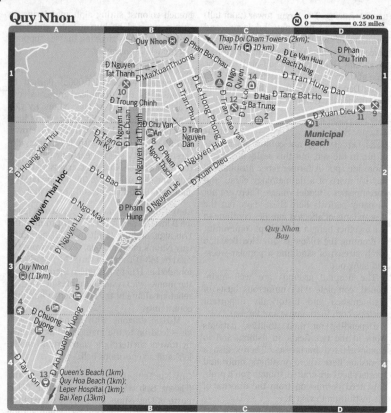

Quy Nhon

⊙ Top Sights
1 Municipal Beach D1

⊙ Sights
2 Binh Dinh Museum C1
3 Long Khanh Pagoda C1

⊕ Activities, Courses & Tours
4 Zen Spa A3

🛏 Sleeping
5 Anh Vy Hotel A3
6 Anya Hotel Quy Nhon A3
7 John & Paul Inn A4

8 Kim House B2

⊗ Eating
9 C.ine D1
10 Gia Vy 2 .... B1
11 Nha Hang Lien Thanh D1
12 Sisters Tavern & Pizzeria C1

⊖ Drinking & Nightlife
Den 2 .... (see 8)
13 Quy Nhon Sports Bar A4

⊕ Shopping
14 Lon Market C1

🛏 Sleeping

New guesthouses and hostels have revital-
ised the Quy Nhon accommodation scene.
Most travellers prefer to base themselves at
nearby Bai Xep Beach, but there are several
inexpensive places in town.

★ **Nhon Hai Beach Hostel**   HOSTEL **$**
(☎ 088 855 5368; www.facebook.com/nhonhai
hostel; Hai Nam, Nhon Hai; dm/r US$5/17; ﷯﷯)
Beachside in a fishing village 17km east
of the city, this locally owned hostel has
good-quality accommodation and kind

hosts. The air-conditioned dorm has an en suite, while the attractive private rooms enjoy sea views. Rent a kayak, snorkelling gear or scooter, or take a boat trip along the peninsula. Delicious meals are 50,000d to 100,000d.

Kim House HOSTEL $
(☑ 0902 343 635; www.facebook.com/pg/den 2coffee; 25 Đ Le Xuan Tru; dm 132,000d, d 297,000-330,000d; ❋ 🛜) Fine fairly new hostel on a side road with cosy six-bed dorms and decent private rooms that have high ceilings and solid wooden furniture. Showers are clean and there's a great cafe downstairs for your free breakfast, as well as good coffee and beers.

John & Paul Inn HOSTEL $
(☑ 0256-651 7770; http://johnandpaulinn.com; 63 Đ Chuong Duong; dm US$5-6, r US$16; ❋ 🛜) Popular hostel in the south of town with clean dorms (including a female-only option) and good private rooms with cable TV and balcony. The name references the Beatles, though you're more likely to hear heavy rock and metal in the busy downstairs restobar.

Anh Vy Hotel HOTEL $
(☑ 0256-384 7763; anhvy08@gmail.com; 8 Đ An Duong Vuong; s/d/tr from 220,000/260,000/320,000d; ❋ @ 🛜) A long-running place operated by a friendly couple who speak English and offer excellent travel information. They also have bikes and scooters for hire at fair rates. The rooms are looking a little tired these days but all have hot-water bathrooms; those with sea views cost a little more.

Anya Hotel Quy Nhon HOTEL $$$
(☑ 0256-653 6728; https://en.anyahotel.com; 3 Đ Nguyen Trung Tin; r US$62-108, ste US$145; ❋ 🛜 🏊) This luxury hotel is set just inland from the beach. All rooms are designed in a contemporary style, with subtle greys and pale wood colour schemes. The pool area, fitness centre and spa impress, too.

Crown Retreat
Quy Nhon Resort RESORT $$$
(☑ 0256-653 8538; https://crownretreat.com; Trung Luong, Cat Tien; villas from US$96; ❋ 🛜 🏊) This classy hotel 25km north of Quy Nhon enjoys a stunning location on a white-sand beach, with a choice of hillside, sea-view or beachfront thatched bungalows. Attention to detail is excellent, with classy wooden furniture and attractive tiling. The pool area

has uninterrupted ocean views and there's good local and Western food available. Phu Cat airport is 30 minutes away.

 Eating

Quy Nhon is one of the best places in Vietnam to indulge in a seafood session. A lot of the bayside places have been cleared for large construction projects, but Đ Xuan Dieu still has several options.

Gia Vy 2 VIETNAMESE $
(14 Đ Dien Hong; meals 40,000d; ⊗ 7am-9.45pm) Enjoy rolling your own meal! Head to this local joint for lipsmackingly authentic *banh xeo* pancakes: grab some rice paper and make an envelope with a shrimp or beef pancake, salad leaves, green mango, sliced cucumber and a dash of chilli sauce, and savour the flavour.

★**C.ine** SEAFOOD $$
(☑ 0256-651 2675; 94 Đ Xuan Dieu; dishes 40,000-180,000d; ⊗ 11am-10.30pm) Excellent seafood restaurant with gingham tablecloths and views over the bay. Prices are higher than some on this strip but worth it: try the sweet soft-shell crab, scallops with butter and garlic, grilled fish and snail dishes. There's some inaccuracy with English translations on the menu.

Sisters Tavern & Pizzeria ITALIAN $$
(www.facebook.com/SistersQuyNhon; 81 Đ Hai Ba Trung; mains 69,000-159,000d; ⊗ 11am-9.15pm; 🛜) An inviting little bar-restaurant serving terrific pizza (try the sausage arrabbiata), filling pasta dishes, tasty salads, paninis and ribs. You'll find a fine selection of brews to enjoy, too, including craft beers from Heart of Darkness, while Chilean wine is 69,000d a glass.

Nha Hang Lien Thanh SEAFOOD $$
(104 Đ Xuan Dieu; meals 70,000-150,000d; ⊗ 11am-9.30pm) A local seafood place on the bay that serves up fine prawn dishes and marinated (or barbecued) squid. There's no English-language menu, so bring your phrasebook.

🥤 **Drinking & Nightlife**

Cafe culture is alive and kicking in Quy Nhon, while the city's bar scene is steadily growing, too. Đ Hai Ba Trung is lined with cafes frequented by young Vietnamese students and there's quite a buzz about this area, day and night.

Den 2

CAFE

(Kim House, 25 Đ Le Xuan Tru; ☻24hr; 🛜) This branch of Den Coffee at Kim House hostel is going strong, serving premium arabica and quality robusta beans from Vietnam, Ethiopia and around the globe. A perfect espresso is 25,000d, while a *caphe den* (black Vietnamese drip-style coffee) costs 13,000d. Juices, snacks and meals are available.

Quy Nhon Sports Bar

SPORTS BAR

(92 Đ An Duong Vuong; ☻noon-11pm; 🛜) Aussie-owned sports bar in the south of town offering Rooster and East West craft beers, with a lively street terrace and roof bar with sea views. The menu features Western comfort grub, while TVs beam live and recorded sport coverage from around the world.

🛍 Shopping

Lon Market

MARKET

(Cho Lon, Đ Tang Bat Ho; ☻6am-4pm) A bustling central market where street sellers spill over into the surrounding roads. Great for photo opportunities.

ⓘ Getting There & Away

Quy Nhon has decent bus connections to other cities along the coast and a train station and airport nearby.

AIR

Phu Cat airport is 31km northwest of the city.

Vietnam Airlines, VietJet, Bamboo Airways and Jetstar offer connections to Ho Chi Minh City and Hanoi.

BUS

Quy Nhon Bus Station (☑0256-384 6246; Đ Tay Son) is on the south side of town, with frequent buses to Quang Ngai (from 85,000d, 3½ hours), Nha Trang and towns in the central highlands including Pleiku (90,000d, four hours, seven daily).

Son Tung operates two to three daily minibuses/buses (170,000d, six hours) between Quy Nhon and Hoi An. No open-tour buses stop at Quy Nhon.

TRAIN

The nearest mainline station is Dieu Tri, 10km west of the city. Only very slow local trains stop at **Quy Nhon Train Station** (☑0256-382 2036; Đ Le Hong Phong).

From Dieu Tri, destinations include Quang Ngai (108,000d, three hours) and all major towns on the main north–south line.

ⓘ Getting Around

All the airlines offer minibus transfers (50,000d) to/from the city and airport.

From central Quy Nhon to Dieu Tri train station it costs 165,000d in a taxi or about 60,000d on a *xe om*. A taxi to/from Phu Cat airport costs 480,000d. Grab motorbikes are in Quy Nhon but not Grab taxis.

Scooters (from 120,000d per day) are widely available for rent from guesthouses.

Bai Xep

☑0256 / POP 2500

An isolated fishing village just a few years back, the pretty bay of Bai Xep now attracts a steady stream of independent travellers. It's still quite remote, 13km south of Quy Nhon, but this beach's relaxed appeal is considerable and its beauty undeniable.

Bai Xep consists of two small coves. The northernmost cove, **Bai Truoc** ('Front Beach'), is a busy little fishing port with a warren of lanes of tightly packed houses and a small bay strewn with fishing tackle and boats. Just to the south is larger, more attractive **Bai Sau** ('Back Beach'), which has an expanding range of accommodation, each place facing a stunning crescent-shaped sandy bay that offers wonderful swimming.

It's easy to lose track of time here, chilling in a hammock, socialising with locals and fellow travellers, and exploring the stunning coastline and islands offshore.

QUY NHON TRANSPORT CONNECTIONS

DESTINATION	AIR	BUS	CAR/MOTORBIKE	TRAIN (SOFT SEAT)
Danang	n/a	190,000-275,000d, 6½hr, 8 daily	6/8hr	from 187,000d, 6-7hr, 6 daily
Hanoi	from 428,000d, 1½hr, 6-7 daily	from 390,000d, 19hr, 6 daily	around 22/25hr	from 610,000d, 21-24hr, 5 daily
HCMC	from 520,000d, 1hr, 5-6 daily	240,000-380,000d, 12hr, 8-10 daily	13/18hr	from 319,000d, 11-14hr, 7 daily

OFF THE BEATEN TRACK

GANH DA DIA

A smaller version of Ireland's Giant's Causeway, Ganh Da Dia is a spectacular outcrop of volcanic rock that juts into the ocean south of Quy Nhon. Half the fun is simply getting there, as the scenery in this coastal region is superb.

Consisting of hundreds of interlocked columns of volcanic rock, Ganh Da Dia was created millions of years ago as fluid molten basalt cooled. Some of the best sections are formed of incredibly regular pentagonal- and hexagonal-sided horizontal rocks. The Vietnamese call this place 'the cliff of stone plates', and it's regularly used by Buddhist monks for ceremonies.

You can bathe in the tiny rocky cove next to Ganh Da Dia, but the drop-dead gorgeous sandy beach on the south side of the bay, a five-minute walk away, is even more inviting. Overpriced fresh coconuts and snacks are sold by local villagers at the car park.

Ganh Da Dia is signposted from the small town of Chi Thanh, 68km south of Quy Nhon. Heading down Hwy 1, take the turning just past the river bridge on the northern side of town. The route to the coast meanders for 13km through a delightful pastoral landscape of rice paddies and farming villages.

Continuing south (and avoiding Hwy 1) you can take a lovely coastal road to Tuy Hoa. Head inland (west) from Ganh Da Dia for 3.5km and then a side (paved) road heads south through sand dunes, past cacti and agave to the fishing village of An Hai, where a row of seafood restaurants faces the O Loan estuary and makes an ideal pit stop.

From An Hai, it's 27km south to Tuy Hoa. The route has a few twists and turns, but the kilometre waymarks (which indicate the distance to Tuy Hoa) help guide you the right way.

Activities

Guesthouses can arrange island-hopping boat trips including some snorkelling (120,000d per person), cooking classes (150,000d per person) and motorbike hire. Villagers offer massages (around 120,000d per hour) or check out the **spa** (☎0256-384 0132; www.avanihotels.com/en/spa; Avani Quy Nhon Resort & Spa; 1hr massage from 1,200,000d; ⏲9am-9pm) at the Avani resort.

There's some surf here between October and March (Alex, owner of Haven guesthouse, rents out boards to guests). In the rainy season, walks to local waterfalls are rewarding, too.

Sleeping

The Bai Xep region has sleeping choices ranging from dorm beds to luxurious oceanfront villas. More hotels are under construction – including an outlandish, vaguely arty high-rise complete with a boat's bow built into its roof.

★Life's a Beach Backpackers HOSTEL $
(☎086-895 8843; www.lifesabeachvietnam.com; 2km north of Xuan Hai; dm/huts/r from US$5/14/18; ❄📶) This party hostel enjoys a sublime setting on a lovely, private sandy cove beach, with accommodation (good-quality dorms, bungalows and camping) scattered around a shady hillside. There's a restobar for boozing and munchies, and ample hammocks for horizontal chilling. Lots of activities are offered, from kayak hire to karaoke sing-offs. Located 5km south of Bai Xep.

Banana Sea Homestay HOMESTAY $
(☎0931 123 227; www.bananahomestay.com; Bai Sau; dm 160,000d, r 450,000d, huts 500,000-650,000d; ❄📶) Creeping up the hillside behind Back Beach, this super-hospitable Swiss-Vietnamese homestay is as welcoming a base as you could wish for. There's a selection of cute barrel-roofed huts to choose from, some with air-con and all with hot-water en suites and fine views. The clean dorm has air-con. Great food and travel info is available in the cafe below.

★Haven GUESTHOUSE $$
(☎0982 114 906; www.havenvietnam.com; To 2, Khu Vuc 1, Bai Sau; dm 160,000d, r incl breakfast 850,000-1,200,000d; ❄📶) This homey shorefront guesthouse has undergone a serious revamp, with a new block adding an additional eight rooms and a four-bed dorm; most accommodation enjoys a sea view. The welcome and atmosphere remain as warm as ever thanks to the Australian-Vietnamese owners, who've been in Bai Xep for years

and can advise about local excursions and trips. Breakfast is served in the delightful adjoining Big Tree Bistro.

Life's a Beach
GUESTHOUSE $$

(☑0162 993 3117, 0963 289 096; www.lifesabeach vietnam.com; Bai Sau; dm US$7, r incl breakfast US$20-55; ✿🛜) 🏄 British-run place with a prime beachfront slot that's perfect for meeting others and kicking back. Barbecues, board games and pub quizzes ensure a social vibe. There's a choice of digs including big family-friendly units, bungalows, a tree house, bamboo dorm and two smart apartments (located separately on Front Beach). Service is efficient and friendly.

Avani Quy Nhon Resort & Spa
RESORT $$$

(☑0256-384 0132; www.avanihotels.com; 700m south of Bai Xep; r/ste incl breakfast from US$140/165; ✿🛜🏊) All set up for a memorable stay, this stylish beachfront hotel boasts well-designed rooms, all with ocean vistas, natural materials and contemporary mod cons. Tai chi, yoga, snorkelling and fishing trips are offered. There's a lovely pool, fine-dining options and the spa is the best in the region.

Anantara Quy Nhon Villas
LUXURY HOTEL $$$

(☑0256-384 0132; www.anantara.com; 1km south of Bai Xep; villas from US$458; ✿🛜🏊) Opened in 2018, this sublime resort consists of 26 villas, all equipped with private pools and contemporary style, and surrounded by lush tropical landscaping. In-house Sea.Fire.Salt restaurant has a reputation as the best in the entire Quy Nhon district, and the astonishing wellness facilities include a Thai massage pavilion overlooking the ocean.

🍴 Eating

Banana Sea
VEGETARIAN $

(www.bananahomestay.com; Bai Sau; meals from 45,000d; ⊗7am-10pm; 🛜🏄) This happy homestay has a meat-free menu of tempting local and Western food with vegan, lactose-free and gluten-free dishes available. Join in for breakfast or a family-style dinner. Cocktails and beers are also served.

Big Tree Bistro
INTERNATIONAL $$

(www.havenvietnam.com/bigtreebistro; Haven, To 2, Khu Vuc 1, Bai Sau; most mains 100,000-169,000d; ⊗6am-9pm; 🛜) Pizza from a wood-fired oven is the speciality at this casual, sociable hotel restaurant that enjoys terrific vistas over Back Beach. You'll also find good

salads and excellent barbecued meats such as whole roast chicken on the menu.

Bau Huy
SEAFOOD $$

(Bai Sau; meals 60,000-160,000d; ⊗10am-9pm) This small local seafood place serves ocean-fresh crab, shellfish and fish dishes – just peruse what's on offer in the bubbling tubs.

Sea.Fire.Salt
INTERNATIONAL $$$

(☑0256-384 0077; www.anantara.com; Anantara Quy Nhon Villas, 1km south of Bai Xep; meals from 320,000d; ⊗6.30am-10.30pm; 🛜) Anantara's signature restaurant is a supremely elegant (and expensive) affair, and offers Vietnamese and Western dishes. It's the latter that impresses the most, with innovative creations like seafood and steak dishes cooked on salt bricks; try the locally sourced lobster cooked in its own shell with garlic-parsley butter.

❶ Getting There & Away

Bai Xep is 13km south of Quy Nhon and connected by local buses: T11 (9000d) runs roughly hourly from the Metro mall between 5.30am and 5pm (with a break for lunch). A taxi from Quy Nhon is 190,000d. Many travellers arrive by motorbike.

Tuy Hoa

☑0257 / POP 219,000

Tuy Hoa is steadily being transformed into a vast new city, with a large plaza and multi-laned boulevards. It's a possible overnight stop to break up a longer journey, especially for cyclists brave enough to tackle Hwy 1, but most visitors are just passing through.

⊙ Sights

The few sights the town has are all on hilltops visible from the main highway. Tuy Hoa's sandy beach is huge, stretching for miles along a largely empty shoreline.

Nhan Cham Tower
TEMPLE

(off Ð Le Trung Kien) FREE To the south of town, the 20m-high Nhan Cham Tower is an impressive sight, particularly when illuminated at night. The climb up to the tower, which dates from the 14th century, takes you through a small botanic garden and you'll be rewarded with great views from the hilltop.

War Memorial
MEMORIAL

(off Ð Le Trung Kien) FREE This striking white war memorial in the south of town has been

VUNG RO BAY

A spectacular natural harbour ringed by forested peaks, Vung Ro Bay is a remote, wildly beautiful lagoon-like expanse of turquoise water 25km south of Tuy Hoa. It's celebrated as Vietnam's most easterly point on the mainland.

A crooked finger of land protects the bay from the worst South China Sea (East Sea) storms, allowing a floating village and fish farms to flourish in its sheltered waters. On the northeast side of Vung Ro, the coastal road passes an exquisite undeveloped sandy cove, **Bai Mon**, the perfect spot for a swim. From this beach a steep path leads up to a 19th-century lighthouse, built by the French, from where there are ocean vistas of the Vung Ro coastline.

This part of Vietnam hit the headlines back in February 1965 when a US helicopter detected the movement of a North Vietnamese supply ship in the area. Vung Ro was part of the alternative Ho Chi Minh Sea Trail and was being used to smuggle arms into South Vietnam for Viet Cong forces. The discovery of a sea supply route from north to south confirmed US suspicions and was used as justification to ramp up US involvement in the war.

Today the isolation and raw beauty of the Vung Ro coast is under threat by a plan for a giant oil refinery and billion-dollar resort complex and marina. This development project was proposed years ago, but the investment licence for the Vung Ro refinery was revoked in March 2018. However, negotiations are continuing and the project could yet be back on.

designed with overlapping sails that are vaguely reminiscent of the Sydney Opera House.

🛏 Sleeping

Coast Homestay HOMESTAY $
(☑ 078 222 8444; www.facebook.com/Coast. Homestay; 236 Đ Ba Trieu; r with shared/private bathroom from US$7/9; ❄🛜) This homestay has very well-presented neat rooms with good-quality wood furnishings, some with shared bathrooms. There's a guest kitchen and lounge. Our only observation is that it's not that close to the coast (the beach is 600m away).

My Ha Hotel HOTEL $
(☑ 0257-368 6970; C13 Đ Hoang Van Thu; r US$11-20; ❄🛜) Offering fine value, this welcoming minihotel has smart, spotless, well-equipped rooms with good air-conditioning, flat-screen TVs and quality beds and linen (though the cheapest rooms are windowless). The friendly staff rent scooters (130,000d per day) and help out travellers. It's 500m from the beach.

Nhiet Doi Hotel HOTEL $
(☑ 0257-382 2424; www.nhietdoihotel.com; 216 Đ Nguyen Hue; r 220,000-350,000d; ❄🛜) The 16 rooms here have attractive furnishings; all but the cheapest are quite spacious. Staff speak little English but will help with

motorbike rentals. Tasty meals (30,000d to 50,000d) are available.

⭐ **Sala Tuy Hoa Beach Hotel** HOTEL $$
(☑ 0257-368 6666; www.salatuyhoabeach.com; 51 Doc Lap; r US$40; ❄🛜🏊) This newcomer enjoys a prime beachfront location and its spacious rooms are in fine shape, some with ocean views. There's a sense of style about the whole operation and facilities are good with a cafe, restaurant, two pools (the larger one is across the street) and landscaped grounds. Staff go the extra mile to assist guests. Excellent value all round.

🍴 Eating & Drinking

You'll find a glut of simple restaurants and street vendors along the main highway and Đ Tran Hung Dao. Seafood shacks and *bia hoi* (draught beer) joints are on the beach. For cafes, fast food and Korean-style meat restaurants head to the **Vincom Plaza** (https://vincom.com.vn; Hung Vuong; ⊙ 9am-10pm).

Ca Phe Mai Ngoi VIETNAMESE $
(277 Đ Le Duan; meals 25,000-65,000d; ⊙ 8am-8.30pm) This twin-level artistically designed cafe-restaurant has plenty of greenery and mismatched seating. It offers hearty breakfasts, full-flavoured soups and noodle dishes, and serves up a mean *com ga* (chicken and rice).

Cav Coffee CAFE
(Vincom Plaza, Hung Vuong; ⊗9am-10pm; ☎) If you're in need of a caffeine fix, this cafe will satisfy your cappuccino cravings and espresso needs. Tea, juices and snacks also served.

🛈 Getting There & Away

AIR

Vietnam Airlines (☑0257-382 6508; www.vietnamairlines.com; 353 Đ Tran Hung Dao; ⊗8am-4.30pm Mon-Sat) and **VietJet** (www.vietjetair.com) operate flights to Hanoi (from 726,000d), while VietJet and **Jetstar** (www.jetstar.com) cover the connection to HCMC (from 483,000d). There's always at least one daily flight to both cities. The airport, sometimes called Dong Tac, is 8km south of town.

BUS

From Tuy Hoa, there are regular buses to Quy Nhon (49,000d, two hours) and Nha Trang (72,000d, three hours).

TRAIN

Tuy Hoa Train Station (Đ Le Trung Kien) is on the road parallel to the highway. Destinations include Danang (from 222,000d, seven to eight hours) and Nha Trang (from 58,000d, two hours).

Tuy Hoa to Nha Trang

☑0258

The spectacular coast between Tuy Hoa and Nha Trang takes in the easternmost points of mainland Vietnam, a craggy landscape of wind-lashed capes, fishing villages and cove beaches. Exploring the coastal road you'll see tantalising glimpses of a number of remote and beautiful spots, while others are hidden behind jungle, along promontories or on secluded islands. Money-changing facilities and ATMs are thin on the ground, so cash up first in Nha Trang, Tuy Hoa or Quy Nhon.

🛈 Getting There & Away

Regular buses connect Tuy Hoa with Nha Trang via Hwy 1. To make the most of this remote region you'll need your own transport; a motorbike is ideal.

Dai Lanh Beach

Crescent-shaped Dai Lanh Beach has a split personality. A scruffy fishing village occupies the northern end, but it yields to an attractive beach shaded by casuarina trees – there's good swimming in the sheltered bay here.

The fishing village can be interesting to explore and there's a small early morning market, but for most travellers it's all about the beach. There are ample restaurants on the highway and affordable minihotels, such as **Le Plateau** (☑097 349 9986; Hwy 1; r 250,000d; ❄☎), athough none really stand out.

Dai Lanh is 32km south of Tuy Hoa and 83km north of Nha Trang on Hwy 1.

Whale Island

About 1km south of Dai Lanh, a vast sand-dune causeway connects the mainland to the Hon Gom Peninsula, which is almost 30km in length.

Boats for Whale Island (Hon Ong) leave from Hom Gom's main village, Dam Mon, set on a sheltered bay. The island is a 15-minute boat ride away. It's a tiny speck on the map, with only one place to stay, the **Whale Island Resort** (☑096 135 1877; www.whaleislandresort.com; d/villa incl breakfast from US$40/90; ☎), a fine place to enjoy barefoot living. Transfers are free for guests.

Doc Let Beach

Stretching for 18km, the chalk-white sands and shallow turquoise waters of Doc Let ensure it ranks among Vietnam's best beaches. However, in the last few years developers have moved in big time, and busloads of tourists are herded here on tours from Nha Trang.

This giant bay can be divided into three sections. The northern part is where most of the tourism action is, with a cluster of beachfront hotels and cheaper guesthouses inland. Looming over the central section is the giant Hyundai shipyard and port, an important local employer but a real blight on the landscape.

The southern part is backed by a wooded promontory and has the best stretch of sand. This part was totally tranquil until late 2017, but with the influx of developers and day-trippers (and jet skis), the character of the place has changed.

🛌 Sleeping & Eating

Virtually all the hotels here have restaurants. There are very few eating options otherwise.

Light Hotel HOTEL $
(☑088 645 3069; Ha Huy Tap, Dong Cat; r 320,000-450,000d; ❄☎) Around 400m inland from the beach, this hotel has clean,

inviting rooms with efficient air-con. It's well managed by the affable Trung who looks after his guests well and can help out with transport.

⭐**Some Days of Silence** BOUTIQUE HOTEL $$$

(☑0258-367 0952; www.somedaysresort.com; Dong Cat; r US$115-125, bungalow incl breakfast from US$200; ❄@🤖☎) This stunning, artistically designed place feels more like an in-the-know retreat than a mere hotel. Elegant bungalows and rooms are lovingly decorated and feature four-poster beds and bathrooms with pebble-detailing. There's a sublime tropical garden, a good spa and service is great. The pagoda-style restaurant and terrace make a lovely setting for healthy, creative meals (US$12).

❶ Getting There & Away

Hourly No 3 buses (25,000d, 1½ hours) leave from Đ Nguyen Thien Thuat in Nha Trang for Dong Cat village on the northern end of Doc Let Beach.

By road, the turn-off for Doc Let is signposted from Hwy 1. From here continue 10km past photogenic salt fields, looking out for the signs to the resorts. Most of the hotels and resorts also offer some sort of transfer service for a fee.

There's a separate, direct (paved) road to Doc Let's southern section via the shipyard from the same Hwy 1 turn-off.

Ninh Van Bay

Welcome to an alternate reality populated by European royalty, film stars and the otherwise rich and secretive. For the average punter not able to afford an uberluxurious hotel, this place doesn't exist. Well, at least not before 2017, when the mother-of-all flashpacker retreats opened here on a private bay.

Ninh Van Bay is all about get-away-from-it-all beach bliss, and there's a sprinkling of exquisite sandy coves you can reach by kayak, SUP or boat. There's only very limited road access to the region; some resorts are only reachable by boat.

🛏 Sleeping & Eating

⭐**Ninhvana** HOSTEL $

(☑0258-364 9569; www.vietnambackpackerhostels.com; dm/d from 150,000/915,000d; ❄🤖☎) This astonishing travellers' 'resort' takes flashpacking to a different level. If you've ever dreamt of finding *The Beach* (like Leonardo DiCaprio), well, this could be the place. Ninhvana has now wisely dropped its all-inclusive model and offers affordable pay-as-you-go pricing. Dorms and private rooms are excellent and there are twice-daily shuttle bus links to Nha Trang.

With two pools, a private white-sand shoreline, yoga, kayaks/SUPs and lots of evening activities (from karaoke to Mexican fiestas), you'll have a lot of fun. There's also an outdoor cinema, basketball court and beach volleyball.

⭐**Six Senses Ninh Van Bay** RESORT $$$

(☑0258-352 4268; www.sixsenses.com; villa US$920-3230; ❂❄🤖☎) With a magical setting on a secluded cove and elegant traditionally inspired villas, each with its own swimming pool, Six Senses makes an astonishing base camp for unwinding and indulging. This is not a place to watch your dong or dollars, for rates are some of the highest in Vietnam, but the attention to detail and service are superb.

Facilities include a wonderful Six Senses Spa and restaurants featuring Western and Asian cuisine. For the ultimate experience book the Rock Villa, set in its own private bay over dramatic rock formations. It even has a wine cellar.

An Lam Retreat RESORT $$$

(☑0258-372 8388; www.anlam.com; villa US$330-740; ❂❄🤖☎) With natural materials, handcrafted furniture and earthy colours, this retreat tempts visitors with its back-to-nature ethos. You can't miss the astonishing globular restaurant that juts into the bay, a fine piece of contemporary architecture, though the menu (mains from US$20) is pricey. Villas are beautifully presented and there are kayaks for coastal exploring. Only accessed by boat; no children.

L'Alyana Villas Ninh Van Bay RESORT $$$

(☑0258-362 4777; http://lalyana.com; villa US$385-1090; ❂❄🤖☎) All guests approach this enclave of luxury in a speedboat, skimming across a turquoise bay fringed by forested hills. On arrival settle in to a life of sybaritic tropical living. The thatched villas (the smallest a mighty 90 sq metres) have private plunge pools. Personal butlers, complimentary yoga, kayaking and hiking only add to L'Alyana's allure.

ⓘ Getting There & Away

Only Ninhvana is reachable by road. All other hotels organise boat transfers from private docks 15km north of Nha Trang.

Nha Trang

🗐 0258 / POP 441,000

The high-rise, high-energy beach resort of Nha Trang enjoys a stunning setting: it's ringed by a necklace of hills, with a turquoise bay dotted with tropical islands.

A sweeping crescent beach of white sand defines the shoreline, backed by an impressive promenade dotted with parks and sculpture gardens. Inland there's a cosmopolitan array of boutiques and dining options.

As restaurants wind down, nightlife cranks up – central Nha Trang is a party town at heart. Until a few years ago a lot of the bar action was geared at the backpacker market, but today it's mainly aimed at the burgeoning numbers of Asian and Russian package tourists.

There are more sedate activities on offer, too. Try an old-school spa treatment with a visit to a mudbath, book a river cruise or explore the ancient Cham towers north of the centre.

ⓘ When to Go

Nha Trang has its very own microclimate and the rains tend to come from October until December, a time best avoided if you are into lazing on the beach or diving in the tropical waters.

◎ Sights

Don't miss the impressive Cham towers just north of the city.

★ Nha Trang Beach   BEACH
(Map p248) Forming a magnificent sweeping arc, Nha Trang's 6km-long golden-sand beach is the city's trump card. Sections are roped off and designated for safe swimming (where you won't be bothered by jet skis or boats). The turquoise water is very inviting, and the promenade a delight to stroll.

Two popular lounging spots are the Sailing Club (p258) and Louisiane Brewhouse (p257). If you head south of here, the beach gets quieter and it's possible to find a quiet stretch of sand.

The best beach weather is generally before 1pm, as the afternoon sea breezes can whip up the sand.

During heavy rains, run-off from the rivers at each end of the beach flows into the bay, gradually turning it a murky brown. Most of the year, however, the sea is just like it appears in the brochures.

★ Po Nagar Cham Towers   BUDDHIST TEMPLE
(Thap Ba, Lady of the City; Map p247; north side of Xom Bong Bridge; admission 22,000d, guide 50,000d; ⊘ 6am-6pm) Built between the 7th and 12th centuries, these impressive Cham towers are still actively used for worship by Cham, Chinese and Vietnamese Buddhists. Originally the complex had seven or eight towers, but only four remain, of which the 28m-high North Tower (Thap Chinh; 817 CE), with a terraced pyramidal roof, vaulted interior masonry and vestibule, is the most magnificent.

The towers stand on a granite knoll 3km north of central Nha Trang, on the northern bank of the Cai River.

It's thought this site was first used for worship as early as the 2nd century CE. The original wooden structure was razed to the ground by attacking Javanese in 774 CE, but was replaced by a stone-and-brick temple (the first of its kind) in 784.

The towers serve as the Holy See, honouring Yang Ino Po Nagar, the goddess of the Dua (Liu) clan, which ruled over the southern part of the Cham kingdom. There are inscribed stone slabs scattered throughout the complex, most of which relate to history or religion and provide insight into the spiritual life and social structure of the Cham.

All the temples face east, as did the original entrance to the complex, which is to the right as you ascend the hillock. In centuries past, worshippers passed through the pillared meditation hall, 10 pillars of which can still be seen, before proceeding up the steep staircase to the towers.

In 918, King Indravarman III placed a gold *mukha-linga* (carved phallus with a human face painted on it) in the North Tower, but it was taken by Khmer raiders. This pattern of statues being destroyed or stolen and then replaced continued until 965, when King Jaya Indravarman IV replaced the gold *mukha-linga* with the stone figure, Uma (Shakti, or the female consort of Shiva), which remains to this day.

Above the entrance to the North Tower, two musicians, one of whose feet is on the head of the bull Nandin, flank a dancing

Nha Trang

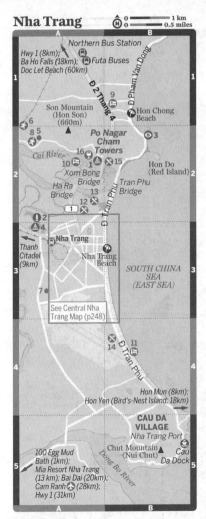

other towers and has little ornamentation; the pyramidal roof lacks terracing or pilasters, although the interior altars were once covered with silver. There is a lingam inside the main chamber.

The South Tower (Mieu Dong Nam), at one time dedicated to Sandhaka (Shiva), still shelters a lingam, while the richly ornamented Northwest Tower (Thap Tay Bac) was originally dedicated to Ganesh. To the rear of the complex is a less-impressive museum with a few examples of Cham stonework.

This site has a continuing religious significance, so be sure to remove your shoes before entering and wear respectful clothing.

Long Son Pagoda BUDDHIST TEMPLE
(Map p247; off Đ 23 Thang 10; ◷ 7.30-11.30am & 1.30-5.30pm) FREE Climb steep steps up to this striking pagoda, founded in the late 19th century. The entrance and roofs are decorated with mosaic dragons constructed of glass and ceramic tile, while the main sanctuary is a hall adorned with modern interpretations of traditional motifs. From the hilltop above, crowned with a large,

four-armed Shiva. The sandstone doorposts are covered with inscriptions, as are parts of the walls of the vestibule. A gong and a drum stand under the pyramid-shaped ceiling of the antechamber. In the 28m-high pyramidal main chamber there is a black-stone statue of the goddess Uma with 10 arms, two of which are hidden under her vest; she is seated and leaning back against a monstrous beast.

The Central Tower (Thap Nam) was built partly of recycled bricks in the 12th century on the site of a structure dating from the 7th century. It is less finely constructed than the

Central Nha Trang

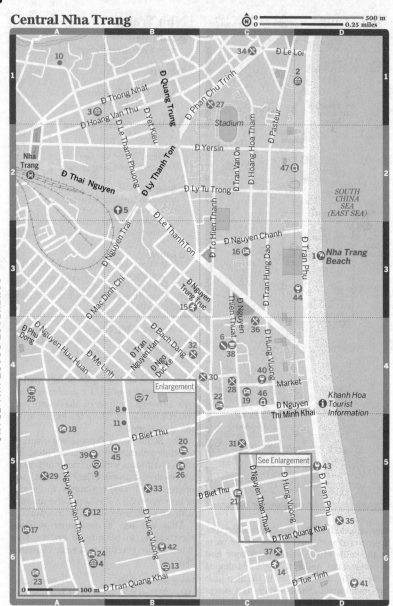

white seated Buddha (p250), there are excellent city views.

Beggars congregate within the complex, as do a number of scam artists. There's a persistent scam here, where visitors are approached by children (and adults) with pre-printed name badges claiming to 'work for the monks'. Others try to sell incense sticks at vastly overpriced rates. Ignore them all. If you do want to make a contribution towards the upkeep of the complex, leave it in the donation boxes.

Central Nha Trang

SOUTHEAST COAST NHA TRANG

The pagoda is located about 400m west of the train station. Modest dress should be worn, with shoulders and knees covered.

Alexandre Yersin Museum　MUSEUM
(Map p248; ☎0258-382 2355; 10 Đ Tran Phu; 20,000d; ◷7.30-11.30am & 2-4.30pm Mon-Fri, 7.30-11.30am Sat) This small museum is dedicated to the scientist Dr Alexandre Yersin (1863–1943), who founded Nha Trang's Pasteur Institute in 1895. The Swiss-born Yersin introduced rubber- and quinine-producing trees to Vietnam, and discovered the rat-borne microbe that causes bubonic plague.

You can browse Yersin's library and view displays including laboratory equipment (such as astronomical instruments) and a fascinating 3D photo viewer.

There's information in English, French and Vietnamese, with a short film on Yersin's life.

Long Thanh Gallery　GALLERY
(Map p248; ☎0258-382 4875; www.longthanh art.com; 126 Đ Hoang Van Thu; ◷8am-5.30pm Mon-Sat) FREE This gallery exhibits the work of Long Thanh, one of Vietnam's most prominent photographers, who shoots powerful black-and-white images of everyday Vietnamese moments and compelling portraits. Prints start at around 2,000,000d.

Mai Loc Gallery　GALLERY
(Map p248; ☎090 515 6711; https://mailoc photographer.com; 247 Đ Nguyen Thien Thuat; ◷8-11am & 2.30-10.30pm) FREE The fine monochrome photography of Mai Loc, a native of Nha Trang, is showcased at this gallery. Ask him about his life story (he's an ex-gold miner, *cyclo* driver and tour guide). He also leads photography tours.

Nha Trang Cathedral　CHURCH
(Nha Tho Nui; Map p248; cnr Đ Nguyen Trai & Đ Thai Nguyen) FREE Built between 1928 and 1933 in

French Gothic style, complete with stained-glass windows, Nha Trang Cathedral stands on a small hill overlooking the train station. It's a surprisingly elegant building given that it was constructed of simple cement blocks. Some particularly colourful Vietnamese touches include the red neon outlining the crucifix, the pink backlighting on the tabernacle and the blue neon arch and white neon halo over the statue of St Mary.

Buddha   MONUMENT

(Map p247; Kim Than Phat To) FREE On a hilltop behind the Long Son Pagoda, this huge white Buddha is seated on a lotus blossom and visible from all over the city. Around the statue's base are fire-ringed relief busts of Thich Quang Duc and six other Buddhist monks who died in self-immolations in 1963, in protest against the repression of Buddhists by the South Vietnamese Government. The platform around the 14m-high figure has great views of Nha Trang and nearby rural areas.

Hon Chong Promontory   LANDMARK

(Map p247; 22,000d) The narrow granite promontory of Hon Chong offers fine views of the mountainous coastline north of Nha Trang and the nearby islands.

The beach here has a more local flavour than Nha Trang Beach, but the rubbish is unpleasant and it attracts some tour groups. Still, it's fun to watch local kids do Acapulco-style swan dives into the ocean.

There is a reconstructed Ruong house (a wooden residence handmade in the traditional style of the region) and a great cafe (Map p247; http://coffeehonchong.weebly.com; ⊙6am-8pm).

🏃 Activities

The Nha Trang area is a prime diving, surfing, wakeboarding, parasailing, white-water rafting and mountain-biking centre. Boat trips around the bay and up the Cai River are also a great day out.

There's also plenty of spa, pampering and yoga action.

Spas & Thermal Baths

Locals swear that the only way to get really clean is to get deep down and dirty in a natural mudbath, and there are now several places around Nha Trang where you can get stuck in (the mud). Try to avoid weekends, which get very busy indeed.

If you'd prefer a more conventional spa, there are plenty that fit the bill nicely.

★ I Resort   THERMAL BATHS

(Map p247; ☑ 0258-383 8838; www.i-resort.vn; 19 Đ Xuan Ngoc, Vinh Ngoc; packages from 300,000d; ⊙8am-8pm) Upmarket thermal spa that's the most attractive of the mud-fests around Nha Trang, with hot mineral mudbaths (private tub 700,000d for two people), bathing pools and even nine mineral waterfalls. The rural setting is gorgeous, with distant mountain views, and there's a decent restaurant, spa/massage salon and gift shop. All kinds of mud and spa packages are available.

Located 7km northwest of the centre, it's worth spending at least half a day here. Call for a shuttle (20,000d one way).

100 Egg Mud Bath   THERMAL BATHS

(Tam Bun Tram Trung; ☑ 0258-371 1733; www.tramtrung.vn; Đ Nguyen Tat Thanh, Phuoc Trung; public/private egg per person 250,000/300,000d; ⊙8am-7pm) This place is named after its egg-shaped private pods where you can indulge in a little mud play. All kinds of mud plastering, wraps and scrubs are offered. You'll find pools and tubs (that can be filled with herbs and essential oils) scattered around this huge complex, which also has Jacuzzis, a huge swimming pool, a restaurant and a waterfall. Located 6km southwest of Nha Trang.

Xanh Spa   SPA

(☑ 0258-398 9666; www.mianhatrang.com; Mia Resort Nha Trang, Bai Dong, Cam Hai Dong; massages from US$45; ⊙9am-9pm) With Zen-like treatment rooms high above the ocean, this high-end hotel's spa enjoys a dramatic setting. Staff are superbly trained, and responsive to client requests. Scrubs, massages, pedicures and manicures are all excellent; try an aloe vera body wrap.

Vy Spa   SPA

(Map p248; ☑ 093 374 7058; off Đ Nguyen Thien Thuat; ⊙9am-10pm) Choose from Vietnamese, Thai or Swedish massages or beauty treatments at this simple salon. Massages start at 160,000d per hour, a facial is 230,000d.

Su Spa   SPA

(Map p248; ☑ 0258-352 3242; www.suspa.com.vn; 93 Đ Nguyen Thien Thuat; ⊙8am-9.30pm) Classy spa in the heart of town with a relaxed ambience that will soothe the travel-weary. This stylishly designed place offers good scrubs (from 392,000d), rubs, tubs, waxing, facials (from 476,000d) and body massages (from 483,000d).

Thap Ba Hot Spring Center   THERMAL BATHS
(Map p247; ☑ 0258-383 5345; https://tambun thapba.vn; 15 Đ Ngoc Son; ☺ 7am-7.30pm) The original hot thermal mud centre remains good value. Private rooms work out to be pricey so consider the communal mudbath (200,000d; 15 minutes maximum time); there are also mineral-water swimming pools. Lots of other packages are offered; on-line discounts available. It's 7km northwest of Nha Trang (130,000d by taxi); call for a shuttle bus pick-up (30,000d one way).

To get here under your own steam, follow the signpost on the second road to the left past the Po Nagar Cham Towers and continue along the winding road for 2.5km.

Diving

Scuba-diving is popular although conditions are not that rewarding for experienced divers. Visibility averages 15m but can be as much as 30m, depending on the season. February to September is considered the best time to dive, while October to December is the worst time of year.

There are around 25 dive sites in the area. There are no wrecks to visit, but some sites have good drop-offs and there are a few small underwater caves to explore. Frankly, it's not world-class diving, but the waters support a variety of soft and hard corals, and a reasonable number of small reef fish. You can expect to see clownfish, pufferfish and trumpetfish, as well as cuttlefish and octopus.

A full-day outing including boat transport, two dives and lunch typically costs between US$60 and US$85 with a professional dive school. Snorkellers can usually tag along for US$15 to US$20.

Most dive operators also offer a range of dive courses, including a 'discover diving' programme for uncertified first-time divers to experience the underwater world with the supervision of a qualified dive master. PADI Open Water courses cost roughly US$350 to US$400, SSI courses a little less.

There are around 20 dive operators in Nha Trang, including the odd dodgy set-up not following responsible diving practices (and even using fake PADI/SSI accreditation). These tend to charge ridiculously cheap prices. Don't compromise on safety, and stick to reputable operators.

Freediving has also now arrived in Nha Trang. Vietnam Active (p252) offers a US$65 trial, while a Level 1 SSI course is US$250.

Angel Dive   DIVING
(Map p248; ☑ 0258-352 2461; www.angel divevietnam.com; 10 Đ Nguyen Thien Thuat; 2 dives US$60) Experienced SSI dive shop with English, French and German instruction, good courses for kids and Nitrox diving. Dive day trips include marine park fee, lunch and drinks. Snorkelling costs US$20 per person.

Oceans 5   DIVING
(Map p248; ☑ 0258-352 2012, 0258-381 1969; www. oceans5.co; 49/06 Đ Hung Vuong; 2 dives US$75) SSI scuba-diving school providing training courses and well-organised fun dives. Gear is in good condition. A photographer speciality

SOUTHEAST COAST NHA TRANG

NHA TRANG'S BEST DIVE SITES

Most of the best dive action is around Hon Mun Island, which is an officially designated marine park.

Moray Beach On the south side of Hon Mun, with healthy hard and soft corals, including a giant table coral formation. Two species of moray eel, lionfish, leaf fish and scorpionfish can be spotted. Maximum depth is 18m.

Coral Garden An array of impressive hard corals including gorgonians. Expect to see Moorish idols, nudibranchs and pufferfish. It's on the east side of Hon Mun.

Madonna Rock Off tiny Hon Rom, this site has a resident 1.5m grouper, and barracudas and unicornfish are encountered. There are great swim-throughs. Also known as Octopus Rock.

Light House A deep dive at the tip of Hon Tre Island where barracuda, stingrays, triggerfish and snapper are seen. For experienced divers.

Green Canyon Off the northeast coast of Hon Mun with a steep drop-off suitable for deep diving. It's a good spot to see lionfish, nudibranchs and passing snapper.

BOAT TRIPS ON THE BAY

The 71 offshore islands around Nha Trang are renowned for the remarkably clear water surrounding them. Trips to these islands have been a huge draw for years now, and virtually every hotel and travel company in town books island-hopping boat tours.

Back in the day (well the 1990s), party-boat tours involved a ride out to sea on a leaky fishing boat, copious joints and rice-wine shots in a 'floating bar' (a tube in the ocean). Unsurprisingly, local party officials deemed the ganja and drinking games a bit too counter-revolutionary for their tastes.

Today there's more of a choice – with everything from backpacker booze cruises to family-geared outings.

Frankly, most of these trips are extremely touristy, involving whistle-stop visits to the run-down Tri Nguyen Aquarium, some snorkelling on a degraded reef, and a bit of beach time (admission fee charged). The booze cruises feature (very) organised entertainment with a cheesy DJ on the deck (or a tacky boy band) and lots of drinking games. Expect 20 or 30 people packed on a small boat. If this sounds like your idea of hell, well, you've been warned.

In recent years upmarket options have increased, with everything from private charters to cruises on traditional junks now available.

Keep the following tips in mind:

➡ Choose the right tour. Some are geared towards Asian families, others are booze cruises aimed solely at the backpacker market.

➡ Remember sunscreen and drink plenty of water.

➡ Entrance charges to the aquarium and beach are not usually included.

➡ If you're more interested in snorkelling than drinking, the dive schools' trips will be more appropriate.

There are a few decent boat-trip operators.

Sailing Center Vietnam (Map p247; ☑ 0258-387 8714; www.sailing.vn; 7 Đ Hien Luong; half-day trips from US$300) These professionals organise bespoke trimaran and catamaran charters to the islands off Nha Trang. Trips include some snorkelling time, lunch and refreshments.

Emperor Cruises (☑ 012-3666 8879; http://emperorcruises.com; cruise adult/child US$85/65) Offers memorable day or dinner trips on traditional wooden junks around Nha Trang bay and islands. The cuisine, drinks and service are first class.

Mojzo Tours (Map p248; ☑ 098 887 9069; www.facebook.com/pg/mojzodormhostel; 76 Đ Nguyen Thi Minh Khai) This hostel offers inexpensive tours designed for budget-watching backpackers, including a four-island bay trip (200,000d) and a snorkelling tour (350,000d).

---

course is US$195, and accommodation packages are also available.

Sailing Club Divers DIVING
(Map p248; ☑ 0258-352 2788; www.sailingclubdivers.com; 72-74 Đ Tran Phu) This PADI five-star centre provides professional instruction, modern equipment and multilingual instructors, and aims to offer quality over quantity. The dive boat is superb. An Open Water course is 8,000,000d.

Rainbow Divers DIVING
(Map p248; ☑ 0258-352 4351; www.dievietnam.com; 19 Đ Biet Thu; PADI Open Water course US$400) This established PADI dive school

offers instruction in many languages. Courses include Naturalist, Nitrox and Digital Photography. A boat trip with two dives is US$75, while two try dives cost US$80.

Vietnam Active DIVING
(Map p248; ☑ 0258-352 8119; www.vietnamactive.com; 115 Đ Hung Vuong) Offers scuba diving (one-day trial US$70) and freediving (taster US$65).

Adventure Sports

Shamrock Adventures RAFTING
(Map p248; ☑ 0905 150 978; www.shamrockadventures.vn; Đ Phan Dinh Giot; trips per person incl lunch from US$45) Specialises in fishing

trips (including deep-sea and fly) and also runs white-water rafting excursions (which can be combined with some mountain biking) along the Serapok River.

River & Island Boat Trips

Island tours can be fun, but choose your trip carefully.

Pham Tours BOATING

(Map p248; ☑0914 047 406; www.nhatrangriver tour.com; 120/1/6 Đ Hung Vuong; per person from US$50) Boat tours that concentrate on cultural sights and cottage industries (rice-paper making, mat weaving, embroidery) along the Cai River and include a hot spring and mudbath session. Countryside tours by bike or car are also available. English and French spoken.

Hon Mun SNORKELLING

(Ebony Island) Pretty Hon Mun Island is Nha Trang's most famous snorkelling and dive site. The coral is in fair condition and visibility is usually good, but it can get very crowded as it's on the main day-tripping agenda.

Hon Yen BOATING

(Bird's-Nest Island) Also known as Salangane Island, this is the lumpish landmass visible from Nha Trang Beach. These and other islands off Khanh Hoa province are the source of Vietnam's finest *salangane* (swiftlet) nests; locals climb up tottering bamboo ladders to fetch them. There is a small, secluded beach here. The 17km trip takes three hours or so by small boat from Nha Trang; boats leave from Cau Da dock.

Hon Mot SNORKELLING

Sandwiched neatly between Ebony Island and Hon Tam (Silkworm Island) is tiny Hon Mot, a popular place for snorkelling.

Yoga

There are always several freelance yoga instructors based in Nha Trang; check noticeboards in cafes and restaurants, including LIVINCollective (p256), for class details.

Yoga Victoria YOGA

(Map p248; ☑0258-352 8119; 14 Đ Nguyen Trung Truc; per class 150,000d) Yoga Victoria has a large, air-conditioned studio and offers hatha and ashtanga classes.

Tours

★**Lanterns Tours** CULTURAL

(Map p248; ☑0258-247 1674; www.lanterns vietnam.com; 30a Đ Nguyen Thien Thuat) This

nonprofit organisation offers fine-value street-food tours (250,000d per person, minimum two) of Nha Trang featuring seven dishes including *banh tai vac* (tapioca shrimp dumplings). It also offers a tour to Ninh Hoa (from US$35), a nontouristy town, which takes in a local market and lunch with a family. Cooking classes (US$27), too.

Sinh Tourist TOURS

(Map p248; ☑0258-352 2982; www.thesinhtour ist.vn; 90c Đ Hung Vuong; ☺6am-10pm) Reliable, professional agency for inexpensive local trips, including a city tour for 649,000d as well as open-tour buses, train and flight bookings.

Easy Rider Trips TOURS

(Map p247; ☑090 538 4406; http://easyrider trips.com; 15 Đ Ngoc Son) These motorbike (or car) tours get good feedback. It costs US$65 to US$75 per day to sit on the back of a bike. The Nha Trang–Dalat route is very popular, and takes one to three days depending on your itinerary.

🛏 Sleeping

Nha Trang has a very wide selection of hotel rooms, from dorms to luxury suites. Most are within a block or two of the beach. During high season (July and August) prices increase and it can be tough to find a place to stay.

There's a cluster of cheapies on an alleyway at 64 Đ Tran Phu, very close to the beach; all offer similar air-conditioned rooms for US$15 or so. Hostel-style places tend to be located inland from the beach.

Luxury hotels line Đ Tran Phu, the waterfront boulevard. The area's most exclusive resort hotels are out of town, in Ninh Van Bay to the north. More and more new four- and five-star places are being constructed on Bai Dai Beach, along the airport road.

★**Sunny Sea** HOTEL **$**

(Map p248; ☑090 574 6506, 0258-352 2286; www.facebook.com/nangbienhotel; 64b/9 Đ Tran Phu; r 250,000-350,000d; ❈☎) Run by a local couple (a doctor and nurse) and their staff, this very welcoming minihotel is in the heart of town and just off the beach. Rooms are in great shape: very clean, with springy mattresses, minibar and modern bathrooms (some have a balcony, though no sea views).

★ Mojzo Inn Boutique

HOSTEL $

(Map p248; 📞 0988 879 069; www.facebook.com/mojzoInn; 120/36 Đ Nguyen Thien Thuat; dm US$7, r US$19-23; ☕❄🛜) Staff really make an effort to welcome guests at this funky hostel, providing travel tips, free local maps and transport info. There are well-designed dorms, a lovely cushion-scattered lounge area, huge breakfasts, free water refills and a cool rooftop.

Cafune Coffee Culture Homestay

HOSTEL $

(Map p247; 📞 097 290 7279; www.facebook.com/cafunent; 73/4 Bac Son; dm/d US$5/18; ☕❄🛜) Perfect for java-heads or budding baristas, this likeable cafe doubles as a hostel. Double rooms have king-size beds and dorms have en suites. Cafe staff are more than happy to share their blending, extracting and tamping know-how. There's a guest kitchen and yard for hanging out. Located 5km north of the town centre, 500m inland from the beach.

Mojzo Dorm

HOSTEL $

(Map p248; 📞 0258-625 6568; www.facebook.com/mojzodormhostel; 76 Đ Nguyen Thi Minh Khai; dm US$5; ❄🛜) This alt Mojzo follows the same successful formula as the original, with very welcoming and engaging staff, a free breakfast, free afternoon tea and free beer (5pm to 6pm) on the rooftop. Oh, and the comfy dorms and communal bathrooms are well kept, too. Lots of tours (snorkelling, river cruises) are offered at cheap rates.

iHome

HOSTEL $

(Map p248; 📞 0258-352 1239; http://ihome-nha-trang.business.site; 31e2, Đ Biet Thu; dm/d incl breakfast US$6/20; ❄🛜) A hedonist's heaven, this party hostel has all bases covered with unlimited free beer during happy hour and a vibing atmosphere. Staff are lots of fun and there are tons of tours and activities, an awesome rooftop bar, a lounge for TV viewing and a good buffet breakfast.

Happy Angel Hotel

BOUTIQUE HOTEL $

(Map p248; 📞 0258-352 5006; www.happyangelhotel.com; 11 Đ Nguyen Thien Thuat; dm/d US$7/20; ❄🛜) The designer touches found in the sleek furniture, bright bathrooms and cute balconies will make you happy at these prices. It's quietly tucked off the main drag, yet walking distance to the beach. Rates drop considerably in the low season.

Carpe DM Hotel

HOTEL $

(Map p248; 📞 0258-352 7868; 120/62 Đ Nguyen Thien Thuat; r US$20-30; ❄🛜) South of the centre, this well-managed place has bright rooms with a contemporary touch, all very well equipped and attractively furnished with large flat-screen TVs. The more expensive options have a balcony.

Hotel An Hoa

GUESTHOUSE $

(Map p248; 📞 0258-352 4029; 64b/6 Đ Tran Phu; r with fan/air-con US$12/16; ❄📶🛜) Cleanliness standards are excellent at this well-run place and the staff are all smiles and eager to help. Rooms vary from small and windowless to bigger and better options with larger bathrooms and a smarter trim. It's a short walk from the beach.

Binh An Hotel

GUESTHOUSE $

(Map p248; 📞 090 514 3548; www.binhanhotel.com; 102 Đ Hoang Hoa Tham; r US$18-23; ❄📶🛜) A family run, welcoming place where the owners look after guests well and provide travel tips and fresh fruit daily. Its 10 rooms are spotless, spacious and have good air-conditioning and fast wi-fi. There's a lift, and a filling breakfast is available for 60,000d.

Rosaka Hotel

HOTEL $$

(Map p248; 📞 0258-383 3333; www.rosakahotel.com; 107a Đ Nguyen Thien Thuat; r US$52-78, ste from US$90; ❄🛜🏊) Offering fine value, this hotel is located 400m inland from the beach and has spacious, very well-kept rooms with wooden floors and gorgeous en suites. You'll love the stunning rooftop infinity pool and welcoming staff, gym and spa.

Summer Hotel

HOTEL $$

(Map p248; 📞 0258-352 2186; www.thesummerhotel.com.vn; 34c Đ Nguyen Thien Thuat; r US$36-82, ste incl breakfast US$96; ❄📶🛜🏊) The Summer is a good midranger with affordable prices. Rooms have high comfort levels and comfortable trim, though the cheapest are windowless (or have a view of the stairwell). You'll love the rooftop pool.

Galliot Hotel

HOTEL $$

(Map p248; 📞 0258-352 8555; http://galliothotel.com; 61a Đ Nguyen Thien Thuat; r US$45-68; ❄📶🛜🏊) There are 135 rooms to choose from at this 16-storey hotel, all well presented, though avoid the very cheapest, which don't have a window. The rooftop pool is a delight and staff are efficient and helpful. The location is convenient, with restaurants just steps away and the beach a five-minute walk.

★ Mia Resort Nha Trang HOTEL $$$
(☎ 0258-398 9666; www.mianhatrang.com; Bai Dong, Cam Hai Dong; condos/villas from US$195/230;) Mia has an exceptional setting, on a secluded, private sandy beach, and the villas are supremely spacious and contemporary, with vast bathtubs and either ocean or garden views. There's a fine spa and a choice of great restaurants (Sandals for international fare, La Baia for Italian), while Mojito's is the perfect spot for (you've guessed it) that famous Cuban cocktail.

Staff love to chat with guests here. The next bay to the north has now been developed by Mia and has a collection of huge villas (some with five bedrooms), but the shoreline here is rocky not sandy.

Champa Island Resort RESORT $$$
(Map p247; ☎ 0258-382 7827; http://champaislandresort.vn; 304 Đ 2/4, Vinh Phuoc; r/ste from US$72/96;) Spread over two islands in the Cai River, yet only 3km north of the centre, this large resort hotel makes a tranquil base and has all the facilities you could want: huge pool, large gym, ample dining options and fine spa. There's a wide choice of accommodation including two-bed suites, which are great value for families.

Evason Ana Mandara Resort & Spa RESORT $$$
(Map p247; ☎ 0258-352 2522; www.sixsenses.com; Đ Tran Phu; villa US$270-610;) Part of the Six Senses group, this oceanside hotel has a distinctly colonial feel thanks to the classic furnishings and four-poster beds. It's the only city hotel on the shore side of the beach, so you snooze to lapping waves rather than roaring traffic. Facilities include two swimming pools, Western and Vietnamese restaurants, an excellent spa and free guest bikes.

Eating

There's an array of cosmopolitan flavours, from Japanese to Greek, in the central tourist zone around Đ Tran Quang Khai and Đ Biet Thu. Nha Trang has a burgeoning cafe scene, too.

For more authentic Vietnamese cuisine, head away from the beach to where the locals live; the north of the city is a good hunting ground.

Yen Vegetarian Restaurant VEGETARIAN $
(Map p248; www.facebook.com/Yen-Vegetarian-Restaurant-and-Yoga; 46/9 Đ Le Thanh Ton; meals 45,000-90,000d; ⏱ 7am-9pm;) This intimate place is perfect for a budget veggie feed with good seaweed fried rice, bitter melon salad and green mango salads. The bamboo seating and pot plants add to its charm. Located down a little alley off Đ Le Thanh Ton; there's also a yoga school here.

Au Lac VEGETARIAN $
(Map p248; 28c Đ Hoang Hoa Tham; meals 15,000-32,000d; ⏱ 10am-7pm;) No-frills vegan/vegetarian place where a mixed plate

NHA TRANG STREET FOOD

Rents and real-estate prices are high in central Nha Trang, which is not a great place for cheap local grub. All these street-food experiences are north of the centre.

Banh Xeo Stand (Map p247; Đ 2 Thang 4; meals 30,000-60,000d; ⏱ 11am-7.30pm) Over the road from the Cham towers, this food stand is worked by a feisty older woman who cooks up great *banh xeo* (savoury rice-flour pancakes with shrimp and bean sprouts) on a smoking griddle.

Seafood Street (Map p247; Thap Ba; meals 75,000-230,000d; ⏱ 6-10pm) Thap Ba is famous for its evening-only seafood places, which produce fine steamed or barbecued clams, crab and prawns.

79 Dung Lin (Map p248; 29 Đ Phan Chu Trinh; meals 75,000-130,000d; ⏱ 6-9.30pm) Simple local joint that's famous for its wonderfully flavoursome barbecued duck (half a duck with salad, dips and rice 100,000d).

Nem Vu Thanh An (Map p248; 15 Đ Le Loi; meals 40,000-60,000d; ⏱ 7.30am-9pm) Inexpensive local place that serves up the best *nem nuong* (grilled minced pork marinated with shallots and spices) in the city. It's served with dipping sauce, green mango strips, herbs and salad.

Lanterns (p256) Serves some Viet street-food classics in restaurant surrounds.

(20,000d) is just about the best-value meal you can find in Nha Trang. Just point, take a seat and a plate will arrive. Surrounds are simple, with steel tables and plastic stools.

Culture Cafe
CAFE $

(Map p248; ☏ 077 890 8606; www.facebook.com/pg/CafeCultureNhaTrang; 31/7a Đ Biet Thu; meals 79,000-150,000d; ⊗8am-10pm Wed-Mon; 🛜) Owned by a welcoming Englishman, this tiny cafe down a little alley is tricky to find but well worth seeking out for fry-up breakfasts, muffins (including smoked salmon) and eggs Benedict. It also does a roaring trade in pizza (call for delivery) and serves fine espressos, coconut lattes (55,000d) and smoothies.

Andao
CAFE $

(Map p248; 164 Đ Bach Dang; cakes from 30,000d; ⊗noon-8pm Mon-Sat; 🛜) For the best cakes in town head straight to Andao. Made on the premises, choices include wonderfully indulgent triple chocolate cake and coconut cake. It also sells bars of artisan chocolate and the coffee is excellent, too.

Omar's Indian Restaurant
INDIAN $

(Map p247; 96a/8 Đ Tran Phu; mains 55,000-136,000d, set meals 160,000d; ⊗9am-10.30pm; 🛜) Authentic Indian restaurant where you can't go wrong with a set meal, which includes a bhaji, poppadoms, a veggie or chicken curry, rice and a beer. It also serves great vegetable samosas, thalis and flatbreads including nan and chapatti. Halal.

Dam Market
VIETNAMESE $

(Map p247; Đ Trang Nu Vuong; meals 15,000-50,000d; ⊗6am-4pm) For a traditional local experience, try Dam Market, which has a colourful collection of stalls, including *com chay* (vegetarian) options, in the 'food court'.

★ Lac Canh Restaurant
VIETNAMESE $$

(Map p247; 77 Đ Nguyen Binh Khiem; meals 45,000-150,000d; ⊗11am-8.45pm) Lac Canh has shifted across the road from its original location but remains a memorable dining experience, a somewhat scruffy-looking barbecue joint filled with smoke and laughter. Locals feast on meat (beef, richly marinated with spices, is the speciality, but there are chicken cuts and seafood, too), which you grill over charcoal at your table. Note: it closes quite early.

★ Mix
GREEK $$

(Map p248; ☏ 0165 967 9197; www.mix-restaurant.com; 77 Đ Hung Vuong; meals 120,000-240,000d; ⊗11am-10pm Thu-Tue; 🛜🍴) You will have to wait for a table at busy times, such as this bustling, sociable Greek place's popularity. Freshly prepared and beautifully presented dishes include 'mix dips' (with hummus and tzatziki), feta and watermelon salad, *patzarosalata* (beetroot salad with fresh herbs, Greek yoghurt, garlic and onion) and fine-value platters (from 190,000d).

LIVINCollective
AMERICAN $$

(Map p248; ☏ 091 863 8349; http://livincollective.tumblr.com; 77 Đ Bach Dang; mains 100,000-250,000d; ⊗10am-10pm Mon-Sat; 🛜) This hugely popular restaurant/store/hang-out serves delicious North American food including smoked barbecued meats (pork ribs) and the best burgers in town in a yard-like setting. There are a few veggie options like quesadillas. Wash it down with a craft beer, glass of wine or cider and browse the store while you're here.

This is the venue for the Collective Market, held every few months, which draws independent food vendors and art and craft designers.

Lanterns
VIETNAMESE $$

(Map p248; ☏ 0258-247 1674; www.lanternsvietnam.com; 30a Đ Nguyen Thien Thuat; dishes 55,000-235,000d; ⊗7am-10.30pm; 🛜🍴🏠) Ever-popular ethical restaurant that supports local orphanages and provides scholarship programmes. Flavours are predominantly Vietnamese – order a set menu (from 140,000d) and you'll get a good selection, or try a street-food classic like *goi buoi* (pomelo salad with pork and shrimp). International offerings include pasta, salads and sandwiches, and there are several good-value breakfast combos (from 50,000d).

Yen's Restaurant
VIETNAMESE $$

(Map p248; ☏ 0933 766 205; www.facebook.com/yensrestaurant; 3/2a Đ Tran Quang Khai; meals 80,000-210,000d; ⊗10am-10.30pm; 🛜) An atmospheric restaurant with subtle lighting, stylish seating and a winning line-up of flavoursome clay-pot, curry, noodle, rice and stir-fry dishes. Service is excellent, with well-trained English-speaking staff.

Nha Trang Xua
VIETNAMESE $$

(☏ 0258-389 6700; www.facebook.com/NhahangNhaTrangXua; Thai Thong, Vinh Thai; meals 90,000-230,000d; ⊗9am-9pm; 🛜🏠) This classic Vietnamese restaurant is set in a traditional house in the countryside, 7km west of town, surrounded by rice paddies and a lotus pond. The chunky wooden tables and rustic ambience set a nice tone though service can be distracted. On the menu are Vietnamese salads, beef in bamboo, fish and frog dishes.

★**Kiwami**   JAPANESE **$$$**
(Map p248; ☑ 0956 130 933, 0258-351 6613; 136 Đ Bach Dang; meals 200,000-600,000d; ⏰ noon-10pm Thu-Tue; ✴) One of the best Japanese restaurants in coastal Vietnam, this is an intimate affair with a specialist sushi chef: perch on a bar stool and watch the master at work, or sit in one of the side alcoves. The sashimi and sushi sets are divine, or try some meats from the roaster grill. Sake and Sapporo beer available. Book ahead.

★**Sailing Club**   INTERNATIONAL **$$$**
(Map p248; ☑ 0258-352 4628; www.sailingclub nhatrang.com; 72-74 Đ Tran Phu; mains 180,000-390,000d; ⏰ 7.30am-11pm; ✆) A beachfront in-stitution: people-watch from elegant seating by day, sip on a cocktail at sundown, dine on gourmet food under the stars and then burn it all off on the dance floor. There are three separate menus – Vietnamese, international and Indian. Highlights include linguine with Atlantic mussels and chorizo, and sailfish masala.

🍷 **Drinking & Nightlife**

Nha Trang was once famous for its hedon-istic backpacker party scene, but these days there are far fewer Western travellers in town and it's the Asian market that's the most lively. Sleek skybars, smart lounges and boisterous beach parties draw huge crowds of young Chinese, Korean and local tourists. The party entertainment tends to be orchestrated with DJs and MCs ordering the crowd to 'put your hands in the air'.

If a mellower vibe is more your scene, there are a few quirky bars around and plen-ty of good coffee shops.

★**Alpaca Homestyle Cafe**   CAFE
(Map p248; www.facebook.com/alpacanhatrang; 10/1b Đ Nguyen Thien Thuat; ⏰ 8.15am-9.30pm Mon-Sat; ✆) This hip little cafe with an artis-tic interior is famous for its coffee (sourced in Dalat), which comes in espresso, French press, drip (Chemex and Hario) or cold-brewed options. Iced teas, juices (45,000d) and great Mediterranean and Mexican food are also offered.

★**Sunshine Bar**   BAR
(Map p247; ☑ 0120 791 8901; www.facebook.com/ sunshinebar.nhatrang; 35/48 Đ Ngo Den; ⏰ 11am-9pm Tue-Sun; ✆) Ramshackle bar on the riverbank owned by a hospitable Japanese couple who speak great English. Music is very well selected, with DJ Alan Ritchie spinning reggae on Sundays. There's great food, too; try *okonomiyaki* (a savoury pan-cake). It's walking distance from the Cham towers, accessed by a narrow lane (walking or scooter access only).

Louisiane Brewhouse   BREWERY
(Map p248; www.louisianebrewhouse.com.vn; 29 Đ Tran Phu; ⏰ 7am-midnight; ✆) This shorefront microbrewery has it all – you can cool off in the swimming pool or enjoy the sea breeze before sampling one of the seven craft brews, which include red ale and a witbier. There's a full food menu.

Skylight Bar   BAR
(Map p248; http://skylightnhatrang.com; Best Western Premier Havana Nha Trang, 38 Đ Tran Phu; admission incl drink 180,000-250,000d; ⏰ 4.30pm-midnight; ✆) Nha Trang's best vistas are from this skybar-club-lounge on the 43rd floor. There's a killer cocktail list (130,000d upwards), shishas and DJs spin party anthems to a packed dance floor of mainly Asian visitors. On Wednesdays it's 2-4-1 and Tuesdays is ladies' night (free admission).

Deja Brew   BAR
(Map p248; www.facebook.com/dejabrewnha trang; 46 Hung Vuong; ⏰ 7am-10pm Mon, Tue & Thu, 9am-5pm Wed, 9am-10pm Fri-Sun; ✆) Yes, the name's a tad cheesy but the craic is strong at this bohemian hole-in-the-wall cafe-bar on a little alley near the night market. Run by friendly folk and serves great coffee, juices, smoothies and cheap cocktails.

Qui   LOUNGE
(Map p248; http://quilounge.com/nhatrang; 62 Đ Tran Phu; ⏰ 9am-2am; ✆) Stylish and expen-sive lounge bar boasting a prime beach-facing terrace where the funky house sounds create a sociable vibe. Delve into the cocktail list ('Nha Trang Calling' blends coconut te-quila, cachaca, lime, a touch of mango and tonic; 140,000d) or sip a scotch. There's also an interesting food menu featuring seafood and Wagyu beef. Happy hour 5pm to 8pm weekdays.

Crazy Kim Bar   BAR
(Map p248; http://crazykimvietnam.wordpress.com; 19 Đ Biet Thu; ⊙9am-late; 🛜) This place is home to the commendable 'Hands off the Kids!' campaign, working to prevent paedophilia – part of the profits go towards the cause. Crazy Kim's has regular themed party nights, cheap beer and tasty pub grub. There are happy hour promos throughout the night, including two-for-one cocktails between 4.30pm and 10.30pm.

Sailing Club   BAR, CLUB
(Map p248; www.sailingclubnhatrang.com; 72-74 Đ Tran Phu; ⊙7am-2am; 🛜) This beach club is a mecca for party people with DJs and bands, and draws huge crowds for its legendary Saturday-night events. Expect mainstream-chart sounds, with predictable party banter ('yo ready for dis?!') from an MC. During the week there are live bands.

Nghia Bia Hoi   BEER GARDEN
(Map p248; 7g/3 Đ Hung Vuong; ⊙11am-10pm) Popular *bia hoi* joint that pulls in a loyal local (and backpacker) crowd. It serves a light lager and a darker brown beer, as well as snacks.

 Shopping

Fashion boutiques selling everything from sarongs to sunglasses are concentrated along Đ Nguyen Thi Minh Khai.

⭐**LIVINCollective**   CLOTHING, ART
(Map p248; http://livincollective.tumblr.com; 77 Đ Bach Dang; ⊙10am-10pm Mon-Sat; 🛜) A huge space showcasing art and design from local, independent producers: from fashion (check out Sinhtolina) to photographs, organic beauty products to customised motorbike helmets, and gourmet chocolate to chilli sauces. You can also grab a coffee, beer or a bite to eat.

Lemongrass House   COSMETICS
(Map p248; http://fb.com/lemongrasshouse.vn; 38 Đ Nguyen Thi Minh Khai; ⊙10am-10pm) 🌿 This Thai brand sells lotions, body creams and scrubs, masks, hair products, essential oils and even some teas. All products are sourced from natural ingredients and made in small batches.

Nha Trang Centre   MALL
(Map p248; www.nhatrangcenter.com; Đ 20 Tran Phu; ⊙9am-10pm) Beachfront mall complex with dozens of local and international fashion stores including the likes of Farah, Levi's and Saga du Mekong. There's also a supermarket, food mall, restaurants and cafes.

Bambou   CLOTHING
(Map p248; www.bambolucompany.com; 15 Đ Biet Thu; ⊙8.30am-10pm) Casual clothing from natural materials (like bamboo and raw cotton) for men, women and kids. Many have Vietnamese motifs and prices are affordable.

ⓘ Getting There & Away

AIR
All the main domestic airlines fly to Cam Ranh, and there are also international links to cities across East Asia.

Cam Ranh International Airport (☏0258-398 9913) is 35km south of the city via a beautiful coastal road.

Vietnam Airlines (Map p248; ☏0258-352 6768; www.vietnamairlines.com; 91 Đ Nguyen Thien Thuat) connects Nha Trang with Hanoi, HCMC and Danang daily and also has flights to many Chinese cities including Nanjing and Nanning. Bamboo Airways (www.bambooairways.com) links Nha Trang with Danang, Haiphong and Hanoi. VietJet Air (www.vietjetair.com) has links to Danang, Hanoi and HCMC daily and also flights to Seoul and several cities in China including Shanghai and Chengdu. Jetstar (www.jetstar.com) offers good connections with Hanoi and HCMC.

NHA TRANG TRANSPORT CONNECTIONS

DESTINATION	AIR	BUS	CAR/MOTORCYCLE	TRAIN
Dalat	n/a	US$7, 5hr, 11 daily	4-5hr	n/a
Danang	from US$42, 1hr, 2 daily	US$11-14, 11-12hr, 12 daily	11hr	US$14-18, 9-11hr, 7 daily
Ho Chi Minh City	from US$26, 1hr, 14-16 daily	US$9-13, 11-12hr, 16 daily	10hr	US$11-16, 7-9hr, 7 daily
Mui Ne	n/a	US$8, 5hr, 2 daily	5hr	n/a
Quy Nhon	n/a	US$6.50, 6hr, every 2hr	6hr	US$5.50-7.50, 3½-4½hr, 7 daily

WORTH A TRIP

BAI DAI BEACH

South of Nha Trang, a spectacular coastal road leads to Cam Ranh Bay, a gorgeous natural harbour, and the airport. Virtually the entire shoreline south of Mia Resort forms Bai Dai (Long Beach), a breathtaking sandy coast.

Until recently the Vietnamese military controlled the entire area, restricting access to all but the odd fishing boat. However, times have changed and now the entire strip has been earmarked for development. Several giant resort hotels have already opened and many others are under construction.

You may not find virgin sands any longer, but some of the best surf breaks in Vietnam are still here on Bai Dai.

At the northern tip of the coastline, **Coco's Surf Kitchen Lounge** (☑083 694 7813; www.facebook.com/cocosbarbaidainhatrang; Bai Dai Beach; meals from 90,000d; ☺9am-7pm; ☎) offers great food, hires surfboards, SUPs and kayaks (all 200,000d per hour) and provides surf lessons for 800,000d. Irregular 'Beach Beats' parties here are a lot of fun; check its Facebook page for information. There are also lots of local seafood restaurants, all with near-identical menus on this strip.

A one-way journey in a taxi to the north end of Bai Dai costs around 280,000d, or you can catch an airport-bound bus (50,000d, every 30 minutes) and jump off anywhere along the coast.

Other usual international links include an Air Asia flight to/from Kuala Lumpur and Bangkok, Korean Air to/from Seoul, and Bangkok Airways to/from Bangkok.

BOAT

Cau Da Dock (Map p247) Public boats depart here for the islands.

BUS

Nha Trang has no main bus station of much use to travellers. The smallish **Northern Bus Station** (Ben Xe Phia Bac; Map p247; Dien Bien Phu) is inconveniently located 5.5km north of the centre. It's used by **Futa Buses** (Map p247; ☑1900 6067; https://futabus.vn; Dien Bien Phu), which provides a good service to cities including Dalat (135,000d, four hours, six daily), Buon Ma Thuot (140,000d, five hours, two daily), HCMC (225,000d, 12 hours, eight daily) and Danang (240,000d, 12 hours, two daily). Contact the bus company to hop aboard a shuttle bus from the centre of town.

Sinh Tourist (p253) is reliable and very popular with travellers; buses leave from its office in the centre. Services head north to Hoi An (250,000d, 11 hours, one daily). It also offers connections to Mui Ne (115,000d, five hours, two daily), Dalat, Buon Ma Thuot and HCMC.

Nha Trang is a major stopping point for all open-tour buses.

Note: we've heard reports of travellers being off-loaded from buses at a dusty parking lot on Đ Nguyen Thien Thuat (near the old airfield in the south of town). Book a Grab or take a taxi from here, as waiting xe om drivers routinely overcharge arriving travellers.

CAR & MOTORCYCLE

One of the best trips to experience is the mountain pass from Nha Trang to Dalat, a stunning journey by car or motorbike. Throw the mountain road back down from Dalat to Mui Ne into the mix and you have a great loop.

Based in Nha Trang, rates for Easy Rider Trips (p253) start at around US$65 per day for the Nha Trang–Dalat journey (which can be covered in one to three days depending on stops).

TRAIN

The **Nha Trang Train Station** (Map p248; ☑0258-382 2113; Đ Thai Nguyen; ☺ticket office 7-11.30am, 1.30-6pm & 7-9pm) is in the centre of town. It's on the main north–south line with good connections to destinations including Dieu Tri (for Quy Nhon), Danang and HCMC. There's no line to Dalat.

❶ Getting Around

TO/FROM THE AIRPORT

Shuttle buses (50,000d, 45 minutes) connect the airport with Nha Trang roughly every 30 minutes between 6am and 6.30pm. They pass through the heart of town, stopping at points along the coastal road Đ Tran Phu.

Departing town, taxis are a convenient option. **Nha Trang Taxi** (☑0258-382 6000) charges 400,000d from the airport to downtown. It's cheaper in the other direction, around 300,000d, if you fix a price ahead rather than use the meter.

BICYCLE

Nha Trang city is pretty flat, so it's easy to get around all the sights by bicycle. Hotels have bikes to rent from 30,000d per day.

TAXI & XE OM

Always use a metered taxi from a reputable company such as **Mai Linh** (☏ 0258-382 2266) or Nha Trang Taxi (p259). Grab is another good option.

Nha Trang has an excessive number of *xe om* drivers. A motorcycle ride anywhere in the centre shouldn't cost more than 25,000d. Be careful at night, when some less-reputable drivers moonlight as pimps and drug dealers.

Around Nha Trang

The three waterfalls and refreshing pools at Ba Ho Falls (Suoi Ba Ho; 100,000d; bike parking 5000d; ☺ 7am-5.30pm) are in a forested area 23km north of Nha Trang and about 2km west of Phu Huu village. Turn off Hwy 1 just north of Quyen Restaurant and you'll find them a 20-minute walk from the parking area. It's fun clambering upstream through the pools, though they are slippery; good footwear is recommended as it takes an hour of tough trekking to see all three falls.

Around 11km west of Nha Trang, and dating from the 17th-century Trinh dynasty, the Thanh Citadel (Thanh co Dien Khanh; ☺ 9am-5pm) was rebuilt by Prince Nguyen Anh (later Emperor Gia Long) in 1793 during his successful offensive against the Tay Son Rebels. Only a few sections of the walls and gates remain.

Phan Rang & Thap Cham

☏ 0259 / POP 192,000

This really is a tale of two cities: Phan Rang hugging the shoulders of Hwy 1 and Thap Cham straddling Hwy 20 as it starts its long climb to Dalat. Anyone travelling Vietnam from north to south will notice a big change in the vegetation when approaching the joint capitals of Ninh Thuan province. The familiar lush green rice paddies are replaced with sandy soil supporting only scrubby plants. Local flora includes poinciana trees and prickly-pear cacti with vicious needles.

With two major highways (1A and 20) intersecting in the town, this area makes a possible pit stop on the coastal run. As the twin towns of Phan Rang and Thap Cham are both industrial and not particularly attractive, consider basing yourself at nearby Ninh Chu Beach, 6km to the east.

◉ Sights

The area's best known sight is the group of Cham towers known as Po Klong Garai, from which Thap Cham (Cham Tower) derives its name. There are many more towers dotted about the countryside in this area and the province is home to tens of thousands of Cham people.

★ Po Klong Garai Cham Towers
HINDU SITE

(Thap Cham; 15,000d; ☺ 7am-5pm) These imposing Cham towers date from the end of the 13th century. Built from brick as Hindu temples, they stand on a platform at the top of Cho'k Hala, an exposed granite hill. It can be furnace-hot here.

Over the entrance to the largest tower (the *kalan*, or sanctuary) is a beautiful carving of a dancing Shiva with six arms. Note the inscriptions in the ancient Cham language on the doorposts. These tell of past restoration efforts and offerings of sacrifices and slaves.

Inside the *kalan*'s vestibule is a statue of the bull Nandin, vehicle of the Hindu god Shiva. Nandin is also a symbol of the agricultural productivity of the countryside. To ensure a good crop, farmers would place an offering of fresh greens, herbs and areca nuts in front of Nandin's muzzle. Under the main tower is a *mukha-linga* sitting under a wooden pyramid. Liquor is offered and incense burned here.

Inside the smaller tower opposite the entrance to the sanctuary you can get a good look at some of the Cham's sophisticated building technology; the wooden columns that support the lightweight roof are visible. The structure attached to it was originally the main entrance to the complex.

Po Klong Garai is just north of Hwy 20, at a point 6km west of Phan Rang towards Dalat. The towers are on the opposite side of the tracks to Thap Cham Train Station. Some of the open-tour buses running the coastal route make a requisite pit stop here.

Po Ro Me Cham Tower
HINDU SITE

(donations welcome) FREE Po Ro Me is one of the most atmospheric of Vietnam's Cham

CHAM KATE FESTIVAL

Po Klong Garai is a great place to observe the *kate* celebrations, which take place in the seventh month of the Cham calendar (around September/October). The festival commemorates ancestors, Cham national heroes and deities such as the farmers' goddess Po Ino Nagar.

On the eve of the festival, a procession guarded by the mountain people of Tay Nguyen carries King Po Klong Garai's clothing to the accompaniment of traditional music. The procession lasts until midnight. The following morning the garments are carried to the tower, once again accompanied by music, along with banners, flags, singing and dancing. Notables, dignitaries and village elders follow behind. This colourful ceremony continues into the afternoon.

The celebrations then carry on for the rest of the month, as the Cham attend parties and visit friends and relatives, honour their ancestors and worship Cham deities. They also use this time to pray for good fortune.

towers, thanks in part to its isolated setting on top of a craggy hill with sweeping views over the cactus-strewn landscape. The temple honours the last ruler of an independent Champa, King Po Ro Me (r 1629–51); his image and those of his family are found on the external decorations. It's 18km southwest of Phan Rang.

Cham Cultural Centre MUSEUM
(Thap Cham; ⊙7am-5pm) FREE This large modern structure is dedicated to Cham culture. There's some superb photography of Cham people, village life and customs exhibited here, as well as paintings, pottery, traditional dress and agricultural tools. There are also numerous souvenir stalls.

It's a good reminder that while the Cham kingdom is long gone, the Cham people remain in the region. It's located below the Cham towers.

Bau Truc Village VILLAGE
This Cham village is known for its pottery and you'll see several family shops in front of the mud and bamboo houses. It's around 4km northwest of Phan Rang's centre, off the main road to the Cham temples. The Cham Cultural Centre has set up music classes here so villagers can learn to play traditional Cham musical instruments (drums and the *saranai* flute). A heritage trail is also being developed.

🛏 Sleeping & Eating

Traffic congestion and heavy industry do not make for a peaceful environment. Nearby Ninh Chu Beach is more tranquil (though huge hotel construction projects are planned here, including the mega-storey Sunbay Park complex).

Com ga (chicken with rice) is a local speciality, as is roasted or baked *ky nhong* (gecko), served with fresh green mango. If you prefer self-catering and have quick reflexes, most hotel rooms have a ready supply.

Phan Rang is the grape capital of Vietnam. Stalls in the market sell fresh grapes, grape juice and dried grapes (too juicy to be called raisins).

Ho Phong Hotel HOTEL $
(☑0259-392 0333; 363 Đ Ngo Gia Tu; r 300,000-620,000d; ❀@☎) A welcoming hotel with spacious, well-furnished rooms sporting cable TV, minibar and modern en-suite bathrooms. Scooters are available for rent and staff speak some English.

Big Dog Homestay HOMESTAY $
(☑090 497 5751; www.facebook.com/pg/BigDog-Homestay; Đ Le Thanh Ton; dm/r 120,000/230,000d; ❀☎) Decorated with local textiles, this attractive hostel-like homestay has large rooms filled with bunk beds, a guest kitchen and yard for barbecues and chatting. Cleanliness is good and scooters can be rented at fair rates.

Phuoc Thanh VIETNAMESE $
(3 Đ Tran Quang Dieu; mains 30,000-60,000d; ⊙8am-9pm) The best *com ga* restaurant on Đ Tran Quang Dieu.

❶ Getting There & Away

BUS
Phan Rang Bus Station (opposite 64 Đ Thong Nhat) is on the northern side of town. Regular buses head north to Nha Trang (50,000-65,000d, two hours, every 45 minutes), northwest to Dalat (80,000d, three

SOUTHEAST COAST PHAN RANG & THAP CHAM

MY HOA: KITING MECCA

Around 17km north of Ninh Chu via a pretty coastal road, the beachside village of My Hoa is fast becoming the Phan Rang region's kitesurfing hotspot. Between November and March you can expect sunny skies and onshore trade winds of between 20 and 30 knots.

Two kite camps have opened with no doubt more to follow, though the scene is still mellow and emerging. So if you'd rather chill under the stars on a relatively undeveloped shoreline than base yourself in a booming tourist resort like Mui Ne, head to My Hoa. There's no public transport here; a taxi from Phan Rang town costs 200,000d and takes 40 minutes or so. Places to stay include:

Vietnam Surf Camping (☑083 907 3705; http://kitesurfing-vietnam.com; My Hoa; tent/hut US$15/40; ﹡🛇) Here hardcore kiters can live the dream, sleeping under canvas and waking up to the sound of the ocean. It's a peaceful camp run by dedicated kitesurfers; lessons and courses are offered. Bell tents are spacious and sleep two, while the fan-cooled detached huts (with en suites) are very comfortable and cute. Long-stay discounts available.

Phi Kite School (☑094 576 6192; www.phikiteschool.com; My Hoa; dm US$15, bungalow US$30-65; ﹡🛇) Around 17km north of Ninh Chu, this cool kitesurfing camp is perfect for those wanting to dodge the crowds in Mui Ne. It's very well set up indeed, with a beachfront location and choice of accommodation options: eight-bed dorms, containers and smart, spacious sea-view bungalows. The bar-resto serves up delicious Western and Vietnamese grub (and grog) and there are regular barbecues. Kiting courses are offered and there's quality equipment for rent.

---

hours, hourly) and south to Ca Na (25,000d, one hour, every 30 minutes) and Phan Thiet (85,000d, three hours, every 40 minutes). For Mui Ne change in Phan Thiet.

TRAIN

Thap Cham Train Station (7 Đ Phan Dinh Phung) is about 6km west of Hwy 1, within sight of Po Klong Garai Cham towers, and is served by several daily express trains. Destinations include Nha Trang (from 101,000d, around 1½ hours), Muong Man (for Mui Ne; from 75,000d, around two hours) and HCMC (from 211,000d, six to seven hours).

Ninh Chu Beach

☑0259

East of Phan Rang, the giant bite-shaped bay of Ninh Chu is popular with Vietnamese tourists on weekends and holidays, but relatively tranquil the rest of the time. Some litter blights the scene, but the 10km-long sandy beach is attractive and makes a relaxed base for visiting the nearby Cham towers of Po Klong Garai. Conditions are great for kitesurfing here; a kiting community is steadily being established locally, and in My Hoa up the coast.

 Activities

Phi Kitesurfing   KITESURFING
(☑094 576 6192; www.phikiteschool.com; My Hoa; 7hr beginner course US$350) This professional kitesurfing school offers instruction (US$50 per hour) and kite-gear hire (US$30 per hour) on the Phan Rang coast in season (roughly November to March). It now has a permanent base in My Hoa, 17km from Ninh Chu.

Sleeping

Hotels are scattered along the shoreline in Ninh Chu with budget accommodation concentrated at the north end of the bay in the fishing village. Kitesurfers congregate on My Hoa beach to the north.

★**Minh Duc Guesthouse**   GUESTHOUSE $
(☑097 737 1737; www.facebook.com/minhduc guesthousephanrang; 24a An Duong Vuong; dm 100,000d, r 230,000-450,000d; ﹡🛇) This excellent guesthouse, steps from the beach in the fishing village, has inexpensive, simple air-conditioned rooms (some with two double beds) with hot-water en suites, as well as a decent dorm. Bach, the English-speaking owner, can help out with travel connections,

bicycle and scooter rental, motorbike maintenance and onward transport.

Duc Chinh Hotel GUESTHOUSE $
(☑ 091 270 7470; 354/5 Đ Truong Chinh; r 200,000-380,000d; ❀🛜) A stone's throw from the shore in the fishing village, this fine place is run by hospitable owners who speak decent English and prepare delicious Vietnamese food for guests. Rooms are in good shape with flat-screen TVs and crisp white linen.

Lan Anh Hotel HOTEL $
(☑ 0259-389 0009; www.hotellananh.com.vn; 66 Đ Yen Ninh; r incl breakfast 300,000-580,000d; ❀🛜) Inexpensive, good-value rooms with smart modern decor and cable TV; some have sea views. Murals add a splash of artistic colour, and prices are affordable for the beachside location.

★ Amanoi RESORT $$$
(☑ 0259-377 0777; www.aman.com; Vinh Hy village; villa US$790-1240; ❀@🛜🏊) Amanoi enjoys a spectacular location on a private cove north of Ninh Chu; its 36 pavilions have ocean or national park views. The trad-hip design echoes Buddhist temple architecture, and service and facilities are stupendous, including a 20m clifftop infinity pool, fitness centre, spa, and yoga, Pilates and meditation classes. The ambience is supremely relaxing. This really is a very special luxury escape.

✖ Eating

There's a row of beachfront seafood restaurants in the fishing village. All the hotels and guesthouses have restaurants or provide meals.

Thuy Tien Restaurant SEAFOOD $$
(beachfront; mains 40,000-150,000d; ◷ 7.30am-9pm) Popular beachside seafood place in the fishing village where you can catch ocean breezes and feast on delicious clams, crab, shrimp, squid and grilled fish.

ℹ Getting There & Away

Ninh Chu is 7km east of Phan Rang; local buses are infrequent. *Xe om* charge around 30,000d or a metered taxi is around 85,000d.

Ca Na

☑ 0259 / POP 6200
During the 16th century, princes of the Cham royal family would fish and hunt tigers, elephants and rhinoceros in the Ca Na region. Today this busy little fishing port is better known for its white-sand beaches, which are dotted with huge granite boulders and quite popular with domestic tourists. The best of the beach is just off Hwy 1, a kilometre north of the centre. It's a beautiful spot, but it's tough to ignore the constant honking and rumble of trucks.

🛏 Sleeping & Eating

All the hotels along Hwy 1 have restaurants featuring plenty of seafood.

Pandaran Hotel HOTEL $
(☑ 068 376 1955; https://pandaranhotel.word press.com; Hwy 1; s 230,000d, d from 270,000d; ❀🛜) Built on stilts almost above the waves, this marine blue-and-white place has 20 good-value if smallish rooms in good shape; those facing the ocean enjoy refreshing sea breezes. Chinese and local food is available at fair rates.

Ca Na Hotel HOTEL $
(☑ 0259-376 0922; Hwy 1; r 350,000-450,000d; ❀🛜) This hotel's all-about location, which is both a blessing (beachside) and a curse (abutting Hwy 1 – expect thunderous traffic noise). Accommodation varies: older bungalows are poorly maintained while newer constructions are in reasonable shape. There's a roadside restaurant for meals.

Hon Co Ca Na Resort RESORT $$
(☑ 0259-376 0999; http://honcocana.com; Hwy 1; r 900,000-1,600,000d; ❀🛜) This resort has clean standard rooms with few frills and much fancier deluxe options that offer space and a dash of contemporary style. It's located on a private stretch of beach, though the roar of Hwy 1 is omnipresent.

ℹ Getting There & Away

Ca Na is 32km south of Phan Rang. Most long-haul buses cruising Hwy 1 will drop off or pick up people here.

Mui Ne

☑ 0252 / POP 18,000
Once upon a time, Mui Ne was an isolated stretch of shoreline where pioneering travellers camped on the sand. Times have changed and it's now a string of beach resorts that have fused into one long coastal strip. These resorts are, for the most part, mercifully low-rise and set amid pretty gardens by the sea.

Mui Ne Beach

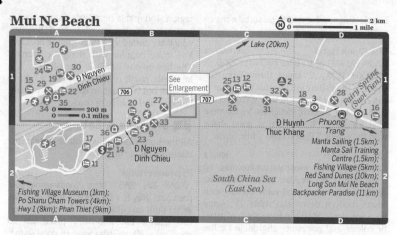

Mui Ne Beach

◉ Sights
1	Fairy Spring	D1
2	Hoi Tinh Pagoda	C1
3	Market	D1

✪ Activities, Courses & Tours
4	Botanica Spa	B1
5	Bun Khoang Mui Ne	A1
6	Easy Rider Mui Ne	B1
7	Forester Beach Spa	A1
	Jibes	(see 35)
	Mui Ne Cooking School	(see 4)
	Sailing Club Kite School	(see 21)
8	Sealinks Golf & Country Club	A2
	Surfpoint Kiteboarding School	(see 23)
9	Tropical Minigolf Mui Ne	B2
	Xanh Spa	(see 21)
10	Yoga Dom Na Gore	A1

🛌 Sleeping
11	Allez Boo Resort	A2
12	Cargo Remote	C1
13	Cat Sen Auberge	C1
14	Cham Villas	B2
15	Coco Sand Hotel	A1
16	Duy An Guesthouse	D1
17	Herbal Hotel & Spa Mui Ne	A2
18	Minhon Hotel	D1
19	Mui Ne Backpacker Village	A1
20	Mui Ne Hills Budget Hotel	B1

21	Sailing Club	B2
22	Shades Resort	A1
23	Sunsea Resort	B2
24	Xin Chao	A1

✗ Eating
25	Bi Bo	C1
26	Bo Ke	C1
27	Choi Oi	B1
28	Com Chay Vi Dieu	D1
	Dong Vui Food Court	(see 3)
29	Lam Tong Quan	A1
30	Modjo Bar & Restaurant	A1
31	Nhu Bao	C1
	Sandals	(see 21)
32	Sindbad	C1
33	Villa Aria Mui Ne	B1

🍸 Drinking & Nightlife
	Dragon Beach	(see 26)
34	Joe's Café	A1

🛍 Shopping
35	Jibes	A1
36	Lemongrass House	B2

ℹ Information
	Sinh Tourist	(see 31)

The original fishing village is still here, but tourists outnumber locals these days. There is a handful of luxury hotels (and a smattering of cheap guesthouses) but Mui Ne is mainly a midrange resort.

Kitesurfing is a huge draw – there are several excellent schools and world-class wind conditions between late October and April. One major problem the area faces is the steady creep of coastal erosion, particularly around Km 12.

It's almost impossible to get lost in Mui Ne, as everything is spread out along a 10km stretch of highway.

ℹ️ When to Go

Mui Ne sees only about half the rainfall of nearby Phan Thiet. The sand dunes help protect its unique microclimate, and even during the wet season (from June to September) rains tend to be fairly light and sporadic. High season is from mid-December through to late February; the rest of the year Mui Ne is rarely busy.

◉ Sights

Mui Ne has a pagoda or two and some Cham temples worth investigating, but for most visitors the towering sand dunes east of town are the main attraction.

Sand Dunes
BEACH

Mui Ne is famous for its enormous red and white sand dunes. The 'red dunes' *(doi hong)* are conveniently located north of the main strip, but the 'white dunes' *(doi cat trang)*, 24km northeast, are the more impressive – the near-constant oceanic winds sculpt the pale-yellow sands into wonderful Saharaesque formations. But as this is Vietnam (not deepest Mali) there's little chance of experiencing the silence of the desert.

Prepare yourself for the hard sell as children press you to hire a plastic sledge to ride the dunes. Unless you're very light, it can be tricky to travel for more than a few metres this way.

Quad bikes and dune buggies also destroy the peace. Expect some litter, too; periodically there's a clean-up, but the tide of plastic keeps returning.

If you're booking a sand dune tour be careful to agree on an itinerary, preferably in writing. We hear complaints, particularly about 'sunset tours' that are cut short with the sun high in the sky.

Fishing Village Museum
MUSEUM

(📷 0901 111 1666; www.seagull.vn; 360 Đ Nguyen Thong; incl guide 100,000d; ⊗ 9am-6pm) This museum is dedicated to the fishing industry in the Mui Ne and Phan Thiet region, and has 14 interactive exhibits depicting its 300-year history. The process of traditional fish-sauce-making is explained in English, Vietnamese, Russian and Chinese. It's at the western end of the main strip.

Fairy Spring
RIVER

(Suoi Tien; off Đ Huynh Thuc Khang; 15,000d) This stream flows through a patch of dunes and past some interesting sand and rock formations. It's a pleasant walk wading from the sea up the creek to its source, a spring. You can do the trek barefoot, but if you're heading out into the big sand dunes after, you'll need proper footwear. Expect some rubbish and souvenir stands along the way.

Po Shanu Cham Towers
HINDU SITE

(Km 5; adult/child 15,000/7000d; ⊗ 7.30-11.30am & 1-4.30pm) Around 6km west of Mui Ne, these Cham towers occupy a hillside with sweeping views of nearby Phan Thiet and a cemetery filled with candy-like tombstones. Dating from the 9th century, this complex consists of the ruins of three towers, none of which are in very good shape. There's a small pagoda on-site, too.

Market
MARKET

(Đ Nguyen Dinh Chieu) Mui Ne's main market is a traditional nontouristy affair where locals shop for food and essentials.

Hoi Tinh Pagoda
BUDDHIST TEMPLE

(Đ Nguyen Dinh Chieu) This Buddhist pagoda is above the road on the eastern end of the Mui Ne strip.

🏃 Activities

Mui Ne is the adrenaline capital of southern Vietnam. There's no scuba-diving or snorkelling to speak of, but when Nha Trang and Hoi An get the rains, Mui Ne gets the waves: surf's up from August to December.

★ Manta Sail Training Centre
BOATING

(📷 090 840 0108; www.mantasailing.org; 108 Đ Huynh Thuc Khang; sailing instruction per hour US$66) One of Southeast Asia's best sailing schools, British-run Manta offers instruction and training (from beginner to advanced racing). Speak to staff about wakeboarding (US$100 per hour), SUP hire

> ### WATERSPORTS
>
> For kitesurfers and windsurfers, the strongest gales blow from late October to late April, when swells can stir things up big time.
>
> Consider investing in a short kitesurfing lesson before opting for a multiday course, as it's a tricky skill to master. Bear in mind it is an extreme sport and most places will not offer a refund for anyone who drops out.
>
> Mui Ne also has an excellent sailing school and plenty of places rent out SUPs and kayaks.

(US$20 half day) and boat tours. The centre also has budget rooms available right by the beach.

★ Mui Ne Hot Air Balloon   BALLOONING
([☑]0120 853 6828; www.vietnamballoons.com; from US$165) The first hot-air balloon experience in Vietnam is a professionally run, European-owned operation that sees you either soaring over the spectacular white sand dunes and desert lakes east of Mui Ne, or alternatively over the bustling fishing harbour of Phan Thiet. Prepare yourself for a magical flight at sunrise.

Yoga Dom Na Gore   YOGA
(Yoga on the Hill; [☑]081 325 9143, 0903 970 1629; www.yogadomnagore.com; 133a Đ Nguyen Dinh Chieu; class 250,000d; ☺Nov-Apr) This hilltop yoga centre has classes by experienced instructors conducting hatha, ashtanga, Iyengar and aerial yoga classes in English and Russian. Massages, Pilates, meditation and martial arts sessions are also available.

Tropical Minigolf Mui Ne   MINIGOLF
(www.minigolfmuine.com; 97 Đ Nguyen Dinh Chieu; 1 round 100,000-120,000d; ☺10am-11pm) This attractive shady crazy golf course is dotted with craggy rock formations to challenge your putting skills. There's a bar and restaurant here, too.

Easy Rider Mui Ne   ADVENTURE SPORTS
([☑]098 444 4129; http://easyridermuine.com/booking; 138 Nguyen Dinh Chieu; 1-day trip from US$65) An experienced collective of Easy Riders offering local coastal rides and extended trips to Dalat, Nha Trang, HCMC and the southwest highlands.

Bun Khoang Mui Ne   SWIMMING
(Tien Dat; www.bunkhoangmuine.com; 133 Đ Nguyen Dinh Chieu; adult/child 80,000/50,000d; ☺7.30am-6.30pm) This hilltop leisure complex has a 30m pool plus a smaller kids' pool and sunloungers (and pounding music...). There are also hot mineral baths and mud pools. However, the concrete tubs (620,000d for two people) filled with hot mud aren't that tempting.

Sealinks Golf & Country Club   GOLF
([☑]0252-374 1777; www.sealinksvietnam.com; Km 8; 18 holes 1,800,000d) Sealinks is a fine 7671yd course with ocean views and a challenging layout that includes lots of water hazards. Discounted late afternoon rounds are also available. The complex includes a pro shop, hotel and driving range.

Kitesurfing

Sailing Club Kite School   KITESURFING
([☑]062 384 7440; www.sailingclubkiteschool.com; Sailing Club, 24 Đ Nguyen Dien Chieu; ☺8am-6pm) Experienced and patient instructors and quality equipment are the draw at this fine kiting school. A two-hour Discover Kite (Level 1) course is 2,500,000d, while the 10-hour Zero to Hero is 11,300,000d.

Surfpoint Kiteboarding School   KITESURFING, SURFING
([☑]0167 342 2136; www.surfpoint-vietnam.com; 52a Đ Nguyen Dinh Chieu; 5hr course incl all gear US$250; ☺7am-6pm) One of Mui Ne's best-regarded kite schools. A three-hour starter course costs US$150/120 for one/two people. Surfing lessons on soft boards are also offered (from US$50) when waves permit.

Jibes   KITESURFING, WATER SPORTS
([☑]0252-384 7405; www.jibesbeachclub.com; 84-90 Đ Nguyen Dinh Chieu; ☺7.30am-6pm) Mui Ne's original kitesurfing school, Jibes offers instruction (US$65 per hour) and gear including windsurfs (US$55 per day), SUPs (US$20 per half-day), surfboards, kitesurfs and kayaks for hire. Catamaran sailing also offered. Accommodation deals are possible.

Spas & Massage

If playing in the waves sounds like too much hard work, you can simply lounge around on the beach or indulge in a spa treatment. There's an excess of spa/massage places – at least 25 or so – along the Mui Ne strip. Most are low quality, offering body massages from as little as US$8 per hour.

Xanh Spa   SPA
([☑]062-384 7440; www.sailingclubmuine.com; Sailing Club, 24 Đ Nguyen Dinh Chieu; 1hr massage from 710,000d; ☺10am-9pm) This gorgeous spa offers the full gamut of massages, facials (from 600,000d), body treatments, steam sessions, wraps, manicures and pedicures. Essential oils and natural products are used.

Forester Beach Spa   SPA
([☑]0252-374 1899; 82 Đ Nguyen Dinh Chieu; 1hr massage from 406,000d; ☺10am-9pm) Well-designed spa with bamboo massage cabins right by the shore, so you can tune into rolling waves while you're being pampered. Staff are professional and discounts are often available. A 30-minute back massage is 259,000d.

Botanica Spa SPA

(📞094 887 7203; 83b Đ Nguyen Dinh Chieu; 1hr massage from 300,000d; ⊙noon-midnight) Good-value spa perfect for a soothing massage, treatment, manicure or pedicure.

🎓 Courses

Mui Ne Cooking School COOKING

(📞091 665 5241; www.muinecookingschool. com; 1st fl, 85 Đ Nguyen Dinh Chieu; 2½hr class US$30-35; ⊙classes 9am-12.30pm Mon-Sat) Well-regarded Vietnamese cooking classes with two different menus, depending on the day. Dishes include *pho bo* (Vietnamese beef noodle soup) and *banh xeo* (crispy pancakes with bean sprouts and sweet-and-sour dipping sauce). Food tours (US$25) to Phan Thiet at night are also great fun.

🎉 Festivals & Events

Mui Ne Street Food Festival FOOD & DRINK

(www.facebook.com/muinestreetfoodfestival) Mui Ne hosts a popular street food festival three times a year (usually January, April and July), featuring local dishes from Phan Thiet in addition to national and international classics. It's held on the main drag by Blue Ocean Resort and there's also live music.

🛏 Sleeping

Most accommodation is either right on the coastal road or just off it, with a few good-value places in the hills behind town. Wherever you are, you won't be far from the beach.

Really rock-bottom rates are tricky to find, but Mui Ne does have a few hostels with dorm beds.

★Minhon Hotel HOTEL $

(📞0252-651 5178; www.facebook.com/MiNhon MuineHotel; 210/5 Đ Nguyen Dinh Chieu; r from 260,000d; ⊜❄🛜🏊) 🚗 It's difficult to find fault with this exceptional hotel, which offers outstanding value and reflects traditional Vietnamese architecture. Staff are welcoming and helpful, and the rooms very spacious and well furnished. The location is excellent, down a little lane near the Dong Vui Food Court. It's solar powered and bikes are free for guests to use.

★Mui Ne Backpacker Village HOSTEL $

(📞0252-374 1047; www.muinebackpackervillage. com; 137 Đ Nguyen Dinh Chieu; dm/r from US$5/ 20; ⊜❄🛜🏊) More village than hostel, this huge, modern backpacking palace is very

well designed around an inviting swimming pool. Thanks to the bar-restaurant, pool table, darts and table football there's a social vibe. Dorms (four to 12 beds) all have air-conditioning, while private rooms have cable TV and a balcony or patio. The hostel runs lots of good-value tours, books transport and does laundry.

Coco Sand Hotel GUESTHOUSE $

(📞0127 364 3446; www.cocosandhotel.com; 119 Đ Nguyen Dinh Chieu; r US$15-28; ❄🛜) Down a little lane, Coco Sand has excellent-value rooms with air-conditioning, cable TV, fridge and private bathroom. There's a shady courtyard garden (with hammocks) to enjoy and the friendly owners hire out motorbikes at fair rates.

Long Son Mui Ne Beach Backpacker Paradise HOSTEL $

(📞0252-383 6056; www.longsonmuine.com; Long Son; tents & dm from US$3; ❄🛜) Right on the beach, this travellers' delight is very well set up for long days lounging by the shore and even longer nights lounging around the bar (it's open 24 hours!). Yes, expect lots of drinking and partying action at this social hostel. Digs consist of dorms and tents. It's 13km northeast of central Mui Ne.

Manta Sailing HOSTEL $

(📞090 840 0108; http://mantasailing.org; 108 Đ Huynh Thuc Khang; r US$20-25; 🛜) Right on the beach, these five simple fan-cooled rooms (all with en suites) are located in a sailing school. Based in a rambling building at the far eastern end of the strip, there's a guest kitchen and a very hospitable, helpful British owner.

Duy An Guesthouse GUESTHOUSE $

(📞0252-384 7799; www.duyanguesthouse.com; 87a Đ Huynh Thuc Khang; r 260,000-600,000d; ❄@🛜) In a shady compound at the eastern end of the main drag, this traditional guesthouse (and restaurant) is run by friendly folk who look after their guests well. The 16 rooms include family-size options ideal for sharers.

Mui Ne Hills Budget Hotel HOTEL $

(📞0252-374 1707; www.muinehills.com; 69 Đ Nguyen Dinh Chieu; dm/r from US$5/28; ❄🛜🏊) Around 300m off the main strip, via an incredibly steep access road, this popular spot has several air-conditioned dorms (eight to 12 beds) with en suites and lockers. Private rooms have quality furnishings and contemporary design touches.

★**Cargo Remote** BOUTIQUE HOTEL **$$**
(☑077 625 2825; www.facebook.com/pg/cargo
remotemuine; 201/88 Đ Nguyen Dinh Chieu; s/d/
tr US$50/60/70; ☻🛜💻) 🍃 Eco-retreat built
high on a hilltop above central Mui Ne with
a stunning natural pool, al-fresco restobar
and gorgeous accommodation crafted from
shipping containers and kitted out with
recycled furniture. Expect live music some
evenings (there's a recording studio on-site).
A spa and restaurant with fine local food
seal the deal.

Cargo is building a bar on the beach be-
low, from where buggies will run up to the
hotel.

Cat Sen Auberge B&B **$$**
(☑0122 323 3673; http://catsen.simdif.com; 195 Đ
Nguyen Dinh Chieu; r/bungalows from US$35/48;
✳🛜💻) A wonderfully relaxing place to
stay, Cat Sen Auberge has well-constructed
rooms and lovely bungalows dotted around
extensive, coconut-tree-studded grounds.
There's a great pool and lots of space, with
hammocks for lounging and free drinking
water.

Shades Resort APARTMENT **$$**
(☑0252-743 236; http://shadesmuine.com; 98a
Đ Nguyen Dinh Chieu; r/apt incl breakfast from
1,000,000/1,400,000d; ✳🛜💻) This well-
managed resort has a wide selection of
modish rooms (some with ocean views) and
some supremely spacious apartments that
are ideal for families or sharers. Breakfast
is good and it's centrally located, though
there's no beach on this stretch.

Herbal Hotel & Spa Mui Ne HOTEL **$$**
(☑094 242 7911; http://herbalhotelmuinevietnam.
com; 21 Đ Nguyen Dinh Chieu; r 480,000-880,000d;
✳🛜) Fine-value, spacious, well-presented
and immaculately clean rooms set in
manicured gardens on the west end of the
strip. There's a decent spa here, too.

Xin Chao BOUTIQUE HOTEL **$$**
(☑0252-374 3086; www.facebook.com/xinchao
hotel; 129 Đ Nguyen Dinh Chieu; r US$35-55;
✳@🛜💻) This boutiquey hotel is close
to the heart of Mui Ne, with ample cafes
and restaurants close by. Attractive rooms
are grouped around a pool at the rear and
there's a roadside bar-restaurant.

★**Sailing Club** BOUTIQUE HOTEL **$$$**
(☑0252-384 7440; www.sailingclubmuine.com;
24 Đ Nguyen Dinh Chieu; r/bungalows incl breakfast from US$162/188; ☻✳🛜💻) An intimate
beach retreat with superb attention to detail, the Sailing Club (formerly the Mia) has
gorgeous bungalows built from natural materials scattered around wonderful tropical
gardens. The oceanside pool is small but the
spa is one of the best in Mui Ne; staff are
efficient and super-welcoming. You'll love
Sandals, the in-house restaurant, for Vietnamese, Asian and Western meals.

There's a kids' club, and yoga twice-weekly.

Allez Boo Resort RESORT **$$$**
(☑0252-374 3777; www.allezbooresort.com; 8
Đ Nguyen Dinh Chieu; r US$80-180; ✳@🛜💻)
This classy beachside hotel has a delightful
ambience thanks to its French-colonial-style
architecture and wonderful grounds, which
spill down to the shore, where you'll find
a pool and huge (shaded) Jacuzzi. It's fine
value given the facilities.

Cham Villas BOUTIQUE HOTEL **$$$**
(☑0252-374 1234; www.chamvillas.com; 32 Đ
Nguyen Dinh Chieu; r incl breakfast US$180-266;
☻✳🛜💻) A well-established, refined place
where lovely villas are dotted around a
stunning, shady garden; the secluded pool
area is delightful. It's located on a lovely section of beach, and there's a good in-house
restaurant.

Sunsea Resort BOUTIQUE HOTEL **$$$**
(☑0252-384 7700; www.sunsearesort-muine.com;
50 Đ Nguyen Dinh Chieu; r incl breakfast US$121-
166; ✳@🛜💻) The elegant accommodation
at this very attractive hotel blends natural
materials (thatch, lacquerware and rose-
wood) with modern design. Some of the
cottages are very smart indeed, with ocean
views and Jacuzzis, espresso machines and
sound systems. There's an infinity pool and
a second (partly shaded) pool, too.

✗ Eating

The incredible selection of restaurants is
mostly geared to the cosmopolitan tastes
of its visitors, with Russian, Italian, Thai
and Indian cuisine. Sometimes it's trickier
to find good authentic Vietnamese food,
though seafood is always fresh and flavour-
some. The goat restaurants in Ham Tien,
around Km 18, are a good local experience,
featuring barbecued goat or goat hotpot,
herbs and all.

Wherever you dine, expect to pay more
than you'd expect elsewhere in southern
Vietnam – Mui Ne is an expensive place to
eat out.

DRAGON FRUIT

Arrive at night in the Mui Ne district and you'll be greeted with the eerie sight of field after field filled with lanterns, each light illuminating a bizarre-looking tropical bush. These lights are used to maintain heat around dragon fruit (also known as *pitaya*), which are native to Latin America but thrive in the arid conditions and sandy soil along this stretch of Vietnam's coastline.

There are three main types of dragon fruit, each roughly the size of a large mango: pink skin with red flesh, pink skin with white flesh, and yellowish skin with white flesh. The dragon fruit belongs to the succulent family (related to cacti) and is lauded as a 'superfood' by some nutritionists for its high level of vitamin C content, digestive properties and natural antioxidants. In Mui Ne you'll find dragon-fruit-flavoured cocktails and mocktails.

Dragon fruit plants only bloom at night and the flower (of white petals around a golden centre) only lasts for one day. Vietnam is the world's leading exporter of the fruit, with revenues topping US$1 billion annually.

★**Dong Vui Food Court** FOOD HALL $
(www.facebook.com/DongVuiMuiNe; 246 Đ Nguyen Dinh Chieu; meals 45,000-170,000d; ☺8am-11pm) This attractive open-air food court has loads of independently run cook stations offering everything from Punjabi cuisine to paella, German sausages and Thai curries – plus plenty of Vietnamese options. Just grab a seat and order what you fancy. There's also great craft beer on tap and live music some weekends. It's far busier in the evenings.

Sindbad MIDDLE EASTERN $
(233 Đ Nguyen Dinh Chieu; meals 50,000-120,000d; ☺11am-10.30pm; 🐾) Serves tasty, great-value Greek-ish cuisine including mean *shawarma* (beef or chicken doner kebabs), shish kebabs and great salads (Greek, Italian, garden). For a feast, order the Mediterranean Delight, which includes lots of mini plates including hummus and bruschetta.

Com Chay Vi Dieu VEGETARIAN $
(15b Đ Huynh Thuc Khang; mains 25,000-30,000d; ☺7am-9pm; 🐾) A simple roadside place perfect for inexpensive Vietnamese vegetarian dishes (curries, noodle soup and fried rice dishes); it also serves great smoothies (20,000d) and dragon-fruit juice. Almost no English is spoken.

Lam Tong Quan VIETNAMESE, SEAFOOD $
(92 Đ Nguyen Dinh Chieu; meals 25,000-140,000d; ☺7.30am-10pm) Popular with backpackers, this huge no-frills seafront place has tables right by the shore. There's a wide choice of dishes including lots of seafood and you can fill up for very little (fried rice with veg is 25,000d). Very limited English spoken.

Choi Oi VIETNAMESE $
(☑0252-374 1428; www.facebook.com/choioires taurant; 115 Đ Nguyen Dinh Chieu; meals from 80,000d; ☺8.30am-7.30pm; 🐾) A modern Viet restaurant run by welcoming staff who will guide you through the tempting menu: dishes include tofu with coconut and bamboo with steamed rice (90,000d). Cooking classes also hosted here.

★**Sandals** INTERNATIONAL $$
(☑0252-384 7440; www.sailingclubmuine.com; Sailing Club, 24 Đ Nguyen Dinh Chieu; meals 120,000-380,000d; ☺7am-10pm; 🐾) For a memorable meal in Mui Ne head straight to Sandals in the Sailing Club hotel. It's particularly romantic at night, with tables set around the shoreside pool and subtle lighting. The menu is superb, with everything from Vietnamese platters to pasta. You can enjoy wine by the glass.

Modjo Bar & Restaurant EUROPEAN $$
(☑091 818 9014; https://modjo-muine.business. site; 139 Đ Nguyen Dinh Chieu; meals 100,000-300,000d; ☺11am-11pm; 🐾) Serving Swiss and French fare in stylish surrounds Modjo makes a fine choice for a gourmet meal. Specials include fondue, raclette and steak cooked on a hot-stone plate. Deli ingredients including cheese and salami are imported from Europe and meat from Australia. Quality cocktails, too.

Bi Bo SEAFOOD $$
(191 Đ Nguyen Dinh Chieu; meals 80,000-250,000d; ☺10.30am-9.45pm) On the inland side of the main strip this popular seafood restaurant is consistently recommended by locals. Browse the tanks outside or consult the

menu; think satay squid, red snapper with spring onion, or grilled rock lobster with salt and chilli sauce.

Villa Aria Mui Ne
INTERNATIONAL $$

(www.villaariamuine.com; 60a Đ Nguyen Dinh Chieu; meals 115,000-280,000d; ⊙7am-9.30pm; 🛜) Tables are set on a shore-side deck here and the tempting menu includes seafood, salads, soups and pasta. There's a good wine selection available.

Nhu Bao
SEAFOOD $$

(📋0914 531 767; 146 Đ Nguyen Dinh Chieu; meals 70,000-200,000d; ⊙9am-9.30pm) No-nonsense Vietnamese seafood place: step past the bubbling tanks and there's a huge covered terrace that stretches down to the ocean. Crab or squid, fish or shrimp, all dishes are delicious.

Bo Ke
SEAFOOD $$

(Đ Nguyen Dinh Chieu; mains 45,000-190,000d; ⊙5-10pm) This group of seafood shacks on the shore features little more than plastic furniture and neon strip lights, but the fish and seafood are superfresh. Check prices carefully before you eat, as billing errors are not uncommon.

🍸 Drinking & Nightlife

There's a cluster of bars and beachside clubs around Km 15 on the strip and more bars around the Dong Vui Food Court.

Joe's Café
BAR

(www.joescafemuine.com; 86 Đ Nguyen Dinh Chieu; ⊙7am-1am; 🛜) This very popular pub-like place has live music (every night at 7.30pm) and a gregarious vibe. During the day it's a good place to hang, too, with seats set under a giant mango tree, magazines to browse, a pool table and an extensive food menu. Serves local, imported, draught and craft beers.

Dragon Beach
BAR, CLUB

(120-121 Đ Nguyen Dinh Chieu; ⊙5pm-4am) This beachfront club has a cool location by the waves with a chill-out deck scattered with cushions and a lively dance floor. Musically, expect EDM and banging techno. Staff are notoriously unprofessional – don't expect much in the way of service.

🛍 Shopping

Lemongrass House
COSMETICS

(https://lemongrasshouse.com.vn; 53 Đ Nguyen Dinh Chieu; ⊙10am-10pm) Excellent natural

beauty products, including body lotions and creams, scrubs, essential oils and perfumes. Prices start at around 250,000d.

Jibes
CLOTHING

(www.jibesbeachclub.com; 84 Đ Nguyen Dinh Chieu; ⊙9.30am-7.30pm) Good-quality water-sports gear for kitesurfers and windsurfers, surfers and SUP enthusiasts. All clothing is original.

❶ Information

Sinh Tourist (📋098 925 8060; 144 Đ Nguyen Dinh Chieu; ⊙7am-10pm) Operates open-tour buses to HCMC, Nha Trang, Dalat and Vung Tau. Has a computerised booking system.

Vietinbank ATM (Đ Nguyen Dinh Chieu) Towards the western end of the Mui Ne strip.

❶ Getting There & Away

BUS

Open-tour buses are the most convenient option for Mui Ne, as most public buses only serve Phan Thiet. Several companies have daily services to/from HCMC (110,000d to 135,000d, six hours), Nha Trang (115,000d, five hours) and Dalat (from 118,000d, four hours). Sleeper open-tour night buses usually cost more.

Phuong Trang (http://futabus.vn; 97 Đ Nguyen Dinh Chieu), also known as Futa, has very regular, comfortable buses running between Mui Ne and HCMC (140,000d). Its depot is just west of the Fairy Spring river. Sinh Tourist operates four daily buses on the HCMC route and also serves Vung Tau (four hours, two daily).

Local buses (9000d, 45 minutes, frequent) make trips between Phan Thiet Bus Station and Mui Ne, departing from the Coopmart, on the corner of Đ Nguyen Tat Thanh and Đ Tran Hung Dao.

CAR

It costs around US$100/130 to rent a car/minivan for the run to HCMC (five to six hours).

If you've a little more time, consider hiring a car to take you along the scenic coastal road to Vung Tau, perhaps stopping at the Ke Ga lighthouse en route. A one-way trip (five to six hours for a leisurely drive) costs around US$110. Regular buses and ferries connect Vung Tau with HCMC.

MOTORCYCLE

Easy Riders (p266) operates from Mui Ne, although there are not as many riders as in Dalat or Nha Trang. One of the best trips to experience by motorbike is actually the triangle between these three destinations, as the mountain roads from Mui Ne to Dalat and on to

SOUTHEAST COAST MUI NE

Nha Trang are some of the most dramatic in the south. A *xe om* ride from Phan Thiet to Mui Ne will cost around 80,000d.

TRAIN

The nearest train station on the main north–south line is Muong Man, 29km west of Mui Ne. It's not served by public transport; a taxi costs 475,000d to/from Mui Ne.

ⓘ Getting Around

The local police fine tourists riding motorbikes in Mui Ne without the correct documentation. However, dozens of visitors still rent scooters, which cost from 120,000d per day.

Traffic moves very fast along the main strip. Take care.

Xe om drivers charge 25,000d or so for a short hop. **Mai Linh** (☑ 0252-389 8989) operates reliable metered taxis.

Phan Thiet & Around

☑ 0252 / POP 194,000

The bustling port city of Phan Thiet is traditionally known for its *nuoc mam* (fish sauce), producing millions of litres of the stuff per annum. There's not much to see in town, but the riverside fishing harbour is always chock-a-block with brightly painted boats and there are sights nearby including the Ke Ga lighthouse and Ta Cu Mountain.

The long promenade on the east side of town is attractive, as is the fishing harbour in the heart of town.

For travellers, the city acts as a gateway to the nearby beach resort of Mui Ne.

◉ Sights

Ke Ga Lighthouse   LIGHTHOUSE

(5000d; ⊗ 7am-4.30pm) Around 30km south of Phan Thiet, the spectacular Ke Ga lighthouse dates from the French era. Constructed in 1899, it sits on a rocky islet some 300m from the shore, towering almost 40m above the ocean. It's just possible to swim (or even wade) across if the tide is very low, but most visitors hire a boat operator (from 100,000d return) to get across.

You're no longer allowed to ascend the lighthouse.

Still, there are fine vistas from the islet east across the ocean and back towards inland hills. Note: guards routinely overcharge foreigners for entrance tickets.

Van Thuy Tu Temple   TEMPLE

(231 Đ Ngu Ong; 10,000d; ⊗ 7am-6pm) Vietnam's whale-worship cult is thought to have originated in early Cham times. Fishing communities in southern Vietnam revere whales as near-divine beings who offer protection against storms, and there are whale temples

SOUTHEAST COAST PHAN THIET & AROUND

WORTH A TRIP

THE ROAD FROM PHAN THIET TO LONG HAI

A beautiful road parallels the coast between Phan Thiet and Long Hai, passing some memorable scenery and the impressive Ke Ga lighthouse. Traffic is light. There are pockets of tourism development, but for now most of the coastline is a beguiling mix of giant sand dunes, fishing villages, wide ocean views and some near-deserted beaches. This region makes a great day trip from Vung Tau or Mui Ne. There's limited public transport so a motorbike or car is the way to go. Savvy travellers use this road to avoid tackling the nightmarish Hwy 1.

Immediately south of Phan Thiet, the first section of the road is beautiful, with a casuarina-lined shoreline and the ocean to the east, while the inland scenery is dominated by rust-red sand dunes. After 30km or so you reach the majestic Ke Ga lighthouse, which clings to a tiny island offshore.

South of Ke Ga, the coastal road pushes southwest, passing fields bursting with dragon fruit (the main crop), reaching La Gi, 22km down the road. La Gi is an isolated market town, but it does have hourly bus connections (35,000d, two hours) to Long Hai and a good homestay in the hills behind town.

Continuing southwest of La Gi, the coastal road keeps on snaking its way along the shoreline, with towering sand dunes on the inland side. Chunks of the near-virgin coast have been parcelled off here and there, awaiting future hotel resorts and mass tourism, but it's not hard to park and find a bit of beach for a revitalising dip. The section 7km north of Ho Coc is particularly scenic and worth investigating, the lonely (for now) road hugging the shore.

dotted along the coast. This one is particularly fascinating to visit as it contains the skeleton of a 19m whale. The temple itself is said to date back to 1762 and also contains other cultural relics.

Ta Cu Mountain
MOUNTAIN

(admission & cable car 250,000d) The highlight here is the white reclining Buddha (Tuong Phat Nam). At 49m long, it's the largest in Vietnam. The pagoda was constructed in 1861, but the Buddha was only added in 1972. It has become an important pilgrimage centre for Buddhists.

The mountain is just off Hwy 1, 31km southwest of Phan Thiet. From the highway it's a beautiful two-hour trek, or a 10-minute cable-car ride and a short but steep hike.

✗ Eating

Phan Thiet has some excellent seafood restaurants off its seafront promenade.

Nha Hang Chay Vien Chau
VEGETARIAN $

(154 Đ Tran Quy Cap; meals 55,000-125,000d; ⊙7am-9pm; 🐾) This large vegetarian restaurant is situated on the western side of the city and has a choice of dining areas including formal table seating and a garden terrace. There's a diverse menu of Vietnamese dishes, all priced moderately.

Song Bien
SEAFOOD $$

(162 Đ Le Loi; mains 60,000-210,000d; ⊙9am-8pm; 🐾) At the western end of the beach promenade this very popular, utilitarian seafood place offers a wide selection of fish, shrimp and crab dishes and also has an outstanding selection of vodka. Note it closes quite early.

❶ Getting There & Away

Phan Thiet Bus Station (Đ Tu Van Tu) is on the northern outskirts of town. Local bus 9 (35,000d) meets the train from HCMC and heads right along the Mui Ne strip stopping at hotels on the way.

Phan Thiet train station is on a spur off the north–south line. The nearest main-line train station is 12km west of town in Muong Man.

Ho Coc Beach

📞 0254 / POP 1680

With golden sands, rolling inland dunes and clear waters, this beach – which stretches for almost 10km north of Ho Tram – makes a tempting place to stop. Ho

Coc is getting increasingly busy with visitors from Saigon but on weekdays it still remains peaceful.

Huong Phong
Ho Coc Beach Resort
CAMPGROUND $

(📞0254-387 8145; http://huongphonghococcbeach resort.com; tent per person 140,000d, r from 1,070,000d; ❄️ 🐾 🕸️) This large resort complex has a campground perfectly priced for shoestringers, allowing you to stay in a tent (provided) for very little and get the full run of facilities, beach access, restaurants and pool. There are also somewhat bland but functional rooms.

Hotel Ven Ven
HOTEL $$

(📞0254-379 1121; r 700,000d-1,000,000d; ❄️@🕸️) This tasteful, vaguely Spanish-looking hotel has classy, well-appointed rooms with flat-screen TVs; many have a balcony or terrace. Set in lush gardens and has a fine restaurant (meals from 75,000d; try the claypot dishes).

Ho Tram Beach

📞 0254 / POP 1490

Around Ho Tram, the coastal road unexpectedly becomes a four-lane highway to facilitate access to the gargantuan Grand Ho Tram Strip, a vast casino resort complex popular with Chinese tourists.

Casino aside, Ho Tram is very low key – until very recently it consisted of nothing more than a tiny fishing village, scruffy open-air market and a fine, though rubbish-strewn, beach.

However, vastly improved road links to Saigon have opened up this stretch of coastline to development and more and more new places are being constructed.

🛏️ Sleeping & Eating

You'll find simple guesthouses near the fishing village and some very fancy resort complexes along the shore. Sleeping under canvas is also an option as there are several campgrounds.

Local villagers steam, fry and grill fresh seafood right on the beach in Ho Tram. Make sure you try the delicious clams or mussels served with a topping of peanuts, spring onion, lime and chilli; a portion of six costs around 30,000d.

Hoa Bien Motel
HOTEL $

(📞0254-378 2279; r 360,000-680,000d; ❄️🕸️) Steps from the shore in the fishing village, the simple yet well-presented rooms here have modern facilities and bathrooms, though the cheapest options are very compact. The helpful owners speak some English and there's a restaurant for breakfast and seafood.

Beach House GUESTHOUSE **$**
(☑0254-378 1678; www.beachhousehotram.com; tent rental 100,000d, bungalows from US$56; ❄🅿) The Beach House is actually a large hotel complex in a tranquil location on a sandy spit of land between a riverbank and the beach. There's a wide choice of rooms and bungalows plus a shady campground (tents are provided). Rates rise on weekends.

River Ray Estates RESORT, CAMPGROUND **$$**
(☑0254-378 1460; http://riverrayestates.com; Ben Cat; r US$49-131, villa from US$90, camping per person 95,000d; ❄🅿🏊) In extensive grounds and a short walk from the beach, River Ray has a fine location, choice of wooden cabins and villas (some sleep up to eight) and a campground (you'll need your own tent). The in-house restaurant has good Thai and Vietnamese dishes.

Sanctuary RESORT **$$$**
(☑0254-378 1631; www.sanctuary.com.vn; villa from 15,000,000d; ❄@🅿🏊) This resort complex is home to gorgeous contemporary villas, each with private pool, open-plan kitchens and hip furnishings. It's just off a stunning, broad sandy beach and the resort's cafe-restaurant is great for a healthy Western or local meal. There's a floodlit tennis court (and a golf course 3km away).

Ho Tram BBQ Restaurant BARBECUE **$$**
(meals 60,000-160,000d; ⏱11am-9pm) This large, bustling place specialises in delicious barbecued meat and fish dishes. Wash them down with a cold Saigon or 333 beer. It's located around 2km inland from Ho Tram village.

❶ Getting There & Away

There's irregular public transport on this coastline. Slow local buses trundle between Vung Tau and Ba Ria. However, it's perfect terrain for exploring on two wheels; scooters are available from hotels and guesthouses.

Vung Tau

☑0254 / POP 222,000

A popular weekend escape from HCMC, Vung Tau rocks at weekends when beach-starved locals and expats descend in numbers, but it is relatively quiet during the week. The city enjoys a spectacular location on a peninsula, with ocean on three sides; the light and sea air make it a refreshing break from sultry Saigon.

Vung Tau is a remarkably civilised-looking city of broad boulevards and imposing colonial-era buildings. Few travellers

---

ANZAC SITES AROUND VUNG TAU

Nearly 60,000 Australian soldiers were involved in the American War throughout the 1960s and 1970s. The **Long Tan Memorial Cross** commemorates a particularly fierce battle that took place on 18 August 1966 between Australian troops and Viet Cong fighters. Originally erected by Australian survivors of the battle, the current cross is a replica installed by the Vietnamese in 2002. It's located about 18km from Ba Ria town or 55km from Vung Tau, near the town of Nui Dat. Permits to visit the Long Tan memorial are no longer necessary, and trips can be combined with the seldom-visited **Long Phuoc tunnels**, an underground network that is a much smaller version of the more famous tunnels at Cu Chi.

At Minh Dam, 5km from Long Hai, there are **caves** with historical connections to the Franco–Viet Minh and American Wars. Although the caves are little more than spaces between the boulders covering the cliff face, VC soldiers bunked here off and on between 1948 and 1975; you can still see bullet holes in the rocks from the skirmishes that took place. Steps hewn into the rock face lead up to the caves, with spectacular views over the coastal plains at the top.

Nearby there is a **mountain-top temple** with more great panoramic views of the coastline.

Tommy's (p274) operates good tours of the key sites geared for returning vets. Otherwise hook up with a taxi driver and expect to pay US$75 or so for a full-day tour.

bother to visit the city, but it makes a good place to start (or end) an intriguing coastal road trip to Mui Ne and beyond.

◎ Sights

★ Robert Taylor
Museum of Worldwide Arms MUSEUM
(📞 0254-381 8369; http://baotangroberttaylor.com; 98 Đ Tran Hung Dao; 100,000d; ◷ 8am-6pm) Come here for a stupendous private collection of military arms, uniforms and paraphernalia from across the globe. One section is dedicated to the conflict in Vietnam, another to the French Colonial period and there are Chinese, European and even Zulu exhibits.

Robert Taylor, who has spent more than 50 years amassing and curating the collection, is often at hand to provide explanations. The attention to detail is superb and there are excellent descriptions in English and Vietnamese.

Giant Jesus MONUMENT
(Tuong Dai Chua Kito Vua; parking 2000d; ◷ 7.15-11.30am & 1.30-5pm) **FREE** Atop Small Mountain with his arms outstretched to embrace the South China Sea (East Sea), this 32m giant Jesus is one of the biggest in the world – taller than his illustrious Brazilian cousin. It's possible to ascend to the arms for a panoramic view of Vung Tau. Note you cannot enter the actual statue in vest-tops or shorts.

French Field Guns LANDMARK
FREE These six massive cannons, all with support trenches, demonstrate how strategically important Cap St Jacques was to the colonial authorities (it guarded access to Saigon). To reach them take Đ Tran Phu beyond Mulberry Beach and look for Hem 444 in the fishing village, about 6km from Vung Tau. Turn right up a narrow, rough track manageable by motorbike or on foot.

White Villa MUSEUM
(Bach Dinh, Villa Blanche; Đ Tran Phu; 15,000d; ◷ 7am-4.30pm) The weekend retreat of French governor Paul Doumer (later a French president), this gorgeous, grand colonial-era residence has extensive gardens bursting with frangipani. The interior is oddly empty (besides the odd piece of furniture and some Ming pottery retrieved from shipwrecks off the coast). It sits about 30m above the road, up a winding lane.

🏃 Activities

Vung Tau is not a major watersports centre, but if the weather gods are smiling, some residents surf and kitesurf.

Surf Station SURFING, WINDSURFING
(📞 0163 290 0040, 0254-526 101; 8 Đ Thuy Van; ◷ 8am-6pm) Based at the **Vung Tau Beach Club** (www.vungtaubeachclub.com; 8 Đ Thuy Van; ◷ 9am-late; 🖥), Surf Station offers board rental and kitesurfing and surfing classes. The equipment is good and instructors are professional.

☞ Tours

Tommy's Tours HISTORY
(📞 0254-351 5181; www.tommysvietnam.com; 3 Đ Le Ngoc Han; day tour US$125) Tommy's runs highly informative tours of the military sites around Vung Tau, which are popular with Aussie and Kiwi veterans. Tours take in the Long Phuoc tunnels, Long Tan Memorial Cross and key battle zones. Half-day or full-day tours can be arranged.

Pioneer Travel TOURS
(📞 093 777 5838; https://pioneertravel.com.vn; 171 Đ Pham Ngu Lao, HCMC; from US$90; ◷ 7am-7pm) This HCMC-based company runs good guided day trips from the city to the battle sites (Long Tan Memorial Cross, Long Phuoc tunnels, Nui Dat) around Vung Tau.

🛏 Sleeping

Most foreigners prefer to stay on Front Beach where the restaurants and bars are found, while the majority of Vietnamese visitors head for Back Beach.

On weekends and holidays Vung Tau heaves with local tourists, so book ahead.

★ Gecko Hostel HOSTEL $
(📞 098 897 8785; www.facebook.com/Gecko hostelvn; 75 Đ Tran Dong; dm US$5, r US$16-20; ❄🖥) This is a social hostel that is popular with both foreigners and young Vietnamese. It has pizza-making evenings and beer-downing sessions on weekends. Staff will direct you to Vung Tau's sights and have a useful map. Breakfast is available for just 20,000d.

Sakura Hotel HOTEL $
(📞 0254-357 0465; thachhoapa@yahoo.com.vn; Phan Huy Chu; r weekdays/weekends from 300,000/400,000d, apt 440,000/800,000d; ❄🖥) This hotel is very popular thanks to its ever-

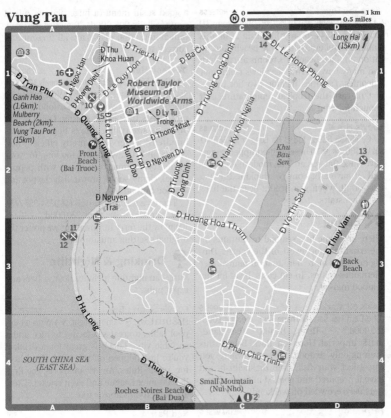

Vung Tau

SOUTHEAST COAST VUNG TAU

helpful owner, who speaks good English, rents out scooters and bikes and can advise travellers about onward transport. The well-furnished rooms are in decent shape, or you can opt for a spacious apartment with a kitchenette.

Vung Tau Riva Hotel HOTEL $$
(☑ 0254-361 2556; www.vungtaurivahotel.com; 3 Đ Thuy Van; r US$44-76; ✳ 🛜) Built in 2018, this slimline hotel enjoys a prime beachfront location on Back Beach. Its rooms are modern and many have terrific sea views from their balconies. Facilities include two hot tubs – just in case the tropical temperature isn't enough for you!

Lucy's Hotel HOTEL $$
(☑ 0254-385 8896; 138 Đ Ha Long; r US$35-40, apt US$60; ✳ 🛜) These well-equipped rooms have huge flat-screen TVs, modern en suites and all have a balcony overlooking the bay. Best of all, when you need a beer, the bar's just downstairs.

✕ Eating

There are some fine seafood restaurants on the coastline northwest of the centre. Dining out costs more here than in many other Vietnamese cities. To cut costs, head for the seafood market.

Seafood Market SEAFOOD $
(Cho Dem Hai San; Đ Thang Tam; meals 45,000-180,000d; ⊙5-11pm) Behind the landmark Imperial Hotel on Back Beach, this evening-only seafood market is where you can select your fish, crab or shellfish and have it prepared and cooked in front of you. Gets *very* crowded on weekends.

Ferry Cafe VIETNAMESE $
(Ferry Terminal, Đ Ha Long; meals 38,000-90,000d; ⊙7am-9pm) Located somewhat incongruously inside the ferry terminal building, this bustling open-sided place catches the sea breeze and serves up tasty noodles and meat dishes. Try the steak cooked in a skillet.

Bistrot 9 FRENCH $$
(https://bistroninevungtau.com; 9 Đ Truong Vinh Ky; snacks/meals from 50,000/100,000d; ⊙6am-10pm; ✳ 🛜) A chic, casual French bistro-deli with a fine pavement terrace. It's the best place in town for a Western breakfast or brunch (try the pancakes or eggs Benedict). Classics like coq au vin (225,000d) will satisfy your Gallic cravings later. Bread is baked daily on the premises.

Sushi Tokyo JAPANESE $$
(http://sushitokyo.vn; 201 Đ Thong Nhat; meals 75,000-200,000d; ⊙10am-2pm & 5-10pm) Intimate, relatively inexpensive Japanese with a good sushi menu (a huge plate of mixed *maki* rolls is 298,000d). Tempura, teriyaki, ramen and udon dishes are all present and correct, too.

★**Ganh Hao** SEAFOOD $$$
(☑ 0254-355 0909; 3 Đ Tran Phu; meals 140,000-450,000d; ⊙11am-9.30pm; 🛜) With tables by the ocean, this wonderful seafood restaurant boasts the perfect setting. Don't be put off by its size (Ganh Hao is huge and seats hundreds) as service is pretty efficient and you shouldn't have to wait too long for your meal. Try sublime crab (great with pepper sauce), clams, squid, prawn, fish claypot and seafood hotpots.

There's a second **branch** (☑ 0254-357 7777; ferry terminal; meals from 220,000d; ⊙10am-10pm) by the ferry terminal but we prefer the original's setting and ambience.

🍷 Drinking & Nightlife

Vung Tau nightlife includes hostess bars and expat pubs.

Lucy's Sports Bar SPORTS BAR
(138 Đ Ha Long; ⊙7am-midnight; 🛜) With a busy pool table, a great sea-facing terrace and a sociable vibe, Lucy's is great for a drink if you've just hopped off the ferry. Head here for Aussie Rules, American sports, the English Premier League and even cricket. There are good rooms above, too.

Red Parrot PUB
(6 Đ Le Quy Don; ⊙noon-midnight; 🛜) This popular expat pub has a heavy-duty clientele of war veterans, oil workers and working girls.

ℹ Information

International SOS (☑ 0254-385 8776; www.internationalsos.com; 1 Đ Le Ngoc Han; ⊙24hr) A well-respected clinic with international standards and international prices.

Vietcombank (27-29 Đ Tran Hung Dao; ⊙7.30am-3.30pm) Exchanges dollars and offers credit-card advances.

ℹ Getting There & Away

BOAT
Note sailing schedules for all boats are liable to change due to weather conditions.

Hydrofoils connect HCMC (200,000d to 250,000d, 90 minutes) with Vung Tau, a very mellow way to travel. **Greenlines** (☑ 098 690 8907; www.greenlines-dp.com; pier; adult/child 250,000/120,000d) runs four to six daily services. Book ahead for weekend travel. In Vung Tau, the boat leaves from Cau Da Pier.

Ferries also connect Con Son Island with Vung Tau, with sailings approximately every three days. Boats do not leave when seas are rough (and conditions aboard the boats are pretty rough, too). Ferries depart at 5pm from Vung Tau port, about 15km west of the city; the journey takes around 12 hours.

BUS

Futa Phuong Trang buses (115,000d, three hours, 16 daily) connect HCMC with Vung Tau from Mien Tay bus terminal.

There are also minibuses from Mien Dong Bus Station in HCMC (90,000d, 1½ hours, frequent) between 5am and 7pm to Vung Tau.

From HCMC airport, regular shuttle vans (160,000d, 2½ hours), operated by a number of companies, head to Vung Tau.

AT A GLANCE

POPULATION
Dalat: 184,000

FAST FACT
Buon Ma Thuot is
Vietnam's caffeine
capital, hosting
a biennial Coffee
Festival (p294)

**BEST WILDLIFE
EXPERIENCE**
Wild Gibbon
Trek (p282)

BEST DORMS
Mooka's Home
(p288)

**BEST COFFEE
ROASTERY**
La Viet Coffee (p291)

WHEN TO GO
Mar Great for Buon
Ma Thuot's biennial
Coffee Festival.

Oct Autumn in
Dalat, the perfect
time for exploring or
adrenaline-pumping
activities.

Dec Trek or cycle
through Cat Tien
National Park in
cooler temperatures,
visiting the wild
gibbons.

Datanla Falls (p286)
SAIKO3P/SHUTTERSTOCK ©

Southwest Highlands

Few parts of Vietnam stir the imagination with the lure of adventure quite like the highlands. The ribbon-like Ho Chi Minh Hwy winds its way past coffee plantations, pine-studded mountains, enormous reed-covered lakes and deeply traditional ethnic minority villages, laying down the challenge of an epic two-wheeled journey. Protected jungle in the remoter corners hosts singing gibbons, pygmy lorises, wild elephants and incredible numbers of birds. Active travellers take to the mountains, forests, waterfalls and rivers in cycling, hiking, rafting and abseiling adventures, and the former French hill station of Dalat beguiles with its cool climate, the palaces of the last emperor of Vietnam and bars for after-dark thrills.

Cat Tien National Park

📞 0251 / ELEV 700M

Wonderful Cat Tien (Vuon Quoc Gia Cat Tien; Map p348; 📞 0251-366 9228; www.namcattien.vn; incl ferry ride adult/child 60,000/10,000d; ⊙ 7am-10pm) 🏊 comprises an amazingly biodiverse area of lowland tropical rainforest. The 720-sq-km park is one of Vietnam's outstanding natural treasures – a true jungle – and the hiking, mountain biking and birdwatching are the best in the south of the country. Try to avoid weekends and public holidays, when the park gets very busy with domestic tourists.

Fauna in the park includes 100 types of mammal, including elephants, leopards, the bison-like guar and primates such as gibbons, pygmy lorises and langurs. There are also 79 types of reptile, 41 amphibian species, plus an incredible array of snakes, spiders and insects, including around 400 butterfly species. Of the 350-plus birds, rare species include the orange-necked partridge and Siamese fireback.

Bear in mind that the larger animals, including elephants and leopards, are very retiring. You're most likely to see primates, birds and reptiles.

Dry season in the park is from November to April. Be prepared for leeches during the rainy months of May to October.

⊙ Sights & Activities

Cat Tien National Park can be explored on foot, on mountain bike, by 4WD and by boat along the Dong Nai River. It's worth calling ahead to book a guide and the most popular excursions.

There are several well-established hiking trails in the park, ranging from 2km to 26km in length. Some are flat and paved, while others are demanding, muddy slogs that require crossing streams.

Guides charge 400,000/800,000d for a half-day/day's trekking or birdwatching, regardless of group size. Take plenty of insect repellent and water. 'Anti-leech socks' are provided by the guides.

Hotels such as Green Bamboo Lodge (p282) offer boat trips at dawn or dusk for 250,000d per person.

★ Dao Tien Endangered Primate Species Centre WILDLIFE RESERVE

(Map p348; www.go-east.org; Cat Tien National Park; adult/child incl boat ride 300,000/100,000d; ⊙ tours 8.30am & 2pm) Set on an island in the Dong Nai River, this rehabilitation centre with a stellar reputation hosts golden-cheeked gibbons, pygmy lorises (both endemic to Vietnam and Cambodia), black-shanked doucs and silvered langurs that were illegally trafficked. The eventual goal is to release the primates back into the forest. You can view gibbons in a semiwild environment and hear their incredible calls.

Hundreds of native fruit-tree saplings were planted on the island to provide the primates with foraging territory and encourage them to learn the necessary skills to move around the forest canopy. The centre's current focus is preserving the pygmy loris from extinction. Sadly, several of the rescued animals will never be released into the wild, as hunters tore out their poisonous teeth, without which they can't fend for themselves. The Dao Tien website allows you to sponsor individual primates. Check online for opening times.

Crocodile Lake LAKE

(Bau Sau; Map p348; Cat Tien National Park; 140,000d) Crocodile Lake is home to 200 crocs and is one of Cat Tien National Park's highlights. Getting here involves a 9km drive or bicycle ride from the park headquarters and then a 5km hike to the swamp; the walk takes about three hours return. A vehicle to the hiking start point costs 250,000d each way. Alternatively, you can trek all the way with a guide from the park headquarters along a jungle route criss-crossed by streams.

Kayaks can be rented at the lake for 150,000d per hour, but be careful not to disturb the crocs and be aware that these are wild animals and that you paddle at your own risk. For the best chance of seeing crocs (unlikely during the heat of the day) book an overnight stay with park rangers at their lakeshore station (double 600,000d to 700,000d, suite 1,400,000d).

Centre of Rescue and Conservation of Species WILDLIFE RESERVE

(Map p348; Cat Tien National Park; adult/child 150,000/50,000d; ⊙ 7.30am-4pm) South of the park headquarters, this rescue centre is home to a selection of sun bears and black bears, rescued from poachers and/or bear bile farms, as well as a few other animals. Conditions are not ideal, though the bears share a large outdoor area in which they're let loose every morning. There are hour-long tours of the facility at 8.30am, 10am, 1.30pm and 3pm.

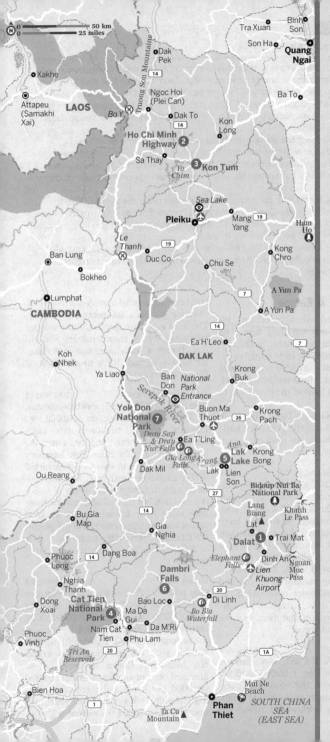

Southwest Highlands Highlights

1 Dalat (p283)
Cranking up the adrenaline with a canyoning, white-water rafting, cycling or hiking adventure.

2 Ho Chi Minh Highway (p293)
Revving up a motorbike and riding the twists and turns.

3 Kon Tum (p299)
Exploring indigenous culture and customs in the surrounding Bahnar, Sedang and Jarai villages.

4 Cat Tien National Park (p280) Tracking down wild gibbons in the early morning, then seeking out crocodiles by torchlight at night.

5 Lak Lake (p293)
Hiking or boating to the minority villages around the biggest lake in the highlands.

6 Dambri Falls (p287) Getting drenched in spray at this 90m-high waterfall.

7 Yok Don National Park (p297) Trekking into the jungle for birdwatching and elephant spotting.

DON'T MISS

WILD GIBBON TREK

Golden-cheeked gibbons have been reintroduced into Cat Tien and this experience offers a rare insight into the lives of these charismatic primates. The four-hour **trek** (Map p348; www.go-east.org; Cat Tien National Park; per person 1,050,000d, maximum 4 people) runs daily from the park HQ and involves a 4.30am start to get out to the gibbons in time for their dawn chorus – you have a chance to watch two separate gibbon families go about their everyday business.

Golden-cheeked gibbons are very territorial, with dominant females, and live in nuclear family groups, with the young staying with their mother for up to eight years. As with most other endangered creatures in Vietnam, they're hunted for the illegal pet trade, with parents killed and babies abducted, and also for dubious traditional-medicine purposes.

It's a reasonably easy hike, but it's not suitable for kids under the age of 12. The trip includes a guided tour of the Dao Tien Endangered Primate Species Centre (p280), typically done at 8.30am, straight after the trek. If staying outside the park you'll have to pay an extra 50,000d for an early river ferry crossing.

The wild gibbon trek is run by the park authorities, with the support of Go East. All proceeds go back into the national park and assist rangers in their protection efforts. Book well in advance.

Sleeping & Eating

As there are good overnight options, it's worth spending two full days here. The national park has reasonable accommodation that is handy for early morning excursions; you'll also avoid paying repeat park-entrance fees. There are better guesthouses on the east bank of the river, close to the park entrance.

The village of Nam Cat Tien, a 10-minute walk from the park entrance, has a few basic noodle and rice joints, but most people eat at their guesthouse.

★ **Green Bamboo Lodge** LODGE $
(Map p348; ☑ 0973 343 345; cattien_vung@yahoo.com; Nam Cat Tien; r 150,000-350,000d, stilt houses 600,000-800,000d; ❋ ᯤ ⌁) A 150m walk from the ferry crossing, on the east bank of the river, this popular cluster of thatched bamboo-and-brick bungalows comes in a dozen good-value configurations, most of which offer riverside views. The most expensive stilt houses come with air-con and tree-house-style balconies overlooking the chocolate-brown river. Reception can arrange onward transport and tours, and the riverside restaurant is good.

Green Hope Lodge GUESTHOUSE $
(Map p348; ☑ 0972 184 683; www.greenhopelodge.com; Nam Cat Tien; r 115,000-500,000d; ❋ ᯤ) Well-organised and good-value riverside guesthouse run by an amenable family. The wood-roofed, brick-walled rooms are large and set around a garden strewn with riverside pavilions for post-trek lounging. The most expensive rooms are in a wooden stilt house with a shared balcony and air-con. There's a restaurant, and motorbikes for getting around. It's a 10-minute stroll from the ferry crossing.

Ta Lai Long House GUESTHOUSE $
(Map p348; ☑ 0974 160 827; www.talai-adventure.vn; Cat Tien National Park; dm 500,000d; ᯤ) Excellent, unique, traditional-style lodge managed by Westerners and locals from the S'Tieng and Ma minorities. The dormitory accommodation is in two well-constructed timber longhouses, with good, screened bedding, modern facilities and plenty of activities on offer, but it's probably not for those who value their privacy. Avoid weekend school team-building events like the plague. It's 12km southwest of the park HQ.

A third of the profits goes to local charity projects.

Green Cat Tien GUESTHOUSE $
(Map p348; ☑ 0251-366 9228; cattienvietnam@gmail.com; Cat Tien National Park; standard r 350,000-400,000d, superior r 500,000-600,000d, camping per person 50,000d; ❋ ᯤ) Rooms at the national park's HQ are old fashioned but sizeable, with TVs and fridges and acceptable bathrooms. Guides and treks can be arranged here, mountain bikes can be hired (30,000d per hour) and there's the relaxing riverside **Yellow Bamboo Restaurant** (meals 60,000-100,000d; ⊙7am-9pm; ᯤ).

★**Forest Floor Lodge**   LODGE $$$
(Map p348; 🖬 0251-669 890; www.forestfloor lodges.com; Cat Tien National Park; r or luxury tents €115; 🕸🖥) This ecolodge, 1.5km north of park HQ, sets the standard for atmospheric accommodation in Vietnam's protected areas. There are comfortable tented rooms overlooking the Ben Cu river rapids, and larger, stylish rooms set in traditional wooden houses, as well as a decent restaurant. The lodge is across the river from the Dao Tien primate centre, so you'll hear the gibbons in the morning.

ℹ Information

Guides and tours are booked at the park headquarters on the west bank of the river. A ferry makes frequent crossings of the Dong Nai River between 6.30am and 7pm. Park entry (which includes river crossings) is paid at the **ticket booth** (Map p348; ⊘ 6.30am-7pm) near the ferry.

ℹ Getting There & Away

All buses between Dalat and Ho Chi Minh City (every 30 minutes) pass the junction to Nam Cat Tien village (180,000d, four hours) and the park, 6km south of Ma Da Gui town on Hwy 20 at kilometre marker 142. It's best to call ahead to your guesthouse to ask them to send a motorbike/taxi to meet you (150,000/250,000d). Otherwise you're at the mercy of the *xe om* (motorbike-taxi) drivers at the junction, who ask for 200,000d to cover the remaining 18km to the park.

Smaller local buses to HCMC (80,000d to 100,000d, four hours) leave Nam Cat Tien village hourly until 3pm. Your guesthouse can book seats on a passing sleeper bus to Dalat or HCMC, but you'll have to first take a taxi to the road junction.

A private car to HCMC costs around 2,000,000d.

ℹ Getting Around

Guesthouses either rent or provide bicycles free of charge. You can also rent bicycles at park headquarters for 30,000d per hour or 100,000/150,000d per half-day/day. You'll need to pay 100,000d to take a non-park bike across the ferry into the park.

Dalat & Around

🖬 0263 / POP 184,755 / ELEV 1475M

Dalat is an alternative Vietnam: the weather is spring-like instead of tropically hot, the town is dotted with French-colonial villas rather than socialist architecture, and the surrounding farms cultivate strawberries, coffee and flowers in place of rice.

The French came here first, fleeing the heat of Saigon for average daily temperatures that hover between 15°C and 24°C. They left behind their holiday homes and a resort vibe, which the Vietnamese have added to with their own unique touches. Dalat is Vietnam's honeymoon capital and extremely popular with domestic tourists.

For foreign visitors, the moderate climate has made Dalat the adventure-sports capital of southern Vietnam, with canyoning, mountain biking, white-water rafting and treks into the surrounding hills all available.

December to March is the busiest time for foreign visitors, with most Vietnamese coming between May and August to escape the heat.

History

Home to hill tribes for centuries, 'Da Lat' means 'river of the Lat tribe' in the Lat language. The city was established in 1912 and quickly became fashionable with Europeans – at one point during the French colonial period, 20% of Dalat's population was foreign, and grand villas remain scattered around the city, particularly along Tran Hung Dao in the city's southeast.

During the American War, Dalat was spared by the tacit agreement of all parties concerned. Indeed, it seems that while South Vietnamese soldiers were being trained at the city's military academy and affluent officials of the Saigon regime were relaxing in their villas, Viet Cong cadres were doing the same thing not far away (also in villas). On 3 April 1975 Dalat fell to the North without a fight.

⊙ Sights

⊙ Dalat

Dalat's sights are spread around town, and are most easily visited by *xe om* or taxi or by renting a motorbike.

★**Hang Nga Crazy House**   ARCHITECTURE
(🖬 0263-382 2070; 3 Đ Huynh Thuc Khang; adult/child 60,000/20,000d; ⊘ 8.30am-7pm) A freewheeling architectural exploration of surrealism, Hang Nga Crazy House is a joyously designed, outrageously artistic private home. Imagine sculptured rooms connected by superslim bridges rising out of a tangle of concrete greenery, an excess of cascading lava-flow-like shapes, wild colours, spiderweb windows and an almost organic quality

Central Dalat

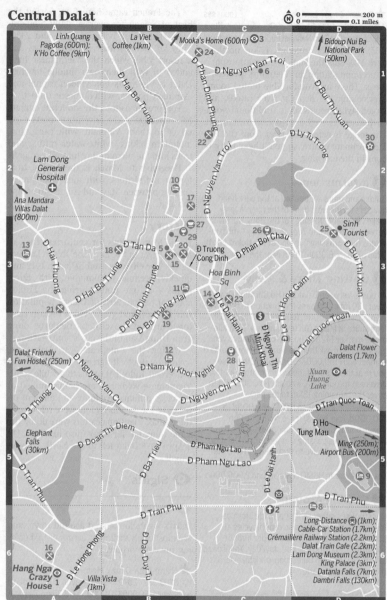

Long-Distance (1km);
Cable-Car Station (1.7km);
Crémaillère Railway Station (2.2km);
Dalat Train Cafe (2.2km);
Lam Dong Museum (2.3km);
King Palace (3km);
Datanla Falls (7km);
Dambri Falls (130km)

to it all, with the swooping handrails resembling jungle vines. Think of Gaudí and Tolkien dropping acid together and designing their own version of Disneyland.

The brainchild of owner Mrs Dang Viet Nga, the Crazy House has been an imaginative work in progress since 1990. Hang

Nga, as she's known locally, has a PhD in architecture from Moscow and has designed a number of other buildings around Dalat. Her father, Truong Chinh, succeeded Ho Chi Minh as Vietnam's second president from 1981 until his death in 1988, which is perhaps one reason that planning permission

Central Dalat

doesn't seem to be a problem. There's a shrine to him in the ground-floor lounge.

A note of caution for those with young kids: the Crazy House's maze of precarious tunnels, high walkways with low guard rails and steep ladders is not at all child-safe.

King Palace PALACE
(Dinh 1; ☑ 0263-358 0558; Hung Vuong; adult/child 50,000/20,000d; ☺ 7am-5pm) Built by a French merchant in 1929, the surprisingly modest but attractive royal residence of Bao Dai (1913–97), Vietnam's last emperor, beckons visitors with its beautiful tree-lined avenue. It was home to Bao Dai and his family until they went into exile in France in 1954. The house was subsequently taken over by then Prime Minister Ngo Dinh Diem.

Highlights are the emperor's coronation photos and the easily missed secret doorway, disguised as a bookcase, that leads through tunnels to a parked Huey helicopter. For 40,000d you can have your photo taken next to a waxwork likeness of Bao Dai.

**Crémaillère
Railway Station** HISTORIC BUILDING
(Ga Da Lat; 1 Đ Quang Trung; ☺ 6.30am-5pm) FREE From Dalat's wonderful art deco train station you can ride one of the nine scheduled trains that run to Trai Mat (return from 108,000d, 30 minutes) daily between 6.55am and 4.39pm; a minimum of 25 passengers is required. A *crémaillère* (cog railway) linking

Dalat and Thap Cham from 1928 to 1964 was closed due to VC attacks. A Japanese steam train is on display alongside a collection of old carriages.

At Trai Mat you can visit the impressively kitsch Linh Phuoc Pagoda (p286), just a couple of hundred metres from the station.

Lam Dong Museum MUSEUM
(☑ 0263-381 2624; 4 Đ Hung Vuong; admission 15,000d; ☺ 7.30-11.30am & 1.30-4.30pm) This hillside museum is a stampede through Dalat's history, with a side trip into natural history, complete with outrageously bad taxidermy, and plenty of propaganda. Highlights include evocative photos of the Ma, K'Ho and Churu people and displays of their traditional dress, musical instruments and ceremonial altars. Check out the remarkable stone xylophones dating back more than 3000 years.

Linh Son Pagoda ARCHITECTURE
(Chua Linh Son; 120 Đ Nguyen Van Troi; ☺ dawn-dusk) Built in 1938, the Linh Son Pagoda is a lovely ochre-coloured building that fuses French and Chinese architecture. The giant bell is said to be made of bronze mixed with gold, with its great weight making it too heavy for thieves to carry off.

Dalat Flower Gardens GARDENS
(Vuon Hoa Thanh Pho; ☑ 0263-382 2151; Đ Tran Nhan Tong; adult/child 50,000/25,000d; ☺ 7.30am-4pm) These gardens were established in 1966

and include hydrangeas, fuchsias and orchids, the last of these in shaded buildings to the left of the entrance. Like any good Vietnamese park, the gardens have been embellished with a riot of topiary.

Dalat Cathedral
CATHEDRAL

(Đ Tran Phu; ⊙ Mass 5.15am & 5.15pm Mon-Fri, 5.15pm Sat, 5.15am, 8.30am & 6pm Sun) The gingerbread-style Dalat Cathedral was built between 1931 and 1942 for use by French residents and holidaymakers. The cross on the spire is topped by a weathercock, 47m above the ground. The church is irregularly open outside Mass times.

Linh Quang Pagoda
BUDDHIST TEMPLE

(Chua Linh Quang; 133 Đ Hai Ba Trung; ⊙ dawn-dusk) Flanked by enormous coiling concrete dragons rearing out of a pond, and with a fabulously decorative outdoor tableau featuring the young Buddha atop a lotus flower, this is Dalat's oldest and most colourful pagoda. Founded in 1931 it had to be extensively restored after the American War.

Xuan Huong Lake
LAKE

Created by a dam in 1919, this banana-shaped lake was named after an anti-authoritarian 17th-century Vietnamese poet. It has become a popular icon of Dalat and a magnet for joggers and honeymooners. The lake can be circumnavigated on a scenic 7km path.

⊙ Around Dalat

Sights outside town are most easily visited as out-and-back trips, preferably with your own transport. Linking them neatly together isn't easy.

Truc Lam Pagoda
BUDDHIST TEMPLE

(Ho Tuyen Lam; Truc Lam Yen Tu; ⊙ dawn-dusk) FREE The Truc Lam Pagoda enjoys a hilltop setting and has immaculately tended flower and bonsai gardens. It's an active monastery, though the grounds frequently teem with tour groups. Be sure to arrive by cable car (1 way/return adult 60,000/80,000d, child 40,000/50,000d; ⊙ 7.30-11.30am & 1-4.30pm Mon-Fri, 7.30am-4.30pm Sat & Sun), which soars over majestic pine forests; the terminus is 3km south of Dalat centre, up a short road next to the long-distance bus station.

The pagoda can also be reached by road via turn-offs from Hwy 20.

K'Ho Coffee
FARM

(⌨ 0989 722 184; www.khocoffee.com; Lat Village; ⊙ by appointment 8am-4pm Mon-Sat) ⏴ This coffee farm has been in the family of Rolan since the 1860s. It's part of a K'Ho coffee-growing cooperative that ensures profits directly support K'Ho minority farmers. The beans are arabica, including varieties grown in Africa, which are rarely found in Vietnam. If you call Josh and Rolan in advance, you can stop by to see the plantation and pick up some Fair Trade, locally roasted beans.

It also stocks beautiful traditional weavings done by the K'Ho women in the community. Predominantly blue and intricately embroidered, each takes weeks to complete; prices start from 1,200,000d.

The farm is 10km north of Dalat near Lat, a collection of nine hamlets made up of Chill, Ma and K'Ho people and worth a visit.

Datanla Falls
WATERFALL

(adult/child 30,000/15,000d; ⊙ 7am-5pm) This is the closest waterfall to Dalat, so expect crowds. You can reach the cascade (which is pretty but quite modest) either by walking down or taking a short bobsled-on-rails ride (adult/child 80,000/40,000d). A longer alpine roller coaster (adult/child return 150,000/80,000d) also runs from a few hundred metres away.

Datanla is 7km south of Dalat. Take Hwy 20 and turn right about 200m past the turn-off to Truc Lam Pagoda and Tuyen Lam Lake.

Linh Phuoc Pagoda
BUDDHIST TEMPLE

(Trai Mat; ⊙ dawn-dusk) This complex comprises a large prayer hall, a dragon made from more than 10,000 beer bottles, a seven-storied pagoda, a massive Bodhisattva of Compassion made from flowers and an adjoining hall with an impressive standing Bodhisattva. Everything is covered in enough coloured tiles to give kitsch a bad name. Pretty it's not, but it is certainly impressive in its extravagance.

It's 10km east of Dalat centre, near Trai Mat, and best visited after a scenic train ride from Dalat's old train station.

Bidoup Nui Ba National Park
NATIONAL PARK

(⌨ 0944 125 715, 0263-374 7449; www.bidoupnui-ba.gov.vn; adult/child 40,000/20,000d) Occupying a densely forested highland plateau, this little-visited national park encompasses coniferous woodlands, bamboo groves and grasslands at altitudes between 650m and 2288m. It is also home to various primates, black bears and the vampire flying frog. Possible hikes include Thien Thai Waterfall (3.5km), Lang Biang Peak (9km) and an

DAMBRI FALLS

One of the highest (90m), most magnificent and easily accessible waterfalls in Vietnam, **Dambri Falls** (☑0263-375 1517; www.dambri.com.vn; adult/child 200,000/120,000d; ☺7am-5pm) are worth visiting even in dry season. For some incredible views, ride the vertical cable car (more of an elevator, really), or trudge up the steep path, to the top of the falls.

A second path leads down some steep stairs to the front of the falls for more great views, and carries on down to the smaller Dasara Falls, or you can take the alpine coaster from the centre at the entrance to the falls. The surrounding complex includes a hotel, Ferris wheel and water slides.

The falls are 130km southwest of Dalat. The road to them branches off Hwy 20, 18km north of Bao Loc. Buses travelling between Dalat and Ho Chi Minh City will drop you at the junction. From there, you'll have to negotiate with a *xe om* driver for a ride to the falls. Expect to pay 150,000d.

overnight camping trip to Bidoup mountain. The park is 50km north of Dalat and most people visit on a motorbike tour. English-speaking staff can be elusive.

Elephant Falls   WATERFALL
(Thac Voi; admission 20,000d;   ☺7.30am-5pm) Named after a large rock that allegedly resembles an elephant's head, these powerful curved falls are reached by a steep ascent along uneven, very slippery stone steps with intermittent railings. You can squeeze through a cave to get behind the falls and be doused with bracing spray. The falls are near Nam Ban village, 30km southwest of Dalat.

Local buses (20,000d, one hour) leave for Nam Ban from behind Dalat's main square every 40 minutes or so between 6am and 6pm.

☞ Tours

Adventure outfits offer trekking, mountain biking, kayaking, canyoning and abseiling, as well as downhill bike rides to the coast. Compare prices, but make sure you're comfortable with all the equipment and safety procedures. Three tourists died while canyoning at Datania in 2016.

★**Phat Tire Ventures**   ADVENTURE
(☑0263-382 9422; www.ptv-vietnam.com; 109 Đ Nguyen Van Troi; ☺8am-7pm) A highly professional and experienced operator with mountain-biking trips from US$40, trekking from US$39, kayaking from US$39 and canyoning (US$72), plus rapelling (US$57) and white-water rafting (US$67) in the rainy season. Multiday cycling trips are available.

Pine Track Adventures   ADVENTURE
(☑0263-383 1916; www.pinetrackadventures.com; 72b Đ Truong Cong Dinh; ☺8am-8.30pm) Run by an enthusiastic and experienced local

team, this operator offers canyoning (from US$55), white-water rafting (from US$68), trekking (from US$35), cycling (from US$41) and some excellent multisport packages. A six-day bike tour from Dalat to Hoi An costs from US$650.

Dalat Happy Tours   FOOD & DRINK
(☑0336 546 450; www.dalathappytours.com; street-food tour per person US$22) After all the active exertions around Dalat, replenish your calories by taking an entertaining, nightly street-food tour with friendly Lao and his guides. Start from the central Hoa Binh cinema and proceed to sample *banh xeo* (filled pancakes), buffalo-tail hotpot, delectable grilled skewers, 'Dalat pizza', rabbit curry, hot rice wine and more. Food costs are included.

**Groovy Gecko
Adventure Tours**   ADVENTURE
(☑0263-383 6521; www.groovygeckotours.net; 65 Đ Truong Cong Dinh; ☺7.30am-8.30pm) Long-running agency that offers a unique (for Dalat) canyoning adventure that includes abseiling down a remote 65m-high waterfall (US$72) at Dasar. Also does mountain-bike trips (from US$35) and day hikes (from US$28), as well as a one-day downhill cycle to Nha Trang or quieter Mui Ne (US$75).

☆ Festivals & Events

Dalat Flower Festival   CULTURAL
(☺Dec-Jan) Taking place every two years, occasionally annually, between late December and early January, this festival celebrates and promotes the abundance of flowers grown around Dalat. Events happen at a number of venues, including Dalat Flower Gardens (p285) and around Xuan Huong Lake, and go beyond flowers to feature

fashion shows and art. The festival attracts many domestic tourists, so finding a hotel room at this time can be hard.

🛏 Sleeping

Dalat has an ever-growing number of accommodation options covering every possible budget. The temperate climate means air-conditioning isn't really necessary.

★ **Villa Doc May**   GUESTHOUSE $

(📞 0263-382 5754, 0363 978 225; villadocmaydalat@gmail.com; 16/3 Đ Nam Ky Khoi Nghia; r 450,000-850,000d; ❄🛜) More a homestay than a guesthouse, with just four individually decorated rooms, all comfortable, as well as pleasant communal areas and an upstairs Middle Eastern–style shisha cafe. The cheaper ground-floor rooms don't have windows but are still pleasant. Owner Yom is helpful with restaurant suggestions and scooter rental. Find it up a steep alley off the street, on the left.

An overspill hotel a few doors further down offers brighter, spacious rooms (double 350,000d to 450,000d) with balcony but less of a homestay vibe.

★ **Mooka's Home**   HOSTEL $

(📞 0932 579 752; mookahome@gmail.com; 2 Co Loa; dm 105,000d, r 290,000-400,000d; ❄@🛜) Big and light dorms come with sparkly bathrooms at this popular place, and there are five spacious private rooms. There's a roof terrace and a downstairs communal area. Group dinners or barbecues (120,000d, every other day) take place on the roof terrace and everyone gets a free evening beer. The friendly staff can arrange tours, bus tickets, motorbike rental and laundry.

Dalat Friendly Fun Hostel   HOSTEL $

(📞 0973 393 891; dalatfriendlyfun@gmail.com; 18 Mac Dinh Chi; dm incl breakfast US$5; 🛜) This place lives up to its name with a warm welcome and helpful staff who organise nightly group dinners (US$3), as well as recommending decent tour operators. Dorms are huge and bright, with curtained beds and inside bathrooms.

Villa Pink House   HOTEL $

(📞 0263-381 5667; www.facebook.com/VillaPinkHouseDalat; 7/8 Đ Hai Thuong; r standard/deluxe 450,000/500,000d; @🛜) A well-run, family-owned place in a quiet location down an alley across from Dalat Hospital. Rooms are comfortable, all have balconies and some have great views. It's managed by the affable

Mr Rot, who can arrange day trips to the countryside around Dalat.

Dreams Hotel   HOTEL $$

(📞 0263-383 3748; www.dreamshoteldalat.vn; 138-140 Đ Phan Dinh Phung; r incl breakfast US$30-35; ❄❋🛜) This reliable place runs a couple of hotels in town. All rooms have high-quality mattresses and decent bathrooms, and some have balconies. There's a free Jacuzzi, a steam room and a sauna from 4pm to 7pm. The only downer is the location on a traffic-heavy street, but the double glazing works well. It also has some long-term apartments.

Tulip Hotel I   HOTEL $$

(📞 0263-351 0995; www.tuliphotelgroup.com; 26-28 Ba Thang Hai; d 430,000-980,000d; ❄🛜) Reliable midrange choice in the heart of Dalat. The best rooms are spacious and light, the cheapest are small and without much natural light, but all are well kept with comfortable beds and a central location. It's on a noisy street, so shun the balcony and ask for a room at the back.

★ **Ana Mandara Villas Dalat**   BOUTIQUE HOTEL $$$

(📞 0263-355 5888; www.anamandara-resort.com; Đ Le Lai; r 2,000,000-3,000,000d; ❄❋🛜) Elegant, secluded property spread across seven lovingly restored French-colonial villas in the peaceful western suburbs. Finished in period furnishings, which can appear a little spartan compared to modern-day ones, the villas have the option of private dining. Most come with an ornamental fireplace and all have wonderful views. The spa, pool and restaurant are all excellent.

★ **Villa Vista**   BOUTIQUE HOTEL $$$

(📞 0263-351 2468; www.facebook.com/villavistadalat; 40 Ngo Thi Sy, Phuong 4; r US$65-95; ❄🛜) Look down from this villa on the hill and the whole of Dalat opens up in the valley. There are only four rooms, decorated in 19th-century French fashion (albeit with flat-screen TVs and rain showers). Delightful owners Tim and Huong prepare remarkable breakfasts, and they can hook you up with Easy Riders or motorbike rental and will share their Dalat knowledge. Discounts of 30% in the low season.

Dalat Palace   HISTORIC HOTEL $$$

(📞 0263-382 5444; www.royaldl.com; 2 Đ Tran Phu; r 6,200,000-7,800,000d; ❄❋🛜) With unimpeded views of Xuan Huong Lake, this grande dame of Dalat hotels has vintage

THE ONGOING BATTLE FOR THE HIGHLANDS

The uneasy relationship in the central highlands between the hill tribes and the Vietnamese majority dates back centuries, when Vietnamese expansion pushed the tribes up into the mountains. While French-colonial rule recognised the hill tribes as a separate community, known as Montagnards, South Vietnam later attempted to assimilate them through such means as abolishing traditional schools and courts, prohibiting the construction of stilt houses and appropriating their land.

In response the minority peoples formed nationalist guerrilla movements, the best-known of which was the Front Unifié de Lutte des Races Opprimées (FULRO) or the United Front for the Struggle of the Oppressed Races. In the 1960s the hill tribes were courted by the US as allies against North Vietnam, and were trained by the CIA and US Special Forces.

The hill tribes paid dearly for this after the war, when government policies brought more ethnic Vietnamese into the highlands, along with clampdowns on education in native languages and religious freedom (often, hill-tribe peoples belong to unauthorised churches). Many of the minorities have been relocated to modern villages, partly to discourage slash-and-burn agriculture. It also speeds up assimilation.

In 2001 and 2004 protests erupted, notably in Gia Lai and Dak Lak provinces (Pleiku and Buon Ma Thuot), which the government quickly and, according to human rights organisations, violently suppressed. International human rights groups point to more deaths than the government admits to, and thousands of hill-tribe people fled to Cambodia or the US afterwards. What happens in the central highlands all too often remains behind closed doors, both for outsiders and international observers, and also for many ordinary Vietnamese. Talk to any organisation that works with the minority people and you'll hear a story of continuing government surveillance, harassment and religious persecution, with tensions remaining over land rights especially.

Citroën cars in its sweeping driveway, and lashings of wood panelling and period class. The opulence of French-colonial life has been splendidly preserved – claw-foot tubs, fireplaces, chandeliers and oil paintings – though in low season the cavernous, silent hallways feel like something out of *The Shining*. Look for online deals.

The hotel was originally built as the Lang Bien Palace Hotel in 1922 and was restored in the 1990s by Larry Hillblom, then joint-owner of DHL.

Dalat Hotel du Parc HOTEL **$$$**

(☑ 0263-382 5777; www.royaldl.com; 15 Đ Tran Phu; r 1,000,000-2,000,000d, ste 2,500,000d; ❄ ☎) A respectfully refurbished 1932 building that offers a dash of colonial-era style at enticing prices. The grand lobby lift sets the tone and the rooms, while looking their age, include some period furnishings and polished wooden floors. It's bristling with facilities, from a spa and fitness centre to a decent restaurant. Deluxe rooms are worth the extra money.

🍴 Eating

Dalat's restaurants offer everything from noodles to traditional highland food and an increasing number of decent international choices. The city has a wealth of vegetables plucked from the hectares of greenhouses surrounding the city. Look out for fantastic avocado ice cream and shakes.

Toasted rice-paper *banh trang nuong* (often called 'Dalat pizza') can be found on many street corners. It's tasty, though some people prefer it without the processed cheese.

⭐ **Tau Cao Wonton Noodles** NOODLES **$**

(☑ 0263-382 0104; 217 Đ Phan Dinh Phung; noodles 40,000d; ⊙ 6am-8pm) This humble eatery is famed throughout Dalat and is always heaving with locals, who come for the noodle wonton soup. It's served with thin slices of pork on top and a sprinkling of mincemeat. Add chilli, lime and bean sprouts to taste and you're good to go. Classic Asian street eats. No English spoken.

⭐ **Trong Dong** VIETNAMESE **$**

(☑ 0263-382 1889; 220 Đ Phan Dinh Phung; meals 80,000-150,000d; ⊙ 11am-9pm; ☎) Intimate restaurant, run by a very hospitable team, where the creative menu includes spins on Vietnamese delights such as shrimp paste on a sugar-cane stick, beef wrapped in *la lot* leaf, and fiery lemongrass-and-chilli squid. The English menu makes life easy.

Quan Trang
VIETNAMESE $

(☑0263-382 5043; 15 Đ Tang Bat Ho; dishes 35,000d; ⊙10.30am-8pm) The local speciality *banh uot long ga* here is among the best in town. The rice noodles are saucy not soupy and the fresh shredded chicken, herbs and chilli lift the dish. Delicious – people certainly aren't here for the plastic decor. Several other places nearby offer the same dish.

Goc Ha Thanh
VIETNAMESE $

(☑0263-355 3369; 53 Đ Truong Cong Dinh; meals 55,000-110,000d; ⊙noon-10pm; 🛜🌱) Casual, popular, foreigner-friendly place with bamboo furnishings run by a welcoming Hanoi couple. Strong on dishes such as coconut curry, mango chicken, fish clay pots, tofu stir-fries and the signature artichoke and stewed-pork soup (180,000d). Plenty of vegetarian options.

One More Cafe
CAFE $

(☑0129 934 1835; www.facebook.com/pg/one morecafe77; 77 Đ Hai Ba Trung; meals 85,000-115,000d; ⊙8am-9pm, closed Wed; 🛜🌱) Comfy chairs, eclectically decorated peach walls and a glass display full of house-baked cakes and seven-seed bread greet you at this cosy, Aussie-owned cafe. The menu offers Western classics – burgers, soups, sandwiches and Caesar salad – as well as a recommended all-day breakfast. Fine for a coffee, tea or smoothie, too.

Thai Corner
THAI $

(Đ Le Dai Hanh; meals 120,000-180,000d; ⊙10am-10pm) Authentic and tasty, this place serves up a great papaya salad, tom yum soup and the best green curry we've had in Vietnam, with picturesque views over Dalat's night market below. Service is excellent. The open-air restaurant can get chilly at night, so bring a layer.

★ Restaurant Ichi
JAPANESE $$

(☑0263-355 5098; 17-19 Đ Hoang Dieu; rolls 60,000-130,000d, meals 150,000-260,000d; ⊙5.30-10pm Tue-Sun, closed every 2nd Tue) Dalat's only truly genuine Japanese restaurant is compact, with subdued lighting and jazz in the background. Spicy tuna rolls, chicken yakitori and tempura are all fantastic, the bento boxes are a bargain and there's even *natto* (fermented soybeans) for aficionados. Perch at the bar to watch sushi-master Tomo at work.

Ganesh Indian Restaurant
INDIAN $$

(☑0263-355 9599; www.ganesh.vn; 1f Đ Nam Ky Khoi Nghia; meals 110,000-150,000d; 🛜🌱) All your subcontinental favourites are here – tandoori chicken, South Indian coconut curries, huge nan breads and set-meal thalis (180,000d to 210,000d) – and they're all excellent. Try the boneless chicken *kadahi* (a tomato and onion sauce) – it's not on the menu, but they'll make it and it's delicious. If it's too cramped inside, sit at the outdoor terrace bar.

Oz Burger
BURGERS $$

(☑0902 475 923; 61 Đ Ba Thang Hai; meals 95,000-190,000d; ⊙8am-10pm) Popular with backpackers, Asian tourists and even a few locals, this Australian-run joint isn't cheap but serves up delicious burgers, along with toasted sandwiches and vegetarian options. Add fries and a beer for 60,000d.

Le Chalet Dalat
VIETNAMESE $$

(☑0967 659 788; 12b Huynh Thuc Khang; meals 100,000-150,000d; ⊙9am-9pm Mon-Fri, 7am-9pm Sat & Sun; 🛜) Strategically located almost opposite Dalat's most popular tourist sight, Hang Nga Crazy House (p283), this partially open-air, artfully decorated garden bistro makes a useful lunch or breakfast stop. The menu ranges across Vietnamese classics, with healthy soups and a great papaya, mango and peanut salad, and a separate menu for shared dishes.

V Cafe
INTERNATIONAL $$

(☑0263-352 0215; www.vcafedalatvietnam.com; 1/1 Đ Bui Thi Xuan; meals 135,000d; ⊙8am-10.30pm; 🛜🌱) This bistro-style place is a key hang-out for Dalat expats. It serves international cuisine, such as a Vietnamese grapefruit salad with peanuts and shrimp, veg lasagne, beef goulash and Mexican-style quesadillas, with lots of veg options and good breakfasts. There's a covered terrace with pub tables and mellow live piano in the evenings, and happy hour from 4pm to 6pm.

Nhat Ly
VIETNAMESE $$

(☑0263-382 1651; 88 Đ Phan Dinh Phung; meals 80,000-190,000d; ⊙10am-10pm) This place serves hearty highland meals on tartan tablecloths (something of a Dalat restaurant theme), including sumptuous hotpots, grilled meats and seafood. Try the steamed crab in beer. Draws plenty of locals – always a good sign.

Dalat Train Cafe
INTERNATIONAL $$

(☑0263-381 6365; www.dalattrainvilla.com; 1 Đ Quang Trung; meals 80,000-160,000d; ⊙8am-

10pm; 🐦📶) Calling all trainspotters! Don't miss the opportunity to step inside this lovingly resorted French-era railway carriage for a meal in a unique setting, surrounded by images of trains worldwide and serenaded by train-themed 1950s blues music. The blue-cheese burger, spicy tofu and veg lasagne are all sound choices.

From Dalat train station, turn right, walk up the hill, look for the sign on the left and curve around the alleyway.

★**Le Rabelais**　　　　FRENCH $$$
(☑0263-382 5444; www.royaldl.com; 2 Đ Tran Phu; meals 400,000-1,600,000d; ⊘7am-10pm) The signature restaurant at the Dalat Palace (p288) is *the* colonial-style destination, with the grandest of dining rooms and a spectacular terrace that looks down to the lake shore. Set dinner menus (1,300,000d to 1,700,000d) offer the full experience. Otherwise treat yourself to flawless à la carte dishes, such as seared duck breast with orange or roast rack of lamb. There's little for vegetarians.

Alternatively come for an indulgent afternoon tea (350,000d) on the terrace between 2.30pm and 5pm.

Ming　　　　　　　CHINESE $$$
(☑0263-381 3816; 7 Tran Hung Dao; meals 150,000-850,000d; ⊘10am-2pm & 5-9pm) Refined Chinese restaurant housed in a nicely restored, colonial-era villa, with lake views from its terrace and a pleasant garden. Scroll through the iPad menu to select dishes such as dim sum, Peking duck, pork ribs with honey sauce, fried beef on iron plate, and flower crab with ginger and scallion. The set meals (240,000d to 620,000d) are good value.

🍷 **Drinking & Nightlife**

Coffee houses are everywhere here. Dalat wine can be found all over town (and elsewhere in Vietnam). The reds are pleasantly light, while the whites tend to be heavy on the oak. Dalat has a limited but energetic night scene with bars clustered together on Đ Truong Cong Dinh, as well as a number of live-music venues.

★**La Viet Coffee**　　　　COFFEE
(☑0263-398 1189; www.facebook.com/coffeela viet; 200 Đ Nguyen Cong Tru; coffee 35,000-60,000d; ⊘7am-10.30pm; 🐦) Caffeine fiends will want to head to this unique mix of coffee shop, farm and factory. In a warehouse-like

building with industrial design touches, and surrounded outside by coffee plants, you can either sip the excellent brews on offer at a table or go on a 10-minute tour of the facility and have the coffee-roasting and -washing processes explained to you.

The shop sells everything connected to coffee, from beans to Vietnamese-style *phin* filters. It also serves sandwiches, waffles and special coffee cocktails. It's located in Dalat's northern suburbs.

District I　　　　　CRAFT BEER
(34 Nguyen Chi Thanh; ⊘3pm-midnight) This two-storied bar offers a dozen craft beers on tap, mostly from Saigon's Rooster Beers, along with bottles from Belgium, Germany and the Czech Republic, in a hip, welcoming atmosphere.

100 Roofs Café　　　　　BAR
(Duong Len Trang; 57 Đ Phan Boi Chau; ⊘8am-midnight; 🐦) A surreal drinking experience. The owners claim Gandalf and his hobbit friends have drunk here, and the labyrinth of rooms with multiple nooks and crannies, multilevel grottoes and fantastical sculptures does resemble a Middle Earth location. A happy hour (6pm to 8pm) and Wonderland-like rooftop garden add to the wide-eyed fun. Fittingly, it's also called the Maze Bar.

Fog Bar　　　　　　BAR
(76 Đ Truong Cong Dinh; ⊘4pm-midnight; 🐦) Dalat's hipster hang-out (for alcohol imbibers, anyway), with a DJ every night in the small dark interior and a nicer outside terrace at which to sip pretty good cocktails (from 70,000d). It's very much a local scene, but foreigners are welcomed, too.

Bicycle Up Cafe　　　　COFFEE
(82 Đ Truong Cong Dinh; ⊘7am-10pm) Is it an antique store? Is it a cafe? This tiny corner beguiles with its riot of old bicycle parts, bird cages, vintage telephones and antique pianos. Find a corner to perch in to sip some seriously good coffee and smoothies.

☆ **Entertainment**

★**Escape Bar**　　　　　LIVE MUSIC
(☑0263-369 5666; www.facebook.com/The EscapeBarDalat; 94 Đ Bui Thi Xuan, Golf Valley Hotel; ⊘10am-midnight; 🐦) Expect top-notch improvised covers of Hendrix, the Eagles, the Doors and other classics at this live-music bar owned by blues guitarist Curtis King; travelling musicians are

welcome to jam. Food is served and there's a pool table and spacious terrace. Happy hour is from 6pm to 8pm; music starts at around 9.30pm.

ℹ Information

Lam Dong General Hospital (☏ 0263-382 1369; 4 Đ Pham Ngoc Thach; ☺24hr) Emergency medical care.

Main Post Office (14 Đ Tran Phu; ☺7am-6pm)

Vietcombank (6 Đ Nguyen Thi Minh Khai; ☺7.30am-3pm Mon-Fri, to 1pm Sat) Changes travellers cheques and foreign currencies.

ℹ Getting There & Away

AIR

Lien Khuong Airport (☏ 0263-384 3373) is 30km south of Dalat. There are regular flights with **Vietnam Airlines** (☏ 0263-383 3499; www.vietnamairlines.com; 2 Đ Ho Tung Mau), VietJet Air and Jetstar, including five daily to Ho Chi Minh City, four daily to Hanoi and four flights a week to Danang.

BUS

Dalat is a major stop for open-tour buses. **Sinh Tourist** (☏ 0263-382 2663; www.thesinhtourist.vn; 22 Đ Bui Thi Xuan; ☺8am-7pm) has daily buses at 7.30am and 1pm to Nha Trang and at 8am and 9.30pm to Ho Chi Minh City, and offers city tours.

Dalat's **long-distance bus station** (Ben Xe Lien Tinh Da Lat; Đ 3 Thang 4) is 1.5km south of Xuan Huong Lake, and is dominated by reputable **Phuong Trang** (Futabus; www.futabus.vn) buses that offer free hotel pick-ups and drop-offs and cover all main regional destinations.

CAR & MOTORCYCLE

From Nha Trang, high road 27C offers spectacular views – a dream for motorcyclists and cyclists – hitting 1700m at Hon Giao mountain and following the breathtaking 33km Khanh Le pass.

Another dramatic drive from the coast is from Phan Rang via Ngoan Muc Pass, 43km southeast of Dalat. On a clear day you can see the ocean, 55km away.

Hwy 27 to Buon Ma Thuot is scenic but pot-holed in places. A major new road is being built between Dalat and Buon Ma Thuot that bypasses the airport.

ℹ Getting Around

TO/FROM THE AIRPORT

The Vietnam Airlines bus between Lien Khuong Airport and Dalat (40,000d, 40 minutes) is timed around flights. It leaves from in front of the Ngoc Phat Hotel (10 Đ Ho Tung Mau) two hours before each departure. Your lodgings can organise to have it pick you up, but include an extra 30-minute buffer for the bus to pick everybody else up, too!

Taxi companies in Dalat offer fixed 180,000d to 250,000d fares to the airport, which is much cheaper than a metered or Grab taxi. Your hotel can book this.

BICYCLE

The hilly terrain makes it sweaty work getting around Dalat. Several hotels rent out bicycles (100,000d per day) and some provide them free to guests.

CAR

Daily rentals (with driver) start at US$50.

MOTORCYCLE

For short trips around town (around 20,000d), xe om drivers can be found around the Central Market area. Motorbike hire starts at 100,000d per day.

TAXI

Try the ubiquitous and reliable green **Mai Linh** (☏ 0263-352 1111; www.mailinh.vn) taxis, or use Grab.

BUSES FROM DALAT

DESTINATION	COST (D)	TIME (HR)	FREQUENCY	DISTANCE (KM)
Buon Ma Thuot	180,000	5	4 daily	200
Can Tho	360,000	12	7am & 8pm	461
Danang	285,000	12	5 daily between 2-6pm	660
HCMC	240,000	7	hourly 6am-midnight	306
Hue	345,000	14	4pm	760
Kon Tum	270,000	10	6am & 7pm	272
Nha Trang	135,000	4	6 daily 7am-5pm	136
Pleiku	240,000	9	6am & 7pm	760

THE HO CHI MINH TRAIL

This legendary route was not one but many paths that formed the major supply link for the North Vietnamese and VC during the American War. Supplies and troops leaving from the port of Vinh in north-central Vietnam headed inland along mountainous jungle paths, crossing in and out of Laos, and eventually arrived near Saigon. With all the secrecy, propaganda and confusion regarding the trail, it's hard to say how long it was in full – estimates range from over 5500km (suggested by the US military) to more than 13,000km (claimed by the North Vietnamese).

While elephants were initially used to cross the Truong Son Mountains into Laos, eventually it was sheer human power that shouldered supplies down the trail, sometimes supplemented by ponies, bicycles or trucks. Travelling from the 17th parallel to the vicinity of Saigon took about six months in the mid-1960s; years later, with a more complex network of paths, the journey took only six weeks, but it was still hard going.

Each person started out with a 36kg pack of supplies, as well as a few personal items (eg a tent, a spare uniform and snake antivenin). What lay ahead was a rugged and mountainous route, plagued by flooding, disease and the constant threat of American bombing. At their peak, more than 500 American air strikes hit the trail every day and more ordnance was dropped on it than was used in all the theatres of war in WWII.

Despite these shock-and-awe tactics and the elaborate electronic sensors placed along the McNamara Line, the trail was never blocked. Most of it has returned to the jungle, but you can still follow sections of the trail today. Note that this is mostly the more developed trail from the early 1970s, as the older trail was over the border in Laos. The **Ho Chi Minh Highway**, a scenic mountain road running along the spine of the country, is the easiest way to get a fix. Starting near Hanoi, it passes through some popular tourist destinations and former battlefields, including the Phong Nha caves, Khe Sanh, Aluoi, Kon Tum and Buon Ma Thuot on its way to Saigon. The most spectacular sections include the roller-coaster ride through Phong Nha-Ke Bang National Park, where looming karsts are cloaked in jungle.

Travel this route by car (or 4WD), motorbike or even bicycle if you're training for the King of the Mountains jersey, or arrange a tour through the Easy Riders (http://easyridertrips.com) in Dalat or one of the leading motorbike touring companies in Hanoi. **Explore Indochina** (Map p64; 0913 093 159; www.exploreindochina.com; 27 P Hang Trong, Hoan Kiem district, Hanoi) specialises in trail tours. Hoi An Motorbike Adventures (p211) offers shorter rides along sections between Hoi An and Phong Nha and a loop from Hoi An to Hue via the Hai Van Pass.

Lak Lake

The largest natural body of water in the central highlands, Lak Lake (Ho Lak) is surrounded by rural scenery. You can get paddled out onto the blue, reed-covered expanse in a long boat. While the lake is pretty at sunrise and sunset, the real draws here are the three M'nong villages scattered around it.

Accommodation is centred on **Le** village, which is really now a neighbourhood of Lien Son town. Nearby **Jun** village and slightly more removed **M'lieng** village (3km from Le) on the southwestern shore are more traditional and can be reached by boat or dirt road.

Unfortunately all hotels and tour agencies here offer elephant rides, which are popular with the domestic tourists who make up most visitors to Lak Lake. We strongly advise against riding elephants, as it is detrimental to their health.

 Activities

Cafe Duc Mai can arrange a day hike that takes in a waterfall, a local village and coffee and pepper farms with a guide, lunch and transport for US$65 for two people, and also rents bicycles (50,000d per half-day). Both Duc Mai and Van Long can organise short canoe paddles (200,000d per hour).

Sleeping & Eating

Van Long HOTEL $
(0262-358 5659; www.dulichvanlong.com; 3 Y Jut, Buon Le; mattress in longhouse 100,000d, r 300,000-350,000d;) Right by the lake, this is the most comfortable place to stay. Rooms are fresh and clean, and the corner VIP rooms have lake views. Alternatively you can bed down in its upmarket longhouse, which has dorm mattresses on the floor with mozzie nets and fans. There's a pleasant on-site restaurant (meals 80,000d).

Cafe Duc Mai
VIETNAMESE $

(☎ 0905 371 633, 0262-358 6280; ducmaicoffee@
yahoo.com; Y Jut, Buon Le; meals 100,000d; 🛜)
Run by Mr Duc and his English-speaking
daughter and son, this place serves tasty local spreads; there's no menu, just say what
you like or don't like. The cafe can also arrange a mattress in a traditional longhouse
(100,000d per night) a few doors away or
homestays in neighbouring villages.

ℹ️ Getting There & Away

Five daily sleeper buses connecting Dalat
(180,000d, four hours) and Buon Ma Thuot pass
through Lien Son, a 15-minute walk from the
lake. There are also hourly local buses (No 12)
between Lien Son and Buon Ma Thuot (25,000d,
one hour) and plusher limousine minibuses
(35,000d). All tour agencies in Buon Ma Thuot
offer day tours.

Buon Ma Thuot
☎ 0262 / POP 211,891 / ELEV 451M

Buon Ma Thuot can trace its origins back
to a simple rural settlement: the Ede name
translates as 'Thuot's father's village'. But
Buon Ma Thuot (pronounced 'boon me tote')
has long outgrown its rustic origins and is
now a thoroughly modern city. That's largely down to its coffee, which was introduced
by the French between 1915 and 1920 and is

THE MATRILINEAL EDE

The Ede people of Dak Lak province
are unusual for their matrilineal family
structure and the powerful position that
Ede women wield in the family. Young
women generally choose their husband,
who then moves into their wife's family
longhouse, which is owned by the family
matriarch. Children take the mother's
surname, and family property is passed
down from mother to daughter (sons get
no inheritance), giving the women important economic power. The wife is generally responsible for the family budget.
The centuries-old matrilineal system
is changing in the face of Vietnam's
rapid economic transitions, but remains
largely intact in remoter rural areas.

The Ede are also the largest of Vietnam's minority ethnic groups living in
the United States, largely due to their
role fighting alongside US troops during
the American War.

---

some of the best in Vietnam. Surrounding
Dak Lak province exports more coffee than
any other in Vietnam.

Most travellers stop here en route to
nearby attractions: Yok Don National Park
(p297), a few striking waterfalls and heaps
of minority villages that are home to 44
ethnic groups, the dominant ones being the
Ede, Jarai, M'nong and Lao.

◎ Sights

⭐**Ethnographic Museum**
MUSEUM
(Bao Tang Tinh Daklak; Đ Y Nong; admission
30,000d; ☺8am-5pm Tue-Sun) This excellent
museum takes you through the history of
Dak Lak province, from stone tools and
bronze burial drums to the American War
and its aftermath, written from the North
Vietnamese perspective. The ethnography
section introduces the matriarchal Ede,
M'nong and Jarai people through outstanding photography, displays of traditional
clothing, musical instruments and ritual objects such as the buffalo sacrifice pole. Entry
is from the north side.

Victory Monument
MONUMENT
This monument commemorates the events
of 10 March 1975 when VC and North Vietnamese troops liberated the city. It's an interesting piece of socialist-realist sculpture,
consisting of a column supporting a central
group of figures holding a flag, with a modernist arch forming a rainbow over a concrete replica tank.

🎆 Festivals & Events

Coffee Festival
CULTURAL
(☺Mar) With Buon Ma Thuot home to some
of the finest coffee in Vietnam, this biennial
festival – next held in 2023 – is designed to
promote the local beans and normally takes
place in March at various venues around
town. There are music and stilt-walking performances, while many coffee shops offer
free coffee during the festival.

🛏️ Sleeping

Ngoc Mai Guesthouse
HOTEL $
(☎0262-385 3406; www.chdtravel.com; 9
Nguyen Binh; s 190,000d, d 250,000-270,000d;
❄🛜) It's not a hostel, but this cheapie
attracts international travellers with its
English- and French-speaking family who
can arrange tours of the area and onward
transport. Rooms are plain but clean (the
singles are small), with decent mattresses,

Buon Ma Thuot

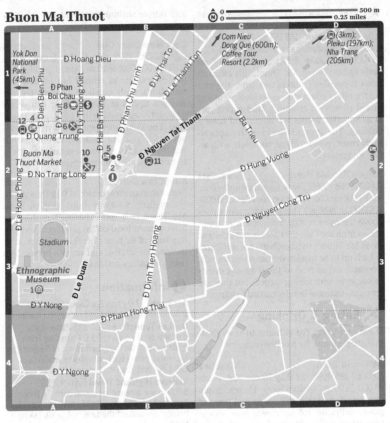

Buon Ma Thuot

and are fine for a night or two. Motorbikes (75,000/150,000d per half/full day) can be rented. Only the more expensive streetside rooms with balcony have much natural light.

Eden Hotel   HOTEL $
(☏0262-384 0055; www.edenhotelbmt.com. vn; 228 Đ Nguyen Cong Tru; r 350,000-650,000d;

⌗ ☏) This budget joint is popular with Easy Riders and their clients. Rooms are characterless, but clean and big enough, though ask for a back-block room with shared balcony and view, rather than the windowless cheaper rooms. Staff are helpful and some English is spoken. It's a 20-minute walk from the centre of town.

★ **Coffee Tour Resort** DESIGN HOTEL $$
(Legend Coffee Resort; ☑ 0262-357 5575; www.
coffeetourresort.com; 149-153 Ly Thai To; r incl
breakfast standard/superior/deluxe 580,000/
650,000/1,100,000d; ❄ ☎) Something of an
oasis in busy Buon Ma Thuot, this efficient
hotel a couple of kilometres from the city
centre offers comfortable, spotless, sensibly
priced rooms set around a landscaped gar-
den. Superior rooms are larger and have a
balcony. The grounds include the appeal-
ingly rustic 'coffee village', complete with an
Ede longhouse.

Saigon Ban Me Hotel HOTEL $$$
(☑ 0262-368 5666; www.saigonbanmehotel.com.
vn; 1-3 Đ Phan Chu Trinh; r incl breakfast 1,150,000-
2,300,000d; ❄ ☎ ▨) This gleaming tower rises
above the most central intersection in town,
across from the Catholic Church, but guests at
Buon Ma Thuot's swishest hotel are sufficient-
ly high up to be insulated from street sounds.
Rooms aren't as flash as the imposing exteri-
or suggests, with ageing carpets, but they are
spacious, business-hotel-standard lodgings.

✗ Eating & Drinking

Đ Nguyen Cong Tru is home to several atmospheric joints for a coffee or beer.

★ **Thanh Tram** VIETNAMESE $
(☑ 0262-385 4960; 22 Đ Ly Thuong Kiet; meals
25,000-35,000d; ⊙ 10am-9pm) There's really
only one dish at this welcoming and popular
place: delicious, roll-your-own *nem nuong*
(rice-paper rolls, with salad, crudites, herbs
and pork sausage, served with peanut sauce).

Bun Rieu Cua NOODLES $
(71 Đ Ly Thuong Kiet; noodles 20,000d) For a fabulous quick lunch or breakfast, this roadside
stall does fantastic crab noodle soup. Throw
in the provided green leaves, lime, fish sauce
and purple shrimp paste and mix it all together for a taste explosion.

Com Nieu Dong Que VIETNAMESE $$
(☑ 0262-395 7505; 18e Đ Ngo Quyen; meals
60,000-200,000d; ⊙ 10am-10pm) Upscale Viet-
namese cuisine in refined but relaxed sur-
roundings, with excellent service. Try the
clay-pot dishes or the excellent fish soups
delicately seasoned with basil and tama-
rind. The Vietnamese menu has many more
options if you can navigate it, but neither
has many choices for vegetarians. It's a
15-minute walk from the centre.

Kinh Chau Coffee CAFE
(www.kinhchaucoffee.com.vn; 91 Đ Ly Thuong Kiet;
⊙ 6am-10pm; ☎) Every third shop in Buon
Ma Thuot is a coffee house, but this one
from a rated local coffee producer (you can
buy bags of its beans here) stands out, with
its spacious interior and smooth brews. Also
does smoothies and tea.

ⓘ Information

Agribank (37 Đ Phan Boi Chau; ⊙ 7.30am-
2.30pm Mon-Sat) ATM and money exchange.
DakLak Tourist (☑ 0262-385 2246; www.
daklaktourist.com.vn; 1-3 Đ Phan Chu Trinh;
⊙ 8am-5pm) On the ground floor of Saigon Ban
Me Hotel; offers tours of villages, waterfalls,
Lak Lake and Yok Don National Park.
Vietnam Highland Travel (☑ 0262-385
5009; www.luhanhcaonguyen.com; 24 Đ Ly
Thuong Kiet; ⊙ 8am-6pm) Experienced guides,
homestays and off-the-beaten-track trekking
trips.

ⓘ Getting There & Away

AIR
Buon Ma Thuot Airport (Cang Hang Khong
Buon Ma Thuot; Hoa Thang) is 8km east of
town; a taxi should cost 150,000d. There are

SOUTHWEST HIGHLANDS BUON MA THUOT

JARAI DEATH RITUALS

The Jarai minority of the Pleiku and Kon Tum areas honour their dead in graveyards set
up like miniature villages. These graveyards are located to the west of villages, where the
sun sets.

Each grave is marked with a shelter or bamboo stakes. Carved wooden figures are
placed along the edge, often pictured in squatting positions with their hands over their faces
in an expression of mourning. A jar is placed on the grave that represents the deceased
person, and objects that the deceased might need in the next world are buried with them.

For seven years after the death, relatives bring food to the grave and pass death
anniversaries at the grave site, mourning and celebrating the deceased by feasting and
drinking rice wine. After the seventh year, the spirit is believed to have moved on and the
grave is abandoned after an elaborate tomb-abandonment ceremony of animal sacrifice
and gong music that finally cuts the connection between the living and the dead.

BUSES FROM BUON MA THUOT

DESTINATION	COST (D)	TIME (HR)	FREQUENCY (DAILY)	DISTANCE (KM)
Dalat	110,000-140,000	5	5	201
Danang	280,000	11	5 (overnight)	558
Hanoi	650,000-700,000	16	5 (overnight)	1280
HCMC	180,000-245,000	8-9	10	319
Kon Tum	130,000 (200,000 limousine)	5	10	229
Nha Trang	110,000-140,000	4½	12	196
Pleiku	90,000-100,000	4	7	197

daily flights with Vietnam Airlines, VietJet Air and Jetstar to HCMC (three daily), Hanoi (two daily) and Danang.

BUS

The **bus station** (Ben Xe Lien Tinh Dak Lak; 71 Đ Nguyen Chi Thanh) is about 4km northeast of the centre; a taxi costs 60,000d. On bus time-tables, Buon Ma Thuot is often called 'Dak Lak' (the province in which it is located).

The pink-and-green local **bus No 15** (Đ Le Hong Phong) for Yok Don National Park leaves around the corner from the Ngoc Mai Hotel. Blue-and-white **bus No 12** (Đ Nguyen Tat Thanh) to Lak Lake also leaves from the centre of town. Both cost 25,000d and take around one hour.

Yok Don National Park

The largest of Vietnam's nature reserves, **Yok Don National Park** (☑ 0262-378 3049; www.yokdonnationalpark.vn; Buon Don; adult/child 60,000/10,000d; ☺ 7am-10pm) has been gradually expanded and today encompasses 115,000 hectares of mainly dry deciduous forest. The park runs all the way to the border with Cambodia, with the beautiful Sere-pok River flowing through it.

Unfortunately, deforestation and poaching are ongoing issues, meaning its 46 mammal species, including elephants, leopards and rare red wolves, hide deep in the jungle and are virtually never encountered by visitors. More commonly seen wildlife includes muntjac deer, monkeys and snakes. Some 300 bird species live in the park, including storks and two types of hornbills.

Four villages lie within the park, predominantly home to M'nong people but also with communities of Ede and Lao people.

High season is the dry season from October to March.

 Activities

The park offers various activities, as well as overnight packages (US$90/155 for one/two people) that include meals, accommodation, guided birdwatching and the elephant experience.

Book tours and activities at the **National Park Ecotourism Centre** (☑ 0262-378 3049, Mr Gioi 0905 229 436; www.yokdonnationalpark.vn; ☺ 7am-5pm) at the park entrance. There are only two English-speaking guides, so book in advance

Cooking Course COOKING
(per person 350,000d) Immerse yourself in Ede life in Jang Lanh village by signing up for a four-hour cooking course with a local family before 9am. You'll assist the family with dinner (lunch on request) preparation and share the meal with them afterwards. Book at the Ecotourism Centre.

Elephant Experience WILDLIFE
(Yok Don National Park; adult 600,000d; ☺ 8am & 1.30pm) Aimed at foreign visitors and with elephant concern at the fore, this three-hour tour leaves twice a day and allows you to view on foot three free-roaming pachyderms, who were previously used for rides. Full-day trips are also possible. Beware of nearby private sanctuaries that offer elephant rides.

Hiking

There are various hiking trails inside the national park forest, and guided treks can be arranged, ranging from five hours to two days (including overnight camping). For two people, expect to pay 600,000d for a day hike and 1,200,000d for two days' worth of forest adventure, including food and tents.

Guided birdwatching walks in the jungle cost 800,000d for two people for a morning.

Cycling

Guided cycling tours can take in waterfalls, rapids and Drang Phok Lake. A half-day excursion costs 100,000/450,000d per bike/guide.

Sleeping & Eating

A canteen by the park office offers meals (100,000d to 140,000d) if pre-ordered.

Yok Don Guesthouse   GUESTHOUSE **$**
(☑0262-378 3049; Yok Don National Park; s/d 350,000/400,000d; ❄) Just inside the park entrance, near the Ecotourism Centre, this guesthouse offers 14 clean, tiled rooms with TVs, a pleasant terrace and ancient air-con.

Getting There & Away

Local bus No 15 heads from Buon Ma Thuot to Yok Don National Park (25,000d, one hour) every 30 minutes or so. The last bus back is around 5.30pm.

There is a daily overnight sleeper bus from nearby Ban Don direct to Ho Chi Minh City (250,000d, eight hours), leaving at 7.30pm; the Ecotourism Centre can arrange for it to pick you up at the park entrance.

Pleiku

☑0269 / POP 162,051 / ELEV 785M

Pleiku, the capital of Gia Lai province, is best known for its role as a strategic American and South Vietnamese base during the American War. Torched by departing South Vietnamese soldiers in 1975, the city was rebuilt in the 1980s with help from the Soviet Union. The temple and museum are worth exploring if you're here on a short visit.

◉ Sights

★ Minh Thanh Temple   BUDDHIST TEMPLE
(Chua Minh Thanh; 348 Nguyen Viet Xuan; ⊙dawn-dusk) **FREE** Built only in 2014, this large and splendid Buddhist temple, surrounded by water features and bonsai trees, sits south of the city centre. Its proudest feature is a gorgeous nine-tiered pagoda that's lit up at night. Fearsome dragons curl up from the corners of the roof of the main temple building.

Gia Lai Museum   MUSEUM
(Bao Tang Gia Lai; 20 Đ Tran Hung Dao; admission 10,000d; ⊙8-11am & 1.30-4.30pm Tue-Sun) Pleiku's museum features some vaguely interesting Bahnar artefacts, from fine woven baskets and a coat made from tree bark to a replica tomb house, as well as copies of some 15th-century Cham-era stone reliefs. There's the obligatory badly stuffed wildlife, and a history gallery dedicated to Pleiku's role during the French and American wars.

Next to the museum is the large **Dai Doan Ket** (Great Solidarity) square, featuring an 11m-tall statue of Ho Chi Minh and a 58m-long sculpture depicting Vietnam's ethnic groups.

Sleeping & Eating

Duc Long Gia Lai 2 Hotel   HOTEL **$**
(☑0269-374 8777; duclonghotel@duclonggroup.com; 117-119 Đ Tran Phu; r 400,000-550,000d; ❄🖥) This high-rise 18-storey block offers fine views over Pleiku, as well as comfortable business-class digs at affordable rates in a central location (and a ground-floor cafe). Rooms come with decent beds and small balconies. 'Old floor' rooms are huge but old fashioned. Twin rooms are noticeably bigger than the one-bed options. Not much English is spoken.

❶ GETTING TO CAMBODIA: PLEIKU TO BAN LUNG

Getting to the border Remote and rarely used by foreigners, the **Le Thanh–O Yadaw border crossing** lies 90km west from Pleiku and 64km east from Ban Lung, Cambodia. From Pleiku, there are direct minibuses to Ban Lung (150,000d, four hours) at 7am, 9am and 1pm. Otherwise take the daily minivan (75,000d, two hours, 7am) from the Noi Tinh bus station at the main market car park to the Cambodian border at Le Thanh.

At the border Cambodian visas (US$30) are issued at the border; you may end up overpaying by a few dollars or be made to wait. Vietnamese visas need to be organised in advance.

Moving on From O Yadaw, on the Cambodia side of the border, local buses (around US$10) or motorbikes (around US$25) head to Ban Lung. There are far fewer transport options in the afternoon.

BUSES FROM PLEIKU

DESTINATION	COST (D)	TIME (HR)	FREQUENCY (DAILY)	DISTANCE (KM)
Attapeu, Laos	200,000	6	8am	246
Buon Ma Thuot	100,000-200,000 (limousine)	4	2 (limousine 3)	215
Dalat	220,000-250,000	9	5pm & 6pm	383
Danang	140,000-220,000	7½	4	340
HCMC	220,000-400,000	11-12	4	509
Kon Tum	25,000	1	half-hourly 5am-6pm	48
Nha Trang	140,000-220,000	7	7pm	297

HAGL Hotel Pleiku HOTEL $$
(Hoang Anh Gia Lai; ☑0269-371 8450; 1 Phu Dong; s/d incl breakfast from 780,000/950,000d; ❉ ☎) The marble-rich lobby of this four-star hotel sets the tone, and the 117 rooms are large, inviting and well equipped with comfy beds, big bathrooms, safety boxes and balconies. There's also the good Acacia Restaurant and a basic spa.

Com Ga Hai Nam VIETNAMESE $
(73 Đ Hai Ba Trung; meals small/large 35,000/55,000d; ⊙10am-8.30pm) This busy, simple place specialises in delicious crispy chicken and rice with a side salad of lettuce, tomato and onion.

Acacia Restaurant INTERNATIONAL $$
(1 Đ Phu Dong; meals 150,000d; ⊙6am-10pm; ☎☑) The menu at this welcoming restaurant, inside the HAGL Hotel, is a stampede through a variety of Asian (read: Chinese), Western and Vietnamese dishes. The last of these – from snake-head fish soup to grilled squid with prawn paste – work best, and there's even wild boar, but you'll have to block out the hotel muzac.

ⓘ Information

Gia Lai Eco-Tourist (☑0913 157 462, 0269-376 0898; www.gialaiecotourist.com; 82 Đ Hung Vuong; ⊙8-11am & 1.30-5pm Mon-Sat) Day or multiday tours through the highlands, including to remote Chu Mom Ray and Kon Ka Kinh National Parks and overnight trips to minority villages. It can also book limousine minivans and buses to Cambodia.

ⓘ Getting There & Away

AIR
Vetnam Airlines, VietJet Air and Jetstar together offer three flights daily to HCMC, two daily to Hanoi and three a week to Danang.

Pleiku Airport (www.pleikuairport.vn; Thong Nhat) is 5km northeast of town and accessible by taxi (60,000d to 80,000d). Minibuses between Pleiku and Kon Tum stop briefly at the airport.

BUS
Gia Lai Bus Station (Ben Xe Duc Long Gia Lai; 45 Đ Ly Nam De) Pleiku's main bus station is 2.5km southeast of town. It serves most destinations, including Laos, but has no buses to Kon Tum. Pleiku is known as Gia Lai on most bus timetables.

Noi Tinh Bus Station (Ben Xe Noi Tinh; Đ Tran Phu) Buses to Kon Tum and minivans to Cambodia run from this informal bus station in the main market car park in central Pleiku.

TAXI
A taxi from Pleiku to Kon Tum costs around 350,000d

Kon Tum

☑0260 / POP 86,362 / ELEV 525M
Kon Tum's relaxed ambience, river setting and relatively traffic-free streets make it a great stop for travellers intent on exploring the surrounding hill-tribe villages, of which there are around 700 dotting the area – mostly Bahnar, but also Sedang and Jarai. This is a far better base than Pleiku for delving into indigenous culture, and there are a few intriguing sights in Kon Tum itself.

The region saw its share of combat during the American War. A major battle between the South and North Vietnamese took place in and around Kon Tum in the spring of 1972, when the area was devastated by American B-52 raids.

⊙ Sights

★**Kon Tum Museum** MUSEUM
(Bao Tang Kon Tum; ☑0260-359 0698; 659 Đ Nguyen Hue; adult/child 10,000/5000d; ⊙7-11am

Kon Tum

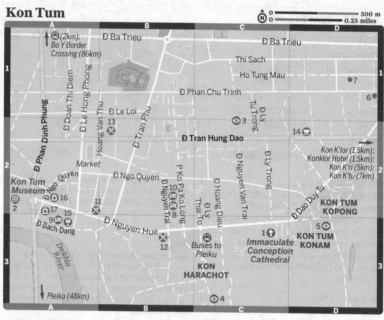

Kon Tum

& 1-5pm) This museum is one of the region's best, with good lighting and clear English text detailing local religious and spiritual life, including displays on the iron forges of the Sedang (Xo Dang) people and the significance of gongs to Vietnam's hill communities (Vietnam's gong culture is included in Unesco's List of the Intangible Cultural Heritage of Humanity). Highlights include an impressive log coffin and a musical instrument known as a *trung* (a marimba made from bamboo tubes).

★ **Immaculate Conception Cathedral**   CHURCH
(Ð Nguyen Hue; ⊙ dawn-dusk) Built entirely from wood, this stunning cathedral from the French era has a dark frontage, gold trim and wide colonnades. Known to the locals as the 'wooden church', it's light, airy and elegant inside, with incredible interlocking beams. The heart of the 160-year-old Kon Tum diocese, it primarily serves the ethnic minority community, and the altar is bedecked in traditional woven fabrics.

Catholic Seminary   NOTABLE BUILDING
(Ð Tran Hung Dao; ⏰7.30-11am & 2-5pm Wed-Mon) **FREE** This lovely old Catholic seminary was built in 1934. The upstairs normally functions as an absorbing museum of hill-tribe life, but was closed for renovation during our visit. Outside, to the left of the building, note the sculpture of Mary and baby Jesus, with Mary dressed in traditional clothing and carrying a Bahnar-style backpack.

👉 Tours

⭐**An Nguyen**   CULTURAL
(☑0905 672 442, 0260-386 2944; evacoffee@ymail.com; 5 Ð Phan Chu Trinh; day tours US$85) Based at the bohemian Eva Cafe, local sculptor An is a knowledgeable guide who can arrange anything from day tours of Bahnar villages, to multiday, in-depth explorations of indigenous cultures, complete with local homestays. Contact him in advance, as he's always busy.

⭐**Highlands Eco Tours**   CULTURAL
(☑0260-391 2788, 0905 112 037; www.vietnamhighlands.net; 41 Ð Ho Tung Mau; ⏰7am-7pm) Long-time guide Mr Huynh speaks decent English and really knows the area. He specialises in minority-village trips, homestays in off-the-beaten-track communities, trekking and battlefield visits, including a day trip to visit the Sodra people. From US$35 to US$45 per day if going by motorbike. He's popular, so call or email in advance.

🛏 Sleeping

⭐**Hnam Chang Ngeh**   HOTEL $
(☑0868 981 031; www.hnam-changngeh.org; 16a Ð Nguyen Trai; s/d incl breakfast 350,000/450,000d, ste 650,000d; ❇🛜) Excellent hotel that was set up to train local minority teenagers to work in the hospitality industry (the name means 'House of Hope' in the Bahnar language). There are 10 comfortable, individually decorated (but dimly lit) rooms, all spacious and stylish, spread over three floors, and a pleasant restaurant. The staff are super helpful and motorbike rental is available.

Thinh Vuong Hotel   HOTEL $
(☑0260-391 4729; thinhvuonghotel.kontum@gmail.com; 17 Ð Nguyen Trai; r 250,000-350,000d; ❇🛜) On a quiet central street, next to the Hnam Chang Ngeh, this friendly hotel gets extra points for the helpfulness of its staff and the large, spotless rooms at bargain prices. The beds are strangely low, but that's our only minor quibble. It does laundry and motorbikes are available for hire (150,000d per day).

Konklor Hotel   HOTEL $
(☑0260-386 1555; www.konklorhotel.vn; 38 Bac Can; r 190,000-350,000d; ❇🛜) This resort-like place offers clean, neat duplexes that feel lifted from a picket-fenced suburb. The superior rooms are great value, but avoid the cheapest singles without a window. Friendly staff speak English, and there's a restaurant and motorbikes for rent (150,000d) – you'll need one as the hotel is 2km east of town

---

ℹ GETTING TO LAOS: KON TUM TO ATTAPEU

Getting to the border The **Bo Y/Phou Keua border crossing** lies 86km northwest of Kon Tum and 119km northeast of Attapeu (Laos). Attapeu-bound buses depart from Pleiku bus station at 6am or 7am, passing through Kon Tum around 7am or 8am. Hotels can arrange a ticket to either Attapeu (250,000d, five hours) or Pakse (350,000, 10 hours). Crossing the border independently can be a challenge. On the Vietnam side, the nearest major town is Ngoc Hoi (Plei Can), 68km west of Kon Tum, which can be reached by minibus (60,000d, two hours) from the same station as minibuses to Pleiku. You'll have to catch a minibus from Ngoc Hoi to the border (15,000d, 30 minutes). There are also morning buses from Ngoc Hoi directly to Attapeu; get there as early as possible. On the Laos side, things are even quieter and you'll be at the mercy of passing traffic to hitch a ride onwards.

At the border Vietnamese visas aren't available at this border, but Lao visas are available for most nationalities (between US$30 and US$40, depending on your nationality).

Moving on The bus from Pleiku arrives in Attapeu around 1pm and then continues to Pakse, five hours away. There are also hourly buses from Attapeu to Pakse.

(close to Kon K'lor village), away from restaurants and cafes.

Indochine Hotel
HOTEL $$

(☏0260-386 3335; www.indochinehotel.vn; 30 Đ Bach Dang; r inc breakfast 700,000-800,000d, ste 1,100,000d-1,500,000d; ✸🖥) Right on the bank of the Dakbla River, this concrete three-star block has rooms that look a little tired, though the renovated luxury rooms are noticeably fresher and the best enjoy great river views.

✗ Eating & Drinking

Pho Ca
NOODLES $

(Đ Nguyen Hue; noodles 25,000d; ⊙7am-8pm) A great place to try the local speciality, *pho hai*, a noodle dish served in two bowls. One contains dry noodles topped with fried ground pork, onion, lettuce, bean sprouts and chilli garlic sauce. The other holds a salty-sweet broth with sliced beef or meatballs. Delicious.

Quan 69
VIETNAMESE $

(511 Đ Nguyen Hue; meals 60,000d; ⊙10am-11pm) Big groups pack this hangar-like space. The beer is disappointingly unchilled but the (Vietnamese-only) menu offers lots of choice and our *bo toi chanh* (beef salad) and *ga sot me* (chicken in tamarind sauce) were excellent.

Rita
INTERNATIONAL $

(☏0989 530 604; 42 Đ Tran Quang Khai; meals 50,000d-110,000d; ⊙7am-10pm) Tucked up a small street off Đ Tran Hung Dao, this

---

MINORITY VILLAGES AROUND KON TUM

There are several clusters of Bahnar villages on the peripheries of Kon Tum. Village life here centres on the traditional *rong* house (*nha-rong*), a tall thatched-roof community house built on stilts. The *rong* is the focal point for festivals and doubles as a village meeting house, spiritual centre, court and school. *Rong* roofs typically have decorations on top, or even woven into them. The stilts were originally there to provide protection from elephants, tigers and other animals. The traditional houses are also on stilts, with livestock residing underneath.

Further away are more isolated Sedang villages and Jarai villages. The latter still practise traditional customs, such as the feeding of the dead in traditional cemeteries, as do the 'Hilltop' Bahnar; the rest have converted to Catholicism – they only bury their dead once and don't 'feed' them. The prefix 'kon' in a place name generally denotes a Bahnar village; 'plei' is most likely a Jarai community.

Generally the local people welcome tourists and it's fine to explore the villages around Kon Tum under your own steam, but ask permission before pointing a camera at people's faces or homes.

Guided day trips to villages are available from around US$35 per person for a guide/motorbike driver, depending on the places visited.

If you have time to spend several days here, An Nguyen (p301) and Highlands Eco Tours (p301) can arrange village homestays. The guides are careful not to intrude too frequently on any one village, so visitors are always welcomed and it's possible to participate in daily activities.

Closest to Kon Tum town, and just a short walk from the Hnam Chang Ngeh hotel, is the beautiful *rong* of **Kon Harachot**, next to a rustic football field. A little further east is the harder-to-find *rong* at **Kon Tum Konam**. Both villages are essentially suburbs of Kon Tum.

Nine kilometres southeast of Kon Tum, the village of **Kon K'tu** is reachable across the Kon K'lor suspension bridge and along a potholed road. There's a beautiful riverside *rong* here, near the Catholic church, as well as a couple of simple homestays. You can watch locals transporting crops along the river in rafts made of tyres.

En route you'll pass a second *rong* at **Kon K'lor**, next to the suspension bridge. You can return to Kon Tum via a second *rong* at the nearby village of **Kon K'ri**.

Ya Chim (Ia Chim) is the collective name for a group of eight Jarai villages that start 17km southwest of Kon Tum. In them you'll find traditional *nghia trang* (cemeteries) complete with wooden mourning figures. You may see villagers 'feeding' the dead by putting food down bamboo tubes leading into the graves.

BUSES FROM KON TUM

DESTINATION	COST (D)	TIME (HR)	FREQUENCY	DISTANCE (KM)
Buon Ma Thuot (Dak Lak)	150,000	5	7am, noon, 1.30pm	188
Dalat	270,000	10	4.30pm	433
Danang	150,000-180,000	6½	6 daily	293
HCMC	270,000-450,000	12	5 daily (all afternoon)	550
Hue	210,000	8½	5 daily	445
Nha Trang	220,000	8	6pm	344
Pleiku (Noi Tinh)	25,000	1	hourly	48
Quy Nhon	100,000	4½	hourly until 10am	190

friendly, unpretentious place is your best bet if you are craving Western comfort food. There's a few pizza and pasta options, as well as steaks, sandwiches and salads.

Gac Mang Re Cafe
CAFE

(www.facebook.com/gacmangrekontum; 86 Tran Hung Dao; ⏰7am-10pm; 🛜) The best cafe in town, with stylish patio seating in a quiet corner of town. For a pick-me-up try the *sinhto* bowl, a smoothie with pieces of custard apple, green apple, spinach, mango, passion fruit, walnuts and chia seeds. It also does meals (40,000d to 120,000d), from chicken curry to salads, pizza and cakes.

Indochine Coffee
BAR

(Ca Phe Dong Duong; 30 Đ Bach Dang; ⏰6am-10pm) Join Kon Tum's cashed-up locals for a tea, *ca phe sua da* (iced milk coffee) or cold Saigon beer at this modernist cafe, shaded by strikingly arranged bamboo pillars, attached to the Indochine Hotel. Prices are surprisingly reasonable.

🛍 Shopping

★ Dakbla's
ARTS & CRAFTS

(620 Đ Nguyen Hue; ⏰10am-8pm) The anthropologically inclined will enjoy this shop that has walls festooned with Bahnar and Sedang artefacts – nipple gongs, funeral masks, drums, weaponry, woven hunter backpacks, jewellery, and traditional clothing. There are also some superb photos for sale.

Shop
ARTS & CRAFTS

(Đ Phan Dinh Phung; ⏰10am-8pm) This nameless shop stocks some choice (but pricey) Sedang and Bahnar hunter backpacks (US$50 to US$75), antique weavings, gongs and more.

ℹ Getting There & Away

Buses to Pleiku (via Pleiku Airport) and Ngoc Hoi depart from a stand just off Đ Nguyen Hue.

Kon Tum's main **bus station** (Ben Xe Kon Tum; 279 Đ Phan Dinh Phung), inconveniently located 2.5km northwest of the centre, handles long-distance services. For Hoi An, take a Danang bus or minivan and change there.

Faster limousine minivans run to Buon Ma Thuot (200,000d). They're useful because they drop you in the centre of town, not in the distant bus station; get your hotel to book these.

AT A GLANCE

POPULATION
8.4 million

TALLEST BUILDING
Vincom Landmark
81 (461m)

**BEST SKYHIGH
RESTAURANT**
Towa (p334)

**BEST HOT-STONE
MASSAGE**
Aveda (p323)

BEST LOCAL IPA
Pasteur Street
Brewing Company
(p338)

WHEN TO GO
Feb Hardly any rain,
the least humidity,
and a city filled with
blooms for the Tet
celebrations.

Mar Low rain and
humidity persist, plus
there's the annual
cyclo challenge.

Dec December is a
whisper cooler than
normal for HCMC and
comparatively dry.

CHỢ BẾN THÀNH

Ben Thanh Market (p341)
RICHIE CHAN/SHUTTERSTOCK ©

Ho Chi Minh City

Ho Chi Minh City (HCMC) is Vietnam at its most dizzying: a high-octane city of commerce and culture that has driven the country forward with its pulsating energy. From the finest of hotels to the cheapest of guesthouses, the classiest of restaurants to the tastiest of street stalls, the choicest of boutiques to the scrum of the markets, HCMC has it all. Known as Saigon until the Communist victory in 1975, here the ghosts of the past live on in buildings like the Reunification Palace, which only a generation ago witnessed a nation in turmoil. It's also easy to time-travel even further back to the Indochine era, with stunning architectural reminders of the city's French-colonial period everywhere, many now converted into museums and grand hotels.

History

Originally part of the kingdom of Cambodia, Saigon was a relatively small port town known as Prey Nokor until the late 17th century (when its population was mainly Khmer). As ethnic Vietnamese settlers pushed south the city became the base for the Nguyen Lords, who were the rulers of southern Vietnam from the 16th to the 18th centuries.

During the Tay Son Rebellion in the 18th century, a group of Chinese refugees established a settlement nearby, which became known by their Vietnamese neighbours as Cholon (Big Market). After seeing off the rebels, Nguyen Anh constructed a large citadel here (roughly where the American and French embassies now stand).

In 1859 Saigon and Cholon were captured by the French (who destroyed the citadel in the process) and Saigon became the capital of Cochinchina a few years later. It wasn't until 1931, after the neighbouring cities had sprawled into each other, that they were officially combined to form Saigon-Cholon (the name Cholon was dropped in 1956).

The city served as the capital of the Republic of Vietnam from 1956 until 1975, when it fell to advancing North Vietnamese forces and was renamed Ho Chi Minh City.

Today HCMC is the financial and commercial engine of the Vietnamese economy, with a growth rate way above the national average and eye-watering land prices. The city is also the most culturally dynamic in the country, with a liberal identity that can irritate conservatives in the governmental departments of Hanoi.

◎ Sights

With pockets of French-colonial grandeur and a ceaseless hubbub on its chaotic streets, Ho Chi Minh City has rewarding sights for temple- and museum-goers, market hounds, history junkies, architecture fans, park lovers or simply anyone addicted to vibrant city life. Three days should be sufficient to get a handle on the main sights.

◎ Dong Khoi Area

This well-heeled area, immediately west of the Saigon River, is both the heart of old Saigon and a 21st-century enclave of designer shops and skyscrapers. Running from the river to Notre Dame Cathedral via the Opera House (Municipal Theatre), ritzy Đ Dong Khoi is the main shopping strip and lends its name to the encircling civic centre and central business district. Yet it's the wide, tree-lined boulevards of ĐL Le Loi and ĐL Nguyen Hue that leave more of an impression. It's in these grand thoroughfares that French-colonial elegance and urban modernity fashion an alluring concoction.

★ Notre Dame Cathedral   CHURCH
(Map p312; Đ Han Thuyen) Built between 1877 and 1883, Notre Dame Cathedral enlivens the heart of Ho Chi Minh City's government quarter, facing Đ Dong Khoi. A red-brick, neo-Romanesque church, it has twin bell towers that are both topped with spires and crosses that reach 60m. This Catholic cathedral, named after the Virgin Mary, was closed for renovation at the time of research, but when it reopens you'll be able to admire its stained-glass windows and interior walls inlaid with devotional tablets.

★ HCMC Museum   MUSEUM
(Bao Tang Thanh Pho Ho Chi Minh; Map p312; www.hcmc-museum.edu.vn; 65 Đ Ly Tu Trong; 30,000d; ⊘ 7.30am-5pm) A grand neoclassical structure built in 1885 and once known as Gia Long Palace (and later the Revolutionary Museum), HCMC's city museum is a singularly beautiful and impressive building, telling the story of the city through archaeological artefacts, ceramics, old city maps and displays on the marriage traditions of its various ethnicities. The struggle for independence is extensively covered, with most of the upper floor devoted to it.

Deep beneath the building is a network of reinforced concrete bunkers and fortified corridors. The system, branches of which stretch all the way to Reunification Palace, included living areas, a kitchen and a large meeting hall. In 1963 President Diem and his brother hid here before fleeing to Cha Tam Church (p319). The network is not open to the public because most of the tunnels are flooded.

In the gardens are various pieces of military hardware, including the American-built F-5E jet used by a renegade South Vietnamese pilot to bomb the Presidential Palace (now Reunification Palace) on 8 April 1975.

★ Central Post Office   HISTORIC BUILDING
(Map p312; 2 Cong Xa Paris; ⊘ 7am-7pm Mon-Fri, to 6pm Sat, 8am-6pm Sun) The city's landmark French-era post office is a period classic, designed by Marie-Alfred Foulhoux (though

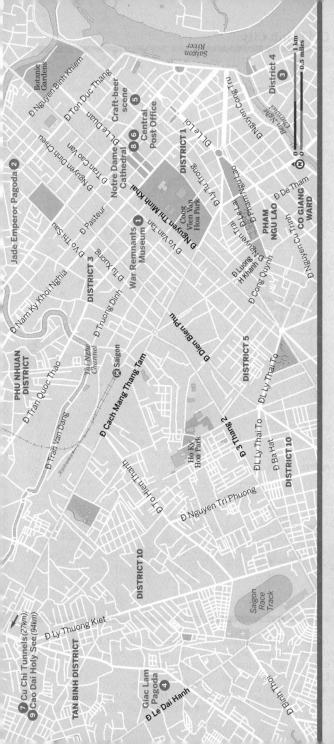

Ho Chi Minh City Highlights

1 War Remnants Museum (p311) Learning about the turbulence of conflict.

2 Jade Emperor Pagoda (p316) Passing through clouds of incense in this mystical world.

3 Street food in District 4 (p315) Chowing down in this atmospheric neighbourhood.

4 Giac Lam Pagoda (p322) Losing yourself at this ancient Chinese temple.

5 Craft-beer scene (p338) Quaffing ales with the locals in the city's many brewhouses.

6 Central Post Office (p306) Checking out the striking interior of this French-era classic.

7 Cu Chi Tunnels (p349) Crawling through the wartime warren of the Viet Cong.

8 Notre Dame Cathedral (p306) Seeing highlights of the city's French-colonial architecture.

9 Cao Dai Holy See (p350) Joining fantastically garbed worshippers at this astonishing temple in Tay Ninh.

Greater Ho Chi Minh City

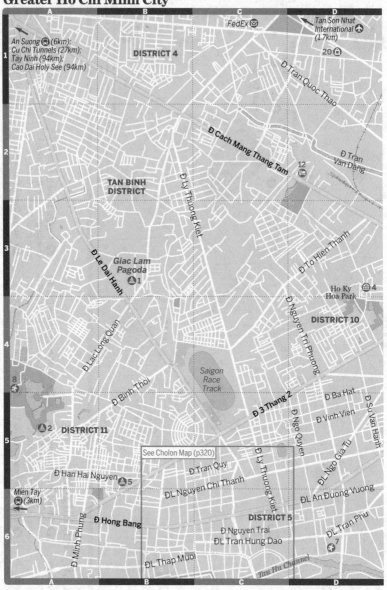

An Suong 🚌 (6km);
Cu Chi Tunnels (27km);
Tay Ninh (94km);
Cao Dai Holy See (94km)

FedEx ✉

Tan Son Nhat
International ✈
(1.7km)

20 🏠

DISTRICT 4

Đ Tran Quoc Thao

Đ Cach Mang Thang Tam

Đ Tran Van Dang

12 🏛

TAN BINH
DISTRICT

Đ Ly Thuong Kiet

Đ To Hien Thanh

Đ Le Dai Hanh

Giac Lam
Pagoda
🏛 1

Ho Ky 🏛 4
Hoa Park

DISTRICT 10

Đ Lac Long Quan

Đ Nguyen Tri Phuong

Đ Binh Thoi

Saigon
Race
Track

Đ 3 Thang 2

Đ Ba Hat

Đ Su Van Hanh

Đ Vinh Vien

8 ✚

Đ Ngo Quyen

ĐL Ngo Gia Tu

🏛 2   DISTRICT 11

See Cholon Map (p320)

Đ Tran Quy

ĐL Ly Thuong Kiet

Đ Han Hai Nguyen 🏛 5

ĐL Nguyen Chi Thanh

ĐL An Duong Vuong

Mien Tay
🚌 (3km)

Đ Minh Phung

Đ Hong Bang

DISTRICT 5

ĐL Tran Phu

Đ Nguyen Trai
ĐL Tran Hung Dao

🐟 7

ĐL Thap Muoi

Tau Hu Channel

often credited to Gustave Eiffel) and built between 1886 and 1891. Painted on the walls of its grand concourse are fascinating historical maps of South Vietnam, Saigon and Cholon, while a mosaic of Ho Chi Minh takes pride of place at the end of its barrel-vaulted hall.

Note the magnificent tiled floor of the interior and the copious green-painted wrought iron.

Fine Arts Museum　　　　　　　GALLERY
(Bao Tang My Thuat; Map p312; www.baotang mythuattphcm.com.vn; 97a Đ Pho Duc Chinh;

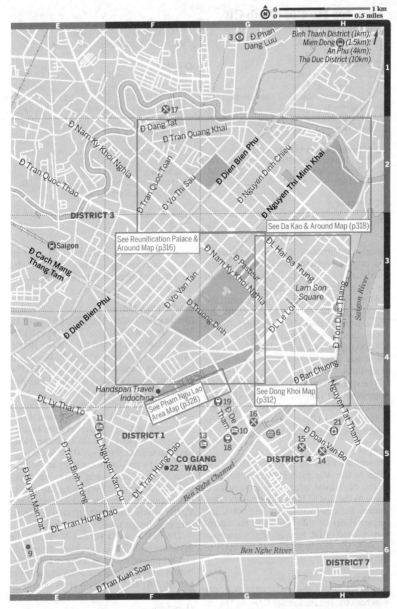

30,000d; ⊘8am-5pm Tue-Sun) With its airy corridors and verandas, this elegant 1929 colonial-era, yellow-and-white building is stuffed with period details; it is exuberantly tiled throughout and home to some fine (albeit deteriorated) stained glass, as well as one of Saigon's oldest lifts. Hung from the walls is an impressive selection of art, including thoughtful pieces from the modern period.

As well as contemporary art, much of it (unsurprisingly) inspired by war, the museum displays pieces dating back to the 4th century. These include elegant

Greater Ho Chi Minh City

Funan-era sculptures of Vishnu, the Buddha and other revered figures (carved in both wood and stone), and Cham art dating from the 7th century to the 14th century.

More statuary is scattered around the grounds and in the central courtyard (accessed from the rear of the building). There's a selection of lovely prints for sale (from 150,000d) at the shop. Building No 2 alongside hosts lesser-known works and stages exhibitions.

The space on the pavement in front of the impressive old Railway Office, up the road between Đ Ham Nghi and ĐL Le Loi and facing the roundabout, was used for public executions in the early 1960s.

People's
Committee Building   NOTABLE BUILDING
(Hôtel de Ville; Map p312; ĐL Nguyen Hue) One of the city's most prominent landmarks is home to the Ho Chi Minh City People's Committee. Built between 1901 and 1908, the former Hôtel de Ville decorates the northwestern end of ĐL Nguyen Hue, but unfortunately the ornate interior is not open to the public.

Opera House   THEATRE
(Nha Hat Thanh Pho; Map p312; ☑ 028-3823 7419; www.hbso.org.vn; Lam Son Sq) Gracing the intersection of Đ Dong Khoi and ĐL Le Loi, this grand colonial edifice with a sweeping staircase was built in 1897 and is one of the city's most recognisable buildings. Officially known as the Municipal Theatre, the Opera House captures the flamboyance of France's belle époque. Performances range from ballet and opera to modern dance and musicals. Check the website for English-language listings and booking information.

Ho Chi Minh Museum   MUSEUM
(Bao Tang Ho Chi Minh; Map p312; 1 Đ Nguyen Tat Thanh, District 4; 10,000d; ◎ 7.30-11.30am & 1.30-5pm Tue-Sun) Nicknamed the 'Dragon House' (Nha Rong), this former customs house was built by the French authorities in 1863. The museum houses many of Ho Chi Minh's personal effects, including some of his clothing, his sandals and spectacles. Information is available in English. It's on the waterfront, just across Ben Nghe Channel from District 1; reach it on foot by heading south along the Saigon River then over the bridge.

The museum covers the story of the man born Nguyen Tat Thanh – from his childhood to his political awakening, his role in booting out the French and leading North Vietnam, and his death in 1969 – mainly through photographs.

The link between Ho Chi Minh and the museum building is tenuous: 21-year-old Ho, having signed on as a stoker and galley boy on a French freighter, left Vietnam from here in 1911 and began 30 years of exile in France, the Soviet Union, the UK, China and elsewhere.

◎ Reunification Palace & Around

Straddling District 1 and District 3, this grid of busy streets encloses the inviting spaces of Tao Dan Park and the pristine grounds of the Reunification Palace. It's here that you'll find some of Ho Chi Minh City's most popular sights and best restaurants.

★ War Remnants Museum   MUSEUM
(Bao Tang Chung Tich Chien Tranh; Map p316; ☑ 028-3930 5587; http://warremnantsmuseum.com; 28 Đ Vo Van Tan, cnr Đ Le Quy Don; adult/child 40,000/20,000d; ☺ 7.30am-6pm) To understand the context of the war with the USA, and its devastating impact on Vietnamese civilians, this remarkable, deeply moving museum is an essential visit. Many atrocities documented here were well publicised, but rarely do Westerners hear the victims of military action tell their own stories. While some displays are one-sided, many of the most disturbing photographs illustrating atrocities are from US sources, including those from the My Lai massacre. Allow at least a couple of hours for your visit.

The museum primarily deals with the American War, but the French-colonial period and conflicts with China are also documented. US armoured vehicles, artillery pieces, bombs and infantry weapons are on display outside. One corner of the grounds is devoted to the notorious French and South Vietnamese prisons on Phu Quoc and Con Son islands. Artefacts include that most iconic of French appliances, the guillotine, and the notoriously inhumane 'tiger cages' used to house war prisoners.

The ground floor of the museum is devoted to a collection of posters and photographs showing support for the antiwar movement internationally. This somewhat upbeat display provides a counterbalance to the horrors upstairs.

Even those who supported the war are likely to be horrified by the photos of children affected by US bombing and napalm. You'll also have the rare chance to see some of the experimental weapons used in the war, which were at one time military secrets, such as the *flechette*, an artillery shell filled with thousands of tiny darts.

Upstairs, look out for the **Requiem Exhibition**. Compiled by legendary war photographer Tim Page, this striking collection documents the work of photographers killed during the course of the conflict, on both sides, and includes works by Larry Burrows and Robert Capa.

The War Remnants Museum is in the former US Information Service building. It was previously called the Museum of Chinese and American War Crimes. Captions are in Vietnamese and English.

★ Reunification Palace   HISTORIC BUILDING
(Dinh Thong Nhat; Map p316; ☑ 028-3829 4117; www.dinhdoclap.gov.vn; Đ Nam Ky Khoi Nghia; adult/child 40,000/20,000d; ☺ 7.30-11am & 1-4pm) Surrounded by royal palm trees, the dissonant 1960s architecture of this landmark government building and the eerie ambience of its deserted halls make it an intriguing spectacle. The first Communist tanks to arrive in Saigon rumbled here on 30 April 1975 and

HO CHI MINH CITY IN...

One Day
Slurp up a steaming bowl of *pho* (rice-noodle soup) and then take a walk from the Saigon River up along ĐL Nguyen Hue, the city's most impressive boulevard north, to the **HCMC Museum** (p306). Next explore the area around the **Ben Thanh Market** (p341), take lunch at **Bep Me In** (p331) then head to the **War Remnants Museum** and after that the **Reunification Palace**. In the evening sample a bold craft beer at **Heart of Darkness** (p338) before a meal at **Quan Bui** (p331) or **Hum Vegetarian Cafe & Restaurant** (p334).

Two Days
Spend the morning in **Cholon** (p318), wandering around the market and historic temples. Catch a taxi up to District 3 for lunch at **Banh Xeo 46A** (p335) or **Chay Garden** (p335) and then walk through Da Kao ward to the **Jade Emperor Pagoda** (p316) and **History Museum** (p318). It's your last night in HCMC, so make the most of it. Start your evening with a drink in a sky bar and then have dinner at **Cuc Gach Quan** (p335) or **Quince** (p334) before catching the vibe at a live-music venue like **Acoustic** (p341), **Rogue Saigon** (p338) or the **Old Compass Cafe** (p331). If you're ready for the evening to descend into a very Saigon state of messiness, and it's a weekend night, continue on to **Observatory** (p339).

Dong Khoi

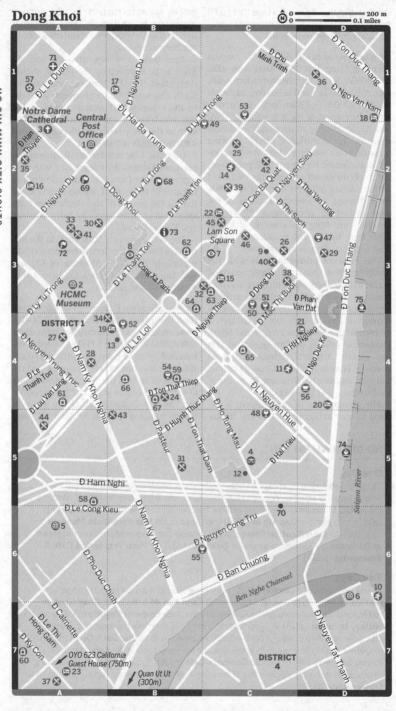

Dong Khoi

it's as if time has stood still since then. The building is deeply associated with the fall of the city in 1975, yet it's the kitsch detailing and period motifs that steal the show. It's also known as the Independence Palace.

After crashing through the wrought-iron gates – in a dramatic scene recorded by photojournalists and shown around the world – a soldier ran into the building and up the stairs to unfurl a VC flag from the balcony. In an ornate reception chamber,

General Minh, who had become head of the South Vietnamese state only 43 hours before, waited with his improvised cabinet.

In 1868 a residence was built on this site for the French governor-general of Cochinchina and gradually it expanded to become Norodom Palace. When the French departed, the palace became home to the South Vietnamese president Ngo Dinh Diem. So unpopular was Diem that his own air force bombed the palace in 1962 in an unsuccessful attempt to kill him, and most of the colonial-era structure was damaged.

The president ordered a new modernist residence to be built on the same site, this time with a sizeable bomb shelter in the basement. Work was completed in 1966, but Diem did not get to see his dream house as he was killed by his own troops in 1963.

The new building was named Independence Palace and was home to the succeeding South Vietnamese president, Nguyen Van Thieu, until his hasty departure in 1975. Designed by Paris-trained Vietnamese architect Ngo Viet Thu, it is an outstanding example of 1960s architecture, with an airy and open atmosphere.

The ground floor is arranged with meeting rooms, while upstairs is a grand set of reception rooms, used for welcoming foreign and national dignitaries. In the back of the structure are the president's living quarters; check out the model boats, horse tails and severed elephants' feet. The 2nd floor contributes a shagadelic card-playing room, complete with a cheesy round leather banquette, a barrel-shaped bar, hubcap light fixtures and three-legged chairs set around a flared-legged card table. There's also a cinema and a rooftop nightclub, complete with helipad: James Bond/Austin Powers – eat your groovy baby heart out.

Perhaps most fascinating of all is the basement with its telecommunications centre, war room and warren of tunnels, where hulking old fans chop the air and ancient radio transmitters sit impassively. Towards the end are rooms where videos appraise the palace and its history in Vietnamese, English, French, Chinese and Japanese. The national anthem is played at the end of the tape and you are expected to stand up – it would be rude not to.

The Reunification Palace is open to visitors as long as official receptions or meetings aren't taking place. English- and French-speaking guides are on duty during opening hours.

Norodom Palace Gatehouse GALLERY
(Van Phong Chinh Phu Hoi Truong Thong Nhat; Map p316; ☑ 028-3822 3652; https://trungbay.dinhdoclap.gov.vn/en; 106 Đ Nguyen Du; ◷ 7.30am-5.30pm) The only surviving structure from the original Norodom Palace (which was bombed in 1962 and replaced with today's Reunification Palace) is this impressive French-colonial-era gatehouse. Good-quality art history exhibitions are held here; the last ticket is issued at 4.30pm.

Salon Saigon ARTS CENTRE
(Map p316; ☑ 0848 3933 3242; www.salonsaigon.com; 6d Đ Ngo Thoi Nhiem; ◷ 9am-noon & 1-6pm Tue-Sat) Housed in a splendidly restored French-colonial mansion – a building that was the home of US Ambassador Henry Cabot Lodge from 1963 to 1967 – Salon Saigon is a venue for art exhibitions and cultural and musical events. The spacious downstairs lounge also includes an excellent library with English, French and Vietnamese books on the history and culture of the country. Check the website for upcoming events and exhibitions.

Xa Loi Pagoda BUDDHIST TEMPLE
(Chua Xa Loi; Map p316; 89 Đ Ba Huyen Thanh Quan, District 3; ◷ 7-11am & 2-8pm) The inner walls of this sanctuary, famed as the repository of a sacred relic of the Buddha, are adorned with paintings depicting the Buddha's life. However, this 1956 building is most notable for its dramatic history. In August 1963 truckloads of armed men attacked the temple, which had become a centre of opposition to the Diem government. Today it's again a peaceful Buddhist refuge, with a large seated Buddha statue and a 32m-high seven-tier tower in its complex. Visitors must wear appropriate clothing (no shorts).

In 1963 the temple was ransacked by soldiers, a raid organised by President Diem's brother, and 400 monks and nuns, including the country's 80-year-old Buddhist patriarch, were arrested. This raid and others elsewhere helped solidify opposition to the regime among Buddhists, a crucial factor in the US decision to support the coup against Diem. The pagoda was also the site of several self-immolations by monks protesting against the Diem regime and the American War.

The etymology of the temple name points to its significance. The Chinese characters on the front of the temple – 'Sheli Si' (舍利寺; Sheli Temple), pronounced 'xa loi chua' in Vietnamese – mean 'Sarira Temple', from the Sanskrit word for 'Buddhist relic'.

WORTH A TRIP

EXPLORING DISTRICT 4

Just south of the glitzy Dong Khoi area, it's a short walk over the Ben Nghe Channel to working-class District 4. Here the ambience is far more Saigonese, with little or no concession to tourism, and with narrow lanes, street markets and shabby concrete apartment blocks. Order a coffee here and expect a drip-fed Vietnamese coffee that resembles engine oil rather than a frothy cappuccino.

District 4 is the best area in the city to sample authentic street food, with dozens of places on Đ Vinh Khanh. For great seafood at affordable prices, try **Oc Dao 2** (Map p308; 232 Đ Vinh Khanh; most mains 30,000-100,000d; ☻3pm-late). HCMC is a city in love with snails, and District 4 is something of a magnet for snail eaters, with many fine places on the buzzing alley Lo J KTT, including **Oc Po** (Map p308; 224 Lo J KTT; dishes from 30,000d; ☻4-11.30pm), which is always packed.

This district, bordered by canals and the Saigon River, was always one of the city's most flood-prone, until the government implemented a land-filling program that removed many small canals. A generation ago, parts of District 4 had a reputation as a hotbed for drug-dealing, illegal gambling dens and the red-light trade, and there were battles between gangsters and police for control of the streets. However, it's now considered a safe area to explore: just use your common sense, avoid dark lanes late at night and perhaps take a taxi home at the end of the evening.

Sights in D4 are few, but you will find the Ho Chi Minh Museum (p310) in the north of the district, while **Xom Chieu Market** (Map p308; 1 Dinh Le; ☻5am-5pm) is a deeply traditional affair and very much geared to local tastes, especially fresh fruit and inexpensive clothing.

Tour operators use District 4 as a destination for their street-food excursions, but it's possible to investigate the area on your own and head here on foot or by cab (a taxi here from District 1 is around 45,000d). From the southern end of Đ Pasteur in District 1, cross the Ben Nghe Channel via the pedestrianised 19th-century Mong Bridge, built by the French, and you can walk along the canal bank, then south down Đ Vinh Khanh. After you've crossed the canal it's not exactly scenic, however, and traffic is heavy.

Women enter the main hall of Xa Loi Pagoda, which houses a giant golden Sakyamuni (the historical Buddha), by the staircase on the right as you come in the gate; men use the stairs on the left. Behind the main hall, a further hall contains a painting of Bodhidharma, an Indian monk celebrated as the father of Zen Buddhism. He stayed at the Shaolin Temple in China, developing the exercises that would become Shaolin Boxing. He is depicted here carrying a shoe on a stick (the story goes that when Bodhidharma's coffin was opened after his death, it was empty apart from one shoe).

Chanting and meditation classes are held here every Wednesday evening. A monk preaches every Sunday from 8am to 10am. On full- and new-moon days, special prayers are held from 7am to 9am and from 7pm to 8pm.

Mariamman Hindu Temple　HINDU TEMPLE
(Chua Ba Mariamman; Map p316; 45 Đ Truong Dinh; ☻7.30am-7.30pm) Only a small number of Hindus live in HCMC, but this colourful slice of southern India is also considered sacred by many ethnic Vietnamese and Chinese. Reputed to have miraculous powers, the temple was built at the end of the 19th century and dedicated to the Hindu goddess Mariamman. Remove your shoes and ignore any demands to buy joss sticks and jasmine.

**Venerable Thich
Quang Duc Memorial**　MONUMENT
(Map p316; cnr Đ Nguyen Dinh Chieu & Đ Cach Mang Thang Tam) This peaceful memorial park is dedicated to Thich Quang Duc, the Buddhist monk who self-immolated in protest at this intersection not far from the Presidential Palace (today's Reunification Palace) in 1963. The memorial was inaugurated in 2010, displaying Thich Quang Duc wreathed in flames before a bas-relief.

Tao Dan Park　PARK
(Map p316; Đ Nguyen Thi Minh Khai) One of the city's most attractive green spaces is 10-hectare Tao Dan Park, its bench-lined walks shaded with avenues of towering tropical trees, including flame trees and huge Sao Den and So Khi trees. It's fascinating to visit in the early morning and late afternoon

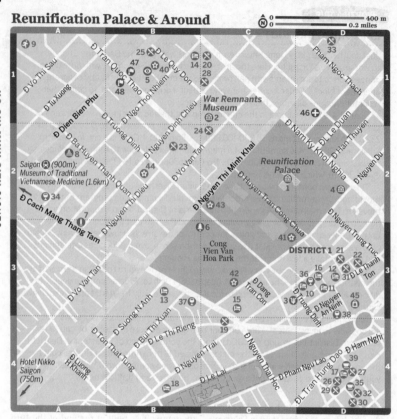

when thousands of locals exercise. The city's bird lovers (mainly elderly gentlemen) also flock here, cages in hand, to what is universally known as the bird cafe.

◉ Da Kao & Around

This old District 1 ward, directly north of the city centre, is home to most of the consulates and some beautiful buildings dating from the French-colonial period. Hidden within its historic streets (and those bordering it in the eastern corner of District 3) are good new restaurants and bars, along with some of the city's best traditional eateries.

★ **Jade Emperor Pagoda** TAOIST TEMPLE
(Phuoc Hai Tu, Chua Ngoc Hoang; Map p318; 73 Đ Mai Thi Luu; ⊙7am-6pm daily, plus 5am-7pm 1st & 15th of lunar month) FREE Built in 1909 in honour of the supreme Taoist god (the Jade Emperor or King of Heaven, Ngoc Hoang), this is one of the most atmospheric temples

in Ho Chi Minh City, stuffed with statues of phantasmal divinities and grotesque heroes. The pungent smoke of incense *(huong)* fills the air, obscuring the exquisite woodcarvings. Its roof is encrusted with elaborate tile work, and the temple's statues, depicting characters from both Buddhist and Taoist lore, are made from reinforced papier mâché.

Inside the main building are two especially fierce and menacing Taoist figures. On the right (as you face the altar) is a 4m-high statue of the general who defeated the Green Dragon (depicted underfoot). On the left is the general who defeated the White Tiger, which is also being stepped on.

Worshippers mass before the ineffable Jade Emperor, who presides – draped in luxurious robes and shrouded in a dense fug of incense smoke – over the main sanctuary. He is flanked by his guardians, the Four Big Diamonds (Tu Dai Kim Cuong), so named because they are said to be as hard as diamonds.

Reunification Palace & Around

HO CHI MINH CITY SIGHTS

Out the door on the left-hand side of the Jade Emperor's chamber is another room. The semi-enclosed area to the right (as you enter) is presided over by Thanh Hoang, the Chief of Hell; to the left is his red horse. Other figures here represent the gods who dispense punishments for evil acts and rewards for good deeds. The room also contains the famous Hall of the Ten Hells, carved wooden panels illustrating the varied torments awaiting evil people in each of the Ten Regions of Hell. Women queue up at the seated effigy of the City God, who wears a hat inscribed with Chinese characters that announce 'At one glance, money is given'. In a mesmerising ritual, worshippers first put money into a box, then rub a piece of red paper against his hand before circling it around a candle flame.

On the other side of the wall is a fascinating little room in which the ceramic figures of 12 women, overrun with children and wearing colourful clothes, sit in two rows of six. Each of the women exemplifies a human characteristic, either good or bad (as in the case of the woman drinking alcohol from a jug). Each figure represents a year in the 12-year Chinese astrological calendar. Presiding over the room is Kim Hoa Thanh Mau, the Chief of All Women. Upstairs is a hall to Quan Am, the Goddess of Mercy, opposite a portrait of Dat Ma, the bearded Indian founder of Zen Buddhism.

The multifaith nature of the temple is echoed in the shrine's alternative name Phuoc Hai Tu (福海寺; Sea of Blessing Temple), whose message is clearly Buddhist. Similarly, the Chinese characters (佛光普照; Phat Quang Pho Chieu) in the main temple hall mean 'The light of Buddha shines on all'.

Outside, a small pond seethes with turtles, some of which have shells marked with auspicious inscriptions.

Da Kao & Around

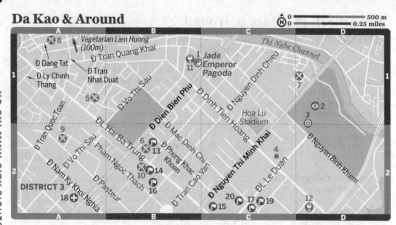

Da Kao & Around

⊙ Top Sights
1 Jade Emperor Pagoda	B1

⊙ Sights
2 Botanic Gardens	D1
3 History Museum	D1

⊕ Activities, Courses & Tours
4 University of Social Sciences & Humanities	C2

✴ Eating
5 Banh Xeo 46A	A1
6 Blanc Restaurant	B2
7 Bloom Saigon	D1
8 Cuc Gach Quan	A1
9 Pho Hoa	A2
10 Tib	B2

⊙ Drinking & Nightlife
11 Indika Saigon	B1
12 Lush	D2

⊙ Entertainment
Saigon Water Puppet Theatre	(see 3)

⊙ Information
13 Cambodian Consulate	B2
14 Chinese Consulate	B2
15 French Consulate	C2
16 German Consulate	B2
17 Netherlands Consulate	C2
18 Raffles Medical Group	A2
19 UK Consulate	C2
20 US Consulate	C2

History Museum   MUSEUM
(Bao Tang Lich Su; Map p318; Đ Nguyen Binh Khiem;
30,000d; ⊗8-11.30am & 1.30-5pm Tue-Sun) Built
in 1929, this notable Sino-French museum
houses a rewarding collection of artefacts
illustrating the evolution of the cultures of
Vietnam, from the Bronze Age Dong Son civilisation (which emerged in 2000 BCE) and
the Funan civilisation (1st to 6th centuries
CE) to the Cham, Khmer and Vietnamese.
Highlights include valuable relics taken
from Cambodia's Angkor Wat and a fine
collection of Buddha statues. There's good
English information. Parts of the museum
are being renovated.

Botanic Gardens   GARDENS
(Thao Cam Vien; Map p318; 2 Đ Nguyen Binh Khi-
em; incl zoo 50,000d; ⊗7am-7pm) One of the

first projects undertaken by the French after
establishing Cochinchina as a colony was
founding these fantastic, lush gardens. Once
one of the finest such gardens in Asia, they're
very agreeable for strolling beneath giant
tropical trees. Skip the miserable zoo though.

⊙ Cholon

Rummage through Cholon (District 5) and
lift the lid on a treasure trove of historic
temples and Chinese flavours. Ho Chi Minh
City's Chinatown is less Chinese than it
once was, largely due to the 1978–79 anti-
capitalist and anti-Chinese campaign, when
many ethnic Chinese fled the country, taking with them their money and entrepre-
neurial skills. A lot of those refugees have
since returned (with foreign passports) to

explore investment possibilities. Full-form written Chinese characters (as opposed to the simplified system used in mainland China) decorate shopfronts and temples in abundance, adding to the sensation that you have strayed into a forgotten corner of the Sino world. Finding a Mandarin-speaker isn't hard, although most Hoa-Kieu (Vietnamese-Chinese) residents chat in southern Chinese dialects.

Cholon means 'big market' and during the American War it was home to a thriving black market. Like much of HCMC, Cholon's historic shopfronts are swiftly disappearing under advertising hoardings or succumbing to developers' bulldozers, but some traditional architecture survives, and an atmospheric strip of traditional herb shops (p321) thrives between Đ Luong Nhu Hoc and Đ Trieu Quang Phuc, providing both a visual and an olfactory reminder of the old Chinese city. A taxi from Pham Ngu Lao to Cholon costs around 110,000d, or hop on bus 1 from Ben Thanh Market. Saigon- and Cholon-heritage buff Tim Doling features excellent essays on the area's changing face on his website www.historicvietnam.com.

★ **Binh Tay Market** MARKET
(Cho Binh Tay; Map p320; www.chobinhtay.gov. vn; 57a ĐL Thap Muoi; ⊙6am-7.30pm) Cholon's main market has a great clock tower and a central courtyard with gardens. Much of the business here is wholesale but it's popular with tour groups. The market was originally built by the French in the 1880s; Guangdong-born philanthropist Quach Dam paid for its rebuilding and was commemorated by a statue that is now in the Fine Arts Museum (p308). Very little English is spoken but expect a friendly welcome if you take breakfast or coffee with the market's street-food vendors.

★ **Phuoc An Hoi Quan Pagoda** TAOIST TEMPLE
(Quan De Mieu; Map p320; 184 Đ Hong Bang) FREE Delightfully fronted by greenery and opening to an interior blaze of red, gold, green and yellow, this is one of the most beautifully ornamented temples in town, dating from 1902. Of special interest are the elaborate brass ritual ornaments and weapons, and the fine woodcarvings on the altars, walls, columns, hanging lanterns and incense coils. From the exterior, look out for the ceramic scenes, each containing innumerable small figurines, that decorate the roof.

To the left of the entrance stands a life-size figure of the sacred horse of Quan Cong. Prior to departing on a journey, people make offerings to the equine figure before stroking its mane and ringing the bell around its neck. Behind the main altar, with its stone and brass incense braziers, is a statue of Quan Cong, to whom the temple is dedicated; other shrines are dedicated to Ong Bon (the guardian who presides over happiness and wealth) and Nam Ba Ngu Hanh.

Khanh Van Nam Vien Pagoda TAOIST TEMPLE
(Map p320; 269/2 Đ Nguyen Thi Nho) Built between 1939 and 1942, this temple is said to be the only pure Taoist temple in Vietnam and is unique for its colourful statues of Taoist disciples. Features to seek out include the unique 150cm-high statue of Laotse – the supreme philosopher of Taoism and author of the *Dao De Jing* (The Classic of the Way and its Power) – located upstairs.

Laotse's mirror-edged halo is rather surreal, while off to his left are two stone plaques with instructions for Taoist inhalation and exhalation exercises. A schematic drawing represents the human organs as a scene from rural China. The diaphragm, agent of inhalation, is at the bottom; the stomach is represented by a peasant ploughing with a water buffalo. The kidneys are marked by four yin and yang symbols, the liver is shown as a grove of trees and the heart is represented by a circle with a peasant standing in it, above which is a constellation. The tall pagoda represents the throat and the broken rainbow is the mouth. At the top are mountains and a seated figure that represent the brain and imagination, respectively.

The temple operates a home for several dozen elderly people. Next door is a free medical clinic also run by the pagoda. Leave a donation with the monks if you wish.

Thien Hau Pagoda TAOIST TEMPLE
(Ba Mieu, Pho Mieu, Chua Ba Thien Hau; Map p320; 710 Đ Nguyen Trai) FREE This gorgeous 19th-century temple is dedicated to the goddess Thien Hau, and always attracts a mix of worshippers and visitors, who mingle beneath the large coils of incense suspended overhead. It is believed that Thien Hau can travel over the oceans on a mat and ride the clouds to save people in trouble on the high seas.

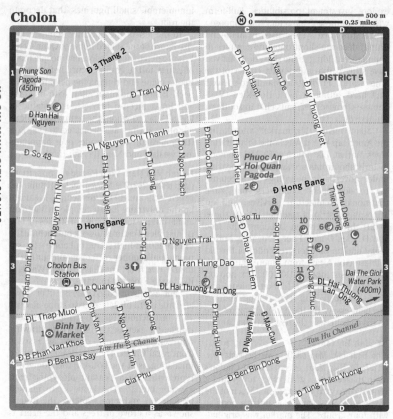

Cholon

◎ Top Sights

◎ Sights

Cha Tam Church   CHURCH
(Nha Tho Cha Tam; Map p320; 25 Đ Hoc Lac;
⊙7am–noon, 2-6pm & 7-9pm) **FREE** Built
around the turn of the 19th century, this de-
caying light-caramel-painted church exudes
a sleepy, tropical feel. A pew in the church

is marked with a small plaque identifying
the spot where President Ngo Dinh Diem
was seized after taking refuge here with his
brother Ngo Dinh Nhu on 2 November 1963,
after fleeing the Presidential Palace.

When their efforts to contact loyal military officers (of whom there were almost
none) failed, Diem and Nhu agreed to surrender unconditionally and revealed where
they were hiding. The coup leaders sent an
M-113 armoured personnel carrier to the
church and the two were taken into custody.
However, before the vehicle reached central
Saigon the soldiers had killed Diem and Nhu
by shooting them at point-blank range and
then repeatedly stabbing their bodies.

When news of the deaths was broadcast
on radio, Saigon exploded with jubilation.
Portraits of the two were torn up and political prisoners were set free. The city's
nightclubs, which had closed because of the
Ngos' conservative Catholic beliefs, were

reopened. Three weeks later the US president, John F Kennedy, was assassinated. As his administration had supported the coup against Diem, some conspiracy theorists speculated that Diem's family orchestrated Kennedy's death in retaliation.

The mint-green and white church interior is decorated with images of the Stations of the Cross, while holy water is dispensed from huge clam shells. The statue in the tower is of François Xavier Tam Assou (1855–1934), a Chinese-born vicar apostolic (delegate of the pope) of Saigon. Today the church has a congregation of around 3000 ethnic Vietnamese and 2000 ethnic Chinese. Masses are held daily.

Quan Am Pagoda   BUDDHIST TEMPLE
(Chua Quan Am; Map p320; 12 Đ Lao Tu) `FREE` One of Cholon's most active and colourful temples, this shrine was founded in the early 19th century. It's named after the Goddess of Mercy, whose full name is Quan The Am Bo Tat, literally 'the Bodhisattva Who Listens to the Cries of the World' (觀世音菩薩 in Chinese characters), in reflection of her compassionate mission.

The goddess's name is usually shortened to Quan Am (she is also worshipped in China, Korea and Japan) and her statue lies hidden behind a remarkably ornate exterior. In Tibet, where she is also widely worshipped, the goddess – who was once male – finds earthly form in the Dalai Lama. Fantastic ceramic scenes decorate the roof, depicting figures from traditional Chinese plays and stories. Other unique features of this temple are the gold-and-lacquer panels of the entrance doors.

Tam Son Hoi Quan Pagoda   TAOIST TEMPLE
(Chua Ba; Map p320; 118 Đ Trieu Quang Phuc) Retaining much of its original rich ornamentation, this 19th-century temple – a guildhall named after Sanshan (Three Mountains) in China's seaboard Fujian province – is dedicated to Me Sanh, the Goddess of Fertility, entreated by local women praying for children. Thien Hau – the Goddess of Seafarers – is also revered within the main shrine.

Ong Bon Pagoda   TAOIST TEMPLE
(Chua Ong Bon, Nhi Phu Mieu; Map p320; 264 ĐL Hai Thuong Lan Ong) This atmospheric temple is crammed with gilded carvings, smoking incense and the constant hubbub of kids from the large school next door. Built by Chinese immigrants from Fujian province,

it's dedicated to Ong Bon, the guardian who presides over happiness and wealth, and who is seated in a gilded cabinet sparkling with LED lights, an intricately carved and gilded wooden altar before him.

Cholon Jamail Mosque   MOSQUE
(Map p320; 641 Đ Nguyen Trai) The clean lines and minimal ornamentation of this mosque contrast starkly with nearby Chinese and Vietnamese Buddhist temples. Note the pool for ritual ablutions in the courtyard and the tiled mihrab (niche) in the wall of the prayer hall, indicating the direction of Mecca. This mosque was built by Tamil Muslims in 1935 but since 1975 it has served the Malaysian and Indonesian Muslim communities.

Traditional Herb Shops   AREA
(Map p320; Đ Hai Thuong Lan Ong) While you're roaming the area, stroll over to the strip of traditional herb shops between Đ Luong Nhu Hoc and Đ Trieu Quang Phuc for an olfactory experience you won't soon forget. The streets here are filled with amazing sights, sounds and rich herbal aromas.

Nghia An Hoi Quan Pagoda   TAOIST TEMPLE
(Map p320; 678 Đ Nguyen Trai) Noteworthy for its gilded woodwork, this temple has a large carved wooden boat hanging over its entrance and inside, to the left of the doorway, an enormous representation of Quan Cong's red horse with its groom. The temple is more accurately a guildhall (Hoi Quan), built in the early 19th century by Chinese from Yian (Nghia An) in China's Guangdong province.

◉ District 11

Immediately west of Cholon, the main enticements of District 11 are a couple of interesting old pagodas and a popular water park.

Giac Vien Pagoda   BUDDHIST TEMPLE
(Map p308; Đ Lac Long Quan; ⊘ 7-11.30am & 1.30-7.30pm) In a land where so many ancient temples have been 'restored' in concrete and neon, it's a joy to discover one that looks its age. The temple has an atmosphere of scholarly serenity, and its secluded location down an alley near Dam Sen Lake means it is less visited than other temples in nearby Cholon. It was founded by Hai Tinh Giac Vien in the late 1700s and it is said that Emperor Gia Long, who died in 1819, used to worship here.

Hidden behind a warren of winding lanes, the approach to the pagoda has several impressive tombs on the right – a popular playground for local kids. The pagoda itself has some 100 lavish carvings of divine beings.

The main sanctuary is on the other side of the wall behind the Hai Tinh Giac Vien statue. The dais is set behind a fantastic brass incense basin with fierce dragon heads emerging from each side. The Guardian of the Pagoda is against the wall opposite the dais.

Phung Son Pagoda   BUDDHIST TEMPLE

(Phung Son Tu, Chua Go; Map p308; 1408 ĐL 3 Thang 2; ☺ prayers 4-5am, 4-5pm & 6-7pm) Built between 1802 and 1820 on the site of structures from the Funan period, dating back at least to the early centuries of Christianity, this Buddhist temple is extremely rich in gilded, painted and beautifully fashioned bronze, wood, ceramic and beaten-copper statuary. The main dais, with its many levels, is dominated by a large gilded A Di Da Buddha (the Buddha of Infinite Light; Amitābha). The main entrances are locked most of the time, but the side entrance is open during prayer times.

◉ Other Neighbourhoods

Saigon is a vast city and there are pockets of interest spread around the outer (and emerging inner) suburbs. District 2, an upmarket area that's very popular with expats, is definitely worth visiting for its restaurants and bars, while Tan Binh District has an interesting temple. A short walk south of District 1, check out District 4 (p315) for street eats.

★ Giac Lam Pagoda   BUDDHIST TEMPLE

(Chua Giac Lam; Map p308; 118 Đ Lac Long Quan, Tan Binh District; ☺ 4am-noon & 2-9pm) FREE Believed to be the oldest temple in HCMC (1744), Giac Lam is a fantastically atmospheric place set in peaceful, garden-like grounds. The Chinese characters that constitute the temple's name (覚林寺) mean 'Feel the Woods Temple' and the looming bodhi tree (a native fig tree, sacred to Buddhists) in the front garden was the gift of a Sri Lankan monk in 1953. Prayers are held daily from 4am to 5am, 11am to noon, 4pm to 5pm and 7pm to 9pm.

Next to the tree stands a gleaming white statue of compassionate Quan The Am Bo Tat (also known as the Goddess of Mercy) on a lotus blossom, a symbol of purity.

As at many Vietnamese Buddhist temples, aspects of both Taoism and Confucianism

can be found here. For the sick and elderly, the pagoda is a minor pilgrimage sight, as it contains a bronze bell that, when rung, is believed to answer the prayers posted by petitioners.

The main sanctuary lies in the next room, filled with countless gilded figures. On the dais in the centre of the back row sits the A Di Da Buddha, easily spotted by his colourful halo. The fat laughing fellow, seated with five children climbing all over him, is Ameda, the Buddha of Enlightenment, Compassion and Wisdom.

About 3km from Cholon, Giac Lam Pagoda is best reached by taxi or *xe om* (motorbike taxi).

Museum of Traditional Vietnamese Medicine   MUSEUM

(Map p308; www.fitomuseum.com.vn; 41 Đ Hoang Du Khuong, District 10; adult/child 120,000/60,000d; ☺ 8.30am-5pm) A lovely piece of traditional architecture in itself, this absorbing and very well-stocked museum with over a dozen exhibition rooms affords fascinating insights into local medical practices, which are heavily influenced by China. While you're here, catch the short film about Vietnamese medicine, *A Century of Health Care Experiences,* and be sure to delve into the world of East Asian potions and remedies through the ages. Don't miss the Cham tower at the top, equipped with a fertility symbol.

San Art   GALLERY

(Map p308; ☎ 0163 981 1696; www.san-art.org; Millennium Masteri, 132 Đ Ben Van Don, District 4; ☺ 10.30am-6.30pm Tue-Sat) This inspiring, independent, nonprofit gallery was founded by artists, giving other local artists the opportunity to display and develop their intriguing work. There's an excellent open-resource reading room with a great selection of contemporary art books. The gallery tends to shift location quite regularly, so check their website for updates.

The Factory   GALLERY

(☎ 028-3744 2589; www.factoryartscentre.com; 15 Nguyen U Di, Thao Dien, District 2; adult/child under 16yr 50,000d/free; ☺ 10am-7pm Tue-Sun) HCMC's best contemporary art space is in District 2 on the east side of the Saigon River. Interesting exhibitions and showcases of local artists are partnered with talks and there's a lively program of events. In the compound is a Thai restaurant operating from a shipping container enlivened with colourful street art. Check the website for upcoming exhibitions. You can reach District 2 by the waterbus service from the city centre.

Le Van Duyet Temple TEMPLE

(Map p308; Đ Dinh Tien Hoang, Binh Thanh district) Dedicated to Marshal Le Van Duyet (1763–1831), this shrine is also his burial place, alongside that of his wife. The marshal was a South Vietnamese general and viceroy who helped defeat the Tay Son Rebellion and re-unify Vietnam. Among the items on display are a portrait of Le Van Duyet, personal effects including European-style crystal goblets, two life-size horse statues and a stuffed, mounted tiger. The temple is reached by heading north from Da Kao on Đ Dinh Tien Hoang.

Activities

River Cruises

Boats can be chartered from **Bach Dang Jetty** (Map p312; Đ Ton Duc Thang) to tour the Saigon River, but this option is definitely becoming less commonplace due to the water-bus service and as the waterfront is being gentrified. Prices should be around US$25 per hour for a small boat. It's best to set an itinerary and a time limit at the start.

Les Rives BOATING

(Map p312; 0128 592 0018; www.lesrivesexperi ence.com; 4th fl, 43-45 Đ Ho Tung Mau; adult/child sunset cruise 1,399,000/980,000d, Mekong Delta cruise 2,499,000/1,799,000d) Runs sunset boat tours (minimum two people) at 4pm along canals beyond the city edges, and a Mekong Delta speedboat trip that departs at 8am and takes eight hours.

Les Rives can also convey you to the Cu Chi Tunnels by boat. Other options incorporate scooter trips and cooking classes. Call for a pick-up.

Indochina Junk BOATING

(Map p312; 028-3895 7438; www.indochinajunk. com.vn; 5 Đ Nguyen Tat Thanh, District 4) Lunch and dinner cruises with set menus (from 350,000d) in an atmospheric wooden junk on the Saigon River, departing from next to the Ho Chi Minh Museum in District 4.

Massage & Spa

Ho Chi Minh City offers some truly fantastic hideaways for pampering and treatments – the perfect antidote to a frenetic day spent dodging motorbikes.

★ Aveda SPA

(028-3519 4679; www.avedaherbal.com; Villa 1, 21/1 Đ Xuan Thuy; ⊙9am-8pm Wed-Mon) This wonderful District 2–based spa is Indian-owned and offers sublime, professional and keenly priced Ayurvedic spa treatments: try a head massage (500,000d) or a wonderful hot-stone massage (from 400,000d). Herbal hair care and henna treatments (both from 400,000d) are offered too. You can reach it from District 1 by waterbus or taxi (around 160,000d).

L'Apothiquaire SPA

(La Maison de L'Apothiquaire; Map p316; 028-3932 5181; www.lapothiquaire.com; 64a Đ Truong Dinh, District 3; ⊙9am-9pm) One of the city's most elegant spas, L'Apothiquaire is housed in a beautiful white mansion tucked down a quiet alley, with a pool and sauna. A four-hour Gentleman's Care package (2,770,000d) takes in foot and body treatments, facial, meal and free pick-up. L'Apothiquaire also makes its own line of lotions and cosmetics.

There is another centrally located branch in **District 1** (Artisan Beauté; Map p312; 028-3822 2158; www.lapothiquaire.com; 41 Đ Dong Khoi; ⊙9am-9pm).

Spa Gallery SPA

(Map p312; 028-6656 9571; www.booking spavietnam.com; 15b Đ Thi Sach; 1hr massage from 330,000d; ⊙10am-11.30pm) Spa Gallery has a reputation for offering excellent massages and treatments from well-trained staff. Facials and scrubs are fine value, or try the Gallery Special (630,000d), which includes a body massage with hot stones and a salt scrub.

Swimming Pools & Water Parks

Several inner-city hotels, including the Park Hyatt Saigon (p326) and Majestic Hotel (p326), offer nonguests access to their pools for a fee.

Dam Sen Water Park WATER PARK

(Map p308; www.damsenwaterpark.com.vn; 3 Đ Hoa Binh, District 11; adult/child before 4pm 170,000/130,000d, after 4pm 150,000/110,000d; ⊙9.30am-6pm Mon-Sat, 8.30am-6pm Sun) With wave pools and water slides, rivers with rapids (or slow currents) and rope swings, this is a good escape for families if the kids are getting tired of the city's incessant pace.

Dai The Gioi Water Park WATER PARK

(Map p308; www.daithegioiwaterpark.com.vn; Đ Ham Tu, Cholon; 45,000-85,000d; ⊙8am-9pm Mon-Fri, 10am-9pm Sat & Sun) Has a large pool with slides and lanes for lap swimming.

HO CHI MINH CITY ACTIVITIES

🎓 Courses

Grain Cooking Classes
COOKING

(Map p312; ☑ 028-3827 4929; www.grainbyluke.com; Level 3, 71-75 ĐL Hai Ba Trung; US$48; ⊙ 9am-noon & 2-5pm Mon-Sat) Cooking classes designed and coordinated by Vietnamese-Australian celebrity chef Luke Nguyen. Four-course menus change regularly to reflect seasonal produce, and Luke himself is on hand for some classes throughout the year.

Saigon Cooking Class
COOKING

(Map p312; ☑ 028-3825 8485; www.saigoncook ingclass.com; 74/7 ĐL Hai Ba Trung; 909,000d; ⊙ 10am & 2pm Tue-Sun) Watch and learn from the chefs at Hoa Tuc restaurant as they prepare three mains and a dessert. Dishes change daily: on Thursdays one of them is *bo la lot* (chargrilled beef wrapped in betel leaves with lemongrass). Kids can also participate for discounted rates (from 575,000d).

Vietnam Silver House
ARTS & CRAFTS

(Map p308; ☑ 028-3924 6568; www.vietnam silverhouse.com; 68 Đ Nghia Thuc, District 5; US$35; ⊙ 8am-8pm) At this jewellery workshop you can spend a challenging and enjoyable half-day with an instructor sawing, annealing, filing, soldering, hammering and polishing your own .950 silver ring to take home as a keepsake. The mini-museum charts the fascinating evolution of silversmithing in Vietnam, and expertly crafted silver items can be seen in the ground-floor retail space.

Mai Home
COOKING

(Saigon Culinary Arts Center; Map p328; ☑ 028-3838 6037; www.cookingsaigon.com; 269 Đ Nguyen Trai; US$38-45) Market visits and popular cooking classes held a short walk from the Pham Ngu Lao backpacker area. Special vegetarian menus are available.

University of Social Sciences & Humanities
LANGUAGE

(Dai Hoc Khoa Hoc Xa Hoi Va Nhan Van; Map p318; ☑ 028-3822 5009; www.hcmussh.edu.vn; 12 Đ Dinh Tien Hoang) This uni's group classes are a reasonably priced way to learn the language. Prices start at 65,000d per person per hour.

👉 Tours

Before you sign up for a standard, middle-of-the-road travel-agent tour of the city – the cheapest of which are available from agencies in the Pham Ngu Lao area – consider one of the far more imaginative and fun tours covering everything from street food and hidden cafes, to Chinatown, the art scene and Saigon after dark. Motorbike/scooter tours usually arrange pick-ups from your accommodation.

★ Old Compass Travel
TOURS

(Map p312; ☑ 028-3823 2969; www.oldcom passtravel.com; 3rd fl, 63/11 Đ Pasteur; from US$40) Excellent city tours lead by passionate Saigon residents who are experts on Vietnamese culture and architecture. Tales of the City is a heritage walking tour that takes in many of the sights along ĐL Le Duan and into the heart of District 1. Religious Architecture and Art tours are both very rewarding too. Based at the excellent Old Compass Cafe (p331). Consider their 'alternative' Cu Chi Tunnels tour too (which is not the typical tourist experience) or owner Mark Bowyer's superb 15-day Vietnam tours.

Sophie's Art Tour
TOURS

(☑ 0933 752 402; www.sophiesarttour.com; US$65; ⊙ 9am-1pm Tue-Sat) Art expert Sophie Hughes was based in Hue at the time of research but still leads occasional art tours in HCMC; check the website for updates. Tours visit private collections and contemporary art spaces, and explain the influence of Vietnamese history on artistic style and technique.

Vespa Adventures
TOURS

(Map p328; ☑ 0122 299 3585; www.vespaadventures.com; 169a Đ De Tham; from US$78) Entertaining guided city tours on vintage scooters, as well as day trips to the Mekong Delta (US$95). Embracing food, drink and music, the Saigon After Dark tour is brilliant fun, and the Saigon Craft Beer Tour is essential for travelling hopheads.

Saigon 2CV Tour
DRIVING

(☑ 090 978 9884; www.saigon2cvtour.com; adult/child from 1,200,000/900,000d) Explore the city in vintage open-topped Citroën vehicles. Options include an evening street food tour and a morning tour taking in HCMC's highlights.

Saigon Street Eats
FOOD & DRINK

(☑ 090 844 9408; www.saigonstreeteats.com; US$49-65) Excellent three- to four-hour scooter foodie tours around the streets and backstreets of town with Barbara and her husband, Vu. Select your tour according to taste: morning *pho* tours, lunchtime veggie tours or evening seafood tours. Bespoke tours can also be arranged.

Back of the Bike Tours
TOURS

(☑ 093 504 6910; www.backofthebiketours.com; from US$42) Cheaper than other scooter tours, this outfit offers a wildly popular four-hour Street Food tour and a good Night Rider tour that takes in seven districts. The speedboat trips to Cu Chi Tunnels (per person US$80) are also great.

Vietnam Photo Adventures
TOURS

(☑ 0913 236 876; www.vietnamphotoadventures. com; from US$99) These tours are curated by an experienced photographer who is also a long-term resident of Vietnam. Produce your own photographic memories on excursions focusing on Saigon landmarks, and street life of Cholon and local neighbourhoods. Saigon Scoot 'n' Shoot (US$199) is a tour from the back of a motorbike. Longer one- and two-night trips in the Mekong Delta are also available.

XO Tours
CULTURAL

(☑ 0933 083 727; www.xotours.vn; from US$52) Wearing *ao dai* (traditional dress), these women run scooter/motorbike foodie, sights and Saigon by Night tours: they're super-hospitable and fantastic fun.

Detoured
TOURS

(☑ 090 346 4383; www.detouredasia.com; US$55) Good walking tours exploring Saigon's street-art scene and heritage apartment blocks (maximum group size is eight). Standard tours of the city and regional highlights can also be arranged.

★ Festivals & Events

Tet
NEW YEAR

(☉ 1st day of 1st lunar month) The whole city parties and then empties out for family breaks. Đ Nguyen Hue features a huge flower exhibition, blooms fill Tao Dan Park and adults give 'lucky money' to children.

⌂ Sleeping

District 1 is the obvious lodging choice given its proximity to the airport and almost everything of interest. Within District 1, head east towards Đ Dong Khoi to be close to the best restaurants and bars, west towards Pham Ngu Lao for budget accommodation, or for somewhere midrange, try around Ben Thanh Market. Be aware, however, that traffic and pollution are punishing all over District 1.

District 3, just north of District 1, is also a convenient location for sights and is a little more leafy. There are also several interesting riverside properties in District 2, around 20 minutes from central HCMC by taxi (or waterbus).

At the lower end, a few dollars can be the difference between a dank, stuffy, windowless shoebox and a pleasant, well-appointed room with air-conditioning and ventilation. For rock-bottom prices, Pham Ngu Lao has rooms for US$15 or so. Dorms are available for as little as US$4 a night, but security can be an issue in the cheapest of places, so reckon on paying upwards of US$8 for a decent hostel bed.

More discerning budget travellers can book ahead for similar places at slightly lower rates in the surrounding areas, such as the Co Giang and Nguyen Thai Binh wards.

At the top end, some of the city's best hotels occupy period, character-filled buildings where standards are international, as are the prices.

⌂ Dong Khoi Area

Home to Ho Chi Minh City's top-notch hotels, the Dong Khoi area is also sprinkled with attractive midrange options. You'll find a few budget options on the fringe of this zone too.

Saigon Central Hostel
HOSTEL $

(Map p312; ☑ 028-3914 1107; saigoncentralhostel@gmail.com; 54/6 Đ Ky Con; dm/d US$7/27; ❄@🛜) Friendly guesthouse located in a quiet lane in an emerging area of town – it's walking distance from Pham Ngu Lao and Dong Khoi. Dorms have decent air-con, the breakfast is good and there's a rooftop terrace.

Town House 23
GUESTHOUSE $

(Map p316; ☑ 028-3915 1491; www.townhousesaigon.com; 23 Đ Dang Thi Nhu; dm US$11, r US$32-37; ❄@🛜) Located in a quiet cafe-lined street a short walk from the bustle of Pham Ngu Lao, Town House 23 is a modern and well-designed combination of hostel and guesthouse. The decor is particularly stylish and the team at reception is very helpful. Not all rooms have windows.

★ Myst
BOUTIQUE HOTEL $$$

(Map p312; ☑ 028-3520 3040; www.themystdongkhoihotel.com; 6-8 Đ Ho Huan Nghiep; r US$130-180; ❄🛜≋) Very popular, this hip hotel is just a short stroll from the riverside and good shopping along Đ Dong Khoi. Decor combines retro Indochinese style with a dash of 1930s art-deco influence. The quirky exterior is enlivened by a living wall of tropical shrubbery. There's a compact rooftop lap pool, and Bar Bleu, on the 14th floor, has extensive city views.

Park Hyatt Saigon
HOTEL $$$

(Map p312; 028-3824 1234; www.saigon. park.hyatt.com; 2 Lam Son Sq; r from US$320; ✸@🛜🏊) This luxury hotel is one of HCMC's very best. A prime location opposite the Opera House combines with exemplary service, fastidiously attired staff and lavishly appointed rooms. Relaxation opportunities include an inviting pool and the acclaimed Xuan Spa. Highly regarded (yet affordable) restaurants include Opera, for Italian, and Square One (www.saigon.park. hyattrestaurants.com/squareOne; meals from 280,000d; ⊙noon-2.30pm & 5.30-10.30pm; 🛜), serving Vietnamese and international fare.

Le Méridien
HOTEL $$$

(Map p312; 028-6263 6688; www.lemeridien saigon.com; 3c Đ Ton Duc Thang; d from US$222; ⊖✸@🛜🏊) Le Méridien's sleek contemporary design and stellar facilities (including a pool, spa, and five different bars, cafes and restaurants) make it a fine choice. Many rooms have excellent river views, and the dining scene on Đ Ngo Van Nam is nearby.

Intercontinental Asiana Saigon
HOTEL $$$

(Map p312; 028-3520 9999; www.intercontinen tal.com; cnr ĐL Hai Ba Trung & ĐL Le Duan; r from US$235; ✸@🛜🏊) One of the city's premier addresses, the Intercontintental is modern and tasteful without falling into generic blandness. Rooms have a dash of design class, including Eames-style chairs and sculpted free-standing baths, and many enjoy supreme views. A neighbouring tower of apartment-style residences caters to longer stays.

Liberty Central Saigon Citypoint
HOTEL $$$

(Map p312; 028-3822 5678; www.libertycen tralsaigoncitypoint.com; 59 Đ Pasteur; d from US$135; ✸@🛜🏊) Liberty is a Vietnamese hotel brand with a reputation for value and service. Rooms feature chic decor and spacious bathrooms, and relaxation options include a rooftop pool with views to the Saigon River, and an excellent spa. Some of the city's best eating and drinking options are nearby.

Caravelle Hotel
HOTEL $$$

(Map p312; 028-3823 4999; www.caravelle hotel.com; 19 Lam Son Sq; r from US$182; ✸@🛜🏊) One of the first luxury hotels to reopen its doors in postwar Saigon, the five-star Caravelle remains a classic operation. Rooms in the modern 24-floor block are quietly elegant; the priciest rooms and suites are in the historic 'signature' wing. The rooftop Saigon Saigon Bar (⊙11am-2am; 🛜) is a spectacular cocktail spot.

Majestic Hotel
HOTEL $$$

(Map p312; 028-3829 5517; www.majestic saigon.com; 1 Đ Dong Khoi; r US$132-195; ⊖✸🛜🏊) This 1925 city landmark enjoys an unmatched location on the Saigon River and its graceful facade, marrying art-nouveau and French-colonial styles, is illuminated at night. Majestic's rooftop bar is the perfect spot for a cocktail on a breezy evening. However, rooms are perhaps a little ordinary given the grand address.

🛏 Reunification Palace & Around

This area encompasses a lot of greenery, with Tao Dan Park at its core. There are many fine midrange options around Ben Thanh Market.

Coco Hostel
HOSTEL $

(Map p312; 090 311 8216; www.facebook.com/ cocohostelbar; 178/4b Đ Pasteur; dm US$8-10, r US$27-32; ⊖✸🛜) This small hostel is run by a friendly team and has an enviable location in an upmarket corner of District 1 near parkland and the Reunification Palace. Dorm beds all have reading lights and privacy curtains, and all accommodation is air-conditioned. There's a guests' kitchen and breakfast is included.

Vietnam Backpacker Hostel
HOSTEL $

(Map p316; 028-3925 4348; www.vietnam backpackerhostels.com; 200 Đ Le Lai; dm from 119,000d, r 886,000d; ⊖✸🛜) This lively place remains a good choice if you want to socialise and be in the heart of things. The building is a sprawling, multistorey affair offering good-value dorms (with eight to 12 beds) and spacious private rooms. It has a rooftop bar and offers lots of fun nights: quizzes, games and even a 'shit shirt' evening!

★Nguyen Shack
GUESTHOUSE $$

(Map p316; 028-3822 0501; www.nguyen shack.com; 6/15 Đ Cach Mang Thang Tam; r

900,000-1,150,000đ; ✿✽⊙) Down a quiet residential lane a shortish walk from Pham Ngu Lao and Ben Thanh Market, Nguyen Shack's first city opening incorporates a rustic look, with bamboo furniture and ample greenery, spotless and spacious rooms (some sleeping four), and a leafy, shared downstairs area. Breakfast and water refills are complimentary.

Avanti Hotel Saigon   HOTEL **$$**
(Map p316; ☑0838 228 066; https://avanti hotel.business.site; 186 Đ Le Thanh Ton; r US$45-75; ✿✽⊙) Located at the northern end of Ben Thanh Market, this hotel is perfect for those on a retail mission, and there are some superb restaurants within walking range too. Rooms are smallish but neat and well-appointed, and staff are eager to please.

Sanouva   HOTEL **$$**
(Map p316; ☑028-3827 5275; www.sanouvahotel. com; 177 Đ Ly Tu Trong; r from US$65; ✿✽@⊙) The Sanouva channels a chic Asian vibe and has a good location just two blocks back from Ben Thanh Market. Rooms are well presented with Vietnamese furnishings and colourful accents. Book direct for the best rates.

Anpha Boutique Hotel   BOUTIQUE HOTEL **$$**
(Map p316; ☑028-3823 8890; www.anphabou tiquehotel.com; 202 Đ Le Thanh Ton; d US$54-101; ✿✽⊙) Close to the Ben Thanh Market, Anpha Boutique features stylish rooms with super-comfortable beds, coffee-making facilities and flat-screen TVs. The staff are helpful and friendly, and while breakfast on the roof terrace could be better, consolation comes with views of Saigon's Bitexco Financial Tower.

★Ma Maison Boutique Hotel   HOTEL **$$$**
(Map p308; ☑028-3846 0263; www.mamaison. vn; 656/52 Đ Cach Mang Thang Tam, District 3; s US$65-75, d US$80-125; ✽@⊙) Classy Ma Maison is halfway between the airport and the city centre, and partly in the French countryside, decor-wise. Wooden shutters soften the exterior of the modern, medium-rise block, while in the rooms, painted French-provincial-style furniture and first-rate bathrooms add a touch of panache.

★Fusion Suites Saigon   DESIGN HOTEL **$$$**
(Map p316; ☑028-3925 7257; www.saigon. fusion-suites.com; 3-5 Đ Suong Nguyet Anh; r US$137-234; ✿✽⊙) In a relatively quiet street lined with tall, decades-old trees,

Fusion Suites Saigon offers spacious rooms decked out in warm natural wood and enlivened with monochrome images of Vietnamese life. Rainforest showers in the bathrooms, an excellent rooftop restaurant, and a modern ground-floor cafe and juice bar are all good reasons to make this your Saigon base.

Spa and wellness services are also available, but there's no swimming pool. Ask for a room on the higher floors as the primary school across the road can get pretty lively.

Mai House Saigon   HOTEL **$$$**
(Map p316; ☑028-7303 9000; www.maihouse. com/saigon; 157 Đ Ngo Thoi Nhiem, District 3; r from US$120; ✿✽⊙⊠) This fine luxury choice has a whiff of colonial glamour, with French Indochinese design touches, dark-wood furniture and sumptuous furnishings. Options include spacious rooms, suites and serviced apartments. There's a fine pool, a gym (open 24 hours) and a spa. It's around the corner from the Reunification Palace in District 3.

Adora Art Hotel   HOTEL **$$$**
(Map p316; ☑028-2253 9316; www.adorahotel benthanh.com; 189-191 Đ Ly Tu Trong; r US$95-120, ste from US$155; ✿✽⊙⊠) Very conveniently located, the Adora Art is steps from the Ben Thanh Market and a stroll from Tao Dan Park. Rooms are presented beautifully, with plush furnishings, and the rooftop pool enjoys panoramic views of the city.

Lavender Hotel   HOTEL **$$$**
(Map p316; ☑028-2222 8888; www.lavender hotel.com.vn; 208 Đ Le Thanh Ton; r 2,100,000-2,900,000đ; ✿✽⊙) Eschewing the nanna-ish connotations of its name, Lavender drapes itself stylishly in creamy marble and muted tones. The location, right by Ben Thanh Market, is excellent. Note that the two smallest room categories do not have windows.

🏨 Pham Ngu Lao Area

Pham Ngu Lao is Ho Chi Minh City's budget zone and it's easy to hunt for a hotel or guesthouse on foot here. Four streets (Đ Pham Ngu Lao, Đ De Tham, Đ Bui Vien and Đ Do Quang Dau), along with a warren of intersecting alleys, form the heart of this backpacker ghetto, with more than 100 accommodation choices available. Even midrange travellers can find excellent deals here, often at budget prices. Basic breakfasts are usually included.

Among the options are many family-run guesthouses (US$15 to US$35 per night) and minihotels (US$30 to US$60), and even a few dorms (decent options from US$8).

Lily's Hostel
HOSTEL **$**

(Map p328; ☑028-3920 9180; lilyhostel.hcm@ gmail.com; 35/5 Đ Bui Vien; dm/d US$8/28; ❄✳🛜) Lily's has a warm and welcoming ambience courtesy of its hip, modern decor. Located in a lane just off bustling Đ Bui Vien, it easily bridges the gap between hostel and boutique guesthouse. Some private rooms have a flat-screen TV and minibar.

Diep Anh
GUESTHOUSE **$**

(Map p328; ☑028-3836 7920; dieptheanh@ hcm.vnn.vn; 241/31 Đ Pham Ngu Lao; r US$21-26; ❄✳@🛜) A step above most PNL options, figuratively and literally (with thousand-yard stairs), Diep Anh's tall and narrow shape makes for light and airy upper rooms. Clean, safe and secure, this is a very welcoming guesthouse run by a hands-on couple.

Hong Han Hotel
GUESTHOUSE **$**

(Map p328; ☑028-3836 1927; www.honghan hotelhcm.com; 238 Đ Bui Vien; r incl breakfast US$25-35; ❄✳@🛜) A well-run family-owned guesthouse where you can opt for front rooms with ace views, or smaller, quieter and cheaper rear options; all en suites are small and functional. There are seven floors, with no lift, however.

Hideout Hostel
HOSTEL **$**

(Map p328; ☑028-3838 9147; www.hideout hostels.asia/saigon.html; 281 Đ Pham Ngu Lao; dm US$7; ✳@🛜) A modern PNL hostel with an emphasis on good times and meeting other travellers. Dorms (one for females) are spick and span with bright colours, and a free beer per day is on offer in the rooftop bar (which has a pool table and foosball). The hostel runs bar crawls three nights a week (free for guests).

Giang Son
GUESTHOUSE **$**

(Map p328; ☑028-3837 7547; 283/14 Đ Pham Ngu Lao; r US$20-32; ✳🛜) On a back alley off Pham Ngu Lao, tall and thin Giang Son has three rooms on each floor, a roof terrace and charming service; the sole downer is that there's no lift. Consider upgrading to a room with a window.

Long Hostel
HOSTEL **$**

(Map p328; ☑028-3836 0184; longhomestay@ yahoo.com; 373/10 Đ Pham Ngu Lao; dm/d US$8/20; 🛜) This popular, simple and clean

Pham Ngu Lao Area

guesthouse is run by a pleasant and helpful family. Rooms are small but clean and four-bed dorms are available; however, there's only one shower room per floor so expect a wait in the morning. All guests get a couple of free beers.

Bich Duyen Hotel
GUESTHOUSE $

(Map p328; ☑028-3837 4588; www.bich duyenhotel.net; 283/4 Đ Pham Ngu Lao; r US$20-28; ❇@♠) In the heart of the action, this efficiently run guesthouse offers a welcoming stay. The more expensive rooms are worth the extra money for a window. No lift.

Pham Ngu Lao Area

Liberty Hotel Saigon Greenview
HOTEL $$

(Map p328; ☑028-3836 9522; www.libertysaigon greenview.com; 187 Đ Pham Ngu Lao; r from US$42; ❇@♠) Refurbished in a cool and classy mix of soothing neutral colours and natural wood, Liberty's Saigon Greenview is one of Pham Ngu Lao's better accommodation options. Rooms at the front have views of the 23/9 Park on the northern edge of Saigon's backpacker district, though they do suffer a degree of traffic noise.

C-Central Hotel
HOTEL $$

(Map p328; ☑028-3837 8087; www.ccentral hotels.com; 216 Đ De Tham; r US$58-86; ➖❇♠) C-Central is a sleek, modernist hotel with comfortable, compact rooms and a lift. However, it's bang smack in the very centre of the Pham Ngu Lao backpacking scene so expect chaos and commotion round the clock.

Blue River Hotel
HOTEL $$

(Map p328; ☑028-3837 6483; www.facebook. com/blueriverphamngulao; 283/2c Đ Pham Ngu Lao; r US$28-52; ❇♠) A refurbished, welcoming little hotel with decent, spacious rooms, each with modern furnishings, minibar, flat-screen LCD TVs and a safe. A kitchen for guest use is available.

Duc Vuong
HOTEL $$

(Map p328; ☑028-3920 6991; www.ducvuong hotel.com; 195 Đ Bui Vien; d US$32-58; ❇@♠) The Duc Vuong has good-value rooms with ample space and wooden floors, plus friendly staff and a rooftop restaurant that effortlessly morphs into a bar for sunset drinks.

Elios Hotel
HOTEL $$

(Map p328; ☑028-3838 5584; www.elioshotel.vn; 233 Đ Pham Ngu Lao; r US$52-82; ❇@♠) This three-star hotel's swish entrance, with its aquariums and elegant design, sets a classy tone. Elios' 81 dark-wood rooms are inviting, with safes and writing desks, and many have fine city vistas. Breakfast is served in the rooftop restaurant.

Beautiful Saigon 1
HOTEL $$

(Map p328; ☑028-3836 4852; www.beautiful saigonhotel.com; 62 Đ Bui Vien; r US$40-70; ❇@♠) A tall and skinny minihotel, with a modern reception run by staff wearing red *ao dai*. A lift ascends to the tidy rooms, the cheaper of which are small and windowless.

Cat Huy Hotel
HOTEL $$

(Map p328; ☑028-3920 8716; www.cathuy hotel.com; 353/28 Đ Pham Ngu Lao; r US$30-42; ❇♠) Stuffed away down an alley in Pham

Ngu Lao, this established 10-room hotel has decent twin, double and triple rooms with flat-screen TVs and minibars. The cheapest rooms are without windows, others have balconies. There's no lift.

🛏 Co Giang

For a quieter alternative to Pham Ngu Lao, there's a string of guesthouses in Co Giang ward (District 1) in a quiet alley connecting Đ Co Giang and Đ Co Bac. This is an emerging area, gritty in parts but with a burgeoning array of hipster cafes and trendy restaurants.

OYO 623 California

Guest House   GUESTHOUSE $

(Map p308; ☑ 028-3837 8885; www.oyorooms.com/vn; 171đ Co Bac; s/d US$16/22; ❄@ 🤶) There's no mirrors on the ceiling or pink champagne on ice, but at the guesthouse California, now rebranded under the OYO umbrella, there's a guests' kitchen, roof garden and further rooms across the way.

⭐**Chez Mimosa Boutique Hotel**   HOTEL $$

(Map p308; ☑ 028-3838 9883; www.chezmimosa.com; 71 Đ Co Giang; r 1,000,000-1,600,000d; ⊝❄🤶) Expect a warm welcome from the well-trained staff at this attractive hotel. Rooms are light, airy and presented with white furniture and style. It's located in an interesting district that's fast becoming one of HCMC's most fashionable. Laundry is free for guests, but there's no lift. There are other Mimosa branches nearby.

🛏 District 2

This is the perfect location if HCMC's pollution and traffic are a real concern. It's an upmarket zone home to expats and wealthy Saigonese. To get to the centre you'll be relying on taxis or the waterbus.

Glenwood City Resort   HOTEL $$

(☑1800 1117; www.glenwood.asia; 243 Đ Nguyen Van Huong; r from US$65; ❄🤶🈸) Offering good value for pricey District 2, this place is a good choice for those who favour a peaceful base. There's attractive, spacious accommodation and a fitness centre, while D2's many bars, cafes and restaurants are on your doorstep. Weekly and monthly rates are available.

⭐**River Cottage**   BOUTIQUE HOTEL $$$

(☑ 028-3744 3555; www.rivercottage.com.vn; 18 Đ Duong 6; r US$90-140; ⊝❄🤶) Set in verdant gardens on the banks of the Saigon River, this hotel is a uniquely peaceful retreat from the energy of the city. Eight rooms – some riverside – blend modern design with handmade furniture, beds with luxe linen, wooden daybeds and expansive windows. There's all-day dining, with fine Western and local cuisine available.

Villa Song   BOUTIQUE HOTEL $$$

(☑ 028-3744 6090; www.villasong.com; 187/2 Đ Nguyen Van Huong; r US$180-260, ste US$385-445; ⊝❄🤶🈸) In a District 2 garden location with river views, this French-inspired boutique hotel is one of HCMC's most relaxing places to stay. Very romantic rooms and suites are filled with heritage Indochinese style and contemporary Vietnamese art, and the property's Song Vie bistro has an absolute riverside location. The spa is also very well regarded. A free minibus shuttle – around 30 minutes – to central HCMC is available.

🛏 Other Neighbourhoods

Hotel Nikko Saigon   HOTEL $$$

(Map p308; ☑ 028-3925 7777; www.hotelnikkosaigon.com.vn; 235 Đ Nguyen Van Cu, District 1; d from US$110; ❄@🤶) The location is a bit stranded for sightseers, so you'll be taking taxis to the centre, but this is reflected in the rates, which are fine value given the quality of rooms and facilities. Expect faultless service, an obsessive attention to detail and some of the best Japanese food in town.

🍴 Eating

Hanoi may consider itself more cultured, but Ho Chi Minh City is Vietnam's culinary capital. Delicious regional fare is complemented by a well-developed choice of international restaurants, with Indian, Japanese, Thai, Italian and East–West fusions well represented. Unsurprisingly, given its heritage, HCMC has a fine selection of French restaurants, from the casual bistro to haute cuisine.

There are also a few escapes further afield for those willing to explore, including District 2, which scores highly for international cuisine. For a really local experience head south to District 4 (p315), particularly for seafood and snails.

🍴 Dong Khoi & Ben Thanh Market

Dong Khoi, as well as bordering sections of District 3, has a high concentration of top-quality restaurants. In recent years the

Ben Thanh Market area has taken off, with a food court and lots of quirky independent places.

Maison Saigon Marou   CAFE $
(Map p316; ☑028-7300 5010; www.maison marou.com; 167-169 Đ Calmette; snacks from 60,000d; ⊙9am-10pm Mon-Thu, to 11pm Fri-Sun; 🚇) 🍴 This stylish and colourful cafe is home base for Marou, an artisan chocolate producer. Watch Marou's skilled team tempering and moulding chocolate crafted from local fair-trade cacao, and enjoy drinks (hot chocolate from 90,000d) and snacks also incorporating the stellar ingredients. Try the iced chocolate with cinnamon and chilli.

Secret Garden   VIETNAMESE $
(Map p312; ☑090 990 4621; www.facebook.com/ secretgarden158pasteur; 4th fl, 158 Đ Pasteur; meals 70,000-120,000d; ⊙8am-10pm; 🚇🍴) You pass through a motorbike parking lot then negotiate the stairs of a faded HCMC apartment building to reach this wonderful rooftop restaurant. Rogue chickens peck away in the herb garden, Buddhist statues add ambience, and delicious homestyle dishes are served with city views. Service can sometimes be a little *too* casual, but it's worth persevering for the great flavours.

Huong Lai   VIETNAMESE $
(Map p312; ☑028-3822 6814; www.huonglai 2001saigon.com; 38 Đ Ly Tu Trong; meals 80,000-200,000d; ⊙11.30am-3pm & 6-10pm) A must for finely presented, traditional Vietnamese food, the airy and high-ceilinged loft of an old French-era shophouse is the setting for dining with a difference. Staff are from disadvantaged families or former street children, and receive on-the-job training, education and a place to stay.

Ralf's Artisan Gelato   ICE CREAM $
(Map p316; ☑097 932 7905; www.facebook.com/ ralfsartisangelato; 39 Đ Dang Thi Nhu; ice cream from 75,000d; ⊙1-10pm Tue-Sun) This specialist gelato outlet run by a lively Austrian offers a raft of flavours including green tea, pistachio and lemongrass. Ralf's sundaes are actually more like a mini-meal, and good coffee is also on offer.

Ben Thanh
Street Food Market   STREET FOOD $
(Map p316; ☑090 688 1707; www.facebook.com/ pg/BenThanhstreetfoodmarket; 26-30 Đ Thu Khoa Huan; meals from 45,000d; ⊙9am-midnight) Grab a table at the front of the market, order up some cold beers from the adjacent bar, then go exploring to put together a mini-feast of well-priced street food. Highlights include fresh oysters from Nha Trang and Korean-style meat treats. There's live music on Tuesdays and Saturdays.

★Quan Bui   VIETNAMESE $$
(Map p312; ☑028-3829 1515; www.quan-bui.com; 17a Đ Ngo Van Nam; meals 80,000-250,000d; ⊙8am-11pm) Stylish Indochinese decor features at this slick place where the focus is on authentic local cuisine. Many dishes feature the more hearty flavours of northern Vietnam; offerings include delicious *heo quay Quan Bui* (roasted pork served with pickle). Cocktails – from the associated bar across the lane – are among HCMC's best, and upstairs there's an air-conditioned and smoke-free dining room.

★Bep Me In   VIETNAMESE $$
(Map p316; ☑028-6866 6128; www.facebook. com/bepmein; 136/9 Đ Le Thanh Ton; mains 60,000-150,000d; ⊙11am-11pm; 🚇🍴) At the rear of a nail-bar alley near Ben Thanh Market, this superb resto offers rustic, honest dishes from rural Vietnam in hip surrounds. On the ground floor there are big shared tables, and the quirky decor includes colourful wall paintings and a vintage motorcycle rickshaw doubling as a drinks station. The upstairs dining room is more quiet and refined.

★Old Compass Cafe   CAFE $$
(Map p312; ☑090 390 0841; www.facebook. com/oldcompasscafe; 3rd fl, 63 Đ Pasteur; meals 150,000d; ⊙10.30am-10pm Sun-Thu, to 11pm Fri & Sat; 🚇) This cafe/cultural centre is a gem. It's tricky to find: off busy Đ Pasteur, along an alley and then up steep stairs in a somewhat rundown apartment building. But persevere and you'll enter a gorgeous all-day cafe that often segues into a live-music and performance space at night. Relax over coffee, wine or craft beer or opt for a fine-value lunch deal.

There are ample books to browse while you're lounging on a sofa, plus well-chosen tunes on the stereo and a character or two is always around. Check Facebook for listings of events.

★Hum Lounge
& Restaurant   VEGETARIAN $$
(Map p312; ☑028-3823 8920; www.humviet nam.vn; 2 Đ Thi Sach; meals 100,000-220,000d; ⊙10am-10pm; 🚇🍴) Excellent Vietnamese-inspired vegetarian cuisine in a central garden location. Settle into the elegant space with subtle lighting and classy furnishings

in a lane off the riverfront. Delectable dishes include calabash and seaweed soup (85,000d) and beetroot salad with passion fruit (140,000d).

Padma de Fleur
VIETNAMESE $$

(Map p316; ☑090 300 9873; www.cafe.padma defleur.vn; 55/6 Đ Le Thi Hong Gam; meals 150,000-220,000d; ☺9am-10pm Tue-Sun, set meals 11.30am-2pm & 5-10pm; ☎) This wonderful florist-cafe is run by an artistic owner who takes as much care with her bouquets as she does with her cooking. The food is healthy, nutritious and delicious, with lots of Vietnamese salad leaves and tasty morsels to savour. Located on a backstreet in an emerging hipster corner of town south of Pham Ngu Lao.

The space is open throughout the day for drinks (and flowers!), but food is only served at set times. Cocktails are also available in the evening (from 5pm to 10pm); reservations required.

Secret House
VIETNAMESE $$

(Map p316; ☑0911 877 008; www.facebook.com/ secrethousevn; 55/1 Đ Le Thi Hong Gam; meals 100,000-180,000d; ☺7am-10pm) Secret House offers a stylish take on homestyle Vietnamese cooking close to Ben Thanh Market. The main dining room features mud-and-straw walls and rustic lamps fashioned from fish traps, while outside tables overlook a herb garden. The extensive menu includes some countryside specialities, such as *nuoc mam kho quet*, a caramelised fish sauce used as a dip. Flavours and presentation are top-notch.

It's located on a wide alleyway (marked with number 55) off Đ Le Thi Hong Gam.

Nha Hang Di Mai
VIETNAMESE $$

(Map p316; ☑090 867 2388; www.nhahang dimai.com; 136-138 Đ Le Thi Hong Gam; meals 100,000-160,000d; ☺7.30am-10pm; ☎☑) This colourful restaurant offers a diverse taste of flavours from around Vietnam in air-conditioned comfort. Vintage decor with a touch of Indochine style is the setting for zingy salads, excellent noodle dishes and good seafood. Try the refreshing juices, iced teas and smoothies.

Cafe Marcel
BRASSERIE $$

(Map p312; ☑090 987 8096; www.facebook. com/cafemarcelsaigon; 96 Đ Nam Ky Khoi Nghia; meals 160,000-240,000d; ☺9am-10pm Tue-Sun; ☎) For the best brunch in the city look no further: this stylish little cafe serves Gallic classics with a twist – try a *croque marcel*,

a spicy *shakshouka* (eggs poached in tomato, pepper and garlic) or one of their many sourdough options. Sides include smashed avocado and bacon. Located on the 1st and 2nd floors.

Temple Club
VIETNAMESE $$

(Map p312; ☑028-3829 9244; www.templeclub. com.vn; 29 Đ Ton That Thiep; meals 140,000-220,000d; ☺noon-midnight; ☎☑) This restaurant is housed on the 2nd floor of a beautiful colonial-era house decorated with spiritual motifs and elegant Chinese characters. It has a refined atmosphere, with exposed brick walls and classy seating, and offers a huge selection of Vietnamese dishes (including vegetarian specialities) and fine cocktails.

Sky 28
INTERNATIONAL $$

(Map p312; ☑028-3822 9888; www.sedonaviet nam.com; 28th fl, Sedona Suites tower, 94 Đ Nam Ky Khoi Nghia; meals from 180,000d; ☺7am-10.30pm; ☎) Expect some of Saigon's best views from the tables of this 28th-floor upmarket hotel cafe-restaurant. It serves tasty international food, including burritos, club sandwiches and shawarma kebabs, and offers a three-course lunch deal for 189,000d. During happy hour (5pm to 8pm) beers cost just 40,000d. Or just grab a coffee and savour the cityscape.

Xu
VIETNAMESE $$

(Map p312; ☑028-3824 8468; www.xusaigon. com; 1st fl, 75 ĐL Hai Ba Trung; 3-course set lunch Mon-Fri 295,000d, meals 115,000-320,000d, tasting menus 900,000-1,300,000d; ☺11.30am-midnight) This superstylish restaurant-lounge serves a menu of Vietnamese-inspired fusion dishes. It's pricey, but well worth the flutter for the top service and classy wine list. The lunch menu includes classics like *com tam* ('broken' rice, grilled pork and lightly pickled vegetables) and there are innovative Viet tapas and top-notch cocktails too.

3T Quan Nuong
BARBECUE $$

(Map p312; ☑028-3821 1631; 29 Đ Ton That Thiep; meals 85,000-280,000d; ☺5-11pm) This breezy alfresco Vietnamese barbecue restaurant on the rooftop of the Temple Club is in many a HCMC diner's diary: choose your meat, fish, seafood and veggies and flame them up right there on the table. It's a lot of fun.

Propaganda
VIETNAMESE $$

(Map p312; ☑028-3822 9048; www.propaganda bistros.com; 21 Đ Han Thuyen; meals 125,000-580,000d; ☺7.30am-11pm; ☎) Colourful murals and retro socialist posters brighten up this popular bistro with park views. The menu focuses on street-food classics from around Vietnam, all enjoyed with a bustling and energetic ambience. Salads are particularly good and there are tempting 'Discovery' menus (from 510,000d), which include four courses, wine and tea.

Nha Hang Ngon
VIETNAMESE **$$**

(Map p312; ☑ 028-3827 7131; 160 Đ Pasteur; meals 70,000-300,000d; ☺ 7am-10pm; ☎) Thronging with locals and foreigners, this is one of HCMC's most popular spots, with a large range of the very best street food on offer in stylish surroundings across three levels. It's set in a leafy garden ringed by food stalls, with each cook serving a specialised traditional dish, ensuring an authentic taste of Vietnamese, Thai, Japanese, Chinese or Korean cuisine.

Relish & Sons
BISTRO **$$**

(Map p312; ☑ 012 0721 4294; www.relishandsons.com; 44 Đ Dong Du; meals 120,000-250,000d; ☺ 10am-11pm; ☎) Relish & Sons brings a versatile Melbourne vibe to Saigon. Highlights include gourmet burgers, and craft beer and cider on tap. Later in the evening try one of their cocktails with an Asian spin (like a Lemongrass Fizzle).

5Ku Station
BARBECUE **$$**

(Map p312; www.facebook.com/5kuStation; 29 Đ Le Thanh Thon; meals from 130,000d; ☺ 4pm-late) Hopping with evening diners, this branch of a chain of makeshift-looking alfresco barbecue restaurants is fun, boisterous and outgoing. Grab yourself a wooden box seat and a cold beer, and chow down on tasty barbecue and hotpot alongside a mix of locals, travellers and expats. Veggie dishes, including cauliflower stir-fried with garlic (65,000d), are also available.

Refinery
BISTRO **$$**

(Map p312; ☑ 028-3823 0509; www.therefinerysaigon.com; 74/7c ĐL Hai Ba Trung; meals 185,000-385,000d; ☺ 11am-late; ☎) Formerly an opium refinery, this lovely bistro and wine bar has winning cocktails and appetising food with a French and Mediterranean accent. Menu highlights include fine platters (try a cold cut), pasta and meat cooked on the charcoal grill. Set lunches are great value, with three courses and coffee costing 265,000d.

L'Usine
CAFE **$$**

(Map p312; ☑ 028-6674 9565; www.lusinespace.com; 151/1 Đ Dong Khoi; meals from 140,000d; ☺ 7.30am-10.30pm; ☎) This elegant cafe is set above a high-end clothing store, with decor combining industrial-style seating and vintage photos of old Saigon. The appetising

cafe menu features French-inspired comfort food, sandwiches, burgers, pasta and excellent all-day breakfasts (from 160,000d). Baked goods are made fresh in their central kitchen.

Barbecue Garden
VIETNAMESE **$$**

(Map p312; www.barbecuegarden.com; 135a Đ Nam Ky Khoi Nghia; meals 80,000-200,000d; ☺ 11am-11pm) Trees festooned with fairy lights, outdoor tables and a laid-back ambience make this the ideal spot for groups. Fire up the tabletop grills to barbecue different meats and seafood, and partner it all with tasty Vietnamese salads and cold beer. Weekday lunch specials are good value.

Soulburger
BURGERS **$$**

(Map p312; ☑ 0122 517 1261; www.facebook.com/soulburgersaigon; 4 Đ Phan Boi Chau; burgers 215,000-410,000d; ☺ 4-10pm Mon-Thu, 11am-10pm Fri & Sat, 11am-9pm Sun; ☎) Head up the narrow staircase here for some of Saigon's best burgers. They're all named after music legends like Little Richard and James Brown, and sides of chicken wings, onion rings and poutine complete the North American focus. Grab a balcony table for Ben Thanh Market views, and be surprised by the good range of German and Belgian beers also available.

Pizza 4P's
PIZZA **$$**

(Map p316; ☑ 028-3622 0500; www.pizza4ps.com; 8 Đ Thu Khoa Huan; meals 170,000-380,000d; ☺ 10am-2am Mon-Sat, to 11pm Sun) Close to Ben Thanh Market, Pizza 4P's has an interesting mix of pasta and Japanese-influenced pizza – trust us, the combinations work – and is partnered with excellent craft beer from HCMC's Heart of Darkness brewery.

Jake's BBQ
BARBECUE **$$**

(Map p312; ☑ 028-3825 1311; www.jakesamericanbbq.com; 50 Đ Pasteur; meals 150,000-350,000d; ☺ 10.30am-10.30pm) Park yourself at the bar and combine comfort grub and cold brews with US and Canadian sports on the TV. Standouts are the smoky ribs with a rich St Louis–style barbecue sauce and pulled-pork parfait (layered with mashed potatoes and baked beans). There are wraps and sandwiches too.

Annam Gourmet Market
CAFE **$$**

(Map p312; ☑ 028-3822 9332; www.annam-gourmet.com; 16 ĐL Hai Ba Trung; sandwiches from 90,000d, meals from 170,000d; ☺ 7am-9pm Mon-Fri, to 9.30pm Sat; ☎) A quiet, relaxing and neat place for breakfast, brunch, a salad, bruschetta or baguette sandwich, this stylish coffee shop on the upper floor of a delicatessen has lime-green sofas, a curved glass window and snappily dressed snackers and diners. There are plenty of gourmet goodies on sale if you're self-catering or planning on a picnic.

La Fiesta
TEX-MEX $$

(Map p316; ☑0944 291 697; www.facebook.com/lafiestavietnam; 33 Đ Dang Thi Nhu; meals 135,000-210,000d; ⊙11am-10pm Tue-Sun; ☎) Tacos, burritos and enchiladas all feature at this colourful restaurant where the decor features cacti and *lucha libre* (Mexican wrestling) masks. Well-crafted margaritas and sangria seal the deal – especially when served by the jug. *¡Olé!*

★ Quince
INTERNATIONAL $$$

(Map p312; www.facebook.com/quincesaigon; 37 Đ Ky Con; meals from 1,300,000d; ⊙5.30-11pm Mon-Sat; ☎) Saigon's hottest ticket is a resolutely urbane, happening space with an open kitchen, distressed brick walls, cool tunes and a slightly edgy location close to the Saigon River. The vibe is reminiscent of East London or New York, with prices and a wine list to match. The regularly changing menu traverses the globe with aplomb, raiding Asia, Europe and the Americas for influence.

Seafood options might include Hokkaido scallop sashimi with citrus-based marinade, Dalat tomatoes and puffed heirloom quinoa, while meat eaters will rejoice at dishes like barbecued smoked duck breast with burnt cabbage, black vinegar dressing and Sichuan chilli oil. Small plates are available and are a good way to go, as there's so much to savour here.

Racha Room
THAI $$$

(Map p312; ☑0908 791 412; www.facebook.com/theracharoom; 12-14 Đ Mac Thi Buoi; meals 260,000-450,000d; ⊙3pm-midnight; ☎) This bar-resto has cool clientele, playlists of lounge and house music and a fine layout with an elongated bar in the heart of the action. The menu features Thai street snacks (75,000d to 280,000d), shared plates (from 180,000d) and dumplings, and effortlessly stretches to include the fare of neighbouring countries as well.

Towa
JAPANESE $$$

(Map p312; ☑1800 234 579; www.towavn.com; 28th fl, Sedona Suites tower, 94 Đ Nam Ky Khoi Nghia; lunch/dinner from 250,000/550,000d; ⊙11.30am-2pm & 6-10.30pm Mon-Thu, 11.30am-3pm & 6-11pm Fri-Sun; ☎) For astonishing city vistas Towa can't be matched from its perch on the 28th floor. One of HCMC's best Japanese restaurants, this is the natural habitat for the city's elite and high rollers from Tokyo. Prices are as eye-watering as the views but lunchtime deals (two/three courses are 189,000/219,000d) offer fine value. Sushi and sashimi platters and cocktails are simply sublime. Book ahead. Alfresco tables are also available.

Skewers
MEDITERRANEAN $$$

(Map p312; ☑028-3822 4798; www.shgsaigon.com; 9a Đ Thai Van Lung; meals 280,000-500,000d; ⊙11.30am-2pm & 6-10pm; ☎) With a winning line in perfectly done skewered meats, the Mediterranean menu here takes in all stops from the Maghreb to Marseilles. It's strong on atmosphere, has an open-plan kitchen and draws a crowd; book ahead.

✗ Reunification Palace & Around

Banh Mi Huynh Hoa
VIETNAMESE $

(Map p316; 26 Đ Le Thi Rieng; banh mi 44,000d; ⊙2.30-11pm) This hole-in-the-wall *banh mi* joint is busy day and night with locals zipping up on motorbikes for stacks of the excellent baguettes stuffed with pork, pork and more pork, in tasty ways you may not have known existed. Street standing room only.

Beefsteak Nam Son
VIETNAMESE $

(Map p316; 157 Đ Nam Ky Khoi Nghia; meals from 50,000d; ⊙6am-10pm; ☎) For first-rate, affordable steak in a simple setting, this is a superb choice. Local steak, other beef dishes (such as the spicy beef soup *bun bo Hue*), imported Australian fillets and even cholesterol-friendly ostrich are on the well-priced menu.

Vegetarian Lien Huong
VEGETARIAN $

(Com Chay Lien Huong; Map p308; ☑093 348 5064; 10d Đ Tran Nhat Duat; meals 60,000-120,000d; ⊙8am-10pm; ☑) It's moved to this new location in the north of District 1, but the creative flavours are still there. Standouts include green-banana and mushroom hotpot with lemongrass and rice noodles. The English-language menu has excellent descriptions of the health benefits of each dish. Great value.

★ Hum Vegetarian Cafe & Restaurant
VEGETARIAN $$

(Map p316; ☑028-3930 3819; www.humvegetarian.com; 32 Đ Vo Van Tan, District 3; meals 130,000-

240,000d; ⊙10am-10pm; 🌱) This serene and elegant vegetarian restaurant requires your attention. Everything – from the charming service to the delightful Vietnamese dishes and peaceful outside tables – makes dining here an occasion to savour. Try the tofu in fermented bean sauce or the grilled pumpkin salad. There's also an equally laid-back and more central location (p331).

★ Chay Garden VEGETARIAN $$
(Map p316; 📞028-9885 5667; www.chaygarden. com; 52 Ð Vo Van Tan; meals 65,000-200,000d; ⊙7am-10pm; 🎍🌱) When you need a respite from Saigon's teeming streets, this lovely vegetarian restaurant is the perfect choice. Tucked down a quiet lane near the War Remnants Museum, Chay Garden consists of several dining rooms around a courtyard garden. Breakfast choices include *bun Hue* (vegan royal noodle soup), and you'll find salads, hotpots and soups for lunch and dinner.

Maria VIETNAMESE, SEAFOOD $$
(Map p316; 📞028-3930 2379; www.facebook.com/ marinasaigonseafoodrestaurant; 172 Ð Nguyen Dinh Chieu; meals 140,000-600,000d; ⊙7am-10pm) Ask a sample of well-to-do Saigonese where to go for seafood and chances are they will recommend this place. It's definitely geared to local tastes (bright lights, TVs playing sports, and piped music), but the food is delicious, particularly the baby salt-and-pepper squid (210,000d) and steamed clams (163,000d).

★ Jardin des Seins FRENCH $$$
(Map p316; 📞028-3930 3394; www.jdspourcel. com; 251 Ð Dien Bien Phu; mains from 820,000d; ⊙noon-2pm & 6-10pm) Opened by three-Michelin-starred twin chefs Jacques and Laurent Pourcel, this heritage villa in the city centre offers Mediterranean French gastronomy with wonderfully unexpected pairings like shrimp carpaccio with a Dijon-vinaigrette sorbet. Look for subtle winks to local cuisine, such as the offal spring roll that accompanies stewed Miéral pigeon.

The weekday lunch specials are excellent value at 630,000d for three courses. Dinner is also served in the minimalist Glass Box next to the villa, while drinks and caviar are available until 2am at the Caviar Bar.

Blanc Restaurant FUSION $$$
(Map p318; 📞028-6266 3535; www.blancres taurant.vn; 178/180d ÐL Hai Ba Trung; meals 300,000-500,000d; ⊙11am-11pm; 🎍) Housed in a beautifully restored French colonial-era building, Blanc serves refined Vietnamese fusion amid an eclectic collection of antiques and artwork. Thought is given to innovative flavours and textures, as in the Norwegian salmon atop a bed of coconut cut into noodles. The twist: the staff are hearing impaired, and diners are encouraged to interact with them using pictographs of Vietnamese sign language.

Shri Restaurant & Lounge INTERNATIONAL $$$
(Map p316; 📞028-3827 9631; www.shri.vn; 23rd fl, Centec Tower, 72-74 Ð Nguyen Thi Minh Khai; meals 450,000-1,400,000d; ⊙11am-midnight Mon-Fri, from 4pm Sat & Sun; 🎍) Atop an office block, romantic Shri has some of the best views in town. Book ahead for a terrace table or settle for the industrial-chic dining room. Look forward to international spins on steak and seafood – with international prices to match – or a cheaper pasta and paella menu. Also consider Shri for a sunset cocktail.

✕ Da Kao & Around

Banh Xeo 46A VIETNAMESE $
(Map p318; 📞028-3824 1110; 46a Ð Dinh Cong Trang; regular/extra large 80,000/120,000d; ⊙10am-9pm; 🌱) This renowned spot, acclaimed by Anthony Bourdain, serves some of the best *banh xeo* (Vietnamese rice-flour pancakes stuffed with bean sprouts, prawns and pork) in town. Vegetarian versions are available too. Other dishes include excellent *goi cuon* (fresh summer rolls with pork and prawn).

Pho Hoa VIETNAMESE $
(Map p318; http://phohoapasteur.restaurantsnap shot.com; 260c Ð Pasteur; meals 60,000-80,000d; ⊙6am-midnight) This long-running *pho* joint is more upmarket than most but is definitely the real deal. Tables come laden with herbs, chilli and lime, as well as *gio chao quay* (fried Chinese bread), *banh xu xe* (glutinous coconut cakes with mung-bean paste) and *cha lua* (pork-paste sausages wrapped in banana leaves).

★ Cuc Gach Quan VIETNAMESE $$
(Map p318; 📞028-3848 0144; www.cucgach quan.com.vn/en; 10 Ð Dang Tat; meals 110,000-240,000d; ⊙9am-midnight; 🌱) It comes as little surprise to learn that the owner of this place is an architect when you step into this cleverly renovated old villa. The decor is both rustic and elegant, which is also true

of the food, with many veggie options available. Despite its tucked-away location in the northernmost reaches of District 1, this is no secret hideaway: book ahead.

Tib
VIETNAMESE $$

(Map p318; ☑028-3829 7242; www.tibrestaurant.com.vn; 187 ĐL Hai Ba Trung; meals 180,000-440,000d; ☺11am-2pm & 5-10pm; 🗟🖉) Visiting presidents and prime ministers have slunk down the lantern- and fairy-light-festooned alley into this atmospheric old house to sample Tib's imperial Hue cuisine. Although you could probably find similar food for less money elsewhere, the courtyard setting is enchanting.

Bloom Saigon
FUSION $$$

(Map p318; ☑028-3910 1277; www.bloom-saigon.com; 3/5 Hoang Sa; meals 110,000-460,000d; ☺10.30am-10.30pm) In a lovingly restored heritage mansion, Bloom combines fusion flavours with the good-news story of offering culinary training for disadvantaged youth. Meals are firmly based in Vietnam, but tinged with subtle Western influences. Interesting menu options include the beef rolls in mustard greens (150,000d).

✖ Pham Ngu Lao Area

Pham Ngu Lao's eating options are good value but can attempt to satisfy every possible culinary whim, so don't expect super-authentic food.

Five Oysters
VIETNAMESE $

(Map p328; ☑090 301 2123; www.fiveoysters.com; 234 Đ Bui Vien; meals from 50,000d; ☺9am-11pm) With a strong seafood slant and friendly service, light and bright Five Oysters in back-packerland is frequently full of travellers feasting on oysters (25,000d to 30,000d), which are served with spring onion and garlic, wasabi, or even cheese (it works!). The octopus, shrimp dishes, seafood soup, snails, *pho* and grilled mackerel with chilli oil are also great.

Asiana Food Town
STREET FOOD $

(Map p328; ☑090 377 0836; www.facebook.com/asianafoodtown; 4 Đ Pham Ngu Lao; meals 50,000-120,000d; ☺8.30am-10pm; 🖉) A handy location near Pham Ngu Lao's accommodation, air-con and a huge selection of street food from around Vietnam and the rest of Asia are the highlights of this excellent undercover food court. There's a convenient supermarket, a pharmacy and an English-language bookshop as well.

Coriander
THAI $

(Map p328; www.coriander-ngo-ri.com; 16 Đ Bui Vien; dishes 59,000-259,000d; ☺10am-2pm & 5-10pm; 🗟) The cheap decor does Coriander few favours, but the menu is stuffed with authentic Siamese delights. The lovely fried *doufu* (tofu) is almost a meal in itself, the green curry is zesty, and salads like *som tum chae* (green-papaya salad with tomato) are satisfying and authentic.

Café Zoom
BURGERS $

(Map p328; www.facebook.com/cafezoomsaigon; 169a Đ De Tham; meals 70,000-160,000d; ☺7am-2am) Paying homage to the classic Vespa, this buzzing place has a perfect location for watching the world go by. The menu includes great burgers with original toppings, plus excellent ribs (from 20,000d) and Vietnamese favourites. Quiz night on Wednesdays (from 9pm) is always popular.

Bookworm's Coffee
CAFE $

(Map p328; 4 Đ Do Quang Dau; meals from 50,000d; ☺7am-11pm; 🗟🖉) Browse the books at the rear of this cafe then settle down to order British comfort grub like the full English breakfast, cottage pie, bangers 'n' mash or fish 'n' chips with a mug of Yorkshire tea. It also does vegan versions of many dishes.

Pho Quynh
VIETNAMESE $

(Map p328; 323 Đ Pham Ngu Lao; pho 60,000d; ☺24hr) Occupying a bustling corner on Đ Pham Ngu Lao, this place is often packed out. As well as regular *pho*, it specialises in *pho bo kho*, a stewlike broth.

Melbourne Cafe
CAFE $

(Map p328; www.themelbournecafesaigon.com; 254c Đ Bui Vien; meals 55,000-120,000d; ☺8.30am-midnight Mon-Sat, 10am-midnight Sun; 🗟) The Melbourne is a classic cafe downstairs, where you can sip a perfect espresso, while upstairs is more local. There's a wide-reaching Vietnamese menu featuring seafood, chicken, pork and beef dishes; try their *mi hoanh thanh* (wonton noodle soup).

Pho Hung
VIETNAMESE $

(Map p328; 241 Đ Nguyen Trai; meals 45,000-75,000d; ☺6am-3am) Popular *pho* place near backpackersville, open till the wee hours.

Dinh Y
VEGAN $

(Map p328; 171b Đ Cong Quynh; meals from 36,000d; ☺6.30am-7pm; 🖉) Run by a friendly Cao Dai family, this humble vegan spot looks like a simple canteen. The food is delicious and cheap; try one of their daily set menus ('special dinners' cost 40,000d, served from 3pm to 9pm). Located near Thai Binh Market.

Quan Ut Ut
BARBECUE **$$**

(Map p308; ☑028-3914 4500; www.quanutut. com; 168 Đ Vo Van Kiet; meals 180,000-320,000d; ⊙11am-10.30pm; 🐾) With a name roughly translating to the 'Oink Oink Eatery', this casual place with river views celebrates everything porcine with an American-style barbecue spin. Huge streetside grills prepare great ribs, spicy sausages and pork belly, and tasty sides include charred sweetcorn and roasted pumpkin and beetroot. The owners make their own flavour-packed craft beers.

Baba's Kitchen
INDIAN **$$**

(Map p328; ☑028-3838 6661; www.babaskitchen.in; 274 Đ Bui Vien; meals 80,000-210,000d; ⊙11am-10.30pm; 🍴) Baba's sets Đ Bui Vien alight with the fine flavours, aromas and spices of India. There's ample vegetarian choice and the atmosphere is as inviting as the cuisine is delectable. Highlights include delicious *paneer kadai* (Indian cheese, peppers and onion in a thick tomato sauce). Rather excellent service, too.

Vittorio
ITALIAN **$$**

(Map p328; 137 Đ Bui Vien; meals 85,000-200,000d; ⊙9am-11pm) One of the better options along bustling Đ Bui Vien, with a friendly atmosphere, decent wood-fired pizza and other Italian-inspired dishes.

✖ District 2

The Thao Dien neighbourhood of District 2 is popular with expat diners and wealthy Viets. A taxi from District 1 should cost around 180,000d to 220,000d and take around 20 minutes. Or you can take the waterbus.

Family Garden 2
VIETNAMESE **$**

(☑091 366 2887; www.familygarden.vn; 28 Đ Thao Dien; meals from 70,000d; ⊙10am-2pm & 5-9pm) This simple-looking spot looks like it belongs in a Mekong Delta village rather then inner HCMC, with its thatched roof, chunky wooden tables and forested surrounds. Expect earthy, punchy flavours from a menu that changes regularly. Limited English spoken and it's tricky to find, down a lane opposite AIS Sports Center.

★Mekong Merchant
CAFE, BISTRO **$$**

(☑028-3744 7000; www.mekongmerchant.com; 23 Đ Thao Dien; meals 130,000-360,000d; ⊙7am-11pm; 🐾🍴) Thatched-roof buildings clustered around a courtyard provide an atmospheric setting for this informal but upmarket cafe-bistro-bar. Phu Quoc seafood is delivered directly and chalked up on the blackboard menu daily. Mekong Merchant serves the best eggs Benedict in HCMC, but there's so much else of interest here too, including signature dishes like beef Tiger Beer pot pie with baked mash potato, carrot and peas.

Boat House
BISTRO **$$**

(☑028-3744 6790; www.facebook.com/boat housevietnam; 40 Lily Rd, APSC Compound, 36 Đ Thao Dien; bar snacks from 65,000d, meals 160,000-340,000d; ⊙7.30am-10pm) This versatile spot features many riverside options: enjoy a leisurely lunch at the outside tables, sit at the bar for a few beers or graduate to cocktails on the daybeds. Food runs from bar snacks to burgers, salads and wraps, and weekdays from 4.30pm to 6.30pm there are good happy-hour specials. There's live music every Friday and Sunday (5pm to 9pm).

MAD House
BISTRO **$$**

(☑028-3519 4009; www.madhousesaigon.com/home; 6/1/2 Đ Nguyen U Di; meals 150,000-300,000d; ⊙8am-10pm; 🐾🍴) Highlights here include an innovative menu blending Scandinavian and Vietnamese influences – MAD House translates to 'Food House' in Danish. There's also excellent coffee, robust cocktails, wine by the glass (from 85,000d) and craft beer. Look forward to stunning tropical decor and a lovely garden area that's a perfect retreat from the bustle of the city.

★Lubu
MEDITERRANEAN **$$$**

(☑028-6281 8371; www.luburestaurant.com; 97b Đ Thao Dien; meals 240,000-600,000d; ⊙8.30am-10pm; 🐾🍴) Shared tables and a sunny whitewashed interior combine with excellent Mediterranean cuisine at this District 2 favourite. Spanish, Moroccan, Greek and Italian are the main culinary touch points, with menu highlights including paella, souvlaki and tapas, along with some of the city's very best brunch options like green *shakshouka* (eggs baked in a spicy spinach, kale, Swiss chard and coriander sauce for 200,000d).

Deck
FUSION **$$$**

(☑028-3744 6632; www.thedecksaigon.com; 33 Đ Nguyen U Di, Thao Dien; tapas 80,000-350,000d, meals 185,000-695,000d; ⊙8am-midnight; 🐾) Deck is housed in an architecturally impressive pavilion set between an elegant garden and the river. You could happily linger here all afternoon, knocking off a few bottles of wine, portions of dim sum (from 195,000d) and 'small plates' like tuna carpaccio with mojito dressing (240,000d). Mains combine European cooking styles with the flavours of Asia.

Drinking & Nightlife

Happening HCMC is concentrated around the Dong Khoi area, with everything from dives to designer bars open until 1am. Pham Ngu Lao stays open later, and Pham Ngu Lao's Đ Bui Vien is a pedestrian-only street from 7pm to 2am on Saturdays and Sundays. Dance clubs usually kick off after 10pm; ask around at popular bars about the latest and greatest places.

Dong Khoi Area

Many of Dong Khoi's coolest bars are also restaurants. Restaurants like Racha Room (p334) also double as bars.

★ Heart of Darkness   CRAFT BEER

(Map p312; ☑090 301 7596; www.heartofdark nessbrewery.com; 31D Đ Ly Tu Trong; ⊙11am-midnight) This premier craft brewery has an always-interesting selection of innovative beers on tap. The selection varies as the Heart of Darkness brewers are always trying something, but the Dream Alone pale ale and Sacred Fire golden ale are great drops.

★ Pasteur Street
Brewing Company   CRAFT BEER

(Map p312; www.pasteurstreet.com; 144 Đ Pasteur; ⊙11am-10pm; ☜) Pasteur Street Brewing turns out a fine selection of craft beer. Brews utilise local ingredients including lemongrass, rambutan and jasmine, and up to six different beers are always available (small/large beers from 45,000/95,000d). There are great bar snacks too (try the spicy Nashville fried chicken), also served in the brewery's hip space. There's a second, larger **branch** (Map p312; 26a Đ Le Thanh Ton; ⊙11am-1am; ☜) in District 1.

Rogue Saigon   CRAFT BEER

(Map p312; ☑090 236 5780; www.facebook.com/roguesaigon; 11 Đ Pasteur; ⊙4pm-midnight) Live music and Vietnamese craft beers combine on Rogue's rooftop terrace in a gritty building on the riverside edge of District 1. You'll find good beers such as Lac Brewing's Devil's Lake IPA, and music with an acoustic, blues or rock vibe. There are DJ sessions on Saturday and also jams and quiz nights.

Malt   BAR

(Map p312; ☑091 848 4763; www.maltsaigon.com; 46-48 Đ Mac Thi Buoi; ⊙2pm-1am Mon-Fri, noon-1am Sat & Sun; ☜) Malt is one of the city's cosiest and most welcoming bars, and has a no-smoking policy (a rarity in HCMC). There's always a well-curated selection of local craft brews on tap – the savvy bar staff can make good beer recommendations – and there's moreish comfort food, including mac 'n' cheese and sliders. Darts and a vintage shuffleboard table are added attractions.

Alley Cocktail Bar & Kitchen   COCKTAIL BAR

(Map p312; ☑093 565 3969; www.facebook.com/thealleysaigon; 63/1 Đ Pasteur; ⊙5pm-midnight Mon-Wed, to 1am Thu-Sat; ☜) Good luck finding this place (turn left just after the Liberty Central Saigon Citypoint hotel and follow the signs), but when you do discover it, celebrate with a classic cocktail, craft beer or whisky. The eclectic approach to music stretches from live music on acoustic Thursdays to DJs on Friday and Saturday nights. The generous happy hour is from 5pm to 8pm. The snacks menu takes in tapas and fresh spring rolls.

Layla   COCKTAIL BAR

(Map p312; ☑028-3827 2279; www.facebook.com/LaylaEateryandBarHCM; 2nd fl, 63 Đ Dong Du; ⊙4pm-1am Sun-Thu, to 2am Fri & Sat) With a long bar – we're talking 10m-plus here – Layla is a laid-back spot that's perfect for the first or last cocktails of the night. Don't be surprised if the combination of a chic ambience, super-comfy sofas and Med-style bar snacks sees you staying longer than planned.

Workshop   COFFEE

(Map p312; www.facebook.com/the.workshop. coffee; 10 Đ Ngo Duc Ke; ⊙8am-9pm; ☜) Coffee-geek culture comes to HCMC at this spacious upstairs warehouse space. Single-origin, fair-trade roasts from Dalat feature, and there's a great display of black-and-white photos of old Saigon to peruse while you're waiting for your Chemex or cold brew. Cold-pressed juices and good snacks (80,000d to 190,000d) are available too.

Apocalypse Now   CLUB

(Map p312; ☑028-3824 1463; www.facebook.com/apocalypsenowsaigon; 2c Đ Thi Sach; ⊙7pm-4am) 'Apo' has been around since 1991 and remains one of the must-visit clubs in town. It's a sprawling place with a big dance floor and a courtyard, and its eclectic cast combines travellers, expats, Vietnamese movers

COFFEE CULTURE

HCMC's coffee culture is deep and established, and can be witnessed (and partaken in) on most streets in the city where there's a traditional Vietnamese cafe serving treacle-thick drip coffee.

New-wave coffee shops are now mushrooming throughout the city, with Workshop a key venue in the centre of town. In the mean hipster streets south of Pham Ngu Lao we rate quirky independents **Chat Coffee Roasters** (Map p316; www.facebook.com/Chat-Coffee-Roasters; 55/1 Ð Le Thi Hong Gam; ⊙7am-midnight; 🛜) and **Saigon Coffee Roastery** (Map p316; www.facebook.com/saigoncoffeeroastery; 12 Ð Dang Thi Nhu; ⊙7am-10pm; 🛜).

Further afield, the sleek contemporary surrounds of **Bosgaurus Coffee** (www.bosgaurus coffee.com; Saigon Pearl complex, D6, off Ð Nguyen Huu Canh; ⊙7am-9pm; 🛜), on the Saigon River 2km north of the centre, are well worth a caffeine pilgrimage, while over in District 2 **Dolphy** (www.facebook.com/dolphycafe; 28 Ð Thao Dien; ⊙6am-10pm; 🛜) is a reliable bet.

and shakers, plus the odd working girl. Expect pounding techno. There are (cheesy) live bands on Saturday nights.

Lush BAR
(Map p318; www.facebook.com/LushSaigon; 2 Ð Ly Tu Trong; ⊙9pm-3am Tue-Sun) Once you're done chatting in the garden bars, move to the central bar for serious people-watching and arse-shaking. The decor is very manga, with cool graphics plastering the walls. DJs spin most nights, with Bass on Saturdays pulling in the crowds.

Broma: Not a Bar BAR
(Map p312; ☎0126 387 2603; 41 ÐL Nguyen Hue; ⊙5.30pm-2am) This rooftop bar overlooking busy Ð Nguyen Hue has a good selection of international beers, live gigs, and DJs with a funk, hip-hop and electronica edge.

Phatty's SPORTS BAR
(Map p312; ☎028-3821 0796; www.facebook. com/Phattysbarsaigon; 46-48 Ð Ton That Thiep; ⊙8am-midnight; 🛜) This sports bar is renowned for its convivial atmosphere, good grub and big screens. English soccer, rugby and Australian Rules football are all screened on a regular basis.

Reunification Palace & Around

★BiaCraft CRAFT BEER
(Map p316; ☎028-3933 0903; www.biacraft.com; 11 Ð Le Ngo Cat, District 3; ⊙11am-11pm; 🛜) With almost 40 taps, BiaCraft is an essential destination for thirsty souls. Complementing its own creations are ales and ciders from craft breweries in HCMC and Hanoi; it's possible to take out freshly sealed cans of all available beers. Combine a tasting paddle with

probably the city's best bar food, with quirky offerings like drunken baby potatoes and Nashville hot quail.

There are other BiaCrafts around town, including a (less impressive) **branch** (90 Ð Xuan Thuy, Thao Dien, District 2; ⊙3-11pm Mon-Thu, 11am-11pm Fri-Sun; 🛜) in the District 2 area.

★Observatory CLUB
(Map p316; www.facebook.com/theobservatory hcmc; 85 Ð Cach Mang Thang Tam; ⊙6pm-4am Thu, to 6am Fri & Sat; 🛜) This excellent musical cooperative now has a permanent location in a block with a skyline view for its DJ events and gigs featuring emerging electronic musicians and bands. It's one of the best places to check out the underground scene in HCMC. Check the Facebook page for listings.

East West Brewing CRAFT BEER
(Map p316; ☎0913 060 728; www.eastwestbrew ing.vn; 181-185 Ð Ly Tu Trong; ⊙11am-midnight) All beers are brewed on-site at this impressive microbrewery (or should that be megamicrobrewery) near Ben Thanh Market. Ales include a Far East IPA with American and New Zealand hops and every month a seasonal brew or two is released, including Oktoberfest lagers. There's also decent burgers, salads and seafood.

OMG BAR
(Map p316; www.facebook.com/omgsaigon; Tan Hai Long Hotel, 15-19 Ð Nguyen An Ninh; ⊙5pm-1am) OMG is a decent rooftop bar near Ben Thanh Market that's less pretentious than some other sky bars around town. Beers/cocktails cost from 90,000/160,000d. Happy hour is from 5pm to 7.30pm. Food-wise, there's an adventurous spirit evident with tasty tapas.

SKY-HIGH SAIGON

To get to grips with the layout of HCMC you really need to head up high. The most famous viewpoint is the Skydeck on the 49th floor of the **Bitexco Financial Tower** (Map p312; www.bitexcofinancialtower.com; 2 Đ Hai Trieu; adult/child 200,000/130,000d; ⏲9.30am-9.30pm), a 262m-high, Carlos Zapata–designed skyscraper in the heart of the city, but frankly the crowds and costs involved do not add up to a great visitor experience. Similarly, **Skyview** (☎028-3639 9999; www.landmark81skyview.com; Landmark 81, off Đ Nguyen Huu Canh, Binh Thanh; child/adult 405,000/810,000d; ⏲8.30am-10pm) at Landmark 81, which opened in 2019 and is Southeast Asia's tallest structure, is overpriced and quite a distance from the city centre.

Sky bars and sky restos (not viewing decks) are perhaps the best way to really savour the high life. **Air 360 Sky Lounge** (Map p316; www.facebook.com/Air360SkyLounge; 21st fl, 136-138 Đ Le Thi Hong Gam, Ben Thanh Tower; ⏲5.30pm-2am) is handy for the backpacker district of Pham Ngu Lao and has a good happy hour (from 5.30pm to 8pm). At **Social Club Saigon** (Map p316; www.hoteldesartssaigon.com; Hotel des Arts, 76-78 Đ Nguyen Thi Minh Khai, District 3; ⏲9am-1pm; 📶) you can mix with the city's elite, 24 storeys above District 3, while neighbouring Shri (p335) serves some of the best cocktails in town and good tapas. In the heart of Dong Khoi you can't beat Sky 28 (p332) for a pocket-friendly sky-high experience, while the adjacent Japanese restaurant Towa (p334) is one of the city's finest and shares the same astonishing vistas.

Pham Ngu Lao Area

Whiskey & Wares BAR

(Map p308; ☎0163 279 4179; www.facebook.com/WhiskeyandWares; 196 Đ De Tham; ⏲4.30pm-1.30am Tue-Sun; 📶) 🌿 Fine whisky, good cocktails and local craft beer all appeal at this sophisticated bar a short hop from Pham Ngu Lao. It's also a top spot to purchase local artisanal goods. It's LGBT-friendly but welcoming to all.

Tipsy Unicorn GAY & LESBIAN

(Map p308; ☎028-7307 3647; www.facebook.com/TipsyUnicornSaigon; 37 Đ De Tham; ⏲4pm-2am; 📶) One of the city's very few openly gay bars, drawing a loyal crowd of locals with a fun, welcoming vibe. There's plenty going on, with quiz nights, DJs on Saturdays, live bands and even drag-queen bingo (Sundays at 9pm).

Ong Cao BAR

(Map p328; ☎091 199 6160; www.facebook.com/ongcaosaigon; 240 Đ Bui Vien; ⏲5-11.15pm; 📶) A hoppy cut above the backpacker bars lining Đ Bui Vien, Ong Cao is your best bet for craft brews in Pham Ngu Lao. Bar snacks, including cheese and charcuterie plates, partner well with 16 taps serving mainly local beers.

Other Neighbourhoods

★Saigon Outcast BAR

(www.saigonoutcast.com; 188 Đ Nguyen Van Huong, District 2; ⏲10am-11.30pm Tue-Sat, to 10.30pm Sun) This District 2 venue has a diverse combination of live music, DJs, cinema nights and good times amid street art. Cocktails, craft beer and local ciders are available in the raffish garden bar, and there are outdoor flea and farmers markets here bimonthly. There's a rock-climbing wall that will keep kids occupied for hours. Check the website for what's on.

Indika Saigon BAR

(Map p318; ☎0122 399 4260; www.facebook.com/IndikaSaigon; 43 Đ Nguyen Van Giai; ⏲4pm-midnight; 📶) Tucked down a narrow laneway, the off-the-radar Indika Saigon dubs itself the 'House of Curiosity'. It is definitely worth venturing to, with a barbecue joint and beer bar at the front and the labyrinthine premises used for concerts, open-mic sessions, movie nights and DJs. Check out the Facebook page for listings. Cash only.

☆ Entertainment

Consult the Saigoneer (www.saigoneer.com) to find out what's on during your stay in Ho Chi Minh City. Copies of *Asialife HCMC* (www.asialifemagazine.com/vietnam), available in hotels, are also worth a look.

Live Music & Performances

Ho Chi Minh City has an enthusiastic live-music scene, with all styles of bands hitting the city's stages. Just off Đ Pasteur, the Old Compass Cafe (p331) and the Alley Cocktail Bar & Kitchen (p338) attract live performers most weekends. Saigon Outcast and Rogue Saigon (p338) also showcase an eclectic mix of expat and international performers on a regular basis. Check their Facebook pages for listings.

Acoustic
LIVE MUSIC

(Map p316; ☑ 028-3932 2239; www.facebook.com/acousticbarpage; 6e1 Ð Ngo Thoi Nhiem, District 3; ☺7pm-midnight; ☎) Don't be misled by the name: most of the musicians are fully plugged in and dangerous when they take to the intimate stage of the city's leading live-music venue. And judging by the numbers that pack in, the local crowd just can't get enough. It's at the end of the alley by the upended VW Beetle.

Yoko
LIVE MUSIC

(Map p316; ☑ 028-3933 0577; www.facebook.com/Yokocafesaigon; 22a Ð Nguyen Thi Dieu; ☺8am-5pm Mon, 8am-midnight Tue-Sat, 4pm-midnight Sun; ☎) This live-music venue hosts anything from funk rock to metal, acoustic to indie, kicking off at around 9pm nightly. Check Facebook for what's on.

AO Show
LIVE PERFORMANCE

(Map p312; www.luneproduction.com; Opera House, Lam Son Sq; from 700,000d; ☺6pm or 8.30pm most days) This tourist-oriented showcase of Vietnamese music, dance and flying acrobats is held in the spectacular, recently renovated Opera House, a French-colonial structure dating from 1897.

Municipal Theatre
CONCERT VENUE

(Opera House; Map p312; ☑ 028-3829 9976; Lam Son Sq) The landmark French-era Opera House is home to the HCMC Ballet and the Ballet & Symphony Orchestra (www.hbso.org.vn), and hosts performances by visiting artists.

Conservatory of Music
CONCERT VENUE

(Nhac Vien Thanh Pho Ho Chi Minh; Map p316; ☑ 028-3824 3774; http://hcmcons.vn; 112 Ð Nguyen Du) Performances of both traditional Vietnamese and Western classical music are held here. Check the English-language section of the website to see what's scheduled.

Water Puppets

Although it originates in the north, the art of water puppetry migrated south to Ho Chi Minh City to satiate tourist demands.

Golden Dragon
Water Puppet Theatre
PUPPET THEATRE

(Map p316; ☑ 028-3930 2196; 55b Ð Nguyen Thi Minh Khai; tickets 270,000d) Saigon's main

water-puppet venue, with shows starting at 6.30pm and 8.30pm and lasting about 50 minutes.

Saigon Water
Puppet Theatre
PUPPET THEATRE

(Map p318; History Museum, Ð Nguyen Binh Khiem; 100,000d) Within the History Museum (p318), this small theatre has performances at 9am, 10am, 11am, 2pm, 3pm and 4pm, lasting about 20 minutes.

Cinemas

Lotte Cinema Diamond
CINEMA

(Map p312; www.lottecinemavn.com; 13th fl, Diamond Department Store, 34 ÐL Le Duan; tickets 90,000-150,000d) Three screens here show films in their original language with Vietnamese subtitles.

Galaxy
CINEMA

(Map p316; www.galaxycine.vn; 116 Ð Nguyen Du; tickets 90,000-150,000d) One of the best cinemas in town, with Hollywood blockbusters and local hits.

🛍 Shopping

Junk is energetically peddled to tourists on the city's teeming streets, but plenty of great finds can be uncovered in bustling markets, antique stores, silk boutiques and speciality shops selling ceramics, ethnic fabrics, lacquered bamboo and custom-made clothing.

🛍 Dong Khoi Area

Any shopping journey should start along gallery- and boutique-lined Ð Dong Khoi and its intersecting streets, where high-quality handicrafts and gifts can be found.

★ Chung Cu 42 Ton That Thiep
CLOTHING

(Map p312; 42 Ð Ton That Thiep; ☺most shops 9am-9pm) Come for the apartment building partially converted into cool boutique shops, and linger for the young, social-media-savvy fashion labels that produce stylish but affordable clothing. Triple T is a great store here selling linen menswear. Head upstairs, and also through to the back to the second building.

Ben Thanh Market
MARKET

(Cho Ben Thanh; Map p316; ÐL Le Loi, ÐL Ham Nghi, ÐL Tran Hung Dao & Ð Le Lai; ☺5am-6pm) Ben Thanh and its surrounding streets comprise one of HCMC's liveliest areas. Everything that's commonly eaten, worn or used by the Saigonese is piled high, and souvenirs can be found in equal abundance. Vendors are determined and prices are usually higher than elsewhere (though restaurant stalls are reasonable), so bargain vigorously and ignore any 'Fixed Price' signs.

Good restaurant stalls are usually open until mid-afternoon. Once the indoors market closes, a small night market just outside takes over until midnight.

Ben Thanh is an area where it pays to be extra vigilant about looking after personal items and electronics.

Mekong Quilts
ARTS & CRAFTS
(Map p312; ☑ 028-2210 3110; www.mekongquilts. com; 68 ĐL Le Loi; ☺9am-7pm) 🍃 Beautiful handmade silk quilts, sewn by the rural poor in support of sustainable incomes. Bags, scarves, bowls and even very cool bamboo bikes are also sold.

Saigon Kitsch
GIFTS & SOUVENIRS
(Map p312; 33 Đ Ton That Thiep; ☺9am-10pm) Specialises in reproduction propaganda items, emblazoning its revolutionary motifs on coffee mugs, coasters, jigsaws and T-shirts. Laptop and tablet covers fashioned from recycled packaging, posters and Vietnamese cookbooks are also stocked.

L'Usine
CLOTHING, HOMEWARES
(Map p312; www.facebook.com/Lusinespace; 151/1 Đ Dong Khoi; ☺7.30am-10.30pm) Marrying shopping and dining, this smooth upstairs outlet, next to the restaurant-cafe of the same name, has an eye-catching line in stylish threads and colourful bags. There's another classy L'Usine cafe and design combo on Đ Le Loi (Map p312; 70b Đ Le Loi; ☺7.30am-10.30pm).

Sadec
HOMEWARES
(Map p312; www.sadecdistrict.com; 91 Đ Mac Thi Buoi; ☺8.30am-8.30pm) Worth browsing for stylish homewares (including lovely wooden kitchen utensils made from acacia and teak), clothing, art and fabrics from all around the Mekong River region.

Mystere
ARTS & CRAFTS
(Map p312; ☑ 028-3823 9615; 141 Đ Dong Khoi; ☺9am-10pm) Attractive lacquerware, textiles (embroidered and batik), ceramics and jewellery sourced from ethnic minority peoples and hill tribes throughout Vietnam, with an emphasis on the north and northeast regions. Also has its own range of silver jewellery.

Mai Lam
CLOTHING
(Map p312; www.mailam.com.vn; 132-134 Đ Dong Khoi; ☺9am-9pm) Mai Lam is inspired by Vietnamese street style; head here for vibrant, innovative (but pricey) hand-stitched men's and women's clothing and accessories.

Annam Gourmet Market
MARKET
(Map p312; www.annam-gourmet.com; 16 ĐL Hai Ba Trung; ☺7am-9pm) This large, fabulously stocked deli sells imported cheeses, wines, chocolates and other delicacies over two floors, with a fine cafe-restaurant crammed into the corner of the 1st floor.

Nhu Y Oriental Lacquer Wares
ARTS & CRAFTS
(Map p312; www.nhuylacquer.com; Level 3, 90 ĐL Nguyen Hue, District 1; ☺9am-9.30pm) Gorgeous collection of eye-catching handmade boxes, Chinese lacquered couplets, inscribed pictures and more.

Saigon Centre
SHOPPING CENTRE
(Map p312; www.saigoncentre.com.vn; 65 ĐL Le Loi; ☺9.30am-9.30pm) A sleek multilevel mall with flashy international shops, cafes and a Japanese-style food court in its basement level. On the 4th floor, tiNiWorld has a playground and activities for children.

🏠 Pham Ngu Lao Area

The city's backpacker district has stores replete with all the travel essentials you might need.

Ginkgo
CLOTHING
(Map p328; www.ginkgo-vietnam.com; 254 Đ De Tham; ☺8am-10pm) With two branches in the PNL area, this fun upmarket shop sells exuberant, brightly coloured T-shirts and hoodies, with a quirky Asian and Vietnamese focus.

🏠 Nguyen Thai Binh & Around

Antique hunters can head to Đ Le Cong Kieu, directly across the road from the Fine Arts Museum. There's no guarantee objects for sale are actually old, so purchase with care.

Antique Street Saigon
ANTIQUES
(Map p312; ☑ 0168 481 0093; 38 Đ Le Cong Kieu; ☺10am-5pm Mon-Sat) This is the best of the arts and antiques stores along Đ Le Cong Kieu near the Fine Arts Museum. The shop overflows with interesting discoveries and art painted by the owner.

Dan Sinh Market
MARKET

(Map p312; 104 Đ Yersin; ⊙most stalls 7am-5pm) Also known as the War Surplus Market, head here for authentic combat boots or rusty (and perhaps less authentic) dog tags among the overflowing hardware stalls. There are also rain jackets, mosquito nets, canteens, duffel bags, ponchos and boots. Check out Steven's Shop (open 9.30am to 4.30pm) for quirky one-off and vintage discoveries.

🏠 District 2

This upmarket area is replete with delis and design stores and has some excellent clothing boutiques.

Chula Fashion
CLOTHING

(☑089 885 4412; www.chulafashion.com; 32 Tran Ngoc Dien, District 2; ⊙10am-6pm) Beautifully crafted garments (mostly for women) in silk, linen and wool. Bold prints and geometric patterns are joined by stylised elements taken from Vietnamese food, art and culture.

In the Mood
HOMEWARES

(☑096 877 3862; www.facebook.com/inthemoodsaigon; 32 Tran Ngoc Dien, District 2; ⊙10am-7pm) Head to this little store in District 2 for fine-quality basketry, carvings, linen and cotton cushions and bags, copper water bottles, natural soaps and essential oils.

🏠 Other Neighbourhoods

Mai Handicrafts
ARTS & CRAFTS

(Map p308; ☑028-3844 0988; www.maihandicrafts.com; 298 Đ Nguyen Trong Tuyen, Tan Binh District; ⊙9am-5pm Mon-Sat) 🍃 A fair-trade shop dealing in ceramics, ethnic fabrics and other gift items that, in turn, support disadvantaged families and street children. To get here, head northwest on ĐL Hai Ba Trung, which becomes Đ Phan Dinh Phung, and turn left on Đ Nguyen Trong Tuyen.

SC Vivo City
MALL

(www.scvivocity.com.vn; 1058 Đ Nguyen Van Linh; ⊙10am-10pm) A sprawling international mall for those seeking retail therapy.

ℹ️ Information

LGBTIQ+ TRAVELLERS

There are few openly gay venues in town, but most of Ho Chi Minh City's popular bars and clubs are generally gay-friendly. Out and proud Tipsy Unicorn (p340) is perhaps the best place to start, an openly LGBT bar, while not far away **Thi Bar** (Map p328; www.facebook.com/thibarsaigon; 224 Đ De Tham; ⊙5pm-late; 🛜) and Whiskey & Wares (p340) both attract a mixed crowd. Check Utopia (www.utopia-asia.com) for gay happenings and nightlife tours around HCMC.

MEDICAL SERVICES

Columbia Asia (Map p316; ☑028-3823 8888; www.columbiaasia.com/saigon; 8 Đ Alexandre de Rhodes; ⊙emergency 7.30am-9pm Mon-Fri, 8am-5pm Sat & Sun) Centrally located near Notre Dame.

FV Hospital (Franco-Vietnamese Hospital; ☑028-5411 3500; www.fvhospital.com; 6 Đ Nguyen Luong Bang, District 7; ⊙24hr) French-, Vietnamese- and English-speaking physicians; superb care and equipment, and 24-hour emergency service.

HCMC Family Medical Practice (Map p312; ☑24hr emergency 028-3822 7848; www.vietnammedicalpractice.com; rear, Diamond Department Store, 34 ĐL Le Duan; ⊙24hr) Well-run practice, also with branches in Hanoi and Danang.

Raffles Medical Group (Map p318; ☑028-3824 0777; www.rafflesmedicalgroup.com; 167a Đ Nam Ky Khoi Nghia; ⊙24hr) Has an international team of doctors who speak English, French, Japanese and Vietnamese.

POST

Central Post Office (p306) Right across from Notre Dame Cathedral.

SAIGON FOR KIDS

At first glance, Ho Chi Minh City's hectic streets might not look that kiddie-friendly, but sky decks (p340) and high-rise viewpoints are usually popular. Water parks, swimming pools, water-puppet shows, leafy parks and ice-cream shops are other options. Cooking classes (p324) can be great fun, and most places offer discounts for children. Avoid the city's miserable zoo though. Saigon Outcast (p340) is a very cool spot with a climbing wall and lots going on. Amusement centre **tiNiWorld** on the 4th floor of the Saigon Centre is worth considering to keep the kids entertained. Beyond the city is **Dai Nam Theme Park** (Lac Canh Dai Nam Van Hien; ☑0274 351 2660; www.laccanhdainamvanhien.vn; adult/child 100,000/50,000d; ⊙8am-6pm), the closest thing to Disneyland in Vietnam.

FedEx (Map p308; ☑ 028-3948 0370; www.fedex.com; 6 Đ Thang Long, Tan Binh District; ⊙7.30am-6pm Mon-Fri, to 4.30pm Sat) Private freight carrier.

SAFE TRAVEL

➤ Be careful at all times but especially in the Dong Khoi area, around Pham Ngu Lao and the Ben Thanh Market, and along the riverfront. Around these areas you're more likely to be targeted by motorbike 'cowboys' specialising in snatching bags, cameras, laptops and tablets.

➤ It's always best to leave your passport in your hotel room, and try to be prudent and careful when you use your smartphone on the street.

➤ The pollution and traffic are awful. Consider wearing a face mask.

TRAVEL AGENCIES

There's a plethora of travel agencies in town, virtually all of them joint ventures between government agencies and private companies.

Ho Chi Minh City's official government-run travel agency is **Saigon Tourist** (Map p312; ☑ 090 928 4554; www.saigontourist.net; 45 Đ Le Thanh Ton; ⊙8-11.30am & 1-5.30pm). However, it's not useful for independent travel advice and is more concerned with business ventures.

Private agencies can rent out cars, book air tickets and extend visas. Nearly all have multilingual guides.

Most tour guides and drivers are not paid that well, so if you're happy with their service, tipping is common. Plenty of cheap tours – of varying quality – are sold around Pham Ngu Lao and Ben Thanh Market. Another option is a customised private tour with your own car, driver and guide, which allows maximum flexibility and can be surprisingly affordable.

Buffalo Tours (☑ 028-3827 9170; www.buffalotours.com; 40 Đ Mac Thi Buoi; ⊙8.30am-5pm Mon-Fri, to 2.30pm Sat) Top-end travel agency.

EXO Travel (☑ 028-3519 4111; www.exotravel.com; 41 Đ Thao Dien; ⊙8.30am-6pm Mon-Sat) Excellent Indochina specialists.

Ez Pass (Map p312; 89/17 Đ Ham Nghi) Competent all-rounder for domestic and international travel and visa services.

Handspan Travel Indochina (Map p308; ☑ 028-3925 7605; www.handspan.com; 10th fl, Central Park Bldg, 208 Đ Nguyen Trai) High-quality tours, including off-the-beaten-path options.

Innoviet (Map p308; ☑ 096 793 1670; https://innoviet.com; 40 Đ Tran Hung Dao; ⊙9.30am-5pm Mon-Fri) Budget travel agency that does a lot of Mekong Delta trips.

Kim Tran Travel (Map p328; ☑ 028-3836 5489; www.thekimtourist.com; 270 Đ De Tham; ⊙7am-9.30pm) Small-group day trips and over-nighters around HCMC and the Mekong area.

Sinh Tourist (Map p328; ☑ 028-3838 9593; www.thesinhtourist.vn; 246 Đ De Tham; ⊙6.30am-10.30pm) Popular budget travel agency offering great private-bus services.

Sinhbalo Adventures (Map p328; ☑ 028-3837 6766; www.sinhbalo.com; 283/20 Đ Pham Ngu Lao; ⊙7.30am-noon & 1.30-6pm Mon-Sat) For customised tours this is a great choice. Sinhbalo specialises in cycling trips, but also arranges innovative special-interest journeys to the Mekong Delta, central highlands and further afield.

❶ Getting There & Away

AIR

Ho Chi Minh City is served by **Tan Son Nhat International Airport** (☑ 028-3848 5383; www.tsnairport.hochiminhcity.gov.vn/vn; Tan Binh District), located 7km northwest of central HCMC. A number of airlines offer many domestic routes.

Bamboo Airways (www.bambooairways.com) Flies to/from destinations including Danang, Dong Hoi, Halong City, Hanoi and Quy Nhon.

Jetstar Pacific Airlines (☑1900 1550; www.jetstar.com/vn/en/home) Flies to/from destinations including Buon Ma Thuot, Chu Lai, Dalat, Danang, Dong Hoi, Hanoi, Hue, Nha Trang, Phu Quoc, Quy Nhon, Thanh Hoa and Tuy Hoa.

VietJet Air (www.vietjetair.com) Flies to/from destinations including Chu Lai, Dalat, Danang, Dong Hoi, Hai Phong, Halong City, Hanoi, Hue, Nha Trang, Phu Quoc, Quy Nhon and Thanh Hoa.

Vietnam Air Service Company (Vasco; ☑ 028-3845 8017; www.vasco.com.vn) Flies to/from Ca Mau, Con Dao Islands and Rach Gia.

Vietnam Airlines (☑ 028-3832 0320; www.vietnamairlines.com) Flies to/from 15 domestic airports including Hanoi and Phu Quoc.

BOAT

Greenlines (Map p312; ☑ 098 800 9579; www.greenlines-dp.com; Bach Dang Terminal; 1 way adult/child 240,000/120,000d) operates a ferry service linking HCMC to Vung Tau. Booking ahead is recommended for Friday to Saturday sailings. Journeys take around 90 minutes to two hours and can occasionally be delayed or cancelled due to weather and sea conditions. Advance bookings can be made online around a week to 10 days before departure dates. There are four daily departures, or six on Saturdays and Sundays.

BUS

Intercity buses operate from three large stations on the city outskirts, all well served by local bus services from near Ben Thanh Market. Ho Chi Minh City is one place where the open-tour buses really come into their own, as most

GETTING TO CAMBODIA: HCMC TO PHNOM PENH

Getting to the border The busy **Moc Bai/Bavet border crossing** is the fastest land route between Ho Chi Minh City and Phnom Penh. Pham Ngu Lao travel agencies sell bus tickets (US$10 to US$16) to Phnom Penh; buses leave from Pham Ngu Lao between 6am and 4pm, and again just before midnight. Allow seven to eight hours for the entire trip, including time spent on border formalities. For bus journeys to Siem Reap allow 12 to 13 hours, and 14 hours to Sihanoukville.

At the border Cambodian visas (US$30) are issued at the border (you'll need a passport-sized photo). Moc Bai is two hours from HCMC by bus and is a major duty-free shopping zone. It's a short walk from Moc Bai to Bavet (the Cambodian border) and its enclave of casinos.

Moving on Most travellers have a through bus ticket from HCMC to Phnom Penh, which is a further four-hour bus ride away.

depart and arrive in the very convenient Pham Ngu Lao area, saving the extra local bus journey or taxi fare.

Any of the travel agencies around town can book open-tour buses. The rates for open-tour buses with Sinh Tourist are 527,000d for Hoi An or Hue and 776,000d for Hanoi.

Mien Tay Bus Station (Ben Xe Mien Tay; ✆ 028-3825 5955; Đ Kinh Duong Vuong) Serves all areas south of HCMC, essentially the Mekong Delta. This huge station is about 10km west of HCMC in An Lac. A taxi here from Pham Ngu Lao costs around 210,000d. Buses and minibuses from Mien Tay serve most towns in the Mekong Delta using air-con express buses and premium minibuses.

Mien Dong Bus Station (Ben Xe Mien Dong; ✆ 028-3829 4056) Buses to locations north of HCMC leave from this huge and busy station in Binh Thanh district, about 5km from central HCMC on Hwy 13. Note that express buses depart from the east side, and local buses connect with the west side of the complex.

An Suong Bus Station (Ben Xe An Suong; District 12) Buses to Tay Ninh, Cu Chi and other points northwest of HCMC depart from this dirty, crowded terminal, but it's not really worth using them as the Cu Chi Tunnels are off the main highway and are a nightmare to navigate. The station is close to the flyover for Quoc Lo 1 (Hwy 1).

Buses to Cambodia

Plenty of international bus services connect HCMC and Cambodia, most with departures from the Pham Ngu Lao area. Book online or check out the travel agencies at the western end of this backpacker area – especially around **Lac Hong Tours** (Map p328; ✆ 028-3920 5852; www.lachongtours.com; 305 Đ Pham Ngu Lao; ⏱ 6.30am-10pm) – for frequent bus departures to Phnom Penh (from 240,000d), Siem Reap and Sihanoukville (both from 400,000d).

CAR & MOTORBIKE

Enquire at almost any hotel, tourist cafe or travel agency to arrange car hire; this will always include a driver. Agencies in the Pham Ngu Lao area generally offer the lowest prices.

Motorbikes are available in the Pham Ngu Lao area from US$7. However, given the insane traffic and lack of road signs these are not a wise idea.

TRAIN

Trains from **Saigon Train Station** (Ga Sai Gon; ✆ 028-3823 0105; 1 Đ Nguyen Thong, District 3; ⏱ ticket office 7.15-11am & 1-3pm) head north to various destinations: Danang (490,000d to 570,000d, 15½ to 19 hours, six daily); Hue (500,000d to 620,000d, 18½ to 22½ hours, six daily) and Nha Trang (240,000d to 350,000d, seven to nine hours, eight daily).

Book online at www.baolau.com or www.dsvn.vn. You can also purchase tickets from travel agents, or directly at the train station.

Getting Around

BICYCLE

It's not a great idea to cycle around central HCMC; the traffic is appalling and very few locals attempt it these days.

BOAT

The **Saigon Waterbus** (Map p312; ✆ 1900 636 830; www.saigonwaterbus.com; Bach Dang waterbus terminal; tickets 15,000d; ⏱ 7am-7.30pm) links the city centre with District 2; the trip takes just 15 minutes to Binh An station. There are 10 daily departures, with five additional services on weekends. It's a great, inexpensive way to see the Saigon River.

BUS

Local buses are cheap and plentiful, serving more than 130 routes around greater HCMC. However, very few visitors bother with them, preferring to walk or take taxis, which are very inexpensive.

Useful lines from Ben Thanh include 109 or 49 to Tan Son Nhat International Airport, 149 to Saigon Train Station, 1 to Binh Tay Market and **Cholon Bus Station** (Map p320; District 5), 102 to Mien Tay Bus Station and 26 to Mien Dong Bus Station. Most buses have air-con; tickets start at 7000d. Buy your ticket on-board from the attendant.

CAR & MOTORBIKE

Travel agencies, hotels and tourist cafes all hire cars (with drivers) and motorbikes. Even though motorbike travel is the fastest way to get around the city it's best not to attempt riding yourself, as this is one of the toughest and most dangerous cities in the world to navigate by road. Very few travel insurance policies offer cover, too.

If you plan to ride around Vietnam, try **Saigon Scooter Centre** (✆ 028-3848 7816; www. saigonscootercentre.com; 151 Luong Dinh Cua, District 2; ◷ 9am-5.30pm Mon-Sat) for classic Vespas, new scooters and trail bikes. Daily rates start from US$10. For an extra fee it's possible to arrange a one-way service, with a pick-up of the bikes anywhere between HCMC and Hanoi.

CYCLO

A vanishing icon of HCMC, there are very few *cyclos* (pedicabs or bicycle rickshaws) remaining in the city today and they are now prohibited from many central streets. If you do manage to find one, short hops around the city centre will cost around 50,000d.

GOING UNDERGROUND

Ho Chi Minh City sorely needs a metro system to help marshal the transport chaos above ground. First proposed in 2001, the system will run to an estimated five or six lines, with the 20km (part-underground, part-elevated) first line – linking Ben Thanh Market, District 2 and Suoi Tien in the east – under construction. Up to 88% of the scheme is being paid for by the Japanese government. Long delays have affected the project, however, with work suspended for many months as constructors and authorities have argued over funding.

Sandwiched between Đ Dong Khoi and Đ Nguyen Hue, the central station is taking shape near the Opera House. You'll also notice significant construction work and road closures at the western end of ĐL Le Loi and Ben Thanh Market.

MOTORBIKE TAXI

For traffic-dodging speed and convenience, the *xe om* is, for many, the way to go. *Xe om* drivers usually hang out on their parked bikes on street corners, touting for passengers. The accepted rate is around 30,000d for short rides (Pham Ngu Lao to the Dong Khoi area, for instance).

Almost all travellers use the excellent Grab smartphone app these days, which works out cheaper and is less hassle.

TAXI

Metered taxis cruise the streets, but it is worth calling ahead if you are off the beaten path. The flagfall is around 12,000d for the first kilometre; expect to pay around 35,000d from Dong Khoi to Pham Ngu Lao. Some companies have dodgy taxi meters, rigged to jump quickly, but both **Mai Linh Taxi** (✆ 028-3838 3838) and **Vinasun Taxi** (✆ 028-3827 2727) can be trusted. Using Grab is another good option.

AROUND HO CHI MINH CITY

Beyond the urban buzz and excitement of Ho Chi Minh City, the attractions of the surrounding region include fascinating cultural and historical sights such as the Cu Chi Tunnels and the Cao Dai Holy See temple at Tay Ninh. Also worth exploring is the Unesco-accredited area around Can Gio, especially the extensive mangrove forests that were an integral part of the Viet Cong resistance effort during the American War.

Cu Chi

✆ 028 / POP 19,800

If the tenacious spirit of the Vietnamese can be symbolised by a place, few sites are more symbolic than Cu Chi. At first glance there is scant evidence today of the fighting and bombing that convulsed Cu Chi during the war. To see what went on, you have to dig deeper – underground.

The tunnel network of Cu Chi became legendary during the 1960s for facilitating VC control of a large rural area only 30km to 40km from HCMC. At its peak, the tunnel system stretched from the South Vietnamese capital to the Cambodian border; in the district of Cu Chi alone more than 250km of tunnels honeycomb the ground. The network, parts of which were several storeys deep, included countless trapdoors, constructed living areas, storage facilities, weapon factories, field hospitals, command centres and kitchens.

Cu Chi has become a place of pilgrimage for Vietnamese schoolchildren and Communist Party cadres.

History

When the Viet Cong's National Liberation Front (NLF) insurgency began in earnest in around 1960, old tunnels built by the Viet Minh in the 1940s were repaired and new extensions were excavated. Within a few years the tunnel system assumed enormous strategic importance, and most of Cu Chi district and the nearby area came under VC control.

The tunnels of Cu Chi were built over a period of 25 years, beginning sometime in the late 1940s. They were the improvised response of a poorly equipped peasant army to its enemy's high-tech ordnance, helicopters, artillery, bombers and chemical weapons.

The Viet Minh built the first tunnels in the red earth (soft during the rainy season, rock-hard during dry months) of Cu Chi during the war against the French. The excavations were used mostly for communication between villages and to evade French army sweeps of the area.

In early 1963 the Diem government implemented the Strategic Hamlets Program, under which fortified encampments, surrounded by many rows of sharp bamboo spikes, were built to house people who had been 'relocated' from Communist-controlled areas. The first strategic hamlet was in Ben Cat district, next to Cu Chi. However, the VC used the tunnels to access the hamlets and control them from within, so that by the end of 1963 the first showpiece hamlet had been overrun.

The series of setbacks and defeats suffered by the South Vietnamese forces in the Cu Chi area rendered a complete VC victory by the end of 1965 a distinct possibility. In the early months of that year, the guerrillas boldly held a victory parade in the middle of Cu Chi town. VC strength in and around Cu Chi was one of the reasons the Johnson administration decided to involve US troops in the war.

The tunnels facilitated communication and coordination between the VC-controlled enclaves, isolated from each other by South Vietnamese and American land and air operations. They also allowed the VC to mount surprise attacks wherever the tunnels went – even within the perimeters of the US military

WORTH A TRIP

ONE PILLAR PAGODA OF THU DUC

Officially known as Nam Thien Nhat Tru, this Buddhist temple is often called the **One Pillar Pagoda of Thu Duc** (Chua Mot Cot Thu Duc; 1/91 Đ Nguyen Du, Thu Duc district). Modelled on Hanoi's One Pillar Pagoda, the structure is similar but not identical, consisting of a small, one-room temple hall rising on a pillar above a pond, containing a multi-armed image of Quan Am, Goddess of Mercy. At the rear of the compound are tombs holding urns containing bones of monks and other Buddhist faithful.

The pagoda is 15km northeast of central HCMC. Traveller cafes and travel agencies in HCMC should be able to put together a customised tour to the pagoda or arrange a car and driver for you.

base at Dong Du – and to disappear suddenly into hidden trapdoors without a trace.

In addition, Cu Chi was used as a base for infiltrating intelligence agents and sabotage teams into Saigon. The audacious attacks in the South Vietnamese capital during the 1968 Tet Offensive were planned and launched from Cu Chi.

Over the years the VC developed simple but effective techniques to make their tunnels difficult to detect or disable. Wooden trapdoors were camouflaged with earth and branches; some were booby-trapped. Hidden underwater entrances from rivers were constructed. To cook they used 'Dien Bien Phu kitchens', which exhausted the smoke through vents many metres away from the cooking site. Trapdoors were installed throughout the network to prevent tear gas, smoke or water from moving from one part of the system to another. Some sections were even equipped with electric lighting.

When the Americans began using German shepherd dogs, trained to use their keen sense of smell to locate trapdoors and guerrillas, the VC began washing with American soap, which gave off a scent the canines identified as friendly. Captured US uniforms were put out to confuse the dogs further. Most importantly, the dogs were not able to spot booby traps. So many dogs were killed or maimed that their horrified handlers then refused to send more into the tunnels.

HO CHI MINH CITY CU CHI

Around Ho Chi Minh City

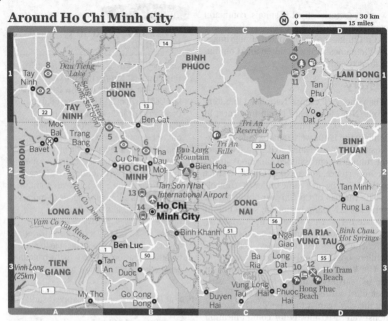

Around Ho Chi Minh City

To deal with the threat posed by VC control of an area so near the South Vietnamese capital, one of the USA's first actions was to establish a large base camp in Cu Chi district. Unknowingly, they built it right on top of an existing tunnel network. It took months for the 25th Division to figure out why they kept getting shot at in their tents at night.

The US and Australian troops tried a variety of methods to 'pacify' the area around Cu Chi, which came to be known as the Iron Triangle. They launched large-scale ground operations involving tens of thousands of troops but failed to locate the tunnels. To deny the VC cover and supplies, rice paddies were defoliated, huge swathes of jungle bulldozed, and villages evacuated and razed. The Americans also sprayed chemical defoliants on the area aerially and a few months later ignited the tinder-dry vegetation with gasoline and napalm. But the intense heat interacted with the wet tropical air in such a way as to create cloudbursts that extinguished the fires. The VC remained safe in their tunnels.

Unable to win this battle with chemicals, the US army began sending men down into the tunnels. These 'tunnel rats', who were often involved in underground fire fights, sustained appallingly high casualty rates.

The USA declared Cu Chi a free-strike zone: little authorisation was needed to shoot at anything in the area, random artillery was fired into the area at night, and pilots were told to drop unused bombs and napalm there before returning to base. But the VC stayed put.

Finally, in the late 1960s, American B-52s carpet-bombed the whole area, destroying most of the tunnels along with everything else around. The gesture was almost symbolic by then because the USA was already on its way out of the war. The tunnels had served their purpose.

The villages of Cu Chi have been presented with numerous honorific awards, decorations and citations by the government since the end of the American War, and many have been declared 'heroic villages'. Since 1975 new hamlets have been established and the population of the area has exploded; however, chemical defoliants remain in the soil and water, and crop yields are still poor.

The VC guerrillas serving in the tunnels lived in extremely difficult conditions and suffered serious casualties. Only about 6000 of the 16,000 cadres who fought in the tunnels survived the war. Thousands of civilians in the area were also killed. Their tenacity was extraordinary considering the bombings, the claustrophobia of living underground for weeks or months at a time, and the deaths of countless friends and comrades.

This district of greater Ho Chi Minh City now has a population of about 360,000, but during the American War it had about 80,000 residents. Mangold and Penycate's *Tunnels of Cu Chi* is a powerful book documenting the story of the tunnels and the people involved on both sides.

☉ Sights

Cu Chi Tunnels
HISTORIC SITE

(adult/child 120,000/35,000d) Two sections of this remarkable tunnel network (which are enlarged and upgraded versions of the real

thing) are open to the public. One is near the village of Ben Dinh and the other is 15km beyond at Ben Duoc. Most tourists visiting the tunnels end up at Ben Dinh, as it's easier for tour buses to reach. Even if you stay above ground, it's still an interesting experience learning about the region's ingenious and brave resistance activities.

Both sites have gun ranges attached where you can shell out a small fortune to fire genuine AK-47s and machine guns. You pay per bullet so be warned: if you're firing an automatic weapon, they do come out pretty fast.

Ben Dinh
HISTORIC SITE

(www.diadaocuchi.com.vn; ☉7am-6pm) The most visited of the tunnel sites, this small, renovated section is near the village of Ben Dinh, about 50km from HCMC. In one of the classrooms at the visitors centre a large map shows the extent of the network while another shows cross-section diagrams of the tunnels. The section of the tunnel system presently open to visitors is a few hundred metres south of the visitors centre. It snakes up and down through various chambers along its 50m length.

The tunnels are about 1.2m high and 80cm across, and are unlit. Some travellers find them too claustrophobic for comfort. A knocked-out M-41 tank and a bomb crater are near the exit, which is in a reforested eucalyptus grove.

Be warned that this site tends to get crowded and you can feel like you're on a tourist conveyor belt most days.

Ben Duoc
HISTORIC SITE

The tunnels here have been enlarged to accommodate tourists, although they're still a tight squeeze. Inside the underground chambers are bunkers, a hospital and a command centre that played a role in the 1968 Tet Offensive. The set pieces include tables, chairs, beds, lights, and dummies outfitted in guerrilla gear.

The massive Ben Duoc temple, built in 1993 in memory of the Vietnamese killed at Cu Chi, is flanked by a nine-storey tower with a flower garden at the front. You'll only be permitted to enter if you're dressed appropriately – although temple wear (long trousers etc) may not be conducive to clambering through earthen tunnels.

Cu Chi War History Museum
MUSEUM

(Nha Truyen Thong Huyen Cu Chi; DT8, Cu Chi; ☉7.30am-4.30pm Mon-Sat) FREE The small Cu

CAO DAISM

A thought-provoking fusion of East and West, Cao Daism (Dai Dao Tam Ky Pho Do) is a religion born in 20th-century Vietnam that embraces disparate elements of Buddhism, Confucianism, Taoism, native Vietnamese spiritualism, Christianity and Islam – with a dash of secular enlightenment thrown in for good measure. The term *Cao Dai* (meaning 'high terrace'; 高台) is a euphemism for God; an estimated two to three million followers of Cao Daism exist worldwide.

Cao Daism was founded by the mystic Ngo Minh Chieu (also known as Ngo Van Chieu; born 1878), a civil servant who once served as district chief of Phu Quoc Island. Widely read in Eastern and Western religious works, he became active in seances and in 1919 began receiving revelations that became the tenets of Cao Daism.

Much of Cao Dai doctrine is drawn from Mahayana Buddhism, mixed with Taoist and Confucian elements (Vietnam's 'Triple Religion'). Cao Dai ethics are based on the Buddhist ideal of 'the good person' but incorporate traditional Vietnamese beliefs as well. The ultimate goal of the Cao Dai disciple is to escape the cycle of reincarnation. This can only be achieved by refraining from killing, lying, luxurious living, sensuality and stealing.

Chi War History Museum is not actually at the tunnel sites but just off the main highway in the central part of Cu Chi town. Like most similar museums, its displays consist mainly of photographs (some quite graphic) and large chunks of rusting military hardware. The subject is covered much more comprehensively in the War Remnants Museum in HCMC.

☞ Tours

As public transport to Cu Chi is a pain, by far the easiest way to get to the tunnels is by guided tour. The competition is stiff, so prices are reasonable (from US$12 per person for a standard tour).

For something different consider a tour (US$80 person, minimum two people) by Old Compass Travel (p324), which will give you far more background and takes in a Viet Cong cemetery, a war memorial and the Saigon River. Or hop on a boat to the Cu Chi Tunnels with Les Rives (p323); boats depart twice daily (at 7am and 11am) and rates include hotel pickup, meals, refreshments, guide and admission fees. Another option is a motorbike tour with **Saigon Riders** (☎ 0919 767 118; www.saigonriders.vn), which costs US$89 per person.

ⓘ Getting There & Around

Cu Chi district covers a large area, parts of which are as close as 30km to central HCMC. The Cu Chi War History Museum is closest to the city, while the Ben Dinh and Ben Duoc tunnels are about 50km and 65km, respectively, from central HCMC.

To explore Cu Chi beyond the tunnels, consider hiring a car and driver through a travel agent, a relatively cheap option when shared between a few people. The roads here can be confusing, so make sure your driver knows the way.

Tay Ninh

☑ 0276 / POP 155,800

Tay Ninh town, the capital of Tay Ninh province, serves as the headquarters of one of Vietnam's most intriguing indigenous religions, Cao Daism. The Cao Dai Great Temple at the sect's Holy See is one of Asia's most unusual and astonishing structures. Built between 1933 and 1955, the temple is a rococo extravaganza blending the dissonant architectural motifs of a French church, a Chinese temple and an Islamic mosque.

Tay Ninh province, northwest of Ho Chi Minh City, is bordered by Cambodia on three sides. The Vam Co River flows from Cambodia through the western part of the province. The area's dominant geographic feature is Nui Ba Den (Black Lady Mountain), which towers above the surrounding plains.

◉ Sights

Cao Dai Holy See   TEMPLE

Home to the Cao Dai Great Temple (Thanh That Cao Dai), the Cao Dai Holy See, founded in 1926, is 4km east of Tay Ninh in the village of Long Hoa. As well as the Great Temple, the complex houses administrative offices, residences for officials and adepts, and a hospital of traditional Vietnamese herbal medicine that attracts people from all over the south for its treatments.

Prayers are conducted four times daily in the Great Temple (suspended during Tet). It's worth visiting during prayer sessions (the one at noon is most popular with tour groups from HCMC) but don't disturb the worshippers. Only a few hundred adherents, dressed in splendid garments, participate in weekday prayers, but during festivals several thousand may attend.

The Cao Dai clergy have no objection to visitors photographing temple objects, but do not photograph people without their permission, which is seldom granted. However, it is possible to photograph the prayer sessions from the upstairs balcony, an apparent concession to the troops of tourists who come here daily.

It's important that guests wear modest and respectful attire inside the temple, which means no shorts or sleeveless T-shirts. Set above the front portico of the Great Temple is the 'divine eye'. Lay women enter the Great Temple through a door at the base of the tower on the left. Once inside they walk around the outside of the colonnaded hall in a clockwise direction. Men enter on the right and walk around the hall in an anticlockwise direction. Hats must be removed upon entering the building. The area in the centre of the sanctuary is reserved for Cao Dai priests.

A mural in the front entry hall depicts the three signatories of the 'Third Alliance between God and Man': the Chinese statesman and revolutionary leader Dr Sun Yat-sen (Sun Zhongshan; 1866–1925) holds an ink stone, while the Vietnamese poet Nguyen Binh Khiem (1492–1587) and French poet and author Victor Hugo (1802–85) write 'God and humanity' and 'Love and justice' in Chinese and French (Nguyen Binh Khiem writes with a brush, Victor Hugo uses a quill pen). Nearby signs in English, French and German each give a slightly different version of the fundamentals of Cao Daism.

The main hall is divided into nine sections by shallow steps, representing the nine steps to heaven, with each level marked by a pair of columns. Worshippers attain each new level depending on their years as Cao Dai adherents. At the far end of the sanctuary, eight plaster columns entwined with multicoloured dragons support a dome representing the heavens. Under the dome is a giant star-speckled blue globe with the 'divine eye' on it.

The largest of the seven chairs in front of the globe is reserved for the Cao Dai pope, a position that has remained vacant since 1933. The next three chairs are for the three men responsible for the religion's law books. The remaining chairs are for the leaders of the three branches of Cao Daism, represented by the colours yellow, blue and red.

On both sides of the area between the columns are two pulpits similar in design to the minbar in mosques. During festivals the pulpits are used by officials to address the assembled worshippers. The upstairs balconies are used if the crowd overflows.

Up near the altar are barely discernible portraits of six figures important to Cao Daism: Sakyamuni (Siddhartha Gautama, the founder of Buddhism), Ly Thai Bach (Li Taibai, a fairy from Chinese mythology), Khuong Tu Nha (Jiang Taigong, a Chinese saint), Laotse (the founder of Taoism), Quan Cong (Guangong, Chinese God of War) and Quan Am (Guanyin, the Goddess of Mercy).

Nui Ba Den
TEMPLE, MOUNTAIN

(Black Lady Mountain; gondola one way/return adult 85,000/165,000d, child 50,000/90,000d) Located 15km northeast of Tay Ninh, Nui Ba Den rises 850m above the rice paddies, corn, cassava (manioc) and rubber plantations of the surrounding countryside. Over the centuries it has served as a shrine for various peoples of the area, including the Khmer, Cham, Vietnamese and Chinese, and there are several interesting cave temples here.

❶ Getting There & Away

Tay Ninh is on Hwy 22 (Quoc Lo 22), 96km from HCMC. The road passes through **Trang Bang**, the place where the famous photograph of a severely burnt young girl, Kim Phuc, screaming and running, was taken during a napalm attack in the American War. Read more about her story in The Girl in the Picture (1999) by Denise Chong.

The easiest way to get to Tay Ninh is via one of the Tay Ninh/Cu Chi tours leaving from District 1. Consider leaving one of the cheaper tours at the Holy See, and then taking a taxi or xe om from there to Nui Ba Den (around 120,000d). You'll need to arrange to meet your bus back at Tay Ninh to get return transport to HCMC.

BUS

By public transport from HCMC, bus 65 travels from the Ben Thanh Bus Station to the An Suong Bus Station (9000d). From there catch a bus to the Tay Ninh Bus Station (85,000d), from where you can arrange a taxi or xe om (around 130,000d) to Nui Ba Den.

AT A GLANCE

POPULATION
Can Tho: 1.57 million

FAST FACT
The Mekong River is the 10th longest in the world (4909km)

BEST BOAT TRIP
An Thoi Islands (p379)

BEST DIVING & SNORKELLING
Con Dao Islands (p403)

BEST SEAFOOD
Phu Quoc Night Market (p385)

WHEN TO GO
Jan While folks shiver up north, Phu Quoc's beaches stay temperate and dry.

Mar A March visit avoids the Tet madness, as well as the summer heat and rain.

Nov The dry season starts, with Khmer longboat festivals in Tra Vinh and Soc Trang.

Floating market, Can Tho (p365)
HADYNYAH/GETTY IMAGES ©

Mekong Delta

The 'rice bowl' of Vietnam, the Mekong Delta is carpeted in a dizzying variety of greens. It's a water world that moves to the rhythms of the mighty Mekong, where boats, houses and markets float upon the innumerable rivers, canals and streams that criss-cross the landscape. The bustling commerce of the delta's towns contrasts sharply with the languid pace of life in the countryside. Here buffalo wallow in rice paddies, coconut- and fruit-laden boats float along the mud-brown waters, and two-wheeled exploration of the narrow lanes is rewarded with a true taste of rural hospitality. Elsewhere, mangrove forests teem with bird life and bristle with the remains of Viet Cong bunkers, ornate Khmer pagodas and Buddhist temples, while out to sea, islands offer white-sand beaches and tropical hideaways.

History

Once part of the Khmer kingdom, the Mekong Delta was the last region of modern-day Vietnam to be annexed and settled by the Vietnamese. Cambodians, mindful that they controlled the area until the 18th century, still call the delta Kampuchea Krom, or 'Lower Cambodia'.

The Khmer Rouge attempted to reclaim the area by raiding Vietnamese villages and killing their inhabitants. This provoked the Vietnamese army to invade Cambodia on 25 December 1978 and oust the Khmer Rouge from power.

Most of today's inhabitants of the Mekong Delta are ethnic Vietnamese, but significant populations of ethnic Chinese and Khmer, as well as a smaller Cham community, also exist.

When the government introduced collective farming to the delta in 1975, production fell significantly and food shortages hit Saigon, though farmers in the delta easily grew enough to feed themselves. The Saigonese would head down to the delta to buy sacks of black-market rice, but to prevent profiteering the police set up checkpoints and confiscated rice from anyone carrying more than 10kg. All this ended in 1986 and farmers in the region have since transformed Vietnam into the world's third-largest rice exporter.

Getting There & Away

Many travellers visit the Mekong Delta on convenient organised tours. Those travelling on their own will have greater access to little-visited, off-the-beaten-track areas.

The ease of border crossings between Vietnam and Cambodia, including the river border at Vinh Xuong (near Chau Doc) and the land border at Xa Xia (near Ha Tien), has increased traveller traffic along these delta routes. Cambodian visas (officially US$30) are available on arrival at all border crossings.

AIR

Flights connect Can Tho with Con Dao, Dalat, Danang, Haiphong, Hanoi, Nha Trang, Phu Quoc, Thanh Hoa and Vinh; Rach Gia with Ho Chi Minh City (HCMC); and Ca Mau with HCMC. Phu Quoc Island's international airport offers connections to Hanoi, HCMC, Can Tho, Danang and Haiphong, with international connections including Bangkok, Hong Kong, Kuala Lumpur and Seoul. Can Tho is also now an international airport with budget flights to Bangkok and Kuala Lumpur.

BUS

In HCMC, delta buses leave from Mien Tay bus station, 10km west of the centre.

TOURS

Dozens of tours head from HCMC to the Mekong Delta, either as day trips or longer jaunts. This is a good option if you're short on time, but it means abdicating control of your itinerary and choice of hotels.

The cheapest tours are sold around HCMC's Pham Ngu Lao area. Shop around before you book, talk to other travellers and consult internet forums. Pricey tours are not necessarily better, but often 'rock bottom' means travelling with dozens of other tourists and being shuffled from one souvenir stall to another. Rewarding motorbike and scooter tours of the delta are run by Vespa Adventures (p324) and Saigon Riders (p350).

Getting Around

BOAT

Some delta towns have boat connections between them, although with road improvement and the building of bridges, passenger travel on water is declining. The journey between Ca Mau and Rach Gia is particularly scenic. Fast passenger boats and car ferries to Phu Quoc Island leave from Ha Tien and Rach Gia. Cargo boats and infrequent passenger boats head to the remote southern islands.

BUS

It's easy to travel the delta using public transport, and bus connections are excellent. Each urban centre has a main bus station for both buses and minibuses – although it's usually located on the edge of town, requiring a short xe om (motorbike taxi) or taxi ride to your hotel. Minibuses and window-cooled local buses tend to stop more frequently than large buses and some are very cramped.

The most comfortable buses between towns tend to be the plush air-conditioned ones; the most extensive network is run by **Phuong Trang** (www.futaexpress.com). Bus companies sometimes depart from their own bus terminals; most lodgings in the delta can suggest the best bus company for your journey and book tickets in advance, so that a free shuttle delivers you from your hotel to the bus station. If Phuong Trang stops near but not in a town (like Ben Tre), it's sometimes still more convenient to get out a few kilometres away and catch a taxi rather than taking a slow local bus, although you still pay the full bus fare to/from HCMC.

Coming from HCMC, delta buses leave from Mien Tay bus station, 10km west of the centre. To avoid the slight inconvenience of reaching Mien Tay, consider booking one of the cheap day tours to My Tho departing from Đ Pham Ngu Lao and abandoning the tour after the boat trip.

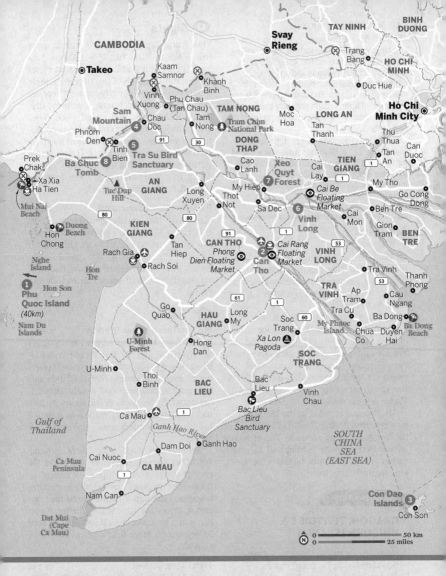

Mekong Delta Highlights

1 Phu Quoc Island (p377) Exploring jungle back roads on a motorbike before watching sunset from a beautiful beach.

2 Can Tho (p365) Witnessing the floating markets come alive with trade at sunrise.

3 Con Dao Islands (p403) Relaxing on these remote tropical islands that once housed political prisoners.

4 Sam Mountain (p398) Hopping from temple to temple in the bucolic countryside around Chau Doc.

5 Tra Su Bird Sanctuary (p395) Watching clouds of storks and egrets at an excellent birdwatching site.

6 Vinh Long (p364) Getting a taste of rural river life at a homestay.

7 Xeo Quyt Forest (p402) Ducking into old Viet Cong bunkers and boating around enchanted waterways.

8 Ba Chuc Tomb (p393) Paying respects to the victims of a Khmer Rouge massacre.

CAR, MOTORBIKE & BICYCLE

The most flexible transport option is private car, bicycle or rented motorbike. Two-wheeling around the delta is good fun, especially along the maze of country roads and on Phu Quoc, although motorbike accidents do occur with inexperienced riders. The delta is quite flat, but be prepared for toll roads and ferry crossings, although these are gradually being replaced with new bridges.

Ferries are cheap and frequent. If you don't wish to cycle solo, **Sinhbalo Adventure Travel** (☑ 028-3837 6766; www.sinhbalo.com) and **Vietnam Backroads** (☑ 028-3837 0532; www.mekongbiketours.com) offer multiday jaunts around the delta.

My Tho

☑ 0273 / POP 272,000

Gateway to the Mekong Delta, My Tho is the capital of Tien Giang province and an important market town, although for the famous floating markets you'll need to continue on to Can Tho.

My Tho's proximity to HCMC means it's a popular day-trip destination for a taste of river life: a flotilla of boats tour the local islands and their cottage industries daily, though many bypass the town itself. The riverfront makes for a pleasant stroll, and the town, including the lively market (Đ Trung Trac), is easily explored on foot.

My Tho was founded in the 1680s by Chinese refugees fleeing Taiwan after the fall of the Southern Ming dynasty. The economy is based on tourism, fishing and the cultivation of rice, coconuts, bananas, mangoes, longans and citrus fruit.

WORTH A TRIP

DRAGON, TORTOISE & UNICORN ISLANDS

Famed for its longan orchards, **Dragon Island** (Con Tan Long) makes for a pleasant stop and stroll, just a five-minute boat trip from My Tho. Some of the residents of the island are shipwrights and the lush, palm-fringed shores are lined with wooden fishing boats. The island has some small restaurants and cafes.

Tortoise Island (Con Qui) and **Unicorn Island** (Thoi Son) are popular stops for their coconut-candy and banana-wine workshops.

◉ Sights

Vinh Trang Pagoda BUDDHIST TEMPLE
(60a Đ Nguyen Trung Truc; ⊙9-11.30am & 1.30-5pm) **FREE** Giant Buddha statues tower over the beautiful grounds of this peaceful temple around 1km east of the city centre, where the monks maintain an ornate sanctuary, decorated with carved and gilded wood. They also provide a home for children in need; donations welcome. To get here, head north on Le Loi, turn right onto Nguyen Trai and cross the bridge. After 400m turn left onto Nguyen Trung Truc. The entrance is 200m from the turn-off, on the right-hand side.

Phoenix Island Sanctuary HISTORIC SITE
(Con Phung; http://conphungtourist.com; 5000d; ⊙8-11.30am & 1.30-6pm) This island sanctuary is a faded version of its former glory, but if you love kitsch, come for the model Apollo rocket inexplicably mixed among Buddhist statues. Private boat tours can include the island.

☞ Tours

My Tho Tourist Boat Station BOATING
(8 Đ 30 Thang 4) In a prominent building on the riverfront, the My Tho Tourist Boat Station is home to several tour companies offering cruises to the neighbouring islands and through the maze of small canals. Depending on what you book, destinations usually include a coconut-candy workshop, a honey farm (try the banana wine) and an orchid garden.

A 2½-hour boat tour costs around 400,000d for one person or 500,000d for two. If you're a day tripper, it's easiest to book your package (including connecting transport) through a HCMC-based tour operator. Prices are significantly better if you can join a group, although you may be able to negotiate a more flexible itinerary if you go it alone.

Tien Giang Tourist BOATING
(Cong Ty Du Lich Tien Giang; ☑093-289 6699; www.tiengiangtourist.com; 8 Đ 30 Thang 4) Reliable boat operator. Three-hour tours to Thoi Son and Phoenix Island cost 670,000d for up to three people.

☷ Sleeping

Song Tien Annex HOTEL $
(☑0273-387 7883; www.tiengiangtourist.com; 33 Đ Thien Ho Duong; r from 400,000d; ❄☷☎) This place offers river views from the balconies,

My Tho

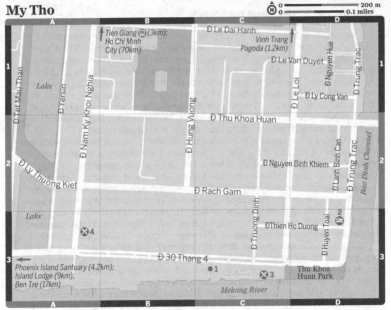

a central location, bathrooms with free-standing, claw-foot bathtubs (rare as unicorn eggs in Vietnam) and friendly, helpful staff, but the fixtures and fittings are showing their age.

Hong Thai Homestay   HOMESTAY **$$**
(📱091-455 7386; 16c Ap 2 Quoi Son, Chau Thanh; s/d US$20/32; ❄️🛜) Mr Thai and his wife make a formidable team: he arranges excursions for his guests amid the coconut groves around their countryside home, and she cooks delicious local staples to feed them. Rooms are simple, fan-cooled and tiled. Located across the river from My Tho; arrange pickup with the owner.

⭐ **Island Lodge**   BOUTIQUE HOTEL **$$$**
(📱0273-651 9000; www.theislandlodge.com.vn; 390 Ap Thoi Binh, Xa Thoi Son; r US$215; ❄️🛜🏊) It's hard to imagine a more tranquil place than this intimate island hideaway. The occupants of its 12 rooms are cheerfully attended to by professional staff, and you can watch the goings-on on the river from the pool, indulge in gourmet cuisine, or retreat to your light, bright room, complete with contemporary art and bamboo-framed beds.

After crossing the bridge from My Tho in the Ben Tre direction, take the turn towards Thoi Son and travel another 3km or so.

My Tho

🎯 **Activities, Courses & Tours**

🛏️ **Sleeping**

🍴 **Eating**

🍴 Eating

My Tho is known for its vermicelli soup, *hu tieu My Tho*, garnished with fresh and dried seafood, pork, chicken, offal and fresh herbs. It's served either with broth or dry and can be made vegetarian. Although *hu tieu* is ubiquitous here, don't miss the speciality restaurants: **Hu Tieu 44** (📱0273-388 3044; 44 Đ Nam Ky Khoi Nghia; soup 25,000d; ⏱8am-9pm) for carnivores, and **Hu Tieu Chay Cay Bo De** (24 Đ Nam Ky Khoi Nghia; mains 15,000-24,000d; ⏱8am-9pm; 🍴) for vegetarians. The latter is on a street with places serving meat versions of the dish and a few other vegetarian restaurants.

THE RIVER OF THE NINE DRAGONS

The Mekong River is one of the world's great rivers and its delta is one of the world's largest. It originates high in the Tibetan plateau, flowing 4500km through China, between Myanmar (Burma) and Laos, through Laos, along the Laos–Thailand border, and through Cambodia and Vietnam on its way to the South China Sea (East Sea). At Phnom Penh (Cambodia), the Mekong River splits into two main branches: the Hau Giang (Lower River, also called the Bassac River), which flows via Chau Doc, Long Xuyen and Can Tho to the sea; and the Tien Giang (Upper River), which splits into several branches at Vinh Long and empties into the sea at five points. The numerous branches explain the Vietnamese name for the river: Song Cuu Long (River of Nine Dragons).

The Mekong's flow begins to rise around the end of May and reaches its highest point in September. A tributary of the river that empties into the Mekong at Phnom Penh drains Cambodia's Tonlé Sap Lake. When the Mekong is at flood stage, this tributary reverses its direction and flows into Tonlé Sap, acting as one of the world's largest natural flood barriers. Unfortunately, deforestation in Cambodia is disturbing this delicate balancing act, resulting in more flooding in Vietnam's portion of the Mekong River basin.

Sporadic seasonal flooding claims the lives of hundreds and can force tens of thousands of residents to evacuate from their homes. Floods cause millions of dollars' worth of damage and have a catastrophic effect on regional rice and coffee crops.

Living on a floodplain presents some technical challenges. Lacking any high ground to escape flooding, many delta residents build their houses on bamboo stilts to avoid the rising waters. Many roads are submerged or turn to muck during floods; all-weather roads have to be built on raised embankments, but this is expensive. The traditional solution has been to build canals and travel by boat. There are thousands of canals in the Mekong Delta – keeping them properly dredged and navigable is a constant but essential chore.

A further challenge is keeping the canals clean. The normal practice of dumping all garbage and sewage directly into the waterways behind the houses that line them is taking its toll. Many of the more populated areas in the Mekong Delta are showing signs of unpleasant waste build-up. The World Wildlife Foundation (WWF) is one organisation that's working with local and provincial governments to help preserve the environment.

Perhaps the biggest current challenge is managing the impact of hydropower dams already operating or under construction on the river. Dams on the Chinese and Laotian stretches of the river have been blamed for reduced water levels, and environmentalists have voiced concerns that additional dams will disrupt the breeding cycles of dozens of fish species. There are also fears that reduced flows will lead to further saline intrusion (exacerbated by recent droughts) downstream in Vietnam, having a catastrophic effect on rice production.

New dams upstream in Laos, such as the massive Xayaburi Dam in northern Laos and the Don Sahong Dam at Si Phan Don in the south, are combining with climate change to create serious downstream challenges for Cambodia and Vietnam. For more on such issues, check out the Mekong River Commission (www.mrcmekong.org), which oversees the dam developments; Save the Mekong Coalition (https://savethemekong.net); and WWF (http://wwf.panda.org).

Chuong Dong Restaurant VIETNAMESE $
(Nha Hang Chuong Duong; ☎ 0273-388 2352; 10 Đ 30 Thang 4; meals 50,000-820,000d; ☺ 7am-11pm) The Vietnamese seafood-focused dishes (ginger clams, fried fish, crab congee, shrimp cakes, spicy sea snails) at this busy restaurant are all good, with some passable Western dishes, too, though what most people come for are the views across the river. Groups also come to be merry and sing, which is not so great for the attached hotel's guests.

❶ Getting There & Away

Major bridges and highways have considerably shortened travel distances to My Tho. If heading to Ben Tre, a taxi (around 260,000d) or xe om (around 120,000d) will be considerably faster than a bus. Buses head to Ben Tre (15,000d, 25 minutes, frequent), Can Tho (60,000d to 90,000d, 2½ hours, several daily) and HCMC (70,000d to 110,000d, 1½ hours, hourly).

Tien Giang Bus Station (Ben Xe Tien Giang; 42 Đ Ap Bac) is 2.3km northwest of town, on the main Hwy 1A towards Ho Chi Minh City. A xe om into town should cost around 40,000d.

Ben Tre

📞 0275 / POP 260,000

The picturesque little province of Ben Tre was always one ferry beyond the tourist traffic of My Tho and consequently developed at a more languid pace, although new bridges connecting Ben Tre with My Tho and Tra Vinh have funnelled more visitors into the area. The town's waterfront, lined with ageing villas, is easy to explore on foot, as is the rustic settlement across the bridge to the south of the centre. This is also a good place to arrange boat trips in the area, particularly for those wanting to escape the tour-bus bustle. Plus, the riverside promenade and the narrow lanes on both sides of the river are ideal for two-wheeled exploration.

The Ben Tre area is famous for its *keo dua* (coconut candy). Many local women work in small factories making these sweets, spending their days boiling cauldrons of the sticky coconut goo before rolling it out and slicing sections into squares.

👉 Tours

★ Mango Cruises — TOURS

(📞 0967 683 366; www.mangocruises.com) Unlike cookie-cutter tours from HCMC, Mango Cruises focuses on the less-visited back roads and canals around Ben Tre and beyond. Day tours comprise a nice mix of cycling, dining on local specialities and observing how rice paper and other local staples are made. Longer tours include outings on its day cruisers and multiday boat trips in the delta.

🛏 Sleeping

The best places to stay have river views. There are only a few flashy hotels for now, and more atmospheric guesthouse-type options offering meals are near Ben Tre rather than in the town proper.

★ Mango Home Riverside — BOUTIQUE HOTEL $$

(📞 0275-351 1958; www.mangohomeriverside.com; d/ste from US$55/75; ❄ 🛜) Set amid coconut and mango trees along the bank of a Mekong tributary, this delightful mango-coloured B&B, run by a Canadian-Vietnamese couple, provides a welcome place to unwind. Spacious rooms have air-con, some have outdoor bathrooms, and there are hammocks for lounging. The food is excellent and at night there's complete silence. It's 10km out of town; call for pickup.

Oasis Hotel — HOTEL $$

(📞 0275-246 7799; http://bentrehoteloasis.com; 151c My An C, My Thanh An; d/f US$32/48; ❄ 🛜 ♿) There's always a warm welcome at this popular, bright-yellow hotel with bar and pool, run by a very helpful Kiwi-Vietnamese couple. It's in the village south of the river and best reached by taxi. Bicycle-rental services facilitate countryside exploration.

🍴 Eating

For ultra-cheap eats, head to the market, where plenty of **food stalls** (cnr Nguyen Binh Khiem & Đ Hung Vuong; dishes around 15,000d; ⏱ 7-10pm) await.

Thuy Pizza — PIZZA $

(51 Đ Ngo Quyen; meals from 65,000d; ⏱ noon-10pm) Adding a welcome touch of innovation

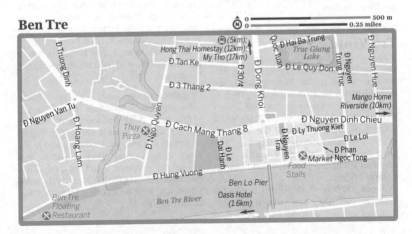

Ben Tre

0 — 500 m
0 — 0.25 miles

Đ Truong Dinh
🚌 (5km);
Hong Thai Homestay (12km);
My Tho (17km)
Đ Tan Ke
Quoc Tuan
Đ Hai Ba Trung
Trúc Giang Lake
Đ Le Quy Don
Đ Nguyen Trung Truc
Đ Nguyen Hue
Đ 3 Thang 2
Đ 30/4
Đ Dong Khoi
Đ Nguyen Van Tu
Đ Hoang Lam
Thuy Pizza
Đ Ngo Quyen
Đ Cach Mang Thang 8
Đ Le Da Hanh
Mango Home Riverside (10km)
Đ Nguyen Dinh Chieu
Đ Ly Thuong Kiet
Đ Nguyen Trai
Đ Le Loi
Đ Phan Ngoc Tong
Market
Food Stalls
Đ Hung Vuong
Ben Lo Pier
Ben Tre Floating Restaurant
Ben Tre River
Oasis Hotel (1.6km)

BUSES FROM BEN TRE

DESTINATION	COST (D)	TIME	FREQUENCY	DISTANCE (KM)
Can Tho	70,000	3hr	several daily	126
HCMC	80,000	2¼hr	hourly	87
My Tho	10,000	30min	frequent	16
Tra Vinh	70,000	2¼hr	several daily	86
Vinh Long	20,000	1½hr	several daily	44

to Ben Tre's largely uninspiring dining scene, this friendly place attracts a healthy contingent of travellers and curious locals. The pizza is as good as can be expected in small-town delta, and owner Thuy is friendly and keen to practise her English.

Ben Tre Floating Restaurant   VIETNAMESE $$
(☑ 075-382 2492; near Đ Hung Vuong; meals 50,000-200,000d; ☉10am-10pm; ☎) This rather grand-looking floating restaurant is set on a giant dragon boat and features three floors. The menu includes a dizzying array of Vietnamese dishes, including seafood, clay pots and hotpots. Prices are on the high side, but it's a good location to draw the river breeze.

❶ Getting There & Away

Buses to Vinh Long drop you at Pha Dinh Kao, the ferry port across the river from town; take the ferry across.

Buses stop at the **bus station** (Ben Xe Thanh Pho Ben Tre; Đ Dong Khoi), located 5km north of the town centre. The last buses to HCMC depart at about 5pm; Thinh Phat and Phuong Trang are among the most comfortable services. From Tra Vinh you can catch a Phuong Trang bus headed to HCMC and prearrange to be dropped off near Ben Tre bus station.

Tra Vinh

☑ 0294 / POP 160,000

The boulevards of Tra Vinh, one of the prettiest towns in the Mekong Delta, are still lined with shady trees, harking back to an earlier era. With more than 140 Khmer pagodas dotting the province, Tra Vinh is a quiet place for exploring the Mekong's little-touted Cambodian connection. The town itself sees a little more tourist traffic now that it's linked to Ben Tre and beyond by large bridges.

About 300,000 ethnic Khmer live in Tra Vinh province. They may seem an invisible minority, as they all speak fluent Vietnamese and there's nothing outwardly distinguishing about their clothing or lifestyle. Dig a bit deeper and you'll discover that Khmer culture is alive and well in this part of Vietnam.

There is also a small but active Chinese community in Tra Vinh, one of the few such communities that remain in the Mekong Delta region.

◉ Sights

Hang Pagoda   BUDDHIST TEMPLE
(Chua Hang, Kampongnigrodha; Đ Dien Bien Phu; ☉dawn-dusk) FREE This modern Khmer pagoda is also known as the stork pagoda after the birds that nest in the tall trees here. It's a beautiful, peaceful complex, and watching dozens of white egrets and storks wheeling overhead is an attraction in itself, but bring a hat due to the frequent bird droppings. You may get to see the orange-robed monks beat the enormous drum in the courtyard. The pagoda is located 6km south of town, 300m past the bus station.

Kampong Ksan   BUDDHIST PAGODA
(Đ Dhong Koi; ☉dusk-dawn) FREE The newest of Tra Vinh's Khmer pagodas is best appreciated from the other side of the river on Kho Dau. From there, the golden peaks reach into the sky reminiscent of riverside Wat Arun in Bangkok. It's a very photogenic scene. Monks are happy for you to take a look around the gold halls when they are not being used.

Ong Met Pagoda   BUDDHIST PAGODA
(Chua Ong Met, Bodhisalaraja; 50/1 Đ Le Loi; ☉dawn-dusk) FREE The most central of Tra Vinh's Khmer pagodas is active, with monks sweeping, studying in the library and going about their business. They will show you around the buildings, if you ask nicely. First established in 711 CE, Ong Met is well maintained and kept brilliantly gold among the eucalyptus trees.

Tra Vinh

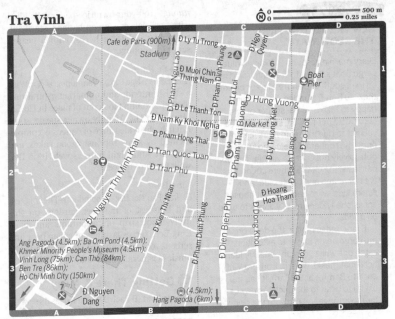

Cafe de Paris (900m)
Đ Ly Tu Trong
Stadium
Đ Ngo Quyen
Đ Muoi Chin
Thang Nam
Đ Le Loi
Đ Hung Vuong
Boat Pier
Đ Le Thanh Ton
Đ Nam Ky Khoi Nghia
Market
Đ Pham Hong Thai
Đ Tran Quoc Tuan
Đ Tran Phu
Đ Hoang Hoa Tham
Đ Kien Thi Nhan
Đ Nguyen Dang
Ang Pagoda (4.5km); Ba Om Pond (4.5km);
Khmer Minority People's Museum (4.5km);
Vinh Long (75km); Can Tho (84km);
Ben Tre (86km);
Ho Chi Minh City (150km)
(4.5km);
Hang Pagoda (6km)

MEKONG DELTA TRA VINH

Ong Pagoda
TAOIST TEMPLE

(Chua Ong & Chua Tau; 44 Đ Dien Bien Phu; ⊙dawn-dusk) **FREE** The very ornate, brightly painted Ong Pagoda is a fully fledged Chinese pagoda and a very active place of worship. The red-faced god on the altar is deified general Quan Cong, who is believed to offer protection against war and is based on a 3rd-century soldier.

Ba Om Pond
BUDDHIST TEMPLE

(Ao Ba Om; Square Lake; ⊙dawn-dusk) **FREE** Five kilometres southwest of Tra Vinh, this large, lotus-filled, square pond is a favourite with local picnickers, and a spiritual site for the Khmers. It would have once served as a bathing pond for the 10th-century Angkor-era temple that was situated here, but it is definitely not recommended to swim in its murky waters today!

Also at this site are the **Ang Pagoda** (Chua Ang) **FREE** and, opposite its entrance, is the nicely presented **Khmer Minority People's Museum** (Bao Tang Van Hoa Dan Tac; ⊙8am-5pm) **FREE**.

🛏 Sleeping

Hoan My Hotel
HOTEL **$**

(☑074-862 211; 105 ĐL Nguyen Thi Minh Khai; r 320,000-450,000d; ❋🐱) This mini-hotel is a friendly spot to stay, with good-value rooms

Tra Vinh

◎ Sights
1 Kampong Ksan	C3
2 Ong Met Pagoda	C1
3 Ong Pagoda	C2

🛏 Sleeping
| 4 Hoan My Hotel | A3 |
| 5 Hotel Gia Hoa 2 | C2 |

✕ Eating
| 6 Bun Nuoc Leo Kim Tuyen | C1 |
| 7 Quan Bun Nem Nuong | A3 |

◎ Drinking & Nightlife
| 8 King Beer | B2 |

featuring functional air-con, hot-water showers and cable TV. There is a lift should you opt for a room on the upper floors, and a secure car park beneath the building.

Hotel Gia Hoa 2
HOTEL **$**

(☑0294-385 8008; 50 Đ Le Loi; r 320,000-580,000d; ❋🐱) Hard to miss due to its central location, its height and its bright-yellow exterior, this brash hotel is surprisingly pleasant inside. Expect large rooms, separate shower stalls and a lift to haul up your luggage.

BEN TRE TO TRA VINH THE SLOW WAY

Every morning around 9.30am, a blue cargo boat sets off to Tra Vinh from Ben Lo Pier, south of Ben Tre Market beside the Cau Ben Tre bridge. The owner is happy to take on a passenger or two (120,000d per person, six hours) and you get to ride in the upstairs 'cabin' or on the roof amid the cargo, un-obtrusively observing river life. The boat passes along canals where coconuts are harvested and processed, and where kids swim beneath stilt houses, occasionally docking in villages to drop off goods.

Every bridge built in the delta brings the cargo boats closer to extinction, so catch one while you can. A nearly iden-tical boat makes the trip from Tra Vinh dock to Ben Tre at 9.30am. It can be useful to head to the dock the day be-fore to arrange the trip with the owner.

Eating & Drinking

Tra Vinh's local speciality is *bun nuoc leo*, a Cambodian-influenced noodle soup made from fermented fish, chicken and coco-nut juice. Another favourite, sold at street stalls, is *banh tet* – sticky rice, mung beans, pork, preserved egg and other ingredients wrapped in banana leaves. Buy a roll and cut it into slices.

There are stacks of good local seafood restaurants along Đ Tran Phu Noi Dai. Just drift up and down and see where the locals are at.

Bun Nuoc Leo Kim Tuyen   CAMBODIAN $
(Đ Ly Thuong Kiet; noodle soup from 15,000d; 6.30am-6.30pm) This unfancy local insti-tution is known for its Tra Vinh speciality dish, *bun nuoc leo*, a Khmer-style, rice-noodle soup with Chinese and Vietnamese influences. Slices of juicy pork, crackling and all, arrive in paper, which you unwrap and slip into the soup of banana flowers and garlic chives in a broth of fermented fish, chicken, coconut juice and lemon-grass. Heaven.

Quan Bun Nem Nuong   VIETNAMESE $
(12 ĐL Nguyen Dang; meals 40,000d; 11am-10pm) South of the centre, this informal joint is justifiably popular with locals for its *nem*

nuong – roll-your-own rice-paper rolls filled with pork sausage, green banana, star fruit, cucumber and fresh herbs, with a peanut sauce for dipping.

Cafe de Paris   CAFE
(118b Đ Pham Ngu Lao; 7am-10pm; ❄) With a stylish interior and upmarket aspirations, this cafe wouldn't look out of place in Ho Chi Minh City. The friendly owner speaks some English, the wide range of coffees is comple-mented by some seriously good cakes, and there are some light bites as well. It's a 1km walk north of the centre.

King Beer   BEER GARDEN
(Đ Tran Phu Noi Dai; 5pm-1am) The biggest and brashest of the beer gardens on this lively night strip of restaurants and bars, King Beer serves lashings of cheap beer and screens football games at the weekend. The music is generally turned up to 11.

Getting There & Away

A **cargo boat** (Đ Bach Dang) still plies its slow way between Tra Vinh and Ben Tre and can take on passengers.

Most buses leave from the **main bus station** (Ben Xe Khach Tra Vinh; QL 54), which is about 5km south of the town centre on Hwy (QL) 54 (the continuation of the main street, Đ Dien Bien Phu), though some operators have their own departure points.

Buses go to the following destinations:

Ben Tre (70,000d, 2¼ hours, several daily, 86km)

Can Tho (65,000d to 90,000d, 2½ hours, hourly, 84km)

HCMC (100,000d to 130,000d, 4 hours, hourly, 150km)

Vinh Long (50,000d, 1½ hours, several daily, 75km)

Phuong Trang offers free shuttle-bus pickup from your hotel to the bus station but makes many stops. Enquire when booking your ticket.

Vinh Long
📞 0270 / POP 200,000

The capital of Vinh Long province, plonked about midway between My Tho and Can Tho, is a major transit hub. It's a gateway to island life, Cai Be floating market, abundant orchards and rural homestays. The town it-self, however, has little of interest to the visi-tor and most people are passing through on the way to aquatic adventures.

Sights

Vinh Long's main draws are the tranquil islands dotting the river, with houses built on stilts and slow-paced agricultural life.

Van Thanh Mieu Temple   TEMPLE
(Phan Thanh Gian Temple; Đ Tran Phu; ⊙ 5-11am & 1-7pm) Sitting in pleasant grounds across from the river, this temple is southeast of town. Confucian temples such as this are rare in southern Vietnam. The front hall honours local hero Phan Thanh Gian, who led an uprising against the French colonists in 1930. When it became obvious that his revolt was doomed, Phan killed himself rather than be captured by the colonial army. The rear hall, built in 1866, has a portrait of Confucius above the altar.

Cai Be Floating Market   MARKET
(⊙ 5am-noon) This river market is still the principal attraction on a boat tour from Vinh Long, although it has shrunk considerably due to new bridges and roads replacing river transport of goods. The market is at its best around 6am, though still might comprise only a handful of boats. Wholesalers on big boats moor here, each specialising in different types of fruit or vegetables, hanging samples of their goods from tall wooden poles. It's an hour by boat from Vinh Long.

An Binh   ISLAND
The most popular and easiest island to visit is An Binh. You can take the public ferry across and cycle around on your own, but it's better to be on the water and organise a boat trip. Most island homestays organise half-day cruises along narrow canals for around US$20, taking in the floating market and the picturesque backwaters.

☞ Tours

Cuu Long Tourist   BOATING
(🖉 0270-382 3616; 2 Đ Phan B Chau; ⊙ 7am-5pm) Offers a variety of boat tours, ranging from three hours to three days. Destinations include small canals, fruit orchards, brick kilns, a conical-palm-hat workshop and the Cai Be Floating Market.

⊨ Sleeping

Since Vinh Long's biggest draws are its islands, where there are some great homestays and resorts hidden away, there isn't much point in staying in town when Can Tho is only a short drive down the road.

Minh Khue Hotel   HOTEL $
(🖉 0270-382 6688; minhkhuehotel.vinhlong@gmail.com; 38 Đ Trung Nu Vuong; s 250,000-350,000d, tw 400,000-500,000d, VIP from 600,000d; ❄ ☎) Probably the friendliest and smartest among

MEKONG DELTA VINH LONG

Vinh Long

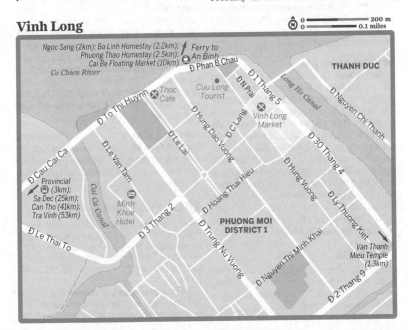

HOMESTAYS AROUND VINH LONG

For many travellers, the chance to experience river life and get to know a local family is a highlight of a Mekong visit. Perhaps 'homestay' is the wrong word: in most cases you will actually be staying in specially constructed rustic hostels and guesthouses.

Some homestays have large communal rooms with bunks, while others offer basic bungalows with shared facilities and some even have rooms with en suites. Breakfast is usually included; in some places you'll share a meal with the family, while in bigger places there are simple restaurants. Interaction with the family can be minimal with long-time hosts. The only constant is a verdant, rustic setting and a taste of rural life.

Although many tourists book through group tours in HCMC, you can just take the ferry from Vinh Long and then a *xe om* to your preferred choice. Some hosts don't speak much English, but welcome foreign guests just the same.

Ngoc Sang (☑ 096 936 7636; homestayngocsang@yahoo.com.vn; 95/8 Binh Luong, Dao Trinh Nhat, An Binh; per person 250,000d; ☎) Most travellers love this friendly, canal-facing rustic homestay. The grandmother cooks up some wonderful local dishes, free bikes are available, the owner runs decent early-morning boat tours and there's a languid atmosphere about the place. The family seems shy when it comes to hanging out with guests, though. Free pickup from the ferry pier, 15 minutes' walk away.

Phuong Thao Homestay (☑ 070-383 6854; www.en.phuongthaohomestay.com; An Binh; dm/d from 200,000/500,000d; ❄☎) Tucked away by the river, around 1.5km from the An Binh boat landing, this rustic guesthouse is run by a friendly family who can rent you bicycles and motorbikes to explore the island. Stay in the large, thatch-walled dorms with mosquito nets, or the two concrete doubles. There's a good ratio of guests per bathroom.

Ba Linh Homestay (☑ 0270-385 8683, 090-726 7377; balinhhomestay@gmail.com; 95 An Thanh, An Binh; r 500,000d; ☎) Run by friendly Mr Truong, this traditional-looking and popular place has six simple, high-roofed, partitioned rooms in a line, all with fan. Breakfast and dinner is included in the price and you may get to try such local specialities as rice-field rat.

a new block of hotels near the riverfront and park on Ð Trung Nu Vuong. Rooms feature contemporary trim bathrooms and smart TVs. Some English is spoken.

★**Mekong Riverside Resort & Spa** RESORT **$$$**
(☑ 0273-392 4466; www.mekongriversideresort.vn; Hoa Qui Ward, Hoa Khanh, Cai Be district; r US$100-130; ❄☎☒) With a magnificent sense of seclusion, this four-star resort has lovely thatched bungalows and stunning views across the vast river. Angle for fish from your balcony, or sit back and watch the riverboats cruise the Mekong at night. With free canoes and a bird-watching tower, the resort offers the chance to fully experience the riverine world of the Mekong Delta.

It's 2km west of Cai Be along the river; offers pickup from HCMC.

 Eating

Flee the mayhem by heading to the riverfront, where a handful of cafes and restaurants afford respite. Vinh Long Market is good for budget eating.

Thoc Cafe CAFE **$**
(☑ 0270-388 7979; www.facebook.com/thoc cafevinhlong; 19 Ð Le Lai; mains 20,000-75,000d; ☺6am-10pm; ☎) Occupying a prime location overlooking the river and the adjacent gardens, this is an inviting al-fresco cafe with an upstairs terrace for river breezes. The menu is primarily snacks and light bites, but locals flock here for coffees, shakes, juices and the views.

Vinh Long Market VIETNAMESE **$**
(Cho Vinh Long; Ð 3 Thang 2; meals from 20,000d; ☺6am-6pm) Great spot for local fruit and inexpensive street snacks, such as *nem* (fresh spring rolls).

ⓘ Getting There & Away

Buses leave hourly for Can Tho (40,000d, one hour) and HCMC (105,000d, three hours), though popular Phuong Trang buses leave only twice daily. There are several daily buses to Sa Dec (15,000d, one hour) and Tra Vinh (50,000d, 1½ hours).

The main **provincial bus station** (Ben Xe Khach Vinh Long; Hwy 1A) has frequent long-distance services to HCMC and other delta destinations. It's 2.5km south of town on the way to Can Tho. A taxi to the station costs around 130,000d. Coming from HCMC, the larger bus companies Phuong Trang and Mai Linh provide a free shuttle bus to town.

There are frequent car/passenger **ferries** (Pha An Binh) across the river to An Binh.

Can Tho & Around

📞 0292 / POP 1.57 MILLION

The epicentre of the Mekong Delta, Can Tho is the largest city in the region and will feel like a metropolis if you've just spent a few days exploring the backwaters. As the political, economic, cultural and transport centre of the Mekong Delta, it's a buzzing town with a lively waterfront lined with sculpted gardens, an appealing blend of narrow backstreets and wide boulevards, and perhaps the greatest concentration of foreigners in the delta. It is also the perfect base for visiting nearby floating markets, the major draw for tourists who come here to boat along the many canals and rivers leading out of town.

Can Tho has the best selection of hotels, guesthouses, homestays, restaurants, cafes and bars in the Mekong Delta, so it's a good place in which to indulge after some rural delta adventures.

🅾 Sights

★**Cai Rang Floating Market** MARKET
(⊙5am–noon) **FREE** The biggest floating market in the Mekong Delta, Cai Rang is 6km from Can Tho in the direction of Soc Trang. There's a bridge here that serves as a great vantage point for photography. The market is best around 6am to 7am, and it's well worth getting here early to beat the boatloads of tourists and the heat. This is a wholesale market, so look at what's tied to the long pole above the boat to see what they're selling.

Cai Rang can be seen from the road, but getting here is far more interesting by boat (US$10 to US$15). From the market area in Can Tho it takes about 45 minutes by boat to the market, or you can drive to the Cau Dau Sau boat landing (about 4km southwest of Can Tho by the Dau Sau Bridge), skipping the least interesting section of river, from where it takes only about 10 minutes to reach the market.

★**Ong Temple** TEMPLE
(32 Đ Hai Ba Trung; ⊙6am–8pm) **FREE** In a fantastic location facing the Can Tho River and decorated with huge, constantly burning incense coils, this Chinese temple is set inside the **Guangzhou Assembly Hall**, and wandering through its fragrant, smoke-filled

MEKONG DELTA CAN THO & AROUND

ℹ FLOATING MARKET TOURS

The undisputed highlight of any visit to Can Tho is taking a boat ride to a **floating market**, but Can Tho is also the only place in the delta where you might experience hassle from would-be guides – they'll accost you as soon as you get off the bus and even turn up at your lodgings after asking your *xe om* or taxi driver where you're headed. When choosing who you go with, consider the following:

➡ What does the tour include? Is it a 40-minute dash to Cai Rang, returning to Can Tho straight away, or a half-day tour taking in smaller waterways?

➡ How big is the boat? Larger boats come equipped with life jackets, have roofs and get to the markets faster, but you'll be in a large group. Smaller boats make for a more intimate experience, but not all carry life jackets and may have flimsy roofs (or none at all), so you might end up doing a wet-rat impression in a downpour, or get sun scorched on the return trip.

➡ When does the tour depart? If you start out after 6.30am, you've missed the busiest activity.

➡ Does the guide speak good English? Small boats along the riverside near the giant statue of Ho Chi Minh offer the cheapest deals, but you won't get a commentary on riverside life.

➡ Costs range from around 120,000d per hour (depending on your negotiating skills) for a small boat with the operator speaking a few words of English, to around US$30 per person for a seven-hour tour taking in both markets with a fluent English-speaking guide.

Can Tho

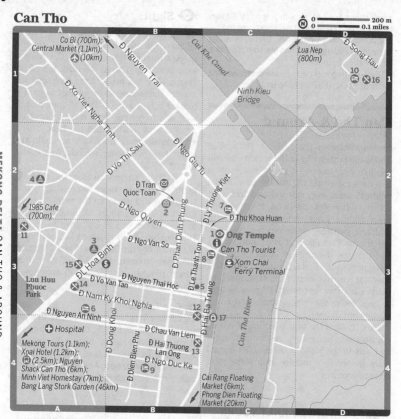

Can Tho

interior is very enjoyable. It was originally built in the late 19th century to worship Kuang Kung, a deity symbolising loyalty, justice, reason, intelligence, honour and cour-age, among other merits. Wait long enough and you'll see how the incense coils are lit and hung on long poles.

Phong Dien Floating Market · MARKET

(⊙5am-noon) FREE An intimate floating market, Phong Dien has more stand-up rowing boats than motorised craft, with local vendors shopping and exchanging gossip. Less crowded than Cai Rang (p365), it has far fewer tourists and less activity. It's most bustling between 5am and 7am, with little to see later. The market is 20km southwest of Can Tho; get here by road or sign up for a six-hour combined Cai Rang–Phong Dien tour, returning to Can Tho through quiet backwaters.

Pitu Kohsa Rangsay Pagoda · BUDDHIST PAGODA

(Chua Pitu Khosa Rangsay; 27/2 Truong Dinh; ⊙dawn-dusk) FREE Trying to hide down a quiet backstreet, but gloriously gilded, this rare three-level Khmer Theravada Buddhist pagoda from 1948 contrasts sharply with the adjacent grey buildings. The carved, detailed wall patterns, painted columns, huge Buddha statue and city views from the balcony are all impressive. Its charitable pursuits include helping disadvantaged youths to study.

Binh Thuy Ancient House · HOUSE

(144 Đ Bui Huu Nghia; donations accepted; ⊙7am-6pm) FREE Dating from 1870, the Binh Thuy house was built by wealthy merchant Duong Chan Ky and extensively renovated in the French-colonial style in the early 20th century. The interior of the house is very much original, with ornate hand-painted floor tiles, elaborate decorative wood carvings and huge floor-to-ceiling display cabinets. The house was a main location in the film adaptation of *The Lover* (L'Amant), directed by Jean-Jacques Annaud in 1992.

Can Tho Museum · MUSEUM

(Bao Tang Can Tho; ☏0292-382 0955; 1 ĐL Hoa Binh; ⊙8-11am & 2-5pm Tue-Thu, 8-11am & 6.30-9pm Sat & Sun) FREE This large, well-presented museum brings local history to life with mannequins and life-size reproductions of buildings, including a Chinese pagoda and a house interior. Displays (with ample English translations) focus on the Khmer and Chinese communities, plant and fish specimens, rice production and, inevitably, various wars.

Munireangsey Pagoda · BUDDHIST TEMPLE

(36 ĐL Hoa Binh; ⊙8am-5pm) FREE This small golden pagoda was originally built in 1946 to serve Can Tho's Khmer community. The ornamentation is typical of Khmer Theravada Buddhist pagodas, with none of the multiple Bodhisattvas and Taoist spirits common in Vietnamese Mahayana pagodas.

🏛 Tours

★ Hieu's Tour · CULTURAL

(☏093-966 6156; www.hieutour.com; 27a Đ Le Thanh Ton) Young, enthusiastic, English-speaking guide Hieu and his team offer excellent, unique tours around Can Tho, from early-morning jaunts to the floating markets (US$35 per person) to cycling tours, food tours and even visits to Pirate Island (p392) further afield. Hieu is keen to show visitors true delta culture, and a floating homestay is in the works.

Mekong Tours · CULTURAL

(☏090-785 2927; www.mekongtours.info; 93 Đ Mau Than) Based at Xoai Hotel, this operator offers highly recommended tours of the floating markets (Cai Rang US$29, Cai Rang plus Phong Dien US$47 per boat for up to three people), as well as an entertaining nightly street-food tour that departs the hotel at 6.30pm.

🛏 Sleeping

Xoai Hotel · HOTEL $

(☏090-765 2927; www.hotelxoai.com; 93 Đ Mau Than; r 220,000-350,000d; ✳@🖸) This friendly, efficient hotel offers fantastic value and has bright, mango-coloured rooms – appropriate given the name means 'Mango Hotel'. Helpful staff speak excellent English and there's a roof terrace with hammocks. Budget tours are also available for those looking to band together.

Thanh Ha · GUESTHOUSE $

(☏0918 183 522; mshaguesthouse@gmail.com; 118/14 Đ Phan Dinh Phung; r from 350,000d; ✳🖸) This guesthouse is hidden down an alleyway thriving with local life. Various large white-tiled rooms have thin curtains and firm beds, but are sparkling clean. Tiny rooms with shared bathroom are slightly cheaper. Ms Ha, the proprietor, is a character, and she can help arrange tours and rent you a bicycle or motorbike.

Nguyen Shack Can Tho · GUESTHOUSE $$

(☏0966 550 016; www.nguyenshack.com; Ong Tim Bridge, Thanh My, Thuong Thanh; d with shared bathroom 500,000d, bungalows from 1,000,000d; 🖸) 🌱 Not a shack, but rather a clutch of rustic thatched bungalows with fans, this great place overlooks the Ong Tim River, 6km from Can Tho. It's the kind of place where backpackers are inspired to linger longer, thanks to the camaraderie between English-speaking staff and guests. The engaging tours and the proximity to Cai Rang floating market are bonuses.

An attached restaurant isn't cheap but serves great food. It's also pretty convenient for the bus station, as it's southwest of the city.

Kim Tho Hotel
HOTEL **$$**

(☑ 0292-381 7517; 1a Đ Ngo Gia Tu; r 900,000-2,100,000d; ❈ 🕾) A smart hotel, verging on the boutique, Kim Tho is decked out with attractive fabric furnishings in the foyer. Rooms are stylish throughout and include designer bathrooms. Cheaper rooms are on lower floors, but superior rooms have hardwood flooring and the pricier river-view rooms are still a great deal. There's also a rooftop coffee bar on the 12th floor.

Tay Ho Boutique Hotel
HOTEL **$$**

(☑ 0292-382 3392; www.canthotourist.vn; 42 Đ Hai Ba Trung; r 450,000-650,000d; ❈ 🕾) This old-timer has been given a facelift and while 'boutique' may be stretching things, it is a good-value option in a great riverfront location. It's set in a cluster of Indochine-era shophouses, but the interior is now contemporary, with smart bathrooms and glistening tiles.

Kim Lan Hotel
HOTEL **$$**

(☑ 0292-0381 7079; http://kimlanhotelcantho. com/; 138a Đ Nguyen An Ninh; r 350,000-600,000d; ❈ @ 🕾) This very clean minihotel has chic, quiet rooms with contemporary furnishings and artwork on the walls. Even the cheapest, windowless standard rooms are small but perfectly formed, and deluxe rooms are a treat. Staff are friendly and helpful. Not among the eating action, but restaurants are a short stroll away.

Minh Viet Homestay
GUESTHOUSE **$$**

(☑ 097-812 3213; 245/1 Phu Quoi, Cai Rang; s/d/q US$15/25/45; 🕾) Closer to Cai Rang floating market than Can Tho, this is a rustic guesthouse consisting of basic rooms with mosquito nets and thatched roofs. Minh and his family are welcoming, congenial hosts, and he's happy to take guests on whirlwind tours of the countryside and the floating markets, or rent out free bicycles to explore the local area. Bring earplugs to block out the chugging of early-morning boats.

★ Victoria Can Tho Resort
RESORT **$$$**

(☑ 0292-0381 0111; www.victoriahotels.asia; Cai Khe Ward; r/ste from US$115/175; ❈ @ 🕾 ☀) Designed with a French-colonial accent, the breezy rooms at this stylish, sophisticated hotel are set amid lush greenery around a pair of inviting swimming pools that overlook the river. Facilities include an excellent restaurant, an open-air bar and a riverside spa. Activities on offer include cycling tours, cooking classes and cruises on the *Lady Hau*, a converted rice barge.

Azerai
RESORT **$$$**

(☑ 0292-362 7888; www.azerai.com; Au Island; r from 4,950,000d; ❈ @ 🕾 ☀) Set on a private island in the middle of the Hau River, Azerai offers the Mekong Delta's most luxurious lodgings. Rooms are set in stunning contemporary pavilions, many looking out on the river, and include a designer touch. There's an idyllic lotus pond and some iconic banyan trees – both favourites for selfie seekers – in the grounds.

Guests arrive by private boat from a welcome lounge near the Victoria Can Tho Resort, and the boat runs 24 hours ondemand for guests.

Nam Bo Boutique Hotel
BOUTIQUE HOTEL **$$$**

(☑ 0292-0381 9139; www.nambocantho.com; 1 Đ Ngo Quyen; ste from 2,300,000d; ❈ 🕾) With a mere seven suites in a colonial-era building, this super-central riverfront hotel revels in traditional presentation and contemporary elegance. The Nam Bo suite is the loveliest, while corner suite No 8 has epic views across to the riverfront. There are excellent restaurants at both the ground level – Nam Bo – and the rooftop – L'Escale.

Can Tho Ecolodge
LODGE **$$$**

(☑ 090-176 3838; https://cantho.ecolodge.asia; Ba Lang Ward; r 2,350,000-4,700,000d; 🕾 ☀) From the same team as the long-running Mai Chau Lodge (p126) in the mountainous far north of Vietnam, this lodge has a completely different setting, on the banks of a river in the pancake-flat Mekong Delta. Rooms are simple yet elegantly decorated with local furnishings and set in rustic two-storey wooden houses. The lodge is about 12km southwest of Can Tho in Ba Lang.

🍴 Eating

The night market is atmospheric and surrounded by cafes and upmarket restaurants. Hotpot Alley, in Hem 1 between Đ Mau Than and Đ Ly Tu Trung, is the place for fish and duck hotpots. Plenty of budget Vietnamese and vegetarian restaurants are spread along Đ De Tham.

Nem Nuong Thanh Van   VIETNAMESE $

(☑0292-0382 7255; cnr Nam Ky Khoi Nghia & 30 Thang 4; meals 45,000d; ⊘8am-9pm) The only dish this locally acclaimed spot does is the best *nem nuong* in town. Roll your own rice rolls using the ingredients provided – pork sausage, rice paper, green banana, star fruit (carambola), cucumber and a riot of fresh herbs – then dip into the peanut-and-something-else sauce, its secret jealously guarded. Simple and fantastic!

Quan Com Chay Cuong   VEGETARIAN $

(9 Đ De Tham; meals from 15,000d; ⊘11am-10pm; ☑) On a street with plenty of eating options, this is one of the better and larger *com chay* (vegetarian) eateries in the city. The vegetable, rice and mock-meat dishes (including mock-chicken hotpot) are nicely prepared and the service is friendly. Order from the English menu or point at what you like at the buffet.

Can Tho Night Market   VIETNAMESE $

(Đ Phan Boi Chau; snacks 5000-30,000d; ⊘5-11pm) Every evening the space between Phan Boi Chau and Phan Chu Trinh streets comes alive with dozens of bustling food stalls selling grilled meats and tofu on skewers, as well as grilled rice-paper *banh trang nuong* ('Vietnamese pizza'), fresh sugar-cane juice and more.

Banh Cong Co Ut   VIETNAMESE $

(So 38 Hem 86; meals from 15,000d; ⊘noon-9pm Mon-Sat) One of Can Tho's culinary claims to fame is this restaurant's *banh cong*, a savoury mung-bean 'muffin' studded with whole shrimp. Three generations of skilled women grate, mix and fry this local favourite. Wrap some in the lettuce and herbs and dunk in the *nuoc mam*. One is enough, but order more just in case.

★Nam Bo   INTERNATIONAL $$

(☑0292-382 3908; http://nambocantho.com; 1 Đ Ngo Quyen, Nam Bo Boutique Hotel; meals 210,000-350,000d; ⊘6.30am-10.30pm; ☎) With a charming, romantic Mediterranean feel, this restaurant does a good mix of Vietnamese and Western dishes. We're fans of the lemongrass chicken and grilled sea bass in banana leaf; bananas flambéed in rice wine add an

alcoholic flourish to the meal. The six-dish set menus (from 210,000d) are a steal.

Lua Nep   VIETNAMESE $$

(☑097-360 6979; www.luaneepresortcantho.com; Song Hau, Cai Khe; mains 50,000-500,000d; ⊘6am-10.30pm; ☎☑) Set under a soaring series of thatched roofs that could be a modernist take on a traditional tribal house, this is the most sophisticated Vietnamese dining experience in Can Tho, set on a private headland jutting into the river. Dishes focus on fresh fish and seafood, but the menu is extensive and includes a good vegetarian selection.

It's packed with local diners most nights and does draw some tour groups, but for good reason. It's large enough to lose yourself from the crowd.

L'Escale   INTERNATIONAL $$

(☑0292-381 9139; http://nambocantho.com; 1 Đ Ngo Quyen, Nam Bo Boutique Hotel; meals 180,000-500,000d; ⊘5-10.30pm; ☑) With tantalising river views from the top of the Nam Bo Boutique Hotel and subdued romantic lighting, this is the place to canoodle with your crush over a sunset cocktail and beautifully executed dishes such as clay-pot fish with pineapple, sautéed garlic shrimp with spinach and smoked-duck salad.

Lighthouse Cafe-Restaurant   INTERNATIONAL $$

(☑0292-381 9994; www.facebook.com/thelighthousecantho; 120 Đ Hai Ba Trung; meals 160,000-460,000d; ⊘6am-11pm; ☎) Set over two floors near the market, this stylish restaurant kicks off with affordable breakfasts, fresh coffee and juices, before moving on to sandwiches and panini for lunch. The main lunch and dinner menu is one of the more sophisticated in town, including cold cuts, oyster gratin, *confit de canard* (duck) and imported steaks and lamb racks.

Spices Restaurant   INTERNATIONAL $$$

(☑0292-0381 0111; Victoria Can Tho Resort, Cai Khe Ward; meals 200,000-680,000d; ⊘6am-10pm; ☎☑) Go for a table overlooking the river at this fine restaurant that's refined without being stuffy, and opt for the beautifully presented trio of salads (green papaya, banana flower, green mango) or the assorted starter for two, before following up with deep-fried elephant fish or pork-stuffed squid. Lamb shanks and seared duck cater to homesick palates and the desserts are divine.

Drinking

Co Bi
CRAFT BEER

(☎093-991 2918; 88 Đ Tran Van Kheo; ⊙4pm-midnight; 🛜) Set slap bang in the middle of Can Tho's naughty nightlife strip, this place is more refined that its surroundings. Draught craft beer (49,000d) includes big-city favourites from Pasteur St and East West breweries, as well as some cheaper bottled options and pricey imports. It even offers 'craft cocktails' from Rogue Spirits.

1985 Cafe
CAFE

(☎0292-389 2626; www.facebook.com/cafe1985 cantho; 138 Đ Huynh Cuong; ⊙6.30am-10pm; 🛜) This cafe and bar stretches across a block, and its 'back door' entrance is made up of a mosaic of old shutters that gives it a dishevelled retro look. The retro theme continues inside with old motorbikes, cassette players and other '80s throwbacks on display. Live music most nights, including open mics, and chilled beers.

Shopping

Old Market
MARKET

(Cho Can Tho; 138 Đ Hai Ba Trung; ⊙6am-9pm) Roofed with terracotta tiles edged with ceramic decorations, this atmospheric French-era market building is the centrepiece of the city's attractive riverfront tourist district. The blood, guts and chaos of the original market have moved north to the **central market** (Đ Tran Van Kheo; ⊙6am-6pm) and to some of the neighbouring streets, leaving upmarket, tourist-orientated stalls selling lacquerware, clothes, pillowslips, postcards and the like.

❶ Information

Can Tho Tourist (☎0292-382 1852; www.canthotourist.com.vn; 50 Đ Hai Ba Trung; ⊙7am-6pm Mon-Fri, 7am-11am & 1-5pm Sat & Sun) Helpful staff speak English and French, and decent city maps are available, as well as general information on attractions in the area and bus information.

Hospital (Benh Vien; ☎0292-382 0071; 4 Đ Chau Van Liem) Offers 24-hour emergency medical care.

Main Post Office (2 ĐL Hoa Binh; ⊙8am-5pm Mon-Sat)

Vietcombank (☎0292-382 0445; 7 ĐL Hoa Binh; ⊙7.30-11am & 1-4.30pm Mon-Fri, plus 7.30-11am Sat) Foreign-currency exchange and a 24-hour ATM.

❶ Getting There & Away

AIR

Can Tho International Airport (www.canthoairport.com; Đ Le Hong Phong) is served by **Vietnam Airlines** (www.vietnamairlines.com) and **Vietjet Air** (www.vietjetair.com), with flights to Con Dao, Dalat, Danang, Haiphong, Hanoi, Nha Trang, Phu Quoc, Thanh Hoa and Vinh. There are also international budget flights to Bangkok and Kuala Lumpur. There are no direct flights to HCMC, as it is a relatively easy drive.

The airport is 10km northwest of the city centre. A taxi into town will cost around 220,000d.

BOAT

Ferries across the river leave from **Xom Chai Ferry Terminal** (Ben Pha Xom Chai) for those looking to explore a more rural side of Can Tho on two wheels.

BUS

All buses depart from the main **bus station** (Ben Xe 91B; Đ Nguyen Van Linh), 2.5km southwest of the centre. A *xe om* into town costs around 50,000d, or around 75,000d in a taxi. Some bus companies will include a shuttle bus that will take you to your lodgings from the station; check when buying the ticket.

BUSES FROM CAN THO

DESTINATION	COST (D)	TIME (HR)	FREQUENCY	DISTANCE (KM)
Ben Tre	70,000	3	several daily	123
Ca Mau	100,000	3¼-4	hourly	149
Cao Lanh	55,000	2½	daily	82
Chau Doc	65,000	4	hourly	120
HCMC	120,000-160,000	3½	every 30min	169
Long Xuyen	50,000	1½	hourly	61
Phnom Penh	340,000	7	6.30am daily	226
Soc Trang	55,000	1½	hourly	62

Soc Trang

☑ 0299 / POP 223,000

Modern Soc Trang is an important centre for the Khmer people, who constitute 30% of the population of the namesake province, the highest proportion in the country. It's a useful base for exploring Khmer temples in the area and acts as the nearest port to the Con Dao islands.

◉ Sights

★ **Xa Lon Pagoda** BUDDHIST TEMPLE
(Chua Sa Lon; Hwy 1A) Originally built in wood in the 18th century, this magnificent Khmer pagoda was completely rebuilt in 1923 but proved to be too small. From 1969 to 1985 the large present-day pagoda was slowly built as funds trickled in from donations. The ceramic tiles on the exterior of the pagoda are particularly impressive.

It's located 12km southwest of Soc Trang, taking Đ Tran Hung Dao towards Bac Lieu.

Buu Son Tu BUDDHIST TEMPLE
(Chua Dat Set; 163 Đ Ton Duc Thang; admission by donation; ☺ dawn-dusk) Buu Son Tu (Precious Mountain Temple) was founded over 200 years ago by a Chinese family named Ngo. The temple is highly unusual in that nearly every object inside is made entirely of clay. The hundreds of statues and sculptures that adorn the interior were hand-sculpted by the monk Ngo Kim Tong. The pagoda is an active place of worship, and totally different from the Khmer and Vietnamese pagodas elsewhere in Soc Trang.

Mahatup Pagoda BUDDHIST TEMPLE
(Chua Doi; Đ Van Ngoc Chinh; ☺ dawn-dusk) FREE
Mahatup Pagoda, also called the Bat Pagoda, is a large, peaceful Khmer monastery compound with a resident colony of fruit bats. Hundreds of these creatures hang from the trees – the largest weigh about 1kg, with a wingspan of about 1.5m. Around dusk hundreds of bats swoop out of the trees to forage in orchards all over the Mekong Delta.

The Bat Pagoda is 2km south of Soc Trang – a 20,000d *xe om* ride.

✨ Festivals & Events

Oc Bom Boc Festival CULTURAL
(Bon Om Touk) Once a year the Khmer community from all over Vietnam and even Cambodia turns out for this festival, with longboat races on the Soc Trang River. Races are held according to the lunar calendar,
on the 15th day of the 10th moon (roughly in November). The races start at noon, but things get jumping in Soc Trang the evening before.

🛏 Sleeping & Eating

Que Huong Hotel HOTEL $$
(☑ 0299-361 6122; 128 Đ Nguyen Trung Truc; r 490,000-790,000d, ste 1,290,000d; ❄ 🛜) Rooms here are in much better shape than the no-nonsense exterior might first suggest. The suites include a sunken bath and a full-size bar, although drinks are not included. Convenient location near the bus station, parks and places to eat.

L'Amour Riverside INTERNATIONAL $$
(☑ 0299-650 8888; 146 Đ Ly Thuong Kiet; meals 20,000-320,000d; ☺ 7am-10pm; ❄ 🛜) This huge restaurant is set over four floors overlooking the river. It may look empty from downstairs, but count the number of motorbikes and you'll know the locals are hanging out upstairs. Noodle soups, pizzas, burgers and hotpots are on offer, plus shakes, iced coffees and cakes.

ℹ Getting There & Away

Buses run hourly from Soc Trang to Bac Lieu (50,000d, 1½ hours), Ca Mau (67,000d, three hours), Can Tho (55,000d, 1½ hours) and HCMC (155,000d, six hours). The **bus station** (Ben Xe Soc Trang; Đ Le Van Tam) is conveniently in the town centre, near the corner of Le Hung Vuong, the main road into town.

For Con Son island, **Superdong** (www.super dong.com.vn) schedules a twice-daily ferry at 8am and 1.15pm (310,000d, 2½ hours) from Tran De port, 33km southeast of Soc Trang. This returns from Ben Dam, Con Son island, at 8am and 1pm.

Phu Quoc Express (www.phuquocexpress boat.com) has one ferry a day from Tran De to the Con Dao Islands (standard/VIP 350,000/500,000d) in each direction, leaving Tran De at 9am and Ben Dam at noon.

These are relatively new services and will not always run, particularly during high winds or heavy seas.

Ca Mau

☑ 0290 / POP 315,000

On the banks of the Ganh Hao River, Ca Mau is the capital and sole city in Ca Mau province, which covers the southern tip of the Mekong Delta. It's a remote and inhospitable area that wasn't cultivated until the

OFF THE BEATEN TRACK

BAC LIEU BIRD SANCTUARY

The **Bac Lieu Bird Sanctuary** (Vuon Chim Bac Lieu; ☑ 0291-383 5991; electric buggy 400,000d; ☺ 6am-6.30pm), 6km southwest of the little-visited town of Bac Lieu, is notable for its 50-odd species of birds, including a large population of graceful white herons. Bird populations peak in the rainy season – approximately May to October – and the birds nest until about January.

Birding guides should be hired at the sanctuary entrance since without them there's a good chance of getting lost; little English is spoken. The **Bac Lieu Tourist** (☑ 0291-382 4272; www.baclieutourist.com; 2 Đ Hoang Van Thu; ☺ 7-11am & 1-5pm) office also arranges transport and guides (at a price markup).

The visit includes an electric-golf-buggy ride around the perimeter of the sanctuary, and guides stop at viewing towers and observation posts along the way. Bring your own binoculars. The guides aren't supposed to receive money, so tip them discreetly.

Cong Tu Hotel (☑ 0291-358 0580; 13 Đ Dien Bien Phu, Bac Lieu; superior/deluxe 400,000/500,000d; ❄ ☎) is by far the most characterful place to stay in Bac Lieu. It's a revamped 1919 colonial gem – the smarter rooms have balconies and high ceilings and are decorated in decadent 19th-century style. The **restaurant** (meals 40,000-100,000d) has an extensive menu and the fish dishes are particularly good.

Part of the old house has been turned into the **Cong Tu Bac Lieu Museum** (20,000d; ☺ 7am-5pm), which offers a mishmash collection of antique furniture, old photographs and a classic Citroen 2CV. It is mainly popular with Vietnamese tourists for period selfies.

Bac Lieu is on the bus route between Soc Trang (1½ hours) and Ca Mau (1½ hours).

late 17th century. Owing to the boggy terrain, the province has the lowest population density in southern Vietnam.

Given that, it's perhaps surprising that Ca Mau city is a relatively pleasant place. With wide boulevards and parks and busy shopping streets, the town has developed rapidly in recent years but sees very few visitors. Improved transport links make for an easy stopover for a slice of delta life untroubled by tourism, but it is a bit much of a southerly diversion from key attractions in the delta to make it really worth the time.

◉ Sights

U-Minh Forest   FOREST
(10,000d; ☺ 6am-5pm closed Mar-May) Bordered by Ca Mau, the largest mangrove forest beyond the Amazon basin covers 1000 sq km. Home to endangered mammals, including the hairy-nosed otter and the fishing cat, and 187 bird species, the forest was a hideout for the Viet Cong (VC) during the American War. Thirty-minute boat trips around the forest cost 140,000d.

Ca Mau Tourism (www.camautourism. vn) arranges all-day boat tours (US$180), but you can get a speedboat to Thu Bay (two hours), then a motorbike to the entrance for 90,000d.

Ca Mau Market   MARKET
(Đ Le Loi) Traditionally Ca Mau life was lived facing the water, and while the floating market has disappeared in recent years, the main market still sprawls along the streets to the west of Phung Hiep Canal, south of Đ Phan Ngoc Hien.

Cao Dai Temple   TEMPLE
(Đ Phan Ngoc Hien; ☺ dawn-dusk) Like all Cao Dai places of worship, this temple (built in 1966) is a riot of colour and ornamentation, though there are more impressive ones elsewhere in the delta.

🍽 Sleeping & Eating

Dong Anh Hotel   HOTEL $
(☑ 0290-357 6666; www.donganhhotel.com.vn; 25 Đ Tran Hung Dao; r from 350,000d; ❄ ☎) A friendly, clean and central hotel. Some rooms share terraces looking down over the main street. A little English is spoken.

Anh Nguyet Hotel   HOTEL $$
(☑ 0290-356 7666; www.anhnguyethotel.com; 207 Đ Phan Ngoc Hien; r 590,000-1,500,000d; ❄ ☎) Romantically translating as the Moonlight Hotel, this place attempts a glitzy look. Rooms are perfectly fine, although walls are thin and the carpets rather cheap. There's a decent buffet breakfast.

Hai San Quat Mo   VIETNAMESE $

(☏ 0290-626 6888; 14 Đ Bui Thi Truong; mains 40,000-150,000d; ⏱ 10am-2am; 🛎) Set on a lively strip of restaurants and bars, this cavernous place specialises in seafood and grills and draws a steady local crowd. Highlights includes anything from grilled scallops in garlic to salted chilli prawns. Cold beers are plentiful.

ℹ Getting There & Away

AIR

Small **Ca Mau Airport** (☏ 0290-383 6436; 93 Đ Ly Thuong Kiet) is 3km east of the centre, on Hwy 1A. Vietnam Airlines has a daily flight to and from HCMC (one hour).

BOAT

One hydrofoil a day travels between Ca Mau and Rach Gia (300,000d, three to four hours) from **Ferry Pier Can Ganh Hao** (Pha Can Ganh Hao), departing at 2pm. The journey time depends on how many stops are made for cargo.

If you're debating whether to take a hydrofoil or a bus, the hydrofoil is less crowded than the basic buses between Ca Mau and Rach Gia and, until more bridges have been built, it's also faster and generally more comfortable. The journey is also more interesting. The boats are low and long, meaning views are just above the waterline.

The trip between Ca Mau and Rach Gia allows you to observe the countryside as it switches from a green, undeveloped section dotted with rattan houses near Ca Mau to a heavily built-up and industrial stretch approaching Rach Gia. If you're cycling around the delta, the hydrofoils can carry your bicycle for an extra fee.

BUS

There are two bus stations. Phuong Trang offers the most comfortable services to HCMC, Can Tho and even Dalat. Express buses leave for HCMC between 5am and 10.30am.

The main **bus station** (Ben Xe Ca Mau; Đ Ly Thuong Kiet) is located 2km east of central

Ca Mau

BUSES FROM CA MAU

DESTINATION	COST (D)	TIME (HR)	FREQUENCY	DISTANCE (KM)
Bac Lieu	50,000	1¾	every 30min	89
Can Tho	100,000	4-5	hourly	151
HCMC	126,000-186,000	9	hourly	329
Rach Gia	120,000	4	several daily	138

Ca Mau. It serves most destinations bar Rach Gia and Ha Tien.

The small **Ca Mau Kien Giang bus station** (Ben Xe Ca Mau Kien Giang; Đ Nguyen Trai) is around 3km northeast of central Ca Mau. Services run to Rach Gia and Ha Tien.

Rach Gia

☑ 0297 / POP 405,000

A thriving port on the Gulf of Thailand, Rach Gia's population includes significant numbers of both ethnic Chinese and ethnic Khmer, and the lively waterfront and bustling backstreets are worth a stroll. The city has expanded massively to the south in the past decade and now merges with Rach Soi.

With its easy access to the sea and its proximity to Cambodia and Thailand, fishing, agriculture and smuggling are profitable trades in this province. The area was once famous for supplying the large feathers used to make ceremonial fans for the Imperial Court.

If you're in town for longer than it takes to catch a boat to Phu Quoc Island, there are a couple of sights worth a quick whizz through: a temple dedicated to local icon Nguyen Trung Truc, an 1860s resistance leader; and a museum housed in a handsome French-era building displaying some Oc-Eo artefacts.

◉ Sights

★ **Hon Son Island** ISLAND

(Lai Son) Hon Son, also known after its main village of Lai Son, is a solitary and beautiful mountain island about 50km southwest of Rach Gia. It is very undeveloped and has some pretty coastline, with a single road circling the island and connecting a handful of communities and remote beaches. Superdong (p376) has boats to Hon Son (150,000d, 1½ hours), departing Rach Gia at 7.30am (continuing to Nam Du for 100,000d around 9am) and returning to the mainland at noon.

The island is ringed by some large rock formations that make popular photo opportunities for Vietnamese selfie fans. In the north, **Bai Bac** and **Bai Bo** are the best beaches, but **Bai Bang**, in the east, is also popular thanks to a horizontal coconut palm and lots of strategically placed swings. Accommodation in the 250,000d-to-500,000d range is available in Lai Son and dotted about the island.

Phu Quoc Express (p376) and Ngoc Thanh Express (www.ngocthanhexpress.com) also take it in turns to service this route.

Nam Du Islands ISLAND

The Nam Du archipelago is a cluster of 20 islands located more than 80km off the coast and ringed with sandy coves. The main island of Hon Lon (Big Island) is popular with young Vietnamese travellers, but sees few foreigners. There's a major litter problem in the dock and around the island's beaches. Superdong (p376) has boats to Nam Du (210,000d, 2½ hours) via Hon Son (100,000d), departing Rach Gia at 7.30am and returning to the mainland at 11am.

Bai Tret is the main village and port. Accommodation in the 300,000d-to-800,000d range is available here and at various beaches about the island. In general, prices are about one-third higher than the mainland and electricity is still sporadic. The best beach is **Bai Cay Men**, in the southwest of the island, where there is a shack selling fresh seafood, coconuts and beer. Seafront shacks in Bai Tret set up dockside tables at night and sell fresh seafood straight from plastic tanks.

As well as Superdong, Phu Quoc Express (p376) and Ngoc Thanh Express (www.ngocthanhexpress.com) take it in turns to service this route.

Nguyen Trung Truc Temple BUDDHIST TEMPLE

(18 Đ Nguyen Cong Tru) This temple is dedicated to Nguyen Trung Truc, a leader of the 1860s resistance campaign against the newly arrived French. The first temple structure

was a simple building with a thatched roof; over the years it has been enlarged and rebuilt several times. In the centre of the main hall is a portrait of Nguyen Trung Truc on an altar.

Among other exploits, Nguyen Trung Truc led the raid that resulted in the burning of the French warship *Espérance*. Despite repeated attempts to capture him, Nguyen Trung Truc continued to fight until 1868, when the French took his mother and a number of civilians hostage and threatened to kill them if he didn't surrender. Nguyen Trung Truc turned himself in and was executed by the French in the marketplace of Rach Gia on 27 October 1868.

Kien Giang Museum MUSEUM
(21 Đ Nguyen Van Troi; ⊗ 7.30-11am & 1.30-5pm Mon-Fri) FREE Housed in an ornate gem of a French-colonial-era building, this museum's collection includes lots of war photos and some Oc-Eo artefacts and pottery. The museum sees few visitors, so don't be surprised if staff are a little lax with the opening hours.

Nguyen Trung Truc Statue LANDMARK
Statue of the 1860s Rach Gia resistance leader against the French.

Rach Gia

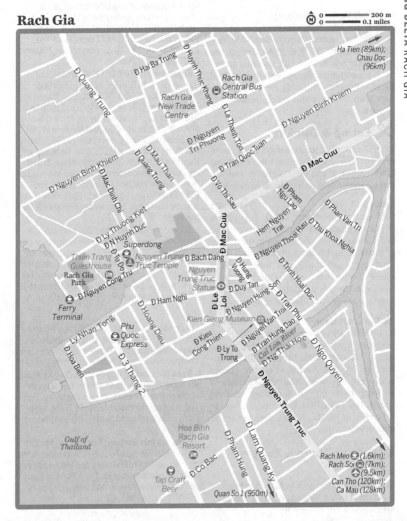

📋 Sleeping

There are clusters of hotels near the bus station on Đ Le Thanh Ton and near the boat pier on Đ Tu Do.

Thien Trang Guesthouse   GUESTHOUSE $
(📱 094-506 5574; 24 Đ Nguyen Cong Tru; r 300,000-450,000d; ❄ 🖥) Walking distance from the ferry terminal, this is a handy place to stay before an early boat to Phu Quoc, Hon Son or Nam Du. Rooms are simple but clean and include hot-water bathrooms and TV. It has a cavernous lobby with motorbike parking – useful if you're exploring the delta on two wheels.

Hoa Binh Rach Gia Resort   HOTEL $$
(📱 0297-355 3355; www.hoabinhrachgiaresort.com.vn; Đ Co Bac; standard/superior/deluxe 850,000/1,100,000/1,200,000d; ❄ @ 🖥 🏊) One of the smartest hotels in Rach Gia, boasting an imposing location on the river to the south of the old city centre. Rooms have a smart business trim befitting the hotel's conference-venue status.

🍴 Eating & Drinking

Rach Gia is known for its seafood, dried cuttlefish, *ca thieu* (dried fish slices), fish sauce and black pepper. It can be inexpensive and you can cook your own on a tabletop barbecue.

Quan So 1   SEAFOOD $
(82 Đ Lac Hong; meals from 75,000; ⏰ 8am-10pm; 🖥) Here's how it works: grab a barbecue and order a wave of seafood to cook in the middle of the table, and wash it all down with some local beers. Staff don't speak English and the menu translations are downright bizarre, but the seafood is delicious and the place is hugely popular with discerning locals.

★ Tap Craft Beer   CRAFT BEER
(📱 089-898 8846; Vincom Plaza, off Đ 3/2; ⏰ 6am-midnight; 🖥) One of the liveliest spots in the Mekong Delta, this cool little craft-beer bar near the river is set over two floors with some street-side seating. There are 15 or more beers on tap, including seasonal specialities from East West and Pasteur St breweries in HCMC. It also turns out coffee and snacks by day.

ℹ Getting There & Away

AIR

Vietnam Airlines has daily flights to and from HCMC and Phu Quoc Island (in the high-season months of November to April).

Rach Gia Airport (www.rachgiaairport.net; 418 Cach Mang Thang Tam) is around 10km southeast of the centre, along Hwy 80. A taxi into town costs around 150,000d and takes about 20 minutes.

BOAT

Boats to Phu Quoc Island leave from the centrally located **ferry terminal** (Ban Tau Rach Gia Phu Quoc; Đ Nguyen Cong Tru) at the western end of Đ Nguyen Cong Tru. One speedboat leaves daily for Ca Mau (300,000d, three hours) from the **Rach Meo ferry terminal** (Ben Tau Rach Meo; 📱 0297-381 1306; Đ Ngo Quyen), about 2km south of town.

Phu Quoc Express (📱 0297-628 7888; https://phuquocexpressboat.com; 16 Đ 3 Thang 2; ⏰ 7am-6pm) departs for Phu Quoc (standard/VIP 340,000/540,000d, child 270,000d, 2½ hours) at 7.20am, 11am and 1.45pm. From the island, it departs at 7.30am, 10.30am and 1.30pm.

Superdong (📱 077-387 7742; www.super dong.com.vn; 14 Đ Tu Do) heads to Phu Quoc (adult/child 340,000/240,000d, 2½ hours) at 8am, 8.30am, 8.45am, 12.40pm and 1pm. Trips from Phu Quoc run at exactly the same times plus a departure at 1.20pm. At the time of writing, Superdong was the only company operating fast boats to Hon Son (150,000d, 1½ hours) and Nam Du (210,000d, 2½ hours) islands, departing at 7.30am and returning at 11am and midday from Nam Du and Hon Son respectively. Phu Quoc Express and Ngoc Thanh Express (www.ngocthanhexpress.com) sometimes also service this route.

Superdong and Phu Quoc Express both operate modern boats, but the latter is slightly more comfortable, particularly if you upgrade to VIP class. Both companies can take motorbikes for a handling fee of about 180,000d each way. For those with their own cars, there are also up to 10 car ferries a day from Rach Gia to Phu Quoc.

BUS

Check which station your bus departs from and whether bus-station transfer is provided when purchasing your ticket. Tickets sold at one station may depart from another station!

Rach Gia Central Bus Station (Ben Xe Khach Rach Gia; Đ Nguyen Binh Khiem) is just north of the city centre and serves primarily Ha Tien. The most comfortable buses are Trang Ngoc Phat, closely followed by Mai Linh and Phuong Trang.

Rach Soi Bus Station (Ben Xe Rach Soi; Ben Xe Tinh Kien Giang; 376 QL63), 7km south of the city, serves Ho Chi Minh City and the majority of delta destinations (bar Ha Tien). Phuong Trang has comfortable regular and sleeper buses to HCMC and Can Tho.

A taxi into town from the central bus station costs around 30,000d. From the Rach Soi bus station, fares are around 150,000d. Phuong Trang provides a free shuttle bus to take you from your hotel to the bus station.

Phu Quoc Island

📞 0297 / POP 115,000

Fringed with white-sand beaches and with large tracts still cloaked in dense tropical jungle, Phu Quoc has rapidly morphed from a sleepy island backwater to a must-visit beach escape for Western expats and sun-seeking tourists. Beyond the resorts lining Long Beach, the rapid development beginning on the northwest coast and the megaresorts in sight of Sao Beach, there's still ample room for exploration and escaping the sometimes-littered waters. Dive the reefs, kayak in the bays, eat up the back-road kilometres on a motorbike, or just lounge on the beach, followed by a massage and a fresh seafood dinner.

Phu Quoc is not really part of the Mekong Delta and its rice production – the most famous, and valuable, crop is black pepper – and the islanders here have traditionally earned their living from the sea. Its claim to fame across Vietnam is the production of high-quality *nuoc mam* (fish sauce).

History

Phu Quoc Island served as a base for the French missionary Pigneau de Behaine during the 1760s and 1780s. Prince Nguyen Anh, who later became Emperor Gia Long, was sheltered here by Behaine when he was being hunted by the Tay Son rebels.

Being a relatively remote and forested island (and an economically marginal area of Vietnam), Phu Quoc was useful to the French-colonial administration as a prison.

The Americans took over where the French left off and housed about 40,000 VC prisoners here. The island's main penal colony, which is still in use today, was known as the Coconut Tree Prison (Nha Lao Cay Dua) and part of it is now open to the public as a historic museum near An Thoi town.

ℹ When to Go

Phu Quoc's rainy season darkens skies from late May to October, when the sea gets rough and a lot of diving stops. The peak season for tourism is midwinter (December and January), when the sky is blue and the sea is calm. It can get pretty damn hot around April and May.

◎ Sights

◎ Duong Dong

The island's main town and chief fishing port on the central west coast is a tangle of budget hotels catering to domestic tourists (although foreigners are allowed), streetside stalls, bars and shops. The old bridge in town is a great vantage point from which to photograph the island's scruffy fishing fleet crammed into the narrow channel, and the filthy, bustling produce market makes for an interesting stroll. Most visitors come for the night market, seafood and the best glimpse at local life on the island.

Fish Sauce Factory FACTORY
(Map p380; www.hungthanhfishsauce.com.vn; Duong Dong; ⊙8-11am & 1-5pm) FREE The distillery of Nuoc Mam Hung Thanh is the largest of Phu Quoc's fish-sauce makers, a short walk from the market in Duong Dong. At first glance, the giant wooden vats may make you think you've arrived for a wine tasting, but one sniff of the festering *nuoc mam* essence jolts you back to reality. Take a guide along unless you speak Vietnamese.

Most of the sauce produced is exported to the mainland for domestic consumption, though an impressive amount finds its way abroad to kitchens in Japan, North America and Europe.

Dinh Cau Temple TAOIST TEMPLE
(Cau Castle; Map p380; Đ Bach Dang, Duong Dong) FREE This combination temple and lighthouse was built in 1937 to honour Thien Hau, the Goddess of the Sea, who provides

> ### GROWING PAINS
> Despite development (an international airport, a Vietnamese version of Disneyland, the world's longest over-sea cable car, five-star hotels, a golf course and new highways), much of Phu Quoc Island is protected since becoming a national park in 2001. Phu Quoc National Park covers close to 70% of the island, an area of 31,422 hectares. However, rubbish is a problem on many beaches, and resorts tend to clean up just their own stretches of shoreline. With more major development slated in the coming years, now is a good time to see Phu Quoc Island before it loses some of its charm.

MEKONG DELTA PHU QUOC ISLAND

Phu Quoc Island

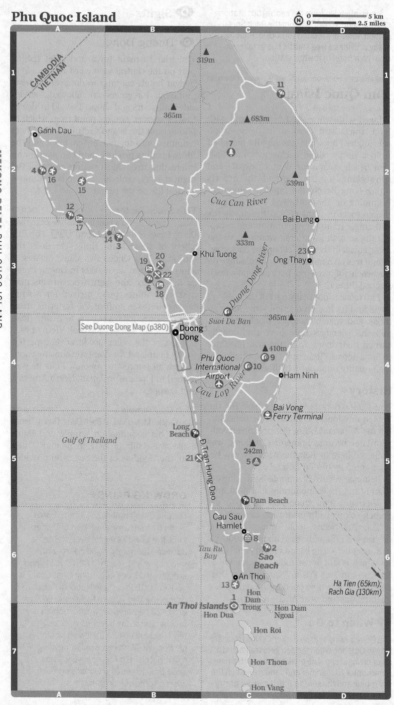

Phu Quoc Island

protection for sailors and fishers. Sometimes called a 'castle', or 'rock temple' for the rocky outcrop it clings to, Dinh Cau gives you a good view of the harbour entrance. The promenade is popular with locals taking a stroll at sunset.

◉ Around the Island

Phu Quoc is Vietnam's largest island and even with much-improved infrastructure, it can still take some time to navigate by motorbike or taxi. Most of the accommodation, wining and dining is concentrated in Duong Dong and the Long Beach strip to its south. Ong Lang beach has a developing scene of its own, but it's more mellow than its southern neighbour. VinPearlLand and the Hon Thom Cable Car are drawing domestic tourists and families to the northwest and south of the island, and the whole southern coast is under development by big hotel chains and megaresorts.

Much of the north and the east remains relatively undeveloped and is best explored by motorbike. Sao Beach in the far southwest remains one of the most beautiful of the island's public beaches.

★ Sao Beach   BEACH
(Bai Sao; Map p378) With picture-perfect white sand, the delightful curve of beautiful Sao Beach bends out alongside a sea of mineral-water clarity just a few kilometres from An Thoi, the main shipping port at the southern tip of the island. There are a couple of beachfront restaurants where

you can settle into a deckchair (50,000d for nonguests), change into bathers (10,000d fee) or partake in water sports.

★ An Thoi Islands   ISLAND
(Quan Dao An Thoi; Map p378) Just off the southern tip of Phu Quoc, these 15 islands and islets are a paradise of white sand and blue waters. They can be visited by chartered boat for a fine day of sightseeing, fishing, swimming and snorkelling. Hon Thom (Pineapple Island) is about 3km in length and is the largest island in the group; it's now connected to Phu Quoc by the Hon Thom Cable Car (p382), the world's longest over-sea ride.

Other islands here include Hon Dua (Coconut Island), Hon Roi (Lamp Island), Hon Vang (Echo Island), Hon May Rut (Cold Cloud Island), the Hon Dams (Shadow Islands), Chan Qui (Yellow Tortoise) and Hon Mong Tay (Short Gun Island). The only real development at this stage is the new Sun World and attached water park Aquapolis on Hon Thom Island.

Most boats depart from An Thoi on Phu Quoc, but you can make arrangements through hotels on Long Beach, as well as with dive operators. Boat trips generally don't run during the rainy season.

Ho Quoc Pagoda   BUDDHIST TEMPLE
(Chua Truc Lam Ho Quoc; Map p378; Thien Vien Truc Lam Ho Quoc) FREE Climb the stairs of this pagoda, on a remote stretch of coastal road 10km north of Sao Beach, for one of the best views from any temple in Vietnam: blue sky and the water off Bai Dam Beach

frame the temple-gate eaves, with green hills lying behind. Ho Quoc was only built in 2012 and features a Quan Am statue and a giant bell. Admirers of Ho Quoc venture here for sunrise and full-moon evenings.

Long Beach
BEACH

(Bai Truong; Map p380) Long Beach is draped invitingly along the west coast from Duong Dong to An Thoi. Development concentrates in the north, near Duong Dong, where the recliners and rattan umbrellas of the various resorts rule; these are the only stretches that are kept garbage-free. With its west-facing aspect, sunsets can be stupendous.

Although not the prettiest, Long Beach is a good budget choice for accommodation and socialising. Duong Dong and its night market are walking distance from the beach's north end.

Thom Beach
BEACH

(Bai Thom; Map p378) The road from Dai Beach to Thom Beach via Ganh Dau is very beautiful, passing through dense forest with tantalising glimpses of the coast below. Thom Beach, located on the northeast tip of the island, is pretty scruffy in places, but there are a couple of guesthouses that serve fresh seafood for lunch if you're touring the island on two wheels.

Ong Lang Beach
BEACH

(Bai Ong Lang; Map p378) Ong Lang Beach has a series of sandy bays sheltered by rocky headlands, and several midrange resorts in the area service those wanting to get away from everything (apart from the comfort of said resorts). The upmarket bubble lacks Long Beach's benefit of being walking distance from town, but some resorts offer shuttle buses to Duong Dong, about 7km to the south.

Phu Quoc Prison
MUSEUM

(Nha Tu Phu Quoc; Coconut Prison; Map p378; http://phuquocprison.org; Nguyen Van Cu; ⏰8-11.30am & 1.30-5pm) **FREE** Not far from Sao Beach (p379) in the south of the island, Phu Quoc's notorious old prison, built by the French in the late 1940s, contains a small museum that narrates (in English) the jail's gruesome history. Much of the site comprises mannequins of Vietnamese soldiers in chilling re-enactments, such as being forced to stand and starve in exposed, outdoor barbed-wire cages. A **war memorial** stands south of the prison, on the far side of the road.

Duong Dong

Duong Dong

Coi Nguon Museum   MUSEUM

(Map p380; 149 D Tran Hung Dao; 20,000d; ⊙8am-5pm) With displays on Vietnamese medicines, Stone Age tools, a boatful of barnacle-encrusted ceramics, oddly compelling shell-covered furniture and a small room devoted to the island prison, this dusty private museum is an oddball introduction to Phu Quoc history and culture. But did the marine fauna section really require the untimely demise of 14 hawksbill turtles? It is located towards the southern end of the main Long Beach strip, about 5km south of Duong Dong.

Phu Quoc National Park   NATIONAL PARK

(Map p378) About 70% of Phu Quoc is forested and the trees and adjoining marine environment enjoy official protection. This is the last large stand of forest in the south, and in 2010 the park was declared a Unesco Biosphere Reserve. The forest is densest in the Khu Rung Nguyen Sinh forest reserve in northern Phu Quoc; you'll need a motorbike or mountain bike to tackle the bumpy dirt roads that cut through it. There are no real hiking trails.

Vung Bau Beach   BEACH

(Bai Vung Bau; Map p378) This is an appealing northern beach accessible via the coastal road. The waves are rough and it's a little neglected, with rubbish in parts, but it means you can have the beach without the crowds. The few resorts here have nothing around them but beach. Visit soon; more development is in the works. A taxi from Duong Dong is about 300,000d.

Cua Can Beach   BEACH

(Bai Cua Can; Map p378) The most accessible of the northern beaches, Cua Can is about 11km from Duong Dong. It remains mercifully quiet during the week, but can get busy at weekends. A ride through the villages around Cua Can is interesting, as they are a world away from the mass tourism of Long Beach.

Suoi Tranh   WATERFALL

(Map p378; ☑0297-384 9863; 5000d; ⊙7am-9pm) Compared with the waterlogged Mekong Delta, Phu Quoc has very little surface moisture, but there are several springs originating in the hills. The most accessible of these is 4m-high Suoi Tranh; look for the entrance sign and concrete tree from the Duong Dong–Vong Beach road. From the ticket counter it's a 10-minute walk through the forest to the falls.

MEKONG DELTA PHU QUOC ISLAND

Suoi Da Ban
WATERFALL

(Map p378; admission 5000d, motorbike 1000d) Suoi Da Ban is a white-water creek tumbling across some attractive large granite boulders. There are deep pools and it's nice enough for a dip. Bring plenty of mosquito repellent. The best time to visit the falls is between May and September, as they dry to a trickle by the height of the dry season. It's located about 15km east of Duong Dong, reached via the hamlet of Ham Ninh.

Dai Beach
BEACH

(Bai Dai; Map p378) A relatively isolated northern beach that retains its remote tropical charm.

Activities

There are several places to rent kayaks along Sao Beach, and its protected, fairly calm waters make for a smooth ride. In addition to locals who hire out boats, you can ask at the beachside restaurants. The going rate is about 80,000d per hour.

★ Hon Thom Cable Car
CABLE CAR

(Map p378; ☑088-677 8686; An Thoi; over/under 1.4m in height 150,000/100,000d; ☺to Hon Thom 8am-noon, to An Thoi 1.30-7.30pm) The world's longest over-sea cable car (7.9km), this is an epic ride over the An Thoi Islands to Hon Thom, with some stunning views of the fishing fleet bobbing below. The 25-minute trip is in Austrian-made Doppelmayr cars carrying up to 30 people. The cable-car embarkation point near An Thoi is designed like a faux Italian village, complete with aged Renaissance houses and a mini-Colosseum ticket office.

Hon Thom is in the process of being transformed into Sun World, a sort of honky-tonk theme park with a huge water park called Aquapolis. The cable-car fee is incredible value when you consider it includes a bus transfer from Duong Dong and an electric buggy ride to the beach at Hon Thom.

VinPearlLand
AMUSEMENT PARK

(Map p378; ☑1900 6677; www.vinpearlland.com; Dai Beach; adult/child 500,000/400,000d; ☺9am-9.30pm; ⚐) Like a Vietnamese version of Disneyland (Visneyland?), complete with faux Cinderella castle, roller coasters and log flumes, this is a good place for some family fun if planning a full-on beach holiday on Phu Quoc. Nearby is a 3000-room resort, golf course and VinPearl Safari, with combo tickets available for adult/child

900,000/750,000d. The water park is one of the highlights if the children have had enough of the beach action.

Sea World
DIVING

(☑0297-282 8888; https://seaworld.vn; Hon May Rut; incl transfer and speedboat 1,190,000d; ☺12.30-4.00pm; ⚐) Find your sea legs with a sea walk around the coral garden near Hon May Rut island in the An Thoi archipelago. It's a good-value option for children who are too young to dive to experience the underwater world. Hotel pickup from Long Beach is included in the price.

Troc's Kitchen
COOKING

(Map p380; ☑098-810 3950; https://trocskitchen andcookingclass.com; 122 Đ Tran Hung Dao; per person US$30-45; ☺10am & 4pm daily) Troc's Kitchen is a fun-filled cooking class based at Phu House Hostel. Classes include a range of Vietnamese classics from south to north, and a special menu (US$45) is offered at weekends. One bottle of Kinh Beer is included for all wannabe chefs.

VinPearl Safari
SAFARI

(Map p378; https://safari.vinpearlland.com; Bai Dai; adult/child 650,000/500,000d; ☺9am-4pm; ⚐) We bet you didn't expect to go on an African safari in Vietnam, but this safari, complete with *Jurassic Park*–style gates, takes you on a tour through the African savannah, as well as packing all sorts of other unexpected exiles such as Madagascan lemurs. It's professionally run, but there is a lot of cheesy razzamatazz, particularly at weekends and holidays.

Combo tickets with VinPearlLand are available for adult/child 900,000/750,000d. It's located in the far northwest of the island, in Ganh Dau commune.

Diving & Snorkelling

Although Nha Trang is arguably the best all-round dive destination in Vietnam, there's plenty of underwater action around Phu Quoc, but only during the dry months (November to May). Two fun dives cost from US$70 to US$90, depending on the location and operator; four-day PADI Open Water courses hover between US$340 and US$380; and snorkelling trips cost US$30 to US$35.

Flipper Diving Club
DIVING

(Map p380; ☑0297-399 4924; www.flipperdiving. com; 60 Đ Tran Hung Dao; ☺7am-7pm) Centrally located, multilingual PADI dive centre for everything from novice dive trips to full instructor courses. Very professional, with plenty of diving experience worldwide, and with instructors who'll put you at ease if you're a newbie.

Rainbow Divers DIVING
(Map p380; ☑ 0913 400 964; www.divevietnam. com; 11 Đ Tran Hung Dao; ⊙ 9am-6pm) This reputable PADI outfit was the first to set up shop on the island and offers a wide range of diving and snorkelling trips. As well as the walk-in office, it's well represented at resorts on Long Beach.

👉 Tours

Book tours through your hotel or resort. Squid fishing at night is popular, and you'll spot the lights of boats (to lure the cephalopods to the surface) on the evening horizon. Specialised companies and individuals offer boat excursions and fishing trips.

The classic tours cover sights just in the north or just in the south for about 420,000d each. Sights vary but all cover pagodas, the prison, a fish-sauce factory and a beach.

Jerry's Jungle Tours ADVENTURE
(Map p380; ☑ 093-822 6021; www.jerrystours. wixsite.com/jerrystours; 106 Đ Tran Hung Dao; day trips from US$30) Archipelago explorations by boat, with snorkelling, fishing, day and multiday trips to islands, motorbike tours, bouldering, birdwatching, hiking and cultural tours around Phu Quoc.

John's Tours BOATING
(Map p380; ☑ 091-893 9111; www.phuquoc trip.com; 4 Đ Tran Hung Dao; tours per person US$15-35) Well represented at hotels and resorts; cruises include snorkelling, island hopping, sunrise fishing and squid-fishing trips.

Viet Sail BOATING
(Map p378; ☑ 077-683 0072; https://sailingschool vietsail.business.site; Chez Carole Resort; 1-2hr 600,000-1,000,000d; ⊙ 7am-7pm) Take to the high seas around Phu Quoc in a catamaran or dinghy with experienced French sailor Pierre. Snorkelling gear is included. It's located at Chez Carole Resort on Cua Can Beach.

Anh Tu's Tours BOATING
(Map p380; ☑ 0913 820 714; anhtupq@yahoo.com) Snorkelling, squid fishing, island tours and motorbike rental.

🛏 Sleeping

Accommodation prices yo-yo depending on the season and visitor numbers. Variations are more extreme than anywhere else in Vietnam, and tend to affect budget and midrange places the most. Some places treble their prices in the December-to-January peak season, when bookings are crucial. Overall, you'll get less for your money than you'd expect for the price.

Some hotels provide free transport to and from the airport; enquire when booking.

🛏 Duong Dong & Long Beach

Long Beach offers the best range of accommodation on the island, from backpacker hostels to luxury hotels and resorts. It's a great option thanks to an excellent range of restaurants and bars and plenty of beach clubs for those without access to a private beach or pool.

★ 9 Station Hostel HOSTEL **$**
(Map p380; ☑ 0297-658 8999; www.9station hostel.com; 91/3 Đ Tran Hung Dao; dm 135,000-225,000d, r from 780,000d; ✱ ⊛ ⊠) The flashpacker hostel has arrived in Phu Quoc with 9 Station, a cracking place to stay, with a range of dorms from four to 12 beds and modern private rooms with attached bathroom. The best features are a huge reception and restaurant-bar with a helpful tour desk and a swimming pool that draws guests like moths to a light.

Langchia Home HOSTEL **$**
(Map p380; ☑ 093-913 2613; 84 Đ Tran Hung Dao; dm 165,000d, r 600,000-1,050,000d; ✱ ⊛ ⊠) A favourite with solo travellers, this hostel gets plenty of praise for the friendliness and helpfulness of its staff, the lively bar with pool table and the swimming pool in which to cool down. Dorm beds come with mosquito nets and individual fans. It's worth paying extra for the decent breakfast.

Phu House Hostel HOSTEL **$**
(Map p380; ☑ 0297-359 7999; www.phuhouse hostel.com; 122 Đ Tran Hung Dao; dm 140,000-230,000d, r 400,000-550,000d; ✱ @ ⊛) Phu House boasts the stylings of a Hoi An family mansion but feels modern with comfy dorm beds, privacy curtains, rain shower, air-con and immaculate cleanliness. It's a social hub thanks to nightly free beer (5pm), regular events, a pool table and a Jacuzzi.

It's living proof that Phu Quoc isn't just for lovebirds and families.

Sleepbox Hostel
GUESTHOUSE $

(Map p380; ☑ 090-762 6519; 57/112 Đ Tran Hung Dao; r 350,000-400,000d; ❉ 🛜) More a guesthouse than a hostel, this small pad offers a big welcome thanks to the friendly owners. The rooms are tastefully decorated with a contemporary flourish and include smart hot-water bathrooms.

Vida Loca Resort
HOTEL $$

(Map p380; ☑ 0297-384 7583; www.vidaloca resort.com; 118/12 Đ Tran Hung Dao; r 1,200,000-2,500,000d; ❉ 🛜 ▣) This friendly place offers redesigned rooms and bungalows amid a leafy garden, set on a prime piece of beachfront. Splurge on a sea-view bungalow if you have the spare dong.

Free Beach Resort
BUNGALOW $$

(Map p380; ☑ 098-112 1210; www.freebeachbun galows.com; Khu Pho 7; bungalows from 700,000d; ❉ 🛜) Located next to one of the few remaining stretches of 'free beach' on the main Long Beach drag, this place offers good-value bungalows with easy access to the sea. They have simple trim, but feature private hot-water bathrooms and small verandas for chilling out.

Sunshine Bungalow
HOTEL $$

(Map p380; ☑ 0297-397 5777; www.sunshine phuquoc.com; Đ Tran Hung Dao; bungalows 300,000-700,000d; ❉ 🛜) Friendly place run by a Vietnamese family, less than 100m from the sea and sand. Large, bright rooms nestle amid lush vegetation and the owners do their best to help. Some English and German spoken.

Lan Anh Garden Resort
RESORT $$

(Map p380; ☑ 077-398 5985; www.lananh phuquoc.com.vn; KP7 Đ Tran Hung Dao; r 750,000-1,450,000d; ❉ 🛜 ▣) Enticing little resort hotel with friendly, professional staff, a clutch of rooms arranged around a small pool, and motorbikes for rent. Nab an upstairs room if you can for the breezy verandas. Book on its website for discounted rates.

Nhat Huy
Garden Guesthouse
GUESTHOUSE $$

(Map p380; ☑ 096-562 3169; http://nhathuy gardenguesthouse.weebly.com; Đ Tran Hung Dao; d/f 750,000/1,200,000d; ❉ 🛜 ▣) Travellers who linger here a few days find themselves treated like family by the gregarious staff and are invited to join impromptu barbecues. Your crash pad is a small bungalow set in a shady garden setting, with a hammock out front for lazing about. It's on the main road and a short walk from the beach.

La Veranda
RESORT $$$

(Map p380; ☑ 0297-398 2988; www.laveranda resort.com; 118/9 Đ Tran Hung Dao; r US$205-330, villas from US$445; ❉ @ 🛜 ▣) Shaded by palms, this Accor resort, designed in colonial style and small enough to remain intimate, is one of the most elegant places to stay on the island. There's an appealing pool, a stylish spa and rooms featuring designer bathrooms. The beach is pristine, and dining options include a cafe on the lawn and the **Pepper Tree Restaurant** (meals 250,000-700,000d; ⊘ 6am-11pm; 🛜 🍴).

Cassia Cottage
RESORT $$$

(Map p380; ☑ 0297-384 8395; www.cassiacot tage.com; 100c Đ Tran Hung Dao; r US$175-245, villa US$445; ❉ 🛜 ▣) Set amid flourishing greenery, this is a seductive two-for-one boutique resort on Long Beach in a sleepy beachside repose. The older section has two pools, pretty beach bar and cottages with private gardens. The newer side has a flashy pool with free sunset yoga, a handsome open restaurant with tables overlooking the sea, and luxe balcony rooms flaunting spice-trader personality.

Famiana Resort & Spa
RESORT $$$

(Map p380; ☑ 0297-398 3366; http://famiana resort.com; Đ Tran Hung Dao; r/villa/ste from 2,000,000/2,500,000/3,750,000d; ❉ @ 🛜 ▣) This refined 60-room resort has splendid seafront villas with mezzanine floors, a large pool, a spotless stretch of private beach and sea kayaks available for active travellers.

🛏 Around the Island

Rockier than Long Beach, Ong Lang, 7km north of Duong Dong, has the advantage of being substantially less crowded and, hence, feels much more like a tropical-island escape. Because of its relative isolation, expect to spend most of your time in and around your resort, although most places can arrange bike or motorbike hire to get you out and about. Definitely book ahead.

Elsewhere around the island, accommodation is very spread out, with many of the beaches occupied by megaresorts or fenced off for development. Sao Beach, in the southeast corner of the island, is one of the best stretches of sand and has some good mid-range resorts. Vung Bau Beach also has some good boutique options for those that want to get away from the crowd.

★ Bamboo Cottages & Restaurant
RESORT $$$

(Map p378; ☑ 0297-281 0345; www.bamboo phuquoc.com; r US$100-155; ✿ @) ✎ Run by a friendly family with a coterie of cheeky dogs, Bamboo Cottages has Vung Bau Beach largely to itself. The focal point is an open-sided restaurant and bar, right by the beach. Set around the lawns, the attractive, lemon-coloured villas have private, open-roofed bathrooms with solar-powered hot water. The family supports an education scholarship for local kids in need.

Guests get timed, free use of kayaks, snorkels and bicycles. Bamboo Cottages is 18km north of Duong Dong.

★ Chen Sea Resort
RESORT $$$

(Map p378; ☑ 0297-399 5895; www.chensea -resort.com; villas US$199-499; ✿ @ 🛜 🏊) Beautiful Chen Sea has stunning villas with sunken baths (some with hot tubs) and deep verandas, designed to resemble ancient terracotta-roofed houses, all decorated with Angkorian art. The large azure rectangle of the infinity pool faces the resort's beautiful sandy beach. The isolation is mitigated by plenty of activities: cycling, kayaking, catamaran outings, in-spa pampering and fine dining. It's located on the southern section of Ong Lang Beach, about 6km north of Duong Dong.

Mango Bay
RESORT $$$

(Map p378; ☑ 077-398 1693; www.mangobay phuquoc.com; bungalows 3,150,000-11,150,000d; @🛜) ✎ A charming, if simple, getaway for those who want some romance in their life. Set around a small cove accessed from a dusty road through a mango orchard, the ecofriendly resort uses solar panels and organic and recycled building materials, and has its own butterfly garden. Strung out along the beautiful beach, airy bungalows come with delightful open-air bathrooms.

It's located on Ong Lang Beach, about 7km north of Duong Dong.

✕ Eating

Local peppercorns and cobia fish are specialities. Many resorts have excellent restaurants with sunset views. Guests at remote resort locations like Ong Lang Beach tend to eat in. Duong Dong town has the night market, seafood restaurants and the best range of options without the markup. Try local seafood restaurants in Ham Ninh fishing village, along the pier at the end of the main road.

✕ Duong Dong & Long Beach

★ Phu Quoc Night Market
SEAFOOD $

(Cho Dem Phu Quoc; Map p380; Đ Bach Dang; meals from 50,000d; ⊙ 4.30pm-3am; ✍) The most atmospheric and best-value place to dine on the island, Duong Dong's busy night market has stalls of snacks, coconut ice cream and a parade of outdoor restaurants serving a delicious range of Vietnamese seafood, grills and vegetarian options. Quality can be mixed, so follow the discerning local crowd. Riverside tables can be a bit whiffy.

A post-meal meander among the stalls of clothes, souvenirs and peppercorns is a tourist ritual.

Khanh Ly Vegetarian
VEGETARIAN $

(Map p380; ☑ 0297-281 0180; 35 Đ Nguyen Trai; meals 20,000-45,000d; ⊙ 8am-8pm; ✍) Pick and choose from a buffet of Vietnamese vegan-vegetarian dishes, such as mock shrimp on sugar cane, to accompany green veg and rice for an excellent-value, delicious plate. Staff are friendly, and there are also hearty noodle soups to tempt carnivores.

Heaven Restaurant
VIETNAMESE $

(Map p380; ☑ 097-554 2769; 141 Đ Tran Hung Dao; meals 40,000-90,000d; ⊙ 8am-11pm; ✍) You may not expect heaven to have basic wooden tables opening onto a road, but it does at this good-value family joint. With fresh, generous servings of Vietnamese dishes such as lemongrass chicken and a very long list of vegetarian options, this is paradise for every taste.

★ Saigonese
FUSION $$

(Map p380; ☑ 093-805 9650; www.facebook. com/saigoneseeatery; 73 Đ Tran Hung Dao; meals 150,000-220,000d; ⊙ 9am-1pm & 5-11pm Wed-Mon) The hippest casual dining on Phu Quoc delights with fusion dishes lifted from designer cookbooks. The seasonal appetisers excel in *bao* (steamed buns filled with pulled beef and beetroot), and squid with avocado cream. Try the caramelised-shrimp clay pot and, for dessert, popcorn banana cake. Manager Thao's experiences abroad show in the chic ambience.

MEKONG DELTA PHU QUOC ISLAND

Spice House at Cassia Cottage
VIETNAMESE $$

(Map p380; www.cassiacottage.com; 100c Đ Tran Hung Dao; meals 190,000-300,000đ; ⊙7-10am & 11am-10pm) Nab a sea-view table, order a papaya salad, grilled garlic prawns, *banh xeo* (savoury-filled pancake), cinnamon-infused okra, a delectable Khmer fish curry or grilled beef skewers wrapped in betel leaves, and time dinner to catch the sunset at this excellent restaurant. There's even a single romantic cabana table right on the sand.

Winston's Burgers & Beer
BURGERS $$

(Map p380; ☑076-390 1093; www.facebook.com/winstonsburgers; 121 Đ Tran Hung Dao; burgers from 135,000đ; ⊙11am-11pm) The name says it all: this bar is about really good burgers, beer and a large selection of cocktails, mixed by the eponymous Winston. Linger for a chat or challenge your drinking companions to a game of Connect 4. It has few vegetarian options.

The Embassy
INTERNATIONAL $$

(Map p380; ☑096-806 7940; www.embassyphuquoc.com; 99a Đ Tran Hung Dao; meals 65,000-200,000đ; ⊙8am-9pm; ❋🐾) This Scandinavian cafe and bakery doubles as a cocktail bar by night, so is a good spot any time of day. Healthy and delicious breakfasts are available, including granola and yogurt combos, before switching to sandwiches and salads at lunch and finishing with cheese and meat platters after dark.

Ganesh
INDIAN $$

(Map p380; ☑0297-399 4917; www.ganeshphuquoc.com; 97 Đ Tran Hung Dao; meals 90,000-225,000đ; ⊙11am-10pm; 🐾) Although the service can be slow, the Indian dishes here are fantastic: the mango prawn curry is a standout. If you are feeling a real hunger, go for a vegetarian/meat/seafood thali set (from 195,000đ).

★ Itaca Resto Lounge
FUSION $$$

(Map p380; ☑077-399 2022; www.itacalounge.com; 119 Đ Tran Hung Dao; tapas 90,000-195,000đ, meals 170,000-550,000đ; ⊙6-11.45pm Thu-Tue; 🐾🐾) This much-applauded restaurant has a creative Mediterranean-Asian fusion menu (with tapas), an inviting al-fresco arrangement and friendly, welcoming hosts. Don't expect sea views, but do expect Wagyu beef burgers, seared tuna with passion fruit, wild-mushroom risotto and a charming ambience.

✖ Around the Island

Alanis Deli
CAFE $

(Map p378; ☑0297-399 4931; 98 Đ Tran Hung Dao; meals from 60,000đ; ⊙8am-10.30pm; 🐾) Fab caramel pancakes, American breakfast combos, plus good (if pricey) coffee and wonderfully friendly service. It's located near the turnoff to Ong Lang Beach, about 6km north of Duong Dong.

Sakura 1
VIETNAMESE $

(Map p378; www.facebook.com/sakuraphuquoc; Đ Le Thuc Nha; meals 50,000-100,000đ; ⊙9am-10pm) This simple wood restaurant is run by the very fluent English-speaking Kiem. In spite of the name, the dishes are Vietnamese rather than Japanese, and standouts include prawns in tamarind sauce and smoked aubergine. If you're with a group, whole red snapper makes a great addition to the meal. Friendly service. It's located in the village of Ong Lang.

★ So True
VIETNAMESE $$

(Map p378; ☑094-342 2226; Đ Le Thuc Nha, Ong Lang; mains 69,000-175,000đ; ⊙1-11pm) Located in the heart of Ong Lang, this restaurant does an excellent turn at mod-Viet cuisine, with signature specialities such as *bo so tru* (beef with green-pepper sauce), squid with lemongrass and kumquat, and cobia fish with dill and turmeric. Phu Quoc draught beer is on tap and there are some interesting photographs from all over Vietnam adorning the walls.

Mango Bay Restaurant
INTERNATIONAL $$

(Map p378; ☑0297-398 1693; http://mangobayphuquoc.com; Mango Bay Resort, Ong Lang Beach; meals 135,000-410,000đ; ⊙7am-9pm; 🐾) One of the best eating experiences around is to sit on the deck at Mango Bay, dining on tamarind blue-swimmer crab and peering out to sea. There are Australian beef steaks, honey duck breast and lots of Thai flavours, too. The calm atmosphere and the bar with a good drinks list add to the pleasure.

Sailing Club
INTERNATIONAL $$$

(Map p378; ☑093-103 1035; www.sailingclubphuquoc.com; Khu Phuc Hop; meals 110,000-900,000đ; ⊙10am-11pm; 🐾🐾) The Nha Trang institution has dropped anchor in Phu Quoc in an impressive setting at the southern end of Long Beach, near the Intercontinental Hotel. The menu is predominantly Asian fusion, but also includes comfort food such as burgers and pizzas, plus an affordable menu for kids. A beautiful spot day or night, it tends to draw a crowd.

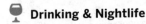 Drinking & Nightlife

The epicentre of Long Beach nightlife is the small lanes around La Veranda (p384). If you don't want a drink but just an urban buzz, Duong Dong's night market (p385) is where it's at.

★House No 1
BAR
(Map p380; https://houseno1phuquoc.com; 12 Đ Le Loi; ⏱5pm-1am; 🛜) One of the few bars in the centre of town, House No 1 is a great spot for evening drinks, including local and craft beers, cocktails and De Spirit, a locally produced refined rice wine. Midweek live music, plus a cool rooftop cafe that's popular with a local crowd.

★Cheeky Traveller
BAR
(Map p380; 118 Đ Tran Hung Dao; ⏱4pm-1am; 🛜) A great little travellers' bar run by a couple of seasoned travellers who have settled on Phu Quoc. Draught beer flows and custom cocktails are available on demand. Bar games such as Jenga towers and beer pong kick off later in the evening, plus it's been known to stay open late into the night. Cheeky!

The Rabbit Hole
IRISH PUB
(Map p380; www.therabbitholeirishbar.com; 118 Đ Tran Hung Dao; ⏱10am-late; 🛜) Enter the rabbit hole and, like Alice, you may lose track of time. A great little bar with a happy hour from 3pm to 7pm, plus classic pub pursuits like darts and a pool table. It also doubles as a reliable sports bar for big games.

Blue Monkey
BAR
(Map p380; www.bluemonkey.vn; 116 Đ Tran Hung Dao; ⏱7pm-4am; 🛜) One of the funkiest bars around Long Beach, this place has live music most nights and stays open later than most bars. Homemade coconut vodka, craft beer on tap and creative cocktails pull a crowd, but watch out for the impromptu karaoke sessions.

Rory's Bar
BAR
(Map p378; ☑0919 333 950; Cay Sao; ⏱9am-midnight; 🛜) Relocated to the remote east side of the island, this huge beach bar is taking a big gamble on drawing day-tripping motorbikers and pulling in punters by night with a free midnight shuttle bus back to Duong Dong. Designed like a giant shipwreck, it's a fun stop for lunch and a top spot to watch big games.

Coco Bar
BAR
(Map p380; 118/3 Đ Tran Hung Dao; ⏱9am-midnight) With chairs and music spilling onto the pavement, Coco is a great place for a roadside bevvy and a chat with the mix of travelling folk, Gallic wayfarers, local drinkers and passing pool sharks.

BEACH CLUBS

Those staying in cheaper digs without beachfront access should check out one of the many happening beach clubs on the Long Beach strip. Most offers sunbeds and umbrellas for around 100,000d to 200,000d per day, including showers and, sometimes, towels. Some places are free if you are only using the sand and buy some food and drink throughout the day.

Blue Bar Beach Club (Map p380; Đ Tran Hung Dao; ⏱9am-late; 🛜) One of the glitziest beach clubs, with a cavernous shaded interior and a well-tended beachfront with sunbeds and beanbags.

Horizon Beach Bar (Map p380; 98 Đ Tran Hung Dao; ⏱10am-midnight; 🛜) A little beach bar near the Doung Dong end of the Long Beach strip, with friendly owners who speak English and offer affordable sunbeds.

Mandala Beach Bar (Map p380; Đ Tran Hung Dao; ⏱9am-late; 🛜) One of the liveliest of the beach clubs, this is a popular place to watch the sun sink over the horizon from the recumbent position of a beanbag.

Oc Sen Beach Bar (Map p380; 118/10 Đ Tran Hung Dao; ⏱10am-late; 🛜) Beach club by day, turning a different kind of club by night with DJs, bonfires and a Thai-islands vibe.

Joe's Bar (Map p380; Long Beach; ⏱8am-11pm; 🛜) A cheap-and-cheerful beach bar behind the Long Beach Centre; it also has a 'Beach Spa' with massages for 200,000d.

Shopping

Phu Quoc Pearls
JEWELLERY

(Map p380; Đ Tran Hung Dao; ⏾8am-5pm) For black, yellow, white, pink or any other colour of pearl, Phu Quoc Pearls is a requisite stop. Displays feature all manner of jewellery made from said pearls.

Avid pearl hunters can find cheaper wares at kiosks in the village of Ham Ninh, but you have a guarantee of authenticity here.

ℹ Information

There are ATMs at the airport, in Duong Dong and in many resorts on Long Beach.

The **post office** (Map p380; Đ 30 Thang 4; ⏾8am-5pm Mon-Fri) is located in downtown Duong Dong.

ℹ Getting There & Away

AIR

Phu Quoc International Airport (Map p378; www.phuquocairport.com) is 10km southeast of Duong Dong. Among the domestic services are daily flights to Can Tho, Danang, Haiphong, Hanoi and HCMC. Useful domestic airlines include **Vietnam Airlines** (www.vietnamairlines.com), **Vietjet Air** (www.vietjetair.com) and **Jetstar** (www.jetstar.com/vn/en).

International flight connections include Bangkok, Guangzhou, Hong Kong, Kuala Lumpur, Seoul and Singapore. There should also be regular chartered flights to destinations in Germany, Italy, Russia and other European cities.

Demand can be high in peak season, so book ahead.

BOAT

Phu Quoc Express (Map p380; ☎0297-628 1888; www.pqe.com.vn; 15 Đ Tran Hung Dao; ⏾7am-9pm) and **Superdong** (Map p380; ☎0297-398 0111; www.superdong.com.vn; 10 Đ 30 Thang 4) offer connections from Ha Tien (1½ hours) and Rach Gia (2½ hours) to Phu Quoc's **Bai Vong** (Pha Bai Vong; Map p378) on the east coast. Phu Quoc Express has the smartest hydrofoils with VIP class, while Superdong is slightly cheaper but also reliable. Phu Quoc travel agents have the most up-to-date schedules and can book tickets. Seas can be rough between June and September. During peak season (December, January and national holidays), there are often extra services.

Phu Quoc Express hydrofoils to Ha Tien (standard/VIP 250,000/350,000d) depart Phu Quoc at 8am, 9.45am. 11.45am, 1.45pm and 3.30pm. From Ha Tien they leave at 6am, 7.45am, 9.45am, 11.45am and 1.45pm. Hydrofoils from Phu Quoc to Rach Gia (standard/VIP 340,000/540,000d) depart at 7.30am,

10.30am and 1.30pm. In the other direction, they depart Rach Gia at 7.20am, 11am and 1.45pm.

Superdong fast boats from Phu Quoc to Ha Tien (230,000d) depart at 8am, 9.45am, 11.45am and 1pm. From Ha Tien they depart at at 7.35am, 8am, 9.45am and 1.45pm. Fast boats between Phu Quoc and Rach Gia (330,000d) leave at 8am, 8.30am, 8.45am, 12.40pm and 1pm in both directions.

From Ha Tien there are also car ferries to Phu Quoc (passenger/motorbike/car 185,000/80,000/700,000d). Some run to Phu Quoc's Da Chong port, in the northeast of the island, with regular departures daily from 4am to 4pm from Ha Tien (3½ hours) and from 5am to 6pm from Da Chong port; some also run to Bai Vong port on the east coast. More car ferries are due to be added to meet booming demand.

To get to the ferry terminals on the east coast of Phu Quoc, Superdong runs its own shuttle buses (30,000d) from its ticket office in Duong Dong. A taxi from Duong Dong costs about 250,000d, while a xe om will cost about 150,000d.

There is a minimart near the ferry terminal at Bai Vong, plus local snack sellers; drinks are sold on board the ferries.

ℹ Getting Around

TO/FROM THE AIRPORT

Expect to pay around 60,000d for a xe om to Long Beach and 110,000d for a taxi. Fares to Duong Dong are about 50% more. You will also have to pay an additional airport toll of 5000d for a xe om, or 20,000d for a taxi.

Phu Quoc Bus 11 (https://busphuquoc.com) runs from Duong Dong to An Thoi via the airport every 20 minutes and costs 20,000d.

Jetstar runs a shuttle bus to Duong Dong town for 50,000d.

BICYCLE

Bicycle rentals are available through most lodgings from 70,000d per day. Depending on where you are, long stretches of open highway may not be pleasant to cycle in the heat.

MOTORBIKE

For short xe om runs, 20,000d should be sufficient. Otherwise figure on around 60,000d for about 5km. From Duong Dong to Bai Vong will cost about 70,000d or so. Agree on a price before setting off.

Motorbikes can be hired from most hotels and bungalows for around 120,000d (semi-automatic) to 150,000d (automatic) per day. Inspect cheaper bikes thoroughly before setting out.

Major highways run south from Duong Dong to An Thoi, the southern tip of the island, as well as to Sao Beach and north as far as Cape Ganh

Dau, the northwest tip of Phu Quoc. A two-lane highway connects Duong Dong with the car-ferry port, but there are still some unsurfaced roads in the far north of the island.

TAXI

Mai Linh (📞 0297-397 9797) is a reliable operator. From Duong Dong it costs about 25,000d to the bars of Long Beach, 160,000d to the coast after the airport, and 250,000d to Bai Vong ferry terminal. Taxi Phu Quoc is the island's very own taxi-booking app.

Ha Tien

📞 0297 / POP 82,000

Ha Tien may be part of the Mekong Delta, but lying on the Gulf of Thailand it feels a world away from the rice fields and rivers that typify the region. There are dramatic limestone formations peppering the area, which are home to a network of caves, some of which have been turned into temples. Plantations of pepper trees cling to the hillsides. On a clear day, Phu Quoc Island is easily visible to the west.

The town itself has a languid charm, with crumbling colonial villas and a colourful riverside market. Already bolstered by the number of Phu Quoc– and Cambodia-bound travellers, visitor numbers are set to soar further as a competing number of ferry companies take advantage of the close proximity to Phu Quoc.

In 2018 it was given city status by the government, so Ha Tien is truly on the map.

⊙ Sights

Thach Dong Cave Pagoda   BUDDHIST TEMPLE
(Chua Thanh Van; 5000d; ⊙ 6.30am-5.30pm) This Buddhist cave temple is 4km northeast of town. Scramble through the cave chambers to see the funerary tablets and altars to Ngoc Hoang, Quan The Am Bo Tat and the two Buddhist monks who founded the temples of the pagoda.

A taxi here from town is 60,000d, but you may need to call for one for the return trip as very few pass by.

Phu Dung Pagoda   BUDDHIST TEMPLE
(Phu Cu Am Tu; Đ Phu Dung; ⊙ dawn-dusk) FREE
This pagoda was founded in the mid-18th century by Nguyen Thi Xuan. Her tomb and that of one of her female servants are on the hillside behind the pagoda. Inside the main hall of the pagoda, the most notable statue on the central dais is a bronze Thich Ca Buddha from China.

WORTH A TRIP

HON GIANG & NGHE ISLANDS

There are many islands along this coast and some locals make a living gathering swiftlet nests (the most important ingredient of that famous Chinese delicacy, bird's-nest soup) from their rocky cliffs. About 15km from Ha Tien and accessible by small boat, Hon Giang Island has a lovely, secluded beach. Hon Giang can be visited by a local boat arranged in the junction town of Ba Hom.

Nghe Island, near Hon Chong, is a favourite pilgrimage spot for Buddhists. The island contains a **cave pagoda** (Chua Hang) next to a large statue of Quan The Am Bo Tat, which faces out to sea. Boats to Nghe Island can be arranged in Hon Chong.

To get here, continue north past the Mac Cuu Tombs and take the first left onto Đ Phu Dung.

Tam Bao Pagoda   BUDDHIST TEMPLE
(Sac Tu Tam Bao Tu; 328 Đ Phuong Thanh; ⊙ dawn-dusk) FREE Founded by Mac Cuu in 1730, Tam Bao Pagoda is home to a community of Buddhist nuns. In front of the splendid, many-tiered pagoda is a statue of Quan The Am Bo Tat (the Goddess of Mercy) standing on a lotus blossom. Within the sanctuary, the largest statue on the dais represents A Di Da (the Buddha of the Past), made of painted brass.

Dong Ho   NATURAL FEATURE
The name translates as East Lake, though Dong Ho is actually an inlet of the sea. It's said to be most beautiful on nights when there is a full or almost-full moon. According to legend, fairies dance here on such nights.

The 'lake' is just east of Ha Tien, bounded to the east by a chain of granite hills known as the Ngu Ho (Five Tigers) and to the west by the To Chan hills.

Ngoc Tien Monastery   BUDDHIST TEMPLE
(Tinh Xa Ngoc Tien; ⊙ dawn-dusk) From Ha Tien's riverfront, this Buddhist monastery is a striking sight – sprawling up the hill on the other side of the river. The buildings themselves are unremarkable, but it's worth making the steep climb for the sweeping views of the town and countryside. Follow the narrow road at its base and the monastery is

Ha Tien

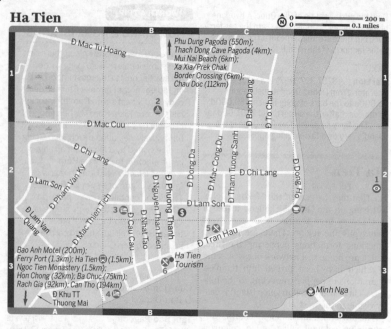

Ha Tien

reached via a tiny lane at number 48; look for the yellow sign topped with a Buddhist swastika (symbolising eternity).

☞ Tours

Mr The Tours   CULTURAL
(☏0918 574 780; oasisbarhatien@hotmail.com; tours US$10-20) The inimitable Mr The (pronounced 'tay') is an intelligent, patient and experienced guide who runs day and half-day tours of Hon Chong and Ha Tien from the back of his motorcycle. He speaks English and can meet at short notice to discuss. Oasis Bar can call him for you. He also sells bus tickets with motorbike transfer to the station.

⊨ Sleeping

Bao Anh Motel   HOTEL $
(Nga Nhi Bao Anh; ☏0166 223 8440; cnr Đ Hong Van Tu & Đ Truong Sa; r Mon-Fri from 350,000d,

Sat & Sun from 400,000d; ✳☎) You could spend days passing anonymously through its characterless halls, but for clean rooms with river views, this hotel is great value. Large front-room windows offer marginal soundproofing (only because they don't open).

Hai Van Hotel   HOTEL $
(☏0297-385 2872; www.khachsanhaivan.com; 55 Đ Lam Son; r 180,000-350,000d; ✳☎) A favourite with tour groups and conventions, the Hai Van offers clean, smart (if somewhat featureless) rooms with polished floors. Some English is spoken, which is useful if you've become used to widespread spoken English in Cambodia.

River Hotel   HOTEL $$
(☏0297-395 5888; www.riverhotelvn.com; Đ Tran Hau; r/ste from 900,000/2,000,000d; ✳☎☒)

With contemporary, spacious and stylish rooms, a towering and sinuous outline and river views, Ha Tien's most glam hotel enjoys an optimum position on the waterfront. Staff are helpful despite limited English, and the place is practically deserted midweek, so discounts are negotiable. Karaoke 'entertainment' takes place on the top floor.

Eating

★ Oasis Bar INTERNATIONAL $

(☑ 0297-370 1553; www.oasisbarhatien.com; 30 Đ Tran Hau; meals 60,000-150,000d; ⊙9am-9pm; ⓢ) Run by a resident Western expat and his Vietnamese wife, this friendly little restaurant-bar is a great spot for a cold beer, plunger coffee, impartial travel information and for leafing through copies of the *Evening Standard,* the *Observer* and the *Daily Mail.* The menu runs to all-day, full-English breakfasts, filled baguettes, Greek salad, mango shakes and more.

There are plans to relocate to a new homestay and bar about 4km from town; details will be available on the website.

Quan Hu Tieu Thuy SOUP $

(☑ 0163 818 1003; 7 Đ Tran Hau; noodle soup 30,000d; ⊙2-9pm) A brightly lit stall, metal tables and a family effort is what creates excellent *hu tieu*, a chicken noodle soup that is the Mekong's pho. Crowds form here for excellent succulent broiled chicken and fat udon-style egg noodles in a clear broth doused in the usual herby Vietnamese favourites. One of the brothers speaks English.

Ha Tien Night Market MARKET $

(Đ So 5; meals from 20,000d; ⊙5-9pm) Some of Ha Tien's cheapest and best eats are available at the night market, which has relocated to the new area of the city to the west. The grilled seafood is fresh and particularly good.

Drinking & Nightlife

Ha Tien's speciality is an unusual variety of purple-skinned coconut – containing no milk, but with delicate and delicious flesh – that can only be found in Cambodia and this region of Vietnam. Restaurants all around the Ha Tien area serve up the coconut flesh in a glass with ice and sugar.

Dong Ho Coffee CAFE

(☑ 0297-385 1828; Đ Dong Ho; ⊙6am-9pm) Dotted with fairy lights and glowing with Chinese lanterns at night, this floating cafe is a breezy choice for a sundowner beer or a *cafe sua* (iced coffee) overlooking the waters of Dong Ho.

Information

Agribank (☑ 0297-385 2055; 37 Đ Lam Son; ⊙7am-5pm Mon-Fri) Has an ATM.

Ha Tien Tourism (☑ 0297-395 9598; Đ Tran Hau; ⊙8am-5pm) This agency handles

---

GETTING TO CAMBODIA: HA TIEN TO KEP

Getting to the border The **Xa Xia/Prek Chak border crossing** connects Ha Tien with Kep and Kampot on Cambodia's south coast, making a trip to Cambodia from Phu Quoc via Ha Tien, or vice versa, that much easier. Several minibus companies leave Ha Tien for Cambodia at around 1pm, heading to Kep (US$9, one hour, 47km), Kampot (US$12, 1½ hours, 75km), Sihanoukville (US$15, four hours, 150km) and Phnom Penh (US$15, four hours, 180km). Bookings can be made through Ha Tien Tourism, which can arrange the Cambodian visa, too.

It's a really good idea to have US dollars on you when crossing into Cambodia; you can pay for the Cambodian visa in dong, but they'll hit you with a really unfavourable exchange rate. On the Cambodian side, you can withdraw dollars from ATMs.

In peak season, when minibuses get booked up way in advance, you can go all the way to Kep or Kampot on the back of a *xe om* if you're travelling light. Oasis Bar can recommend reputable motorbike drivers. If you make an independent arrangement with a *xe om* driver, do not hand over the money until you reach your destination, or else you risk being abandoned at the border.

At the border Cambodian visas officially cost US$30, but be prepared to overpay by around US$5 to join the 'express line', or be made to wait indefinitely.

Moving on It's possible to take a local bus or taxi to the border and then wait for a local bus or arrange a motorbike on the Cambodian side, but since tourist minibuses cost only slightly more and are far comfier, most travellers opt for a through minibus ticket.

transport bookings, including boats to Phu Quoc and buses to Cambodia. Also arranges Cambodian visas (US$35). Look for the neon 'food & drink' sign.

ℹ Getting There & Away

BOAT

Ferries (p388) to Phu Quoc stop across the river from the town.

Minh Nga (☑ 0297-627 4949; ⊙7am-5pm) has boats to Pirate Island (Hai Tac, 50,000d, one hour) at 8.15am and 1pm, returning at 8.30am and 2.30pm.

BUS

Trang Ngoc Phat (www.taxihatien.vn) runs the most comfortable buses to Rach Gia.

The **bus station** (Ben Xe Ha Tien; Hwy 80) is located in large purpose-built facilities 1.5km south of the bridge, next to a hospital. Buses for HCMC depart between 7am and 10am or between 6pm and 10pm.

Around Ha Tien

Tropical islands, white-sand beaches and an evocative war memorial are within reach of Ha Tien.

◉ Sights

★ Pirate Island   ISLAND
(Quan Dao Ha Tien, Hai Tac) This small speck of an island, covered in lush vegetation and with clear blue waters, has a sordid 500-year history as a pirate haven that only came to an end during reunification in 1975. Today the inhabitants make their living from the sea. A paved motorbike trail circles the island; you can hike up to the hill temple and visit the tranquil beach, and if you come with a Vietnamese speaker, you can arrange to go out with the fishers.

Besides the 2000-or-so inhabitants who reside in the four small, scrappy fishing villages, there's an army base on top of the hill, keeping a vigilant eye out for potential invaders from Cambodia. Rumours of pirate treasure have circulated for years, and in 1983 the army promptly expelled from Vietnam a couple of foreign treasure seekers who arrived illegally by boat from Cambodia, equipped with metal detectors.

The best beach on the island is Bai Bac on the northern coast, which also offers some local beach shacks to feast on fresh seafood. A day trip is possible, but there are now several places to stay, including some basic homestays and guesthouses in the 250,000d-to-500,000d range. Boat trips to nearby islands are available for a negotiable 250,000d. Going out on a fishing boat at night, you may see the sparkly shapes of fish shooting through the water, thanks to the phosphorescence phenomenon.

Minh Nga runs boats to Pirate Island (50,000d, one hour) at 8.15am and 1pm from Ha Tien, returning at 8.30am and 2.30pm.

For more on Pirate Island, see the Vietnam Coracle guide at http://vietnamcoracle.com/pirate-islands-dao-hai-tac-travel-guide.

Mui Nai Beach   BEACH
(Stag's Head Peninsula; person/car 5000/10,000d) The best of the Gulf of Thailand beaches, Mui Nai is 8km west of Ha Tien. The water is incredibly warm and becalmed, so great for taking a dip, and the beach is much improved thanks to several tonnes of sand from Phu Quoc Island, all set beneath a canopy of lofty palms. There are beaches on both sides of the peninsula, lined with simple restaurants and guesthouses. A *xe om* from Ha Tien will cost around 60,000d.

Hon Chong
☑ 0297 / POP 2000

Hon Chong is home to photogenic stone grottoes, cave shrines and what would be the nicest stretch of sand on the delta's mainland if it weren't for the dirty water, polluted by town discharge and rubbish. The road to Hon Chong winds its way past Khmer pagodas, Cao Dai temples, pepper farms, grandiose churches and karst outcrops.

◉ Sights

Duong Beach   BEACH
(Bai Duong; 5000d, incl in Hon Phu Thu Tourist Area fee) Just beyond Hon Chong, a headland road hugs grubby Duong Beach for 3km, passing a **Khmer temple**. The sparse karst rock formations in the sea are unusual, but it's no Halong Bay of Hon Chong, as tour guides like to dress it up. An entrance fee to Hon Phu Tu Tourist Area, comprising Hang Cave Pagoda and Father and Son Isle, is charged at the far end of the beach.

Hang Cave Pagoda   BUDDHIST SITE
(Chua Hang; 5000d, incl in Hon Phu Tu Tourist Area fee; ⊙dawn-dusk) You need to walk through the market at the far end of Duong Beach to reach the cave pagoda, set against the base

of a stony headland. The entry to the cave containing **Hai Son Tu** (Sea Mountain Temple) is inside the pagoda. Visitors light incense and offer prayers here before entering the cool grotto itself, the entrance of which is located behind the altar.

Father & Son Isle   LANDMARK

(Hon Phu Tu; 5000d, incl in Hon Phu Tu Tourist Area fee) From Duong Beach, just beyond Hon Chong village, you can see rocky remnants of Father and Son Isle, several hundred metres offshore. It was said to be shaped like a father embracing his son, but the father was washed away in 2006. Boats can be hired at the shore to row out for a closer look at the orphan remains.

🛏 Sleeping & Eating

Plenty of casual seafood shacks line the beach. Loads of stalls with BBQ oysters vie for your attention inside the Hon Phu Tu Tourist Area.

Green Hill Guesthouse   GUESTHOUSE $

(📞0297-385 4369; www.facebook.com/pg/Green HillGuestHouse; r US$15-25; 🖫) In an imposing villa on the northern headland of Duong Beach, this well-maintained and friendly, family-run place has spacious rooms, including the room of choice on the top floor, plus a garden dripping with greenery.

❶ Getting There & Away

Hon Chong is 32km from Ha Tien towards Rach Gia. The access road branches off the Rach Gia– Ha Tien highway at the small town of Ba Hon. Buses can drop you at Ba Hon, from where you can hire a motorbike to continue the journey to Hon Chong (around 80,000d). A motorbike day tour from Ha Tien will cost around US$15.

Chau Doc

📞0296 / POP 163,000

Draped along the banks of the Hau Giang River (Bassac River), Chau Doc sees plenty of travellers washing through on the river route between Cambodia and Vietnam. A likeable little town with significant Chinese, Cham and Khmer communities, Chau Doc's cultural diversity – apparent in the mosques, temples, churches and nearby pilgrimage sites – makes it fascinating to explore even if you're not Cambodia-bound. Taking a boat trip to the Cham communities across the river, or heading to nearby Sam Mountain and Tra Su Bird Sanctuary are highlights, while

the bustling market and intriguing waterfront provide fine backdrops to a few days of relaxation.

◉ Sights

★**Ba Chuc Tomb**   MEMORIAL

(Nha Mo Ba Chuc; ⊗8am-5pm) FREE Ba Chuc's memorial, 40km south of Chau Doc, stands as a ghastly reminder of the horrors perpetrated by the Khmer Rouge. Between 18 April and 30 April 1978, the Khmer Rouge killed 3157 villagers here, leaving only two survivors. The memorial consists of two parts: the **ossuary** housing the skulls and bones of more than 1100 victims; and the **memorial room** next door, displaying wrenching post-massacre photos.

It's possible to organise a tour from Chau Doc (US$30), or a *xe om* from Ha Tien (75km, 400,000d).

In the ossuary, designed to resemble a flowering lotus, the skulls and bones are divided by age group (including the minute skulls of toddlers and babies) and gender. This collection resembles Cambodia's Choeung Ek killing fields, where thousands of skulls of Khmer Rouge victims are on display, but as it's clean, sterile and well lit, with a spot to leave offerings in the centre, it appears almost cheerful compared to what confronts you next door.

The memorial room showcases the weapons used by the Khmer Rouge (knives, bayonets and cudgels) and sticks used for torture, particularly of women. Many of the Ba Chuc victims were tortured to death. The photos are for strong stomachs only.

The bottoms of walls at the **Phi Lai Tu Temple** behind the memorial room are still stained dark with the blood of the slain; more than 300 villagers were slaughtered inside. The Vietnamese government might have had other motives for invading Cambodia at the end of 1978, but certainly outrage at the Ba Chuc massacre was a major one.

Ba Chuc is 4km south of the road running parallel to the Cambodian border between Ha Tien and Chau Doc. The site was extensively renovated to mark the 40-year commemoration of the massacre in 2018.

Between 1975 and 1978 Khmer Rouge soldiers regularly crossed the border into Vietnam and slaughtered innocent civilians. Over the border, things were even worse, with nearly two million Cambodians killed during the period of Pol Pot's Democratic Kampuchea regime.

MEKONG DELTA CHAU DOC

Chau Doc

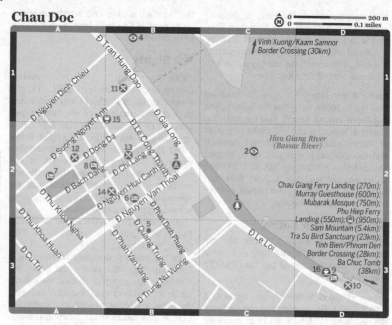

Chau Doc

◎ Sights
1	30 Thang 4 Park	C2
2	Chau Doc Floating Market	C2
3	Chau Phu Temple	B2
4	Floating Houses	B1

◎ Activities, Courses & Tours
5	Mekong Tours	B3

⌂ Sleeping
6	Dai Loi Hotel	B2
7	Hotel Hung Cuong	A2
8	Trung Nguyen Hotel	A2
9	Victoria Chau Doc Hotel	D3

⊗ Eating
10	Bassac Restaurant	D3
11	Bay Bong	B1
12	Cafe Giop Pho	A2
13	Chau Doc Covered Market	B2
14	Thanh Tinh Vegetarian	B2

◎ Drinking & Nightlife
15	Boke Station	B1
	Tan Chau Salon Bar	(see 9)

ⓘ Transport
16	Blue Cruiser	D3
	Hang Chau	(see 16)
	Victoria Speedboat	(see 16)

Floating Houses
HOUSE

(Đ Tran Hung Dao) These rustic houses, the floats of which consist of empty metal drums, are both a place to live and a livelihood for their residents. Under each house, fish are raised in suspended metal nets. The fish flourish in their natural river habitat, and the family can feed them whatever scraps are handy. You can get a close-up look by hiring a tourist boat (p397).

Chau Doc Floating Market
MARKET

(⊘ 5am-noon) You need to get up at the crack of dawn to see the best of this floating market. The action is busiest around 5am to 6am, when locals gather to buy fresh produce wholesale. Less colourful and much calmer than other floating markets in the Mekong Delta.

30 Thang 4 Park
PARK

(Đ Le Loi) Stretching from the main market to the Victoria Chau Doc Hotel, this park is the city's main promenading spot and a superlative area for river gazing. Sculptures and a fountain are framed by manicured lawns and paths, and if you're interested in getting river-borne, women may approach you here offering rides in small boats.

Chau Phu Temple
BUDDHIST TEMPLE

(Dinh Than Nguyen Huu Canh; cnr Đ Nguyen Van Thoai & Đ Gia Long; ☉dawn-dusk) **FREE** This temple was built in 1926 to worship the Nguyen dynasty official Thoai Ngoc Hau, buried at Sam Mountain (p398). The yellow structure is decorated with both Vietnamese and Chinese motifs; inside are funeral tablets bearing the names of the deceased as well as biographical information about them. There's also a shrine to Ho Chi Minh.

Mubarak Mosque
MOSQUE

(Thanh Duong Hoi Giao) The pretty, pastel Mubarak Mosque, where local Cham Muslim children study the Qur'an in Arabic script, is on the riverbank opposite Chau Doc. Visitors are permitted, but you should avoid entering during the calls to prayer (five times daily) unless you are a Muslim. To get there, take the car ferry from Chau Giang ferry landing across the Hau Giang River. From the ferry landing, walk inland from the river for 30m, turn left and walk 50m.

Tuc Dup Hill
HILL

(25,000d) Because of its network of connecting caves, Tuc Dup Hill (216m) served as a strategic base of operations for US soldiers during the American War. *Tuc dup* is Khmer for 'water runs at night' and it is also known locally as 'Two Million Dollar Hill', in reference to the amount of money the Americans sank into securing it.

There isn't much to see (artillery, a view over fields), but you'll pass near it if you're taking the back road through Ba Chuc to Chau Doc.

☞ Tours

Mekong Tours
CULTURAL

(✆098 308 6355; 41 Đ Quang Trung) Local travel agency for booking boat or bus transport to Phnom Penh, boat trips on the Mekong, cars with drivers and day tours. One of the few ways to join a Tra Su Bird Sanctuary group tour (US$12), in comfortable small buses, with pickup from your hotel. Staff speak good English.

Xuan Mai
CULTURAL

(✆0855 8896 11847, 0849 1891 0477; maixuan vn2001@yahoo.com) Friendly English-speaking Mai arranges private tours of the area, either on motorbike or by car. She also makes bookings for speedboat transfers to Cambodia.

⌸ Sleeping

Trung Nguyen Hotel
HOTEL $

(✆0296-356 1561; 86 Đ Bach Dang; s/d 300,000/400,000d; P✳☞) One of the better budget places, with something of a mid-range trim. Rooms are more decorative than the competition, with balconies overlooking the market. It's a busy corner site, so pack earplugs or ask for a room facing the rear. Excellent English spoken.

Dai Loi Hotel
BUSINESS HOTEL $$

(✆0296-356 6619; 68-72 Đ Nguyen Van Thoai; r 450,000-900,000d; ✳☞) This shiny, super-central hotel sparkles with myriad Christmas baubles in the lobby. Rooms are spacious, tiled affairs with firm beds, and the place attracts a mixed crowd of international travellers and Chinese businessmen. English and French spoken.

MEKONG DELTA CHAU DOC

WORTH A TRIP

TRA SU BIRD SANCTUARY

This immense 800,000-hectare **forest** (Rung Tram Tra Su; 120,000d, boat rides per person 75,000d; ☉7am-4pm) is home to an astounding number of wading birds. Much of the wetland is off-limits to visitors so that the birds' breeding grounds are not disturbed, but visits include a short speedboat ride and a tranquil 20-minute paddle along narrow channels through the gnarled and green sunken forest. Even if you only spot a few birds, it's a beautiful, if short, green trip. The sanctuary is 23km west of Chau Doc.

The best time to visit is December to January, when the babies hatch. Motorbike tours from Chau Doc cost around US$20 per person. Group tours organised by Mekong Tours cost US$12 per person, with pickup in comfortable small buses, admission and rides included. While there's a greater likelihood of sharing rowboats on the tour, with three passengers per boat it's hardly a problem.

ⓘ GETTING TO CAMBODIA: CHAU DOC TO PHNOM PENH BY BOAT

Getting to the border One of the most enjoyable ways to enter Cambodia is via the **Vinh Xuong/Kaam Samnor border crossing** just northwest of Chau Doc along the Mekong River. Several companies in Chau Doc sell boat journeys from Chau Doc to Phnom Penh via the Vinh Xuong border. **Hang Chau** (☑ Chau Doc 0296-356 2771, Phnom Penh 855-23 998935; www.hangchautourist.vn; per person $27) boats depart Chau Doc at 7.30am and arrive at 12.30pm. From Phnom Penh they depart at 12.30pm. The more upmarket Blue Cruiser (p398) leaves the Victoria Chau Doc Hotel pier at 7am, costing US$50 (US$44 in the reverse direction, leaving Phnom Penh at 1.30pm). It takes about five hours, including the border check. The price includes a simple lunch and snack. **Victoria Speedboat** (www.victoriahotels.asia/en/victoria-speedboat; Victoria Chau Doc Hotel) is the smartest option to Phnom Penh, departing Chau Doc at 7.30am and Phnom Penh at 1.30pm. It is nearly US$100 per person with taxes, but expect personal service all the way.

At the border If you're coming from Cambodia, arrange a visa in advance, unless you are exempt. Cambodian e-visas are not yet accepted at these land borders. Cambodian visas are available at the crossing, but minor overcharging is common (plan on paying around US$35).

Moving on Hang Chau, Blue Cruiser and Victoria boats take you all the way to Phnom Penh.

Murray Guesthouse　　　GUESTHOUSE $$
(☑0296-356 2108; www.themurrayguesthouse. com; 11 Truong Dinh; d/f from US$32/45; ☺❉🛜) With its walls decorated with indigenous art, collected from around the world by the Kiwi-Vietnamese owners, this wonderful guesthouse outside of the centre sets a high standard. Nice touches include a guest lounge with pool table and bar, a rooftop terrace drowning in greenery, comfortable beds and a tasty *pho* for breakfast. The owners can offer travel advice and loan bicycles.

Hotel Hung Cuong　　　BUSINESS HOTEL $$
(☑0296-356 8111; 96 Đ Dong Da; standard/deluxe 550,000/650,000d; ❉🛜) Stylish modern hotel overlooking a peaceful green square. Rooms come with satellite TV, chic bathrooms and welcome touches of artwork. The Hung Cuong buses to HCMC conveniently depart from just outside the hotel. Rooms facing the front 'benefit' from the ringing of gongs at the temple. Professional, helpful staff speak excellent English.

★ **Victoria Chau Doc Hotel**　　　HOTEL $$$
(☑0296-386 5010; www.victoriahotels.asia; 32 Đ Le Loi; r/ste from US$130/175; ❉🛜≋) Chau Doc's most luxurious option, the Victoria delivers classic colonial charm, overseen by staff clad in *ao dai* (Vietnam's national dress). With a striking riverfront location, the hotel's grand rooms have dark-wood floors and furniture, plus inviting bathtubs. The swimming pool overlooks the busy river and there's a small spa upstairs. A range of tours is available to guests.

🍴 Eating

At night you can try a variety of cool *che* (dessert soups) at *che* stalls around the green square on Đ Bach Dang and Đ Dong Da. There are also lots of other inexpensive food stalls with large whiteboard menus.

Cafe Giop Pho　　　CAFE $
(☑076-626 7888; 86 Đ Dong Da; mains 22,000-85,000d; ☺6am-9pm; ❉🛜) This centrally located cafe is incredibly popular with locals thanks to top coffee creations, cheap international breakfasts and a mash-up of burgers, pizzas and quesadillas. It even serves cocktails to draw an evening crowd.

Thanh Tinh Vegetarian　　　VEGETARIAN $
(Com Chay Tam Tinh; ☑0296-386 5064; 12 Quang Trung; meals 25,000d; ☑) There's vegetarian and then there's exceptional smoky mock chicken, lemongrass tofu and garlic morning glory on a plate with rice, plus a sweet-and-sour soup, for a bargain price. Point and choose from the display out front.

Chau Doc Covered Market　　　VIETNAMESE $
(Cho Chau Doc; Đ Bach Dang; meals 20,000-40,000d; ☺7am-9pm; ☑) Try delicious local specialities, such as grilled glutinous rice

filled with banana, and other stall food in this busy fresh-food market.

Bay Bong VIETNAMESE $
(20 Đ Suong Nguyet Anh; meals 50,000-150,000d; ⊙9am-8pm) This informal spot with metal tables and chairs has so-so service and little is English spoken (but there is an English menu), yet the food is really something, with tasty fish-and-vegetable hotpot, stir-fried rice with seafood, snake-head-fish soup, garlicky morning glory and more.

★**Bassac Restaurant** INTERNATIONAL $$$
(☑0296-386 5010; 32 Đ Le Loi; meals 170,000-450,000d; ⊙6am-10pm; ☑) Chau Doc's most sophisticated dining experience is at the Victoria Chau Doc Hotel where the menu veers between wonderful international dishes (roast rack of lamb, seared duck breast), dishes with a French accent (provençale tart, *gratin dauphinois*) and beautifully presented Vietnamese dishes, such as grilled squid with green peppercorns. The apple pie with cinnamon ice cream makes for a sublime ending.

🍷 Drinking & Nightlife

Tan Chau Salon Bar BAR
(32 Đ Le Loi, Victoria Chau Doc Hotel; ⊙6am-11pm) Sip a cocktail amid elegant Indochine surroundings at this atmospheric bar. The sophisticated establishment is not as expensive as it looks and there's a pool table for some action.

Boke Station CRAFT BEER
(☑090-808 0491; 1 Đ Phan Dinh Phung; ⊙6.30am-10pm; ☎) Cafe by day, serving original Vietnamese coffees brewed by experienced baristas, it turns bar by night and offers a great range of craft beers from Pasteur St and East West in HCMC as well as imports from Belgium, Germany and beyond. The contemporary space is set in a funky old dilapidated shophouse.

❶ Getting There & Away

The most comfortable long-distance buses to Can Tho and HCMC are Phuong Trang (www.futaexpress.com) and the older buses of Hung Cuong. Book tickets in advance through your lodgings. Both companies offer free shuttle buses to your hotel within the city centre in Can Tho; Phuong Trang offers a free shuttle from Mien Tay station to its office in district 10 in HCMC. Enquire when purchasing your ticket and ignore taxi drivers on arrival.

The **bus station** (Ben Xe Chau Doc; Đ Le Loi) is on the eastern edge of town, around 2km out of the centre, where Đ Le Loi becomes Hwy 91. All buses depart from here, with the exception of the Hung Cuong buses to HCMC, which depart from in front of Hotel Hung Cuong. A taxi from the centre to the bus station is 50,000d.

❶ Getting Around

Boats to Chau Giang district (across the Hau Giang River) leave from two docks: vehicle ferries depart from **Chau Giang ferry landing** (Ben Pha Chau Giang), opposite 419 Đ Le Loi; smaller, more-frequent boats leave from **Phu Hiep ferry landing** (Ben Pha FB Phu Hiep), a little further southeast.

Private tourist boats (around 100,000d for two hours), which are rowed standing up, can be hired from either of these spots or from 30 Thang 4 Park (p394), and are highly recommended for seeing the floating houses and visiting nearby Cham minority villages and

MEKONG DELTA CHAU DOC

❶ GETTING TO CAMBODIA: CHAU DOC TO PHNOM PENH BY BUS

Getting to the border Eclipsed by the newer crossing of Xa Xia near Ha Tien, the **Tinh Bien/Phnom Den border crossing** is less convenient for Phnom Penh–bound travellers, but may be of interest to those who savour the challenge of obscure border crossings. A bus to Phnom Penh (US$25, five to six hours) passes through Chau Doc en route from Can Tho at around 7.30am and can be booked through Mekong Tours (p395) in Chau Doc; double-check the pickup point. The roads leading to the border have improved.

At the border Cambodian visas can be obtained here, although you may wish to pay US$35 rather than the official fee of US$30 to be processed quickly. Yes, it's a mild form of extortion, but your time may be more valuable than your money. Cambodian e-visas are not yet accepted at these land borders.

Moving on Most travellers opt for a through bus ticket from Chau Doc.

BUSES FROM CHAU DOC

DESTINATION	COST (D)	TIME (HR)	FREQUENCY	DISTANCE (KM)
Can Tho	65,000	4	hourly	120
Cao Lanh	60,000	3	hourly	90
Ha Tien	60,000	3½-4	5 daily	88
HCMC	105,000-140,000	6-7½	every 30min	245
Long Xuyen	45,000	1½	hourly	62
Vinh Long	80,000	4	hourly	127

mosques. Motorboats (around 250,000d per hour, seat six to eight people) can be hired in the same area. **Blue Cruiser** (☑ HCMC 028-3926 0253, Phnom Penh 855-16 868887; www.blue cruiser.com) charters whole boats.

Sam Mountain

A sacred place for Buddhists, Sam Mountain (Nui Sam, 284m) and its environs are crammed with dozens of pagodas and temples. A strong Chinese influence makes it particularly popular with ethnic Chinese, but Buddhists of all ethnicities visit. Temples at the base and surrounds can show Islamic, Indian and Khmer influences. The views from the top are excellent (weather permitting), ranging deep into Cambodia. There's a military outpost on the summit, a legacy of the days when the Khmer Rouge made cross-border raids and massacred Vietnamese civilians.

◎ Sights

★ **Cavern Pagoda**   BUDDHIST TEMPLE
(Chua Hang; ⊘ 4am-9pm) FREE Also known as Phuoc Dien Tu, this temple is halfway up the western (far) side of Sam Mountain, with amazing views of the surrounding countryside. The lower part of the pagoda includes monks' quarters and two hexagonal tombs in which the founder of the pagoda, a female tailor named Le Thi Tho, and a former head monk, Thich Hue Thien, are buried. The upper section has two parts: the main sanctuary, and an astounding complex of caverns and grottoes.

The main sanctuary features the statues of A Di Da (the Buddha of the Past) and Thich Ca Buddha (Sakyamuni, the Historical Buddha), while in the caverns and grottoes you'll find a host of deities, including a 1000-arm and 1000-eye Quan Am. There's also a mirror room of Buddhas and an effigy of Bodhidharma, the founder of Zen Buddhism.

According to legend, Le Thi Tho came from Tay An Pagoda to this site half a century ago to lead a quiet, meditative life. When she arrived, she found two enormous cobras, one white and the other dark green. Le Thi Tho soon converted the snakes, which thereafter led pious lives. Upon her death, the snakes disappeared, but remain in statue form in one of the dark cavern passages.

Tay An Pagoda   BUDDHIST TEMPLE
(Chua Tay An; ⊘ 4am-10pm) FREE Founded in 1847 on the site of an earlier shrine, Tay An's current structure dates from 1958. Aspects of its eclectic architecture, particularly its domed tower, reflect Hindu and Islamic influences. Its main gate is of traditional Vietnamese design, and on its roofline romp figures of lions and two dragons fighting for possession of pearls, chrysanthemums and lotus blossoms. Coming from Chau Doc on Hwy 91, Tay An Pagoda is located straight ahead at the foot of the mountain.

The temple itself is guarded by statues of a black elephant with two tusks and a white elephant with six tusks. Inside are arrayed fine carvings of hundreds of religious figures, most made of wood and some blinged up with disco-light halos. Statues include Sakyamuni, the 18 *a-la-han* (arhat) and the 12 *muoi hai ba mu* (midwives). The temple's name, Tay An, means 'Western Peace'.

Temple of Lady Xu   BUDDHIST TEMPLE
(Mieu Ba Chua Xu; ⊘ 24hr) FREE Founded in the 1820s to house a statue of Lady Xu that's become the subject of a popular cult, this large temple faces Sam Mountain, on the same road as Tay An Pagoda. Originally a simple affair of bamboo and leaves, the temple has been rebuilt many times, blending mid-20th-century design with Vietnamese Buddhist decorative motifs and plenty of neon.

Tomb of Thoai Ngoc Hau   TOMB
(Lang Thoai Ngoc Hau; ⊘ 5am-10.30pm) FREE A high-ranking official, Thoai Ngoc Hau (1761–1829) served the Nguyen Lords and,

later, the Nguyen dynasty. In early 1829 Thoai Ngoc Hau ordered that a fine tomb be constructed for himself at the foot of Sam Mountain. The site he chose is nearly opposite the Temple of Lady Xu.

The steps are made of red 'beehive' stone *(da ong)*. In the middle of the platform is the tomb of Thoai Ngoc Hau and those of his wives, Chau Thi Te and Truong Thi Miet. There's a shrine at the rear and several dozen other tombs in the vicinity where his officials are buried.

🛏 Sleeping

⭐ **Victoria Nui Sam Lodge**   LODGE **$$$**
(☑ 0296-357 5888; www.victoriahotels.asia/en/ hotels-resorts/nuisam; Sam Mountain; standard/ deluxe/f from 1,450,000/1,650,000/2,400,000d; ❄ @ 🛜 ☒) Set imperiously on the slopes of Sam Mountain, this rustic lodge wouldn't look out of place in the Alps. Rooms are simply yet tastefully furnished with four-poster beds and include balcony terraces for sunset views over the rice fields. The restaurant-bar has prime position at the top of the resort and includes a private dining pavilion for two.

❶ Getting There & Away

Many people get here by rented motorbike or on the back of a xe om (about 50,000d one way from Chau Doc). The best way is to hire a xe om driver to take you, wait and return (about 120,000d). Even without speaking much English, they are used to this arrangement and know you want to see all the temples. Drivers wait outside most hotels, and staff can help you negotiate. The main road to Sam Mountain is one of the widest boulevards in the delta and lined with an impressive variety of stone sculptures.

A rewarding way to get here is to rent a bicycle in Chau Doc and take the smaller road that runs towards the Cambodian border through peaceful rice-paddy scenery. You will have to park your bike and walk from the mountain base.

Walking down is easier than walking up (a not particularly scenic 45-minute climb), so you can get a motorbike to drop you at the summit (about 30,000d from the base of the mountain). The road to the top runs along the east side of the mountain – when driving here, veer left at the base of the mountain and turn right after about 1km where the road begins its climb.

Long Xuyen

☑ 0296 / POP 385,000

The capital of An Giang province has little to detain travellers, especially since Can Tho and Chau Doc are an easy bus ride away. Long Xuyen was once a stronghold of the Hoa Hao sect. Founded in 1939, the sect emphasises simplicity in worship and does not believe in temples or intermediaries between humans and the Supreme Being. Until 1956

Long Xuyen

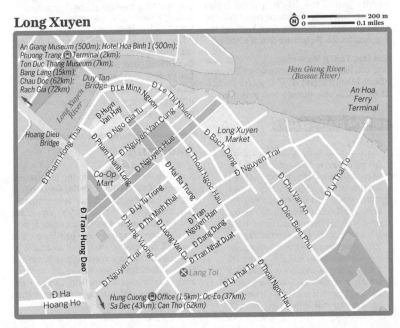

the Hoa Hao had an army and constituted a major military force in this region.

The town's other claim to fame is being the birthplace of Vietnam's second president, Ton Duc Thang, whose childhood home on Tiger Island has become a museum. The An Giang Museum is also well worth a look.

◉ Sights

Bang Lang Stork Garden
BIRD SANCTUARY

(Vuon Co Bang Lang; 10,000d; ⊙5am-6pm) On the road between Can Tho and Long Xuyen, this magnificent 1.3-hectare bird sanctuary has astonishing views of thousands of resident storks and snowy egrets. There is a tall viewing platform to see the birds filling the branches. The best times to view this incredible sight are around dawn and dusk.

Bang Lang is 15km southeast of Long Xuyen, and 46km northwest of Can Tho. A *xe om* from Long Xuyen is about 300,000d for the round trip, including wait time. Otherwise join a tour in Can Tho or jump on a bus to Thoi An hamlet and then a *xe om*.

An Giang Museum
MUSEUM

(Nha Bao Tang An Giang; 11 Đ Ton Duc Thang; 15,000d; ⊙7.30-11am & 1.30-5pm Tue-Sun) Even though the signage is in Vietnamese only, the upstairs exhibition on the Oc-Eo culture is well worth a look, with pottery, fine gold jewellery and a huge lingam (Hindu phallus) forming part of the display. The exhibition on Cham culture is also interesting, while the usual displays on the American War and the war against the French are less absorbing.

Ton Duc Thang Museum
MUSEUM

(Khu Luu Niem Bac Ton Duc Thang; off Đ Nguyen Hue; ⊙7-11am & 1-5pm) FREE If you're a scholar of Vietnamese history, you may wish to visit My Hoa Hung village on Tiger Island, birthplace and childhood home of Ho Chi Minh's successor, Ton Duc Thang. The museum showcases various personal effects, including the leg irons he was clapped in when serving his 16 years in Con Dao prison for plotting against the French.

Take the ferry from Ben Pha O Moi at the end of Đ Nguyen Hue and walk up the road.

🛏 Sleeping & Eating

Hotel Hoa Binh 1
HOTEL $

(✉ 0296-625 0436; http://hoabinhhotel.vn; 130 Đ Tran Hung Dao; r from 350,000d; ❄ 🛜) Large rooms with wooden floors, friendly service and a decent breakfast served on the roof terrace make this large hotel a good overnight option, and popular for wedding receptions.

Lang Toi
SEAFOOD $$

(✉ 0296-372 7727; 33 Đ Tran Nhat Duat; meals from 100,000d; ⊙11am-10pm) Ultra-fresh fish and seafood are served grilled and steamed with a variety of sauces at this professional restaurant. Pick your dinner from the fish tanks.

❶ Getting There & Away

The most comfortable buses to HCMC, Can Tho and Chau Doc are Phuong Trang (www.futa express.com) and Hung Cuong which both depart from their own respective terminals. The Phuong Trang terminal is around 2.5km north of central Long Xuyen; the Hung Cuong office is about 1.5km south of the centre, on the main highway Đ Tran Hung Dao.

There are hourly bus services to the following destinations:

Can Tho (50,000d, 1½ hours, 62km)

Cao Lanh (50,000d, 1½ hours, 46km)

Chau Doc (45,000d, 1½ hours, 62km)

HCMC (135,000d, 5 hours, 187km)

Rach Gia (85,000d, 2 hours, 72km)

OC-EO

During the 1st to 6th centuries CE, when southern Vietnam and southern Cambodia were under the rule of the Indian-influenced Cambodian kingdom of Funan, Oc-Eo (Hwy 943), 37km southwest of Long Xuyen, was a major trading city and important port. In the late 1990s the site was excavated, uncovering skeletons in burial vases, elaborate gold jewellery, weaponry, a wealth of pottery and more. Little remains except building foundations, but it's a beautiful backcountry ride to get there.

Cao Lanh

✍ 0277 / POP 160,000

A newish town carved from the jungles and swamps of the Mekong Delta, Cao Lanh is big for business, but draws few tourists – you may double the foreigner population just by turning up. Cao Lanh's main appeal is as a base to explore Xeo Quyt Forest and Tram Chim National Park, both reachable by boat, but it's also a surprisingly walkable city that's refreshingly untouched by tourism. Pack some mosquito repellent, as Cao Lanh has a higher incidence of dengue fever than other Mekong Delta towns.

Cao Lanh

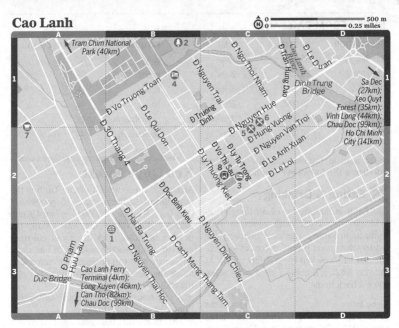

Sights

Van Thanh Mieu PARK

At the heart of the city and encompassing a temple and lake with a topiary outline of Vietnam in the middle, this lush park is a wonderful place to observe local life: from early-morning exercise on the strange-looking contraptions, to the twinkling lights after dark when lovers gather on the benches around the lake, staring at the water and keeping physical contact to a minimum.

Dong Thap Museum MUSEUM

(162 Đ Nguyen Thai Hoc; ⊙ 7.30-11.30am & 1.30-5pm) **FREE** The Dong Thap Museum is among the Mekong's best museums, despite having only limited English captions. The ground floor of the handsome building displays an anthropological history of Dong Thap province, with exhibits of tools, sculptures, models of traditional houses and a few stuffed animals and pickled fish. Upstairs is devoted to war history and Ho Chi Minh.

Sleeping

Hoa Anh HOTEL **$**

(☎ 0277-224 0567; hoaanhhotel@yahoo.com.vn; 38 Đ Ly Tu Trong; d/tw/tr 250,000/300,000/400,000d; 🅿🛜) For the cheapest price you'll

get a tidy, smallish double with a bathroom at this fresh-faced hotel near the bus station. The two-bed rooms are spacious, while the triple rooms can fit a family.

Huong Sen Hotel BUSINESS HOTEL **$$**

(☎ 091 945 3128; 18 Đ Vo Truong Toan; r 700,000d; 🅿🛜) The smartest of Cao Lanh's lodgings and the tallest building in town, Huong Sen overlooks the appealing Van Thanh Mieu park. Rooms are compact with firm beds but comfortable enough, some staff

BUSES FROM CAO LANH

DESTINATION	COST (D)	TIME	FREQUENCY	DISTANCE (KM)
Can Tho	55,000	2¼hr	daily	82
Chau Doc	60,000	3½hr	hourly	99
HCMC	105,000	3½hr	hourly	141
Long Xuyen	50,000	2hr	hourly	46
Sa Dec	15,000	45min	several daily	27
Vinh Long	40,000	1¼hr	several daily	44

speak a little English and the adjoining cafe-bar is the town's evening hotspot.

✖ Eating & Drinking

Cao Lanh is famous for *chuot dong* (rice-field rats), so come with room in your stomach to sample the local delicacy; the tender white meat is reminiscent of – you've guessed it! – chicken (or possibly quail). At the very least, it'll make a great story when you get back home.

Ngoc Lan   VIETNAMESE $
(☑0277-385 1498; 210 Đ Nguyen Hue; dishes from 45,000đ; ☺8am-8pm) The 'Magnolia' is a bright and inviting choice, with fresh and tasty pot-cooked pork and mixed-vegetable soup. There is plenty of outdoor seating for warm evenings. It's illuminated with a red-and-green LED sign at night.

Spicy Noodles MYM   NOODLES $
(Mi Cay MYM; ☑0277-388 7077; 224 Đ Nguyen Hue; meals 18,000-99,000đ; ☺4-8pm) Yes, this Korean-fusion cafe's speciality is spicy, thick rice and tapioca noodles in a crab soup with grilled shrimp, fish cakes and pork, a kimchi take on Vietnamese *banh can cua*. Other Korean numbers include *gimbap* (sushi), *tteokbokki* (rice cakes in sweet chilli sauce), lemongrass fried chicken and dessert drinks.

Cau Vua Coffee   COFFEE
(cnr Nguyen Thi Luu & Thien Ho Duong; ☺7.30am-9pm; 🕾) With a leafy green courtyard, comfy chairs on the patio and a tranquil water feature, this is one of the nicest cafes in which to savour a *ca phe sua da* (iced coffee with condensed milk).

❶ Getting There & Away

Cao Lanh Bus Station (Ben Xe Cao Lanh; 71/1 Đ Ly Thuong Kiet) is conveniently located in the centre of town.

Xeo Quyt Forest

Around 35km southeast of Cao Lanh is the magnificent 52-hectare Xeo Quyt Forest (Xeo Quyt, Xeo Quit; 20,000đ; ☺7am-4.30pm) near My Hiep village. One vast swamp beneath a beautiful thick canopy of tall trees and vines, it hides the remains of Viet Cong bunkers, which can be seen on a canoe tour inside the forest and on foot along the walking trails.

A taxi from Cao Lanh, including waiting time, costs around 800,000đ.

For much of the year, a marvellous 20-minute canoe tour (15,000đ) takes you past old bunkers and former minefields along a narrow canal loop choked with *luc binh* (water hyacinths) beneath the forest canopy. It's an exquisite experience, but splash on the repellent. A walking trail parallels the canal and allows you to duck into the Z- and L-shaped VC bunkers (if you're compact enough) and to admire the expertly hidden, tiny trapdoors through which the VC disappeared underground.

During the American War the VC had a base here, where top-brass VC lived in underground bunkers. Only about 10 VC were present at any given time; they were all generals who directed the war from here, just 2km from a US military base. The Americans never realised the VC generals were living right under their noses. Naturally they were suspicious about the patch of forest and periodically dropped some bombs on it to reassure themselves, but the VC remained safe in their hideouts.

Sa Dec

☑0277 / POP 215,000

The drowsy former capital of Dong Thap province, Sa Dec is a comparatively peaceful city of tree-lined streets and fading colonial villas, ringed with orchards and flower markets. Lining the waterways are flower **nurseries** (Cong Laang Hoa Sa Dec, Vuon Hoa; ⊙7am-5pm) `FREE` you can visit, which are especially popular just before Tet for witnessing a riot of blooms loaded onto boats.

The town's biggest attraction (though it'll only take up about 20 minutes of your time) is the **Huynh Thuy Le Old House** (Nha Co Huynh Thuy Le; ☑093-953 3523; 225a Đ Nguyen Hue; 30,000d; ⊙8am-5pm). This fascinating 1895 riverfront residence of Sino-French design was a setting for the film adaptation of *The Lover* by Jean-Jacques Annaud. Other locations seen in the film include Le's grave and pagoda, and the school where the mother of Marguerite Duras, author of *The Lover,* taught.

🛏 Sleeping & Eating

Thao Ngan Hotel HOTEL $
(☑0277-377 4255; 4 An Duong Vuong; r from 250,000d; ❄🌐) The cleanest and nicest of the local hotels is very centrally located near the market and one of the receptionists speaks good English. The shower cubicles make a nice change at this budget to avoid the all-too-common occurrence of bathroom flooding.

Phuong Nam HOTEL $
(☑0277-386 7867; www.khachsanphuongnam. com; 384a Đ Nguyen Sinh Sac; r 250,000-500,00d; ❄🌐) This decent minihotel is on the main road. Rooms are tiled, clean and have standard-issue, firm Vietnamese beds. The staff are friendly and speak some English.

Night Market VIETNAMESE $
(Đ Nguyen Hue; meals around 50,000d; ⊙5-10pm) The hopping riverside night market has a lively string of hotpot restaurants, as well as stalls selling all manner of grilled things.

Quan Com Thuy VIETNAMESE $
(☑0277-386 1644; 439 Đ Hung Vuong; mains 50,000-90,000d; ⊙9am-9pm) This reputable meat-and-rice joint offers aluminium furniture, bright lights and a menu of local specialities, such as clay-pot eel with rice.

❶ Getting There & Away

From the **bus station** (Ben Xe Sa Dec; Hwy 80) behind the hospital, frequent buses leave for Ho Chi Minh City (60,000d to 95,000d, three hours, hourly), Vinh Long (15,000d, one hour, several daily) and Cao Lanh (15,000d, 45 minutes, several daily).

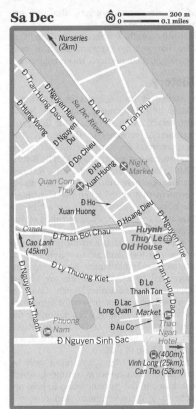

Sa Dec

Con Dao Islands

☑0254 / POP 7400

Isolated from the mainland, the Con Dao islands are one of Vietnam's star attractions. Long the preserve of political prisoners and undesirables, they now turn heads thanks to their striking natural beauty. Con Son, the largest of the chain of 15 islands and islets, is ringed with lovely beaches, coral reefs and scenic bays, and remains partially covered in tropical forests. In addition to hiking, diving and exploring deserted coastal roads, there are excellent wildlife-watching opportunities, with animals such as the black giant squirrel and endemic bow-fingered gecko.

Although it seems an island paradise, Con Son was once hell on earth for the thousands of prisoners who languished in a dozen jails during French rule and the American-backed regime. Many Vietnamese visitors are former soldiers who were imprisoned on the island.

Until recently, few foreigners visited Con Dao, but with the commencement of inexpensive boat connections, this is changing.

History

Occupied at various times by the Khmer, Malay and Vietnamese, Con Son Island also served as an early base for European commercial ventures in the region. The first recorded European arrival was a ship of Portuguese mariners in 1560. The British East India Company maintained a fortified trading post here from 1702 to 1705 – an experiment that ended when the English on the island were massacred in a revolt by the Makassar soldiers they had recruited on the Indonesian island of Sulawesi.

Con Son Island has a strong political and cultural history, and an all-star line-up of Vietnamese revolutionary heroes were incarcerated here (many streets are named after them). Under the French, Con Son was used as a major prison for opponents of colonialism, earning a reputation for routine mistreatment and torture of prisoners. National heroine Vo Thi Sau (p406) was executed here in 1952.

In 1954 the island was taken over by the South Vietnamese government, which continued to use its remoteness to hold opponents of the government (including students) in horrendous conditions.

During the American War, the South Vietnamese were joined here by US forces. The US built prisons and maintained the notorious 'tiger cages' as late as 1970, when news of their existence was broken by a *Life* magazine report.

Increasing numbers of settlers from the mainland and a buoyant tourist sector in recent years are leading to population and environmental pressures.

ℹ When to Go

The driest time to visit Con Dao is from November to February, though the seas are at their calmest from March to July.

The rainy season lasts from June to September, and there are northeast and southwest monsoons from September to November that can bring heavy winds.

September and October are the hottest months, though even then the cool island breezes make Con Dao relatively comfortable.

ℹ Getting There & Away

You've a choice of ferry or plane; book ahead if travelling on a weekend.

AIR

There are several daily flights between Con Son and HCMC (one way US$78), jointly operated by **Vasco** (Map p408; ☑ 038-330 330; www.vasco.com.vn; Đ Ton Duc Thang) and Vietnam Airlines (www.vietnamairlines.com). Con Son is also connected to Can Tho in the Mekong Delta by a daily Vasco/Vietnam Airlines flight (from US$60 one way).

The tiny **Con Dao Airport** (Cỏ Ống Airport; Map p405; ☑ 090-383 1540) is 14km from the town centre. Big hotels provide free transport to and from the airport. Smaller hotels and guesthouses use a shared minibus service (50,000d one-way, book ahead via your accommodation); this includes drop-offs and pickups.

BOAT

Sea connections are not reliable to Con Dao; sailings on all routes are frequently cancelled in heavy seas. All boats leave and depart from Ben Dam port on Con Son.

Superdong (Map p405; ☑ 029-9384 3888; www.superdong.com.vn; Ben Dam port) schedules one daily ferry at 7am or 8am from Tran De, Soc Trang province in the Mekong Delta (adult/child 310,000/220,000d, 2½ hours). It returns from Ben Dam at either 1pm or 2.30pm. This crossing can be rough as the vessel is not large.

There are also **ancient ferries** (Map p408; off Đ Nguyen Hue; ⊙ 7.30-11am & 2-5pm Mon-Sat) connecting Con Son Island with Vung Tau (seats/sleeper berths 200,000/330,000d), with sailings roughly every three days. Facilities are very basic. Boats depart from Ben Dam port at 5pm, taking around 12 hours, and returning from Vung Tau at 5pm.

Ferry tickets can be purchased from travel agents and from an office near Con Son market – look out for the sign on Đ Vo Thi Sau that reads **BQL Cang Ben Dam Huyen Con Dao** (Map p408; ☑ 0254-383 0619; Đ Vo Thi Sau; ⊙ 8-11.30am & 1-5pm).

Shuttle buses (50,000d per person) meet boats and connect Ben Dam with Con Son town. A taxi costs about 260,000d.

Con Son Town

There's nowhere quite like it in all Vietnam. This delightful, pocket-sized island capital, with its litter-free streets, well-kept municipal buildings and air of calm and prosperity, would make a perfect location for a period film.

Con Dao Islands

The main seafront promenade of Đ Ton Duc Thang is a delight to stroll, lined with French-era villas, some crumbling and others renovated as boutique hotels. Nearby is the local market (p410), busiest between 7am and 9am.

Of course, the town's genteel appearance and character is tempered considerably by the presence of several prisons, cemeteries and reminders of the island's historic role as a penal colony. There are ghosts everywhere in Con Son.

◉ Sights

All the former prisons in and around Con Son town share the same opening hours and are covered by a single ticket costing 40,000d. You can purchase this ticket in the Bao Tang Con Dao Museum, which is the logical place to get some historical context before you start a tour of the prisons.

Con Dao Islands

Tiger Cages   HISTORIC BUILDING
(Map p408; off Đ Nguyen Hue; joint ticket 40,000d; ⏰7-11.30am & 1-5pm) The notorious cells dubbed 'tiger cages' were built in 1940 by

the French to incarcerate nearly 2000 political prisoners; the USA continued using them in the 1960s and 1970s. There are 120 chambers with ceiling bars, where guards could poke at prisoners like tigers in a Victorian-era zoo. Prisoners were beaten with sticks from above, and sprinkled with quicklime and water (which burnt their skin and caused blindness).

The tiger cages were deliberately constructed away from the main prison, out of sight, and only accessed by an alleyway. They were unknown to the outside world until 1970, when a US congressional aide, Tom Harkin, visited Con Son and saw evidence of the brutal torture of the prisoners he met there. Harkin had been tipped off about their existence by a former inmate and managed to break away from the pre-arranged tour. Using a map given to him, he discovered the tiger cages behind a vegetable garden, and photographed the cells and prisoners inside. The images were published by Life magazine in July 1970.

Phu Hai Prison   HISTORIC BUILDING

(Map p408; off Đ Ton Duc Thang; joint ticket 40,000d; ⊘ 7-11.30am & 1-5pm) The largest of the 11 jails on the island, this prison dates from 1862. Thousands of prisoners were held here, with up to 200 prisoners crammed into each detention building. During the French era, all prisoners were kept naked and chained together in rows, with one small box serving as a toilet for hundreds. One can only imagine the squalor and stench. Today, emaciated mannequins that are all too lifelike re-create the era.

It's a huge complex, where political and criminal classes were mixed together. 'Solitary' rooms, for prisoners considered to be particularly dangerous, contained as many as 63 inmates, herded together so tightly there was no room to lie down. The prison church dates from the US era, but it was never used.

Bao Tang Con Dao Museum   MUSEUM

(Map p408; Đ Nguyen Hue; 10,000d; ⊘ 7-5pm Mon-Sat) This impressive museum has more than 2000 exhibits, including many rare documents, dioramas and excellent photographs, which comprehensively record the island's history, including the French colonial era and of course the 'prison period'. Modern displays, including audiovisuals, are used. Entrance is free with the 40,000d Con Dao sights ticket.

Hang Duong Cemetery   CEMETERY

(Map p405) Some 20,000 Vietnamese prisoners died on Con Son and 1994 of their graves can be seen at the peaceful Hang Duong Cemetery, located at the northeastern edge of town. Sadly, only 700 of these graves bear the name of the victim interred within.

Vietnam's most famous heroine, Vo Thi Sau, was buried here. On 23 January 1952, she was the first woman executed by a firing squad in Con Son.

In the distance behind the cemetery, you'll see a huge monument symbolising three giant sticks of incense.

Van Son Temple   BUDDHIST PAGODA

(Map p405; ⊘ 6am-8pm) FREE This large hilltop temple complex, 1km southwest of the

---

THE TEENAGE MARTYR

If the breeze is blowing from the north, you can probably smell the incense from a specific grave in Con Son's Hang Duong Cemetery: the tomb of Vo Thi Sau, a national icon.

Vo Thi Sau, a teenage resistance fighter during the French occupation, was politically active from a very early age. She killed a French captain in a grenade attack at the age of 14, and was only captured years later following a second assassination attempt. She was taken to Con Son and executed here, aged 19.

Today's pilgrims come to burn incense and leave offerings at her tomb, such as mirrors, combs and lipstick (symbolic because she died so young). You may even encounter fruit and meals of sticky rice and pork.

Visit the cemetery at midnight and you'll find crowds of people packed around her grave, saying prayers and making offerings. The Vietnamese believe this is the most auspicious time to pay respects and venerate the spirit of this national heroine, who was killed in the early hours of 23 January 1952.

There's also a statue of Vo Thi Sau outside the police headquarters, and the small Museum Vo Thi Sau (Map p408; Đ Le Duan; joint ticket 40,000d; ⊘ 7-11am & 1.30-5pm) dedicated to her in in Con Dao town.

town centre, enjoys fine views over Con Son town and islands offshore to an ocean-filled horizon. A steep staircase (of more than 100 steps) leads up to the traditionally designed pagoda structures, each supported by thick wooden columns and topped with an elaborate tiled roof.

Revolutionary Museum
MUSEUM

(Map p408; Đ Ton Duc Thang; ⊘7-11am & 1.30-5pm) FREE Located in the former French commandant's residence, this museum has exhibits on Vietnamese resistance against the French, communist opposition to the Republic of Vietnam and the treatment of political prisoners. You'll also find a painting of Vo Thi Sau (facing death with her head held high) and some stuffed wildlife: boas, lizards and monkeys.

Phu Binh Camp
HISTORIC BUILDING

(Map p405; joint ticket 40,000d; ⊘7-11.30am & 1-5pm) On the northeastern edge of town, this prison was built in 1971 by the Americans, and had 384 chambers. The cells had corrugated-iron roofs, and were infernally hot. The original structures remain in situ, but there's not that much left to see today. It was known as Camp 7 until 1973, when it closed following evidence of torture.

After the Paris Agreements in 1973, the name was changed to Phu Binh Camp.

🏃 Activities & Tours

For more information on treks and boat trips around the Con Dao Islands, drop by the national park headquarters (p411), just northwest of Con Son town. It costs 60,000d to enter the park by day or 100,000d by night.

Note that some environmentalists in Con Dao were recommending that travellers *do not* join turtle tours in protest at what they see as the inaction of national park staff in protecting nesting turtles, and their eggs, from poachers. If you do decide to go, overnight turtle-watching tours cost around 1,400,000d per person (based on two people; less if there are more of you), which includes an English-speaking guide but not the hire of a boat.

A 50% discount is offered if turtles are not spotted. Bookings can only be made through the national park office. Nesting turtles are very rarely seen outside the main season (from late June to early September).

★ Kitty's Tours
TOURS

(Map p405; ☑090-990 2012; www.facebook.com/tripswithkitty; Mai Homestay, Huynh Thuc Khang; half-day tour per person from 400,000d) Kitty is a Con Son native who is passionate about her island, speaks good English and leads excellent tours. She's highly informed about local sealife, botany and culture. Exact prices depend on numbers; snorkelling trips (including boat hire) start at 800,000d per person.

Hiking

There are lots of treks around Con Son Island, as much of the interior remains heavily forested. A permit is necessary – acquire one at the national park headquarters (p411) – to enter the national park. On some of the longer hikes a guide (200,000d to 300,000d) is mandatory as well.

Bamboo Lagoon
HIKING

(Dam Tre; Map p405) One of the more beautiful walks on the island leads through thick forest and mangroves, past a hilltop stream to Bamboo Lagoon. There's good snorkelling in the bay and you may encounter black squirrels and monkeys en route. The 1½-hour trek starts from near the airport runway. You'll need a permit (from the national-park headquarters), and the first part of the walk (along Vong beach) is very exposed so pack sun cream. A guide is not mandatory.

So Ray Plantation
HIKING

(Map p405) It's a steep climb to the old fruit plantations of So Ray, following a slippery but well-marked trail (lined with information panels about trees and wildlife) through dense rainforest. The former plantation buildings are home to a sociable troop of long-tailed macaques and offer sweeping views over Con Son Town to the other Con Dao islands beyond.

The return hike takes about 1½ hours. A permit is necessary for this hike, but a guide is not mandatory.

Ong Dung Bay
HIKING

(Map p405) The stiff hike (about 20 minutes each way) through rainforest down to Ong Dung Bay begins 2.5km northwest of town; you pass **Ma Thien Lanh Bridge** (Map p405) on the way to the trail. The bay has only a rocky beach, though there is a coral reef about 300m offshore. Snorkelling gear (70,000d) is available from a shoreside lodge, and boat trips to Tre Nho Island can

Con Son

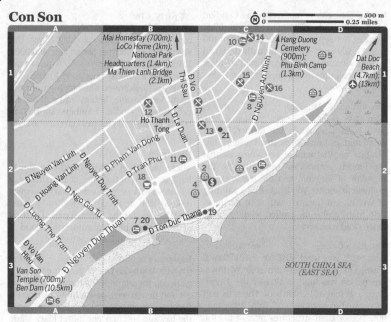

Con Son

◎ Sights
1 Bao Tang Con Dao Museum	D1
2 Museum Vo Thi Sau	C2
3 Phu Hai Prison	C2
4 Revolutionary Museum	B2
5 Tiger Cages	D1

⊕ Activities, Courses & Tours
Con Dao Dive Center	(see 12)

🛏 Sleeping
6 Con Dao Resort	A3
7 Nha Nghi Thanh Xuan	B3
8 Red Hotel	C1
9 Saigon Con Dao Resort	C2
10 Trung Hau Hotel	C1
11 Villa Maison Con Dao Boutique Hotel	B2

✕ Eating
12 Bar200 Con Dao	B1
13 Con Son Market	C2
14 Gia Minh	C1
15 Infiniti Cafe & Lounge	C1
16 Night Market	C1
17 Thu Ba	B1
Villa Maison Con Dao Restaurant	(see 11)

◎ Drinking & Nightlife
18 Cafe Le Condor	B2

ⓘ Transport
19 BQL Cang Ben Dam Huyen Con Dao	C2
20 Vasco	B3
21 Vung Tau Ferry Ticket Office	C2

sometimes be arranged. A permit is not necessary for this hike.

Diving & Snorkelling

Experienced divers who know the waters of Vietnam have long talked up Con Dao as the most pristine marine environment in the country. The waters around the islands are officially protected, and there's abundant healthy coral (table, staghorn and brain corals are all in evidence). Marine life includes green and hawksbill turtles, rays, triggerfish, parrotfish, groupers, cuttlefish and the odd shark.

That said, things could be even better, as official protection is weak. Some skippers still anchor directly on the reef, and illegal fishing affects fish numbers. Every day dive schools clear discarded nets and garbage from reefs.

Diving is possible year-round, but for ideal conditions and good visibility, February to

June is considered the best time, while November and December can see big storms. Rates (around US$160 for two dives, including all equipment) are generally more expensive than at mainland destinations, but the experience is also more rewarding.

Wrecks, including a 65m freighter resting in 30m to 40m with abundant sea life, offer huge potential for more experienced divers.

Cheapo snorkelling excursions are offered by some hotels and freelance guides, but we've heard reports of illegal spearfishing on some of these trips. Dive schools' excursions do cost more, but are environmentally sound.

Con Dao Dive Center   DIVING
(Map p408; ☑️090-3700 8483; http://dive condao.com; Bar200, Đ Nguyen Van Linh; ⏱️7.30am-10pm Feb-Oct) Offers instruction and courses under the PADI umbrella (Open Water is US$550), fun dives (two-dive trips US$160), snorkelling and freediving trips. Owner Rhys is happy to chat about diving options and things to do on Con Dao. The centre is based at Bar200 (p410).

🛏️ Sleeping

There are plenty of guesthouses and minihotels in Con Son town, and even a hostel. Things get busy on weekends, however, when you should book ahead. Options elsewhere on Con Son Island are extremely limited, and none of the others islands have places to stay.

Con Dao is pricey: rates are roughly double what you'd expect to pay on the mainland.

CON SON TOWN

★Mai Homestay   HOMESTAY $
(Map p405; ☑️096-862 0290; www.facebook.com/pg/maihomestaycondao; Huynh Thuc Khang; d 550,000d; ❄️🛜) Very friendly glass-fronted homestay located near the national-park office. Its eight lovely rooms have nice touches, including vintage-style tiling and a dash of art on the walls. There's a guest kitchen and areas in which to chill. The owner, Kitty, was born and raised in Con Dao, runs great island tours (p407) and dispenses excellent travel advice.

LoCo Home   HOSTEL $
(Map p405; ☑️097-996 4089; https://loco-home-vung-tau-vn.book.direct; Đ Le Van Luong, off Đ Huynh Thuc Khang; dm US$8, r from US$22; ❄️🛜) Popular hostel-style spot with choice of female or male dorms (with shared bathrooms) or attractive, light private rooms with terrace and en suite; all accommodation is air-conditioned. It's run by a welcoming couple who offer fishing, snorkelling and camping trips. There's a guest kitchen, free drinking water and breakfast.

Nha Nghi Thanh Xuan   GUESTHOUSE $
(Map p408; ☑️0254-383 0261, 0169 246 2751; 44 Đ Ton Duc Thang; r 365,000-500,000d; 🛜) Painted in marine blue, this guesthouse has rooms with good mattresses; the upstairs options are light and airy. The owners speak little or no English.

Con Dao Resort   HOTEL $$
(Map p408; ☑️0254-383 0939; http://condao resort.vn; 8 Đ Nguyen Duc Thuan; r US$66-100; ❄️@🛜🏊) This hotel faces an invitingly sandy beach, has a large swimming pool and boasts a quiet setting. Rooms are spacious and comfortable; splash out for a sea view. Staff are sweet, and breakfast is mainly Vietnamese fare.

Red Hotel   HOTEL $$
(Map p408; ☑️096-673 0079; http://red-vn.book. direct; 17b Đ Nguyen An Ninh; r from US$24; ❄️🛜) This minihotel has a choice of rooms with hot-water en suites (though expect hard mattresses) and is close to the night market and plenty of eating options. Staff speak limited English but are eager to help and can source rental scooters for exploring the island and organise boat trips.

Trung Hau Hotel   GUESTHOUSE $$
(Map p408; ☑️0254-350 8869; 7 Đ Nguyen Van Linh; r 550,000-750,000d; ❄️🛜) This minihotel has air-conditioned rooms that are in fine shape, all with attractive furniture, good-quality beds and generous bathrooms; many have a balcony, too. It's located on the northeast side of town and has a lift. Almost no English is spoken.

★Villa Maison Con Dao Boutique Hotel   BOUTIQUE HOTEL $$$
(Map p408; ☑️0254-383 0969; www.villamaison condaoboutiquehotel.com; 46 Đ Nguyen Hue; r incl breakfast from US$75; ❄️🛜) Run by a dynamic, caring young Vietnamese couple (who worked for years in five-star resorts), this outstanding hotel in a converted French-era villa offers comfort, style, space and a central location. The spectacular lobby area doubles as a dining room and bar (perfect for memorable meals and cocktails) and

boasts modish furniture and contemporary art. The eight guest bedrooms are immaculately presented.

Saigon Con Dao Resort
HOTEL $$$

(Map p408; ☑ 0254-383 0155; www.saigon condao.com; 18 Ð Ton Duc Thang; r US$85-135, ste from US$195; ❇@🛜🏊) This huge hotel complex occupies several French-era buildings on and off the waterfront. There's a smart (though pricey) wing with a swimming pool and older, somewhat neglected accommodation that's mostly reserved for visiting veterans.

AROUND THE ISLAND

★ Six Senses Con Dao
RESORT HOTEL $$$

(Map p405; ☑ 0254-383 1222; www.sixsens es.com; Dat Doc beach; villas from US$651; ➔❇🛜🏊) This astonishing hotel enjoys a dreamlike location on the island's best beach, 4km northeast of Con Son town. Its 50-or-so ocean-facing, timber-clad beach units fuse contemporary style with rustic chic, each with its own pool and giant bathtub. Eating options include a casual cafe and a magnificent restaurant by the shore.

In the spa centre, you'll find indoor and outdoor rooms for Ayurvedic treatments, while yoga, meditation and wellness sessions are conducted by professional instructors. Diving, sailing trips and trekking can be arranged, too.

★ Poulo Condo Resort
HOTEL $$$

(Map p405; ☑ 0254-383 1500; www.poulocondor resort.com; Vong beach; ste US$240-355, villa from US$410; ➔❇🛜🏊) Terrific hotel built in French-colonial style located in the north of the island next to lovely Vong beach. Swanky suites feature four-poster beds, while the villas all have private pools and sea views. The large infinity pool is stunning and you'll love the tropical gardens, restaurant and spa.

There's a complimentary shuttle-bus service to Con Son town and the airport. Bicycles and kayaks are available for guest use.

✖ Eating

Most restaurants in Con Son are geared to local tastes with Vietnamese classics and seafood, but there are also a couple of Western places. Six Senses Con Dao and Poulo Condo Resort are great choices for a special meal.

If your budget is tight, the small night market (Map p408; snacks 20,000-90,000d; ◷5-10pm) located around the intersection of Ð Tran Huy Lieu and Ð Nguyen An Ninh has cheap eats.

★ Gia Minh
VIETNAMESE $

(Map p408; ☑ 038-356 8789; www.giaminhbistro. com; Ð Nguyen Van Linh; meals 50,000-350,000d; ◷10am-10pm; 🛜) Outstanding place on the outskirts of town run by an accomplished chef. Specialises in handmade noodles, which are available in many delicious guises, with most dishes just 50,000d or so. There are ample choices for vegetarians, who will eat very well here, and also good hotpots (starting at 180,000d), Western food (also from 180,000d) and homemade plum and pineapple wines.

Con Son Market
VIETNAMESE $

(Map p408; Ð Vo Thi Sau; meals 15,000-25,000d; ◷6am-5pm) A good spot for breakfast, with delicious noodle dishes and pancakes churned out at wallet-friendly rates. You can stock up on fruit and snacks here, too.

★ Villa Maison Con Dao Restaurant
INTERNATIONAL $$

(Map p408; ☑ 0254-383 0969; www.villamai soncondaoboutiquehotel.com; 46 Ð Nguyen Hue; mains 140,000-320,000d; ◷10.30am-10pm; 🛜) A supremely relaxing and elegant setting for a meal, this fine hotel restaurant features Asian dishes including mixed Con Dao seafood salad (320,000d) and claypots (190,000d). There's a comprehensive wine list, including options by the glass, as well as superb cocktails and mocktails and usually mellow jazz or classical music in the background.

Thu Ba
SEAFOOD $$

(Map p408; ☑ 0254-383 0255; Ð Vo Thi Sau; meals 80,000-230,000d) Thu Ba is renowned for seafood (consult what's on offer from the tanks by the entrance) and hotpots. The gregarious owner speaks great English and is happy to make suggestions based on what's seasonal and fresh.

Bar200 Con Dao
CAFE $$

(Map p408; http://divecondao.com; Ð Nguyen Van Linh; meals 120,000-220,000d; ◷10am-2pm & 5-10pm; 🛜) This popular cafe is great for coffee (including espresso and cappuccino) or smoothies, plus Western comfort grub, including filling breakfasts, burgers, pizza and sandwiches. After dark the beers and cocktails start flowing. It's run by a friendly team who are clued up on island info and can help plan days out.

Infiniti Cafe & Lounge
CAFE $$

(Map p408; Đ Pham Van Dong; meals 100,000-190,000d; ⊙7am-10pm; 🛜) This hip cafe-bar has an arty vibe with its reclaimed furnishings and quirky decor and boasts a lovely pavement terrace. However, the menu is a little meh, consisting of overpriced sandwiches, mediocre Western grub (pizza and pasta) and mains such as chicken or beef teriyaki.

🍷 Drinking & Nightlife

Cafe Le Condor
CAFE

(Map p408; Đ Nguyen Hue; ⊙6.30am-10.45pm; 🛜) Cool cafe featuring lots of concrete and wood with well-selected music playlists of acoustic and indie Vietnamese artists. Serves the best speciality coffee on the island, including cold brews as well as teas, smoothies and cocktails.

ℹ Information

National Park Headquarters (Map p405; ☑0254-383 0669, 098-383 0669; www.condaopark.com.vn; 29 Đ Vo Thi Sau; ⊙7-11.30am & 1.30-5pm) Located 1km northwest of Con Son Town, this office has information on island-hopping excursions and turtle-watching trips. Pick up a useful free handout on island walks – some hiking trails have interpretive signage in English and Vietnamese. There are also displays on local forest and marine life, environmental threats and conservation activities.

Vietin Bank (Map p408; Đ Le Duan; ⊙8am-2pm Mon-Fri, to noon Sat) Has an ATM; does not change foreign currency.

ℹ Getting Around

Exploring the islands by boat can be arranged through hotels and the national-park office. A 12-person boat costs around 2,300,000d to 5,000,000d per day, depending on stops wanted. Local fishers also offer excursions, but be sure to bargain hard.

This is one of the best places in Vietnam to ride a bike, with little traffic, no pollution and good surfaced roads. There's only one main road, connecting the airport in the north to Ben Dam in the south via Con Son town.

Most hotels rent scooters for US$6 per day. Bicycles cost US$2 per day. There are good coastal cycling routes, such as from Con Son town to Bai Nhat and on to the tiny settlement of Ben Dam. The ups and downs are pretty gentle. Be very careful of the high winds around Mui Ca Map (south of Con Son town).

Con Son Island has several **taxis** (☑0264-361 6161). However, as metered rates are high, negotiate hard for a fixed-price rate to destinations outside Con Son town.

AT A GLANCE

POPULATION
Siem Reap: 195,000

FAST FACT
Around 2.2 million tourists visited Angkor Wat in 2019

BEST MASSAGE
Bodia Spa (p415)

BEST BUZZ
Siem Reap Vespa Adventures (p418)

BEST KHMER FOOD
Cuisine Wat Damnak (p421)

WHEN TO GO
Nov–Feb Humidity is low, there are cool breezes and little rain. Peak season for visitors.

Mar–Jun Temperatures rise and in May or June the monsoon brings rain and humidity.

Jul–Oct The wet season: Angkor is surrounded by lush foliage and the moats are full of water.

Ta Prohm (p428)
MARK READ/LONELY PLANET ©

Siem Reap & the Temples of Angkor (Cambodia)

There is no greater concentration of architectural riches anywhere on earth. Choose from the world's largest religious building, Angkor Wat; one of the world's weirdest, Bayon; or the riotous jungle of Ta Prohm. The monuments are a point of pilgrimage for all Khmers, and no traveller will want to miss their stunning architecture. A short hop away from Angkor is the booming city of Siem Reap, gateway to the temples. Despite the headline act that is Angkor and the sophistication of Siem Reap, Cambodia's greatest treasure is its people. The Khmers have been to hell and back, but they have prevailed and no visitor comes away from this kingdom without a measure of admiration and affection for its inhabitants.

Siem Reap & Around

📱 063 / POP 195,000 (CITY)

The life-support system and gateway for the temples of Angkor, 8km to the north, Siem Reap (*see*-em ree-*ep*; សៀមរាប) was always destined for great things. Visitors come here to see the temples, of course, but there is plenty to do in and around the city when you're templed out. Siem Reap has reinvented itself as the epicentre of chic Cambodia, with everything from backpacker party pads to hip hotels, world-class wining and dining across a range of cuisines, sumptuous spas, great shopping, local tours to suit both foodies and adventurers, and a creative cultural scene that includes Cambodia's leading contemporary circus.

Angkor is a place to be savoured, not rushed, and this is the base from which to plan your adventures. Still think three days at the temples is enough? Think again, with Siem Reap on the doorstep.

◉ Sights

★ **Angkor National Museum** MUSEUM
(សារមន្ទីរជាតិ អង្គរ; ☎ 063-966601; www.angkornationalmuseum.com; 968 Charles de Gaulle Blvd; adult/child under 12 US$12/6; ⊙ 8.30am-6pm May-Sep, to 6.30pm Oct-Apr) Looming large on the road to Angkor is the Angkor National Museum, a state-of-the-art showpiece on the Khmer civilisation and the majesty of Angkor. Displays are themed by era, religion and royalty as visitors move through the impressive galleries. After a short presentation, visitors enter the Zen-like Gallery of a Thousand Buddhas, which has a fine collection of images. Other exhibits include the pre-Angkorian periods of Funan and Chenla; the great Khmer kings; Angkor Wat; Angkor Thom; and the inscriptions.

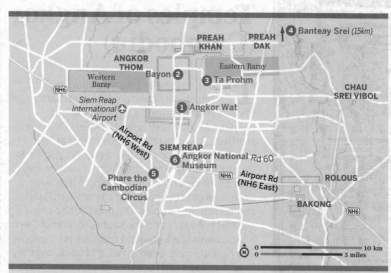

Siem Reap & the Temples of Angkor (Cambodia)

Highlights

❶ Angkor Wat (p423) Watching the sun rise over the holiest of holies, Angkor Wat, the world's largest religious building.

❷ Bayon (p428) Contemplating the serenity and splendour of Bayon, its 216 enigmatic faces staring out into the jungle.

❸ Ta Prohm (p428) Witnessing nature reclaiming the stones at this mysterious ruin, the *Tomb Raider* temple.

❹ Banteay Srei (p431) Staring in wonder at the delicate carvings adorning Banteay Srei, the finest seen at Angkor.

❺ Phare the Cambodian Circus (p421) Seeing a unique performance of the fabulous Cambodian Circus.

❻ Angkor National Museum (p414) Discovering the Khmer civilisation and the majesty of Angkor.

★ **Apopo Visitor Centre**   VISITOR CENTRE

(មជ្ឈមណ្ឌលទស្សនាអាប៉ូប៉ូ; Map p424; ☎081 599237; www.apopo.org; Koumai Rd; US$5; ⊙8.30am-5.30pm Mon-Sat) 🏛 Meet the hero rats that are helping to clear landmines in Cambodia. Apopo has trained the highly sensitive, almost-blind Gambian pouched rat to sniff explosives, which dramatically speeds up the detection of mines in the countryside. The visitor centre gives background on the work of Apopo, with a short video and the chance to meet the rats themselves.

★ **Artisans Angkor –**

Les Chantiers Écoles   ARTS CENTRE

(អាទីសង់អង្គរ; www.artisansdangkor.com; ⊙7.30am-6.30pm) 🏛 FREE Siem Reap is the epicentre of the drive to revitalise Cambodian traditional culture, which was dealt a harsh blow by the Khmer Rouge and the years of instability that followed its rule. Les Chantiers Écoles teaches wood- and stone-carving techniques, traditional silk painting, lacquerware and other artisan skills to impoverished young Cambodians. Free guided tours explaining traditional techniques are available daily from 7.30am to 6.30pm. Tucked down a side road, the school is well signposted from Sivatha St.

★ **Cambodia**

Landmine Museum   MUSEUM

(សារមន្ទីរគ្រាប់មីនកម្ពុជា និងមូលនិធិសង្គ្រោះ; www.cambodialandminemuseum.org; NH67; US$5; ⊙7.30am-5pm) 🏛 Established by DIY deminer Aki Ra, this museum has eye-opening displays on the curse of landmines in Cambodia. The collection includes mines, mortars, guns and weaponry, and there is a mock minefield where visitors can attempt to locate the deactivated mines. Proceeds from the museum are ploughed into mine-awareness campaigns. The museum is about 25km from Siem Reap, near Banteay Srei.

Banteay Srei

Butterfly Centre   WILDLIFE RESERVE

(ស្នូនមេអំបៅបន្ទាយស្រី; www.angkorbutterfly. com; NH67; adult/child US$5/2; ⊙9am-5pm) 🏛 The Banteay Srei Butterfly Centre is one of the largest fully enclosed butterfly centres in Southeast Asia, with more than 30 species of Cambodian butterflies fluttering about. It is a good experience for children, as they can see the whole life cycle from egg to caterpillar to cocoon to butterfly.

Wat Bo   BUDDHIST TEMPLE

(វត្តបូព៌; Tep Vong St; ⊙6am-6pm) FREE This is one of the town's oldest temples and has a collection of well-preserved wall paintings from the late 19th century depicting the *Reamker*, Cambodia's interpretation of the *Ramayana*. The monks here regularly chant sometime between 4.30pm and 6pm, and this can be a spellbinding and spiritual moment if you happen to be visiting.

Preah Ang Chek

Preah Ang Chorm   BUDDHIST SHRINE

(ព្រះអង្គចេក ព្រះអង្គចម; Royal Gardens; ⊙6am-10pm) FREE Located just west of the royal residence is this shrine. Said to represent two Angkorian princesses, these sacred statues were originally housed at the Preah Poan gallery in Angkor Wat, but were moved all over Siem Reap to protect them from invaders, eventually settling here in 1990. Locals throng here to pray for luck, especially newlyweds, and it is an atmospheric place to visit around dusk, as the incense smoke swirls around. Next to the shrine are the tall trees of the Royal Gardens, home to a resident colony of fruit bats (also known as flying foxes). They take off to feed on insects around dusk.

🏃 **Activities**

★ **Bodia Spa**   SPA

(☎063-761593; www.bodia-spa.com; Pithnou St; 1hr massage US$24-36; ⊙10am-midnight) Sophisticated spa near Psar Chaa (the Old Market) offering a full range of scrubs, rubs and natural remedies, including its own line of herbal products.

Cambo Beach Club   SWIMMING

(☎087 466616; www.cambobeachclub.com; Steung Thmey village; per person US$3; ⊙9am-10pm; 🏊) With the only beach in Siem Reap, Cambo Beach Club is a great spot to hang out day or night. The centrepiece is a huge swimming pool complete with floating beanies and a high dive pool. Dining options include lip-smackin' ribs at the Dancing Pig and there is the late-night Underdog Sports Bar for big games.

Angkor Wat Putt   GOLF

(☎012 302330; www.angkorwatputt.com; Chreav District; adult/child US$5/4; ⊙8am-8pm) Crazy golf to the Brits among us, this home-grown minigolf course contrasts with the big golf courses out of town. Navigate minitemples and creative obstacles for 14 holes and win a beer for a hole-in-one. It's now in a more remote location, and is well worth seeking out.

Siem Reap

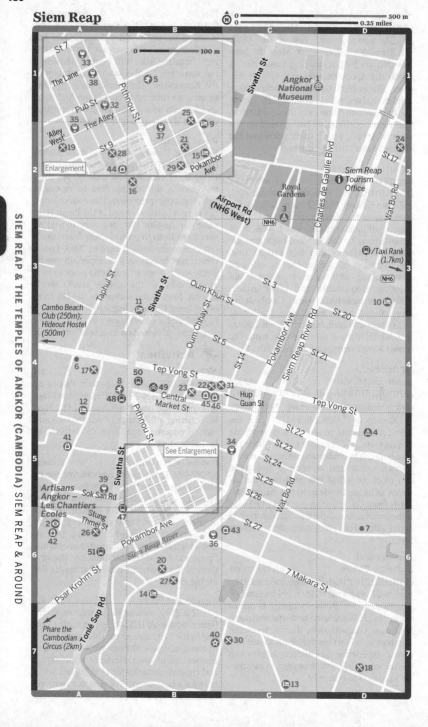

Siem Reap

Boeng Pearaing   BIRDWATCHING
(☑ 085 303050; www.pearaing.org; entry US$10, plus boat fees; ⊙6am-6pm) ✔ This is an up-and-coming birding site based around a natural reservoir just south of the Tonlé Sap lake where it's possible to spot large numbers of rare pelicans, storks and ibis. It is an affordable and accessible birdwatching alternative to Prek Toal Bird Sanctuary, as it lies just half an hour south of downtown Siem Reap. Entry fees go towards conservation and community support.

Peace Cafe Yoga   YOGA
(Map p424; ☑ 063-965210; www.peacecafeangkor.org; Siem Reap River Rd East; per session US$6) This popular community centre and cafe has daily morning and evening yoga sessions, including ashtanga and hatha sessions.

Seeing Hands Massage 4   MASSAGE
(☑ 012 836487; 324 Sivatha St; fan/air-con room US$5/7) ✔ Seeing Hands trains blind people in the art of massage. Watch out for copy-cats, as some of them are just exploiting the blind for profit.

🎓 Courses

**Lily's Secret
Garden Cooking Class**   COOKING
(☑ 016 353621; www.lilysecretgarden.com; off Sombai Rd; per person US$25; ⊙9am-1pm & 3-7pm) This immersive cooking class takes place in a traditional Cambodian house on the outskirts of Siem Reap. Morning and afternoon sessions end in a three-course lunch or dinner. The price includes pickup and drop-off in town at the **Hard Rock Cafe** (☑ 063-963964; www.hardrock.com/cafes/angkor; Siem Reap River Rd East; ⊙11am-midnight; 🕐), as the 'secret garden' cannot be revealed online.

👉 Tours

⭐**Off Track Tours**   CYCLING
(☑ 093 903024; www.kko-cambodia.org; Taphul St; tours US$35-60) ✔ Cycling and *moto* (motorcycle taxi) tours around the paths of Angkor

or into the countryside beyond the Western Baray. Proceeds go towards the Khmer for Khmer Organisation, which supports education and vocational training.

★ **Sam Veasna Center** BIRDWATCHING
(SVC; ☎ 092 554473; www.samveasna.org; St 26; per person from US$100) ✦ Sam Veasna Center, in the Wat Bo area of Siem Reap, is the authority on birdwatching in Cambodia, with professionally trained English-speaking guides, powerful spotting scopes and a network of camps and bird hides scattered throughout north Cambodia. It uses ecotourism to provide an income for local communities in return for a ban on hunting and cutting down the forest.

★ **Siem Reap Food Tours** FOOD & DRINK
(www.siemreapfoodtours.com; per person US$75) Established by an American food writer and an experienced Scottish chef, these tours continue to be a recipe for engaging food encounters despite the founders having moved on. Choose from a morning tour that takes in local markets and the *naom banchok* (thick rice noodles) stalls of Preah Dak, or an evening tour that takes in street stalls and local barbecue restaurants.

Siem Reap Vespa Adventures TOURS
(☎ 012 861610; www.vespaadventures-sr.com; tours per person US$75-126) The modern Vespa is a cut above the average *moto* and is a comfortable way to explore the temples, learn about local life in the countryside or check out some street food after dark, all in the company of excellent and knowledgeable local guides.

🛏 Sleeping

★ **Hideout Hostel** HOSTEL $
(Map p424; ☎ 086 418606; www.hideouthostels. asia/siem-reap; Rose Apple Rd; dm US$3-6, r per person US$10-20; 🕸@🛜🏊) One of the many 'super' hostels that have opened in Siem Reap, in an alternative universe it might have been a boutique hotel. Dorms are super cheap and include free access to the pool. Rooms are pretty swish for the money and some include free-standing bathtubs. Add two free beers from 7pm and it's the real deal.

★ **Onederz Hostel** HOSTEL $
(☎ 063-963525; www.onederz.com; Angkor Night Market St; dm US$5.50-9.50, r US$20-33; 🕸@🛜🏊) Winner of several 'Hoscars' (Hostelworld's Oscars), this is one of the smartest hostels in Siem Reap. Facilities include a huge cafe-bar downstairs, which acts as a giant waiting room for all those coming and going from Siem Reap. Dorms are a little more expensive than some crash pads, but prices include access to the rooftop swimming pool.

★ **Pomme** HOSTEL $
(www.facebook.com/pommesiemreap; Salakamreuk Rd; dm US$5-8; 🕸🛜) Set in a spacious Cambodian wooden house with a lush tropical garden, this is one of the most welcoming hostels in town. Air-con dorms are set behind the main building and include lockers and reading lights. The restaurant and bar attract guests and residents alike, as there is some home comfort food and nightly specials.

Green Home I HOMESTAY $
(☎ 012 221790; www.thegreenhome.org; Chreav Commune; d with fan/air-con from US$8/10; 🕸🛜) Setting the standard for the homestay experience around Siem Reap, the Green Home is set up like a family guesthouse and offers beautiful garden views over the surrounding rice fields. Bathrooms are shared but meticulously clean and the downstairs rooms include air-con. Cooking classes are available, as well as village walks, farm visits and birding trips. It is located about 4km south of town in Chreav District.

Mad Monkey HOSTEL $
(www.madmonkeyhostels.com; Sivatha St; dm US$6.50-9, r US$16-26; 🕸@🛜) The Siem Reap outpost of an expanding Monkey business, this classic backpacker has deluxe dorms with air-con and extra-wide bunk beds, good-value rooms for those wanting privacy and the obligatory rooftop bar – only this one's a beach bar!

★ **1920 Hotel** BOUTIQUE HOTEL $$
(☎ 063-969920; www.1920hotel.com; St 9; r US$50-80; 🕸@🛜) Set in a grand old building near Psar Chaa (the Old Market) dating from, well, we'd hazard a guess at 1920, this is a thoughtfully presented budget boutique hotel with modernist touches in the rooms. The location is great for dining and drinking options in the gentrified alleys nearby.

Babel Guesthouse GUESTHOUSE $$
(☎ 063-965474; www.babelsiemreap.com; 738 Wat Bo village; r US$22.50-35; 🕸@🛜) ✦ This Norwegian-run guesthouse set in a relaxing tropical garden offers service and presentation that are a cut above the nearby budget

places. The Babel owners are keen supporters of responsible tourism.

Rambutan Resort
RESORT $$

(☏063-766655; www.rambutans.info; Wat Dam Nak area; r incl breakfast US$75-100; ❄@🛜🏊) This atmospheric, gay-friendly resort is spread over two stunning villas, each with spacious and stylish rooms and an inviting courtyard swimming pool. It also operates two chic off-site penthouses, which are like having a private apartment.

Shadow of Angkor Residence
GUESTHOUSE $$

(☏063-964774; www.shadowangkorresidence.com; 353 Pokambor Ave; r US$25-55; ❄@🛜🏊) In a grand old French-era building overlooking the river, this friendly place offers stylish air-conditioned rooms in a superb setting close to Psar Chaa.

★Phum Baitang
RESORT $$$

(Map p424; ☏063-961111; www.zannierhotels.com; Neelka Way; villas US$500-720; ❄@🛜🏊) This beautiful resort feels like a boutique Cambodian village. Rooms are set in spacious, elegantly furnished wooden villas, some with private pools, and all connected by extensive wooden walkways over the rice fields. The decor is very designer driftwood. Angelina Jolie stayed here for three months while shooting *First They Killed My Father,* and it's not hard to see what attracted her to the place.

★Montra Nivesha
BOUTIQUE HOTEL $$$

(Map p424; ☏063-760582; www.montranivesha. com; 5 Krom 2; r US$60-150; ❄@🛜🏊) 🍴 A beautiful boutique hotel that gives guests a real sense of Cambodia, Montra Nivesha is set around lush gardens and offers two swimming pools, one suited to laps and one for families. Rooms are decorated with collectables but include modern touches such as smart TV, minibar and safe. The property has an in-house drinking water system to cut the use of plastic.

✗ Eating

★Gelato Lab
ICE CREAM $

(www.facebook.com/gelatolabsiemreap; 109 Alley West; 1/2 scoops US$1.50/2.50; ⊙9am-11pm; 🛜) The great ice cream scooped up here is thanks to the state-of-the-art equipment, all-natural ingredients and – most importantly – plenty of passion courtesy of the Italian owner. Also pours some of the best hand-roasted coffee in town.

Jomno Street Food
CAMBODIAN $

(☏092 762539; https://jomnostreetfood.business. site; Wat Dam Nak village; dishes US$3-7.50; ⊙11am-10pm; 🛜) Earning rave reviews for its original flavour combinations, Jomno promotes its signature platters (from US$7.50) offering a bite-size taste of a range of dishes from the Cambodian street such as *naom banchok* noodles and Battambang sausage. Twists on the classic *amok* (baked fish) include a crispy chicken *amok* salad and a vegan mushroom *amok*. Highly recommended.

Pot & Pan Restaurant
CAMBODIAN $

(☏017 970780; www.thepotandpanrestaurant.com; Stung Thmei St; meals US$2-5; ⊙10am-10pm; 🛜) One of the best-value Khmer restaurants in the downtown area, Pot & Pan specialises in well-presented, authentic dishes at affordable prices. The menu includes spicy soups and subtle salads, and rice is beautifully served in a lotus leaf. Some of the cheapest pizzas in town are, somewhat surprisingly, available here.

Road 60 Night Market
MARKET $

(Map p424; Rd 60; snacks US$1-4; ⊙4-11pm) For a slice of local life, head to the Road 60 Night Market located on the side of the road near the main Angkor ticket checkpoint. Stallholders set up each night, and it's a great place to sample local Cambodian snacks, including the full range of deep-fried insects and barbecue dishes such as quail. Plenty of cheap beer, too.

Peace Cafe
VEGETARIAN $

(Map p424; www.peacecafeangkor.org; Siem Reap River Rd East; mains US$2.50-4.50; ⊙7am-9pm; 🛜🍴) 🍴 This popular garden cafe serves affordable vegetarian meals, while healthy drinks include a tempting selection of vegetable juices. A focal point for community activities, it hosts twice-daily yoga sessions and twice-weekly Khmer classes and monk chanting.

Little Red Fox
CAFE $

(www.thelittleredfoxespresso.com; Hup Guan St; dishes US$3-8; ⊙7am-5pm Thu-Tue; ❄) This foxy little cafe is incredibly popular with long-term residents in Siem Reap, who swear that the regionally sourced Feel Good coffee is the best in town. Add to that designer breakfasts, bagels, salads, creative juices and air-con, and it's easy to while away some time here. The slick upstairs wing is popular with the laptop crowd.

Psar Chaa
CAMBODIAN $

(Old Market; mains US$1.50-5; ⊙7am-9pm) When it comes to cheap Khmer eats, Psar Chaa market has plenty of food stalls on the northwestern side, all with signs and menus in English. These are atmospheric places for a local meal at local-ish prices. Some dishes are on display, others are freshly wok-fried to order, but most are wholesome and filling.

Bugs Cafe
CAMBODIAN $

(☑017 764560; www.bugs-cafe.com; Angkor Night Market St; dishes US$4-9; ⊙5-11pm; ☎) Cambodians were onto insects long before the food scientists started bugging us about their merits. Choose from a veritable feast of crickets, water bugs, silkworms and spiders. Tarantula doughnuts, pan-fried scorpions, snakes – you won't forget this meal in a hurry.

Bayon Pastry School Coffee Shop
BAKERY $

(☑012 604170; http://ecoledubayon.org; off Taphul St; US$1.50-4; ⊙8am-5.30pm) ✔ The Bayon Pastry School has played host to British celebrity chef Nadiya Hussein on her journey of self-discovery in Cambodia, and the coffee shop is the place to sample its fluffy croissant or pain au chocolate and its delightful cakes, all in the good cause of training disadvantaged youths in the art of hospitality.

★Marum
INTERNATIONAL $$

(☑017 363284; www.marum-restaurant.org; Wat Polanka area; mains US$4-9.75; ⊙11am-10.30pm; ☎✔♿) ✔ Set in a delightful wooden house with a spacious garden, Marum serves up lots of vegetarian and seafood dishes, plus some mouth-watering desserts. Menu highlights include beef with red ants and chilli stir-fry, and mini crocodile burgers. Marum is part of the Tree Alliance group of training restaurants; the experience is a must.

★Spoons Cafe
CAMBODIAN $$

(☑076 277 6667; www.spoonscambodia.org; Bambu Rd; mains US$6.25-12; ⊙11.30am-10pm Mon-Sat; ☎) ✔ This excellent contemporary-Cambodian restaurant supports local community outfit EGBOK (Everything's Gonna Be OK), which offers education, training and employment opportunities in the hospitality sector. The menu includes some original flavours such as trey saba (whole mackerel) with coconut-turmeric rice, tiger-prawn curry and tuk kroeung, a pungent local fish-based broth. Original cocktails are shaken, not stirred.

★Pou Kitchen
CAMBODIAN $$

(☑092 262688; www.poukitchen.com; opposite Wat Dam Nak; US$3-6.50; ⊙11am-11pm, closed Wed; ☎) Under the direction of homegrown chef Mengly, Pou Kitchen has taken off as one of the most popular and innovative Cambodian restaurants in town. Choose from grilled beehive salad or chicken with red ant for starters, and move on to Phnom Kulen pork-belly sausage or spicy vegetable-cake curry. Simple surrounds, but far from simple flavours.

★Village Cafe
FRENCH $$

(☑092 305401; www.facebook.com/villagecafe cambodia; 586 Tep Vong St; mains US$5-15; ⊙5pm-late Mon-Sat; ❄☎) Bar, Bites, Beats is the motto at Village Cafe, a happening little bistro that delivers on its promise. Drop in for tapas, wholesome gastropub grub and a glass of wine or four to wash it all down. Features one of the longest bars in Siem Reap. Regular DJ events at weekends draw a crowd.

Le Malraux
FRENCH $$

(☑012 332584; www.lemalraux.com; mains US$5-15; ⊙7am-11pm; ☎) Stunningly located in the network of alleys east of Psar Chaa (the Old Market), Le Malraux is one of the best French restaurants in Siem Reap, and by night this quartier looks like a little corner of France. Eat or drink inside at the bar or al fresco in the street. Meals include a superb pavê of boeuf and succulent fish.

Mahob
CAMBODIAN $$

(☑063-966986; www.mahobkhmer.com; near Angkor Conservation; dishes US$3.50-15; ⊙11am-11pm) The Cambodian word for food is mahob, and at this restaurant it is delicious. Set in a traditional wooden house with a contemporary twist, this place takes the same approach to cuisine as it does to decor, serving up dishes such as caramelised pork shank with ginger and black pepper, or wok-fried local beef with red tree ants. Cooking classes available.

Mamma Shop
ITALIAN $$

(www.facebook.com/mammashop.italian.restau rant; Hup Guan St; mains US$5-10; ⊙11.30am-10.30pm Mon-Sat; ❄☎) A compact menu of terrific homemade pasta is the signature of this bright, friendly Italian corner bistro in the bohemian Kandal village district. Add a selection of piadina romagnola (stuffed flatbread) pizza, a nice wine list and delicious desserts, and this place is highly recommended.

★ **Cuisine Wat Damnak** CAMBODIAN $$$
(🖉 077 347762; www.cuisinewatdamnak.com; Wat Dam Nak area; 5-/6-course set menu US$29/34; ⊘ 6.30-10.30pm Tue-Sat, last orders 9.30pm) Set in a traditional wooden house is this highly regarded restaurant from Siem Reap celeb chef Joannès Rivière. The menu delivers the ultimate contemporary Khmer dining experience. Seasonal set menus focus on market-fresh ingredients and change weekly; vegetarian options are available with advance notice.

🍷 Drinking & Nightlife

★ **Asana Wooden House** BAR
(www.asana-cambodia.com; St 7; ⊘ 6pm-1am; 🛜) This is a traditional Cambodian countryside home dropped into the backstreets of Siem Reap, which makes for an atmospheric place to drink. Lounge on kapok-filled rice sacks while sipping a classic cocktail made with infused rice wine. Khmer cocktail classes (US$15 per person) with Sombai spirits are available at 6pm.

★ **Laundry Bar** BAR
(www.facebook.com/laundry.bar.3; St 9; ⊘ 4pm-late; 🛜) One of the most chilled, chic bars in town thanks to low lighting and discerning decor. Laundry is the place to come for electronica and ambient sounds; it heaves on weekends or when guest DJs crank up the volume. Happy hour until 9pm.

★ **Miss Wong** BAR
(www.misswong.net; The Lane; ⊘ 6pm-1am; 🛜) Miss Wong carries you back to chic 1920s Shanghai. The cocktails are a draw here, making it a cool place to while away an evening, and there's a menu offering dim sum. Gay-friendly and extremely popular with the well-heeled expat crowd.

Beatnik Bar BAR
(www.facebook.com/beatniksiemreap; The Alley; ⊘ 9.30am-1.30am; 🛜) A hip little bar on the corner of The Alley, it's just far enough away from Pub St not to be drowned out by the nightly battle of the bars. Cheap drinks, friendly staff and a convivial crowd add up to a great pit stop.

Angkor What? BAR
(www.facebook.com/theangkorwhatbar; Pub St; ⊘ 5pm-late; 🛜) Siem Reap's original bar claims to have been promoting irresponsible drinking since 1998. The happy hour (to 9pm) lightens the mood for later when

everyone's bouncing along to dance anthems, sometimes on the tables, sometimes under them. Regular DJs and live music add to the party mood.

Barcode GAY
(www.barcodesiemreap.com; Wat Preah Prohm Roth St; ⊘ 5pm-late; 🛜) A superstylin' gay bar that's metrosexual-friendly. The cocktails here are worth the stop, as is the regular drag show at 9.30pm. Happy hour runs from 5pm to 7pm daily.

Score! SPORTS BAR
(www.scorekh.com; 12 Sok San Rd; ⊘ 8am-midnight Sun-Thu, to 2am Fri & Sat) Having expanded from Phnom Penh to Temple Town, Score! commands the entrance to Sok San Rd, beckoning sports fans with an inviting open plan and a ginormous two-storey screen.

☆ Entertainment

★ **Phare the Cambodian Circus** CIRCUS
(🖉 015 499480; www.pharecircus.org; cnr Ring & Sok San Rds; adult/child US$18/10, premium seats US$38/18; ⊘ 8pm) Cambodia's answer to Cirque du Soleil, Phare the Cambodian Circus is so much more than a conventional circus, with an emphasis on performance art and a subtle yet striking social message behind each production. Cambodia's leading circus, theatre and performing-arts organisation, Phare Ponleu Selpak opened its big top for nightly shows in 2013, and the results are unique, must-see entertainment.

Bambu Stage THEATRE
(🖉 097 726 1110; www.bambustage.com; Bambu Rd; show US$24, incl dinner US$38; ⊘ shows from 7pm Mon-Sat; 🛜) Bambu Stage offers an eclectic variety of traditional entertainment, including a nightly shadow puppet show that weaves a historical tale of the Cambodian civil war. Other shows include Temples Decoded (Tuesday) and Snap (Friday), a history of Cambodian photography. The venue also hosts Cambodia Living Arts' all-female drum performance, The Call, on Wednesday, Friday and Sunday at 8pm.

🛍 Shopping

★ **Artisans Angkor** ARTS & CRAFTS
(www.artisansdangkor.com; ⊘ 7.30am-6.30pm; 🛜) 🖉 On the premises of Les Chantiers Écoles (p415) is this beautiful shop, which sells everything from stone and wood reproductions of Angkorian-era statues to household furnishings. It also has a second shop

opposite Angkor Wat in the Angkor Cafe building, and outlets at Phnom Penh and Siem Reap international airports.

All profits from sales go back into funding the school and bringing more young Cambodians into the training programme, which is 20% owned by the artisans themselves.

★ **Angkor Night Market** MARKET
(www.angkornightmarket.com; Angkor Night Market St; ⊙4pm–midnight) Siem Reap's original night market near Sivatha St has sprung countless copycats, but it remains the best and is well worth a browse. It's packed with stalls selling a variety of handicrafts, souvenirs and silks. Island Bar offers regular live music and Sombai offers infused organic rice wines for those who want to make a night of it.

★ **Theam's House** ART
(Map p424; www.theamshouse.com; 25 Veal St; ⊙8am-7pm) After years spent working with Artisans Angkor (p415) to revitalise Khmer handicrafts, Cambodian artist and designer Theam operates his own studio of lacquer creations and artwork. Highly original, this beautiful and creative space can be tricky to find, so make sure you find a driver who knows where it is.

AHA Fair Trade Village ARTS & CRAFTS
(Map p424; ☑078 341454; www.aha-kh.com; Rd 60, Trang village; ⊙10am-7pm) 🖉 For locally produced souvenirs (unlike much of the imported stuff that turns up in Psar Chaa), drop in on this handicraft market. It's a little out of the way, but there are more than 20 stalls selling a wide range of traditional items. There's a Khmer cultural show every second and fourth Saturday of the month, with extra stalls, traditional music and dancing. Two-hour pottery classes are offered here through Mordock Ceramics, one of the stalls.

Soieries du Mekong FASHION & ACCESSORIES
(www.soieriesdumekong.com; 668 Hup Guan St; ⊙10am-7pm) 🖉 Soieries du Mekong is the Siem Reap gallery for a leading handwoven silk project based in remote Banteay Chhmar, which seeks to stem the tide of rural migration by creating employment opportunities in the village. Beautiful silk scarves and other delicate items are for sale.

trunkh GIFTS & SOUVENIRS
(www.trunkh.com; Hup Guan St; ⊙10am-6pm) The owner here has a great eye for the quirky,

stylish and original, including beautiful shirts, throw pillows, jewellery, poster art and T-shirts, plus some offbeat items such as genuine Cambodian water-buffalo bells.

Psar Chaa MARKET
(Old Market; ⊙6am-9pm) When it comes to shopping in town, Psar Chaa is well stocked with anything you may want, and lots that you don't. Silverware, silk, woodcarvings, stone carvings, Buddhas, paintings, rubbings, notes and coins, T-shirts, table mats... the list goes on. There are bargains to be had if you haggle patiently and with good humour.

Made in Cambodia Market MARKET
(www.facebook.com/madeincambodiamarket; Siem Reap River Rd East; ⊙noon-10pm) 🖉 King's Rd hosts the daily Made in Cambodia community market, bringing together many of the best local craftsfolk and creators in Siem Reap, many promoting good causes.

❶ Information

ConCERT (www.concertcambodia.org) Works to build bridges between tourists and good-cause projects in the Siem Reap/Angkor area, with information offices at **Sister Srey Cafe** (www.sistersreycafe.com; 200 Pokambor Ave; mains US$3-6; ⊙7am-6pm Tue-Sun; 🖉) and **New Leaf Book Cafe** (www.newleafeatery.com; near Psar Chaa; mains US$3-6.75; ⊙7.30am-10pm; 🗟). It offers information on anything from ecotourism initiatives to volunteering opportunities.

Royal Angkor International Hospital (☑063-761888; www.royalangkorhospital.com; Airport Rd) This international facility affiliated with the Bangkok Hospital is on the expensive side as it's used to dealing with insurance companies.

Siem Reap Tourism Office (☑063-959600; Royal Gardens; ⊙7am-5pm) Check out the swanky office in the Royal Gardens, which includes a branch of popular Thai coffee chain Inthanin.

Tourist Police (☑012 402424; Rd 60; ⊙6am-6pm) Located at the main ticket checkpoint for the Angkor area, this is the place to lodge a complaint if you encounter any serious problems while in Siem Reap.

❶ Getting There & Away

AIR

All international flights arrive at the **Siem Reap International Airport** (☑063-962400; www.cambodia-airports.com), 7km west of the town centre. Facilities at the airport include cafes, restaurants, bookshops, international ATMs and money-changing services.

There are direct flights from Hanoi, Ho Chi Minh City and Danang in Vietnam with Vietnam Airlines, Cambodia Angkor Air and Lanmei Airlines. There are also seasonal flights connecting Phu Quoc and Nha Trang with Siem Reap.

Demand for seats is high during peak season, so book as far in advance as possible.

BUS

All buses officially depart from the bus station and taxi park, which is 3km east of town and nearly 1km south of NH6. However, tickets are available at bus offices in town, guesthouses, hotels, travel agencies and ticket kiosks. Most bus companies depart from their in-town offices or send a minibus around to pick up passengers at their place of lodging. Upon arrival in Siem Reap, be prepared for a rugby scrum of eager *moto* drivers when getting off the bus at the main bus station.

Bus companies in Siem Reap:

Capitol Tours (☑ 012 830170; www.capitoltourscambodia.com; St 9) Buses to destinations across Cambodia.

Giant Ibis (☑ 095 777809; www.giantibis.com; Sivatha St) Has free wi-fi on board.

Mekong Express (☑ 063-963662; www.catmekongexpress.com; 14 Sivatha St) Upmarket bus company with in-coach attendants and drinks.

Nattakan (☑ 070 877727; nattakan.sr@gmail.com; Concrete Drain Rd) The first operator, and still one of the most reliable, to do direct trips to Bangkok. It's out of the way, so request a free pick-up.

Phnom Penh Sorya (PP Sorya; ☑ 063-969097; www.ppsoryatransport.com.kh; Psar Krom Rd) Most extensive bus network in Cambodia.

Virak Buntham (☑ 017 790440; www.virakbuntham.com) The night-bus specialist to Phnom Penh and Sihanoukville.

ⓘ Getting Around

Guesthouses hire out bicycles, as do a few shops around Psar Chaa (the Old Market), usually for US$1 to US$2 a day. Car hire costs US$30 and up per day, a *moto* (motorcycle taxi) costs from US$10 per day and a tuk tuk about US$15 per day.

Temples of Angkor

Welcome to heaven on earth. The temples of Angkor (ប្រាសាទអង្គរ) are the perfect fusion of creative ambition and spiritual devotion and are a source of inspiration and national pride to all Khmers as they struggle to rebuild their lives after the years of terror and trauma. Today, the temples are a point of pilgrimage for all Cambodians, and no traveller to the region will want to miss their extravagant beauty. Angkor is one of the world's foremost ancient sites, with the epic proportions of the Great Wall of China, the detail and intricacy of the Taj Mahal, and the symbolism and symmetry of the pyramids, all rolled into one.

◉ Sights

◉ Angkor Wat

★**Angkor Wat**   HINDU TEMPLE
(អង្គរវត្ត; incl in Angkor admission 1/3/7 days US$37/62/72; ⊘ 5am-5.30pm) The traveller's first glimpse of Angkor Wat, the ultimate expression of Khmer genius, is matched by only a few select spots on earth. Built by Suryavarman II (r 1112–52) and surrounded by a vast moat, Angkor Wat is one of the most inspired monuments ever conceived by the human mind. Stretching around the central temple complex is an 800m-long series of bas-reliefs, and rising 55m above the ground is the central tower, which gives the whole ensemble its sublime unity.

Angkor Wat is, figuratively, heaven on earth. It is the earthly representation of Mt Meru, the Mt Olympus of the Hindu faith and the abode of ancient gods. The Cambodian god-kings of old each strove to better their ancestors' structures in size, scale and symmetry, culminating in what is believed to be the world's largest religious building, the mother of all temples, Angkor Wat, the 'temple that is a city'.

The temple is the heart and soul of Cambodia: it is the national symbol, the epicentre of Khmer civilisation and a source of fierce national pride. Soaring skyward and surrounded by a moat that would make its European castle counterparts blush, Angkor Wat was never abandoned to the elements and has been in virtually continuous use since it was built.

Simply unique, it is a stunning blend of spirituality and symmetry, an enduring example of humanity's devotion to its gods. Relish the very first approach, as that spine-tingling moment when you emerge on the inner causeway will rarely be felt again. It is the best-preserved temple at Angkor, and repeat visits are rewarded with previously unnoticed details.

Temples of Angkor

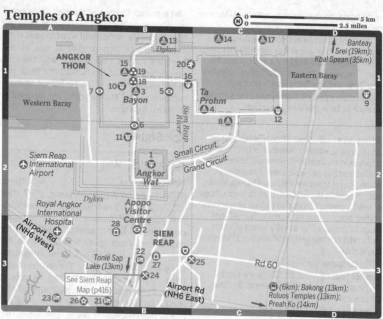

Temples of Angkor

There is much about Angkor Wat that is unique among the temples of Angkor. The most significant fact is that the temple is oriented towards the west. Symbolically, west is the direction of death, which once led a large number of scholars to conclude that Angkor Wat must have existed primarily as a tomb. This idea was supported by the fact that the magnificent bas-reliefs of the temple were designed to be viewed in an anticlockwise direction, a practice that has precedents in ancient Hindu funerary rites. Vishnu, however, is also frequently associated with the west, and it is now commonly accepted that Angkor Wat most likely served both as a temple and as a mausoleum for Suryavarman II.

Angkor Wat is famous for its beguiling apsaras (heavenly nymphs). Almost 2000 apsaras are carved into the walls of Angkor Wat, each of them unique, and there are 37 different hairstyles for budding stylists to check out. Many of these exquisite apsaras have been damaged by centuries of bat droppings and urine, but they are now being restored by the **German Apsara Conservation Project** (GACP; www.gacp-angkor.de; ⊙7am-5pm).

Allow at least two hours for a visit to Angkor Wat and plan a half-day if you want to decipher the bas-reliefs with a tour guide and ascend to Bakan, the upper level, which is open to visitors on a timed ticketing system. The western causeway is currently closed to visitors for an extensive renovation and access is via a floating pontoon, which has become something of a local tourist attraction in itself.

Churning of the Ocean of Milk ARCHAEOLOGICAL SITE
(កូរសមុទ្រទឹកដោះ) The southern section of the east gallery is decorated by the most famous of the bas-relief scenes at Angkor Wat, the Churning of the Ocean of Milk. This brilliantly executed carving depicts 88 asuras on the left, and 92 devas, with crested helmets, churning up the sea to extract from it the elixir of immortality. (Asuras and devas are Vedic-era divine beings.)

Army of Suryavarman II ARCHAEOLOGICAL SITE
(ទ័ពព្រះបាទសូរ្យវរ្ម័នទី២) The remarkable western section of the south gallery depicts a triumphal battle march of Suryavarman II's army. In the southwestern corner about 2m from the floor is Suryavarman II on an elephant, wearing the royal tiara and armed with a battleaxe; he is shaded by 15 parasols and fanned by legions of servants.

⊙ Angkor Thom

It's hard to imagine any building bigger or more beautiful than Angkor Wat, but in **Angkor Thom** (អង្គរធំ; Great City; incl in Angkor admission 1/3/7 days US$37/62/72; ⊙7.30am-5.30pm) the sum of the parts adds up to a greater whole. Set over 10 sq km, the aptly named last great capital of the Khmer empire took monumental to a whole new level.

Centred on Bayon, the surreal state temple of Jayavarman VII, Angkor Thom is enclosed by a formidable *jayagiri* (square wall), 8m high and 13km in length, and encircled by a 100m-wide *jayasindhu* (moat) that would have stopped all but the hardiest invaders in their tracks. This architectural layout is an expression of Mt Meru surrounded by the oceans.

In the centre of the walled enclosure are the city's most important monuments, including Bayon, Baphuon, the Royal Enclosure, Phimeanakas and the Terrace of Elephants. Visitors should set aside a half-day to explore Angkor Thom in depth.

SIEM REAP & THE TEMPLES OF ANGKOR (CAMBODIA) TEMPLES OF ANGKOR

DON'T MISS

THE GATES OF ANGKOR THOM

It is the gates that grab your attention first, flanked by a vast representation of the Churning of the Ocean of Milk, 54 demons and 54 gods engaged in an epic tug of war on the causeway. Each gate towers above the visitor, the magnanimous faces of the Bodhisattva Avalokiteshvara staring out over the kingdom. Imagine being a peasant in the 13th century approaching the forbidding capital for the first time. It would have been an awe-inspiring, yet unsettling, experience to enter such a gateway and come face to face with the divine power of the god-kings.

The **south gate** (ខ្លោងទ្វារទិសខាងត្បូង) is most popular with visitors, as it has been fully restored and many of the heads (mostly copies) remain in place. The gate is on the main road into Angkor Thom from Angkor Wat, and it gets very busy. More peaceful are the east and west gates, found at the end of dirt trails. The **east gate** (ខ្លោងទ្វារខ្លោច) was used as a location in *Lara Croft: Tomb Raider*, where the bad guys broke into the 'tomb' by pulling down a giant polystyrene apsara. The causeway at the **west gate** (ខ្លោងទ្វារតាកោ) of Angkor Thom has completely collapsed, leaving a jumble of ancient stones sticking out of the soil, like victims of a terrible historical pile-up.

Temples of Angkor

THREE-DAY EXPLORATION

The temple complex at Angkor is simply enormous and the superlatives don't do it justice. This is the site of the world's largest religious building, a multitude of temples and a vast, long-abandoned walled city that was arguably Southeast Asia's first metropolis, long before Bangkok and Singapore got in on the action.

Starting at the Roluos group of temples, one of the earliest capitals of Angkor, move on to the big circuit, which includes the Buddhist-Hindu fusion temple of **1 Preah Khan** and the ornate water temple of **2 Preah Neak Poan**.

On the second day downsize to the small circuit, starting with an early visit to **3 Ta Prohm**, before continuing to the temple pyramid of Ta Keo, the Buddhist monastery of Banteay Kdei and the immense royal bathing pond of **4 Sra Srang**.

Next venture further afield to Banteay Srei temple, the jewel in the crown of Angkorian art, and Beng Mealea, a remote jungle temple.

Saving the biggest and best until last, experience sunrise at **5 Angkor Wat** and stick around for breakfast in the temple to discover its amazing architecture without the crowds. In the afternoon, explore **6 Angkor Thom**, an immense complex that is home to the enigmatic **7 Bayon**.

Three days around Angkor? That's just for starters.

TOP TIPS

➡ To avoid the crowds, try dawn at Sra Srang, post-sunrise at Angkor Wat and lunchtime at Banteay Srei.

➡ Three-day passes can be used on non-consecutive days over the course of a week, but be sure to request this.

Bayon
The surreal state temple of legendary king Jayavarman VII, where 216 faces stare down on pilgrims, asserting religious and regal authority.

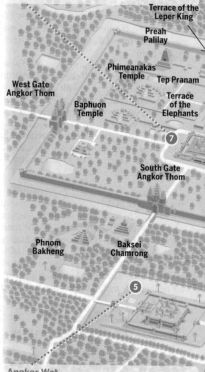

Terrace of the Leper King

Preah Palilay

Phimeanakas Temple

West Gate Angkor Thom

Tep Pranam

Baphuon Temple

Terrace of the Elephants

7

South Gate Angkor Thom

Phnom Bakheng

Baksei Chamrong

5

Angkor Wat
The world's largest religious building. Experience sunrise at the holiest of holies, then explore the beautiful bas-reliefs – devotion etched in stone.

Angkor Thom
The last great capital of the Khmer empire conceals a wealth of temples and its epic proportions would have inspired and terrified in equal measure.

Preah Khan
A fusion temple dedicated to Buddha, Brahma, Shiva and Vishnu; the immense corridors are like an unending hall of mirrors.

Preah Neak Poan
If Vegas ever adopts the Angkor theme, this will be the swimming pool; a petite tower set in a lake, surrounded by four smaller ponds.

North Gate, Angkor Thom

Preah Pithu

Thommanon Temple

6

Prasat Suor Prat

Victory Gate Angkor Thom

East Gate Angkor Thom

Chau Say Tevoda

Ta Keo Temple

Ta Nei Temple

Banteay Srei

3

Banteay Kdei Temple

Roluos, Beng Mealea

4

Prasat Kravan

Bat Chum Temple

Ta Prohm
Nicknamed the *Tomb Raider* temple; *Indiana Jones* would be equally apt. Nature has run riot, leaving iconic tree roots strangling the surviving stones.

Sra Srang
Once the royal bathing pond, this is the ablutions pool to beat all ablutions pools and makes a good stop for sunrise or sunset.

★ **Bayon** BUDDHIST TEMPLE
(បាយ័ន; ⊙ 7.30am-5.30pm) At the heart of Angkor Thom is the 12th-century Bayon, the mesmerising, if slightly mind-bending, state temple of Jayavarman VII. It epitomises the creative genius and inflated ego of Cambodia's most celebrated king. Its 54 Gothic towers are decorated with 216 gargantuan smiling faces of Avalokiteshvara, and it is adorned with 1.2km of extraordinary bas-reliefs incorporating more than 11,000 figures. The upper level of Bayon is under restoration and is scheduled to re-open in 2022.

Baphuon HINDU TEMPLE
(បាពួន; ⊙ 7.30am-5.30pm) Some have called Baphuon the 'world's largest jigsaw puzzle'. Before the civil war the Baphuon was painstakingly taken apart piece by piece by a team of archaeologists, but their meticulous records were destroyed during the Khmer Rouge regime, leaving experts with 300,000 stones to put back into place. After years of excruciating research, this temple has been partially restored. In the 16th century, the retaining wall on the western side of the second level was fashioned into a 60m reclining Buddha.

Terrace of Elephants ARCHAEOLOGICAL SITE
(លានដំរី; ⊙ 7.30am-5pm) The 350m-long Terrace of Elephants was used as a giant viewing stand for public ceremonies and served as a base for the king's grand audience hall. Try to imagine the pomp and grandeur of the Khmer empire at its height, with infantry, cavalry, horse-drawn chariots and elephants parading across Central Square in a colourful procession, pennants and standards aloft. Looking on is the god-king, shaded by multitiered parasols and attended by mandarins and handmaidens bearing gold and silver utensils.

Terrace of the Leper King ARCHAEOLOGICAL SITE
(ព្រះលានស្ដេចគម្លង់; ⊙ 7.30am-5.30pm) The Terrace of the Leper King is just north of the Terrace of Elephants. Dating from the late 12th century, it is a 7m-high platform, on top of which stands a nude, though sexless, statue. The front retaining walls of the terrace are decorated with at least five tiers of meticulously executed carvings. On the southern side of the Terrace of the Leper King, there is access to a hidden terrace with exquisitely preserved carvings.

Preah Palilay BUDDHIST TEMPLE
(ព្រះបាលីឡៃ; ⊙ 7.30am-5.30pm) Preah Palilay is located about 200m north of the Royal Enclosure's northern wall. It was erected during the rule of Jayavarman VII and originally housed a Buddha, which has long since vanished. There are several huge tree roots looming large over the central tower, making for a memorable photo opportunity of a classic 'jungle temple'.

⊙ Other Angkor Temples

★ **Ta Prohm** BUDDHIST TEMPLE
(តាព្រហ្ម; incl in Angkor admission 1/3/7 days US$37/62/72; ⊙ 7.30am-5.30pm) The so-called 'Tomb Raider Temple', Ta Prohm is cloaked in dappled shadow, its crumbling towers and walls locked in the slow muscular embrace of vast root systems. Undoubtedly the most atmospheric ruin at Angkor, Ta Prohm should be high on the hit list of every visitor. Its appeal lies in the fact that, unlike the other monuments of Angkor, it has been swallowed by the jungle, and looks very much the way most of the monuments of Angkor appeared when European explorers first stumbled upon them.

Well, that's the theory, but in fact the jungle is pegged back and only the largest trees are left in place, making it manicured rather than raw like Beng Mealea. Still, a visit to Ta Prohm is a unique, other-worldly experience.

There is a poetic cycle to this venerable ruin, with humanity first conquering nature to rapidly create, and nature once again conquering humanity to slowly destroy. If Angkor Wat is testimony to the genius of

DON'T MISS

ANGKOR ZIPLINE

Angkor provides the ultimate backdrop for this zip-line experience by **Angkor Zipline** (☑ 096 999 9100; www.angkor zipline.com; short/full course US$60/100; ⊙ 6am-5pm), although you won't actually see the temples while navigating the course, despite it being located inside the Angkor protected area. The course includes 10 ziplines, 21 treetop platforms, four skybridges and an abseil finish. There is a panoramic rest stop halfway, and highlights include a tandem line for couples.

MOTIFS, SYMBOLS & CHARACTERS AROUND ANGKOR

The temples of Angkor are intricately carved with myths and legends, symbols and signs, and a cast of characters in the thousands. Deciphering them can be quite a challenge, so we've highlighted some of the most commonly seen around the majestic temples. For more help understanding the carvings of Angkor, pick up a copy of *Images of the Gods* by Vittorio Roveda.

Apsaras Heavenly nymphs or goddesses, also known as *devadasis*; these beautiful female forms decorate the walls of many temples.

Asuras These devils feature extensively in representations of the Churning of the Ocean of Milk, such as at Angkor Wat.

Devas The 'good gods' in the creation myth of the Churning of the Ocean of Milk.

Flame The flame motif is found flanking steps and doorways and is intended to purify pilgrims as they enter the temple.

Garuda Vehicle of Vishnu; this half-man, half-bird creature features in some temples and was combined with his old enemy, the nagas, to promote religious unity under Jayavarman VII.

Kala The temple guardian appointed by Shiva; he had such an appetite that he devoured his own body and appears only as a giant head above doorways. Also known as Rehu.

Linga A phallic symbol of fertility, lingams would have originally been located within the towers of most Hindu temples.

Lotus A symbol of purity, the lotus features extensively in the shape of towers, the shape of steps to entrances and in decoration.

Makara A giant sea serpent with a reticulated jaw; features on the corner of pediments, spewing forth a naga or some other creature.

Naga The multiheaded serpent, half-brother and enemy of garudas. Controls the rains and, therefore, the prosperity of the kingdom; seen on causeways, doorways and roofs. The seven-headed naga, a feature at many temples, represents the rainbow, which acts as a bridge between heaven and earth.

Nandi The mount of Shiva; there are several statues of Nandi dotted about the temples, although many have been damaged or stolen by looters.

Rishi A Hindu wise man or ascetic, also known as *essai*; these bearded characters are often seen sitting cross-legged at the base of pillars or flanking walls.

Vine Another symbol of purity, the vine graces doorways and lintels and is meant to help cleanse visitors on their journey to this heaven on earth, the abode of the gods.

Yama God of death who presides over the underworld and passes judgement on whether people continue to heaven or hell.

Yoni Female fertility symbol that is combined with the lingam to produce holy water infused with the essence of life.

the ancient Khmers, Ta Prohm reminds us equally of the awesome fecundity and power of the jungle.

Built from 1186 and originally known as Rajavihara (Monastery of the King), Ta Prohm was a Buddhist temple dedicated to the mother of Jayavarman VII. It is one of the few temples in the Angkor region where an inscription provides information about the temple's dependents and inhabitants. Almost 80,000 people were required to maintain or attend at the temple, among them more than 2700 officials and 615 dancers.

Ta Prohm is a temple of towers, closed courtyards and narrow corridors. Many of the corridors are impassable, clogged with jumbled piles of delicately carved stone blocks dislodged by the roots of long-decayed trees. Bas-reliefs on bulging walls are carpeted with lichen, moss and creeping plants, and shrubs sprout from the roofs of monumental porches. Trees, hundreds of years old, tower overhead, their leaves

ANGKOR: PLANNING A VISIT

Most budget and midrange travellers prefer to take in the temples at their own pace, and tend to use a combination of transport options, such as car, *remork*, bicycle or minivan. Plan a dawn-to-dusk itinerary with a long, leisurely lunch to avoid the heat of the midday sun. Alternatively, explore the temples through lunch, when it can be considerably quieter than during the peak morning and afternoon visit times. However, it will be hot as hell and the light is not conducive to photography.

One Day

If you have only one day to visit Angkor, arrive at Angkor Wat (p423) in time for sunrise and then stick around to explore the mighty temple while it's quieter. From there continue to the tree roots of Ta Prohm (p428) before breaking for lunch. In the afternoon, explore the temples within the walled city of Angkor Thom (p425) and the beauty of the Bayon (p428) in the late-afternoon light.

Two Days

A second day allows you to include some of the big hitters around Angkor. Spend the first morning visiting petite Banteay Srei, with its fabulous carvings; stop at Banteay Samré (p432) on the return leg. In the afternoon, visit immense Preah Khan, delicate **Preah Neak Poan** (នាគព័ន្ធ; Temple of the Intertwined Nagas; incl in Angkor admission; ⊙ 7.30am-5.30pm) and the tree roots of **Ta Som** (តាសោម; incl in Angkor admission; ⊙ 7.30am-5.30pm), before taking in a sunset at **Pre Rup** (ប្រែរូប; ⊙ 5am-7pm).

Three to Five Days

If you have three to five days to explore Angkor, it's possible to see most of the important sites. One approach is to see as much as possible on the first day or two and then spend the final days combining visits to other sites such as the **Roluos temples** (រលួស; which served as Indravarman I's capital, Hariharalaya, and are among the earliest large, permanent temples built by the Khmers) and Banteay Kdei. Better still is a gradual build-up to the most spectacular monuments. After all, if you see Angkor Wat (p423) on the first day, then a temple like **Ta Keo** (តាកែវ; incl in Angkor admission; ⊙ 7.30am-5.30pm) just won't cut it. Another option is a chronological approach, starting with the earliest Angkorian temples and working steadily forwards in time to Angkor Thom (p425), taking stock of the evolution of Khmer architecture and artistry.

It is well worth making the trip to the 'River of a Thousand Lingas' at Kbal Spean (p432) for the chance to stretch your legs amid natural and human-made splendour, or the remote, vast and overgrown temple of Beng Mealea (p432). Both can be combined with Banteay Srei in one long day.

Visitor Code of Conduct

It is important to remember that the temples of Angkor represent a sacred religious site to the Khmer people, and the authorities have begun cracking down on inappropriate dress at the temples. Expect to be sent back to your guesthouse to change if you are wearing sleeveless tops, hot pants or short skirts. Local authorities have released visitor 'code of conduct' guidelines and a video to encourage dressing appropriately, as well as reminding tourists not to touch or sit on the ancient structures, to pay attention to restricted areas, and to be respectful of monks.

filtering the sunlight and casting a greenish pall over the whole scene.

The most popular of the many strangulating root formations is the one on the inside of the easternmost gopura (entrance pavilion) of the central enclosure, nicknamed the **Crocodile Tree**. One of the most famous spots in Ta Prohm is the so-called 'Tomb Raider tree', where Angelina Jolie's Lara Croft picked a jasmine flower before falling through the earth into...Pinewood Studios.

The temple is at its most impressive early in the day. Allow as much as two hours to visit, especially if you want to explore the maze-like corridors and iconic tree roots.

Preah Khan
BUDDHIST TEMPLE

(ព្រះខ័ន; Sacred Sword; incl in Angkor admission 1/3/7 days US$37/62/72; ⊙7.30am-5.30pm) The temple of Preah Khan is one of the largest complexes at Angkor, a maze of vaulted corridors, fine carvings and lichen-clad stonework. It is a good counterpoint to Ta Prohm and generally sees slightly fewer visitors. Like Ta Prohm it is a place of towered enclosures and shoulder-hugging corridors. Unlike Ta Prohm, however, the temple of Preah Khan is in a reasonable state of preservation thanks to the ongoing restoration efforts of the WMF.

Phnom Bakheng
HINDU TEMPLE

(ភ្នំបាខែង; incl in Angkor admission 1/3/7 days US$37/62/72; ⊙5am-7pm) Located around 400m south of Angkor Thom, the main attraction at Phnom Bakheng is the sunset view over Angkor Wat. For many years, the whole affair turned into a circus, with crowds of tourists ascending the slopes of the hill and jockeying for space. Numbers are now restricted to just 300 visitors at any one time, so get here early (4pm) to guarantee a sunset spot. The temple, built by Yasovarman I (r 889–910), has five tiers, with seven levels.

Banteay Kdei
& Sra Srang
BUDDHIST TEMPLE

(បន្ទាយក្តី និងស្រះស្រង់; incl in Angkor admission 1/3/7 days US$37/62/72; ⊙7.30am-5.30pm) Banteay Kdei, a massive Buddhist monastery from the latter part of the 12th century, is surrounded by four concentric walls. Each of its four entrances is decorated with garudas (eagle-like beings), which hold aloft one of Jayavarman VII's favourite themes: the four faces of Avalokiteshvara. East of Banteay Kdei is a vast pool of water, Sra Srang, measuring 800m by 400m, reserved as a bathing pool for the king and his consorts.

Bakong
HINDU TEMPLE

(បាគង; ⊙7.30am-5.30pm) Bakong is the largest and most interesting of the Roluos group of temples. Built and dedicated to Shiva by Indravarman I, it's a representation of Mt Meru, and it served as the city's central temple. The east-facing complex consists of a five-tier central pyramid of sandstone, 60m square at the base, flanked by eight towers of brick and sandstone, and by other minor sanctuaries. A number of the lower towers are still partly covered by their original plasterwork.

⊙ Further Afield

★Banteay Srei
HINDU TEMPLE

(បន្ទាយស្រី; incl in Angkor admission 1/3/7 days US$37/62/72; ⊙7.30am-5.30pm) Considered by many to be the jewel in the crown of Angkorian art, Banteay Srei is cut from stone of a pinkish hue and includes some of the finest stone carving anywhere on earth. Begun in 967 CE, it is one of the smallest sites at Angkor, but what it lacks in size it makes up for in stature. The art gallery of Angkor, this Hindu temple dedicated to Shiva is wonderfully well preserved, and many of its carvings are three-dimensional.

Banteay Srei means 'Citadel of the Women', and it is said that it must have been built by a woman, as the elaborate carvings are supposedly too fine for the hand of a man.

Banteay Srei is one of the few temples around Angkor to be commissioned not by a king but by a brahman, who may have been a tutor to Jayavarman V. The temple is square and has entrances at the east and west, with the east approached by a causeway. Of interest are the lavishly decorated libraries and the three central towers, which are decorated with male and female divinities and beautiful filigree relief work.

Classic carvings at Banteay Srei include delicate women with lotus flowers in hand and traditional skirts clearly visible, as well as breathtaking re-creations of scenes from the epic *Ramayana* adorning the library pediments (carved inlays above a lintel). However, the sum of the parts is no greater than the whole – almost every inch of these interior buildings is covered in decoration. Standing watch over such perfect creations are the mythical guardians, all of which are copies of originals stored in the National Museum.

Banteay Srei is about 32km northeast of Siem Reap and 21km northeast of Bayon. It is well signposted and the road is surfaced all the way, so a trip from Siem Reap should take about 45 minutes by car or one hour by tuk tuk. Drivers will want a bit of extra cash to come out here, so agree on a sum first.

There's plenty to do in Banteay Srei district as well as several homestays should you wish to stay and explore the area. It is possible to combine a visit to Banteay Srei as part of a long day trip to the River of a Thousand Lingas at Kbal Spean and Beng Mealea. A half-day itinerary might include Banteay Srei, the Cambodia Landmine Museum and Banteay Samre. It takes 45 minutes to explore Banteay Srei temple, but allow 1½ hours to visit the information centre and explore the area.

Banteay Samré
HINDU TEMPLE

(បន្ទាយសំរែ; ☉7.30am-5.30pm) Banteay Samré dates from the same period as Angkor Wat and was built by Suryavarman II. The temple is in a fairly healthy state of preservation due to some extensive renovation work, although its isolation has resulted in some looting during the past few decades. The area consists of a central temple with four wings, preceded by a hall and also accompanied by two libraries, the southern one remarkably well preserved.

Kbal Spean
HINDU SHRINE

(ក្បាលស្ពាន; River of a Thousand Lingas; incl in Angkor admission 1/3/7 days US$37/62/72; ☉7.30am-5.30pm) A spectacularly carved riverbed, Kbal Spean is set deep in the jungle to the northeast of Angkor. More commonly referred to in English as the 'River of a Thousand Lingas', the name actually means 'bridgehead', a reference to the natural rock bridge here. *Lingas* (phallic symbols) have been elaborately carved into the riverbed, and images of Hindu deities are dotted about the area. It was 'discovered' in 1969, when ethnologist Jean Boulbet was shown the area by a hermit.

Phnom Kulen
MOUNTAIN

(ភ្នំគូលែន; www.adfkulen.org; US$20; ☉6-11am to ascend, noon-5pm to descend) Considered by Khmers to be the most sacred mountain in Cambodia, Phnom Kulen is a popular place of pilgrimage on weekends and during festivals. It played a significant role in the history of the Khmer empire, as it was from here in 802 CE that Jayavarman II proclaimed himself a *devaraja* (god-king), giving birth to the Cambodian kingdom. Attractions include a giant reclining Buddha, hundreds of lingams carved in the riverbed, an impressive waterfall and some remote temples.

★ Beng Mealea
BUDDHIST TEMPLE

(បឹងមាលា; US$5; ☉7.30am-5.30pm) A spectacular sight to behold, Beng Mealea, located about 68km northeast of Siem Reap, is one of the most mysterious temples at Angkor, as nature has well and truly run riot. Exploring this *Titanic* of temples, built to the same floor plan as Angkor Wat, is the ultimate Indiana Jones experience. Built in the 12th century under Suryavarman II, Beng Mealea is enclosed by a massive moat measuring 1.2km by 900m.

Koh Ker
HINDU TEMPLE

(កោះកេរ្តិ៍; US$10; ☉7.30am-5.30pm) Abandoned to the forests of the north, Koh Ker, capital of the Angkorian empire from 928 to 944 CE, is within day-trip distance of Siem Reap. Most visitors start at Prasat Krahom where impressive stone carvings grace lintels, doorposts and slender window columns. The principal monument is Mayan-looking Prasat Thom, a 55m-wide, 40m-high sandstone-faced pyramid whose seven tiers offer spectacular views across the forest. Koh Ker is 127km northeast of Siem Reap.

🛈 Getting There & Around

The central temple area is just 8km from Siem Reap, and can be visited using anything from a car or motorcycle to a sturdy pair of walking boots. For the ultimate Angkor experience, try a pick-and-mix approach, with a *moto*, tuk tuk or car for one day to cover the remote sites, a bicycle to experience the central temples, and an exploration on foot for a spot of peace and serenity.

BICYCLE

Cycling is a great way to get around the temples, as there are few hills and the roads are good, so you don't need much experience. You take in more than from out of a car window or on the back of a speeding *moto*.

Many guesthouses and hotels in town rent bikes for around US$1 to US$2 per day. Electric bicycles hired out by **Green e-bikes** (📱095 700130; www.greene-bike.com; Central Market; per 24hr US$11; ☉7.30am-7pm) and others are also a very popular way to tour the temples.

CAR & MOTORCYCLE

A car for the day around the central temples is US$30 to US$35 and can be arranged with hotels, guesthouses and agencies in Siem Reap.

MOTO & TUK TUK

Many independent travellers end up visiting the temples by *moto* (unmarked motorcycle taxi) or tuk tuk. Drivers accost visitors from the moment they set foot in Siem Reap, but they often end up being knowledgeable and friendly, and good companions for a tour around the temples, starting at around US$10 per day for a *moto* and about US$15 to US$20 per day for a tuk tuk.

Tuk tuks are a popular way to get around Angkor as fellow travellers can still talk to each other as they explore (unlike on the back of a *moto*). They also offer some protection from the rain. Slightly cheaper are the smaller Indian-style auto-rickshaws, but they offer a little less breeze than *remork-motos*.

Understand
Vietnam

History

The Vietnamese trace their roots back to the Red River Delta where farmers first cultivated rice. Millennia of struggle against the Chinese then followed. Vietnam only became a united state in the 19th century, but it quickly faced the ignominy of French colonialism and then the devastation of the American intervention. The nation has survived tempestuous times, but strength of character has served it well. Today, Vietnam has benefited from a sustained period of development and increasing prosperity.

The coastal Champa kingdoms were predominantly Hindu, their culture and religion heavily influenced by India. Shiva and the earth goddess Lady Po Nagar were two principal deities.

To get an idea of Vietnam's turbulent history all you have to do is stroll through any town in the country and take at look at the street names. Then try it again somewhere else. You'll soon get déjà vu. The same names occur again and again, reflecting the national heroes who, over the last 2000 years, have repelled a succession of foreign invaders. If the street borders a river, it'll be called Bach Dang (after the battles of 938 and 1288); a principal boulevard will be Le Loi (the emperor who defeated the Chinese in 1427).

The Vietnamese, in the backyard of a giant neighbour, have first and foremost had to deal with China. They've been resisting Chinese domination from as far back as the 2nd century BCE and had to endure a 1000-year occupation. The struggle to nationhood has been immense.

Sure, the American War in Vietnam captured the attention of the West, but for the Vietnamese the Americans were simply the last in a long line of visitors who have come and gone. As far as Ho Chi Minh was concerned, no matter what was required or how long it took, they too would be vanquished.

In centuries past, the Khmers, the Mongols and Chams were all defeated. There was a humbling period of colonialism under the French. As recently as 1979, just after the cataclysmic horrors of the American War, with the country on its knees, Vietnam took on an invading Chinese army – and sent them home in a matter of weeks.

Inevitably all these invaders have left their mark. The Chinese brought Buddhism, Taoism and the principles of Confucianism (community above the individual and a respect for education and family). The French introduced railways, and bequeathed some grand architecture and

TIMELINE	2789 BCE	2000 BCE	300BCE
	The Van Lang kingdom, considered the first independent Vietnamese state, is founded by the Hung Vuong kings. It's referred to by both the Chin and Tang Chinese dynasties.	The Bronze Age Dong Son culture emerges in the Red River Delta around Hanoi, renowned for its rice cultivation and the production of bronze ware, including drums and gongs.	Vietnamese people of the northern region were culturally divided between Au Viet (highland Vietnamese) and Lac Viet (Vietnamese of the plains) who settled the Red River basin.

fabulous cuisine. And though the Americans left a devastated nation, Vietnamese pride remained intact.

In recent years, progress has been remarkable, as Vietnam has become a key member of ASEAN and its economy has boomed – though corruption (Vietnam was ranked 113 out of 176 countries in Transparency International's 2016 corruption index), creaking infrastructure and an anti-democratic ruling party remain. But the country is united, its borders secure, and the Vietnamese people look forward to a lasting period of stability and progress.

The Early Days

Humans first inhabited northern Vietnam about 500,000 years ago, though it took until 7000 BCE for these hunter-gatherers to practise rudimentary agriculture. The sophisticated Dong Son culture, famous for its bronze *moko* drums, emerged some time around the 3rd century BCE. The Dong Son period also saw huge advances in rice cultivation and the emergence of the Red River Delta as a major agricultural centre.

From the 1st to 6th centuries CE, southern Vietnam was part of the Indianised Cambodian kingdom of Funan – famous for its refined art and architecture. Based around the walled city of Angkor Borei, it was probably a grouping of feudal states rather than a unified empire. The people of Funan constructed an elaborate system of canals both for transportation and the irrigation of rice. Funan's principal port city was Oc-Eo in the Mekong Delta, and archaeological excavations here suggest there was contact with China, Indonesia, Persia and even the Mediterranean. Later on, the Chenla empire replaced the Funan kingdom, spreading along the Mekong River.

The Hindu kingdom of Champa emerged around present-day Danang in the late 2nd century CE. Like Funan, it adopted Sanskrit as a sacred language and borrowed heavily from Indian art and culture. By the 8th century, Champa had expanded southward to include what is now Nha Trang and Phan Rang. The Cham were a feisty bunch who conducted raids along the entire coast of Indochina, and thus found themselves

> The people of the Bronze Age Dong Son period were major traders in the region, and bronze drums from northern Vietnam have been found as far afield as the island of Alor, in eastern Indonesia.

IN THE BEGINNING...

Every country has a creation myth and Vietnam is no exception. The Vietnamese claim descent from a union of Dragon Lord Lac Long Quan and the fairy Au Co. Their relationship was fruitful, producing 100 sons, 50 migrating with their mother to the mountains and the other half travelling with their father to the sea. These sons founded the first Vietnamese dynasty, the Hung, who ruled over the kingdom of Van Lang, whose people were the first to be known as the Lac Viet.

250 BCE	111 BCE	40 CE	166
Van Lang is conquered by a Chinese warlord and a new kingdom known as Au Lac is established at Co Loa, close to the modern-day capital of Hanoi.	The Han emperors of China annex the Red River Delta region of Vietnam, heralding 1000 years of Chinese rule. Confucianism prevails as the governing philosophy.	The Trung Sisters (Hai Ba Trung) vanquish the Chinese and proclaim themselves queens of an independent Vietnam.	First contact between Rome and China as envoys pass through the Gulf of Tonkin.

in a perpetual state of war with the Vietnamese to the north and the Khmers to the south. Ultimately this cost them their kingdom, as they found themselves squeezed between these two great powers.

1000 Years of Chinese Occupation

The Chinese conquered the Red River Delta in the 2nd century BCE. Over the following centuries, large numbers of Chinese settlers, officials and scholars moved south, seeking to impress a centralised state system on the Vietnamese.

In the most famous act of resistance, in 40 CE, the Trung Sisters (Hai Ba Trung) rallied the people, raised an army and led a revolt against the Chinese. The Chinese counter-attacked, but, rather than surrender, the Trung Sisters threw themselves into the Hat Giang River. There were numerous small-scale rebellions against Chinese rule – which was characterised by tyranny, forced labour and insatiable demands for tribute – from the 3rd to 6th centuries, but all were defeated.

However, the early Vietnamese learned much from the Chinese, including the advancement of dykes and irrigation works – reinforcing the role of rice as the 'staff of life'. As food became more plentiful the population expanded, forcing the Vietnamese to seek new lands. The Truong Son Mountains prevented westward expansion, as the climate was harsh and the terrain unsuited to rice cultivation, so instead the Vietnamese moved south along the coast. During this era, Vietnam was a key port of call on the sea route between China and India. The Chinese introduced Confucianism, Taoism and Mahayana Buddhism to Vietnam, while the Indian influence brought Theravada Buddhism and Hinduism (to Champa and Funan). Monks carried with them the scientific and medical knowledge of these two great civilisations and Vietnam was soon producing its own doctors, botanists and scholars.

Liberation from China

In the early 10th century, the Tang dynasty collapsed, provoking the Vietnamese to launch a revolt against Chinese rule. In AD 938, popular patriot Ngo Quyen defeated Chinese forces by luring the Chinese fleet up the Bach Dang River in a feigned retreat, only to counter-attack and impale their ships on sharpened stakes hidden beneath the waters. This ended 1000 years of Chinese rule (though it was not to be the last time the Vietnamese would tussle with their mighty northern neighbour).

From the 11th to 13th centuries, Vietnamese independence was consolidated under the emperors of the Ly dynasty, founded by Ly Thai To. This was a period of progress that saw the introduction of an elaborate dyke system for flood control and cultivation, and the establishment of the country's first university. During the Ly dynasty, the Chinese, the Khmer and the Cham launched attacks on Vietnam, but all were repelled.

Dynasties of Vietnam

Ngo 939–965 CE

Dinh 968–980 CE

Early Le 980–1009 CE

Ly 1010–1225

Tran 1225–1400

Ho 1400–1407

Post-Tran 1407–1413

Chinese rule 1414–1427

Later Le 1428–1524

Mac 1527–1592

Trinh Lords of the North 1539–1787

Nguyen Lords of the South 1558–1778

Tay Son 1788–1802

Nguyen 1802–1945

192	225–248	446	602
Emergence of the Hindu Kingdom of Champa.	Female warrior, Trieu Thi Trinh, described as a giant who rode war elephants to battle, confronts the Chinese for decades until defeat and her suicide in 248.	Relations between the kingdom of Champa and the Chinese deteriorate. China invades Champa, sacks the capital of Simhapura and plunders a 50-tonne golden Buddha statue.	Rebellions by leaders including Ly Bon and Trieu Quang Phuc against Chinese rule ultimately fail as the Sui dynasty reconquers Vietnam, with its capital at Dai La Thanh (Hanoi).

Meanwhile, the Vietnamese continued their expansion southwards and slowly but surely began to consolidate control of the Cham kingdom.

Bach Dang Again

Mongol warrior Kublai Khan completed his conquest of China in the mid-13th century. For his next trick, he planned to attack Champa and demanded the right to cross Vietnamese territory. The Vietnamese refused, but the Mongol hordes – all 500,000 of them – pushed ahead. They met their match in the revered general Tran Hung Dao. He defeated them at Bach Dang River, utilising acute military acumen by repeating the same tactics as Ngo Quyen in one of the most celebrated scalps in Vietnamese history.

China Bites Back

The Chinese took control of Vietnam again in the early 15th century, taking the national archives and some of the country's intellectuals back to Nanjing – a loss that was to have a lasting impact on Vietnamese civilisation. Heavy taxation and slave labour were also typical of the era. The poet Nguyen Trai (1380–1442) wrote of this period: 'Were the water of the Eastern Sea to be exhausted, the stain of their ignominy could not be washed away; all the bamboo of the Southern Mountains would not suffice to provide the paper for recording all their crimes'.

Archaeologists conducting excavations at Oc-Eo discovered a Roman medallion dating from 152 CE, bearing the likeness of Antoninus Pius.

Enter Le Loi

In 1418, wealthy philanthropist Le Loi sparked the Lam Son Uprising by refusing to serve as an official for the Chinese Ming dynasty. By 1425, local rebellions had erupted in several regions and Le Loi travelled the countryside to rally the people, and eventually defeat the Chinese.

Le Loi and his successors launched a campaign to take over Cham lands to the south, which culminated in the occupation of its capital Vijaya, near present-day Quy Nhon, in 1471. This was the end of Champa as a military power and the Cham people began to migrate southwards as Vietnamese settlers moved into their territory.

938	1010	1010–1225	1076
The Chinese are kicked out of Vietnam after 1000 years of occupation, as Ngo Quyen leads his people to victory in the battle of the Bach Dang River, when the Chinese fleet is impaled on submerged spikes.	Thang Long (City of the Soaring Dragon), known today as Hanoi, is founded by Emperor Ly Thai To and becomes the new capital of Vietnam.	Under the 200-year Ly dynasty Vietnam maintains many institutions and traditions of the Chinese era including Confucianism and its civil service structure. Wet rice cultivation remains vital.	The Vietnamese military, led by General Ly Thuong, attacks the Sung Chinese and wins a decisive battle near the present-day city of Nanning, and later defeats Cham forces.

The Coming of the Europeans

The first Portuguese sailors came ashore at Danang in 1516 and were soon followed by a party of Dominican missionaries. During the following decades the Portuguese began to trade with Vietnam, setting up a commercial colony alongside those of the Japanese and Chinese at Faifo (present-day Hoi An). With the exception of the Philippines, which was ruled by the Spanish for 400 years, the Catholic Church has had a greater impact on Vietnam than on any other country in Asia.

Lording it over the People

In a dress rehearsal for the tumultuous events of the 20th century, Vietnam found itself divided in two throughout much of the 17th and 18th centuries. The powerful Trinh Lords were later Le kings who ruled the North. To the South were the Nguyen Lords. The Trinh failed in their persistent efforts to subdue the Nguyen, in part because their Dutch weaponry was matched by the Portuguese armaments supplied to the Nguyen. By this time, several European nations were interested in Vietnam's potential and were jockeying for influence. For their part, the Nguyen expanded southwards again, absorbing territories in the Mekong Delta.

Buddhism flourished during the 17th and 18th centuries and many pagodas were erected across the country. However, it was not pure Buddhism, but a peculiarly Vietnamese blend mixed with ancestor worship, animism and Taoism.

Tay Son Rebellion

In 1765 a rebellion broke out in the town of Tay Son near Qui Nhon, ostensibly against the punitive taxes of the Nguyen family. The Tay Son Rebels, as they were known, were led by the brothers Nguyen, who espoused a sort of Robin Hood–like philosophy of take from the rich and redistribute to the poor. It was clearly popular and in less than a decade they controlled the whole of central Vietnam. In 1783 they captured Saigon and the South, killing the reigning prince and his family. Nguyen Lu became king of the South, while Nguyen Nhac was crowned king of central Vietnam.

Continuing their conquests, the Tay Son Rebels overthrew the Trinh Lords in the North, while the Chinese moved in to take advantage of the power vacuum. In response, the third brother, Nguyen Hue, proclaimed himself Emperor Quang Trung. In 1789, Nguyen Hue's armed forces overwhelmingly defeated the Chinese army at Dong Da in another of the greatest hits of Vietnamese history.

In the South, Nguyen Anh, a rare survivor from the original Nguyen Lords – yes, know your Nguyens if you hope to understand Vietnamese history! – gradually overcame the rebels. In 1802, Nguyen Anh proclaimed himself Emperor Gia Long, thus beginning the Nguyen dynasty. When he captured Hanoi, his work was complete and, for the first time in two centuries, Vietnam was united, with Hue as its new capital city.

1288	14th century	1427	1471
The Mongols invade Dai Viet but General Tran Hung Dao repeats history by spearing the Mongol fleet on sharpened stakes on the Bach Dang River.	Cham forces led by king Che Bong Nga kill Viet emperor Tran Due Tong and lay siege to his capital Thang Long in 1377 and 1383.	Le Loi triumphs over the Chinese, declaring himself emperor, the first in the long line of the Le dynasty. He is revered as one of the nation's greatest heroes.	The Vietnamese inflict a humbling defeat on the kingdom of Champa, killing more than 60,000 Cham soldiers and capturing 36,000, including the king and most of the royal family.

The Traditionalists Prevail

Emperor Gia Long returned Vietnam to Confucian values in an effort to consolidate his precarious position, a calculated move to win over conservative elements of the elite.

Gia Long's son, Emperor Minh Mang, worked to strengthen the state. He was profoundly hostile to Catholicism, which he saw as a threat to Confucian traditions, and extended this antipathy to all Western influences.

The early Nguyen emperors continued the expansionist policies of the preceding dynasties, pushing into Cambodia and Lao territory. Clashes with Thailand broke out in an attempt to pick apart the skeleton of the fractured Khmer empire. The return to traditional values may have earned support among the elite at home, but the isolation and hostility to the West ultimately cost the Nguyen emperors as they failed to modernise the country quickly enough to compete with the well-armed Europeans.

For a closer look at China's 1000-year occupation of Vietnam, which was instrumental in shaping the country's outlook and attitude today, try *The Birth of Vietnam* (1983) by Keith Weller Taylor.

The French Takeover

France's military activity in Vietnam began in 1847, when the French Navy attacked Danang harbour in response to Emperor Thieu Tri's imprisonment of Catholic missionaries. Saigon was seized in early 1859 and, in 1862, Emperor Tu Duc signed a treaty that gave the French the three eastern provinces of Cochinchina (the southern part of Vietnam during the French-colonial era). However, over the next four decades the French colonial venture in Indochina faltered repeatedly and, at times, only the reckless adventures of a few mavericks kept it going.

In 1872 Jean Dupuis, a merchant seeking to supply salt and weapons via the Red River, seized the Hanoi Citadel. Captain Francis Garnier, ostensibly dispatched to rein in Dupuis, instead took over where Dupuis left off and began a conquest of the North.

A few weeks after the death of Tu Duc in 1883, the French attacked Hue and the Treaty of Protectorate was imposed on the imperial court. A struggle then began for royal succession that was notable for its palace coups, the death of emperors in suspicious circumstances and heavy-handed French diplomacy.

The French colonial authorities carried out ambitious public works, such as the construction of the Saigon–Hanoi railway and draining of the Mekong Delta swamps. These projects were funded by heavy government taxes that had a devastating impact on the rural economy. Such operations became notorious for the abysmal wages paid by the French and the appalling treatment of Vietnamese workers.

One of the most prominent early missionaries was French Jesuit Alexandre de Rhodes (1591–1660), widely lauded for his work in devising *quoc ngu*, the Latin-based phonetic alphabet in which Vietnamese is written today.

Independence Aspirations

Throughout the colonial period, the desire of many Vietnamese for independence simmered below the surface. Nationalist aspirations often erupted into open defiance of the French. This ranged from the

16th century	1516	1524	17th century
HCMC begins life as humble Prey Nokor, a backwater Khmer village in what was then the eastern edge of Cambodia.	Portuguese traders land at Danang, sparking the start of European interest in Vietnam. They set up a trading post in Faifo (present-day Hoi An) and introduce Catholicism.	A period of instability and warfare ensues as feudal conflicts rage between the Trinh from the north (Thang Long) and the Nguyen from the south (based around Hue).	Ethnic Vietnamese settlers arrive in the Mekong Delta and Saigon region, taking advantage of the weaknesses of the Khmer, who are torn apart by internal strife and Siamese invasions.

publishing of patriotic periodicals to a dramatic attempt to poison the French garrison in Hanoi.

The imperial court in Hue, although allegedly quite corrupt, was a centre of nationalist sentiment and the French orchestrated a game of musical thrones, as one emperor after another turned against their patronage. This culminated in the accession of Emperor Bao Dai in 1925, who was just 12 years old at the time and studying in France.

Leading patriots soon realised that modernisation was the key to an independent Vietnam. Phan Boi Chau launched the Dong Du (Go East) movement that planned to send Vietnamese intellectuals to Japan for study with a view to fomenting a successful uprising in the future. Phan Tru Chinh favoured the education of the masses, the modernisation of the economy and working with the French towards independence. It was at this time that the Roman script of *quoc ngu* came to prominence, as educators realised this would be a far easier tool with which to educate the masses than the elaborate Chinese-style script of *nom*.

Rise of the Communists

The most successful of the anti-colonialists were the communists, who were able to tune into the frustrations and aspirations of the population – especially the peasants – and effectively channel their demands for fairer land distribution.

The story of Vietnamese communism, which in many ways is also the political biography of Ho Chi Minh, is convoluted. The first Marxist grouping in Indochina was the Vietnam Revolutionary Youth League, founded by Ho Chi Minh in Canton, China, in 1925. This was succeeded in February 1930 by the Vietnamese Communist Party. In 1941 Ho formed the Viet Minh, which resisted the Vichy French government, as well as Japanese forces, and carried out extensive political activities during WWII. Despite its nationalist platform, the Viet Minh was, from its inception, dominated by Ho's communists. However, as well as being a communist, Ho appeared pragmatic, patriotic and populist and understood the need for national unity.

WWII & Famine

When France fell to Nazi Germany in 1940, the Indochinese government of Vichy France–collaborators acquiesced to the presence of Japanese troops in Vietnam. The Japanese left the French administration in charge of the day-to-day running of the country and, for a time, Vietnam was spared the ravages of Japanese occupation. However, as WWII drew to a close, Japanese rice requisitions, combined with floods and breaches in the dykes, caused a horrific famine in which perhaps 2 million North Vietnamese people starved to death. The only force opposed to both the French and Japanese presence in Vietnam was the Viet Minh, and

The 1945 Potsdam Agreement failed to recognise Vietnam as an independent state, but partitioned Vietnam at the 16th Parallel (just north of Danang).

1651	1765	1802	1862
The first *quoc ngu* (Romanised Vietnamese) dictionary, the *Dictionarium Annamiticum Lusitanum et Latinum*, is produced, following years of work by Father Alexandre de Rhodes.	The Tay Son Rebellion erupts near Quy Nhon, led by the brothers Nguyen; they take control of the whole country over the next 25 years.	Emperor Gia Long takes the throne and the Nguyen dynasty is born, ruling over Vietnam until 1945. The country is reunited for the first time in more than 200 years.	Following French attacks on both Danang and Saigon, Emperor Tu Duc signs a treaty ceding control of the Mekong Delta provinces to France, renaming them Cochinchina (Cochinchine).

Ho Chi Minh received assistance from the US government during this period. As events unfolded in mainland Europe, the French and Japanese fell out and the Viet Minh saw its opportunity to strike.

A False Dawn

By the spring of 1945 the Viet Minh controlled large swathes of the country, particularly in the north. In mid-August, Ho Chi Minh called for a general uprising, later known as the August Revolution. Meanwhile in central Vietnam, Bao Dai abdicated in favour of the new government, and in the South the Viet Minh soon held power in a shaky coalition with non-communist groups. On 2 September 1945, Ho Chi Minh declared independence at a rally in Hanoi. Throughout this period, Ho wrote many letters to US president Harry Truman and the US State Department asking for US aid, but received no replies.

A footnote on the agenda of the Potsdam Conference of 1945 was the disarming of Japanese occupation forces in Vietnam: Chinese Kuomintang would accept the Japanese surrender north of the 16th Parallel and the British would do so in the south.

When the British arrived in Saigon, anarchy ruled with private militia, the remaining Japanese forces, the French and Viet Minh competing for hegemony. When armed French paratroopers reacted to Ho's declaration of independence by attacking civilians, the Viet Minh began a guerrilla campaign. On 24 September, French general Jacques Philippe Leclerc arrived in Saigon, declaring, 'we have come to reclaim our inheritance'.

In the north, Chinese Kuomintang troops were fleeing the Chinese communists and making their way southward towards Hanoi. Ho tried to placate them, but as the months of Chinese occupation dragged on, he decided to accept a temporary return of the French, deeming them less of a long-term threat than the Chinese. The French were to stay for five years in return for recognising Vietnam as a free state within the French Union.

War with the French

The French had managed to regain control of Vietnam, at least in name. However, following the French shelling of Haiphong in November 1946, which killed hundreds of civilians, the detente with the Viet Minh began to unravel. Fighting soon broke out in Hanoi, and Ho Chi Minh and his forces fled to the mountains to regroup, where they would remain for the next eight years.

In the face of determined Vietnamese nationalism, the French proved unable to reassert their control. Despite massive US aid to halt communism throughout Asia, for the French it was ultimately an unwinnable war. As Ho said to the French at the outset: 'You can kill 10 of my men for every one I kill of yours, but even at those odds you will lose and I will win'.

The 2002 remake of *The Quiet American* (based on the 1955 novel by Graham Greene), starring Michael Caine, is a must-see. Beautifully shot, it is a classic introduction to Vietnam in the 1950s, as the French disengaged and the Americans moved in to take their place.

HISTORY A FALSE DAWN

1883	late 19th century	1905	1925
The French impose the Treaty of Protectorate on the Vietnamese, marking the start of 70 years of colonial control, although active resistance continues throughout this period.	The Romanised *quoc ngu* alphabet for Vietnamese grows in popularity as a means of eradicating illiteracy and promoting education. Traditional Chinese-style scripts are phased out.	The progressive Dong Du ('Go East') movement seeks to modernise the nation by sending Vietnamese students to Japan for education.	Ho Chi Minh moves towards organised political agitation, establishing the Revolutionary Youth League of Vietnam in southern China, an early incarnation of the Vietnamese Communist Party.

After eight years of fighting, the Viet Minh controlled much of Vietnam and neighbouring Laos. On 7 May 1954, after a 57-day siege, more than 10,000 starving French troops surrendered to the Viet Minh at Dien Bien Phu. This defeat brought an end to the French colonial adventure in Indochina. The following day, the Geneva Conference opened to negotiate an end to the conflict, but the French had no cards left to bring to the table. Resolutions included an exchange of prisoners; the 'temporary' division of Vietnam into two zones at the Ben Hai River (near the 17th Parallel) until nationwide elections could be held; the free passage of people across the 17th Parallel for a period of 300 days; and the holding of nationwide elections on 20 July 1956. In the course of the Franco-Viet Minh War, more than 35,000 French fighters had been killed and 48,000 wounded; there are no exact numbers for Vietnamese casualties, but they were certainly higher.

In May 1954, the Viet Minh dug a tunnel network under French defences on Hill A1 at Dien Bien Phu and rigged it with explosives. Comrade Sapper Nguyen Van Bach volunteered himself as a human fuse in case the detonator failed. Luckily for him it didn't and he is today honoured as a national hero.

A Separate South Vietnam

After the Geneva Accords were signed and sealed, the South was ruled by a government led by Ngo Dinh Diem, a fiercely anti-communist Catholic. His power base was significantly strengthened by 900,000 refugees, many of them Catholics, who had fled the communist North during the 300-day free-passage period.

Nationwide elections were never held, as the Americans rightly feared that Ho Chi Minh would win with a massive majority. During the first few years of his rule, Diem consolidated power fairly effectively, defeating the Binh Xuyen crime syndicate and the private armies of the Hoa Hao and Cao Dai religious sects. During Diem's 1957 official visit to the USA, President Eisenhower called him the 'miracle man' of Asia. As time went on Diem became increasingly tyrannical, closing Buddhist monasteries, imprisoning monks and banning opposition parties. He also doled out power to family members (including his sister-in-law Madame Nhu, who effectively became First Lady).

In the early 1960s the South was rocked by anti-Diem unrest led by university students and Buddhist clergy, which included several highly publicised self-immolations by monks that shocked the world. The US began to see Diem as a liability and threw its support behind a military coup. A group of young generals led the operation in November 1963. Diem was meant to go into exile, but the generals executed both Diem and his brother. Diem was succeeded by a string of military rulers who continued his policies.

In Hanoi and the North, Ho Chi Minh created a very effective police state. The regime was characterised by ruthless police power, denunciations by a huge network of secret informers, and the blacklisting of dissidents, their children and their children's children.

A New North Vietnam

The Geneva Accords allowed the leadership of the Democratic Republic of Vietnam to return to Hanoi and assert control of all territory north of the 17th Parallel. The new government immediately set out to eliminate

1930–31	1930s	1940	1941
The Nghe Tinh rebellion against French rule features strikes and protests by Vietnamese farmers, workers and intellectuals against the French regime and local landowners.	Marxism gains in popularity with the formation of three communist parties, which later unite to form the Vietnamese Communist Party with Tran Phu as the first Secretary General.	The Japanese occupation of Vietnam begins, as the pro–Vichy France colonial government offers the use of military facilities in return for continued control over administration.	Ho Chi Minh forms the Viet Minh (short for the League for the Independence of Vietnam), a liberation movement seeking independence from France and fighting the Japanese occupation.

UNCLE OF THE PEOPLE

Father of the nation, Ho Chi Minh (Bringer of Light) was the son of a fiercely nationalistic scholar-official. Born Nguyen Tat Thanh near Vinh in 1890, he was educated in Hue and adopted many pseudonyms during his momentous life. Many Vietnamese affectionately refer to him as Bac Ho ('Uncle Ho') today.

In 1911 he signed up as a cook's apprentice on a French ship, sailing to North America, Africa and Europe. While odd-jobbing in England and France as a gardener, snow sweeper, waiter, photo retoucher and stoker, his political consciousness began to develop.

Ho Chi Minh moved to Paris, where he mastered a number of languages (including English, French, German and Mandarin) and began to promote the issue of Indochinese independence. He was a founding member of the French Communist Party in 1920 and later travelled to Guangzhou in China, where he founded the Revolutionary Youth League of Vietnam.

During the early 1930s, the English rulers of Hong Kong obliged the French government by imprisoning Ho for his revolutionary activities. After his release he travelled to the USSR and China. In 1941 he returned to Vietnam for the first time in 30 years, and founded the Viet Minh, the goal of which was the independence of Vietnam. As Japan prepared to surrender in August 1945, Ho Chi Minh led the August Revolution, and his forces then established control throughout much of Vietnam.

The return of the French compelled the Viet Minh to conduct a guerrilla war, which ultimately led to victory against the colonists at Dien Bien Phu in 1954. Ho then led North Vietnam until his death in September 1969 – he never lived to see the North's victory over the South.

The party has worked hard to preserve the reputation of Bac Ho. His image dominates contemporary Vietnam – no town is complete without a Ho statue, and most cities have a museum in his name. This cult of personality is in stark contrast to the simplicity with which Ho lived his life. For more on Ho, check out *Ho Chi Minh* (2000), the excellent biography by William J Duiker.

those elements of the population that threatened its power. Tens of thousands of landlords, some with only tiny holdings, were denounced to security committees by their neighbours and arrested. Hasty trials resulted in between 10,000 and 15,000 executions and the imprisonment of thousands more. In 1956, the party, faced with widespread rural unrest, recognised that things had spiralled out of control and began a Campaign for the Rectification of Errors.

The North–South War

The communists' campaign to liberate the South began in 1959. The Ho Chi Minh Trail reopened for business, universal military conscription was implemented and the National Liberation Front (NLF), later known as the Viet Cong (VC), was formed.

mid-1940s	1944–45	1945	1945
The combination of Japanese rice requisitions and widespread flooding leads to a disastrous famine in which 10% of North Vietnam's population (around 2 million people) dies.	The Viet Minh receives funding and arms from the US Office of Strategic Services (OSS; today the CIA).	Ho Chi Minh proclaims Vietnamese independence on 2 September in Ba Dinh Square in central Hanoi, but the French aim to reassert their authority and impose colonial rule once more.	A famine kills hundreds of thousands (perhaps over 1 million) in northern Vietnam.

As the NLF launched its campaign, the Diem government quickly lost control of the countryside. To stem the tide, peasants were moved into fortified 'strategic hamlets' in order to deny the VC potential support.

For the South it was no longer just a battle with the VC. In 1964 Hanoi began sending regular North Vietnamese Army (NVA) units down the Ho Chi Minh Trail. By early 1965 the Saigon government was on its last legs. The South was losing a district capital each week, yet in 10 years only one senior South Vietnamese army officer had been wounded. The army was getting ready to evacuate Hue and Danang, and the central highlands seemed about to fall.

Viet Cong and VC are both abbreviations for Viet Nam Cong San, which means Vietnamese communist. American soldiers nicknamed the VC 'Charlie', as in 'Victor Charlie', from the NATO phonetic alphabet.

Enter the Cavalry

The Americans saw France's war in Indochina as an important element in the worldwide struggle against communist expansion. Vietnam was the next domino and could not be allowed to topple. In 1950, US advisers rolled into Vietnam, ostensibly to train local troops – but American soldiers would remain on Vietnamese soil for the next 25 years. As early as 1954, US military aid to the French topped US$2 billion.

A decisive turning point in US strategy came with the August 1964 Gulf of Tonkin incident. Two US destroyers claimed to have come under unprovoked attack off the North Vietnamese coast. Subsequent research suggests that there was a certain degree of provocation: one ship was assisting a secret South Vietnamese commando raid, and according to an official National Security Agency report in 2005, the second attack never happened.

However, on US president Lyndon Johnson's orders, 64 sorties unleashed bombs on the North – the first of thousands of such missions that would hit every single road and rail bridge in the country, as well as 4000 of North Vietnam's 5788 villages. A few days later, the US Congress overwhelmingly passed the Tonkin Gulf Resolution, which gave the president the power to take any action in Vietnam without congressional control. As the military situation of the Saigon government reached a new nadir, the first US combat troops splashed ashore at Danang in March 1965. By December 1965, there were 184,300 US military personnel in Vietnam and 636 Americans had died. By December 1967, the figures had risen to 485,600 US soldiers in the country and 16,021 dead.

For a human perspective on the North Vietnamese experience during the war, read The Sorrow of War (1987) by Bao Ninh, a poignant tale of love and loss that suggests the soldiers from the North had the same fears and desires as most American GIs.

US Strategies

By 1966 the buzzwords in Washington were 'pacification', 'search and destroy' and 'free-fire zones'. Pacification involved developing a progovernment civilian infrastructure in each village, and providing the soldiers to guard it. In some cases, villagers were evacuated so the Americans could use heavy weaponry such as napalm and tanks in areas that were declared free-fire zones.

1946	late 1940s	1949	1954
Strained relations between the Viet Minh forces and the French colonialists erupt into open fighting in Hanoi and Haiphong, marking the start of the eight-year Franco-Viet Minh War.	While the Viet Minh retreat to the mountains to regroup, the French attempt to forge a Vietnamese government under Emperor Bao Dai, last ruler of the Nguyen dynasty.	The Communist victory in China sees increased arms supplies flow across the border to Viet Minh forces, who score notable battle successes against the French.	French forces surrender to Viet Minh fighters as the siege of Dien Bien Phu comes to a dramatic close on 7 May, marking the end of colonial rule in Indochina.

These strategies were only partially successful: US forces could control the countryside by day, while the VC usually controlled it by night. Even without heavy weapons, VC guerrillas continued to inflict heavy casualties in ambushes and through extensive use of mines and booby traps. Although free-fire zones were supposed to prevent civilian casualties, plenty of villagers were nevertheless shelled, bombed, strafed or napalmed. These attacks turned out to be a fairly efficient recruiting tool for the VC.

The Turning Point

In January 1968 North Vietnamese troops launched a major attack on the US base at Khe Sanh in the Demilitarised Zone (DMZ). This battle, the single largest of the war, was in part a massive diversion from the Tet Offensive.

TRACKING THE AMERICAN WAR

The American War in Vietnam was the story for a generation. Follow in the footsteps of soldiers, journalists and politicians on all sides with a visit to the sites where the story unfolded.

Danang Beach The strip of sand (nicknamed 'China Beach' by the Americans) near Danang where US soldiers dropped in for some rest and relaxation.

Cu Chi Tunnels The Vietnamese dug an incredible and elaborate tunnel network to evade American forces, just 30km from Saigon and right under the noses of a US base.

Demilitarised Zone (DMZ) The no-one's land at the 17th Parallel, dividing North and South Vietnam. After 1954 it became one of the most heavily militarised zones in the world.

Ho Chi Minh Trail The supply route to the South; the North Vietnamese moved soldiers and munitions down this incredible trail through the Truong Son Mountains in an almost unparalleled logistical feat.

Hue Citadel The ancient Citadel was razed to the ground during street-to-street fighting in early 1968 when the Americans retook the city from the communists after a three-week occupation.

Khe Sanh This was the biggest smokescreen of the war, as the North Vietnamese massed forces around this US base in 1968 to draw attention away from the coming Tet Offensive.

Long Tan Memorial The Australian contingent who fought in Vietnam, mostly based near Vung Tau in the south, is remembered here with the Long Tan Memorial Cross.

My Lai The village of My Lai is infamous as the site of one of the worst atrocities in the war, when American GIs massacred hundreds of villagers in March 1968.

Vinh Moc Tunnels The real deal: these tunnels haven't been surgically enlarged for tourists and they mark yet another feat of infrastructural ingenuity.

1955	1960	1962	1964
Vietnam is 'temporarily' divided at the 17th Parallel into North Vietnam and South Vietnam and people are given 300 days to relocate to either side of the border.	The National Liberation Front (better known as the Viet Cong) launch a guerrilla war against the Diem government in the South, sparking the 'American War'.	Cuc Phuong National Park, just west of the city of Ninh Binh, is declared Vietnam's first national park as Ho Chi Minh declares 'forest is gold'.	Although the US is not officially at war, it launches Operation Pierce Arrow and bombs North Vietnam for the first time in retaliation for the Gulf of Tonkin incident, in which the US believed it was under attack.

THE COST OF WAR

In total, 3.14 million Americans (including 7200 women) served in Vietnam. Officially, 58,183 Americans were killed in action or listed as missing in action (MIA). The direct cost of the war was officially put at US$165 billion, though its real cost to the economy was likely to have been considerably more.

By the end of 1973, 223,748 South Vietnamese soldiers had been killed in action; North Vietnamese and VC fatalities have been estimated at 1 million. Approximately 4 million civilians (or 10% of the Vietnamese population) were injured or killed during the war. At least 300,000 Vietnamese and 1592 Americans were still listed as MIA by 2019.

The Tet Offensive marked a decisive turning point in the war. On the evening of 31 January, as the country celebrated the Lunar New Year, called Tet, the VC broke an unofficial holiday ceasefire with a series of coordinated strikes in more than 100 cities and towns. As the TV cameras rolled, a VC commando team took over the courtyard of the US embassy in central Saigon. However, the communists miscalculated the mood of the population, as the popular uprising they had hoped to provoke never materialised. In cities such as Hue, the VC were not welcomed as liberators and this contributed to a communist backlash against the civilian population.

Although the US were utterly surprised – a major failure of military intelligence – they immediately counter-attacked with massive firepower, bombing and shelling heavily populated cities. The counter-attack devastated the VC, but also traumatised the civilian population.

The Tet Offensive killed about 1000 US soldiers and 2000 Army of the Republic of Vietnam (ARVN) troops, but VC losses were more than 10 times higher. The VC may have lost the battle, but were on the road to winning the war. The US military had long been boasting that victory was just a matter of time. Watching the killing and chaos in Saigon beamed into their living rooms, many Americans stopped swallowing the official line. While US generals were proclaiming a great victory, public tolerance of the war and its casualties reached breaking point.

Simultaneously, stories began leaking out of Vietnam about atrocities and massacres carried out against unarmed Vietnamese civilians, including the infamous My Lai Massacre. This helped turn the tide and a coalition of the concerned emerged.

The poignant wartime diaries of a young doctor who volunteered for the Viet Cong and was killed during the war, *Last Night I Dreamed of Peace: The Diary of Dang Thuy Tramin*, were only published in 2005, 35 years after her death.

Nixon & His Doctrine

Once elected president, Richard Nixon released a doctrine that called on Asian nations to be more 'self-reliant' in matters of defence. Nixon's strategy advocated 'Vietnamisation' – making the South Vietnamese fight the war without the support of US troops.

1965	1967	1968	1969
To prevent the total collapse of the Saigon regime, US President Lyndon Johnson intensifies bombing of North Vietnam and approves the dispatch of American combat troops to the South.	By the end of the year, there are 1.3 million soldiers fighting for the South – nearly half a million of these are from the US.	The Viet Cong launches the Tet Offensive, a surprise attack on towns and cities throughout the South. Hundreds of Vietnamese civilians are killed by US soldiers in the My Lai Massacre.	After a lifetime dedicated to revolution, Ho Chi Minh dies in Hanoi in September 1969 of heart failure. He's succeeded by a 'collective leadership', headed by Le Duan.

Meanwhile the first half of 1969 saw the conflict escalate further as the number of US soldiers in Vietnam reached an all-time high of 543,400. While the fighting raged, Nixon's chief negotiator, Henry Kissinger, pursued peace talks in Paris with his North Vietnamese counterpart Le Duc Tho.

In 1969, the Americans began secretly bombing Cambodia in an attempt to flush out Vietnamese communist sanctuaries. In 1970, US ground forces were sent into Cambodia and the North Vietnamese moved deeper into Cambodian territory. By summer 1970, they (together with their Khmer Rouge allies) controlled half of Cambodia, including Angkor Wat.

This new escalation provoked violent anti-war protests in the US and elsewhere. A peace demonstration at Kent State University in Ohio resulted in four protesters being shot dead. The rise of organisations such as Vietnam Veterans Against the War demonstrated that it wasn't just those fearing military conscription who wanted the USA out of Vietnam. It was clear that the war was tearing America apart.

In the spring of 1972, the North Vietnamese launched an offensive across the 17th Parallel; the USA responded with increased bombing of the North and by laying mines in North Vietnam's harbours. The 'Christmas bombing' of Haiphong and Hanoi at the end of 1972 was calculated to wrest concessions from North Vietnam at the negotiating table. Eventually, the Paris Peace Accords were signed by the USA, North Vietnam, South Vietnam and the VC on 27 January 1973, which provided for a ceasefire, the total withdrawal of US combat forces and the release of 590 American POWs. The agreement failed to mention the 200,000 North Vietnamese troops still in South Vietnam.

US teams continue to search Vietnam, Laos and Cambodia for the remains of their fallen comrades. In more recent years, the Vietnamese have been searching for their own MIAs in Cambodia and Laos.

The American War in Vietnam claimed the lives of countless journalists. For a look at the finest photographic work from the battlefront, *Requiem: By the Photographers who died in Vietnam* (1977), by Horst Faas and Tim Page, is an anthology of work from fallen correspondents on all sides of the conflict and a fitting tribute to their trade.

Other Foreign Involvement

Australia, New Zealand, South Korea, the Philippines and Thailand also sent military personnel to South Vietnam as part of what the Americans called the 'Free World Military Forces', whose purpose was to help internationalise the American war effort in order to give it more legitimacy.

Australia's participation in the conflict constituted the most significant commitment of its armed forces since WWII. Of the almost 60,000 Australian military personnel who served in the war, casualties totalled 521, with over 3000 soldiers wounded.

Most of New Zealand's contingent, which numbered 548 at its highest point in 1968, operated as an integral part of the Australian Task Force, which was stationed near Baria, just north of Vung Tau.

HISTORY OTHER FOREIGN INVOLVEMENT

1970	1971	1972	1973
Nixon's national security advisor, Henry Kissinger, and Le Duc Tho, for the Hanoi government, start talks in Paris as the US begins a reduction in troop numbers.	The Army of the Republic of Vietnam's (ARVN's) Operation Lam Son, aimed at cutting the Ho Chi Minh Trail in Laos, ends in calamitous defeat as half its invading troops are either captured or killed.	The North Vietnamese cross the Demilitarised Zone (DMZ) at the 17th Parallel to attack South Vietnam and US forces in what becomes known as the Easter Offensive.	All sides put pen to paper to sign the Paris Peace Accords on 27 January 1973, stipulating an end to hostilities, but the conflict rumbles on.

The Fall of the South

The War in Numbers

3689 US fixed-wing aircraft lost

4857 US helicopters downed

15 million tonnes of US ammunition expended

4 million Vietnamese killed or injured

Most US military personnel departed Vietnam in 1973, leaving behind a small contingent of technicians, advisors and CIA agents. The bombing of North Vietnam ceased and the US POWs were released. Still the war rumbled on, only now the South Vietnamese were fighting alone.

In January 1975, the North Vietnamese launched a massive ground attack across the 17th Parallel using tanks and heavy artillery. The invasion provoked panic in the South Vietnamese army, which had always depended on US support. In March, the NVA occupied a strategic section of the central highlands at Buon Ma Thuot. South Vietnam's president, Nguyen Van Thieu, decided on a strategy of tactical withdrawal to more defensible positions. This was to prove a spectacular military blunder.

Whole brigades of ARVN soldiers disintegrated and fled southward, joining hundreds of thousands of civilians clogging Hwy 1. City after city – Hue, Danang, Quy Nhon, Nha Trang – was simply abandoned with hardly a shot fired. The ARVN troops were fleeing so quickly that the North Vietnamese army could barely keep up.

Nguyen Van Thieu, in power since 1967, resigned on 21 April 1975 and fled the country, allegedly carting off millions of dollars in ill-gotten wealth. The North Vietnamese pushed on to Saigon and on the morning of 30 April 1975, their tanks smashed through the gates of Saigon's Independence Palace (now called Reunification Palace). General Duong Van Minh, president for just 42 hours, formally surrendered, marking the end of the war.

Just a few hours before the surrender, the last Americans were evacuated by helicopter from the US embassy roof to ships stationed just offshore. Harrowing images of US marines booting Vietnamese people off their helicopters were beamed around the world. And so more than a quarter of a century of American military involvement came to a close. Throughout the entire conflict, the USA never actually declared war on North Vietnam.

The Americans weren't the only ones who left. As the South collapsed, 135,000 Vietnamese also fled the country; over the next five years, at least half a million of their compatriots would do the same. Those who left by sea would become known to the world as 'boat people'. These refugees risked everything to undertake perilous journeys on the South China Sea (East Sea), but eventually some of these hardy souls found new lives in places as diverse as Australia and France.

The Paris Peace Accords of 1973 included a provision for US reparations to Vietnam totalling US$3.5 billion, and this became the main stumbling block to normalising relations in 1978. No money has ever been paid to Vietnam.

Reunification of Vietnam

On the first day of their victory, the communists changed Saigon's name to Ho Chi Minh City (HCMC). This was just for starters.

The sudden success of the 1975 North Vietnamese offensive surprised the North almost as much as it did the South. Consequently, Hanoi had

1975	1976	1978	1979
On 30 April 1975, Saigon falls to the North Vietnamese, as the last Americans scramble to leave the city.	The Socialist Republic of Vietnam is proclaimed and Saigon is renamed Ho Chi Minh City. Hundreds of thousands flee abroad, including many on boats.	Vietnamese forces invade Cambodia on Christmas Day 1978, sweeping through the shattered country and later overthrowing the Khmer Rouge government on 7 January 1979.	China invades northern Vietnam in February in a retaliatory attack against Vietnam's overthrow of the Khmer Rouge, but the Vietnamese emerge relatively unscathed. Thousands of ethnic Chinese flee Vietnam.

'WE WERE WRONG'

Commentators and historians have since observed that if Washington had allowed Vietnam's long history of successfully repelling invaders to deter it, the extensive tragedy of this war might have been averted, and likewise the resulting social disruption in America, as people sought to come to terms with what had happened in Vietnam. An entire generation of Americans had to assess its conduct. Years later, one of the architects of the war, former Defense Secretary Robert NcNamara, stated in his memoir, 'We were wrong, terribly wrong. We owe it to future generations to explain why'.

no detailed plans to deal with the reintegration of the North and South, which had totally different social and economic systems.

The party faced the legacy of a cruel and protracted war that had fractured the country. There was bitterness on both sides, and a daunting series of challenges. Damage from the fighting was extensive, including anything from unmarked minefields to war-focused, dysfunctional economies; from a chemically poisoned countryside to a population that was physically or mentally scarred. Peace may have arrived, but the struggle was far from over.

Until the formal reunification of Vietnam in July 1976, the South was ruled by the Provisional Revolutionary Government. The Communist Party did not trust the South's urban intelligentsia, so large numbers of Northern cadres were sent southward to manage the transition. This fuelled resentment among Southerners who had worked against the Thieu government and then, after its overthrow, found themselves frozen out.

The party opted for a rapid transition to socialism in the South, but it proved disastrous for the economy. Reunification was accompanied by widespread political repression. Despite repeated assurances to the contrary, hundreds of thousands of people who had ties to the previous regime had their property confiscated and were rounded up and imprisoned without trial in forced-labour camps, euphemistically known as re-education camps. Tens of thousands of business people, intellectuals, artists, journalists, writers, union leaders and religious leaders – some of whom had opposed both the Southern government and the war – were held in terrible conditions.

Contrary to its economic policy, Vietnam sought a rapprochement with the USA, and by 1978 Washington was close to establishing relations with Hanoi. But the China card was ultimately played: Vietnam was sacrificed for the prize of US relations with Beijing, and Hanoi moved into the orbit of the Soviet Union, on which it was to rely for the next decade.

Oliver Stone, never one to shy away from political point-scoring, earns a maximum 10 with *Platoon* (1986), the first of his famous trilogy about Vietnam. It is a brutal and cynical look at the conflict through the eyes of rookie Chris, played by Charlie Sheen, with great performances from Tom Berenger and Willem Dafoe.

1980s >	1986 >	1989 >	1991 >
During the decade Vietnam receives nearly US$3 billion a year in economic and military aid from the Soviet Union and trades mostly with the USSR and Eastern bloc nations.	*Doi moi* (economic reform), Vietnam's answer to *perestroika* and the first step towards re-engaging with the West, is launched with a rash of economic reforms.	Vietnamese forces pull out of Cambodia in September as the Soviet Union scales back its commitment to its communist partners. Vietnam is at peace for the first time in decades.	Vietnam, a hard-currency-starved nation, opens its doors to tourism in a bid to boost its finances. The first backpackers arrive, though tough restrictions apply to travel.

STREET NAMES IN VIETNAM

All Vietnamese street names are controlled by an intensely patriotic Communist Party. These reflect important dates, battles, heroes and heroines.

Hai Ba Trung Two sisters who lead a revolt against Chinese rule in 40 CE.

Le Loi Robin Hood–style rebel leader; vanquished the Chinese in 1427.

Nguyen Thai Hoc Led the Yen Bai revolt against the French.

Quang Trung Ruthless 18th-century military leader, emperor and reformer.

Tran Hung Dao Defeated Kublai Khan and invading Mongol forces.

30 Thang 4 The date (30 April) Communist forces captured Saigon.

China & the Khmer Rouge

Relations with China to the north and its Khmer Rouge allies to the west were rapidly deteriorating. War-weary Vietnam felt encircled by enemies. An anti-capitalist campaign was launched in March 1978, seizing private property and businesses. Most of the victims were ethnic Chinese – hundreds of thousands soon became refugees or 'boat people', and relations with China soured further.

Meanwhile, repeated attacks on Vietnamese border villages by the Khmer Rouge forced Vietnam to respond. Vietnamese forces entered Cambodia on Christmas Day 1978. They succeeded in driving the Khmer Rouge from power on 7 January 1979 and set up a pro-Hanoi regime in Phnom Penh. China viewed the attack on the Khmer Rouge as a serious provocation. In February 1979 Chinese forces invaded Vietnam and fought a brief, 17-day war before withdrawing.

Liberation of Cambodia from the Khmer Rouge soon turned to occupation and a long civil war, which exacted a heavy toll on Vietnam. The command economy was strangling the commercial instincts of Vietnamese rice farmers. War and revolution had brought the country to its knees and a radical change in direction was required.

Neil Sheehan's account of the life of Colonel John Paul Vann, *A Bright Shining Lie* (1988), won the Pulitzer Prize. It is the portrayal of one man's disenchantment with the war, mirroring America's realisation it could not be won.

Opening the Door

In 1985, President Mikhail Gorbachev came to power in the Soviet Union. *Glasnost* (openness) and *perestroika* (restructuring) were in, radical revolutionaries were out. Vietnam followed suit in 1986 by choosing reform-minded Nguyen Van Linh to lead the Vietnamese Communist Party. *Doi moi* (economic reform) was experimented with in Cambodia and introduced to Vietnam. As the USSR scaled back its commitments to the communist world, the far-flung outposts were the first to feel the

1992	1994	1995	2003
A new constitution is drawn up that allows selective economic reforms and freedoms. However, the Communist Party remains the leading force in Vietnamese society and politics.	The US trade embargo on Vietnam, in place in the North since 1964 and extended to the reunified nation since 1975, is revoked as relations begin to normalise.	Vietnam joins the Association of South-East Asian Nations (ASEAN), an organisation originally founded as a bulwark against the expansion of communism in the region.	Crime figure Nam Can is sentenced to death for corruption, embezzlement, kidnap and murder; the case implicates dozens of police and politicians.

pinch. The Vietnamese decided to unilaterally withdraw from Cambodia in September 1989, as they could no longer afford the occupation.

However, dramatic changes in Eastern Europe in 1989 and the collapse of the Soviet Union in 1991 were not viewed with favour in Hanoi. The party denounced the participation of non-communists in Eastern bloc governments, arguing that the democratic revolutions were a counter-attack from imperialists against socialism. Politically, things were moving at a glacial pace, but economically the Vietnamese decided to embrace the market. Capitalism has since taken root, and Vietnam joined ASEAN in 1995.

Relations with Vietnam's old nemesis, the USA, have also vastly improved. In early 1994, the USA lifted its economic embargo, which had been in place against the North since the 1960s. Full diplomatic relations were restored and presidents Bill Clinton, George W Bush, Barack Obama and Donald Trump have subsequently visited Vietnam.

> Vietnam received nearly US$3 billion a year in Soviet Union aid throughout the 1980s, and most of its trade was with other socialist countries, from Cuba to Czechoslovakia. Russian and Vietnamese politicians would seal deals at restaurants such as Maxim's in Ho Chi Minh City with Bulgarian wine and Havana cigars.

A Tough Neighbourhood

While dealings with Washington are much improved, serious tensions remain between Vietnam and China, with the temperature of the relationship veering between simmering and near-boiling point.

Hanoi maintains close economic ties to China, one of its largest trading partners, and the two countries share a close cultural heritage. But serious differences periodically erupt with Beijing over maritime territory. For the Vietnamese, even the name 'South China Sea' is intolerable as it implies China has a claim to the entire body of water – in Vietnam it's always the 'East Sea'.

In May 2014 there were at least 21 deaths during anti-Chinese riots, in response to China deploying an oil rig in the disputed Paracel Islands. Tourism slumped as Chinese nationals cancelled holidays in Vietnam, though relations have subsequently been patched up.

A DEATH IN THE FAMILY

It seemed the entire nation paused for a little self analysis on 13 October, 2013. The collective grief was palpable, as a united country buried its legendary war hero, General Vo Nguyen Giap, commander-in-chief of campaigns against the French, Japanese and Americans. He was 102. Charismatic, honest and brave this wiry, determined, clean-living man had devoted his life to his country; he was a freedom fighter with a popular touch.

For many Vietnamese the contrast between leaders like Giap and the nation's political and business elite was acute. Giap lived a simple life, dedicated to achieving the independence of his people, whereas many members of the latter were tainted by allegations of corruption and nepotism.

2004	2009	2010	2013
The first US commercial flight since the end of the American War touches down in Ho Chi Minh City.	Pro-democracy activists are jailed for 'spreading propaganda against the government' including hanging pro-democracy banners on a road bridge and publishing articles on the internet.	Hanoi celebrates its 1000th birthday in October with exhibitions, and wild celebrations grip the capital; its imperial Citadel is declared a Unesco World Heritage site.	General Giap, architect of the victory at Dien Bien Phu and military commander during the American War, dies at the age of 102. Millions pay their respects across the nation.

Something of a personality conflict between the Viets and the Chinese continues, but business is business. More Chinese tourists (5.8 million in 2019) visit Vietnam than any other nationality. And Chinese is the second-most popular foreign language studied in Vietnam.

Vietnam Today

Vietnam's political system could not be simpler: the Communist Party is the sole source of power. Officially, according to the Vietnamese constitution, the National Assembly (or parliament) is the country's supreme authority, but in practice it's a tool of the Party and carefully controlled elections ensure 90% of delegates are Communist Party members.

Officially, communism is still king, but there can be few party hacks who really believe Vietnam is a Marxist utopia. Market-oriented socialism is the mantra. Capitalism thrives like never before, the dynamic private sector driving the economy. On the street, everyone seems to be out to make a buck.

Vietnam has enjoyed over two decades of consistent growth, matching China as one of the world's fastest-growing economies. Per-capita income increased from just US$98 in 1993 to US$2739 in 2019, with Vietnam joining the ranks of East Asian 'tiger' nations. Record numbers of Vietnamese (8.6 million in 2018) are travelling abroad. The country is a leading agricultural exporter – the second-largest coffee producer in the world – and has a strong industrial and manufacturing base. Tourism was booming (until the Covid-19 pandemic).

Vietnam responded immediately to the Covid-19 pandemic in early 2020, maintaining very tight control of its borders, closing schools and introducing highly effective contact tracing and testing, which prevented mass lockdowns. By late March 2021 Vietnam had reported 2586 coronavirus cases and 35 deaths, from a population of nearly 98 million. However the nation's vaccination programme was very slow off the mark, and fully rebooting the economy (particularly tourism) will present a serious challenge.

2015	2017	2019	2020–21
Vietnam marks the 40th anniversary of reunification with massive military parades.	Danang hosts the APEC (Asia-Pacific Economic Cooperation) summit attended by President Trump and many other heads of state.	Vietnam and the EU sign a Free Trade Agreement.	A very rapid and robust governmental response to the Covid-19 pandemic largely limits the impact of the virus in Vietnam.

People & Culture

Industrious, proud, stubborn and yet mischievous, quick to laugh and fond of a joke, the Vietnamese are a complicated bunch. For Westerners, the national character can be difficult to fathom: direct questions are frequently met with evasive answers. A Vietnamese person would never tell a relative stranger their life story or profound personal thoughts the way people sometimes share feelings in the West. Their deep respect for tradition, family and the state reflects core Confucian principles.

The National Psyche

Historically the national mentality has been to work as a team, in harmony rather than in conflict; but times are changing. If you're on the highway or doing business, it's everyone for themselves. It's these attitudes (towards traffic and commerce) that many outsiders, not just Westerners, find most alien. 'Face' is vital, and Vietnamese people hate giving way, often employing elaborate tactics of bluster and bluff to ensure they get where they want to go.

My Generation

In many ways Vietnam is still a traditional, conservative society, particularly for the older generation, who remember the long, hard years and every inch of the territory for which they fought. Brought up on restraint and moderation, many remain unmoved by 21st-century consumer culture. Yet attitudes are changing rapidly. Vietnam is a young

---

WHEN IN NAM... DO AS THE VIETS

Take your time to learn a little about the local culture in Vietnam. Here are a few tips.

Dress code Respect local dress standards: shorts to the knees, women's tops covering the shoulders, particularly at religious sites. Remove your shoes before entering a temple. Topless or nude sunbathing is totally inappropriate.

It's on the cards Exchanging business cards is an important part of even the smallest transaction or business contact. Hand them out like confetti.

Deadly chopsticks Leaving a pair of chopsticks sitting vertically in a rice bowl looks very much like the incense sticks burned for the dead. This is not appreciated anywhere in Asia.

Mean feet Remove shoes when entering somebody's home. Don't point the bottom of your feet towards other people. Never, ever point your feet towards anything sacred, such as a Buddha image.

Hats off to them As a form of respect to elderly or other esteemed people, such as monks, take off your hat and bow your head politely when addressing them. The head is the symbolic highest point – never pat or touch a person there.

Selfie etiquette Grinning selfies taken at former prisons, war memorials and sites where people have suffered are seen as a sign of disrespect by the Vietnamese. Have a bit of decorum.

country; according to 2018 figures, almost 40% of the population is under 25, and the vast majority were born after the American War had ended. For the new generation, Vietnam is very different: a place to succeed and to ignore the staid structures set by the Communists. And yes, on the surface they show off that gleaming new motorbike, sharp haircut or iPhone, but at heart the youth of Vietnam are as hard working as their parents – more than they'd like to admit.

North–South Divide

The north–south divide lingers on. It's said that Southerners think, then do; while Northerners think, then think some more. Southerners typically reckon Northerners have 'hard faces', that they take themselves too seriously and don't know how to have fun. Northerners are just as likely to think of Southerners as superficial, frivolous and business-obsessed. Caricatures these may be, but they shed light on the real differences between north and south that reach beyond the (very different) regional dialects.

Climate plays its part, too. Life is easier in the south, where the fertile Mekong Delta allows three rice harvests a year. The north endures a long winter of grey skies, drizzle, mist and cool winds. Think of the differences between northern and southern Europe (or Maine and Alabama) and you have a snapshot of how one people can become two. Don't forget that the north has also lived with communism for over half a century, while the south had more than two decades of free-wheelin' free-for-all with the Americans (and today has money pouring in from Vietnamese emigrant investors).

Face

Face is all important in Asia, and in Vietnam it is most important of all. Having 'big face' is synonymous with prestige, which is particularly important. All families, even poor ones, are expected to have elaborate wedding parties and throw their money around like it's water in order to gain face. This is often ruinously expensive, but far less distressing than 'losing face'.

Foreigners should never lose their tempers with a Vietnamese person; this will bring unacceptable 'loss of face' to the individual involved and end any chance of a sensible solution to the dispute. Similarly, it's not culturally acceptable for Vietnamese traders to shout at, tug or pressure tourists when trying to do a deal. If hustlers adopt these tactics during a hard sell, walk on.

Paradise of the Blind (1988), by Duong Thu Huong, was the first Vietnamese novel to be published in the USA. It is set in a northern village and a Hanoi slum, and recalls the lives of three women and the hardships they faced over some 40 years.

Lifestyle

Traditionally, Vietnamese life revolved around family, fields and faith, with the rhythm of rural existence continuing for centuries at the same pace. All this has been disrupted by war, the impact of communism and globalisation. Whilst it's true that several generations may still share the same roof, the same rice and the same religion, lifestyles have changed immeasurably.

Vietnam is experiencing its very own '60s swing, which is creating feisty friction as sons and daughters dress as they like, date who they want via apps and hit the town until all hours. But few young people live on their own and they still come home to mum and dad at the end of the day – arguments might arise, particularly when it comes to marriage and settling down.

Some things never change. Most Vietnamese despise idleness and are early risers. You'll see parks full of t'ai chi devotees as dawn breaks, and offices are fully staffed by 7am. Indeed the whole nation seems supercharged with energy and vitality, no matter how hot and humid it is.

Family

In Vietnam the status of your family is more important than your salary. A family's reputation commands respect and opens doors.

Extended family is important to the Vietnamese and that includes second or third cousins, the sort of family that many Westerners may not even realise they have. The extended family comes together during times of trouble and times of joy, celebrating festivals and successes, mourning deaths or disappointments. This is a source of strength for many of the older generation.

The People of Vietnam

Vietnamese culture and civilisation have been profoundly influenced by the Chinese, who occupied the country for 1000 years and whose culture deeply permeates Vietnamese society.

History has of course influenced the mix of Vietnamese minorities. The steady expansion southwards in search of arable lands absorbed first the kingdom of Champa and later the eastern extent of the Khmer empire; both the Cham and the Khmer are sizeable minorities today.

Traffic was not only one way. Many of the minority groups that live in the far northwest only migrated to these areas from Yunnan (China) and Tibet in the past few centuries. They moved into the mountains that the lowland Vietnamese considered uncultivable, and help make up the most colourful part of the ethnic mosaic that is Vietnam today.

The largest minority group in Vietnam has always been the ethnic-Chinese community, which makes up much of the commercial class in the cities. The government has traditionally viewed them with suspicion, and many left the country as 'boat people' in the 1970s. Today they play a major part in economic development, but the stigma remains, and by law ethnic Chinese are unable to hold positions of power such as police officers, soldiers or Communist Party members.

Minorities

Vietnam is home to 53 ethnic minority groups (over 14 million people). Most live in northern Vietnam, carving an existence out of the lush mountain landscapes along the Chinese and Lao borders.

Some groups have lived in Vietnam for millennia, while the Hmong migrated south from China in the past few centuries. Each has its own language, customs, mode of dress and spiritual beliefs.

The government has long encouraged hill tribes to shift to lower altitudes and adopt wet-rice agriculture and the cultivation of cash crops, tea and coffee, with incentives such as subsidised irrigation, better education and healthcare. But the hill tribes' long history of independence keep many away from the lowlands.

Failing businesses often call in a geomancer (feng shui expert). Sometimes the solution is to move a door or a window. If this doesn't do the trick, it might be necessary to move an ancestor's grave.

PEOPLE & CULTURE THE PEOPLE OF VIETNAM

BROTHERS, BUDDIES OR MATES?

There are few places on earth where terms of address are as important as Vietnam. To use the wrong term can be a gross insult, disrespectful, or just a little too casual depending on the circumstances. Age and status are key factors.

Three men, all strangers, get chatting in a bar. Dzung is in his mid-20s, Vinh in his mid-30s, Huong is in his 40s. They quickly work out they have broadly similar social backgrounds. The correct way for Dzung to refer to Vinh is *anh* (big brother), but he should call Huong *chu* (uncle). He should also refer to himself as *em* (little brother) when speaking to Vinh but *chau* (nephew) to Huong.

Unless they are being very modern (or very merry!) and all decide to use the term *ban* (friend).

ETHNIC MINORITY VILLAGES

Vietnam's minorities are spread throughout highland areas in the north and west of the country.

Sapa (p131) Red Dzao and Black Hmong live in the dramatic valleys around town.

Bac Ha (p141) Famous for its market, which draws Flower Hmong from far and wide.

Mai Chau (p125) Beautiful valley base of the White Thai, with many homestays.

Cao Bang (p123) Rugged highland region where Hmong, Nung and Tay people live.

Kon Tum (p299) Traditional Bahnar settlements and homestays.

In the far north, many hill-tribe women still wear incredible hand-woven costumes – some girls start to learn to embroider before they can walk. In the central highlands attachment to traditional dress is rarer.

Prejudices against hill-tribe people endure. Attitudes are changing slowly but the Vietnamese media can still present them as primitive and exotic. It's also not uncommon for Vietnamese people to still see minorities as subversive (some sided with the USA during the American War).

The reality is that minority people remain at the bottom of the educational and economic ladder. Recent trial programs have attempted bilingual education to bridge cultural gaps, and results have been positive. Despite improvements in rural schooling and regional healthcare, many hill-tribe people marry young (as high as 50% to 60% in some groups), have large poor families and die early. According to 2015 World Health Organization figures, poor minority households account for 50% of Vietnam's poor households (yet only number 14% of the population).

Minority Groups

These are some of the main minority groups in Vietnam:

Tay The Tay (population 1.7 million) live at low elevations between Hanoi and the Chinese border. They adhere closely to Vietnamese beliefs in Buddhism, Confucianism and Taoism, but many also worship *yang* (genies) and local spirits. Tay literature and arts are famous throughout Vietnam.

Thai A large group (population 1.6 million) with origins in southern China, they settled along fertile riverbeds between Hoa Binh and Muong Lay. Villages consist of thatched houses built on bamboo stilts. The Thai minority are usually categorised by colour: Red, Black and White Thai. Black Thai women wear vibrantly coloured blouses and headgear.

Muong Mainly concentrated in Hoa Binh province, the male-dominated Muong (population 1.5 million) live in small stilt-house hamlets and are known for their folk literature, poems and music (performed with gongs, drums, pan pipes, flutes and two-stringed violins).

Hmong Around a million Hmong are spread across the far northern mountains. Most are animists, cultivating dry rice and raising animals. Each Hmong group – Black, White, Red, Green and Flower – has its own dress code.

Nung This tribe (population 820,000) lives in small villages in the far northeastern provinces; their culture combines ancestral worship and a talent for handicrafts, including basketry.

Jarai These people (population 360,000) of the south-central highlands still practise animistic rituals, paying respect to their ancestors and nature through a host or *yang*. Jarai cemeteries are elaborate, including carved totem-style effigies of the deceased.

Sedang The 150,000 Sedang of the south-central highlands do not carry family names, and there's said to be complete equality between the sexes. Sedang customs include ceremonial grave abandonment and giving birth at the forest's edge.

During the American War, many minorities were enrolled in the Civil Irregular Defense Group (CIDG), part of the US Army Special Forces. Some fighters later formed militias and resisted Hanoi rule well into the 1980s.

Religion

Many Vietnamese are not very religious and some surveys indicate that only 20% of the population consider themselves to have a faith. That said, over the centuries, Confucianism, Taoism and Buddhism have fused with popular Chinese beliefs and ancient Vietnamese animism to create the Tam Giao (Triple Religion) that many Vietnamese identify with.

Christianity, present in Vietnam for 500 years, and Cao Daism (unique to the region) are other important religions.

Buddhism

The predominant school of Buddhism in Vietnam is Mahayana Buddhism (Dai Thua or Bac Tong, meaning 'from the North'). The largest Mahayana sect in the country is Zen (Dhyana or Thien), also known as the school of meditation. Dao Trang (the Pure Land school), another important sect, is practised mainly in the south.

Theravada Buddhism (Tieu Thua or Nam Tong) is found mainly in the Mekong Delta region, and is mostly practised by ethnic Khmer.

Taoism

Taoism (Lao Giao or Dao Giao) originated in China and is based on the philosophy of Laotse (Old One), who lived in the 6th century BC.

Understanding Taoism is not easy. The philosophy values contemplation and simplicity. Its ideal is returning to the Tao (the Way, or the essence of which all things are made), and it emphasises *am* and *duong,* the Vietnamese equivalents of yin and yang.

Confucianism

More a philosophy than an organised religion, Confucianism (Nho Giao or Khong Giao) has been an important force in shaping Vietnam's social system and the lives and beliefs of its people.

Confucius (Khong Tu) was born in China around 550 BC. His code laid down a person's obligations to family, society and the state, which remain the pillars of the Vietnamese nation today.

Cao Daism

Cao Daism is an indigenous Vietnamese religion founded in the 1920s that fuses the secular and religious philosophies of both East and West. Its prophets include Buddha, Confucius, Jesus Christ, Moses and Mohammed, and some more unorthodox choices, such as Joan of Arc, William Shakespeare and Victor Hugo.

There are thought to be between two and three million followers of Cao Daism in Vietnam. Its colourful headquarters are in Tay Ninh, northwest of Ho Chi Minh City.

Hoa Hao Buddhism

The Hoa Hao Buddhist Sect (Phat Giao Hoa Hao) was founded in the Mekong Delta in 1939 by Huynh Phu So. His Buddhist philosophies involve simplicity in worship and no intermediaries between humans and the Supreme Being. The government punishes dissenting Hoa Hao groups that deviate from state-sanctioned versions of the sect; members have even been placed under house arrest.

Christianity

Catholicism was introduced in the 16th century by missionaries. Today Vietnam has the second-highest concentration of Catholics (7% of the population) in Asia. Protestantism was introduced to Vietnam in 1911 and most of the 200,000 or so followers today are hill-tribe people in the central highlands.

Vietnamese who have emigrated are called Viet Kieu. They have traditionally been maligned by locals as cowardly, arrogant and privileged. However, attitudes have changed and the official policy is now to welcome them back to the motherland.

PEOPLE & CULTURE RELIGION

In recent years, vast new Buddhist temples have been constructed, including Chua Bai Dinh (near Ninh Binh), while Ho Quoc pagoda looks out to the sea from Phu Quoc Island, and giant new Buddha statues now define the coastline of Danang and Vung Tau.

TET: THE BIG ONE

Tet is Christmas, New Year and birthdays all rolled into one. Tet Nguyen Dan (Festival of the First Day) ushers in the Lunar New Year and is the most significant date in the Vietnamese calendar. It's a time when families reunite in the hope of good fortune for the coming year, and ancestral spirits are welcomed back into the family home. And the whole of Vietnam celebrates a birthday: everyone becomes one year older.

The festival falls between 19 January and 20 February, usually the same dates as Chinese New Year. The first three days after Tet are the official holidays but many people take the whole week off.

Tet rites begin seven days before New Year's Day. Altars, laden with offerings, are prepared to ensure good luck in the coming year. Cemeteries are visited and the spirits of dead relatives invited home for the celebrations. Absent family members return home. It's important that the new year is started with a clean slate: debts are paid and cleaning becomes the national sport. A *cay neu* (New Year's tree) – kumquat, peach or apricot blossom – is displayed to ward off evil spirits.

At the stroke of midnight on New Year's Eve, all problems are left behind and mayhem ensues. The goal is to make as much noise as possible: drums and percussion fill the night air.

The events of New Year's Day are crucial as it's believed they affect the year ahead. People take extra care not to be rude or show anger. Other activities that are believed to attract bad spirits include sewing, sweeping, swearing and breaking things.

It's crucial that the first visitor of the year to each household is suitable – a wealthy married man with several children is ideal. Foreigners may not be considered auspicious!

Apart from New Year's Eve itself, Tet is a quiet family affair – *banh chung* (sticky rice with pork and egg) is eaten at home. Shops are closed, and virtually all transport ceases to run. It's a troublesome time to travel in Vietnam. However, you're sure to be invited to join the celebrations. Just remember this phrase: *chuc mung nam moi* – Happy New Year!

Islam

Around 70,000 Muslims, mostly ethnic Cham, live in Vietnam, mainly in the south of the country. Traditionally most Cham Muslims followed a localised adaptation of Islam (praying only on Fridays), though more orthodox Muslim practices have now been adopted.

Hinduism

There are over 60,000 Cham living in Vietnam who identify themselves as Hindus. They predominantly live in the same region as Cham Muslims, concentrated around Phan Rang on the south-central coast.

Women in Vietnam

As in many parts of Asia, Vietnamese women take a lot of pain for little gain, with plenty of hard work to do but little authority at the decision-making level. Vietnamese women were highly successful as guerrillas in the American War. After the war, their contributions were given much fanfare, and indeed women went on to prop up a country that had lost three million men, but most of the government posts were given to men. Today female parliamentary delegates still make up less than 20% of representatives. In the countryside, you'll see women doing back-breaking jobs, such as crushing rocks at construction sites and carrying heavy baskets.

Education is changing the divide, and today more women are delaying marriage to get an education; while only just over 17% of company directors in Vietnam are women, this is high for Asia's average of just under 8%.

Arts & Architecture

Vietnam has a fascinating artistic and architectural heritage. Historically, the nation has absorbed influences from China, India and the Khmer kingdoms and fused them with indigenous traditions. Then the French, Americans and Soviet Union left their marks. Today, contemporary artists and architects look across the globe for inspiration.

Arts

Traditional Music

Vietnam's traditional music uses the five note (pentatonic) scale of Chinese origin. Folk tunes are usually sung without any instrumental accompaniment (and have been adapted by the Communist Party for many a patriotic marching song).

Indigenous instruments include the *dan bau,* a single-stringed zither that generates an astounding array of tones, and the *t'rung,* a large bamboo xylophone. Vietnam's minorities use distinctive instruments: reed flutes, gongs and stringed instruments made from gourds.

Contemporary Music

Vietnam's contemporary music scene is diverse and influenced by trends in the West and east Asia. As all artists are monitored by the government, subjects that could be deemed subversive are largely avoided (or heavily coded). V-pop girl and boy bands such as 365 with heavily stylised looks and choreographed moves are wildly popular with teenagers.

There's a small but growing hip-hop scene, with Ho Chi Minh City–born Suboi (who has over 1.3 million Facebook likes and two albums under her belt) acknowledged as Vietnam's leading female artist. She raps to eclectic beats including dubstep rhythms on her 2016 track Doi.

Vietnam's electronic-music scene is dominated by commercial DJs playing EDM. However, HCMC's Heart Beat (www.heartbeatsaigon.com) promotes excellent underground dance events, while Bass Republic nights feature beats DJs at venues like Lush. In the north, the Quest Festival (www.questfestival.net) pioneered electronic music for four years until the authorities pulled the plug on the event in 2018.

Popular indie acts include HCMC bands the Children and Ca Hoi Hoang ('Wild Salmon'); the latter headlined the 2019 Coracle Festival. Meanwhile in Hanoi, leading lights include the group Ngot and singer Vu.

Rock music is championed by metal merchants Black Infinity, Little Wings and Unlimited, punk band Giao Chi and also alt-roots outfit 6789.

CONTEMPORARY LGBTIQ+ FILMS

Important Vietnamese films featuring powerful LGBTIQ+ narratives have been released over the past decade. Vu Ngoc Dang's *Lost In Paradise* is an empathetic portrayal of a country boy seeking a new life in HCMC. *Rainbow without Colours,* directed by Nguyen Quang Tuyen, deals with the love affair of two stepsons. The excellent Hanoi-set *Flapping in the Middle of Nowhere*, directed by Nguyen Hoang Diep, deals with sexual obsession and features a transgender character. The latter won best film at the Venice International Film Critics' Week.

BEST IN MUSIC

Ohio (Crosby, Stills, Nash and Young; 1970) Anthem that captures the rage and anger of the anti-war movement.

Ngu Di Con (Trinh Cong Son; 1970s) A mother grieves for her son, a missing soldier.

Saigon Bride (Joan Baez; 1967) Protest song that deals with the horrors of war.

Fortunate Son (Creedence Clearwater Revival; 1969) Fortunate sons avoided the draft.

Doi (Suboi; 2016) Beat-driven, bass-heavy track from Vietnamese hip-hop queen.

19 (Paul Hardcastle; 1985) Electro classic referencing the average age of US soldiers.

Viet-American Trace is an emerging artist whose moody, indie-tronic album *Low* received rave reviews upon release in 2017. Trace is the daughter of soul and disco singer Carol Kim.

Trinh Cong Son, who died in 2001, was a prolific writer-composer of anti-war and reconciliation songs; he was once called the Bob Dylan of Vietnam by Joan Baez.

Dance

Traditionally reserved for ceremonies and festivals, Vietnamese folk dance is again mainstream thanks to tourism. The Conical Hat Dance is visually stunning: women wearing *ao dai* (the national dress of Vietnam) spin around, whirling their classical conical hats.

Theatre

Vietnamese theatre fuses music, singing, recitation, dance and mime into an artistic whole. Classical theatre (*hat boi* in the south or *hat tuong* in the north) is very formal, employing fixed gestures and scenery and has an accompanying orchestra (dominated by the drum) and a limited cast of characters.

Hat cheo (popular theatre) expresses social protest through satire. The singing and verse include many proverbs accompanied by folk melodies. *Cai luong* (modern theatre) shows strong Western influences. *Kich noi* or *kich* (spoken drama), with its Western roots, appeared in the 1920s and is popular among students and intellectuals.

Vietnamese theatre is performed by dozens of state-funded troupes and companies around the country. For a memorable setting, try to catch a performance in the French-colonial Hanoi Opera House (p87) or HCMC's Opera House (p310).

Puppetry

Roi can (conventional puppetry) and the uniquely Vietnamese art form of *roi nuoc* (water puppetry) draw their plots from the same legendary and historical sources as other forms of traditional theatre. Water puppetry was first developed by farmers in northern Vietnam, who manipulated wooden puppets and used rice paddies as a stage. There are water-puppet theatres in Hanoi (p88), HCMC (p341), and other cities.

Painting

Painting on frame-mounted silk dates from the 13th century. It was originally the preserve of scholar-calligraphers, who painted grand works inspired by nature and realistic portraits for use in ancestor worship.

Much recent work has had political rather than aesthetic or artistic motives – some of this propaganda art is now highly collectable. Artists such as Nguyen Manh Hung and Tran Luong have experimented with contemporary subjects. Hanoi and Hoi An have some great galleries.

Literature

Truyen khau (traditional oral literature) includes legends, folk songs and proverbs while Sino-Vietnamese literature was dominated by Confucian and Buddhist texts. From the late-13th century, Chinese-style *nom* characters began to be used: the earliest text written was *Van Te Ca Sau* (*Ode to an Alligator*). One of Vietnam's literary masterpieces, *Kim Van Kieu* (*The Tale of Kieu*) was written by Nguyen Du (1765–1820), a poet, scholar, mandarin and diplomat.

Contemporary writers include Nguyen Huy Thiep, who articulates the experiences of Vietnamese people in *The General Retires and Other Stories* (1987), while Duong Van Mai Elliot's memoir, *The Sacred Willow: Four Generations in the Life of a Vietnamese Family* was nominated for a Pulitzer Prize. Bao Ninh's award-winning *The Sorrow of War* (1987), written in a stream-of-consciousness style, has been translated into 15 languages. Leading Viet Kieu (overseas Vietnamese) writers include Viet Thanh Nguyen, Andrew Lam, Nam Le, Le Ly Hayslip, Monique Truong, Andrew X Pham, Amy Quan Barry and Lan Cao.

Director Nguyen Phan Quang Binh's Mekong Delta–set movie, *Floating Lives* (2010), is a powerful, beautifully shot drama about fate and family based on a famous short story by Nguyen Ngoc Tu.

Cinema

One of Vietnam's earliest efforts at *rap* (cinema) was a newsreel of Ho Chi Minh's 1945 Proclamation of Independence. Prior to reunification, the South Vietnamese movie industry produced a string of sensational, low-budget flicks. Conversely, North Vietnamese film-making efforts were very propagandist.

Dang Nhat Minh is perhaps Vietnam's most prolific film-maker. In *The Return* (1993), he hones in on the complexities of modern relationships, while *The Girl on the River* (1987) tells the stirring tale of a female journalist who joins an ex-prostitute in search of her former lover, a Viet Cong soldier. *When the Tenth Month Comes* (1984) deals with the trials of a woman struggling to raise her son and look after her father-in-law.

For a look at the impact of *doi moi* (economic reform), Vu Xuan Hung's *Misfortune's End* (1996) tells the story of a silk weaver who is deserted by her husband for a businesswoman.

Overseas-Vietnamese films include Tran Anh Hung's touching *The Scent of Green Papaya* (1992), which celebrates the coming of age of a young servant girl in Saigon. *Cyclo* (1995), his visually stunning masterpiece, cuts to the core of HCMC's gritty underworld. Vietnamese-American Tony Bui's exquisite feature debut *Three Seasons* (1999) was set in HCMC, while Nguyen Vo Nghiem Minh's *Buffalo Boy* (2004) and *2030* (2014) have both won prestigious international film awards.

BEST IN PRINT

The Quiet American (Graham Greene; 1955) Classic novel set in the 1950s as the French empire is collapsing.

The Sorrow of War (Bao Ninh; 1987) The North Vietnamese perspective, retold via flashbacks.

Vietnam: An Epic History of a Divisive War (Max Hastings; 2019) Definitive account of the war, based on interviews with key players from the American and Vietnamese sides.

Vietnam: Rising Dragon (Bill Hayton; 2010) A candid, highly insightful assessment of the nation.

The Sympathizer (Viet Thanh Nguyen; 2015) Superbly written spy novel dealing with the aftermath of the American War; 2016 Pulitzer Prize winner.

The Sacred Willow: Four Generations in the Life of a Vietnamese Family (Duong Van Mai Elliot; 1999) Memoir of a middle-class family reflecting the history of Vietnam.

ARTS & ARCHITECTURE ARTS

BEST ON FILM

The Vietnam War (2017) Definitive documentary series that examines the roots of the conflict, war itself and its consequences.

Apocalypse Now (1979) The American War depicted as an epic 'heart of darkness' adventure.

The Deer Hunter (1978) Examines the emotional breakdown suffered by small-town-American servicemen.

Cyclo (*Xich Lo* in Vietnamese; 1995) Visually stunning masterpiece that cuts to the core of HCMC's underworld.

Vertical Ray of the Sun (2000) Exquisitely photographed family saga set in Hanoi.

Architecture

Traditional Vietnamese architecture is unusual, as most important buildings are single-storey structures with heavy tiled roofs based on a substantial wooden framework (to withstand typhoons).

In rural parts, houses are chiefly constructed from timber and built in stilted style, so that the home is above seasonal floods (and away from snakes and wild animals). Homes are usually divided into sections for sleeping, cooking and storage, while livestock live below the house.

Quirky Vietnamese styles include the narrow tube houses of Hanoi's Old Quarter – the government collected tax according to the width of the building, so the slimmer the cheaper.

Consider the Vietnamese saying 'land is gold' as you survey a typical townscape today. Skinny concrete blocks of dubious architectural merit, many up to seven storeys high, soar above empty lots or loom above paddy fields. Planning laws (or the virtual lack of them) allow land owners to build whatever they like, so cement constructions painted lime green or pink, kitted out with mirror windows, and built with vaguely French-inspired ornate balconies or Chinese details are quite common.

Colonial Buildings

Vietnam's French legacy is pronounced in the nation's architecture. Stately neoclassical buildings reinforced notions of European hegemony in the colonial era, and many still line grand city boulevards.

After the 1950s, most of these were left to rot as they symbolised an era that many Vietnamese wished to forget. However, recent renovation programs have led to structures, such as the former Hôtel de Ville, now People's Committee Building (p310) in Ho Chi Minh City, and the Sofitel Legend Metropole Hotel (p78) in Hanoi, being restored to their former glory. In HCMC, stop to admire the spectacular halls and vaulted ceiling of the central post office (p306). Haiphong is another city with wonderful French designs.

In Hanoi's French Quarter, many grand villas have fallen on hard times and are today worth a fortune to developers. Meanwhile in Dalat, French villas have been converted into hotels; these include the classy Ana Mandara Villas (p288); stately Dalat Hotel du Parc (p289) with its grand facade; and the shock-and-awe colonial magnificence of the Dalat Palace (p288).

Colonial churches were built in a range of architectural styles. In Hanoi, the sombre neo-Gothic form of St Joseph (p63) is enhanced by dark grey stone, whereas all the bricks used to construct Ho Chi Minh City's cathedral (p306) were imported from France.

Art deco curiosities built under French rule include Dalat's wonderful train station (p285), with its multicoloured windows, and the sleek Azerai La Residence (p184) hotel in Hue.

Colonial Style

Balconies *On important municipal buildings.*

Louvered windows *Usually green or brown.*

Stucco features *Decorative flourishes.*

Colour *Ochre/pale mustard.*

Terracotta roof tiles *Mediterranean-style.*

Pagodas & Temples

Vietnamese religious structures do not follow a specific national prototype. Pagoda styles echo the unique religious make-up of the nation, with strong Chinese content, while southern Cham temples reflect influences from India, Hindu culture and the Khmer empire.

Chua (pagodas) incorporate Chinese ornamentation and motifs, with buildings grouped around garden courtyards and adorned with statues and stelae. Most have single or double roofs with elevated hip rafters, though there are some with *thap* (multi-tiered towers) like Hue's Thien Mu Pagoda (p187).

Vietnamese pagodas are designed according to feng shui (locally called *phong thuy*) to achieve harmony of surroundings. They're primarily Buddhist places of worship, even though they may be dedicated to a local deity. Most are single-storey structures, with three wooden doors at the front. Inside are a number of chambers, usually filled with statues of Buddhas, bodhisattvas and assorted heroes and deities (Thien Hau, goddess of the sea and protector of seafarers, is popular in coastal towns). Flashing fairy lights, giant smoking incense spirals, gongs and huge bells add to the atmosphere.

Check out Hanoi's Temple of Literature (p65) for a superb example of a traditional Vietnamese temple or the wonderful pagodas in Hue.

Cham Style

The Cham primarily practised the Hindu religion, though some elements of Buddhism were also incorporated. Temple-building commenced as early as the 4th century.

Most Cham temples were built from brick, with decorative carvings and detailing probably added later. Principal features included the *kalan* (tower, the home of the deity), saddle-roofed *kosagrha* temples (which housed valuables belonging to the gods) and the *gopura* (gateway). Dotting the temple sites are stone statues of deities and numerous stelae with inscriptions listing important events. Important Cham sights include My Son (p227), Po Nagar (p246), Po Klong Garai (p260) and Po Shanu (p265).

Soviet Influence

Across Vietnam a Soviet influence is deeply evident in many concrete municipal buildings, marketplaces and apartments blocks. Most Soviet architecture was in the prefabricated style of the mid-1950s, using inexpensive concrete and archetypal modernist lines. Even in small towns you can stumble across reminders of Vietnam's past in the Soviet orbit: an austere concrete cinema facade in Hoi An or an ageing town hall.

Soviet architects and planners, such as Garold Isakovich, spent extended periods in the North Vietnamese capital, designing both Ho Chi Minh's Mausoleum (p66) and the bust of Lenin in Lenin Park. Other prominent Soviet examples in Hanoi include the State Bank, a blend of Soviet and Asian styles; the brutalist-style People's Committee building; and the National Assembly, which shows a Le Corbusier influence.

Meanwhile, in HCMC, there's less Soviet style about (unsurprisingly given the city's history). The one building that stands out is Reunification Palace (p311). Completed in 1966, it's a concrete masterpiece designed by Ngo Viet Thu.

To see the results of communist planning, head to Vinh in north-central Vietnam. Decades of incessant bombing reduced the city to rubble (only two buildings were left standing in 1972). East German architects and planners reinvented the city in the mould of their homeland, with cheap, hastily erected concrete apartment buildings that have aged poorly, suffering from a lack of maintenance. The buildings have a quirky appeal, but remain unpopular with residents.

Pagoda Features

Bodhisattvas *Enlightened earthly figures.*

Cheung Huang Yeh *Feared God of the City.*

Quan Am *Goddess of Mercy.*

Swastika *Sacred symbol signifying the heart of the Buddha.*

Thien Hau *Goddess providing protection at sea.*

ARTS & ARCHITECTURE ARCHITECTURE

The dynamic city of Danang must have one of Asia's best collections of contemporary bridges spread over its Han River. These include the aptly named Dragon Bridge, which spews fire nightly at 9pm.

Environment

Vietnam is one of the most diverse countries on earth, with tropical lowlands, intensely cultivated rice-growing regions, a remarkable coastline and karst mountains. But due to population pressure, poverty and a lack of environmental protection, many regions, and the nation's wildlife, are under threat.

The Landscape

The world's 12th-longest river, the Mekong is 4350km in length and passes through China, Myanmar, Laos, Thailand, Cambodia and Vietnam. It's known as the 'River of the Nine Dragons' in Vietnam.

As the Vietnamese are quick to point out, their nation resembles a *don ganh,* the ubiquitous bamboo pole with a basket of rice slung from each end. The baskets represent the main rice-growing regions of the Red River Delta in the north and the Mekong Delta in the south. The country bulges in the north and south and has a very slim waistline – at one point it's only 50km wide. Mountain ranges define most of Vietnam's western and northern borders.

Coast & Islands

Vietnam's extraordinary 3451km-long coastline is one of the nation's biggest draws and it doesn't disappoint, with sweeping sandy beaches, towering cliffs, undulating dunes and countless offshore islands. The largest of these islands is Phu Quoc in the Gulf of Thailand; others include Cat Ba and Van Don, the 2000-or-so islets of Halong Bay, a spattering of dots off Nha Trang, and the fabled Con Dao Islands way out in the South China Sea (East Sea).

River Deltas

The Red River and Mekong River deltas are both pancake-flat and prone to flooding. Silt carried by the Red River and its tributaries, confined to their paths by 3000km of dykes, has raised the level of the riverbeds above the surrounding plains. The Mekong Delta has no such protection, so when *cuu long* ('the nine dragons', ie the nine channels of the Mekong in the delta) burst their banks, it creates havoc for communities and crops.

WHALE WORSHIP

Coastal communities along virtually the entire Vietnamese coastline have temples dedicated to whales, including sites in the Cham islands, Tam Hai and Phan Thiet – the latter contains the 19m skeleton of a fin whale. Fisherfolk believe whales are marine deities that guide and protect them in the ocean. The origins of this cult are unclear, though it's thought to date back to ancient Khmer and Cham times. When a whale washes ashore, villagers will often pick its bones clean of flesh and bury the remains in a tomb or temple. A ceremonial funeral follows with drumming and offerings of flowers, fruit and ghost money.

Some communities even have annual whale festivals (Le Hoi Cau Ngu) with boat races and prayers, usually in the middle of the first lunar month, to mark the commencement of the fishing season. These include Vung Tau and the Danang region.

RHINO HORN & VIETNAM

A rhinoceros is killed every 10 hours in Africa to fuel demand in East Asia. In one national park alone (Kruger in South Africa) over 800 rhinos were killed in 2018. Poaching gangs – equipped with helicopters, machine guns, armoured vehicles and military-grade infra-red scopes – are backed by professional Vietnamese trafficking syndicates. Rangers describe the park as akin to a war zone.

Demand for rhino horn has increased in recent years in Vietnam, spurred by super-stitions about rhino horn doing everything from increasing libido to curing cancer. Using rhino horn is also considered something of a status symbol for some of the emerging wealthy class. Some utterly deluded individuals even consider it a hangover cure.

Even the tragic news about the extinction of the rhino in Vietnam failed to curb de-mand. With tens of thousands of dollars being paid per kilo of horn, traffickers have simply switched their attention elsewhere.

Media campaigns – public-service announcements on national radio, TV and internet lobbying – have tried to change mindsets and make the consumption of rhino horn unacceptable in Vietnam. Organisations including Save the Rhino International (www.savetherhino.org), Traffic (www.traffic.org) and ENV (Education for Nature-Vietnam; www.env4wildlife.org) have targeted the main consumers – wealthy businessmen from Hanoi and HCMC. Other public-education efforts have sought to reinforce the fact that rhino horn has no beneficial medical properties. However, progress is slow.

Legislation is in place to deter trafficking, but it took until 2018 for the first high-level illegal wildlife trader to be jailed for trading rhino horn in Vietnam. Nguyen Mau Chien (owner of a tiger farm) was sentenced to 13 months in prison, a sentence condemned by ENV as too light and an insufficient deterrent.

Highlands

Much of the country consists of rolling hills (mostly in the south) and mighty mountains (mainly in the north), the highest of which is 3143m Fansipan, close to Sapa. The Truong Son Mountains, which form the southwest highlands, run almost the full length of Vietnam along its borders with Laos and Cambodia. Coastal ranges near Nha Trang and those at Hai Van Pass (near Danang) are composed of granite – giant boulders littering the hillsides are a surreal sight. The western part of the southwest highlands is well known for its fertile, red volcanic soil. However, Northern Vietnam's incredible karst formations are probably the nation's most iconic physical features.

Wildlife

Vietnam has plenty to offer those who are wild about wildlife, but in reality many animals live in remote forested areas and encountering them is extremely unlikely.

We'll start with the good news. Despite some disastrous bouts of deforestation, Vietnam's flora and fauna is still incredibly exotic and varied. With a wide range of habitats – from equatorial lowlands to high, temperate plateaus and even alpine peaks – the wildlife of Vietnam is enormously diverse. There are over 300 species of mammals, over 180 reptiles, 848 birds, hundreds of fish and tens of thousands of invertebrates.

New species are regularly being discovered. Intensive surveys by the World Wildlife Fund (WWF) along the Mekong River (including the Vietnamese section) found a total of 1068 new species between 1997 and 2007, placing this area on Conservation International's list of the top five biodiversity hot spots in the world. A subsequent WWF research trip in 2016 found 65 species new to science in Vietnam, including a crocodile lizard, a frog and two types of moles. And in 2019 silver-backed chevrotain, a 'mouse deer' species not seen for nearly 30 years, were found alive in southern Vietnam.

Tram Chim National Park in the Mekong Delta is one of Vietnam's most important wetland reserves, and home to the giant sarus crane, which can measure up to 1.8m in height.

The other side of the story is that despite this outstanding diversity, the threat to Vietnam's remaining wildlife has never been greater due to poaching, hunting and habitat loss. Three of the nation's iconic animals – the elephant, saola (antelope-like animal) and tiger – are on the brink. The last wild Vietnamese rhino was killed inside Cat Tien National Park in 2010.

And for every trophy animal there are hundreds of other less 'headline' species that are being cleared from forests and reserves for the sake of profit (or hunger). Many of the hunters responsible are from poor minority groups who have traditionally relied on the jungle for their survival.

Endangered Species

Vietnam's wildlife has been in significant decline as forest habitats are destroyed, waterways polluted and hunting continues with minimal checks. Captive-breeding programs may be the only hope for some, but rarely are the money and resources available for such expensive efforts.

Officially, the government has recognised 54 species of mammal and 60 species of bird as endangered. Larger animals at the forefront of the country's conservation efforts include elephant, tiger, leopard, black bear, honey bear, snub-nosed monkey, flying squirrel, crocodile and turtle. In the early 1990s, a small population of Javan rhinoceroses, the world's rarest rhino, was discovered in Cat Tien National Park. Twenty years later they had all been wiped out by poachers.

However, there have been some success stories. The Siamese crocodile, extinct in the wild due to excessive hunting and cross-breeding, has been reintroduced to Cat Tien and is now thriving. Wildlife populations have also re-established themselves in reforested areas, and birds, fish and crustaceans have reappeared in replanted mangroves.

TOP 10 NATIONAL PARKS

PARK	FEATURES	ACTIVITIES	BEST TIME TO VISIT
Ba Be	lakes, rainforest, waterfalls, towering peaks, caves, bears, langurs	hiking, boating, birdwatching	Apr-Nov
Bach Ma	waterfalls, tigers, primates	hiking, birdwatching	Feb-Sep
Bai Tu Long	karst peaks, tropical evergreen forest, caves, hidden beaches	swimming, surfing, boating, kayaking, hiking	Apr-Nov
Cat Ba	jungle, caves, trails, langurs, boars, deer, waterfowl	hiking, swimming, birdwatching	Apr-Aug
Cat Tien	primates, elephants, birdlife, tigers	jungle exploration, hiking	Nov-Jun
Con Dao	dugongs, turtles, beaches	birdwatching, snorkelling, diving	Nov-Jun
Cuc Phuong	jungle, grottoes, primates, birdwatching centre, caves	endangered-primate viewing, hiking, birdwatching	Nov-Feb
Hoang Lien	mountains, birdlife, minority communities	hiking, cycling, birdwatching, mountain climbing	Sep-Nov, Apr & May
Phong Nha-Ke Bang	caves, karsts	boat trips, caving, kayaking, hiking	Apr-Sep
Yok Don	stilt houses, minority communities	hiking	Nov-Feb

> **KARST YOUR EYES**
> ....
> Karsts are eroded limestone hills, the result of millennia of monsoon rains that have shaped towering tooth-like outcrops pierced by fissures, sinkholes, caves and underground rivers. Northern Vietnam contains some of the world's most impressive karst mountains, with stunning landscapes at Halong Bay, Bai Tu Long Bay, around Ninh Binh and in the Phong Nha region. At Halong and Bai Tu Long bays, an enormous limestone plateau has dramatically eroded so that old mountain tops stick out of the sea like bony vertical fingers pointing towards the sky. Phong Nha's cave systems are on an astonishing scale, stretching for tens of kilometres deep into the limestone land mass.

Birds

Even casual visitors in Vietnam will spot a few bird species: swallows and swifts flying over fields and along watercourses; flocks of finches at roadsides and in paddies; and bulbuls and mynas in gardens and patches of forest. Vietnam is on the East Asian–Australasian flyway and is an important stopover for migratory waders en route from Siberian breeding grounds to their Australian winter quarters.

Rare and little-known birds previously thought to be extinct have been spotted in the extensive forests along the Lao border. These include Edwards's pheasant, the white-winged wood duck and the white-shouldered ibis.

National Parks

Vietnam has 33 national parks, from Hoang Lien in the far north to Mui Ca Mau on the very southern tip of Vietnam, and over 150 nature reserves. Officially, over 9% of the nation's territory is protected. Levels of infrastructure and enforcement vary widely but every park has a ranger station.

The management of national parks is a continuing source of conflict, because Vietnam is still figuring out how to balance conservation with the needs of the adjoining rural populations (many of them minority peoples). Rangers are often vastly outnumbered by villagers who rely on forests for food and income. Some parks now use high-tech mapping software to track poaching and logging activity.

If you can, try to visit the more popular parks during the week. For many locals a trip to a park is all about having a good time, and noise and littering can be a part of the weekend scene.

Many parks have accommodation and a restaurant; you should always call ahead and order food in advance.

Halong Bay Issues

Unesco World Heritage Site Halong Bay is one of Vietnam's crown jewels. A dazzling collection of jagged limestone karst islands emerging from a cobalt sea, its beauty is breathtaking.

This beauty has proved a blessing for the tourist industry, yet cursed Halong with an environmental headache. In 2019, an estimated six million people cruised the karsts. In order to accommodate everyone, the authorities have dug up mangroves to build coastal roads and new docks. Inadequate toilet-waste facilities and diesel spills from cruise boats have long contaminated the bay.

A deep-water port in Hon Gai draws hundreds of container ships a year through an international shipping channel that cuts through the heart of Halong. The resulting silt and dust has cloaked the sea grasses and shallow sea bottom, making it a struggle for sea life to survive, and putting the entire marine ecosystem in peril.

Pulitzer Prize finalist William deBuys' *The Last Unicorn: A Search for One of Earth's Rarest Creatures* (2015) is about searching for the saola.

VIETNAM'S CAGED SONGBIRDS

The nation's bird biodiversity is under constant threat from Vietnamese men's passion for keeping songbirds in cages. The international organisation Traffic (www.traffic.org) found 8047 birds from 115 species offered for sale in HCMC and Hanoi during three days of research in 2017. Most of these were being sold legally as there's no legislation preventing their sale. The result is silent forests in the remotest regions of the country – and the busiest streets in Hanoi filled with song from caged birds.

Even more alarming are the gargantuan Cam Pha coal mines and cement factory, just 20km east of Halong City, from which tonnes of coal dust and waste leak into the bay.

There's been some recent progress. Until 2012, untreated water was dumped into rivers and ended up in the bay, but a new treatment plant on the Vang Dang River has eased the flow of pollutants.

However, with the 2019 opening of a nearby international airport (Van Don Airport) and a new Halong–Hanoi highway, tourist numbers are sure to increase further.

Environmental Issues

Vietnam's environment is under threat across the entire nation. While the government signed up to key conservation treaties and hosted an Illegal Wildlife Trade conference in 2016, the state's main priorities are job creation and economic growth. There's minimal monitoring of pollution and dirty industries, while many loggers and animal traffickers escape trouble through bribery and official inaction.

Deforestation

Deforestation is a key issue. While 44% of the nation was forested in 1943, by 1983 only 24% was left and in 1995 it was down to 20%. Recent reforestation projects have increased cover since then, but these mostly consist of monocultural plantations of trees (such as acacia for furniture) in straight rows that have little ecological merit. Plantations accounted for 18% of all forest cover in 2019.

Poaching

Wildlife poaching has decimated animal populations in forests; snares capture and kill indiscriminately, whether animals are common or critically endangered. Figures are very difficult to ascertain, but Traffic estimates that over a million animals are illegally traded each year in Vietnam.

Some hunting is done by minority peoples simply looking to put food on the table, but there's a bigger market (fuelled by domestic and Chinese traders) for *dac san* (bush meat) and traditional medicine. Until recently, a trip to the country for many Vietnamese involved dining on wild game, the more exotic the better, and there were bush-meat restaurants on the fringes of many national parks. Laws to curtail this trade have been passed but enforcement is on a very low level.

ENV (Education for Nature-Vietnam) is a local NGO combating the illegal wildlife trade by lobbying politicians and providing educational programs in schools. It maintains files on restaurants offering bush meat and campaigns against the bear-bile trade and tiger farms.

Industry & Pollution

Vietnam has a serious pollution problem. In Ho Chi Minh City, the air quality is punishing, while Hanoi is the most contaminated city in Southeast Asia (and ranked the worst in the world for a period in October 2019).

Motorbikes are the main culprits, all running on low-quality fuel that has choking levels of benzene, sulphur and microscopic dust (PM10). Particulate matter (dust, grime) in Hanoi is around 150 micrograms per cu metre, whereas the World Health Organization recommends a limit of 20. Less than 10% of Hanoians use public transport.

Water pollution affects many regions, particularly the cities and coastal areas (where groundwater has become saline due to over-exploitation). Manufacturers have flooded into Vietnam to build clothing, footwear and food-processing plants, but most industrial parks have no wastewater treatment plants. The result is that discharge has caused biological death for rivers like the Thi Van.

In 2016, a toxic discharge by the Formosa steel plant caused a catastrophic marine disaster, with hundreds of dead fish washing up on the central Vietnam coastline. Fishing and tourism were affected in four provinces, leading to mass protests. Formosa eventually admitted responsibility and offered $500 million for a clean-up and compensation.

Twitchers with a serious interest in the birdlife of Vietnam should carry a copy of *Birds of Southeast Asia* (2018) by Craig Robson, which includes thorough coverage of Vietnam.

ENVIRONMENT ENVIRONMENTAL ISSUES

Global Warming

Vietnam is ranked by the World Bank as one of the most vulnerable countries in the world in the face of climate change, because rising tides, flooding and hurricanes will likely inundate low-lying areas.

A sea-level rise of only 1m would flood more than 6% of the country and affect up to 10 million people. HCMC already experiences serious flooding every month, and the Saigon River only has to rise 1.35m for its dyke defences to be breached. If monsoons worsen, similar flooding will create havoc in the vast deltas of the Red River.

In the Mekong Delta, the nation's rice bowl, rivers up to 50km inland are seeing increased salinity. Near the mouth of the delta, salinisation of water supplies has seen many families switch from rice cultivation to shrimp farming.

Ecocide: The Impact of War

The American War witnessed the most intensive attempt to destroy a country's natural environment the world has ever seen. Decades later, Vietnam is still in recovery mode, such was the devastation caused. American forces sprayed 72 million litres of defoliants (including Agent Orange, loaded with dioxin) over 16% of South Vietnam to destroy the Viet Cong's natural cover.

ON THE BRINK

Vietnam's native elephant species has been listed as endangered since 1976. The government announced the creation of three conservation areas to help protect wild elephants (in Pu Mat, Cat Tien and Yok Don national parks) in June 2013, but as the Forestry department estimates that less than 100 elephants remain in the wild, many see the action as too little, too late.

Only discovered in 1992, the saola is a large antelope-like wild ox and is only found in the Annamite mountains of Vietnam and Laos. Surviving numbers are thought to be in the hundreds. Conservation groups are working with minority people in the area to remove tens of thousands of snares from their forest habitat. For more information, consult www.savethesaola.org.

It's estimated that less than 350 Indochinese tigers remain in the region, of which between 25 and 60 are in Vietnam. As they are in isolated pockets, their long-term chances are not great. Tigers are particularly vulnerable because of their value in the illegal trade in tiger parts for traditional medicine. There are several legal 'tiger farms' in Vietnam; these operate as something between a zoo and a captive breeding centre.

RESPONSIBLE TRAVEL

➡ Shun elephant rides. Working elephants are still illegally trapped and conservation groups have grave concerns about their living conditions, as well as the detrimental effects elephant rides have on the animals' health.

➡ When snorkelling or diving be careful not to touch coral as this hinders its growth.

➡ Avoid touching limestone formations in caves as it affects their development and turns the limestone black.

➡ Most 'exotic' meats such as porcupine and squirrel have been illegally poached from national parks.

➡ Many civets are kept in appalling conditions to produce 'poo coffee'.

➡ Before downing snake wine or snake blood consider that the reptiles (sometimes endangered species) are killed without anaesthesia and can carry salmonella.

Enormous bulldozers called 'Rome ploughs' ripped up the jungle floor, removing vegetation and topsoil. Flammable melaleuca forests were ignited with napalm. In mountain areas, landslides were deliberately created by bombing and spraying acid on limestone hillsides. Elephants, useful for transport, were attacked from the air with bombs and napalm. By the war's end, extensive areas had been taken over by tough weeds (known locally as 'American grass'). The government estimates that 20,000 sq km of forest and farmland were lost as a direct result of the American War.

Scientists have yet to conclusively prove a link between the dioxin residues of chemicals used by the USA and spontaneous abortions, stillbirths, birth defects and other human health problems. Links between dioxin and other diseases, including several types of cancer, are well established.

Chemical manufacturers that supplied herbicides to the US military paid US$180 million to US war veterans, without admitting liability. However, the estimated four million Vietnamese victims of dioxin poisoning in Vietnam have never received compensation. Court cases brought by the Vietnamese Association of Victims of Agent Orange (http://vava.org.vn) have so far been rejected in the USA.

Journalists and other commentators have asserted that the Vietnamese government has been reluctant to pursue compensation claims for Agent Orange poisoning through the international courts because it has placed a higher priority on normalising relations with the USA.

In December 2014, President Barack Obama authorised funds for a clean-up of a dioxin-saturated former US base at Danang airport, and in 2019 the USA approved a US$183-million detoxification program of Bien Hoa airport near HCMC. The Vietnamese government continues to lobby for US assistance so that other contaminated sites can also be cleaned up.

Survival Guide

Directory A–Z

Accessible Travel

Vietnam is not the easiest of places for travellers with disabilities, despite the fact that many locals are disabled as a result of war injuries. Tactical problems include the chaotic traffic and pavements that are routinely blocked by parked motorbikes and food stalls.

That said, with some careful planning it is possible to enjoy a trip to Vietnam. Find a reliable company to make the travel arrangements and don't be afraid to double-check things with hotels and restaurants yourself.

Some budget and many midrange and top-end hotels have lifts. Note that bathroom doorways can be very narrow; if the width of your wheelchair is more than 60cm you may struggle to get inside.

Train travel is not really geared for travellers with wheelchairs, but open tour buses are doable. If you can afford to rent a private vehicle with a driver, almost anywhere becomes instantly accessible. As long as you are not too proud about how you get in and out of a boat or up some stairs, anything is possible, as the Vietnamese are always willing to help.

The hazards for blind travellers in Vietnam are acute, with traffic coming at you from all directions. Just getting across the road in cities such as Hanoi and Ho Chi Minh City (HCMC) is tough enough for those with 20:20 vision, so you'll definitely need a sighted companion!

The Travellers with Disabilities forum on Lonely Planet's Thorn Tree (www.lonelyplanet.com/thorntree/forums/travellers-with-disabilities) is a good place to seek the advice of other travellers. Alternatively, you could try organisations such as Mobility International USA (www.miusa.org), the Royal Association for Disability Rights (www.disabilityrightsuk.org) or the Society for Accessible Travel & Hospitality (www.sath.org).

Download Lonely Planet's free Accessible Travel guides from https://shop.lonelyplanet.com/categories/accessible-travel.com.

Accommodation

Passports are almost always requested on arrival at a hotel. Reception staff will normally photocopy your passport details and visa, and hand your passport back.

Hotels & Guesthouses

Hotels are called *khach san* and guesthouses *nha khach* or *nha nghi*. Many hotels have a wide variety of rooms (a spread of between US$20 and US$75 is not unusual).

PRACTICALITIES

Laundry You'll find laundry places in all the main tourist areas.

Newspapers & magazines *Vietnam News* (http://vietnamnews.vn) is a state-controlled English-language daily. Popular mags include *AsiaLife* (www.asialifemagazine.com/vietnam).

Smoking Vietnam is a smoker's paradise. People light up everywhere, despite an official ban against smoking in public places, although it's not socially acceptable to smoke on air-conditioned transport.

Vaping There are vape stores in all the main cities.

Weights & measures The Vietnamese use the metric system for everything except precious metals and gems, where they follow the Chinese system.

Often the cheapest rooms are at the end of several flights of stairs or lack a window.

Budget hotels Guesthouses (usually family run) vary enormously; often the newest places are the best. Most rooms in this category are very well equipped, with US$12 to US$18 often bagging you in-room wi-fi, air-conditioning, hot water and a TV. Some places even throw in a free breakfast, too. Towards the upper end of this category, mini-hotels – small, smart private hotels – usually represent excellent value for money. Few budget places have lifts (elevators), however.

Midrange hotels At the lower end of this bracket, many hotels are similar to budget hotels but with bigger rooms or perhaps an in-house restaurant. Flash a bit more cash and the luxury factor rises exponentially, with contemporary design touches and a swimming pool and massage or spa facilities becoming the norm.

Top-end hotels Expect everything from faceless business hotels, colonial places resonating with history and chic boutique hotels in this bracket. Resort hotels are dotted along the coastline. Top beach spots such as Nha Trang and Mui Ne all have a range of sumptuous places. Villa-hotels (where your accommodation has a private pool) are becoming popular, while others even include complimentary spa facilities. You'll find ecolodges in the mountains of the north and around the fringes of national parks.

Homestays

Homestays are a possible option in parts of Vietnam, particularly rural areas. All places have to be officially licensed. Areas that are well set up include the Mekong Delta; the White Thai villages of Mai Chau, Ba Be and Moc Chau; parts of the central highlands; and the Cham Islands.

Hostels & Campgrounds

Vietnam has (relatively recently) embraced hostel culture, and places with

dorm beds and a social vibe are spreading throughout the country. Increasingly, Vietnamese students are now booking into hostels and Vietnamese people (not foreigners) are running hostel establishments.

All the main tourist centres have hostels, and some places now even boast swimming pools and stylish bar-restaurants. Check out Ninhvana (p245) in Ninh Vinh Bay) to see how a hostel can be five-star.

Camping is very rare in Vietnam, but dotted along the southern coastline, around Long Bien and Phan Thiet, there are several campsites geared towards the Vietnamese student market.

Prices & Taxes

Prices are quoted in dong or US dollars based on the preferred currency of the particular property; some charge a percentage fee for paying by card rather than cash. Dorm-bed prices are given individually.

Most hotels at the top end levy a tax of 10% and a service charge of 5%, displayed as ++ ('plus plus') on the bill. Some midrange hotels (and even the odd budget place) also try to levy a 10% tax, though this can often be waived.

Discounts are often available at quiet times of the year.

Some hotels (particularly those on the coast) raise their prices in the main tourist season (July and August) and for public holidays like Tet.

Bargaining

Bargaining is essential in Vietnam, but not for everything and it should be good-natured – don't shout or get angry. Discounts of 60% or more may be possible; in other places it may only be 10% – or prices may be fixed. Haggle hard in marketplaces and most souvenir stores, and for *cyclos* and *xe om* (motorbike taxis). Many hotels offer a discount; restaurant prices are fixed.

Children

Children will have a good time in Vietnam, mainly because of the overwhelming amount of attention they attract and the fact that almost everybody wants to play with them.

➡ Big cities usually have plenty to keep kids interested, though traffic safety and pollution are serious concerns.

➡ Watch out for rip tides along the main coastline. Some popular beaches have warning flags and lifeguards.

→ Local cuisine is rarely too spicy for kids and the range of fruit is staggering. International food (pizzas, pasta, burgers and ice cream) is available, too.

→ Breastfeeding in public is perfectly acceptable in Vietnam.

Check out Lonely Planet's *Travel with Children* for more information and advice.

Practicalities

Baby supplies are available in major cities, but dry up quickly in the countryside. You'll find cots in most mid-range and top-end hotels, but not elsewhere. There are no safety seats in rented cars or taxis, but some restaurants can find a high chair. Pack high-factor sunscreen from home as it's not widely available; antibacterial hand gel is also a great idea.

Climate

Vietnam has very complicated weather patterns. Broadly there are two completely different climate zones.

Anywhere south of Nha Trang is hot and dry between November and March, and the rainy season is roughly late April to October. Conversely, central and northern Vietnam's rainy, cool season is October to March, and summers (April to September) are hot and steamy.

Central Vietnam is most affected by typhoons; August to November are the most stormy months.

Customs Regulations

Enter Vietnam by air and the procedure usually takes a few minutes. If entering by land, expect to attract a bit of interest, particularly at remote borders. Duty limits:

→ 400 cigarettes.

→ 1.5L of spirits.

→ Large sums of foreign currency (US$5000 and greater) must be declared.

Electricity

Type C
220V/50Hz

Embassies & Consulates

Generally speaking, embassies won't be that sympathetic if you end up in jail after committing a crime. In genuine emergencies you might get some assistance.

If you have your passport stolen, it can take time to replace it as many embassies in Vietnam do not issue new passports, which have to be sent from a regional embassy.

Australian Embassy (Map p58; ☑024-3774 0100; www.vietnam. embassy.gov.au; 8 Đ Dao Tan, Ba Dinh District, Hanoi; ☺8.30am-noon & 1.30-4.30pm Mon-Fri)

Australian Consulate (Map p312; ☑028-3521 8100; www. hcmc.vietnam.embassy.gov.au; 20th fl, Vincom Center, Đ 47 Ly Tu Trong, HCMC; ☺9am-1pm Mon-Fri)

Cambodian Embassy (Map p70; ☑024-3825 6473; camemb. vnm@mfa.gov.kh; 71a P Tran Hung Dao, Hanoi; ☺8-11.30am & 2-5.30pm Mon-Fri)

Cambodian Consulate (Map p318; ☑028-3829 2751; camcg. hcm@mfaic.gov.kh; 41 Đ Phung Khac Khoan, HCMC; ☺8.30-11.30am & 2-5pm Mon-Fri)

Canadian Embassy (Map p68; ☑024-3734 5000; www. canadainternational.gc.ca/viet nam; 31 Đ Hung Vuong, Hanoi; ☺8.30-10.30am & 1.30-3.30pm Mon-Thu, 8.30-9.30am Fri)

Canadian Consulate (Map p312; ☑028-3827 9899; www. canadainternational.gc.ca; 10th fl, 235 Đ Dong Khoi, HCMC; ☺8.30-10.30am & 1.30-3.30pm Mon-Thu, 8.30-9.30am Fri)

Chinese Embassy (Map p68; ☑024-8845 3736; http://vn. china-embassy.org/chn; 46 P Hoang Dieu, Hanoi; ☺9am-4pm Mon-Fri)

Chinese Consulate (Map p318; ☑028-3829 2457; http://hcmc. chineseconsulate.org; 175 Đ Hai Ba Trung, HCMC; ☺8.30-11am & 1.45-4pm Mon-Fri)

French Embassy (Map p70; ☑024-3944 5700; www.amba-france-vn.org; 57 P Tran Hung Dao, Hanoi; ☺8.30am-5.30pm Mon-Fri)

French Consulate (Map p318; ☑028-3520 6800; www.consul france-hcm.org; 27 Đ Nguyen Thi Minh Khai, HCMC; ☺9am-noon Mon-Fri)

German Embassy (Map p68; ☑024-3845 3836; https:// vietnam.diplo.de/vn-vi; 29 Đ Tran Phu, Hanoi; ☺8.30-11.30am Mon-Fri)

German Consulate (Map p318; ☑028-3829 1967; https:// vietnam.diplo.de/vn-de; 126 Đ Nguyen Dinh Chieu, HCMC; ☺7.30am-3pm Mon-Fri)

Indian Embassy (Map p70; ☑024-3824 4989; www.ind embassyhanoi.gov.in; Đ 58-60 Tran Hung Dao, Hanoi; ☺9am-5pm Mon-Fri)

Irish Embassy (Map p64; ☑024-3974 3291; www.dfa.ie/ irish-embassy/vietnam; 41a P Ly Thai To, Hanoi; ☺9am-noon Mon-Fri)

Japanese Embassy (Map p58; ☑024-3846 3000; www. vn.emb-japan.go.jp; 27 P Lieu Giai, Ba Dinh District, Hanoi; ☺9am-5.30pm Mon-Fri)

Japanese Consulate (Map p316; ☎028-3933 3510; www.hcmcgj. vn.emb-japan.go.jp; 261 Đ Dien Bien Phu, HCMC; ⊗8.30am-noon Mon-Fri)

Laotian Embassy (Map p70; ☎024-3942 4576; laoembassy hanoi@gmail.com; 40 P Quang Trung, Hanoi; ⊗8.30-11.30am & 1-4pm Mon-Fri)

Laotian Consulate (Map p312; ☎028-3829 7667; cglaohcm@ gmail.com; 93 Đ Pasteur, HCMC; ⊗8-11.30am & 1.30-4pm Mon-Fri)

Netherlands Embassy (Map p64; ☎024-3831-5650; www. nederlandwereldwijd.nl/landen/ vietnam; 7th fl, BIDV Tower, 194 Đ Tran Quang Khai, Hanoi; ⊗8am-5pm Mon-Fri)

Netherlands Consulate (Map p318; ☎028-3823 5932; www. nederlandwereldwijd.nl/landen/ vietnam; Saigon Tower, 29 ĐL Le Duan, HCMC; ⊗8am-noon Mon-Fri)

New Zealand Embassy (Map p64; ☎024-3824 1481; www. mfat.govt.nz; Level 5, 63 P Ly Thai To, Hanoi; ⊗8.30am-noon & 1-5pm Mon-Fri)

New Zealand Consulate (Map p312; ☎028-3822 6907; www. mfat.govt.nz/en/embassies; 8th fl, The Metropolitan, 235 Đ Dong Khoi, HCMC; ⊗8.30am-noon & 1-5pm Mon-Fri)

Singaporean Embassy (Map p68; ☎024-3848 9168; www. mfa.gov.sg/hanoi; 41-43 Đ Tran Phu, Hanoi; ⊗8am-noon & 1-5pm Mon-Fri)

Thai Embassy (Map p68; ☎024-3823 5092; www.thai embassy.org/hanoi; 3-65 P Hoang Dieu, Hanoi; ⊗8.30am-noon & 1-5pm Mon-Fri)

Thai Consulate (Map p316; ☎028-3932 7637; www.thai embassy.org/hochiminh; 77 Đ Tran Quoc Thao, HCMC; ⊗8.30-11.30am & 1.30-3pm Mon-Fri)

UK Embassy (Map p64; ☎024-3936 0500; http:// ukinvietnam.fco.gov.uk; 4th fl, Central Bldg, 31 P Hai Ba Trung, Hanoi; ⊗8.30am-12.30pm & 1.30-4.45pm Mon-Thu, 8.30am-12.30pm & 1-3pm Fri)

> ### EATING PRICE RANGES
>
> The following price ranges refer to a typical meal (excluding drinks). Unless otherwise stated, taxes are included in the price.
>
> **$** less than US$5 (115,000d)
>
> **$$** US$5–15 (115,000d–340,000d)
>
> **$$$** more than US$15 (340,000d)

UK Consulate (Map p318; ☎028-3825 1380; www.gov. uk/world/organisations/british-consulate-general-ho-chi-minh-city; 25 ĐL Le Duan, HCMC; ⊗8.30am-noon & 1-4.45pm Mon-Thu, 8.30am-noon & 12.30-3pm Fri)

US Embassy (Map p58; ☎024-3850 5000; https:// vn.usembassy.gov; 7 P Lang Ha, Ba Dinh District, Hanoi; ⊗8am-5pm Mon-Fri)

US Consulate (Map p318; ☎028-3520 4200; https:// vn.usembassy.gov/embassy -consulates/ho-chi-minh-city; 4 ĐL Le Duan, HCMC; ⊗7am-5pm Mon-Fri)

Food

Eating out is a real highlight of travel in Vietnam. For in-depth information on the subject, consult Eat & Drink Like a Local (p41).

Insurance

Insurance is a must for Vietnam, as the cost of major medical treatment is prohibitive. A travel insurance policy to cover theft, loss and medical problems is the best bet.

Some insurance policies specifically exclude activities like scuba diving (and even trekking). Check that your policy covers an emergency evacuation in the event of serious injury.

You're highly unlikely to be driving a car as virtually all rental options include a driver with your policy (and officially you need a Vietnamese licence and local insurance).

It's also impossible to get a licence on a tourist visa.

Though many travellers drive scooters and motorbikes in Vietnam, most insurance policies will not cover you if you do not have a motorbike licence back home.

Internet Access

Internet and wi-fi are widely available throughout Vietnam. Something like 98% of hotels and guesthouses have wi-fi; only in very remote places (such as national parks) is it not standard. Wi-fi is almost always free of charge. Many cafes and restaurants also have (free) wi-fi. Connection speeds are normally good. Internet cafes are also available, costing 3000d to 7000d per hour.

Most travellers also surf the net using 4G mobile phone connections; 5G is being rolled out too.

Legal Matters
Civil Law

On paper it looks good, but in practice the rule of law in Vietnam is a fickle beast. Local officials interpret the law any way it suits them, often against the wishes of Hanoi. There is no independent judiciary. Not surprisingly, most legal disputes are settled out of court.

Drugs

The country has a very serious problem with heroin and methamphetamine use, and the authorities clamp down hard.

Marijuana and, in the northwest, opium are readily available. Note that there are many plain-clothes police in Vietnam, and if you're arrested the result might be a large fine, a long prison term or both.

Police

Few foreigners experience much hassle from police and demands for bribes from travellers are very rare. If something does go wrong, or if something is stolen, the police can't do much more than prepare an insurance report for a negotiable fee – take an English-speaking Vietnamese person with you to translate.

LGBTIQ+ Travellers

Vietnam is a relatively hassle-free place for gay, lesbian and transgender travellers, who shouldn't expect any problems. There are no official laws prohibiting same-sex relationships, or same-sex sexual acts in Vietnam. There's very little in the way of harassment. VietPride (www.facebook.com/viet pride.vn) marches have been held in Hanoi and HCMC since 2012. The Hanoi event takes place over several days in September and includes film screenings, talks, parties and a bike rally.

Vietnam has more progressive governmental policies than many of its Asian neighbours. In January 2015, a Law on Marriage and Family was passed that officially removes a ban on same-sex marriages (though these partnerships have not yet been legally recognised). Transgender people were granted the right in November 2015 to legally undergo sex reassignment surgery and have their gender recognised.

Hanoi and especially HCMC both have gay scenes. That said, venues still keep a low profile and most gay Vietnamese choose to hide their sexuality from their families.

Checking into hotels as a same-sex couple is perfectly acceptable, though be aware that passionate public displays of affection, by heterosexual or nonheterosexual couples, is not culturally acceptable.

Utopia (www.utopia-asia. com) has useful gay travel information and contacts in Vietnam, and the gay dating app Grindr is popular.

Money

Currency

The Vietnamese currency is the dong (d), which has been pretty stable against hard currencies for many years. Most establishments quote prices in dong, with some (mainly luxury hotels) giving US dollar rates.

There's no real black market in Vietnam.

ATMs

ATMs are very widespread. You shouldn't have any problems getting cash with a regular Maestro/Cirrus debit card, or with a Visa or MasterCard debit or credit card. Watch for stiff withdrawal charges (typically 25,000d to 50,000d) and limits: most are around 2,000,000d, however, MB Bank often allows 6,000,000d and Commonwealth Bank up to 10,000,000d.

Cash

US dollars can be exchanged widely. Other major currencies can be exchanged at banks including Vietcombank and HSBC.

Most land border crossings now have some sort of official currency exchange.

Credit Cards

Visa and MasterCard are accepted in major cities and many tourist centres, but don't expect noodle bars to take plastic. Commission charges (around 3%) sometimes apply.

If you wish to obtain a cash advance, this is possible at

Vietcombank branches in most cities. Banks generally charge at least a 3% commission for this service.

Opening Hours

Hours vary little throughout the year.

Banks 8am to 3pm weekdays, to 11.30am Saturday; some take a lunch break

Offices and museums 7am or 7.30am to 5pm or 6pm; museums generally close on Monday; most take a lunch break (roughly 11am to 1.30pm)

Restaurants 11am to 9pm

Shops 8am to 6pm

Temples and pagodas 5am to 9pm

Photography

Camera supplies are readily available in major cities.

Avoid snapping airports, military bases and border checkpoints. Don't even think of trying to get a snapshot of Ho Chi Minh in his glass sarcophagus!

Photographing anyone, particularly hill-tribe people, demands patience and the utmost respect for local customs. Photograph with discretion and manners. It's always polite to ask first and if the person says no, don't take the photo.

Lonely Planet's Guide to Travel Photography is full of helpful tips for photography while on the road.

Post

Every city, town and village has some sort of *buu dien* (post office).

Vietnam has quite a reliable postal service. For anything important, express-mail service (EMS), available in the larger cities, is twice as fast as regular airmail and everything is registered.

Private couriers such as FedEx, DHL and UPS are reliable for transporting documents or small parcels.

Public Holidays

If a public holiday falls on a weekend, it is observed on the Monday.

New Year's Day (Tet Duong Lich) 1 January

Vietnamese New Year (Tet) January or February; a three-day national holiday

Founding of the Vietnamese Communist Party (Thanh Lap Dang CSVN) 3 February; the date the party was founded in 1930

Hung Kings Commemorations (Hung Vuong) Tenth day of the third lunar month (March or April)

Liberation Day (Saigon Giai Phong) 30 April; the date of Saigon's 1975 surrender is commemorated nationwide

International Workers' Day (Quoc Te Lao Dong) 1 May

Ho Chi Minh's Birthday (Sinh Nhat Bac Ho) 19 May

Buddha's Birthday (Phat Dan) Eighth day of the fourth moon (usually June)

National Day (Quoc Khanh) 2 September; commemorates the Declaration of Independence by Ho Chi Minh in 1945

Safe Travel

All in all, Vietnam is an extremely safe country to travel in.

➡ The police keep a pretty tight grip on social order and there are rarely reports of muggings, robberies or sexual assaults.

➡ Scams and hassles do exist, particularly in Hanoi, HCMC and Nha Trang (and to a lesser degree in Hoi An).

➡ Be extra careful if you're travelling on two wheels on Vietnam's anarchic roads; traffic accident rates are woeful and driving standards are pretty appalling.

Undetonated Explosives

For more than three decades, four armies expended untold energy and resources mining, booby-trapping, rocketing, strafing, mortaring and bombarding wide areas of Vietnam. When the fighting stopped, most of this detritus remained exactly where it had landed or been laid; American estimates at the end of the war placed the quantity of unexploded ordnance (UXO) at 150,000 tonnes.

Since 1975 more than 40,000 Vietnamese have been maimed or killed by this leftover ordnance. The central provinces are particularly badly affected, with more than 8000 incidents in Quang Tri alone.

While cities, cultivated areas and well-travelled rural roads and paths are safe for travel, straying from these areas could land you in the middle of danger. *Never* touch any rockets, artillery shells, mortars, mines or other relics of war you may come across. Such objects can remain lethal for decades. And don't climb inside bomb craters – you never know what undetonated explosive device is at the bottom.

You can learn more about the issue of landmines from the Nobel Peace Prize–winning International Campaign to Ban Landmines (www.icbl.org), or consult the website of the Mines Advisory Group (www.maginternational.org), which clears landmines and UXO in Vietnam.

Shopping

Vietnam has some fantastic crafts, clothing and curios to buy. Hotspots include Hanoi, Hoi An and HCMC, each of which has a tempting selection of everything from propaganda art to traditional textiles.

Best fashion buys include silk and linen creations in designer boutiques, 'almost' antiques, ethnic crafts, fine furnishings, homeware and lacquerware. Made-to-measure clothing is also very tempting, though many tailors' work is of questionable quality.

Art & Antiques

Vietnam has strict regulations on the export of real antiques, so be sure to check beforehand that the items you purchase are allowed out of the country. Reputable shops can provide the necessary paperwork.

Traditional and contemporary paintings and photographic prints are popular items. You'll find good art galleries in Hue, Hoi An, HCMC and Hanoi, while Nha Trang alone has a couple of fine photographic galleries. There are tempting Communist propaganda art galleries in Hanoi, too.

Fake antiques (including ceramics and masks) are widespread. Be very careful when splashing cash.

GOVERNMENT TRAVEL ADVICE

The following government websites offer travel advisories and information on current hotspots.

Australian Department of Foreign Affairs (www.smarttraveller.gov.au)

British Foreign Office (www.gov.uk/foreign-travel-advice)

Canadian Department of Foreign Affairs (www.dfait-maeci.gc.ca)

US Department of State (http://travel.state.gov)

Clothing

Boutiques in Hanoi, HCMC, and, to a lesser extent Hoi An and Nha Trang, stock fine cotton and linen (and some silk) fashion. However, note that almost all brand-label merchandise is fake.

Hoi An is the epicentre of bespoke tailoring (p218) in Southeast Asia. There are some reputable firms, but also many others that knock up clothes in a rush from poor-quality fabrics. Shop around.

Handicrafts

All the main tourist centres stock a selection of fine lacquerware; boxes and wooden screens with mother-of-pearl inlay; ceramics; colourful embroidery; silk greeting cards; hill-tribe textiles; basketry; jewellery; and leatherwork.

Telephone

Domestic Calls

Domestic calls are very inexpensive using a Vietnamese SIM.

Phone numbers in Hanoi, HCMC and Haiphong have eight digits. Elsewhere around the country phone numbers have seven digits. Telephone area codes are assigned according to the province.

International Calls

It's usually easiest to use wi-fi or 4G and an app such as WhatsApp, Skype or Viber. Mobile phone rates for international phone calls can be less than US$0.10 a minute.

Mobile Phones

If you have an unlocked phone, it's virtually essential to get a local SIM card for longer visits in Vietnam. 4G data packages are some of the cheapest in the world at around 200,000d for 5GB; some packages include call time, too. Many SIM card deals allow you to call abroad cheaply (from 2000d a minute) as well.

Get the shop owner (or someone at your hotel) to set up your phone in English or your native language. The three main mobile-phone companies are Viettel, Vinaphone and Mobifone.

Time

Vietnam is seven hours ahead of Greenwich Mean Time/Universal Time Coordinated (GMT/UTC). There's no daylight saving or summer time.

Toilets

➤ The issue of toilets and what to do with used toilet paper can cause confusion. In general, if there's a wastepaper basket next to the toilet, that is where the toilet paper goes (many sewage systems cannot handle toilet paper). If there's no basket, flush paper down the toilet.

➤ Toilet paper is usually provided though it's wise to keep a stash of your own while on the move.

➤ There are still some squat toilets in public places and out in the countryside.

➤ The scarcity of public toilets is more of a problem for women than for men. Vietnamese men often urinate in public. Women might find roadside toilet stops easier if wearing a sarong. You usually have to pay a few dong to an attendant to access a public toilet.

Tourist Information

Tourist offices in Vietnam have a different philosophy from the majority of tourist offices worldwide. These government-owned enterprises are really travel agencies whose primary interests are booking tours and turning a profit. Don't expect much independent travel information.

Vietnam Tourism (www.vietnam tourism.com)

Saigon Tourist (www.saigon-tourist.com)

Online resources, travel agents, backpacker cafes and your fellow travellers are usually a much better source of information.

Visas

Types of Visas

The (very complicated) visa situation has recently changed for many nationalities, and is fluid – always check the latest regulations.

Firstly, if you are staying more than 15 days and are from a Western country, you'll still need a visa (or approval letter from an agent) in advance. If your visit is less than 15 days, some nationalities are now visa-exempt (for a single visit, not multiple-entry trips).

Tourist visas are valid for either one calendar month or three months. A single-entry one-month visa costs US$20, a three-month multiple-entry visa is US$70. Only United States nationals are able to arrange one-year visas.

There are two established methods of applying for a visa: Visa on Arrival (VOA) via online visa agents; or via a Vietnamese embassy or consulate. E-visas are a newish third choice (for a limited number of nationalities).

VISA ON ARRIVAL

Visa on Arrival (VOA) is the preferred method for most travellers arriving by air, since it's cheaper, faster and you don't have to part with your passport by posting it to an embassy. Online visa agencies email the VOA to you directly.

It can only be used if you are flying into one of Vietnam's international airports, not at land crossings. The process is straightforward: you fill out an online application form and pay the agency fee (around US$20). You'll then receive by email a VOA approval letter signed by Vietnamese immigration that you print out and show on arrival, where you pay your visa stamping fee in US dollars (or Vietnamese dong), cash only. The single-entry stamping fee is US$25, a multiple-entry stamping fee is US$50.

There are many visa agents, including some inefficient cut-price outfits and copycats with similar names and websites to reputable companies. It's highly recommended to stick to professional agencies; you don't want to be denied entry at Vietnamese immigration due to incompetence. The following are very efficient:

Vietnam Visa Choice (www.vietnamvisachoice.com) Professional agency with online support from native English speakers. Also guarantees your visa will be issued within the time specified or a refund is issued.

Vietnam Visa Center (www.vietnamvisacenter.org) Competent all-rounder with helpful staff well briefed on the latest visa situation. Offers a two-hour express service for last-minute trips (weekday business hours).

VISAS VIA AN EMBASSY OR CONSULATE

You can also obtain visas through Vietnamese embassies and consulates around the world, but fees are normally much higher than using a visa agent and (depending on the country) the process can be slow. In Asia,

Vietnamese visas tend to be issued in two to three working days in Cambodia. In Europe and North America it takes around a week.

E-VISAS

An e-visa program allows visitors to apply for visas online through the Vietnam Immigration Department (or visa agency). Citizens of over 80 countries are eligible, including those from the UK and the USA.

E-visas are single-entry only, valid for 30 days (non-extendable) and cost US$25 if arranged through the government website. Processing takes three to five days.

However, this government-run e-visa system has not been well implemented. The official website is glitch-prone and often fails to load. We've also heard of several cases where applications have gone AWOL and photos rejected for not being picture-perfect.

There have been reports of visitors being deported due to incorrect details (such as wrong date of birth or misspelt names) on the online application form. If you do apply for an e-visa, double-check that all your information provided is 100% accurate. E-visas can be applied for online at https://evisa.xuatnhapcanh.gov.vn.

Some agents are now licensed to issue e-visas. The

advantage of using a competent agent is that your e-visa should be processed quickly and efficiently. Agents can alert you about any potential mishaps in the application, and you'll have someone to liaise with, answer queries and guide you through the process.

Visa Works (https://visa.works) is a reputable agency run by native English speakers with a wide choice of visa options including e-visas. Its helpful wizard guides you through the application process and communication is reliable.

MULTIPLE-ENTRY VISAS

It's possible to leave Vietnam and re-enter without having to apply for another visa. However, you must hold a multiple-entry visa before you leave Vietnam.

Single-entry visas can no longer be changed to multiple-entry visas inside Vietnam.

VISA EXTENSIONS

Tourist visa extensions officially cost as little as US$10, and have to be organised via agents. The procedure takes seven to 10 days and you can only extend the visa for a month (US$40) or two months (US$60) depending on the visa you hold.

You can extend your visa in big cities, but if it's done in a different city from the

VISA-EXEMPTED NATIONALITIES

At the time of research, citizens of the following countries did not need to apply in advance for a Vietnamese visa (when arriving by either air or land) for certain lengths of stay. Note that if you arrive once using an exemption and want to re-enter Vietnam, then you either have to wait 30 days or arrange a visa (from the time of departure).

COUNTRY	DAYS
Myanmar, Brunei	14
Belarus, Denmark, Finland, France, Germany, Italy, Japan, South Korea, Norway, Russia, Spain, Sweden, UK	15
Philippines	21
Cambodia, Indonesia, Kyrgyzstan, Laos, Malaysia, Singapore, Thailand	30
Chile	90

one you arrived in (oh the joys of Vietnamese bureaucracy!), it'll cost you US$50 to US$70. In practice, extensions work most smoothly in HCMC, Hanoi, Danang and Hue.

It's possible but not at all practical for travellers using a visa exemption to extend their stay at the end of the visa exemption (around US$35). But this can take up to 10 working days and you need to give up your passport during this time so it's not a useful option at all.

Volunteering

Opportunities for voluntary work are quite limited in Vietnam as there are so many professional development staff based here. For information, chase up the full list of nongovernment organisations (NGOs) at the **NGO Resource Centre** (Map p58; ☎024-3832 8570; www.ngocentre.org.vn; Room 201, Bldg E3, Trung Tu Diplomatic Compound, 6 Dang Van Ngu, Dong Da, Hanoi), which keeps a database of all the NGOs assisting Vietnam. Pan Nature (www.nature.org.vn/en) has links to opportunities in the environmental sector.

International organisations offering placements in Vietnam include Voluntary Service Overseas (www.vsointernational.org) in the UK, Australian Volunteers International (www.australianvolunteers.com), Volunteer Service Abroad (www.vsa.org.nz) in New Zealand and US-based International Volunteer

---

WOMEN AT WORK

Vietnam has some of the highest rates of female employment in the world, with 79% of women (aged 15 to 64) in the labour force. Only Sweden, Switzerland and Iceland have a higher percentage in the OECD.

In the neighbouring countries of Malaysia and Indonesia the figure is around 55%, while in the USA and China it's around 67%.

State ideology and policy, which encourages women to work and offers generous maternity leave (six months), are contributing factors.

HQ (www.volunteerhq.org), which has a wide range of volunteer projects in HCMC. The USA org Eli Abroad (www.eliabroad.org) has internship and volunteer opportunities. The UN's volunteer program details are available at www.unv.org.

Women Travellers

Vietnam is relatively free of serious hassles for Western women. There are issues to consider, of course, but thousands of women travel alone through the country each year and love the experience. Most Vietnamese women enjoy relatively free, fulfilled lives and a career; the sexes mix freely and society does not expect women to behave in a subordinate manner.

Many provincial Vietnamese women dress modestly (partly to avoid the sun), typically not wearing sleeveless tops or short shorts and skirts. Women who live in big cities tend to wear what they like.

Work

There's some casual work available in Western-owned bars and restaurants throughout the country. This is of the cash-in-hand variety; that is, working without paperwork. Dive schools and adventure-sports specialists will always need instructors, but for most travellers the main work opportunities are teaching a foreign language. Looking for employment is a matter of asking around – jobs are rarely advertised.

Teaching

English is by far the most popular foreign language with Vietnamese students. There's some demand for Mandarin, French and Russian, too.

Private language centres (US$10 to US$18 per hour) and home tutoring (US$15 to US$25 per hour) are your best bet for teaching work. You'll get paid more in HCMC or Hanoi than in the provinces.

Government-run universities in Vietnam also hire some foreign teachers.

Transport

GETTING THERE & AWAY

Most travellers enter Vietnam by plane or bus, but there are also train links from China and boat connections from Cambodia via the Mekong River. Flights, cars and tours can be booked online at lonelyplanet.com/bookings.

Entering Vietnam

Formalities at Vietnam's international airports are generally smoother than at land borders. That said, crossing overland from Cambodia and China is now relatively stress-free. Crossing the border between Vietnam and Laos can be slow.

Passport

Your passport must be valid for six months upon arrival in Vietnam. Many nationalities need to arrange a visa in advance.

Air

Airports & Airlines

The state-owned carrier Vietnam Airlines (www.vietnamairlines.com) has flights to over 30 international destinations, mainly in East Asia, but also to the USA, UK, Germany, France and Australia. The airline has a modern fleet of Airbuses and Boeings, and has a very good recent safety record.

There are now 17 airports deemed 'international' in Vietnam, but only eight have overseas connections (apart from the odd charter). Departure tax is included in the price of a ticket. Vietnam Airport's main portal (www.vietnamairport.vn) has links to most of the following:

Cam Ranh International Airport Located 36km south of Nha Trang, with an expanding range of flights including to Hong Kong and Seoul.

Can Tho International Airport In the Mekong Delta; flights to Kuala Lumpur, Bangkok and Taipei.

Cat Bi International Airport Near Haiphong; flights to China and South Korea.

Danang Airport International flights to countries including China, South Korea, Japan, Thailand, Malaysia, Cambodia and Singapore.

Noi Bai Airport Serves Hanoi.

Phu Quoc International Airport (www.phuquocairport.com) International flights including Singapore, Bangkok and some charters to Europe.

Tan Son Nhat International Airport For Ho Chi Minh City (HCMC).

Van Don Airport Serves Halong Bay with flights to China.

Tickets

It's hard to get reservations for flights to/from Vietnam during holidays, especially Tet, which falls between late January and mid-February.

Land

Vietnam shares land borders with Cambodia, China and Laos, and there are plenty

CLIMATE CHANGE & TRAVEL

Every form of transport that relies on carbon-based fuel generates CO_2, the main cause of human-induced climate change. Modern travel is dependent on aeroplanes, which might use less fuel per kilometre per person than most cars but travel much greater distances. The altitude at which aircraft emit gases (including CO_2) and particles also contributes to their climate change impact. Many websites offer 'carbon calculators' that allow people to estimate the carbon emissions generated by their journey and, for those who wish to do so, to offset the impact of the greenhouse gases emitted with contributions to portfolios of climate-friendly initiatives throughout the world. Lonely Planet offsets the carbon footprint of all staff and author travel.

of border crossings open to foreigners.

Border Crossings

Standard times that foreigners are allowed to cross are usually 7am to 5pm daily.

There are legal money-changing facilities on the Vietnamese side of most border crossings, which can deal with US dollars and some other currencies. Avoid black marketeers, as they have a well-deserved reputation for short-changing and outright theft.

Travellers at border crossings are occasionally asked for an 'immigration fee' of a dollar or two. It pays to carry low-denomination dollars, to avoid being told 'no change'.

CAMBODIA

Cambodia and Vietnam share a long frontier with seven border crossings. One-month Cambodian visas are issued on arrival at all border crossings for US$30, but overcharging is common at all borders except Bavet.

Cambodian border crossings are officially open daily between 8am and 8pm.

CHINA

There are three main borders where foreigners are permitted to cross between Vietnam and China: Dong Dang–Pingxiang (the Friendship Pass), Lao Cai and Mong Cai.

In most cases it's necessary to arrange a Chinese visa in advance.

Time in China is one hour ahead.

LAOS

There are seven overland crossings between Vietnam and Laos. Thirty-day Lao visas are available at all borders.

The golden rule is to try to use direct city-to-city bus connections between the countries, as potential hassle will be greatly reduced. If you travel step by step using local buses, expect transport scams (eg serious overcharging) on the Vietnamese side. Devious drivers have even stopped in the middle of nowhere to renegotiate the price.

Transport links on both sides of the border can be hit-and-miss, so don't use the more remote borders unless you have plenty of time, and patience, to spare.

Bicycle

There are no specific restrictions on bringing bicycles into Vietnam. However, you can expect plenty of attention on remote border crossings from officials, and be prepared to be asked for an unofficial 'import tax' of a few dollars.

Bus

Bus connections link Vietnam with Cambodia, Laos and China. The most popular way to/from Cambodia is the international buses connecting

BORDER CROSSINGS

Cambodian Border Crossings

CROSSING	VIETNAMESE TOWN	CONNECTING TOWN
Le Thanh–O Yadaw (p298)	Pleiku	Ban Lung
Moc Bai–Bavet (p345)	Ho Chi Minh City	Phnom Penh
Vinh Xuong–Kaam Samnor (p396)	Chau Doc	Phnom Penh
Xa Xia–Prek Chak (p391)	Ha Tien	Kep, Kampot
Tinh Bien–Phnom Den (p397)	Ha Tien, Chau Doc	Takeo, Phnom Penh

Chinese Border Crossings

CROSSING	VIETNAMESE TOWN	CONNECTING TOWN
Lao Cai–Hekou (p140)	Lao Cai	Kunming
Mong Cai–Dongxing (p121)	Mong Cai	Dongxing
Dong Dang–Pingxiang (p122)	Lang Son	Nanning

Main Lao Border Crossings

CROSSING	VIETNAMESE TOWN	CONNECTING TOWN
Bo Y–Phou Keua (p301)	Kon Tum, Pleiku	Attapeu
Cau Treo–Nam Phao (p159)	Vinh	Lak Sao
Lao Bao–Dansavanh (p174)	Dong Ha, Hue	Sepon, Savannakhet
Nam Can–Nong Haet (p159)	Vinh	Phonsavan
Tay Trang–Sop Hun (p131)	Dien Bien Phu	Muang Khua

Vietnam Border Crossings

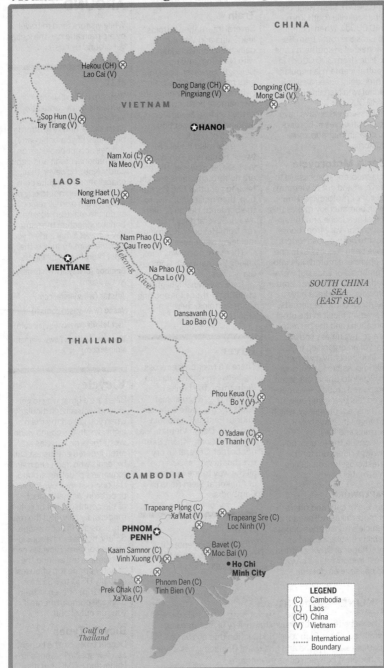

N 0 ————— 200 km
   0 ————— 100 miles

CHINA

Hekou (CH) ⊗
Lao Cai (V)

Dong Dang (CH) ⊗
Pingxiang (V)

Dongxing (CH) ⊗
Mong Cai (V)

VIETNAM

★HANOI

Sop Hun (L) ⊗
Tay Trang (V)

Nam Xoi (L) ⊗
Na Meo (V)

LAOS

Nong Haet (L) ⊗
Nam Can (V)

Nam Phao (L) ⊗
Cau Treo (V)

★ VIENTIANE

Mekong River

Na Phao (L) ⊗
Cha Lo (V)

SOUTH CHINA
SEA
(EAST SEA)

Dansavanh (L) ⊗
Lao Bao (V)

THAILAND

Phou Keua (L) ⊗
Bo Y (V)

O Yadaw (C) ⊗
Le Thanh (V)

CAMBODIA

Trapeang Plong (C) ⊗
Xa Mat (V)

⊗ Trapeang Sre (C)
Loc Ninh (V)

PHNOM
PENH ✪

Kaam Samnor (C) ⊗
Vinh Xuong (V)

Bavet (C)
⊗ Moc Bai (V)

● Ho Chi
Minh City

Prek Chak (C) ⊗
Xa Xia (V)

Phnom Den (C)
Tinh Bien (V)

Gulf of
Thailand

LEGEND
(C)   Cambodia
(L)   Laos
(CH)   China
(V)   Vietnam

······ International
        Boundary

HCMC with destinations including Phnom Penh (from 240,000d), Siem Reap and Sihanoukville (both from 440,000d). When it comes to Laos the route from Savannakhet in southern Laos to Hue (from 300,000d) in central Vietnam is popular. Three daily buses also link Hanoi with Nanning in China (480,000d).

Passengers always have to get off buses at borders to clear immigration and customs.

Car & Motorcycle

It is theoretically possible to travel in and out of Vietnam by car or motorcycle. However, bureaucracy makes this a real headache and the situation can vary from border post to border post. Riders have been successful taking Vietnamese motorbikes into Cambodia or Laos but we've had reports that some border officials inside Laos have demanded import permits. It's very difficult in the other direction (and the permits are costly) unless you are part of an organised tour.

Until recently it was virtually impossible to take any vehicle into China, but some organised groups have managed this by signing up with a Chinese tour agency, which arranges the paperwork, permits and fees.

Consult the forums on www.gt-rider.com for the latest cross-border biking information.

PAPERWORK

Drivers of cars and riders of motorbikes will need the vehicle's registration papers, liability insurance and an International Driving Permit. Most important is a *carnet de passage en douane*,

which acts as a temporary waiver of import duty.

Train

Several international trains link China and Vietnam. A daily train connects Hanoi with Nanning (and on to Beijing!). However, passengers have to leave the train (with all bags) just before the Vietnamese border and again at the Chinese border for scanning and inspection in the dead of night.

You can also travel between Hanoi and Kunming via Lao Cai; however, there are no through trains and you have to get off at Lao Cai station, then make your way to the border at Hekou (2.5km away). Several daily trains run from Hekou to Kunming including a sleeper.

There are no railway lines linking Vietnam with Cambodia or Laos.

Try www.chinahighlights.com/china-trains for booking Chinese trains; there's a small booking fee.

River

There's a river border crossing between Cambodia and Vietnam on the banks of the Mekong. Regular fast boats ply the route between Phnom Penh in Cambodia and Chau Doc in Vietnam via the Vinh Xuong–Kaam Samnor border. Several luxury riverboats with cabins run all the way to the temples of Angkor at Siem Reap in Cambodia.

Sea

Cruise ships excepted, it is not possible to travel to Vietnam by sea.

GETTING AROUND

While visitors tend to travel by air, train and car, the locals get around by bus.

Air

Vietnam has excellent domestic flight connections, with new routes opening up all the time, and very affordable prices (if you book early). Airlines accept bookings on international credit and debit cards. Note, however, that cancellations are quite common. It's safest not to rely on a flight from a small regional airport to make an international connection the same day – travel a day early if you can. Vietnam Airlines is the least likely to cancel flights.

Bamboo Airways (www.bambooairways.com)

Jetstar (www.jetstar.com)

Vasco (www.vasco.com.vn)

VietJet Air (www.vietjetair.com)

Vietnam Airlines (www.vietnamairlines.com)

Bicycle

Bikes are a great way to get around Vietnam, particularly when you get off the main highways. In the countryside, Westerners on bicycles are often greeted enthusiastically by locals who don't see many foreigners pedalling around.

Long-distance cycling is popular in Vietnam. Much of the country is flat or only moderately hilly, and the major roads are in good shape. Safety, however, is a considerable concern. Bicycles can be transported around the country on the top of buses (usually US$1 to US$2 for a short trip) or even in train baggage compartments if you run out of puff.

Bicycle Types

Decent bikes can be bought at a few speciality shops in Hanoi and HCMC, but it's

TOURS

The quality of bottom-end budget tours being peddled in HCMC and Hanoi is often terrible. You tend to get what you pay for. These Vietnam-based operators have a good reputation.

Buffalo Tours (p344) Offers diverse and customised trips, including superb Halong Bay tours and Gourmet Vietnam trips. Based in HCMC.

EXO Travel (p344) Offers a wide range of tours, including cycling, trekking and community tourism. HCMC-based.

Grasshopper Adventures (p211) Well-planned cycling trips, from day rides in the Mekong to bike trips well off the beaten path.

Handspan Travel Indochina (p344) Offers a wide range of innovative, interesting tours to seldom-visited regions including Bac Ha (four days US$387) and alternative destinations such as cycling trips to Phu Luong nature reserve. Other options include jeep tours, trekking and kayaking.

Ocean Tours (p92) Professional tour operator based in Hanoi, with Ba Be National Park options, tours of Halong Bay (overnight from US$115) and adventures around the northeast.

Sinhbalo Adventures (p344) Based in HCMC; specialises in cycling tours to the Mekong Delta and beyond.

better to bring your own if you plan to cycle long distances. Basic cycling safety equipment and authentic spare parts are also in short supply. A bell or horn is mandatory – the louder the better.

Rentals

Hotels and some travel agencies rent bicycles for US$1 to US$3 per day; better-quality models cost from US$6. Cycling is the perfect way to explore smaller cities such as Hoi An, Hue or Nha Trang (unless it's the rainy season!). There are bicycle repair stands along the side of roads to get punctures and the like fixed.

Boat

Vietnam has an enormous number of rivers that are at least partly navigable, but the most important by far is the Mekong and its tributaries. Scenic day trips by boat are possible on rivers in Hoi An, Nha Trang, Danang, Hue, Tam Coc and even HCMC.

Boat trips are also possible on the sea. Cruising Halong Bay is a must for all visitors to northern Vietnam. In central Vietnam the lovely Cham Islands (accessed from Hoi An) are a good excursion, while in

the south, trips to the islands off Nha Trang and around Phu Quoc are recommended. It's possible to reach the Con Dao Islands via boat too. Note many boat trips are seasonal and subject to weather.

Bus

Vietnam has an extensive network of buses that reach the far-flung corners of the country. Modern buses, operated by myriad companies, run on all the main highways. Out in the sticks expect uncomfortable local services.

Most travellers never visit a Vietnamese bus station at all, preferring to stick to the convenient, tourist-friendly open-tour bus network, or use a company like Sinh Tourist (www.thesinhtourist.vn) which has its own terminals.

Whichever class of bus you're on, bus travel in Vietnam is never speedy – plan on just 50km/h on major routes, perhaps 70km/h on Hwy 1 – due to the sheer number of motorbikes, trucks, pedestrians and random animals competing for space.

Bus Stations

Cities can have several public bus stations, and responsibilities can be divided according

to the location of the destination (whether it is north or south of the city) and the type of service (local or long distance).

Bus stations can look chaotic but many now have ticket offices with official prices and departure times clearly displayed.

The better bus companies have their own private terminals.

Deluxe Buses

Modern air-conditioned buses operate between the main cities. You can be certain of an allocated seat and enough space.

Most have comfortable reclining seats, others have padded flat beds for long trips. These sleeper buses can be a good alternative to trains. Deluxe buses are nonsmoking and some even have wi-fi. On the flip side, most of them are equipped with TVs (expect crazy kung fu videos) and some with dreaded karaoke machines. Ear plugs and eye masks are recommended.

Deluxe buses stop at most major cities en route, and for meal breaks.

Sinh Tourist (www.thesinh tourist.vn) Probably the best bus company and most favoured by travellers. Nationwide bus

FARE'S FAIR

For most visitors one of the most frustrating aspects of travelling in Vietnam is the perception that they are being ripped off. Here are some guidelines to help you navigate the maze.

Airfares Fares are dependent on when you book and what dates you want to travel. There is no price difference between Vietnamese and foreigners.

Boat fares Ferries and hydrofoils have fixed prices, but expect to pay more for the privilege of being a foreigner on smaller local boats around the Mekong Delta and to places like the Cham Islands.

Bus fares More complicated. If you buy a ticket from the point of departure (ie the bus station), then the price is fixed and very reasonable. However, should you board a bus along the way, there's a fair chance the driver or conductor will overcharge. In remote areas drivers may ask for four, or even 10, times what the locals pay. Local bus prices should be fixed and displayed by the door, but foreigners are sometimes overcharged on routes such as Danang–Hoi An.

Rail fares Fixed, although naturally there are different prices for different classes.

Taxis Mostly metered and very cheap, but very occasionally some taxis have dodgy meters that run fast. Grab is a good alternative.

Xe oms & cyclos Fares are definitely not fixed and you need to bargain. Hard.

---

services, including sleepers, and you can book ahead online.

Futa (https://futabus.vn) Also known as Phuong Trang, runs modern buses across the country. You can select seats and book online.

Mai Linh Express (www.mailinh express.vn) This reliable, punctual company operates clean, comfortable deluxe buses across Vietnam. Destinations covered include all main cities along Hwy 1 between Hanoi and HCMC. From HCMC buses run to Can Tho, Dalat and other cities in the central highlands.

Local Buses

Short-distance buses depart when full (jam-packed with people and luggage). Don't count on many leaving after about 4pm.

These buses and minibuses drop off and pick up as many passengers as possible along the route; frequent stops make for a slow journey.

Some conductors overcharge foreigners on these services so they're not popular with travellers.

RESERVATIONS & COSTS

Reservations aren't required for most of the frequent, popular services between towns and cities, but it doesn't hurt to purchase the ticket the day before. Always buy a ticket online or from the office, as bus drivers are notorious for overcharging.

On some rural runs foreigners are overcharged. As a benchmark, a typical 100km ride *should* be between US$2 and US$3.

Open-Tour Buses

In backpacker haunts throughout Vietnam, you'll see lots of signs advertising 'Open Tour' or 'Open Ticket'. These are bus services catering mostly to foreign budget travellers. The air-conditioned buses run between HCMC and Hanoi (and other routes) and passengers can hop on and hop off the bus at any major city along the route.

Prices are reasonable. Depending on the operator and exact route, HCMC to Hanoi is US$37 to US$70, while HCMC to Hue is around US$26. The more stops you add, the higher the price. Try to book the next leg of your trip at least a day ahead.

Buses usually depart from central places (often hostels popular with travellers),

avoiding an extra journey to the bus station. Some open-tour buses also stop at sights along the way (such as the Cham ruins of Po Klong Garai).

The downside is that you're herded together with other backpackers and there's little contact with locals. Additionally, it's harder to get off the main 'banana pancake' trail as open-route buses just tend to run to the most popular places. Some open-tour operators also depend on kickbacks from sister hotels and restaurants along the way.

Buying shorter point-to-point tickets on the open-tour buses costs a bit more but you achieve more flexibility, including the chance to take a train, rent a motorbike or simply change your plans.

Nevertheless, cheap open-tour tickets are a temptation and many people go for them. Aside from the main north–south journey, the HCMC–Mui Ne–Dalat–Nha Trang route is popular.

Sinh Tourist (www.the sinhtourist.vn) has a good reputation, with online seat reservations and comfortable buses.

Car & Motorcycle

Having your own set of wheels gives you maximum flexibility to visit remote regions and stop when and where you please. Car hire always includes a driver. Motorbike hire is good value and this can be self-ride or with a driver.

Driving Licences

Unfortunately getting a valid licence to ride a motorbike in Vietnam is impossible for many. The rules and bureaucracy involved are frankly mind-boggling. Foreigners *are* permitted to ride motorbikes in Vietnam with an International Driving Permit (IDP) – you can apply for one online at www.e-ita.org/vietnam. However, this only covers countries that abide by the 1968 Convention on IDPs. There's a full list of eligible countries (which includes most EU countries, UK and Switzerland) at https://en.wikipedia.org/wiki/International_Driving_Permit. But many other nations (including USA, Canada, Australia and New Zealand) are not included. So if you have a 1968 IDP, you can legally ride in Vietnam.

The best source of information is available from local experts Offroad Vietnam (https://vietnammotorbikerental.com).

If you do manage to acquire a hire car without a driver, an IDP is also technically required.

Fuel

Even the most isolated communities usually have someone selling petrol by the roadside. Some sellers dilute fuel to make a quick profit – try to fill up from a proper petrol station.

Hire

The major considerations are safety, the mechanical condition of the vehicle, the reliability of the rental agency, and your budget.

CAR & MINIBUS

Self-drive rental cars are virtually impossible in Vietnam, which is a blessing given traffic conditions, but cars with drivers are popular and plentiful. Renting a vehicle with a driver-cum-guide is a realistic option even for budget travellers, provided there are enough people to share the cost.

Hanoi, HCMC and the main tourist centres have a wide selection of travel agencies that rent vehicles with drivers for sightseeing trips. For the rough roads of northern Vietnam you'll definitely need a 4WD. Approximate costs per day are between US$80 and US$120 for a standard car, or between US$120 and US$135 for a 4WD.

MOTORCYCLE

Many travellers hire a motorbike or scooter for a day or two when in Vietnam. However, unless you've organised an International Driving Permit you may not be covered by insurance.

Motorbikes are usually hired on a very casual basis. Scooters can be hired from virtually anywhere, including cafes, hotels and travel agencies. Some places will ask to keep your passport until you return the bike/scooter. Try to sign some sort of agreement, clearly stating what you are hiring, how much it costs, the extent of compensation and so on.

To tackle the mountains of the north, it is best to get a slightly more powerful model such as a road or trail bike. Plenty of local drivers are willing to act as chauffeur and guide for around US$30 per day.

HIRING A VEHICLE & DRIVER

Renting a car with a driver gives you the chance to design a tailor-made tour. Seeing the country this way is almost like independent travel, except that it's more comfortable, less time-consuming and allows for stops along the way.

Most travel agencies and tour operators can hook you up with a vehicle and driver (most of whom will *not* speak English). Try to find a driver-guide who can act as a translator and travelling companion and offer all kinds of cultural knowledge, opening up the door to some unique experiences. A bad guide can ruin your trip. Consider the following:

➡ Try to meet your driver-guide before starting out and make sure that this is someone you can travel with.

➡ How much English (French or other language) do they speak?

➡ Drivers usually pay for their own costs, including accommodation and meals, while you pay for the petrol. Check this is the case.

➡ Settle on an itinerary and get a copy from the travel agency. If you find your guide is making it up as they go along, use it as leverage.

➡ Make it clear you want to avoid tourist-trap restaurants and shops.

➡ Tip them if you've had a good experience.

The approximate costs per day without a driver are between US$5 and US$8 for a scooter or US$20 and up for trail and road bikes.

INSURANCE

If you're travelling in a tourist vehicle with a driver, the car-hire company organises insurance. If you're using a hired bike, consider carefully that most travel insurance policies will *not cover you* in the event of an accident if you've not got a driving licence valid for motorbike use. Many travellers wing it, but the risks are clear. The cost of treating serious injuries can be bankrupting for budget travellers.

Some policies may even exclude all cover for two-wheeled travel, so if you're riding pillion on a Grab bike or *xe om*, you may not be insured.

Road Conditions & Hazards

Road safety is definitely not one of Vietnam's strong points. The intercity road network of highways is dangerous. High-speed, head-on collisions are a sickeningly familiar sight on main roads.

In general, the major highways are paved and reasonably well maintained, but seasonal flooding can be a problem. A big typhoon can create potholes the size of bomb craters. In some remote areas, roads are not surfaced and transform into a sea of mud when the weather turns bad – such roads are best tackled with a 4WD vehicle or motorbike. Mountain roads are particularly dangerous: landslides, falling rocks and runaway vehicles can add an unwelcome edge to your journey.

EMERGENCIES

Vietnam does not have an efficient emergency-rescue system, so if something happens on the road, it could be some time before help arrives and a long way to even the most basic of medical facilities. Locals might help, but in most cases it will be up to you (or your guide) to get you to the hospital or clinic.

ROAD RULES

Basically, there aren't many or, arguably, any. Size matters and the biggest vehicle wins by default. Be particularly careful about children on the road. Livestock is also a menace; hit a cow on a motorbike and you'll both be hamburger meat.

The police almost never bother stopping foreigners on bikes (except around Mui Ne and sometimes in Nha Trang). However, speeding fines are imposed and the police now have speed 'guns'. In any area deemed to be 'urban' (look out for the blue sign with skyscrapers), the limit is just 50km/h. In cities, there is a rule that you cannot turn right on a red light.

Honking at all pedestrians and bicycles (to warn them of your approach) is not road rage but local etiquette.

Legally, a motorbike can carry only two people, but we've seen up to six on one vehicle...plus luggage! This law is sort of enforced in major cities, but wildly ignored in rural areas.

SPARE PARTS

Vietnam is awash with Japanese (and Chinese) motorbikes, so it is easy to get spare parts for most bikes. But if you are driving something very obscure, bring substantial spares. It is compulsory to wear a helmet when riding a motorbike in Vietnam, even when travelling as a passenger. Consider investing in a decent imported helmet if you are planning extensive rides. Better-quality helmets are from US$35.

Local Transport

Bus

Few travellers deal with city buses due to communication issues and the cheapness of taxis and *xe om*. That said, the bus systems in Hanoi and HCMC are not impossible to

---

MOTORBIKING TIPS

→ Organise an International Driving Permit (IDP) and check your travel insurance policy.

→ Consider joining a tour or hiring a guide who knows the roads and can help with mechanical and linguistic difficulties.

→ Get acquainted with your bike (most are under 250cc) and check current road conditions and routes.

→ Essentials include a good helmet, rain gear and a spare parts and repair kit. Saddle bags are very useful.

→ Decent printed maps are a useful back-up to the Google Maps phone app.

→ Knee, elbow pads and gloves are wise, particularly if off-road.

→ Expect to average about 35km/h.

→ Only use safe hotel parking.

→ Running short on time or energy? Put your bike on the roof of a bus (for a charge).

ROAD DISTANCES (KM)

	Can Tho	Ho Chi Minh City	Mui Ne	Da Lat	Nha Trang	Quy Nhon	Hoi An	Da Nang	Hue	Dong Hoi	Hanoi	Dien Bien Phu	Sapa
Ho Chi Minh City	170												
Mui Ne	370	220											
Da Lat	460	310	150										
Nha Trang	590	440	220	130									
Quy Nhon	800	620	430	340	210								
Hoi An	105	880	720	640	500	300							
Da Nang	1070	900	750	660	530	330	30						
Hue	1150	1000	840	750	620	420	130	100					
Dong Hoi	1320	1160	1000	920	780	580	300	270	170				
Hanoi	1820	1640	1500	1410	1280	1080	790	770	660	500			
Dien Bien Phu	2280	1970	1840	1750	1620	1420	1130	1100	1000	840	430		
Sapa	2140	1960	1820	1730	1590	1390	1100	1080	980	820	320	280	
Mong Cai	2050	1880	1730	1640	1510	1300	1030	990	890	720	310	800	620

negotiate – get your hands on a bus map.

Cyclo

The *cyclo* is a bicycle rickshaw. This cheap mode of transport is steadily dying out, but is still found in some Vietnamese cities.

Groups of *cyclo* drivers always hang out near major hotels and markets. Bargaining is imperative; settle on a fare before going anywhere. Approximate fares are between 15,000d and 25,0000d for a short ride, between 25,000d and 40,000d for a longer or night ride.

However, do consider that there are some dodgy *cyclo* operators out there who target tourists by outrageously overcharging.

Cyclo tours organised by tour operators are sanitised rides around cities.

Taxi

Taxis with meters, found in all major towns and cities, are very cheap by international standards and a safe way to travel around at night. Average tariffs are about 12,000d to 15,000d per kilometre.

However, dodgy taxis with go-fast meters do roam the streets of Hanoi and HCMC; they often hang around bus terminals. Only travel with reputable or recommended companies.

Two nationwide companies with excellent reputations are Mai Linh (www.mailinh.vn) and Vinasun (www.vinasun-taxi.com).

App-based taxis (both car and motorbike) including Grab are available in several Vietnamese cities including HCMC, Hanoi, Danang, Dalat, Hue and Haiphong. Uber is not present in Vietnam.

Xe Om

The *xe om* (zay-ohm) is a motorbike taxi. *Xe* means motorbike, *om* means hug (or hold), so you get the picture. Getting around by *xe om* is easy, as long as you don't have a lot of luggage.

Fares are around 15,000d for a short hop, or from 20,000d in HCMC or Hanoi. Negotiate the price beforehand. There are plenty of *xe om* drivers hanging around street corners, hotels and bus stations. They will find you before you find them…

Train

Operated by national carrier, Vietnam Railways (www.vr.com.vn), the Vietnamese railway system is an ageing but pretty dependable service, and offers a relaxing way to get around the nation. Travelling in an air-conditioned sleeping berth sure beats a hairy overnight bus journey along Hwy 1. And, of course, there's some spectacular scenery to lap up, too.

Check www.seat61.com for the latest information on all trains in Vietnam.

Classes

Trains classified as SE are the smartest and fastest, while those referred to as TN are slower and older. There are four main ticket classes: hard seat, soft seat, hard sleeper and soft sleeper. These are also split into air-conditioned and non-air-conditioned options. Presently, air-con is only available on the faster express trains. Some SE

METRO PROGRESS

Metro lines are under construction in both HCMC and Hanoi, and though both have been delayed, services should start in the next few years. The line in HCMC is a Japanese-Vietnamese partnership; Line 1 was supposed to open in 2020 but is several years behind schedule. Eventually, the plan is for there to be three monorails and six underground lines.

China is the financial muscle behind the Hanoi metro, which has also been beset by construction troubles. Here eight lines are planned, with a total length of 318km. Two lines are currently being built: most work on Line 2A was finished in late 2019, but testing was continuing. It will hopefully be operational by the time you read this.

trains now have wi-fi (though connection speeds, like Vietnamese trains, are not the quickest). Hard-seat class is usually packed and expect plenty of cigarette smoke.

Private Carriages

Comfortable, even luxurious, private carriages tagged onto the back of trains offer a classy way of travelling between Lao Cai and Hanoi: those offered by Orient Express Trains (www.orient expresstrainsapa.com) and Victoria Hotels are renowned and very pricey, but there are many other options including Livitrans (www.livitrans.com). Livitrans, Violette (http:// en.violetexpresstrain.com) and other companies offer luxury carriages between Hanoi and Dong Hoi (US$60), Hue (US$65 to US$80) and Danang (US$70 to US$90), as do several other companies.

Sleepers

A hard sleeper has three tiers of beds (six beds per compartment), with the upper berth cheapest and the lower berth most expensive. Most soft sleepers have two tiers (four beds per compartment) and all bunks are priced the same. 'VIP' two-berth sleepers are now available on trains

SE1 and SE2. Fastidious travellers will probably want to bring a sleeping sheet, sleeping bag and/or pillow case with them, although linen is provided.

Costs

Ticket prices vary depending on the train; the fastest trains are more expensive.

Children under two are free; those between two and nine years of age pay 50% of the adult fare. There are no discounts on the Hanoi–Lao Cai route.

Freight

Bicycles and motorbikes must travel in freight carriages, which will cost around 390,000d for a typical overnight trip.

Reservations

Most travellers use Bao Lau (www.baolau.vn) to book tickets, which is an efficient website with schedules and fares; it details seat and sleeper-berth availability and accepts international cards. E-tickets are emailed to you, which you show when boarding; there's a 40,000d commission per ticket.

You can reserve seats/ berths on long trips 60 to 90 days in advance (less on shorter trips). Most of

the time you can book train tickets a day or two ahead without a problem, except during peak holiday times. For sleeping berths book a week or more before the date of departure. Many travel agencies, hotels and cafes will also buy you train tickets for a small commission.

You could try to buy tickets in advance from the Vietnam Railways bookings site (http://dsvn.vn), however, at the time of writing only Vietnamese credit cards were accepted.

Routes

Aside from the main HCMC–Hanoi run, three rail-spur lines link Hanoi with the other parts of northern Vietnam: one runs east to the port city of Haiphong; a second heads northeast to Lang Son and continues across the border to Nanning, China; a third runs northwest to Lao Cai (for trains on to Kunming, China).

'Fast' trains between Hanoi and HCMC take between 31 and 37 hours.

Safety

Petty crime is rare on Vietnamese trains. Thieves occasionally try to grab stuff as trains pull out of stations. Always keep your bag nearby and lock or tie it to something, especially at night.

Schedules

Several Reunification Express trains depart from Hanoi and HCMC every day. Train schedules change frequently, so check departure times on the Vietnam Railways website (www.vr.com.vn) or Bao Lau's website (www.baolau.vn).

A bare-bones train schedule operates during the Tet festival, when most trains are suspended for nine days, beginning four days before Tet and continuing for four days afterwards.

Health

Health issues (and the quality of medical facilities) vary enormously depending on where you are in Vietnam. The major cities are generally not high risk and have good facilities, though rural areas are another matter.

Travellers tend to worry about contracting infectious diseases in Vietnam, but serious illnesses are rare. Accidental injuries (especially traffic-related) account for most life-threatening problems. That said, a bout of sickness is a relatively common thing.

For information on the COVID-19 pandemic, see p3, p22 and p452.

BEFORE YOU GO

Health Insurance

Don't travel without health insurance – accidents do happen. If your health insurance doesn't cover you for medical expenses abroad, get extra insurance – check our website (www.lonelyplanet.com) for more information. Emergency evacuation is expensive – bills of US$100,000 are not unknown – so make sure your policy covers this.

Medical Checklist

Recommended, but not exhaustive, items for a personal medical kit:

➡ antibacterial cream; eg mupirocin

➡ antihistamines for allergies; eg cetirizine for daytime and promethazine for night

➡ antiseptic for cuts and scrapes; eg iodine solution such as Betadine

➡ DEET-based insect repellent

➡ diarrhoea 'stopper'; eg loperamide

➡ first-aid items, such as scissors, plasters (eg Band-Aids), bandages, gauze, safety pins and tweezers

➡ paracetamol or ibuprofen for pain

➡ steroid cream for allergic/itchy rashes; eg 1% hydrocortisone

➡ sunscreen

➡ antifungal treatments for thrush and tinea; eg clotrimazole or fluconazole

Websites

There's a wealth of travel-health advice on the internet.

www.who.int/ith Publishes a superb book called *International Travel & Health*, which is available free online.

www.cdc.gov Good general information.

www.travelhealthpro.org.uk Useful health advice.

IN VIETNAM

Availability & Cost of Health Care

The significant improvement in Vietnam's economy has brought with it some major advances in public health. However, in remote parts, local clinics will only have basic supplies – if you become seriously ill in rural Vietnam, get to (Ho Chi Minh City) HCMC, Danang or Hanoi as quickly as you can. For surgery or other extensive treatment, don't hesitate to fly to Bangkok, Singapore or Hong Kong.

Private Clinics

These should be your first port of call. They are familiar with local resources and can organise evacuations if necessary. The best medical facilities – in Hanoi and HCMC – have health facility standards that come close to those in developed countries.

State Hospitals

Most are overcrowded and basic. In order to treat foreigners, a facility needs to obtain a special licence and, so far, only a few have been provided.

Self-Treatment

If your problem is minor (eg travellers' diarrhoea) this is an option. If you think you may have a serious disease, especially malaria, do not waste time – travel to the nearest quality facility to receive attention.

Buying medication over the counter is not recommended, as fake medications and poorly stored or out-of-date drugs are common. Check expiry dates on all medicines.

Infectious Diseases

Bird Flu

The bird flu virus rears its head every year in Vietnam. It occurs in clusters, usually among poultry workers. It's rarely fatal for humans. When outbreaks do occur, eggs and poultry are banished from the menu in many hotels and restaurants.

Chikungunya

This virus is mainly transmitted by mosquitoes that bite during the day. Fever, joint pain and rashes are the main symptoms; paracetamol (do not take aspirin) will ease pain. No vaccine or medicine is available, but most patients feel better within a week.

Dengue

This mosquito-borne disease is a real concern in Southeast Asia. It's more common in urban areas, and during rainy season. Several hundred thousand people are hospitalised with dengue haemorrhagic fever in Vietnam every year, but the fatality rate is less than 0.3%. As there is no vaccine available, it can only be prevented by avoiding

mosquito bites. The mosquito that carries dengue bites throughout the day and night, so use insect-avoidance measures at all times. Symptoms include a high fever, a severe headache and body aches (dengue was once known as 'breakbone fever'). Some people develop a rash and experience diarrhoea. There is no specific treatment, just rest and paracetamol – do not take aspirin as it increases the likelihood of haemorrhaging. See a doctor to be diagnosed and monitored.

Hepatitis A

A problem throughout the region, this food- and waterborne virus infects the liver, causing jaundice (yellow skin and eyes), nausea and lethargy. There is no specific treatment for hepatitis A – you just need to allow time for the liver to heal. All travellers to Vietnam should be vaccinated against hepatitis A.

Hepatitis B

The only serious sexually transmitted disease that can be prevented by vaccination, hepatitis B is spread by body fluids, including sexual contact. In some parts of Southeast Asia up to 20% of the population are carriers of hepatitis B, and usually are unaware of this.

HIV

The official figures on the number of people with HIV/AIDS in Vietnam are vague. Health-education messages relating to HIV/AIDS are visible all over the countryside, but the official line is that infection is largely limited to

sex workers and drug users. Condoms are widely available throughout Vietnam.

Japanese B Encephalitis

This viral disease is transmitted by mosquitoes. It's very rarely caught by travellers but vaccination is recommended for those spending extended time in rural areas. There is no treatment; a third of infected people will die while another third will suffer permanent brain damage.

Malaria

For such a serious and potentially deadly disease, there is an enormous amount of misinformation concerning malaria. You must get expert advice as to whether your trip actually puts you at risk.

Many parts of Vietnam, particularly city and resort areas including Danang, Hanoi, HCMC and Nha Trang, have virtually no risk of malaria. For most rural areas, however, the risk of contracting the disease far outweighs the risk of any tablet side effects. Travellers to isolated areas in high-risk regions such as Ca Mau and Bac Lieu provinces, and the rural south, may like to carry a treatment dose of medication for use if symptoms occur. Remember that malaria can be fatal. Before you travel, seek medical advice on the right medication and dosage for you.

Malaria is caused by a parasite transmitted by the bite of an infected mosquito. The most important symptom of malaria is fever, but general symptoms such as headache, diarrhoea, cough or chills may also occur. Diagnosis can only be made by taking a blood sample.

Two strategies should be combined to prevent malaria – mosquito avoidance and antimalarial medications.

PREVENTION

➡ Choose accommodation with screens and fans (if not air-conditioned).

➡ Impregnate clothing with permethrin in high-risk areas.

➡ Sleep under a mosquito net.

➡ Spray your room with insect repellent before going out for your evening meal.

➡ Use a DEET-containing insect repellent on all exposed skin, particularly the ankle area. Natural repellents such as citronella can be effective but must be applied frequently.

➡ Use mosquito coils.

➡ Wear long sleeves and trousers in light colours.

MEDICATION

There are various medications available. Some drugs are not effective in southern regions of Vietnam so always consult a health professional before travel.

Chloroquine and paludrine The effectiveness of this combination is now limited in Vietnam. Generally not recommended.

Doxycycline A broad-spectrum antibiotic that has the added benefit of helping to prevent a variety of tropical diseases, including leptospirosis, tick-borne disease, typhus and melioidosis. Potential side effects include a tendency to sunburn, thrush in women, indigestion and interference with the contraceptive pill. It must be taken for four weeks after leaving the risk area. Effective across the nation.

Lariam (mefloquine) Receives a lot of bad press, some of it justified, some not. This weekly tablet suits many people. Serious side effects are rare but include depression, anxiety, psychosis and seizures. It's around 90% effective in Vietnam.

Malarone (atovaquone/proguanil) Side effects are uncommon and mild, most commonly nausea and headaches. It is the best tablet for scuba-divers and for those on short trips to high-risk areas.

Measles

Measles remains a problem in Vietnam, including the Hanoi area. Many people born before 1966 are immune as they had the disease in childhood. Measles starts with a high fever and rash but can be complicated by pneumonia and brain disease. There is no specific treatment.

Rabies

This uniformly fatal disease is spread by the bite or lick of an infected animal – most commonly a dog or monkey. Seek medical advice immediately after any animal bite and start post-exposure treatment. Having pretravel vaccinations means the post-bite treatment is greatly simplified (but you'll still need to seek medical attention). If an animal bites you, gently wash the wound with soap and water, and apply an iodine-based antiseptic. If you are not vaccinated you will need to receive rabies immunoglobulin as soon as possible.

Schistosomiasis

Schistosomiasis (also called bilharzia) is a tiny parasite that enters your skin after you've been swimming in contaminated water. If you are concerned, you can be tested three months after exposure. Symptoms are coughing and fever. Schistosomiasis is easily treated with medications.

STIs

Condoms, widely available throughout Vietnam, are effective in preventing the spread of most sexually transmitted infections. However, they may not guard against genital warts or herpes. If after a sexual encounter you develop any rash, lumps, discharge or pain when passing urine, seek immediate medical attention.

Travellers' Diarrhoea

Travellers' diarrhoea is by far the most common problem affecting travellers – between 30% and 50% of people will suffer from it within two weeks of starting their trip. In more than 80% of cases, travellers' diarrhoea is caused by a bacteria, and therefore responds promptly to treatment with antibiotics. It can also be provoked by a change of diet, and your stomach may settle down again after a few days.

Treatment consists of staying hydrated, or you could take rehydration solutions.

Loperamide is just a 'stopper' and doesn't get to the cause of the problem. It is helpful if you have to go on a long bus ride, but don't take loperamide if you have a fever or blood in your stools.

AMOEBIC DYSENTERY

Amoebic dysentery is very rare in travellers. Symptoms are similar to bacterial diarrhoea (eg fever, bloody diarrhoea and generally feeling unwell). Treatment involves two drugs: tinidazole or metronidazole to kill the parasite and a second to kill the cysts.

GIARDIASIS

Giardia lamblia is a parasite that is relatively common in travellers. Symptoms include nausea, bloating, excess gas, fatigue and intermittent diarrhoea. 'Eggy' burps are often attributed solely to giardiasis, but they are not specific to this infection. The treatment of choice is tinidazole.

Tuberculosis

Tuberculosis (TB) is very rare in short-term travellers. Medical and aid workers, and long-term travellers who have significant contact with the local population should take precautions. Vaccination is usually only given to children under the age of five, but it is recommended that at-risk adults have pre- and post-travel TB testing. The

REQUIRED & RECOMMENDED VACCINATIONS

The only vaccination *required* by international regulations is yellow fever. Proof of vaccination will only be required if you have visited a country in the yellow-fever zone within six days of entering Vietnam.

The World Health Organization (WHO) recommends the following vaccinations for travellers to Southeast Asia:

Adult diphtheria and tetanus Single booster recommended if you've had none in the previous 10 years.

Hepatitis A Provides almost 100% protection for up to a year; a booster after 12 months provides at least another 20 years' protection.

Hepatitis B Now considered routine for most travellers. A rapid schedule is also available, as is a combined vaccination with hepatitis A. Lifetime protection occurs in 95% of people.

Measles, mumps and rubella Two doses of MMR are required unless you have had the diseases. Many young adults require a booster.

Typhoid Recommended unless your trip is less than a week and only to cities. The vaccine offers around 70% protection and lasts for two or three years.

Most vaccines don't produce immunity until at least two weeks after they're given, so visit a doctor four to eight weeks before departure.

Long-term travellers should also consider Japanese B encephalitis, meningitis, tuberculosis and rabies jabs.

---

main symptoms are fever, cough, weight loss, night sweats and tiredness.

Typhoid

This serious bacterial infection is spread via food and water. It gives a high, slowly progressive fever and headache. Vaccination is recommended for all travellers spending more than a week in Vietnam, or travelling outside of the major cities. Be aware that vaccination is not 100% effective so you must still be careful with what you eat and drink.

Typhus

Murine typhus is spread by the fleas of rodents whereas scrub typhus is spread via a mite. These diseases are rare in travellers. Symptoms include fever, muscle pains and a rash. You can avoid these diseases by following general insect-avoidance measures. Doxycycline will also help prevent them.

Zika

This virus is rare but present in Vietnam. Many infected people have mild to no symptoms (fever, rashes, headaches and joint pain) that last up to a week. It's spread primarily by mosquitoes and sexual intercourse. Infection during pregnancy can cause serious birth defects. There's no specific medicine or vaccine for Zika.

Environmental Hazards

Air Pollution

Air pollution, particularly vehicle pollution, is severe in Vietnam's major cities, especially Hanoi. If you have severe respiratory problems consult your doctor before travelling. See the World Air Quality Index website (https://waqi.info) for Vietnam information.

Bites & Stings

Bedbugs These don't carry disease but their bites are very itchy. Move hotel, and treat the itch with an antihistamine.

Jellyfish In Vietnamese waters most are not dangerous, just irritating. Pour vinegar (or urine) onto the affected area. Take painkillers, and seek medical advice if you feel ill in any way. Take local advice if there are dangerous jellyfish around and keep out of the water.

Leeches Found in humid forest areas. They do not transmit any disease but their bites can be intensely itchy. Apply an iodine-based antiseptic to any leech bite to help prevent infection.

Snakes Both poisonous and harmless snakes are common in Vietnam, though very few travellers are ever bothered by them. Wear boots and avoid poking around dead logs and wood when hiking. First aid in the event of a snake bite involves pressure immobilisation via an elastic bandage firmly wrapped around the affected limb, starting at the bite site and working up towards the chest. The bandage should not be so tight that the circulation is cut off, and the fingers or toes should be kept free so the circulation can be checked. Immobilise the limb with a splint and carry the victim to medical attention. Do not use tourniquets or try to suck the venom out. Antivenom is available only in major cities.

Ticks Contracted during walks in rural areas. If you have had a tick bite and experience symptoms such as a rash (at the site of the bite or elsewhere), fever or muscle aches, you should see a doctor. Doxycycline prevents tick-borne diseases.

Food

Eating in restaurants is the biggest risk factor for contracting travellers' diarrhoea. Ways to avoid it include eating only freshly cooked food, and avoiding shellfish and buffets. Peel all fruit and try to stick to cooked vegetables. Eat in busy restaurants with a high turnover of customers.

Heat

Many parts of Vietnam are hot and humid throughout the year. Take it easy when you first arrive. Avoid dehydration and excessive activity in the heat. Drink rehydration solution and eat salty food.

Heat exhaustion Symptoms include feeling weak, headaches, irritability, nausea or vomiting, sweaty skin and a fast, weak pulse. Cool down in a room with air-conditioning and rehydrate with water containing a quarter of a teaspoon of salt per litre.

Heatstroke This is a serious medical emergency. Symptoms come on suddenly and include weakness, nausea, a temperature of over 41°C, dizziness, confusion and eventually collapse and loss of consciousness. Seek medical help and start cooling treatment.

Prickly heat A common skin rash in the tropics. Stay in an air-conditioned area for a few hours and take cool showers.

Skin Issues

Cuts and scratches Minor cuts and scratches can become infected easily in humid climates and may fail to heal because of the humidity. Take meticulous care of any wounds: immediately wash in clean water and apply antiseptic.

Fungal rashes Common in humid climates. Moist areas that get less air, such as the groin, armpits and between the toes, are often affected. Treatment involves using an antifungal cream such as clotrimazole. Consult a doctor.

Sunburn

➡ Even on a cloudy day, sunburn can occur rapidly.

➡ Always use a strong sunscreen (at least factor 30).

➡ Reapply sunscreen after swimming.

➡ Wear a hat.

➡ Avoid the sun between 10am and 2pm.

Women's Health

Supplies of sanitary products are readily available in urban areas. Birth control options may be limited, so bring adequate stocks.

Pregnant women should receive specialised advice before travelling. The ideal time to travel is in the second trimester (between 16 and 28 weeks), during which time the risk of pregnancy-related problems is at its lowest. Some advice:

Rural areas Avoid remote areas with poor transportation and medical facilities.

Travel insurance Ensure you're covered for pregnancy-related possibilities, including premature labour.

Malaria None of the more effective antimalarial drugs are completely safe in pregnancy.

Travellers' diarrhoea Many diarrhoea treatments are not recommended during pregnancy. Azithromycin is considered safe.

Zika Pregnant women are recommended not to travel to Vietnam because the disease (if rare) can cause serious birth defects.

Language

Vietnamese, or *tiếng Việt* dee·úhng vee·ụht, is the official language of Vietnam and spoken by about 85 million people worldwide, both in Vietnam and among migrant communities around the world. It belongs to the Mon-Khmer language family and has Muong (a hill-tribe language) as its closest relative.

Vietnamese pronunciation is not as hard as it may seem at first as most Vietnamese sounds also exist in English. With a bit of practice and reading our coloured pronunciation guides as if they were English, you shouldn't have much trouble being understood. Note that the vowel a is pronounced as in 'at', aa as in 'father', aw as in 'law', er as in 'her', oh as in 'doh!', ow as in 'cow', u as in 'book', uh as in 'but' and uhr as in 'fur' (without the 'r'). Vowel sounds can also be combined in various ways within a word – we've used dots (eg dee·úh-ng) to separate the different vowel sounds to keep pronunciation straightforward. As for the consonants, note that the ng sound, which is also found in English (eg in 'sing') can also appear at the start of a word in Vietnamese. Also note that đ is pronounced as in 'stop', d as in 'dog' and ğ as in 'skill'.

You'll notice that some vowels are pronounced with a high or low pitch while others swoop or glide in an almost musical manner. This is because Vietnamese uses a system of tones. There are six tones in Vietnamese, indicated in the written language (and in our pronunciation guides) by accent marks above or below the vowel: mid (ma), low falling (mà), low rising (mả), high broken (mã), high rising (má) and low broken (mạ). Note that the mid tone is flat. In the south, the low rising and the high broken tones are both pronounced as the low rising tone. Vietnamese

words are considered to have one syllable, so word stress is not an issue.

The variation in vocabulary between the Vietnamese of the north and that of the south is indicated in this chapter by (N) and (S).

BASICS

Hello.	*Xin chào.*	sin jòw
Goodbye.	*Tạm biệt.*	daạm bee·ụht
Yes.	*Vâng.* (N)	vuhng
	Dạ. (S)	yạ
No.	*Không.*	kawm
Please.	*Làm ơn.*	laàm ern
Thank you.	*Cảm ơn.*	ğaảm ern
You're welcome.	*Không có chi.*	kawm ğó jee
Excuse me./ Sorry.	*Xin lỗi.*	sin lõy

How are you?
Có khỏe không?   ğáw kwả kawm

Fine, thank you. And you?
Khỏe, cám ơn.   kwả ğaảm ern
Còn bạn thì sao?   kwả ğòn baạn teè sow

What's your name?
Tên là gì?   den laà zeè

My name is ...
Tên tôi là ...   den doy laà ...

Do you speak English?
Bạn có nói được   baạn ğó nóy đuhr·ẹrk
tiếng Anh không?   díng aang kawm

I (don't) understand.
Tôi (không) hiểu.   doy (kawm) heẻ·oo

ACCOMMODATION

Where is a ...?	*Đâu có ... ?*	doh ğó ...
hotel	*khách sạn*	kaák saạn
guesthouse	*nhà khách*	nyaà kaák
I'd like (a) ...	*Tôi muốn ...*	doy moo·úhn ...
single room	*phòng đơn*	fòm dern

WANT MORE?

For in-depth language information and handy phrases, check out Lonely Planet's *Vietnamese Phrasebook & Dictionary* and *Hill Tribes Phrasebook & Dictionary*. You'll find them at **shop.lonelyplanet.com**.

double room (big bed)	*phòng giường đôi*	fòm zuhr·èrng đoy

How much is it per night/person?
Giá bao nhiêu một đêm/người? — zaá bow nyee·oo mạwt đem/nguhr·eè

air-con	*máy lạnh*	máy laạng
bathroom	*phòng tắm*	fòm dúhm
fan	*quạt máy*	gwaạt máy
hot water	*nước nóng*	nuhr·érk nóm
mosquito net	*màng*	maàng
sheet	*ra trải giường*	zaa chaỉ zuhr·èrng
toilet	*nhà vệ sinh*	nyaà vẹ sing
toilet paper	*giấy vệ sinh*	záy vẹ sing
towel	*khăn tắm*	kúhn dúhm

DIRECTIONS

Where is ...?
... ở đâu ? — ... ẻr đoh

What is the address?
Địa chỉ là gì? — đee·ụh cheé laà zeè

Could you write it down, please?
Xin viết ra giùm tôi. — sin vee·úht zaa zùm doy

Can you show me (on the map)?
Xin chỉ giùm (trên bản đồ này). — sin jeé zùm (chen baản đàw này)

Go straight ahead.
Thẳng tới trước. — tủhng der·eé chuhr·érk

at the corner	*ở góc đường*	ẻr góp đuhr·èrng
at the traffic lights	*tại đèn giao thông*	đại đèn zow tawm
behind	*đằng sau*	đùhng sow
in front of	*đằng trước*	đùhng chuhr·érk
near (to)	*gần*	gùhn
opposite	*đối diện*	đóy zee·ụhn
Turn left.	*Sang trái.*	saang chaí
Turn right.	*Sang phải.*	saang faỉ

EATING & DRINKING

I'd like a table for ...	*Tôi muốn đặt bàn cho ...*	doy moo·úhn đụht baàn jo ...
(two) people	*(hai) người*	*(hai)* nguhr·eè
(eight) o'clock	*vào lúc (tám) giờ*	vòw lúp (dúhm) zèr

Do you have a menu in English?
Bạn có thực đơn bằng tiếng Anh không? — baạn káw tụhrk đern bùhng díng aang kawm

What's the speciality here?
Ở đây có món gì đặc biệt? — ẻr đay kó món zeè đụhk bee·ụht

I'd like ...
Xin cho tôi ... — sin jo doy ...

Not too spicy, please.
Xin đừng cho cay quá. — sin dùrng jo ğay gwaá

I'm a vegetarian.
Tôi ăn chay. — doy uhn jay

I'm allergic to (peanuts).
Tôi bị dị ứng với (hạt lạc). — doy beẹ zeẹ úhrng ver·eé (haạt laạk)

Can you please bring me ...?
Xin mang cho tôi...? — sin maang jo doy ...

Can I have a (beer), please?
Xin cho tôi (chai bia)? — sin jo doy (jai bee·uh)

Cheers!
Chúc sức khoẻ! — júp súhrk kwẻ

Thank you, that was delicious.
Cám ơn, ngon lắm. — ğaám ern ngon lúhm

The bill, please.
Xin tính tiền. — sin díng dee·ùhn

Key Words

bottle	*chai*	jai
bowl	*bát* (N) *chén* (S)	baát jén
breakfast	*ăn sáng*	uhn saáng
chopsticks	*đôi đũa*	đoy·ee đoõ·uh
cold	*lạnh*	laạng
dessert	*món tráng*	món chaáng
dinner	*ăn tối*	uhn dóy
fork	*cái đĩa* (N) *nĩa* (S)	ğaí deẽ·uh neẽ·uh
glass	*cốc/ly* (N/S)	káwp/lee
hot (warm)	*nóng*	nóm
knife	*con dao*	ğon zow
lunch	*ăn trưa*	uhn chuhr·uh
plate	*đĩa*	đeẽ·uh
restaurant	*nhà hàng*	nyaà haàng
snack	*ăn nhẹ*	uhn nyạ
spicy	*cay*	ğay
spoon	*cái thìa*	ğaí tee·ùh
with	*với*	ver·eé
without	*không có*	kawm ğó

Meat & Fish

beef	*thịt bò*	tịt bò
chicken	*thịt gà*	tịt gaà
crab	*cua*	ğoo·uh
eel	*lươn*	luhr·ern

LANGUAGE EATING & DRINKING

fish	cá	kaá
frog	ếch	ék
goat	thịt dê	tịt ze
pork	thịt lợn (N)	tịt lẹrn
	heo (S)	hay·o
prawns/shrimp	tôm	dawm
snail	ốc	áwp
squid	mực	mụhrk

Fruit & Vegetables

apple	táo/bơm (N/S)	dów/berm
banana	chuối	joo·eé
cabbage	bắp cải	búhp ğaỉ
carrot	cà rốt	ğaà záwt
coconut	dừa	zuhr·ừh
corn	ngô/bắp (N/S)	ngow/búp
cucumber	dưa leo	zuhr·uh lay·o
aubergine	cà tím	ğaà dím
grapes	nho	nyo
green beans	đậu xanh	đọh saang
green pepper	ớt xanh	ért saang
lemon	chanh	chaang
lettuce	rau diếp	zoh zee·úhp
lychee	vải	vaỉ
mandarin	quýt	gweét
mango	xoài	swaì
mushrooms	nấm	núhm
orange	cam	ğaam
papaya	đu đủ	đoo đỏo
peas	đậu bi	đọh bee
pineapple	dứa	zuhr·úh
potato	khoai tây	kwai day
pumpkin	bí ngô	beé ngaw
strawberry	dâu	zoh
sweet potato	khoai lang	kwai laang
tomato	cà chua	ğaà joo·uh
watermelon	dưa hấu	zuhr·uh hóh

Other

chilli sauce	tương ớt	duhr·erng ért
eggs	trứng	chúhrng
fish sauce	nước mắm	nuhr·érk múhm
flat rice noodles	phở	fẻr
fried rice	cơm rang thập cẩm (N)	ğerm zaang tụhp ğủhm
	cơm chiên (S)	ğerm jee·uhn
rice	cơm	ğerm

KEY PATTERNS

To get by in Vietnamese, mix and match these simple patterns with words of your choice:

When's (the next bus)?
Khi nào là (chuyến xe buýt tới)? — kee nòw laà (jwee·úhn sa bweét der·eé)

Where's (the station)?
(Nhà ga) ở đâu? — (nyaà gaa) ẻr đoh

Where can I (buy a ticket)?
Tôi có thể (mua vé) ở đâu? — doy ğó tẻ (moo·uh vả) ẻr đoh

I'm looking for (a hotel).
Tôi tìm (khách sạn). — doy dìm (kaát sạan)

Do you have (a map)?
Bạn có (bản đồ) không? — baạn ğó (baản đàw) kawm

Is there (a toilet)?
Có (vệ sinh) không? — ğó (vẹ sing) kawm

I'd like (the menu).
Xin cho tôi (thực đơn). — sin jo doy (tụhrk dern)

I'd like to (hire a car).
Tôi muốn (xe hơi). — doy moo·úhn (sa her·ee)

Could you please (help me)?
Làm ơn (giúp đỡ)? — laàm ern (zúp đẻr)

I have (a visa).
Tôi có (visa). — doy ğó (vee·saa)

salad	sa lát	saa laát
soup	canh	ğaàng
steamed rice	cơm trắng	ğerm chaáng
ice	đá	đaá
pepper	hạt tiêu	haạt dee·oo
salt	muối	moo·eé
sugar	đường	dur·èrng
thin rice noodles	bún	bún
yellow egg noodles	mì	meè

Drinks

beer	bia	bi·a
coffee	cà phê	ğaà fe
iced lemon juice	chanh đá	jaang đaá
milk	sữa	sũhr·uh
mineral water	nước khoáng (N)	nuhr·érk kwaáng
	nước suối (S)	nuhr·érk soo·eé
orange juice	cam vắt	ğaam vúht
red wine	rượu vang	zee·oọ vaang

	đỏ	đỏ
soy milk	sữa đậu nành	sühr·uh dọh naàng
tea	chè/trà (N/S)	jà/chaà
white wine	rượu vang trắng	zee·oọ vaang chaáng

tourist office	văn phòng hướng dẫn du lịch	vuhn fòm huhr·érng zũhn zoo lịk

EMERGENCIES

Help!
Cứu tôi! — ğuhr·oó doy

There's been an accident!
Có tai nạn! — ğó dai naạn

Leave me alone!
Thôi! — toy

I'm lost.
Tôi bị lạc đường. — doi beẹ laạk đuhr·èrng

Where is the toilet?
Nhà vệ sinh ở đâu? — nyaà vẹ sing ér đoh

Please call the police.
Làm ơn gọi công an. — laàm ern gọy ğawm aan

Please call a doctor.
Làm ơn gọi bác sĩ. — laàm ern gọy baák seẽ

I'm sick.
Tôi bị đau. — doy beẹ đoh

It hurts here.
Chỗ bị đau ở đây. — jãw beẹ đoh ér đay

I'm allergic to (antibiotics).
Tôi bị dị ứng với (thuốc kháng sinh). — doy beẹ zeẹ úhrng ver·eé (too·úhk kaáng sing)

SHOPPING & SERVICES

I'd like to buy ...
Tôi muốn mua ... — doy moo·úhn moo·uh ...

Can I look at it?
Tôi có thể xem được không? — doy ğó tẻ sam đuhr·ẹrk kawm

I'm just looking.
Tôi chỉ ngắm xem. — doy jeẻ ngúhm sam

I don't like it.
Tôi không thích nó. — doy kawm tík nó

How much is this?
Cái này giá bao nhiêu? — ğaí này zaá bow nyee·oo

It's too expensive.
Cái này quá mắc. — ğaí này gwaá múhk

Do you accept credit cards?
Bạn có nhận kó tín dụng không? — baạn kó nyụhn tả dín zụm kawm

There's a mistake in the bill.
Có sự nhầm lẫn trên hoá đơn. — ğó sụhr nyùhm lũhn chen hwaá đern

I'm looking for a/the ...	Tôi tìm ...	doy dìm ...
bank	ngân hàng	nguhn haàng
market	chợ	jẹr

TIME & DATES

What time is it?
Mấy giờ rồi? — máy zèr zòy

It's (eight) o'clock.
Bây giờ là (tám) giờ. — bay zèr laà (dúhm) zèr

morning	buổi sáng	boỏ·ee saáng
afternoon	buổi chiều	boỏ·ee jee·oò
evening	buổi tối	boỏ·ee dóy
yesterday	hôm qua	hawm ğwaa
today	hôm nay	hawm nay
tomorrow	ngày mai	ngày mai\

Monday	thứ hai	túhr hai
Tuesday	thứ ba	túhr baa
Wednesday	thứ tư	túhr duhr
Thursday	thứ năm	túhr nuhm
Friday	thứ sáu	túhr sóh
Saturday	thứ bảy	túhr bảy
Sunday	chủ nhật	jóo nhụht

January	tháng giêng	taáng zee·uhng
February	tháng hai	taáng hai
March	tháng ba	taáng baa
April	tháng tư	taáng tuhr
May	tháng năm	taáng nuhm
June	tháng sáu	taáng sóh
July	tháng bảy	taáng bảy
August	tháng tám	taáng dúhm
September	tháng chín	taáng jín
October	tháng mười	taáng muhr·eè
November	tháng mười một	taáng muhr·eè mạwt
December	tháng mười hai	taáng muhr·eè hai

TRANSPORT

Public Transport

When does the (first)... leave/arrive?	Chuyến ... (sớm nhất) chạy lúc mấy giờ?	jwee·úhn ... (sérm nyúht) jạy lúp máy zèr
boat	tàu/ thuyền	dòw/ twee·ùhn

NUMBERS

1	một	mạwt
2	hai	hai
3	ba	baa
4	bốn	báwn
5	năm	nuhm
6	sáu	sóh
7	bảy	bảy
8	tám	dúhm
9	chín	jín
10	mười	muhr·eè
20	hai mươi	hai muhr·ee
30	ba mươi	ba muhr·ee
40	bốn mươi	báwn muhr·ee
50	năm mươi	nuhm muhr·ee
60	sáu mươi	sów muhr·ee
70	bảy mươi	bảy muhr·ee
80	tám mươi	daám muhr·ee
90	chín mươi	jín muhr·ee
100	một trăm	mạwt chuhm
1000	một nghìn (N)	mạwt ngyìn
	một ngàn (S)	mọt ngaàn

bus	xe buýt	sa beét
plane	máy bay	máy bay
train	xe lửa	sa lúhr·uh

I'd like a ... ticket.	Tôi muốn vé ...	doy moo·úhn vá ...
1st class	hạng nhất	haạng nyúht
2nd class	hạng nhì	haạng nyeè
one-way	đi một chiều	dee mạt jee·oò
return	khứ hồi	kúhr haw·eè

I want to go to ...
Tôi muốn đi ...   doy moo·úhn đee ...

How long does the trip take?
Chuyến đi sẽ   jwee·úhn đee sã
mất bao lâu?   múht bow loh

What time does it arrive?
Mấy giờ đến?   máy zèr đén

bus station	bến xe	bén sa
railway station	ga xe lửa	gaa sa lúhr·uh
the first	đầu tiên	đòw dee·uhn
the last	cuối cùng	ğoo·eé ğùm

the next	kế tiếp	ğé dee·úhp
ticket office	phòng bán vé	fòm baán vá
timetable	thời biểu	ter·eè beé·oo

Driving & Cycling

I'd like to hire a ...	Tôi muốn thuê ... (N)	doy moo·úhn twe ...
	Tôi muốn mướn ... (S)	doy moo·úhn muhr·érn ...
car	xe hơi	sa her·ee
bicycle	xe đạp	sa đạp
motorbike	xe moto	sa mo·to

Is this the road to ...?
Con đường nầy   ğon đuhr·èrng này
có dẫn đến ...?   ğó zũhn đén ...

How many kilometres to ...?
... cách đây bao   ... ğaák đay bow
nhiêu ki-lô-mét?   nyee·oo kee·law·mét

Where's a service station?
Trạm xăng ở đâu?   chaạm suhng ér doh

Please fill it up.
Làm ơn đổ đầy bình.   laàm ern đỏ đày bìng

I'd like ... litres.
Tôi muốn ... lít.   doy moo·úhn ... léet

diesel	dầu diesel	zòh dee·sel
highway	xa lộ	saa lạw
leaded petrol	dầu xăng có chì	zòh suhng ğó jeè
map	bản đồ	baản đàw
unleaded petrol	dầu xăng	zòh suhng

(How long) Can I park here?
Chúng tôi có thể đậu   júm doy ğó tẻ dọh
xe được (bao lâu)?   sa đuhr·ẹrk (bow loh)

I need a mechanic.
Chúng tôi cần thợ   júm doy ğùhn tẹr
sửa xe.   súhr·uh sa

The car/motorbike has broken down (at ...)
Xe bị hư (tại ...).   sa bẹ huhr (daị ...)

The car/motorbike won't start.
(Xe hơi/Xe moto)   (sa her·ee/sa mo·to)
không đề được.   kawm đè đuhr·ẹrk

I have a flat tyre.
Bánh xe tôi bị xì.   baáng sa doy bẹ seè

I've run out of petrol.
Tôi bị hết dầu/xăng.   doy bẹ hét zòh/suhng

I've had an accident.
Tôi bị tai nạn.   doy bẹ dai naạn

GLOSSARY

A Di Da – Buddha of the Past

Agent Orange – toxic, carcinogenic chemical herbicide used extensively during the American War

am duong – Vietnamese equivalent of Yin and Yang

American War – Vietnamese name for what is also known as the Vietnam War

Annam – old Chinese name for Vietnam, meaning 'Pacified South'

ao dai – Vietnamese national dress worn by women

apsaras – heavenly maidens

ARVN – Army of the Republic of Vietnam (former South Vietnamese army)

ba mu – midwife. There are 12 'midwives', each of whom teaches newborns a different skill necessary for the first year of life: smiling, sucking, lying on their stomachs, and so forth

ban – mountainous village

bang – congregation (in the Chinese community)

bar om – literally 'holding' bars associated with the sex industry Also known as 'karaoke om'.

buu dien – post office

cai luong – Vietnamese modern theatre

Cao Daism – indigenous Vietnamese religion

Cham – ethnic minority descended from the people of Champa

Champa – Hindu kingdom dating from the late 2nd century AD

Charlie – nickname for the Viet Cong, used by US soldiers

chua – pagoda

chu nho – standard Chinese characters (script)

Cochinchina – the southern part of Vietnam during the French-colonial era

com pho – rice and rice-noodle soup

crémaillère – cog railway

cyclo – pedicab or bicycle rickshaw

Dai The Chi Bo Tat – an assistant of *A Di Da*

dan bau – single-stringed zither that generates an astounding magnitude of tones

dan tranh – 16-stringed zither

den – temple

Di Lac Buddha – Buddha of the Future

dikpalaka – gods of the directions of the compass

dinh – communal meeting hall

DMZ – Demilitarised Zone, a strip of land that once separated North and South Vietnam

doi moi – economic restructuring or reform, which commenced in Vietnam in 1986

dong – natural caves. Also Vietnamese currency.

dong son – drums

ecocide – term used to describe the devastating effects of the herbicides sprayed over Vietnam during the American War

fléchette – experimental US weapon. An artillery shell containing thousands of darts.

Funan – see *Oc-Eo*

garuda – half human–half bird

gom – ceramics

hai dang – lighthouse

hat boi – classical theatre in the south

hat cheo – Vietnamese popular theatre

hat tuong – classical theatre in the north

ho ca – aquarium

Ho Chi Minh Trail – route used by the North Vietnamese Army and Viet Cong to move supplies to the south

Hoa – ethnic Chinese, one of the largest single minority groups in Vietnam

hoi quan – Chinese congregational assembly halls

huong – perfume

huyen – rural district

Indochina – Vietnam, Cambodia and Laos. The name derives from Indian and Chinese influences.

kala-makara – sea-monster god

kalan – a religious sanctuary

khach san – hotel

Khmer – ethnic Cambodians

Khong Tu – Confucius

kich noi – spoken drama

Kinh – Vietnamese language

Kuomintang – Chinese Nationalist Party, also known as KMT. The KMT controlled China between 1925 and 1949 until defeated by the communists.

li xi – lucky money distributed during the Vietnamese Lunar New Year

liberation – 1975 takeover of the South by the North. Most foreigners call this 'reunification'.

Lien Xo – literally, Soviet Union. Used to call attention to a foreigner

linga – stylised phallus which represents the Hindu god Shiva

manushi-buddha – Buddha who appeared in human form

moi – derogatory word meaning 'savages', mostly used by ethnic Vietnamese to describe hill-tribe people

Montagnards – term meaning highlanders or mountain people, sometimes used in a derogatory way to refer to the ethnic minorities who inhabit remote areas of Vietnam

muong – large village unit made up of *quel* (small stilt-houses)

naga – Sanskrit term for a mythical serpent being with divine powers; often depicted forming a kind of shelter over the Buddha

nam phai – for men

napalm – jellied petrol (gasoline) dropped and lit from aircraft; used by US forces with devastating repercussions during the American War

nguoi thuong – the current government's preferred term for highland people

nha hang – restaurant

nha khach – hotel or guesthouse

nha nghi – guesthouse

nha rong – large stilt house, used by hill tribes as a kind of community centre

nha tro – dormitory

NLF – National Liberation Front, the official name for the VC

nom – Vietnamese script, used between the 10th and early 20th centuries

nu phai – for women

nui – mountain

nuoc mam – fish sauce, added to almost every main dish in Vietnam

NVA – North Vietnamese Army

Oc-Eo – Indianised Khmer kingdom (also called Funan) in southern Vietnam between the 1st and 6th centuries

Ong Bon – Guardian Spirit of Happiness and Virtue

OSS – US Office of Strategic Services. The predecessor of the CIA.

pagoda – traditionally an eight-sided Buddhist tower, but in Vietnam the word is commonly used to denote a temple

phong thuy – literally, 'wind and water'. Used to describe geomancy. Also known by its Chinese name, feng shui.

PRG – Provisional Revolutionary Government, the temporary

Communist government set up by the VC in the South. It existed from 1969 to 1976.

quan – urban district

Quan Cong – Chinese God of War

Quan The Am Bo Tat – Goddess of Mercy

quoc am – modern Vietnamese literature

quoc ngu – Latin-based phonetic alphabet in which Vietnamese is written

rap – cinema

Revolutionary Youth League – first Marxist group in Vietnam and predecessor of the Communist Party

roi can – conventional puppetry

roi nuoc – water puppetry

ruou (pronounced xeo) – rice wine

RVN – Republic of Vietnam (the old South Vietnam)

salangane – swiftlet

sao – wooden flute

saola – antelope-like creature

shakti – feminine manifestation of Shiva

song – river

SRV – Socialist Republic of Vietnam (Vietnam's official name)

Strategic Hamlets Program – program (by South Vietnam and the USA) of forcibly moving peasants into fortified villages to deny the VC bases of support

sung – fig tree

Tam Giao – literally, 'triple religion'. Confucianism, Taoism and Buddhism fused over time with popular Chinese beliefs and ancient Vietnamese animism.

Tao – the Way. The essence of which all things are made.

Tay ba lo – backpacker

Tet – Vietnamese Lunar New Year

thai cuc quyen – Vietnamese for t'ai chi

Thich Ca Buddha – the historical Buddha Sakyamuni, whose real name was Siddhartha Gautama

thong nhat – reunification. Also a commonly used term for the Reunification Express train.

thuoc bac – Chinese medicine

toc hanh – express bus

Tonkin – the northern part of Vietnam during the French-colonial era. Also the name of a body of water in the north (Tonkin Gulf).

truyen khau – traditional oral literature

UNHCR – UN High Commissioner for Refugees

VC – Viet Cong or Vietnamese Communists

Viet Kieu – overseas Vietnamese

Viet Minh – League for the Independence of Vietnam, a nationalistic movement that fought the Japanese and French but later became communist dominated

VNQDD – Viet Nam Quoc Dan Dang. Largely middle -class nationalist party.

xang – petrol

xe lam – tiny three-wheeled trucks used for short-haul passenger and freight transport

xe om – motorbike taxi, also called *Honda om*

xich lo – *cyclo*, from the French *cyclo-pousse*

Behind the Scenes

SEND US YOUR FEEDBACK

We love to hear from travellers – your comments keep us on our toes and help make our books better. Our well-travelled team reads every word on what you loved or loathed about this book. Although we cannot reply individually to your submissions, we always guarantee that your feedback goes straight to the appropriate authors, in time for the next edition. Each person who sends us information is thanked in the next edition – the most useful submissions are rewarded with a selection of digital PDF chapters.

Visit **lonelyplanet.com/contact** to submit your updates and suggestions or to ask for help. Our award-winning website also features inspirational travel stories, news and discussions.

Note: We may edit, reproduce and incorporate your comments in Lonely Planet products such as guidebooks, websites and digital products, so let us know if you don't want your comments reproduced or your name acknowledged. For a copy of our privacy policy visit lonelyplanet.com/privacy.

OUR READERS

Many thanks to the travellers who used the last edition and wrote to us with helpful hints, useful advice and interesting anecdotes:

Alison Lea, Andrea Aurelia Rodríguez Moreno, Ann Lee-Steere, Barney Frost, Bjorn Pelissier, Bob Clayton, C Cartwright, Chen Zhu, Chuang Gao, Erica Maraffino, Eva Langner, Ignacio Mora, Jenean Harris, Jeni Harris, Jens Volmer, Julie Bergeron, Ken Beare, Luis Blanco, M Belanger, Marieluise Gscheidle, Mark Wigginton, Marlyn Kemink, Niamh Cullen, Pascal Tokugawa, Phil France, Renata Pesickova, Steven Pashley, Wolfgang Henk

WRITERS' THANKS

Iain Stewart

Writing a book about Vietnam takes a lot of help on the ground. In HCMC many thanks to Mark Zazula and Lu, Matt Cowan, and Mark and Duong from the Old Compass for their insider knowledge. Up and down the coastline I was helped by Neil and Caroline, Vinh Vu, Mark Wyndham, Alex Leonard, Julia Shaw and my travelling companion and son Louis Stewart.

Damian Harper

Many thanks to all of those who helped along the way on what was an incredible and fascinating journey; much gratitude especially to Ben, Sophie, Kien, Binh, Hu Xuechun, Mai, Anh, Thao, Tam, Priscilla Milis, Matt Bazak, Neil, Paul Mooney, Kim, Tanya Currington, Fabienne, Justine, Thien, Hoang Nguyen, Bradley Mayhew, Truyen and Rosee. Thanks, as ever, to Daisy, Tim and Emma.

Bradley Mayhew

Thanks to Mr Linh for his tips on Ba Be National Park, Nguyen Van Manh in Sapa, Yom at the Doc May in Dalat and Mr Dong at Ngan Nga Bac Ha, who were all incredibly helpful with information. Cheers to QT and Jorgen in Ha Giang for all their help and first-class bike rental. Finally, cheers to Andre for a great couple of weeks riding motorbikes in the far north.

Nick Ray

A big thanks to the people of Vietnam and Cambodia, whose strength and determination have made their countries such fascinating places to visit over the years. Biggest thanks are reserved for my wife, Kulikar Sotho, and our children, Julian and Belle, as without their support and encouragement the adventures would not be possible. Thanks also to Mum and Dad for giving me a taste for travel from a young age. Thanks to fellow travellers and residents, friends and contacts in both countries who have helped shaped my knowledge and experiences there. Thanks also to my co-writers Iain Stewart, Bradley Mayhew and Damian Harper for going the distance to ensure this is a worthy new edition. Finally, thanks to the Lonely Planet team who have worked on this title. The writer may be the public face, but a huge amount of work goes into making this a better book behind the scenes and thanks to everyone for their hard work.

ACKNOWLEDGEMENTS

Climate map data adapted from Peel MC, Finlayson BL & McMahon TA (2007) 'Updated World Map of the Köppen-Geiger Climate Classification', *Hydrology and Earth System Sciences*, 11, 1633–44.

Illustrations p180-1 and p426-7 by Michael Weldon.

Cover photograph: Halong Bay, BODY Philippe/AWL Images ©.

THIS BOOK

This 15th edition of Lonely Planet's *Vietnam* guidebook was researched and written by Iain Stewart, Damian Harper, Bradley Mayhew and Nick Ray. The previous two editions were also researched and written by Iain and Nick, along with Brett Atkinson, Austin Bush, David Eimer and Phillip Tang. This guidebook was produced by the following:

Senior Product Editors Grace Dobell, Sandie Kestell

Regional Senior Cartographer Diana von Holdt

Product Editors Carolyn Boicos, Amanda Williamson

Book Designers Virginia Moreno, Jessica Rose

Assisting Editors Janet Austin, Andrew Bain, Michelle Bennett, Kate Chapman, Nigel Chin, Michelle Coxall, Melanie Dankel, Jodie Martire

Cartographers Mark Griffiths, Corey Hutchison, James Leversha, Anthony Phelan

Cover Researcher Naomi Parker

Thanks to Will Allen, Imogen Bannister, Barbara Delissen, James Hardy, Karen Henderson, Genna Patterson, Oeu Vearyda

Index

Map Legend

Sights

- Beach
- Bird Sanctuary
- Buddhist
- Castle/Palace
- Christian
- Confucian
- Hindu
- Islamic
- Jain
- Jewish
- Monument
- Museum/Gallery/Historic Building
- Ruin
- Shinto
- Sikh
- Taoist
- Winery/Vineyard
- Zoo/Wildlife Sanctuary
- Other Sight

Activities, Courses & Tours

- Bodysurfing
- Diving
- Canoeing/Kayaking
- Course/Tour
- Sento Hot Baths/Onsen
- Skiing
- Snorkelling
- Surfing
- Swimming/Pool
- Walking
- Windsurfing
- Other Activity

Sleeping

- Sleeping
- Camping
- Hut/Shelter

Eating

- Eating

Drinking & Nightlife

- Drinking & Nightlife
- Cafe

Entertainment

- Entertainment

Shopping

- Shopping

Information

- Bank
- Embassy/Consulate
- Hospital/Medical
- Internet
- Police
- Post Office
- Telephone
- Toilet
- Tourist Information
- Other Information

Geographic

- Beach
- Gate
- Hut/Shelter
- Lighthouse
- Lookout
- Mountain/Volcano
- Oasis
- Park
- Pass
- Picnic Area
- Waterfall

Population

- Capital (National)
- Capital (State/Province)
- City/Large Town
- Town/Village

Transport

- Airport
- Border crossing
- Bus
- Cable car/Funicular
- Cycling
- Ferry
- Metro/MTR/MRT station
- Monorail
- Parking
- Petrol station
- Skytrain/Subway station
- Taxi
- Train station/Railway
- Tram
- Underground station
- Other Transport

Routes

- Tollway
- Freeway
- Primary
- Secondary
- Tertiary
- Lane
- Unsealed road
- Road under construction
- Plaza/Mall
- Steps
- Tunnel
- Pedestrian overpass
- Walking Tour
- Walking Tour detour
- Path/Walking Trail

Boundaries

- International
- State/Province
- Disputed
- Regional/Suburb
- Marine Park
- Cliff
- Wall

Hydrography

- River, Creek
- Intermittent River
- Canal
- Water
- Dry/Salt/Intermittent Lake
- Reef

Areas

- Airport/Runway
- Beach/Desert
- Cemetery (Christian)
- Cemetery (Other)
- Glacier
- Mudflat
- Park/Forest
- Sight (Building)
- Sportsground
- Swamp/Mangrove

Note: Not all symbols displayed above appear on the maps in this book

Nick Ray

Mekong Delta, Siem Reap & the Temples of Angkor A Londoner of sorts, Nick comes from Watford, the sort of town that makes you want to travel. He currently lives in Phnom Penh, Cambodia, and has written countless guidebooks on the countries of the Mekong region, including contributing to Lonely Planet's *Cambodia*, *Laos* and *Myanmar* titles. When not writing, he is often out exploring the remote parts of the region as a location scout or line producer for the world of television and film, including the memorable *Top Gear Vietnam*. Cambodia is one of his favourite places on earth and he was excited to revisit some remote corners. He has been travelling to Vietnam since 1995 and was happy to explore some off-the-beaten-track islands on this trip.

OUR STORY

A beat-up old car, a few dollars in the pocket and a sense of adventure. In 1972 that's all Tony and Maureen Wheeler needed for the trip of a lifetime – across Europe and Asia overland to Australia. It took several months, and at the end – broke but inspired – they sat at their kitchen table writing and stapling together their first travel guide, *Across Asia on the Cheap*. Within a week they'd sold 1500 copies. Lonely Planet was born.

Today, Lonely Planet has offices in Tennessee, Dublin and Beijing, with a network of over 2000 contributors in every corner of the globe. We share Tony's belief that 'a great guidebook should do three things: inform, educate and amuse'.

OUR WRITERS

Iain Stewart
Southeast Coast, Ho Chi Minh City Iain trained as a journalist in the 1990s and then worked as a news reporter and a restaurant critic in London. He started writing travel guides in 1997 and has since penned more than 60 books for destinations as diverse as Ibiza and Cambodia. Iain has contributed to Lonely Planet titles including *Mexico; Indonesia; Central America; Croatia; Bali, Lombok & Nusa Tenggara* and *Southeast Asia*. He also writes regularly for the *Independent, Observer* and *Daily Telegraph* and tweets at @iaintravel. He'll consider working anywhere there's a palm tree or two and a beach of a generally sandy persuasion. Iain lives in Brighton (UK) within firing range of the city's wonderful south-facing horizon. Iain also wrote the Plan Your Trip, Understand and Survival Guide chapters.

Damian Harper
Hanoi, Central Vietnam With two degrees (one in modern and classical Chinese from SOAS), Damian has been writing for Lonely Planet for more than two decades, contributing to titles as diverse as *China; Beijing; Shanghai; Thailand; Ireland; London; Mallorca; Malaysia, Singapore & Brunei; Hong Kong* and *Great Britain*. A seasoned guidebook writer, Damian has penned articles for numerous newspapers and magazines, including the *Guardian* and *Daily Telegraph*, and currently makes Surrey, England, his home. A self-taught trumpet novice, his other hobbies include taekwondo, collecting modern first editions and photography. He has had a wide variety of photographs published by Lonely Planet, *National Geographic Traveler*, AA Publishing, Insight Guides and other publishers, periodicals and publications. Follow Damian on Instagram (@damian.harper) or at www.damianharper.com.

Bradley Mayhew
Northern Vietnam, Southwest Highlands Bradley has been writing guidebooks for 20 years now. He started travelling while studying Chinese at Oxford University, and has since focused his expertise on China, Tibet, the Himalaya and Central Asia. He is the co-writer of Lonely Planet guides to *Tibet, Nepal, Trekking in the Nepal Himalaya, Bhutan, Central Asia* and many others. Bradley has also fronted two TV series for Arte and SWR, one retracing the route of Marco Polo via Turkey, Iran, Afghanistan, Central Asia and China, and the other trekking Europe's 10 most scenic long-distance trails.

OVER PAGE MORE WRITERS

Published by Lonely Planet Global Limited
CRN 554153
15th edition – October 2021
ISBN 978 1 78701 793 1
© Lonely Planet 2021 Photographs © as indicated 2021
10 9 8 7 6 5 4 3 2 1
Printed in Singapore